WordPerfect® 6.0

For DOS

Katie Layman
College of San Mateo, San Mateo, California

and

LaVaughn Hart
Chabot College, Hayward, California

PRENTICE HALL   CAREER & TECHNOLOGY
Englewood Cliffs, New Jersey 07632

Library of Congress Cataloging-in-Publication Data

Layman, Katie.
  WordPerfect 6.0/Katie Layman and LaVaughn Hart.
      p. cm.
  Includes index.
  Expanded ed. of: WordPerfect 6.0 made easy. c1993.
  ISBN 0-13-013103-2
      1. WordPerfect (Computer file) 2. Word processing. I. Hart,
  LaVaughan. II. Layman, Katie. WordPerfect 6.0. III. Title.
  IV. Title: WordPerfect six point zero.
  Z52.5.W65L395 1994
  652.5'536--dc20   94-2961
                                                               CIP

Acquisition editor: *Carolyn Henderson*
Editorial/production supervision: *Tally Morgan, WordCrafters Editorial Services, Inc.*
Cover design: *Marianne Frasco*
Buyer: *Ed O'Dougherty*
Editorial assistant: *Jane Avery*

WordPerfect v.6.0 for DOS ©1982, 1993 WordPerfect Corporation. All rights reserved.
Reprinted with permission from WordPerfect Corporation.
WordPerfect is a registered trademark of WordPerfect Corporation.
Button Bar, Grammatik, QuickList, and QuickFinder are trademarks of WordPerfect Corporation.

Printed in the United States of America

10 9 8 7 6 5 4 3 2 1

ISBN 0-13-013103-2

Prentice-Hall International (UK) Limited, *London*
Prentice-Hall of Australia Pty. Limited, *Sydney*
Prentice-Hall of Canada Inc., *Toronto*
Prentice-Hall Hispanoamericana, S.A., *Mexico*
Prentice-Hall of India Private Limited, *New Delhi*
Prentice-Hall of Japan, Inc., *Tokyo*
Simon & Schuster Asia Pte. Ltd., *Singapore*
Editora Prentice-Hall do Brasil, Ltda., *Rio de Janeiro*

CONTENTS

Introduction

The purpose of this textbook is to provide students with simple step-by-step instructions to quickly master WordPerfect 6.0 for DOS, the single most popular word processing program available. Numerous hands-on activities and easy-to-follow instruction lists within the text's chapters allow students to learn by doing. All of these carefully guided walk-throughs are accompanied by thorough, precise explanations of each WordPerfect feature being introduced, making this textbook, **WordPerfect 6.0**, as appropriate for use in individualized instruction programs as it is for use in traditional classrooms.

By focusing on the *tasks* students need to perform with the help of WordPerfect (rather than how WordPerfect "works"), this **WordPerfect 6.0** textbook aids instructors in their efforts to help students acquire the work-ready skills needed to succeed in today's job market. But the book's commitment to students acquisition of these skills does not stop here.

As students work through the text's activities, they are introduced to the proper format for various business documents (memorandums, letters, reports, résumés, newsletters, etc.). What's more, all of the text's activities are based on authentic, real-world documents— "just what students will encounter in everyday life on the job," according to one reviewer. And because students can never have too much training in or reinforcement of their basic English and grammar skills, each chapter includes an *Enriching Language Arts Skills* section and activity.

Finally, the end-of-chapter and end-of-part sections—*The Next Step* and *Checking Your Step* sections, respectively—are designed to fulfill the basic skill requirements that have been identified by the Secretary's Commission on Achieving Necessary Skills (SCANS). *The Next Step* and *Checking Your Step* activities reinforce students' reading, writing, thinking, and decision-making skills. SCANS icons are placed within the text so that instructors and students can quickly identify the activities that build SCANS competencies.

Content Highlights

Above all else, this **WordPerfect 6.0** texbook is committed to providing students with the work-ready skills they need to excel. The book's pedagogical system and the features described in the preceding section have been carefully crafted to achieve this end. Some of the key components of this performance-based system are as follows:

Chapter-opening *Features Covered* sections identify the WordPerfect features introduced in the chapter and provide students with a clear road map of precisely what is to come.

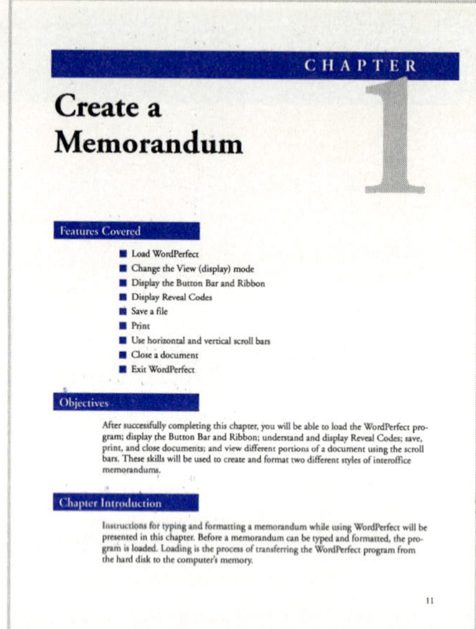

CHAPTER 1

Create a Memorandum

Features Covered

- Load WordPerfect
- Change the View (display) mode
- Display the Button Bar and Ribbon
- Display Reveal Codes
- Save a file
- Print
- Use horizontal and vertical scroll bars
- Close a document
- Exit WordPerfect

Objectives

After successfully completing this chapter, you will be able to load the WordPerfect program; display the Button Bar and Ribbon; understand and display Reveal Codes; save, print, and close documents; and view different portions of a document using the scroll bars. These skills will be used to create and format two different styles of interoffice memorandums.

Chapter Introduction

Instructions for typing and formatting a memorandum while using WordPerfect will be presented in this chapter. Before a memorandum can be typed and formatted, the program is loaded. Loading is the process of transferring the WordPerfect program from the hard disk to the computer's memory.

11

Measurable learning *Objectives* preview chapter material in terms of the actual tasks students will perform as they work through the chapter.

Concise *Chapter Introductions* provide students with succinct narrative overviews of the chapter material.

Numerous screen captures clarify concepts and instructions for students as they proceed through each chapter.

Careful step-by-step instruction lists are provided in the body of the chapter and are accompanied by a *Steps To* icon in the margin to make them easy for students to find when referring back to the text later.

In addition to the step-by-step instruction lists, activity-specific *Start-Up Instructions* and *Finish-Up Instructions* are clearly identified and provide information necessary to the completion of in-chapter activities. This, coupled with the *Steps To* icon, gives students the best of both worlds—detailed, enumerated step-by-step tutorials now, and easy-to-locate generic instruction lists later, when the text needs to function as a reference manual.

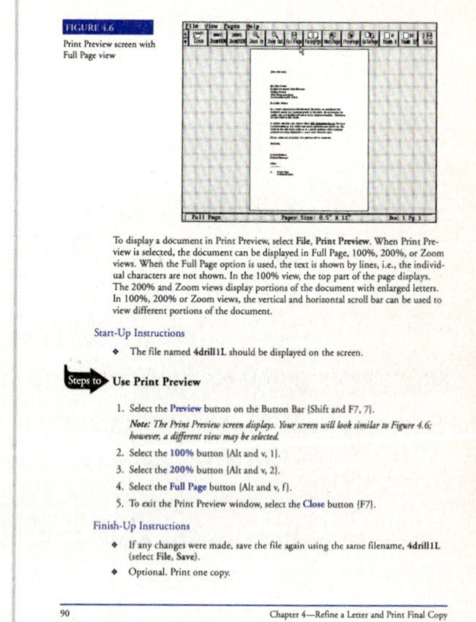

FIGURE 4.6

Print Preview screen with Full Page view

To display a document in Print Preview, select **File, Print Preview**. When Print Preview is selected, the document can be displayed in Full Page, 100%, 200%, or Zoom views. When the Full Page option is used, the text is shown by lines, i.e., the individual characters are not shown. In the 100% view, the top part of the page displays. The 200% and Zoom views display portions of the document with enlarged letters. In 100%, 200% or Zoom views, the vertical and horizontal scroll bar can be used to view different portions of the document.

Start-Up Instructions

- The file named **4drill1L** should be displayed on the screen.

Steps to **Use Print Preview**

1. Select the **Preview** button on the Button Bar {Shift and F7, 7}.
   Note: The Print Preview screen displays. Your screen will look similar to Figure 4.6; however, a different view may be selected.
2. Select the **100%** button {Alt and v, 1}.
3. Select the **200%** button {Alt and v, 2}.
4. Select the **Full Page** button {Alt and v, f}.
5. To exit the Print Preview window, select the **Close** button {F7}.

Finish-Up Instructions

- If any changes were made, save the file again using the same filename, **4drill1L** (select **File, Save**).
- Optional. Print one copy.

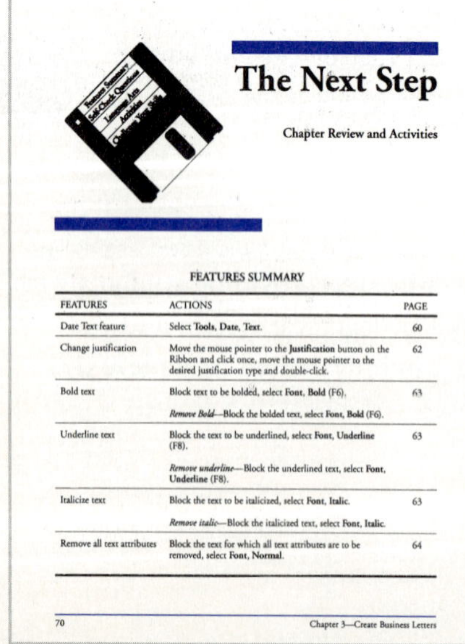

The Next Step

Chapter Review and Activities

FEATURES SUMMARY

FEATURES	ACTIONS	PAGE
Date Text feature	Select **Tools, Date, Text**.	60
Change justification	Move the mouse pointer to the **Justification** button on the Ribbon and click once, move the mouse pointer to the desired justification type and double-click.	62
Bold text	Block text to be bolded, select **Font, Bold** (F6). *Remove Bold*—Block the bolded text, select **Font, Bold** (F6).	63
Underline text	Block the text to be underlined, select **Font, Underline** (F8). *Remove underline*—Block the underlined text, select **Font, Underline** (F8).	63
Italicize text	Block the text to be italicized, select **Font, Italic**. *Remove italic*—Block the italicized text, select **Font, Italic**.	63
Remove all text attributes	Block the text for which all text attributes are to be removed, select **Font, Normal**.	64

Another excellent reference source is the end-of-chapter *Features Summary*, which lists all of the WordPerfect features presented in the chapter and includes page references should the student want to go back to the chapter for additional information.

End-of-chapter *True/False* and *Short Answer* questions enable students to check their understanding of key chapter concepts and procedures (answers for *True/False Questions* are provided at the end of the book).

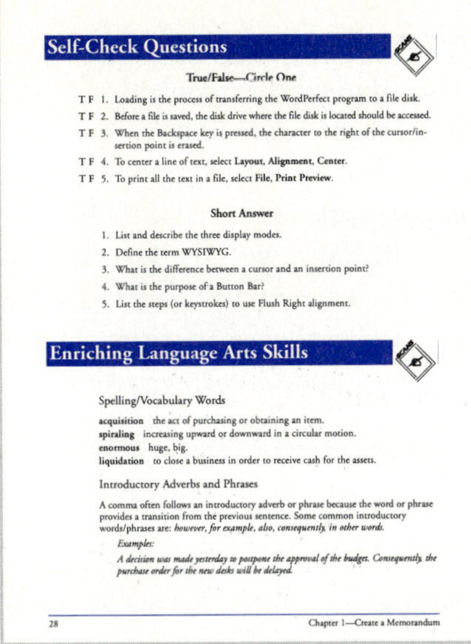

A unique *Enriching Language Arts Skills* section at the end of each chapter reinforces students' spelling and grammar skills—skills the student is called on to use in the chapter's final hands-on *Activity* (correcting mistakes in spelling, punctuation, capitalization, and/or grammar).

Many guided hands-on *Activities* at the close of each chapter let students practice—in a structured, unintimidating environment—what they've learned in the chapter.

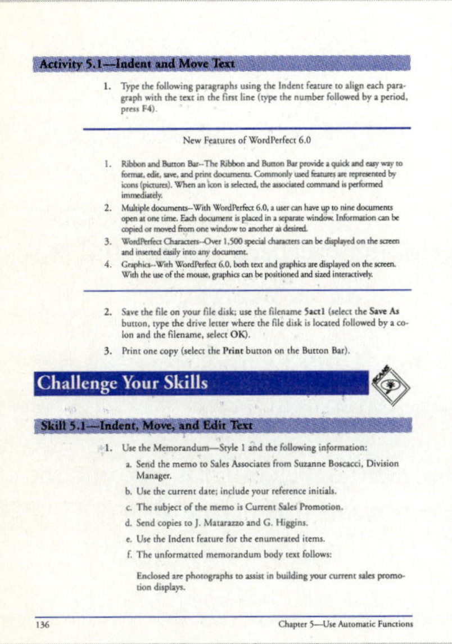

Independent *Challenge Your Skills* activities at the close of each chapter give students ample practice applying what they have learned without the help of guided instructions.

End-of-part *Checking Your Step* production skill-builder activities allow students to stretch their mastery of the program and develop their decision-making and critical thinking skills. The production skill-builder activities can be used for testing, hands-on projects, or as brief office simulation exercises.

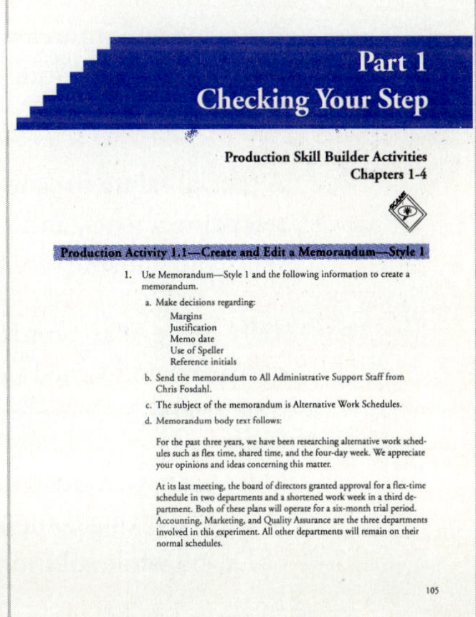

Instructor Support Materials

An **Instructor's Resource Manual** is available that contains teaching suggestions and solutions for the short-answer chapter questions and the practice, end-of-chapter, skill, and production activities. The manual includes a chapter overview, student objectives, lecture notes for the teacher, and one or more additional activities for each chapter. Also provided are production and theory tests. Included with the **Instructor's Resource Manual** are a student disk and an instructor's disk. The student disk includes unformatted files for practice activities, end-of-chapter activities, and challenge activities. The instructor's disk contains formatted files for the practice activities, end-of-chapter activities, challenge activities, and production tests.

Acknowledgments

A genuine thank you to our editor, Carolyn Henderson, for her avid support and eagerness to handle all details and responsibilities that are associated with the creation of a book. Your open-door communication policy to "call whenever needed" is very much appreciated. You are a resourceful, dedicated, and conscientious editor.

Thank you, Jeanette Hartmann, for your meticulous keystroke testing of the *WordPerfect 6.0* manuscript. Your questions and suggestions were extremely useful in creating correct instructions for the hands-on activities and for assisting with the explanation of features. Many thanks too, for writing a comprehensive **Instructor's Resource Manual** and for creating the student and instructor disks. Thank you, Jeanette, for developing excellent teacher and student resources.

We extend a big thank you to Howard Illman, Heald's Business College, and Steve Siu for providing keystroke testing that resulted in accurate step-by-step instructions.

A huge thank you to the many people at Prentice Hall, Inc., who have contributed and continue to contribute outstanding support for the success of this word processing series. Thank you especially Debbie Emry for your constant support and dedication to professional marketing techniques.

A sincere and immense thank you to Liz Kendall, for spear-heading and launching this word processing series. Your support and leadership will always be remembered with much appreciation.

A special salute to Jane Avery for assisting with our many phone calls, swiftly processing contract agreements, and for promptly responding to our numerous requests. Your expert clerical skills and amiable service are highly praised and very much appreciated.

Tally Morgan at WordCrafters, thank you again for applying your expert production skills to our many and varied needs. Your willingness to work days, nights, and weekends to meet our time restraints is measureless!

Once again we extend our thank you to Darrel Dorsett for providing technical assistance and advice for resolving computer hardware complications. Thank you also to Annie for your support of Darrel while solutions were being found for our hardware challenges.

Preface

What is a Microcomputer System?

A microcomputer system is a small computer designed to provide methods for creating, processing, storing and printing data. A system can include the computer, keyboard, mouse, monitor, printer, and software programs. The microcomputer system consists of two basic elements: hardware and software. The physical components of the microcomputer system are called hardware. The programs that instruct the computer to perform functions are called software.

Hardware

The microcomputer hardware includes the monitor (TV-like screen), keyboard, mouse, computer unit, disk drives, and printer. The hardware can be seen, felt, and touched. The IBM PC and compatible computers enclose the disk drive(s) with the computer. The monitor, keyboard, mouse, and printer are attached to the computer via cables (see Figure I.1). The computer unit and the attached hardware make up a computer system.

A computer unit holds the electronic circuitry where the main memory and central processing unit (CPU) reside. The CPU processes and controls information by storing data, performing operations, and transferring information from one location to another. The CPU is often referred to as the "brains" of the computer.

Software

Software programs are lists of instructions that tell the computer what to do. The master program is the disk operating system (DOS). DOS directs the basic operation of the computer system and carries out procedures within application programs. Application programs are more advanced software designed to perform specific tasks. Common applications are word processing, spreadsheet, database, communication, drawing and desktop publishing programs.

DOS and application programs are stored on master disks. A copy of DOS and of an application program can be transferred to the computer's memory when the computer is turned on. Transferring a copy of a program to the computer's memory is

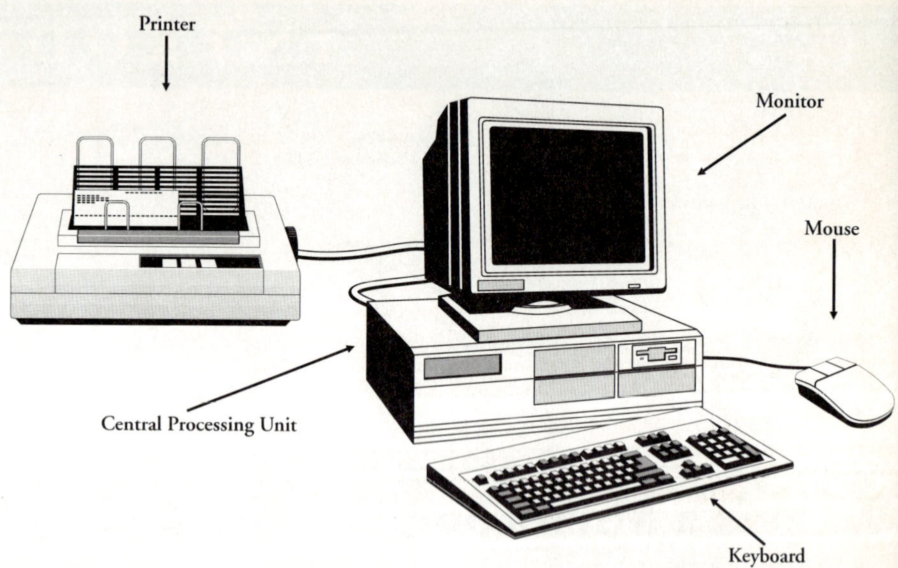

called "loading the program." The disk is being "read" when a copy of a program or other information is transferred from the disk into the computer's memory.

System Requirements and Recommendations

Minimum System Requirements	Recommended System
286 IBM PC or compatible	386 (or higher) IBM PC or compatible
480Kb conventional memory free	520Kb conventional memory free
DOS 3.0 or higher	DOS 6.0 or memory management software
7Mb hard disk space	16 - 18 Mb hard disk space
(Some WordPerfect features will not function in WordPerfect 6.0 when using the minimum system requirements.)	VGA graphics adapter and monitor
	Mouse or other pointer device

WordPerfect provides support for fax boards and fax modems so that documents can be faxed or received directly from the WordPerfect program. Also, WordPerfect supports over 20 sound devices enabling users to create documents that incorporate sound.

Hard disk and floppy disks

What are Disks?

Disks are storage devices. Information that is processed and used by a computer must be stored on either a hard or floppy disk. Since the computer's memory is temporary, all programs and data are erased when the computer is turned off. Therefore disks are used to store programs and data.

A hard disk is rigid, resides inside the computer, and is not removed by the user. Programs are normally stored on a hard disk. A floppy disk is flexible and can be handled by the user. Floppy disks are generally used to store data or files. The most commonly used disk sizes are 5.25 and 3.5 inches (see Figure I.2).

Information that has been created is saved on a floppy or hard disk. A floppy disk is referred to as a file disk or data disk. Information such as a letter, memorandum, or statistical data must be saved. If the information is not saved on a disk, the information will be lost from the computer's temporary memory when the computer is turned off. When a copy of the information is transferred from the computer's memory to a disk, the process is called saving. Saving information to a disk is also called "writing" to a disk.

Care for Floppy Disks

Floppy disks should be labeled using a felt-tip pen. Store disks in a dry, protected location. Avoid dust, smoke, bending and extreme temperatures; keep disks out of the sun and away from beverage containers! Any magnet or magnetized object can damage the data on a disk: avoid using a paper clip on a disk—especially a paper clip that has been stored in a holder with a magnetized ring at the top.

Before information can be saved on a disk, the disk must be formatted (prepared) with electronic instructions to partition the disk into storage areas, create a directory, check for disk defects, etc.

The formatting process is usually performed only once. If a disk is formatted a second time, all information previously saved on the disk is erased.

Steps to ▶ Format a File Disk Using a Hard Disk

1. If necessary, turn on the computer.

2. The C:\ prompt is displayed on the screen.

3. If the disk to be formatted is in drive A, type **format a:**; if the disk to be formatted is in drive B, type **format b:**.

4. Press **Enter**.

5. The message displays: Insert new diskette for drive A: (B:) and press ENTER when ready. Insert a new or used diskette in disk drive A or B.

   Note: If a used disk is formatted, any information on the disk is erased.

6. Press **Enter**.

7. A message displays: Checking existing disk format... or Formatting...; wait a few moments.

   Note: During the formatting process, watch the disk drive light illuminate while instructions are copied from one disk to another.

8. A message displays: Volume label (11 characters, ENTER for none)?

9. Press **Enter**.

10. When formatting is completed, a statement displays indicating that the formatting is complete and a question that asks, Format another (Y/N)?

11. Press **n** for No.

12. Press **Enter**.

    Note: The C:\prompt displays.

What is DOS?

DOS is the disk operating system for IBM PC and compatible microcomputers. DOS is a collection of related programs that control and manage computer operations. DOS is necessary to handle the temporary storage and processing of information and directs the orderly transfer or sharing of information between the computer unit and the disk, monitor, keyboard, printer, etc. In order for the computer to operate, the DOS programs must be accessible when the computer is turned on. Generally, DOS programs are stored on the hard disk.

What are Directories and Paths?

A directory is a named location on a disk where a group of files is stored. A directory is used to keep files organized in separate areas on the disk under different directory names. Application programs such as word processing, spreadsheet, and database programs are usually stored on the computer's hard disk. The files for each application program can be kept together in one directory location under the directory name. For example, all the WordPerfect program files are stored in a directory named WP60.

Other directories can be created under the WP60 directory. Any directories created in the WP60 directory are subdirectories. For example, if the subdirectory named MEMOS was created, MEMOS would be a subdirectory of the WP60 directory.

A path is a route from the DOS prompt to the location of a file. For example, a file named MEM3 that is located in the subdirectory named MEMOS that is in the WP60 directory can be accessed by typing the path from the DOS prompt: C:\WP60\MEMOS\MEM3. However, if using WordPerfect, the various directories and subdirectories can be accessed easily by using the File Manager.

File Names

Every file to be saved is assigned a filename. Filenames can contain one to eight characters and, if desired, a filename extension of one to three characters. The filename extension is separated from the first 1-8 characters by a period. For example, *morris.ltr* or *martin.ltr* are valid filenames. However, morganstern.ltr is not a valid filename because there are more than eight characters before the filename extension.

Any letter (a-z) or number (0-9) and most symbols can be used in a filename. A filename cannot contain spaces, commas, backslashes, asterisks, or a second period.

A filename should represent the information and/or person's name contained in the file. For example, a letter written to Gerry Anderson concerning a tax assessment could be assigned the name *g-andsn.tax* or *anderson.ltr*.

What is WordPerfect 6.0?

The WordPerfect word-processing program is one of the most popular programs in the world. WordPerfect 6.0 is the most current version of WordPerfect in the DOS environment. In addition to the WordPerfect DOS-based program, a WordPerfect for Windows program is available. WordPerfect for DOS and WordPerfect for Windows contain many common elements such as a Menu bar, Button Bars, Ribbon, and dialog boxes that enable the user to more quickly and efficiently perform editing, saving, text formatting, etc.

The Mouse (Pointer Device)

There are various types of pointer devices. The mouse pointer device and the track ball are presently the most popular. The mouse is a hand-held device used to move an arrow or rectangle symbol (pointer symbol) on the screen. The mouse pointer is moved over the screen area until the pointer symbol reaches the item or items to be selected. The left button on the mouse device is pressed to initiate the desired action, such as selecting options, sizing windows, formatting text, or creating objects.

The mouse is held between the thumb and little finger. The index finger or middle finger is used to press the mouse buttons. To maintain consistent control of the mouse, hold the mouse motionless when pressing the mouse buttons.

When the mouse is moved over a flat surface, the pointer symbol moves in the same direction on the screen. When the mouse reaches the edge of the flat surface, the mouse is held firmly, lifted, and relocated. Also, alternating between a short rubbing stroke and lifting the mouse slightly using wrist movement can be very helpful when the mouse reaches the flat surface edge.

The track ball pointer device is stationary and the "ball" is moved by a finger or the palm of the hand. The track ball can be built into the keyboard or can be connected to the computer via a cable.

The mouse pointer changes shape depending on the view mode selected. In Graphics or Page mode view, the pointer is an arrow. The pointer symbol also changes to a two-

Used to choose commands and displays in the Graphics or Page mode views.

Indicates that a graphics box or window can be moved.

Used to choose commands and displays in the text mode view.

Indicates that a graphics box or window can be sized.

headed or four-headed arrow when moving and/or sizing graphics boxes or windows (see chapters 14 and 17). In text mode, the pointer is a highlighted rectangle. The mouse pointer shapes are shown in Figure I.3.

Different techniques are used to initiate an action with the pointer device. The following list shows the basic actions:

Click	Press the left button once and release.
Double-click	Press the left button twice rapidly.
Drag	Press and hold down the left button while moving the mouse or trackball.
Point	Move the pointer to a specific position on the screen.

The WordPerfect Document Window

The WordPerfect document window displays after the program is loaded. Each part of the window is shown in Figure I.4. The menu bar is a list of drop-down menu names that are displayed at the top of the WordPerfect document window after the WordPerfect program is loaded. Each menu in the Menu bar contains commands that are used to instruct WordPerfect to perform specific functions. Each drop-down menu has a list of additional menu commands that are accessed easily by pointing and clicking the mouse or by pressing a designated letter from the keyboard. When a menu "drops down," the first item listed is highlighted. An underline displays beneath one letter in each menu command that can be used to select the option. Some menu commands are followed by three periods (**Save As...**) or a right

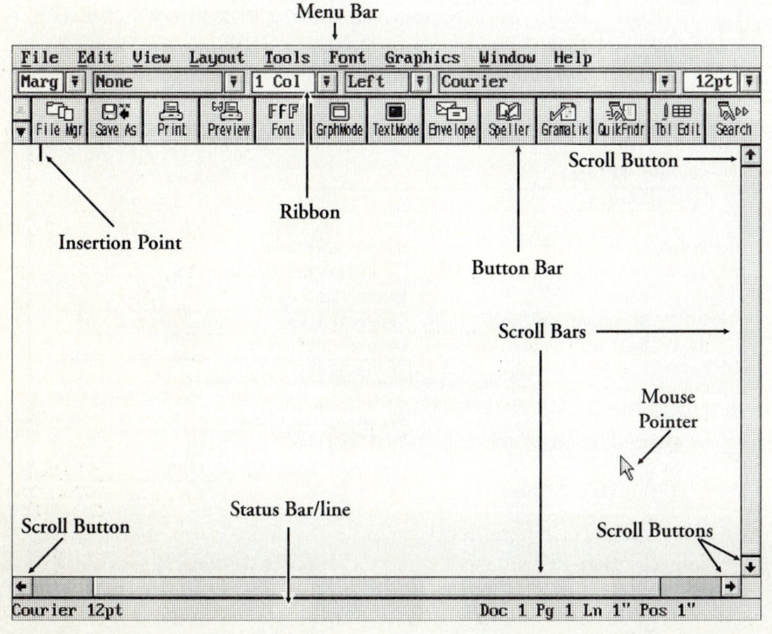

WordPerfect 6.0 document window in graphics mode

arrow to indicate that, if selected, a dialog box or list of additional commands will display.

A Button Bar, usually containing small pictures and text, can be displayed and is used to quickly activate frequently used functions. Once the button is selected, a dialog box displays or the function is performed immediately. (In Text mode view, the Button Bar contains only text, no pictures.)

A Ribbon can be displayed and is used to quickly format text such as fonts, point sizes, columns, and justification. The Ribbon also contains a button to access styles (see Chapter 16) and a button to change the display size of text on the screen.

The Button Bar and Ribbon are not defaulted to display on the screen. However, by selecting the **View** menu the user can choose to display the Button Bar and/or Ribbon. A checkmark beside the bar name in the **View** menu indicates that the bar is displayed. If desired, the Button Bar and/or Ribbon can be removed from the screen in order to see more of a document on the screen. The Button Bar and/or Ribbon can be chosen to display when the program is loaded.

Dialog Boxes

Dialog boxes enable the user to provide WordPerfect with additional instructions. The dialog boxes display after menu commands or Button Bar buttons are selected. For example, when the **Print** button or **File, Print/Fax** is selected, the Print/Fax dialog box displays (see Figure I.5).

In a dialog box, instructions are supplied to the program by selecting from a list of options, and/or by typing information. Often a dialog box contains commands that are followed by three periods (...). When these commands are selected, a second dialog box with additional options displays. The second dialog box allows the user to provide more specific information on how a command is to be accomplished.

Print/Fax dialog box

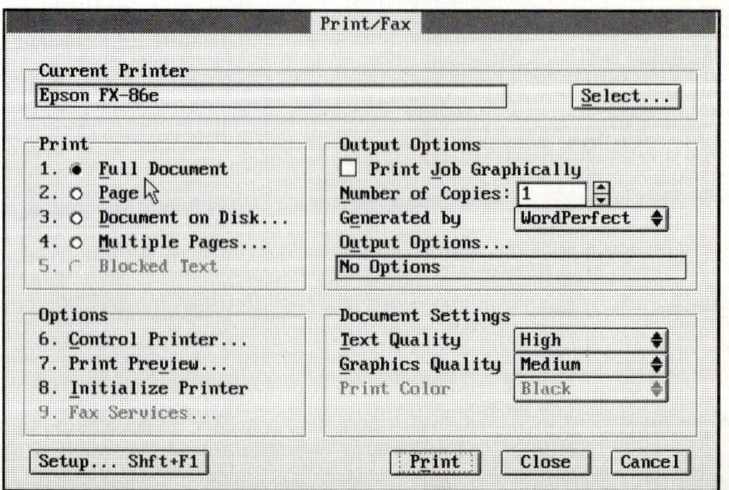

Part 1
The Beginning Step

Create and Edit Business Documents

Chapters 1-4

- Open WordPerfect
- Display the Button Bar and Ribbon
- Center text
- Reveal Codes
- Scroll bars
- Print a document
- Save
- Close a document
- Exit WordPerfect
- Open a document
- Block text
- Delete and insert text
- Undo
- Vertical line spacing
- Justification
- Bold, underline, and italic text attributes
- Help feature
- Change margins
- Font changes
- Print Preview
- Speller

Create a Memorandum

Features Covered

- Load WordPerfect
- Change the View (display) mode
- Display the Button Bar and Ribbon
- Display Reveal Codes
- Save a file
- Print
- Use horizontal and vertical scroll bars
- Close a document
- Exit WordPerfect

Objectives

After successfully completing this chapter, you will be able to load the WordPerfect program; display the Button Bar and Ribbon; understand and display Reveal Codes; save, print, and close documents; and view different portions of a document using the scroll bars. These skills will be used to create and format two different styles of interoffice memorandums.

Chapter Introduction

Instructions for typing and formatting a memorandum while using WordPerfect will be presented in this chapter. Before a memorandum can be typed and formatted, the program is loaded. Loading is the process of transferring the WordPerfect program from the hard disk to the computer's memory.

WordPerfect 6.0 text mode
document window

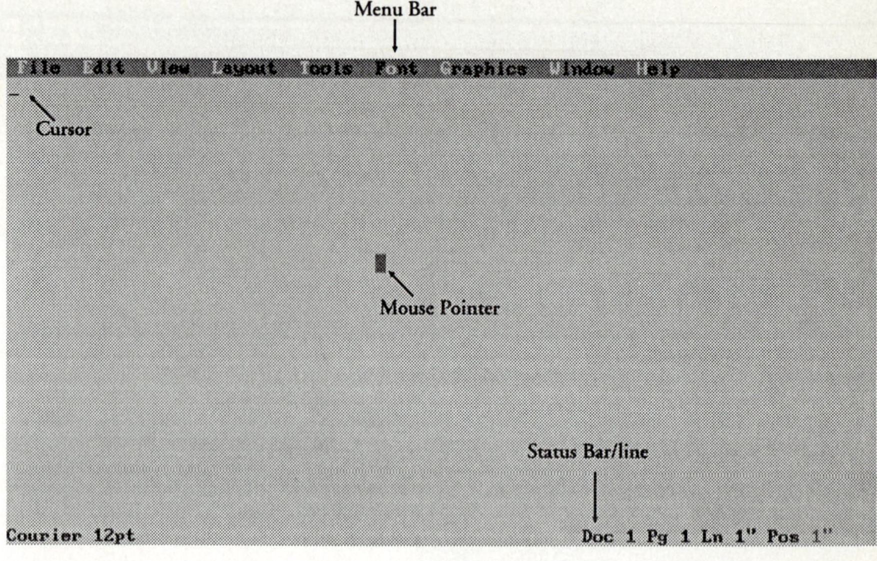

Load WordPerfect

The WordPerfect program is loaded from the C:\ prompt. Usually the WordPerfect program is stored in a directory named WP60. When the WordPerfect 6.0 program is located, the WordPerfect document window displays with a Menu bar at the top of the screen and a Status bar at the bottom of the screen (see Figure 1.1). See the Introduction for additional information concerning the WordPerfect document window.

*Note: The first set of instructions in each step-by-step instruction in this textbook uses the mouse/trackball device. Place the mouse pointer on the option desired; press the left mouse button (click once) to select. The instructions for **using the keyboard keys** immediately follow the instructions for using the mouse and are indicated in braces { }, e.g., {Alt and v, r}.*

Load the WordPerfect Program

1. Turn on the computer and monitor.

2. When the C:\ prompt is displayed on the screen, type **cd wp60** and press **Enter**. Type **wp** and press **Enter** again. (If your computer has a different method for loading the program, see your instructor or instructional assistant.)

   Note: The copyright screen displays briefly, then the WordPerfect document window displays (see Figure 1.1).

3. Place a formatted file disk in drive A or B.

Chapter 1—Create a Memorandum

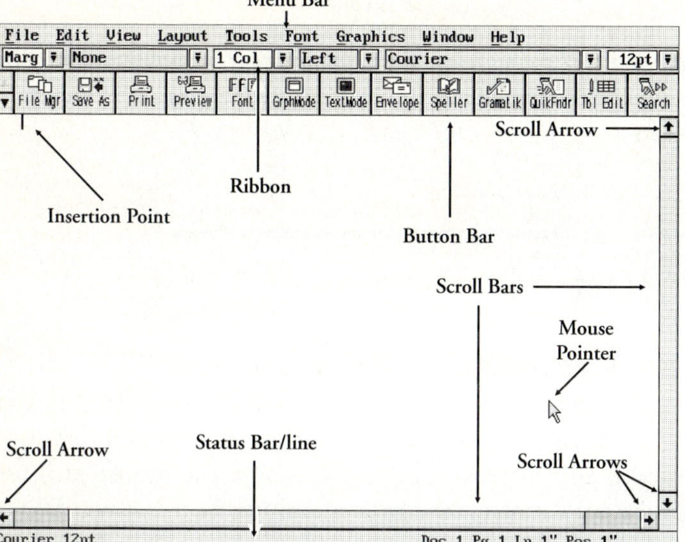

FIGURE 1.2

WordPerfect 6.0 document window in graphics mode

Display Modes

WordPerfect provides three different modes for displaying text on the screen, i.e., text mode, graphics mode, and page mode. Text mode displays characters mono-spaced (each character or symbol occupies the same amount of space) similar to the way characters are displayed when typing commands at the DOS prompt. Graphics mode displays characters as they will print with italic, bold, underline, etc. Also, graphics mode displays pictures that can be sized and moved with the mouse (see Chapter 14). Page mode is similar to graphics mode, displaying the text on the entire page with bold, italic, and underline, etc. Page mode also displays headers, footers, and footnotes that cannot be seen on the screen in either text or graphics mode.

In this book, most activities will be accomplished using the graphics mode because the graphics mode closely illustrates the document as it will appear when printed. The term WYSIWYG, what you see is what you get (pronounced wizzy-wig), is used to describe the display of text and graphics as they will print.

In the text mode, your screen will look similar to Figure 1.1. In the graphics or page mode, your screen will look similar to Figure 1.2. Keep in mind that the Ribbon and Button Bar can be removed *or* displayed on the screen. The buttons on the Button Bar can be customized by the user, and therefore, may appear different from the *WPMAIN* Button Bar shown in Figure 1.3.

Change Display Modes

1. Select the **View** menu {Alt and v}.

   Note: An asterisk displays beside the current mode.

2. Select the desired display mode.

For example, select Graphics Mode {g}.

Note: After a few moments the document window changes from one mode to another. The document window in text mode usually displays with a royal blue background and the graphics and page modes display with a white background.

Cursor/Insertion Point

In the text mode, the cursor appears as a blinking horizontal line. In the graphics or page mode, the cursor appears as a blinking vertical line and is referred to as an insertion point. If a mouse or other pointer device is attached to your computer, a pointer symbol will also display. In the text mode, the mouse pointer is a rectangle, and in the graphics/page modes, the mouse pointer is an arrow. The cursor/insertion point indicates the location where the next action takes place. The cursor displays beneath characters and spaces. The insertion point displays between characters and spaces. The cursor/insertion point will move to characters and lines that have been typed. The cursor/insertion point will not move into blank space unless the **Enter** key or **Spacebar** is pressed. As the **Enter** key or **Spacebar** is pressed or text is typed, the cursor/insertion point moves. See also Steps to Move the Cursor/Insertion Point Quickly From One Point to Another, page 25.

The pointer symbol moves around the screen as the mouse is moved on the desktop. The mouse device can also be used to move the cursor/insertion point by placing the pointer at the desired location and pressing (clicking) the left mouse button once. The direction (arrow) keys on the 10-key numeric keypad are used to move the cursor/insertion point up, down, left, or right one character or line at a time. *NumLock* must be turned off. On many keyboards, a duplicate set of arrow keys is provided on separate keys.

The Button Bar

WordPerfect provides an easy way to access frequently used commands such as **Print** and **Save As** via the *Button Bar* (see Figure 1.3). The Button Bar is a row of buttons that can display below the Menu bar. A mouse must be used to select the Button Bar options.

When WordPerfect is initially placed (installed) on the computer, the Button Bar is not displayed. Many users, however, choose to display the WordPerfect main Button Bar. The main Button Bar is the preset (default) Button Bar that contains options for working more quickly with WordPerfect features. Other Button Bars that contain different options will be accessed in later chapters. Different Button Bars are selected by choosing **View**, **Button Bar Setup**, **Select** to display a list of available Button Bars. Double-click on the desired Button Bar name. The WPMAIN Button Bar is often selected because it contains the buttons for many commonly used features.

The Button Bar

View the Button Bar

1. Select the **View** menu {Alt and v}.
2. Select **Button Bar** {b}.

   Note: When the Button Bar is displayed, a check mark appears beside the Button Bar option in the View menu. By selecting the View, Button Bar option again, the Button Bar will be removed from the screen.

View the Ribbon

ARibbon with option buttons can be displayed on the screen below the Menu bar (see Figure 1.4). The Ribbon option buttons represent commonly used formatting features such as fonts, point size, justification, columns, and paragraph styles. (Styles are discussed in Chapter 16.) A Zoom button is also available to change the display of the text on the screen. When an option on the Ribbon is selected, a drop-down list of choices for that option displays.

When WordPerfect is initially placed (installed) on the computer, the Ribbon does not automatically display. The Ribbon can be set to display by changing the Screen Setup option in the **View** menu.

Display the Ribbon

1. Select the **View** menu {Alt and v}.
2. Select **Ribbon** {r}.

The Ribbon

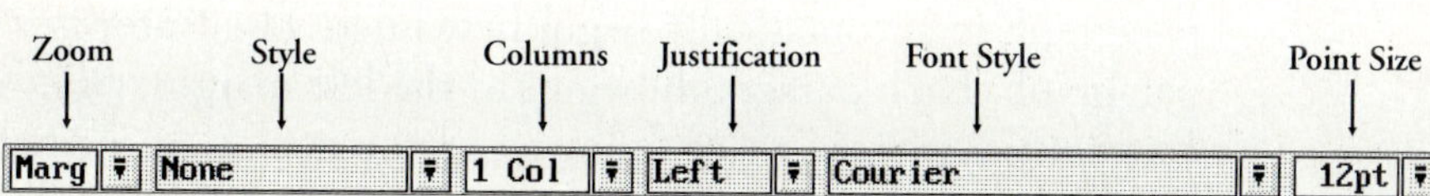

Formatting

ormatting is the process of determining the placement and arrangement of a document when it is printed on a page. The arrangement of a document includes the amount of blank space in the left, right, top, and bottom margins. Formatting also includes alignment, underline/bold text, capitalization, and the number of vertical and horizontal spaces used between words and lines.

The purpose of formatting is to arrange text in a manner that is attractive and easy to read. This textbook includes information on formatting memorandums, letters, tables, reports, mailing labels, newsletters, reports, etc.

In this chapter, formatting using different justification options will be introduced to create memorandum styles. The Center and Flush Right alignment options will be discussed, as well as the format for the main text of a memorandum, called "body text." The justification options and body text format will be used throughout this book.

Wordwrap

One automatic formatting feature of word processing programs is wordwrap. As you type text, the **Enter** key is pressed only at the end of a paragraph or short line. When text reaches the right margin, the cursor/insertion point automatically returns to the beginning of the next line. This automatic return feature is called *wordwrap*.

When wordwrap is used, a hidden code, [SRt] (soft return), is inserted at the end of each line. The hidden code can be viewed by using the Reveal Codes features (see Reveal Codes on page 18). Wordwrap automatically formats the document paragraph to adjust to the margins. If words are inserted or deleted from the paragraph, text automatically readjusts to the margins.

Memorandum—Style 1

here are many acceptable formats for memorandums. In a traditional memorandum, the heading *Memorandum, Memo,* or *Interoffice Correspondence* is typed or preprinted at the top of the page. The memorandum heading is followed by the recipient's name, author's name, date, and subject. The words, *To:, From:, Date:,* and *Subject:* usually precede the recipient's, author's name, the date and subject and are called lead words. The lead words can be typed in the memorandum or preprinted on paper.

The main text of the memorandum (body text) is typed using wordwrap within each paragraph to automatically begin new lines. The **Enter** key is pressed twice after each paragraph. Each paragraph begins at the left margin. After the final paragraph, the **Enter** key is pressed twice followed by the initials of the person typing the memorandum.

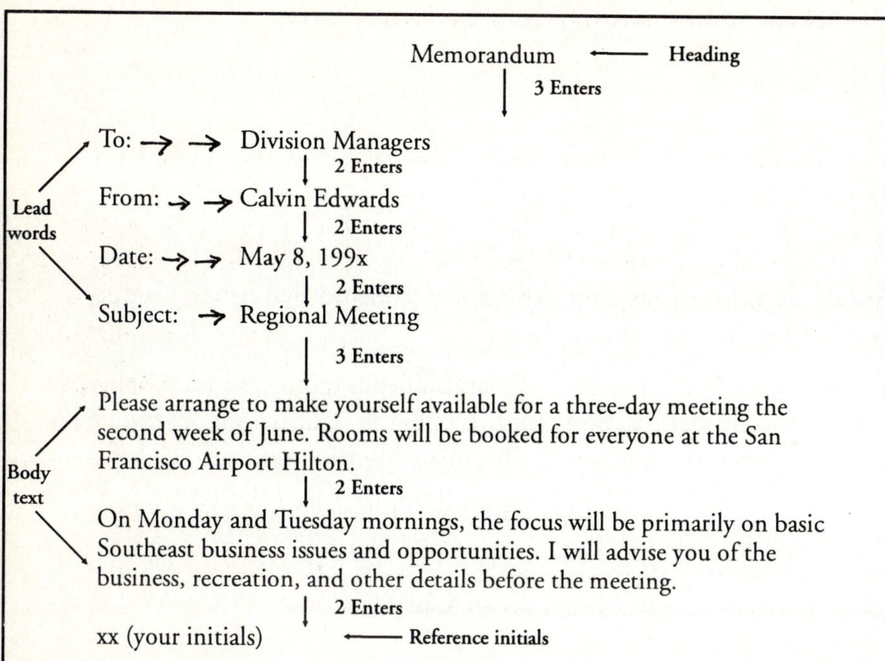

FIGURE 1.5

Memorandum—Style 1

Start-Up Instructions

- ❖ Use the following information to create the memorandum shown in Figure 1.5.
- ❖ The Button Bar and Ribbon should be displayed (select **View**, **Button Bar** and/or **View**, **Ribbon**).

Use Center Alignment (Horizontal Centering)

1. The cursor/insertion point should be located on the left side of the screen.
2. Select **Layout, Alignment, Center** {Shift and F6}.

   Note: The cursor/insertion point moves to the middle of the document window.
3. Type the word(s) to be centered.

   For example, type **Memorandum**.
4. Press **Enter** once.

   Note: The word(s) are now horizontally centered on the screen and a hidden center code is placed in the document. (See Reveal Codes on page 18.) The cursor/insertion point is now located at the left margin one line below the heading.

Start-Up Instructions

- ❖ Press the **Enter** key two more times to create two blank lines after the heading.
- ❖ Backspace to correct errors made while typing. For now, ignore any errors noticed after the memorandum is typed.
- ❖ Use wordwrap when typing the body text paragraphs.

   Note: The paragraph lines may not end with the same words as shown in Figure 1.5.

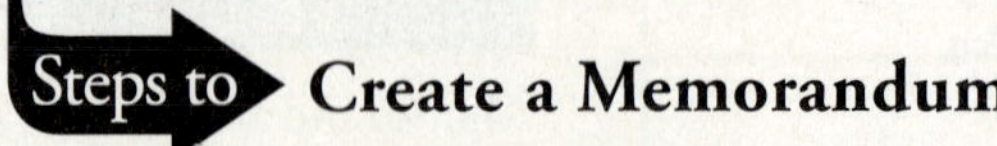 **Create a Memorandum**

1. Press the Tab key once or twice after the lead words as shown in Figure 1.5.

   Note: The Tab key is pressed once or twice after the lead words in order to align the heading information. Visually check that the information following the lead words is aligned.

2. Press the Enter key three times after the subject line and two times after each paragraph including the last paragraph.

3. With the cursor/insertion point at the left margin, begin typing the text of the first paragraph. When the cursor/insertion point reaches the right margin, continue typing. Wordwrap will automatically return the cursor/insertion point to the left margin.

4. Two Enters below the last paragraphs, type your initials in lowercase letters.

Reveal Codes

When formatting options such as Center alignment are selected, WordPerfect places *hidden* codes in the document. To view these codes on the screen, use the Reveal Codes feature. When Reveal Codes is activated, the screen is divided into two sections. The regular document window with the typed document displays at the top of the screen. The document text and formatting (hidden) codes display at the bottom of the screen. This section is known as the Reveal Codes screen. The first code displayed in the Reveal Codes screen is [Open Style:Initial Codes] (see Chapters 15 and 16).

The Reveal Codes screen is routinely used to identify codes. The exact position of the cursor/insertion point is indicated by a shaded or black block. The movement of the shaded/black block in the Reveal Codes screen corresponds to the movement of the cursor/insertion point in the document window.

Two of the most frequently inserted codes are [SRt] and [HRt]. A soft return [SRt] occurs automatically each time wordwrap returns the insertion point to the left margin. A hard return [HRt] occurs each time the Enter key is pressed.

Start-Up Instructions

❖ Press the up arrow key repeatedly to move the cursor/insertion point to the top of the document.

 **Turn on Reveal Codes**

1. Select **View, Reveal Codes** {Alt and F3}.

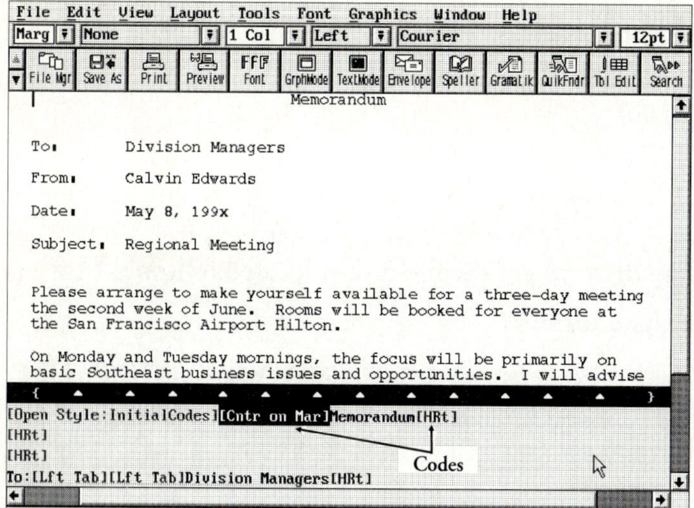

Note: The screen is divided into two sections: the document window at the top and the Reveal Codes screen at the bottom (see Figure 1.6). Notice that the cursor/insertion point in the document window and the shaded/black block in the Reveal Codes screen are located at the exact same position in the document. Press the down arrow key repeatedly to move the cursor/insertion point in the document window and Reveal Codes screen.

Turn Off Reveal Codes

1. When the Reveal Codes screen is displayed on the screen, selecting View, Reveal Codes will remove the Reveal Codes screen {Alt and F3}.

Save a File and Access a Disk Drive

Accessing a disk drive is the process of directing the computer to activate the disk drive where the file disk is located. When a computer with a hard disk is turned on and no disk is in drive A, the computer accesses drive C. Because the file disk is placed in drive A or B, it is necessary to tell the computer to activate drive A or B. Once a disk drive is accessed, the program saves and opens files from the accessed drive.

After a document is created, save the document to the file disk. Saving is the process of transferring the document from the computer's memory to the file disk. Usually, a document is saved to a floppy disk in either drive A or B. When the document is saved, the appropriate drive is accessed.

Access a Disk Drive

1. Place a file disk in the A or B disk drive.

2. Select the File Mgr (File Manager) button on the Button Bar {F5}.

    Note: The current location for saving is displayed in the Specify File Manager List dialog box, e.g., C:\WPDOCS.

3. Press the equals key (=).

    Note: New Directory: C:\WPDOCS displays in the Change Default Directory dialog box.

4. Type the letter of the drive where the file disk is located followed by a colon.

    For example, type a: or b:.

    Note: When a character is typed, the drive letter displayed will be replaced by the character typed.

5. Select OK {press Enter}.

6. Select Cancel {press Esc}.

Steps to ► Save a File

Note: A file disk should be in the A or B disk drive.

1. Select File, Save {press Alt and f, s *or* press Ctrl and F12}

2. Type a filename with eight characters or less (no spaces).

    For example, type **1drill1**. (Do not type the period.)

    *Note: Check the accuracy of the filename before selecting **OK** or pressing **Enter**.*

3. Select OK {press Enter}.

    Note: The document is saved on the file disk that is located in the accessed disk drive. The document name is displayed in the bottom left of the WordPerfect document window, e.g., A:\1DRILL1.

    *Note: If the message displays, "Replace a:\1drill1?", select **Yes** to replace or select **No** to return to the Save Document dialog box and type a new filename.*

Print a Document

A document can be printed by using the **File**, **Print/Fax** command or by selecting the **Print** button on the Button Bar. After **OK** is selected in the Print dialog box, the entire document will be printed. Individual pages or sections of a document can be printed if desired. Additional information concerning printing is discussed in Chapters 5 and 10.

Steps to ► Print a Document

1. The printer should be turned on. If you are sharing a printer, check that the switch box or local area network printer is selected for your printer.

2. The document to be printed is displayed on the screen.

3. Select **File, Print/Fax** {Shift and F7}.

4. Select **Print** to print the document {press Enter}.

Button Bar Shortcut

1. Select the **Print** button on the Button Bar. Select **Print**

Close a Document

Once a document has been typed, saved, and printed, the document is usually cleared from the document window before a new document is begun. However, more than one document window can be displayed on the screen at one time. (See Chapter 17, The WordPerfect Windows.) Closing a document is often referred to as *clearing a document* from the screen. After a document is closed, a blank WordPerfect document window displays and a new document can be typed or an existing document can be opened. If more than one document has been opened, you may need to close additional document windows or select **File**, **New** to obtain a clear document window.

Close a Document

1. Select **File, Close** {press Alt and f, c}. The document will be removed from the document screen.

   Note: If a message displays, "Save changes to...?", select No {press n} to close without saving changes. Repeat Step 1 if more than one window is open.

Memorandum—Style 2

Memorandum—Style 2 illustrates a second acceptable memo format. The lead words and body text format are the same as Memorandum—Style 1. However, the heading "INTEROFFICE CORRESPONDENCE" is used, and the lead words are arranged on only two lines. See Figure 1.7.

In this memorandum style, the date and subject are typed at the right margin. The Flush Right alignment feature is used to move the cursor/insertion point to the right margin. As text is typed, the cursor/insertion point moves back towards the left margin. The final character in the line is located at the right margin. When **Enter** is pressed, the cursor/insertion point returns to the left margin.

The lead word "To:" is followed by the recipient's name or a name that identifies a group of individuals, e.g., sales representatives, district managers, etc. A distribution list can be typed after the body text identifying the individuals who are part of the group. If copies of the memo are to be sent to other individuals, the notation "c:" is typed below the distribution list.

Start-Up Instructions

❖ Use the following steps to type the memorandum shown in Figure 1.7.

❖ Use center alignment (**Shift** and **F6**) before typing the memorandum heading.

Steps to ▶ **Use Caps Lock**

1. Press the **Caps Lock** key once to turn Caps Lock on. With the mouse pointer located below the Button Bar, notice that "POS" in the Status bar at the bottom right side of the screen displays in uppercase letters to show that Caps Lock is turned on.

2. Type the desired text.

   For example, type **INTEROFFICE CORRESPONDENCE.** (Do not type the period.)

3. Press the **Caps Lock** key once to turn Caps Lock off. Notice that "Pos" now displays with a capital "P" and lowercase "os" in the Status bar at the bottom right side of the screen.

4. Press the **Enter** key the desired number of times after the heading.

   For example, press the **Enter** key three times.

5. Type the lead word followed by a colon.

   For example, type **To:**. (Do not type the period.)

6. Press the **Tab** key once or twice and estimate that the text following the lead words will align.

   For example, press the **Tab** key twice.

7. Type the text that will follow the lead word.

   For example, type **Sales Representatives**.

Steps to ▶ **Use Flush Right Alignment**

1. Select **Layout, Alignment, Flush Right** {Alt and F6}.

   Note: The insertion point moves to the right margin. As text is typed, the cursor/insertion point will move back towards the left margin.

2. Type the desired text.

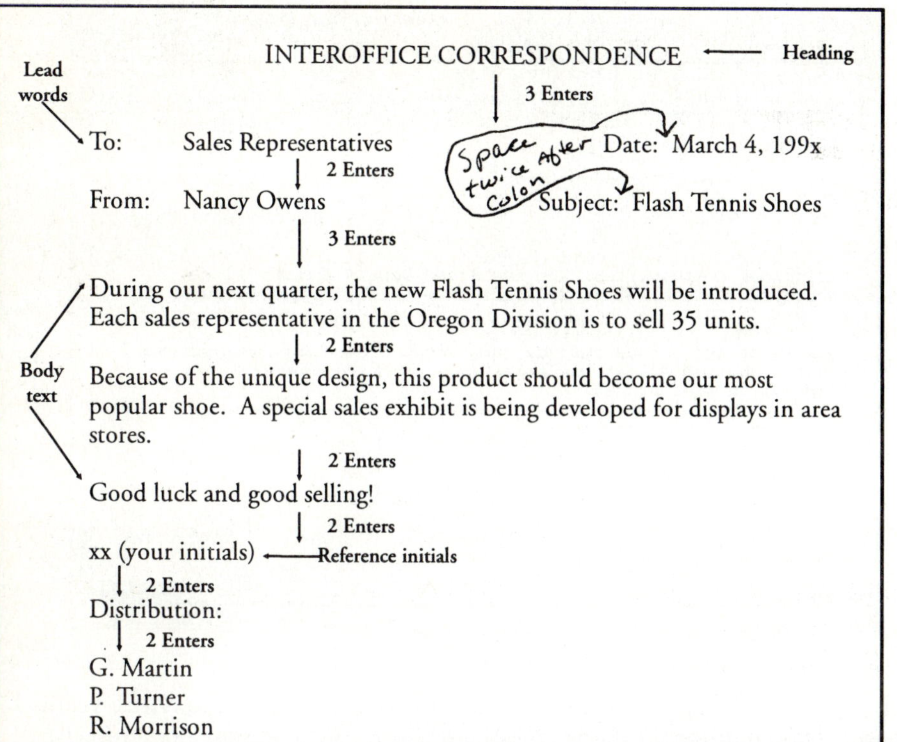

For example, type the lead word **Date** followed by a colon, two spaces, and the current date. Press the **Enter** key twice.

Finish-Up Instructions

- ❖ Continue to type the memorandum with the spacing shown in Figure 1.7.
- ❖ Save the memorandum on your file disk; use the filename **1drill2**—Chapter 1, drill 2. (Select the **File, Save**, type the drive letter where your file disk is located followed by a colon and the filename, select **OK**.)
- ❖ Print one copy (select the **Print** button on the Button Bar, choose **Print**).

Scrolling Horizontally and Vertically

Scrolling is the process of moving text quickly up, down, left, or right in order to view parts of the document not displayed in the document window. A vertical scroll bar can be located at the right of the screen and/or a horizontal scroll bar can be displayed at the bottom of the screen. Each scroll bar contains a scroll box and scroll arrows (controlled by the mouse) that can be used to view various part of a document. See Figure 1.8. Use the **View** menu to display the horizontal and vertical scroll bars. A checkmark displays next to the selected option. If the option is selected again, the checkmark is removed from the option, thus removing the scroll bar from the screen.

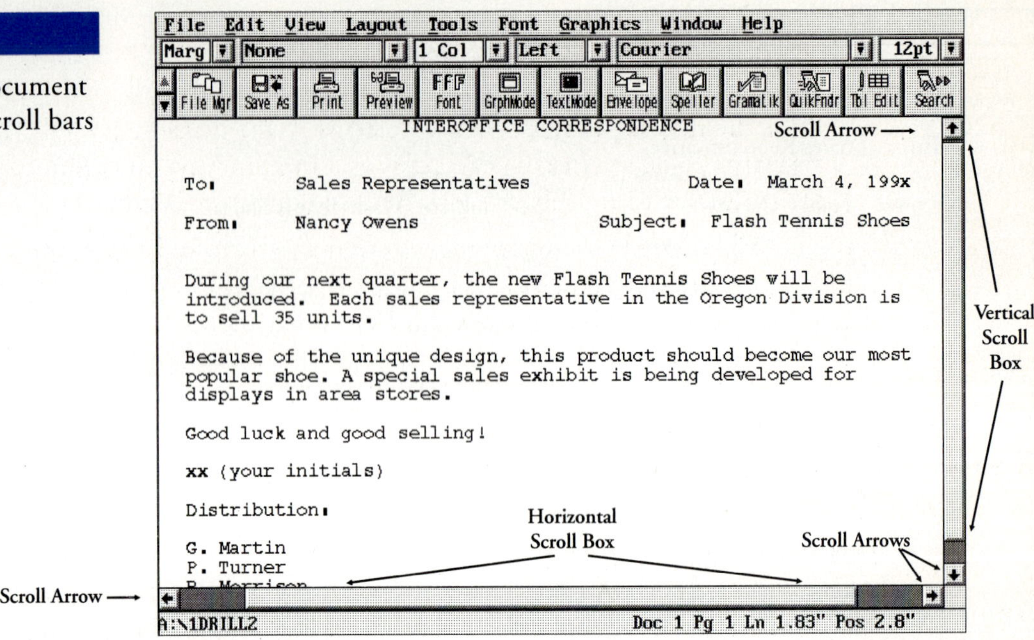

If a document is short, the vertical scroll box can fill (or nearly fill) the entire vertical scroll bar. In this case, clicking on the up or down scroll arrow moves the cursor/insertion point up or down one line. Also, the width of the horizontal scroll box displays the width of the document. By clicking on the left or right horizontal scroll arrows, the cursor/insertion point moves left or right one character.

Start-Up Instructions

❖ With the file named **1drill2** on the screen, use the following steps to practice vertical and horizontal scrolling.

❖ Press the up arrow key repeatedly to move the cursor/insertion point to the top of the document.

View the Horizontal and Vertical Scroll Bars

1. Select **View, Horizontal Scroll Bar** {Alt and v, h}.
2. Select **View, Vertical Scroll Bar** {Alt and v, v}.

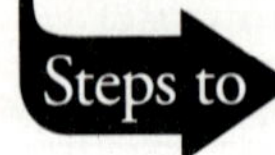
Use the Mouse for Vertical or Horizontal Scrolling

1. Place the mouse pointer on the scroll box in the vertical scroll bar on the right side of the document window; press and hold the left mouse button, then drag the scroll box up or down to scroll. Release the mouse button.

   For example, move the mouse pointer to the vertical scroll box; press and hold the left mouse button while dragging the box down; release the mouse button.

2. Place the mouse pointer on the scroll box in the horizontal scroll bar at the bottom of the document window; press and hold the left mouse button and drag the scroll box to the left or right. Release the mouse button.

    For example, move the mouse pointer to the scroll box in the horizontal scroll bar; press and hold the left mouse button while dragging the box to the right. Release the mouse button.

Moving the Cursor/Insertion Point

To relocate the cursor/insertion point to various parts of the document, use the arrow keys or move the mouse pointer and click at the desired location. For example, the mouse can be used to relocate the cursor/insertion point to any position in the document by pointing on the desired position and clicking once. The up, down, left, and right arrow keys as well as the **Page Up** (PgUp), **Page Down** (PgDn), **Home**, and **End** keys can also be used to relocate the cursor/insertion point.

Move the Cursor/Insertion Point Quickly From One Point to Another

Using the Mouse

1. Move the mouse pointer to any location in the document and click. The cursor/insertion point moves to that location.

    Note: See Steps to Use the Mouse for Vertical and Horizontal Scrolling on page 24.

Using the Keyboard

1. To move the cursor/insertion point to the left side of a line, press the **Home** key and then press the **left arrow** key.

2. To move the cursor/insertion point to the right side of a line, press the **Home** key and then press the **right arrow** key.

    *Shortcut: Press the **End** key.*

3. To move the cursor/insertion point to the first character in the document, press the **Home** key twice and then press the **up arrow** key once.

    *Note: Press the **Home** key three times and then press the **up arrow** key to move the cursor/insertion point to the right of [Open Style:Initial Code] and in front of any inserted codes that could be at the top of the document.*

4. To move the cursor/insertion point to the last character in the document, press the **Home** key twice and then press the **down arrow** key.

5. To move the cursor/insertion point to the top of the document window, press the Home key once and then the up arrow key once.

6. To move the cursor/insertion point to the bottom of the document window, press the Home key once and then press the down arrow key once.

7. To move the cursor/insertion point to the left one word, press the Ctrl and left arrow keys.

8. To move the cursor/insertion point to the right one word, press the Ctrl and right arrow keys.

9. To move the cursor/insertion point to the top of the previous page, press Page Up.

10. To move the cursor/insertion point to the top of the next page, press Page Down.

11. To move the cursor/insertion point to a different page, press Ctrl and Home (Go To), type the page number desired, press Enter.

Exit WordPerfect

After completing your work, the WordPerfect program is exited and the cursor returned to the system prompt, e.g., C:\. Remember to always save your files before exiting the WordPerfect program.

Exit WordPerfect

Note: If necessary, save your file before exiting the WordPerfect program using the Steps to Save a File on page 20.

1. Select File, Exit WP {Home, F7}.

   Note: A list of one or all open documents displays.

2. *If an X displays in the Save box,* click on the X to "unmark" and *not* save the file {press the letter in the Save box}.

   If an X does not display in the Save box, go to Step 3.

3. Select Exit {press Enter}.

   Note: If a message displays, "Do you want to save changes to...?", select Yes to save changes or select No to abandon changes.

The Next Step

Chapter Review and Activities

FEATURES SUMMARY

FEATURES	ACTIONS	PAGE
Load WordPerfect	Type **cd wp60**, press **Enter**, type **wp**, press **Enter** again.	12
Change display modes	Select **View**, choose desired display mode.	13
View the Button Bar	Select **View, Button Bar.**	15
View the Ribbon	Select **View, Ribbon.**	15
Center alignment	Select **Layout, Alignment, Center.**	17
Reveal Codes	Select **View, Reveal Codes** or press **Alt** and **F3.**	18
Access a disk drive	Select the **File Mgr** button, press the = key, type the drive letter where the file disk is located, select **OK**, select **Cancel.**	19
Save a file	Select **File, Save**, type the filename, select **OK.**	20
Print a document	Select **File, Print, Print** or select the **Print** button and choose **Print** or press **Shift** and **F7, Enter.**	20
Close a document	Select **File, Close.**	21
Caps Lock	Press the **Caps Lock** key.	22
Flush Right alignment	Select **Layout, Alignment, Flush Right** or press **Alt** and **F6.**	22

Self-Check Questions

True/False—Circle One

T F 1. Loading is the process of transferring the WordPerfect program to a file disk.

T F 2. Before a file is saved, the disk drive where the file disk is located should be accessed.

T F 3. When the Backspace key is pressed, the character to the right of the cursor/insertion point is erased.

T F 4. To center a line of text, select **Layout**, **Alignment**, **Center**.

T F 5. To print all the text in a file, select **File**, **Print Preview**.

1. List and describe the three display modes.

2. Define the term WYSIWYG.

3. What is the difference between a cursor and an insertion point?

4. What is the purpose of a Button Bar?

5. List the steps (or keystrokes) to use Flush Right alignment.

Enriching Language Arts Skills

Each chapter contains vocabulary/spelling words and basic rules for punctuation, capitalization, or grammar. The last *Challenge Your Skills* activities in each chapter is identified by the ●❖ symbol and has mistakes in spelling, punctuation, capitalization, and/or grammar that are to be corrected. These activities should be proofread and corrected to produce a document that is grammatically accurate and ready for distribution.

Spelling/Vocabulary Words

acquisition   the act of purchasing or obtaining an item.
spiraling   increasing upward or downward in a circular motion.
enormous   huge, big.
liquidation   to close a business in order to receive cash for the assets.

Introductory Adverbs and Phrases

A comma often follows an introductory adverb or phrase because the word or phrase provides a transition from the previous sentence. Some common introductory words/phrases are: *however, for example, also, consequently, in other words.*

> *Examples:*
>
> *A decision was made yesterday to postpone the approval of the budget. Consequently, the purchase order for the new desks will be delayed.*
>
> *The post office requested that we use the new extended zip code. In other words, use the current 5-digit zip code followed by the new 4-digit extension.*

Activities

Activity 1.1—Create a Memorandum—Style 1

1. If necessary, load the WordPerfect program (see page 12).

2. If errors are made while typing, use the **Backspace** key to delete. For this chapter, ignore any errors noticed *after* the memo is typed.

3. Use Memorandum—Style 1 (refer to page 17) and type the following memorandum.

Memorandum

To: Al Lindsay

From: Virginia Ashlan

Date: (Use current date)

Subject: Action Plan Version 5.0

The newest version of the Action Plan program is currently available.

An information bulletin is being sent to all consultants informing them that the instructional materials are now available at all our regional offices. Old versions of Action Plan diskettes and manual contents can be destroyed. The binders can be reused with the new material, and the diskettes can be recycled.

xx (your initials)

---

4. Save the file on your file disk; use the filename **1act1** (Chapter 1, activity 1). (Select **File**, **Save**, type the drive letter where the file disk is located followed by a colon and the filename, select **OK**.)

5. Print one copy (select the **Print** button on the Button Bar, choose **Print**).

6. Close the document to clear the document window (select **File**, **Close**).

Activity 1.2—Create a Memorandum—Style 1

1. If necessary, load the WordPerfect program (see page 12).

2. If errors are made while typing, use the **Backspace** key to delete. For this chapter, ignore any errors noticed *after* the memo is typed.

3. Use Memorandum—Style 1(refer to page 17) and type the following memorandum.

Memorandum

To: All Sales Agents

From: Peter Roth, Division Manager

Date: (Use current date)

Subject: Application Procedures for Multiple Contracts

The purpose of this memorandum is to clarify the procedure for processing exchanges when more than one contract is involved.

The correct procedure is to list each company name along with the policy number for each policy that will be relinquished for the purpose of exchange.

At policy delivery, the policyowner will sign both of the contract forms. Return the forms and policies to the Policy Change Department. If you have questions, please feel free to contact us in Marketing Services.

xx (your initials)

---

4. Save the file on your file disk; use the filename **1act2** (Chapter 1, activity 2). (Select **File**, **Save**, type the drive letter where the file disk is located followed by a colon and the filename, select **OK**.)

5. Print one copy (select the **Print** button on the Button Bar, choose **Print**).

6. Close the document to clear the document window (select **File**, **Close**).

Activity 1.3—Create a Memorandum—Style 2

1. If necessary, load the WordPerfect program (see page 12).

2. If errors are made while typing, use the **Backspace** key to delete. For this chapter, ignore any errors noticed *after* the memo is typed.

3. Use Memorandum—Style 2 (refer to page 23) and type the following memorandum.

To: See Distribution Below   Date: (Use current date)

From: Gene Hunter   Subject: Reimbursement Rates

All offices have been provided with the new fuel reimbursement rates that should be placed into effect immediately. Each office will photocopy a set of the rates and forward the rate sheets to all area representatives.

You will notice that an additional amount for the seasonal adjustment has been added to each rate.

If gasoline prices decline this fall, revised rates will be published to reflect any changes at that time.

xx (your initials)

Distribution:

Stanley Bentley
Lena Jardine
William Moyer

---

4. Save the file on your file disk; use the filename **1act3** (Chapter 1, activity 3). (Select **File**, **Save** button, type the drive letter where the file disk is located followed by a colon and the filename, select **OK**.)

5. Print one copy (select the **Print** button on the Button Bar, choose **Print**).

6. Close the document to clear the document window (select **File**, **Close**).

Challenge Your Skills

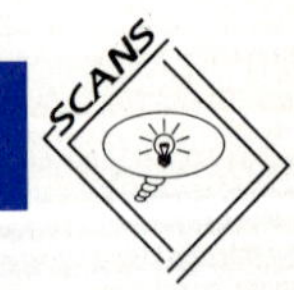

The *Challenge Your Skills* section at the end of each chapter contains a group of activities that reinforce understanding of the chapter's concepts. The activities require decision-making skills. The *Challenge Your Skills* activities should be completed only after completing appropriate chapter drills and activities.

Skill 1.1—Create a Memorandum—Style 1

1. If necessary, load the WordPerfect program.

2. If errors are made while typing, use the **Backspace** key to delete. For this chapter, ignore any errors noticed *after* the memo is typed.

3. Use Memorandum—Style 1 and the following information.

   a. Send the memorandum to MIS Staff from Veronica Pearson. The subject of the memorandum is Network Access Problems.

   b. Use the current date; include your reference initials.

The network has caused loss of productivity in recent weeks. Explanations of known problems are summarized below.

The recent Broadway virus that attacked the entire network caused a productivity loss of two days. MIS took effective action in returning us to operation quickly.

On Monday and Tuesday the network could not be accessed from the IBM PS/2. An unreliable connection was found between the network and the PS/2. Printing could not be accomplished from the Compaq AT. The printer cable had been disconnected from the switch box.

Angelo's computer receives a high number of "Error on Network Server ONEA Abort, Retry?" messages. Jayne Gurry has been notified. This is a recoverable error.

Thanks to all MIS users for your interest in resolving network problems rapidly.

---

4. Save the file on your file disk; use the filename **1skill1** (Chapter 1, skill 1).

5. Print one copy.

6. Close the document to clear the document window.

Skill 1.2—Create a Memorandum—Style 2

1. If necessary, load the WordPerfect program.

2. If errors are made while typing, use the **Backspace** key to delete. For this chapter, ignore any errors noticed *after* the memo is typed.

3. Use Memorandum—Style 2 and the following information.

   a. Send the memorandum to USL Agents from Joyce Bixler. The subject of the memorandum is Purchase of Policies.

   b. Use the current date; include your reference initials.

United Security Life will soon acquire the life and annuity policies of Hampton Insurance Company. Hampton Insurance Company (HIC) is a small-stock life insurer that has experienced financial difficulty and is being liquidated.

As a part of the liquidation process, USL has agreed to purchase HIC's life and annuity policies. This will ensure that all the life and most of the annuity policies continue without loss to the policyholders.

We think that the acquisition of HIC will help us control our unit expenses, which is certainly in everyone's best interest. If you have any questions regarding the acquisition, please contact my assistant, Lois Schloneger.

Distribution:

Russell Crimmins
Catherine Goldfarb
Gerald Pettengill
Marilyn Scutro
Edith Zehr

---

4. Save the file on your file disk; use the filename **1skill2** (Chapter 1, skill 2).

5. Print one copy.

6. Close the document to clear the document window.

∞ Skill 1.3—Create a Memorandum—Style 2; Language Arts

1. If necessary, load the WordPerfect program.

2. If errors are made while typing, use the **Backspace** key to delete. For this chapter, ignore any typing errors noticed *after* the memo is typed.

3. Use Memorandum—Style 2 and the following information.

    a. Send the memorandum to GLI Representatives from I. Arigone, Field Manager. The subject of the memo is Blood Test Limit.

    b. Use the current date; include your reference initials.

    c. The memo is to be distributed to the following persons: T. Deyo; B. Hurwicz; R. Juarez; E. Tang; L. Tolleson; and M. Warrick.

    d. While typing, correct two spelling errors and one punctuation error.

This is a reminder that effective with new business written next month, Global Life Insurance's new blood test rules call for a blood test at $100,000. GLI participated in a recent study involving a large number of the better known insurance companies and a solid majority are requiring blood tests for any policies amounting to $100,000 or greater. Our research combined with the spireling increase in medical costs, makes this adjustment necessary.

We need your full cooperation involving applications for amounts between $95,000 to $99,999, which occur on persons opposed to a blood test. Most people who object to obtaining a blood test are not trying to hide a prior condition. Unfortunately, there is a small segment of people who already know they have a pre-existing condition, and we cannot discern which type of person is objecting. Consequently you are to arrange a blood test on those individuals whose policy amounts barely slide in under the actual rule limits.

It is widely believed that many companies will eventually be forced to increase premiums in order to avoid the consequence of liquidtion. It is our hope that by seeking your cooperation on the above measures, GLI can forestall or avoid sterner remedies later.

---

4. Save the file on your file disk; use the filename **1skill3** (Chapter 1, skill 3).

5. Print one copy.

6. If you have completed your work, exit WordPerfect (select **File**, **Exit WP**).

Edit a Memorandum

Features Covered

- Open a document
- Block text
- Delete text
- Insert text
- Replace text
- Save and rename a file
- Undo
- The disk directory

Objectives

After successfully completing this chapter, you will be able to open a previously created document; delete, insert and replace text; and save a document with a new filename.

Chapter Introduction

Once a memorandum has been created, the author can make revisions to the document. Revisions can include information to be deleted, inserted, or replaced.

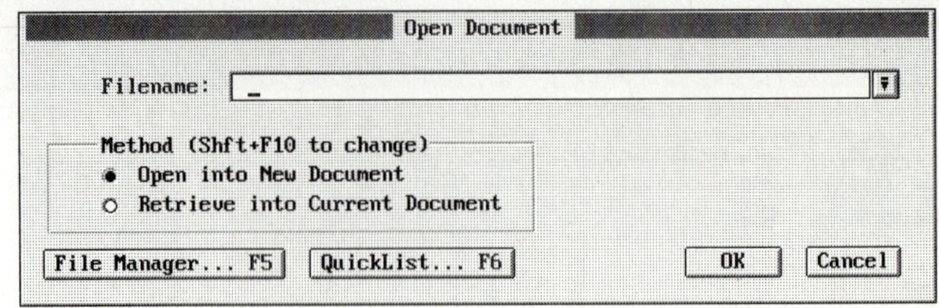

Open or Retrieve a Document

Before a file is edited, the saved document is opened and displayed in the document window. Opening or retrieving a document is the process of transferring a file from the file disk to the computer's memory.

If a saved file is retrieved, the document displays in an empty window or in the current document window where another document is displayed. Select **File, Retrieve** to place a document within a current document that is already displayed on the screen. The retrieved document will be inserted at the location of the insertion point. Retrieving a document is used when two documents are to be combined.

When **File, Open** is used to transfer a saved file from the file disk to the computer's memory, the document displays in a new, empty document window. To avoid combining files accidentally, always use **File, Open** to display a saved document on the screen.

Steps to ▶ **Open a File**

1. Select **File, Open** {Shift and F10}.

   Note: The Open Document dialog box displays (see Figure 2.1).

2. Move the mouse pointer to **File Manager** and click once {F5}.

   Note: The Specify File Manager dialog box displays.

3. Type the drive letter where the file disk is located followed by a colon.

   For example, type **a:** or **b:**. (Do not type the period.)

4. Select **OK** and wait a moment {Enter}.

   Note: The File Manager window displays.

5. Move the mouse pointer to the desired filename and double-click {press the down arrow key to highlight the filename, press Enter}.

   For example, double-click on the file named **1drill1**.

   Note: Wait a moment and the selected file displays in the document window.

Chapter 2—Edit a Memorandum

Delete and Insert Text

Text can be deleted by using the **Backspace** key or the **Delete** (Del) key. When the **Backspace** key is pressed, the character to the left of the cursor/insertion point is erased. When the **Delete** key is pressed, the character or space to the right of the insertion point is erased and the character or space located above the cursor is erased. Text deleted by using the **Backspace** or **Delete** keys can be returned to the screen by using the **Edit, Undo** or **Edit, Undelete** commands (see Undo Erased Text, page 43.

Text can be blocked and deleted. A character, word, sentence, line, paragraph, or entire document can be blocked and deleted. After text is blocked and the **Delete** or **Backspace** key is pressed, the deleted text is placed in WordPerfect's temporary memory (RAM). WordPerfect remembers the last three deletions. Blocked text displays highlighted in Text mode and with a dark background in Graphics/Page mode.

Text is inserted by placing the cursor/insertion point at the location where the new characters are to be typed and typing the characters. As the inserted text is typed, the characters to the right of the cursor/insertion point move over and provide space for the new text.

Block (Select) Text

Using the Mouse

a. *Drag Method:* To block any quantity of text, move the mouse pointer to the beginning of the text to be selected; press and hold the left mouse button while dragging the mouse to highlight the desired text. Release the mouse button.

   *Note: If the blocked text is to be deleted, press the **Delete** key.*

b. *To block a word,* move the mouse pointer to any character in the desired word and double-click.

c. *To block a sentence,* move the mouse pointer to any word in the desired sentence and triple-click.

d. *To block a paragraph,* move the mouse pointer to any location within the paragraph and click four times.

Using the Edit, Select Command

a. *To block a sentence,* place the cursor/insertion point in the desired sentence and choose **Edit, Select, Sentence** {Alt and e, s, s}.

b. *To block a paragraph,* place the cursor/insertion point in the desired paragraph and choose **Edit, Select, Paragraph** {Alt and e, s, p}.

c. *To block a page,* place the cursor anywhere in the desired page and choose **Edit, Select, Page** {Alt and e, s, a}.

Using Keystrokes

1. Place the cursor under (or the insertion point to the left) of the character at the beginning of the text to be blocked.

2. Press **Alt** and **F4**.

   *Note: The words **Block on** display in the bottom left side of the Status bar.*

3. Use any of the following keystrokes.

   a. *To block one character to the right or left*, press the **right arrow** or **left arrow** key.

   b. *To block one line up or down*, press the **up** or **down arrow** key.

   c. *To block to the end of the line*, press **End**.

   d. *To block to the beginning of the line*, press **Home** and then the **left arrow** key.

   e. *To block to the end of the document*, press **Home, Home** and the **down arrow** key.

   f. *To block one screen up*, press - on the numeric keypad.

   g. *To block one screen down*, press + on the numeric keypad.

   h. *To block one page up*, press **Page Up** (PgUp).

   i. *To block one page down*, press **Page Down** (PgDn).

   j. *To block one word to the right or left*, press **Ctrl** and the **left** or **right arrow** key.

   k. *To block one paragraph up or down*, press **Ctrl** and the **up** or **down arrow** key.

   l. *To block to a desired character*, press the desired character.

   m. *To block to the next hard return*, press **Enter**.

   n. *To block to the next hard page* (see Chapter 10), press **Ctrl** and **Enter**.

Turn Off Block

1. To turn off block and remove the highlight from text, click once {Esc or Alt and F4}.

Delete Text

1. Once the desired text has been blocked (selected), press the **Delete** (Del) key.

Shortcuts for deleting text

a. *To delete an entire word,* position the cursor under any character or position the insertion point to the left of any character in the word to be deleted and press **Ctrl** and **Backspace** or **Ctrl** and **Delete**.

b. *To delete from the cursor/insertion point to the beginning of the current word,* press **Home** and **Backspace**.

c. *To delete from the cursor/insertion point to the beginning of the next word,* press **Home** and **Delete**.

d. *To delete from the cursor/insertion point to the end of a line,* press **Ctrl** and **End**.

e. *To delete from the cursor/insertion point to the end of a page,* press **Ctrl** and **Page Down** (PgDn), select **Yes**.

Delete an Enter/Blank Line or Tab Code

1. Turn on Reveal Codes (**Alt** and **F3**).
2. Move the cursor/insertion point to highlight the [HRt] or [Lft Tab] code.
3. Press the **Delete** key.
4. Turn off Reveal Codes (**Alt** and **F3**).

Insert Text or Spaces

1. Place the insertion point to the left of the character or space that will follow the inserted text or space.
2. Type the text or space to be inserted.

   *Note: If text is erased as new text is typed, press the **Insert** (Ins) key once to turn off Typeover. See also the Replace Text section which follows.*

Replace Text

When text is replaced, the original character(s) are deleted and new characters are substituted. For example, if the insertion point is located to the left of the character "b" in the word **band** and the character "s" is typed, the "b" is deleted and the character "s" displays on the screen, changing the word to **sand**. Replacing text is accomplished by first pressing the **Insert** (Ins) key, then typing the new character(s). When the **Insert** key is pressed, the word *Typeover* displays in the Status bar at the bottom left of the screen. When the **Insert** key is pressed again, the word *Typeover* is removed from the Status bar.

> Memorandum
>
> To: Division Managers
>
> From: Calvin Edwards, *Regional Manager*
>
> Date: May 8, 199x
>
> Subject: *Western* Regional Meeting
>
> Please arrange to make yourself available for a three-day meeting the second week of June. Rooms will be booked for everyone at the San Francisco Airport Hilton *for three days and two nights.*
>
> On ~~Monday~~ *Tuesday* and ~~Tuesday~~ *Wednesday* mornings, the focus will be primarily on basic ~~Southeast~~ *west* business issues and opportunities. I will advise you of the business, recreation, and vast details before the meeting. *On Thursday we will join with Joan Hasimi's group to discuss the new marketing promotion.* ¶ *Casual attire will be appropriate for Tuesday and Wednesday.* xx *Thursday's attire will be announced pending the determination of the meeting location.*

Blocked text can be erased and replaced without using the **Delete** or **Backspace** key. The text to be deleted is blocked. When the first character of the new text is typed, the blocked text is deleted.

Steps to ▶ Replace Text

1. Place the insertion point to the left of the first character of the text to be replaced.
2. Press the **Insert** (Ins) key.

   *Note: The word **Typeover** displays on the bottom left side of the Status bar.*
3. Type the new character(s).
4. When you have finished replacing the text, press **Insert** again to turn Typeover off.

   *Note: If desired, select **Edit**, **Undo** to restore the replaced text.*

Start-Up Instructions

❖ The file named **1drill1** typed in Chapter 1 (Figure 1.5) should be opened and displayed on the screen.

❖ Review the steps to block and/or delete text.

❖ Review the steps to replace text.

❖ Make the changes shown in Figure 2.2.

Save and Rename a File

Once a file has been edited, the changed file can be saved using a new file-name. Using a different filename keeps a copy of the original file and saves the changed file under a new filename. If the changed file is saved with the original filename, the original file is erased and replaced by the corrected file.

* ❖ The file named **1drill1** should be displayed on the screen.

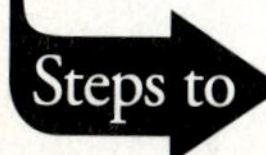

Use Save As to Rename a File

1. With the document displayed on the screen, select the **Save As** button {F10}.

2. Type the new filename (type the drive letter followed by a colon before typing the filename).

    For example, type **a:2drill1r**. (Do not type the period.)

3. Select **OK** {press Enter}.

Finish-Up Instructions

* ❖ Print one copy using the **Print** button on the Button Bar.

* ❖ If additional changes are made to the document, select **File, Save** to save but not rename the document. If no changes are made to the document after printing, clear the screen (select **File, Close**).

Undo Erased Text

Text that has been selected and deleted with the **Delete** or **Backspace** keys can be reinserted (or put back) into the document. When text is reinserted, the deleted text is retrieved to the screen. Reinserting text is referred to as "undo" or "undelete."

There are two methods for reinserting text—**Edit, Undo** and **Edit, Undelete**. When the **Edit, Undo** command is selected, the deleted text is restored to the original location. If **Edit, Undelete** is selected, the text will be restored at the location of the cursor/insertion point. Since WordPerfect remembers the last three deletions, the Edit Undelete command can be used to restore any of the remembered deletions.

The **Undo** command must be selected immediately before another action is attempted. Text that has been reinserted using **Undo** can be deleted again by selecting **Edit, Undo**.

> The Association rules have been updated. The updated rules will be placed
> in your mailboxes over the weekend. The revised rules are easy to read and
> comprehend.

Start-Up Instructions

* ❖ Type the paragraph shown in Figure 2.3.
* ❖ Block and delete the first sentence.

Undo Deleted Text

1. After the text has been blocked and deleted, select **Edit, Undo** {Ctrl and z}. The
   text returns to the screen.

Start-Up Instructions

* ❖ The paragraph typed previously from Figure 2.3 should be displaying on the screen.
* ❖ Block and delete the last sentence.

Undelete Deleted Text

1. After text has been blocked and deleted, move the cursor/insertion point to the
   location where the deleted text is to be restored.

   For example, move the cursor under (or the insertion point to the
   left of) the first character in the second sentence.

2. Select **Edit, Undelete** {Esc}.

   *Note: The deleted text displays highlighted on the screen where the cursor/insertion
   point is located.*

3. Select **Restore** {r}. To abort the undelete process, select **Cancel**.

   Note: If desired, insert one or two spaces after the period in the undeleted sentence.

Finish-Up Instructions

* ❖ Close the document without saving (select **File, Close**).

The Directory

A list of filenames can be displayed on the screen. The list of filenames is called
a directory. The directory is displayed for the disk drive that is accessed. The
accessed disk drive can be changed in order to display a list of filenames for
any disk drive, such as A, B, or C.

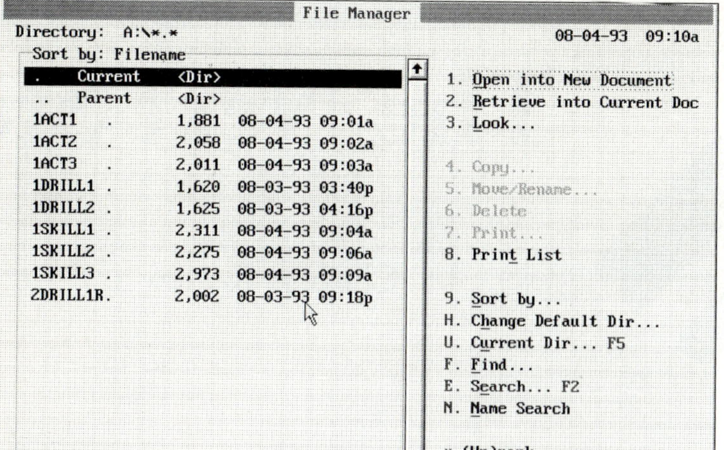

File Manager screen

One method of displaying a disk directory is to select the **File**, **File Manager** command or select the **File Mgr** button on the Button Bar and access the desired drive. The list of the files saved on the selected drive displays. In addition to displaying a disk directory, the File Manager can be used for many other file maintenance functions which are discussed in Chapter 17.

The second method for displaying a disk directory is to use the **File**, **Open** command (see Steps to Open a File on page 38). After reviewing the list of files on the directory, select Close to return to the document window.

Steps to Display the Directory Using the File Manager

Using a Mouse

1. Select the **File Mgr** button on the Button Bar {F5}.

   Note: The Specify File Manager List dialog box displays.

2. Type the drive letter where the file disk is located.

   For example, type **a:**. (Do not type the period.)

3. Select **OK** {Enter}.

   Note: The File Manager screen displays. A list of the filenames on the specified drive is shown on the left side (see Figure 2.4).

4. Select the **Close** button to close File Manager {Esc}.

The Next Step

Chapter Review and Activities

FEATURES SUMMARY

FEATURES	ACTIONS	PAGE
Open a file	Select **File**, **Open**, select the **File Mgr** button, type the drive letter where the file disk is located, select **OK**, move the mouse pointer to the desired filename and double-click.	38
Block text using the mouse		39
Drag method:	Move the mouse pointer to the beginning of the text to be blocked, press and hold the left mouse button while dragging the mouse to highlight the desired text, release the mouse button.	
To block a word:	Move the mouse pointer to any character in the desired word and double-click.	
To block a sentence:	Move the mouse pointer to any word in the desired sentence and triple-click.	
To block a paragraph:	Move the mouse pointer to any location within the paragraph and click four times.	

FEATURES *(cont'd.)*	ACTIONS *(cont'd.)*	PAGE
Block text using the Edit, Select command	*To block a sentence,* place the cursor/insertion point anywhere in the sentence and choose **Edit, Select, Sentence.** *To block a paragraph,* place the cusor/insertion point anywhere in the paragraph and choose **Edit, Select, Paragraph.** *To block a page,* place the cursor/insertion point anywhere in the page and choose **Edit, Select, Page.**	39
Block text using the keyboard	Press **Alt** and **F4**. Use any of the following keystrokes: **Left** or **right arrow** key = one character left or right **Up** or **down arrow** key = one line up or down **End** = end of the current line **Home, Home, left arrow** key = beginning of line **Home, Home, down arrow** key = end of document **Ctrl** and **left** or **right arrow** key = one word left or right **Ctrl** and **up** or **down arrow** key = one paragraph up or down	40
Turn off block	Click once (**Alt** and **F4**).	40
Delete text	Blocked desired text and press **Delete** (Del).	40
Replace text	Press **Insert** (Ins) to turn on Typeover, type the replacement text, press **Insert** again to turn off Typeover.	42
Save and rename a file	Select the **Save As** button, type the new filename, select **OK.**	43
Undo deleted text	After text has been blocked and deleted, select **Edit, Undo.**	44
Undelete deleted text	After text has been blocked and deleted, move the cursor/insertion point to a new location select **Edit, Undelete, Restore.**	44
Display the directory using the File Manager	Select the **File Mgr** button, type the drive letter, select **OK.**	45

Self-Check Questions

True/False—Circle One

T F 1. Once text has been blocked and deleted, it is not possible to undo the deleted text.

T F 2. A file can be opened by selecting **File**, **Open**, **F5**, type the drive letter where the file disk is located followed by a colon, **OK**, double-click on the desired filename.

T F 3. Place the insertion point to the left of a character and press the **Del** key once to delete the character.

T F 4. The **Backspace** key is used to delete characters to the left of the insertion point.

T F 5. When text is replaced, the original characters are deleted and new characters are substituted.

Short Answer

1. List the steps to block and delete a paragraph.

2. State the major difference between opening a document and retrieving a document.

3. State the difference between the **Undo** and the **Undelete** features.

4. What key is pressed to turn Typeover on or off?

5. List the steps to save and rename a file.

Enriching Language Arts Skills

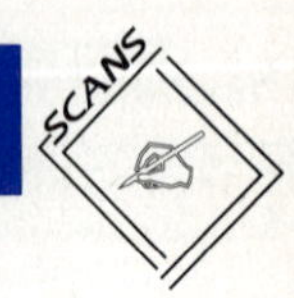

Spelling/Vocabulary Words

commendable   being of high quality; approved of.
nominated   suggested appointment to some position.
negotiations   the process of reaching an agreement.

Introductory Clauses

A comma should follow a dependent clause. (A dependent clause has both a subject and verb but cannot stand alone as a sentence.) An introductory clause often begins with *if, in, when, since,* or *as.*

> *Example:*
>
> *As you prepare your expense report, remember to use the updated gasoline rate schedule.*

Activity 2.1—Edit a Memorandum

1. If necessary, load the WordPerfect program, display the Button Bar and Ribbon, and select the graphics view mode.

2. Open the file named **1act1** that was typed in Chapter 1, page 30 (select **File, Open**, press F5, type the drive letter where the file disk is located followed by a colon, **OK**, double-click on the desired filename).

3. Make the revisions shown.

Memorandum

To: Al Lindsay

From: Virginia ~~Ashlan~~ *Paragon, CSS Director*

Date: (Use current date)

Subject: Action Plan Version 5.0

The newest version of the Action Plan *(version 5.2)* program is currently available.

An information bulletin is being sent to all consultants informing them that the instructional materials are now available at all our regional offices *or from CSS*. Old versions of Action Plan diskettes and manual contents can be destroyed. The binders can be reused with the new material, and the diskettes can be recycled. *If you have binders, please either send them to CSS or let us know the number of binders you have and we will send you the newest contents. ¶ To install Action Plan on a PC, insert Disk 1 in drive A and type A:APINSTAL at the DOS prompt.*

---

4. Proofread and correct any errors.

5. Use the new filename **2act1r** (Chapter 2, activity 1, revised) and save the revised file. (Select the **Save As** button, type the drive letter where the file disk is located followed by a colon and the new filename, select **OK**.)

6. Print one copy (select the **Print** button on the Button Bar, choose **Print**).

7. Close the document to clear the document window (select **File, Close**).

Activity 2.2—Edit a Memorandum

1. If necessary, load the WordPerfect program, display the Button Bar and Ribbon, and select the graphics view mode.

2. Open the file named **1act3** that was typed in Chapter 1, page 32 (select **File, Open**, press **F5**, type the drive letter where the file disk is located followed by a colon, **OK**, double-click on the desired filename).

3. Make the revisions shown.

INTEROFFICE CORRESPONDENCE

To: See Distribution Below   Date: (Use current date)

From: ~~Gene~~ G. Hunter _and B. Wills_   Subject: Reimbursement Rate

All offices have been provided with the new fuel reimbursement rates that should be placed into effect immediately. _We are requesting that_ Each/office will photocopy a set of the rates and forward _division_ the rate sheets to all area representatives.

¶ Also, each sales office has been provided with the rates for all area offices under their authority. Please forward the ~~You will notice that an additional amount for the seasonal adjustment has been added~~ ~~to each rate.~~ _rate sheets to your area operations manager._

If gasoline prices decline this fall, revised rates will be published to reflect any changes at that time.

xx (your initials)

Distribution:

Stanley Bentley   _Penny McManus_
Lena Jardine   _, Ed Salas_
William Moyer

---

4. Proofread and correct any errors.

5. Use the new filename **2act2r** (Chapter 2, activity 2, revised) and save the revised file. (Select the **Save As** button, type the drive letter where the file disk is located followed by a colon and the new filename, select **OK**.)

6. Print one copy (select the **Print** button on the Button Bar, choose **Print**).

7. Close the document to clear the document window (select **File, Close**).

Activity 2.3—Create and Edit a Memorandum

1. If necessary, load the WordPerfect program, display the Button Bar and Ribbon, and select the graphics view mode.

2. Type the following memorandum. Use Memorandum—Style 1 (see Chapter 1, Figure 1.5).

Memorandum

To: See Distribution Below

From: D. P. Crenshaw

Date: (Use current date)

Subject: Employee Changes

Tim will end full-time employment with DPA at the end of the month. He will, however, continue working with us part-time.

Li Jean will be promoted to take over Tim's duties effective immediately.

On behalf of DPA, I want to publicly wish Tim the best of luck in his new life. By next month, we should all see in bookstores one of his creations, HOW TO SURVIVE NETWORKS.

xx (your initials)

Distribution:

Bing Chiou
Isabel Fan
Mike Martinez
Darrell Russo

---

3. Save the file as **2act3** (Chapter 2, activity 3). (Select **File, Save,** type the drive letter where the file disk is located followed by a colon and the filename, select **OK**.)

4. Make the revisions shown.

Memorandum

To: See Distribution Below
From: D. P. Crenshaw, *Human Resources Director*
Date: (Use current date)
Subject: Employee Changes

Tim will end full-time employment with DPA ~~at the end of the month.~~ He will, however, continue working with us part-time.

Li Jean will be promoted to take over Tim's duties effective immediately. *If you have training or graphics needs, please direct your request to Li Jean.*

On behalf of DPA, I want to publicly wish Tim the best of luck in his new life. By next month, we should all see in bookstores one of his creations, HOW TO SURVIVE NETWORKS.

¶ Tim's work at DPA contributed toward our professional-looking courses and slides and to more knowledgeable co-workers on WordPerfect for Windows and PageMaker.

xx *thank you Tim.*

Distribution:

Bing Chiou
Isabel Fan   *Single space*
Mike Martinez
Darrell Russo

---

5. Proofread and correct any errors.

6. Use the new filename **2act3r** (Chapter 2, activity 3, revised) and save the revised file. (Select the **Save As** button, type the drive letter where the file disk is located followed by a colon and the new filename, select **OK**.)

7. Print one copy (select the **Print** button on the Button Bar, choose **Print**).

8. Close the document to clear the document window (select **File, Close**).

Challenge Your Skills

Skill 2.1—Create and Edit a Memorandum

1. If necessary, load the WordPerfect program, display the Button Bar and Ribbon, and select the graphics view mode.

2. Use Memorandum—Style 1 (see Chapter 1, Figure 1.5) and the following information.

   a. Send the memorandum to All Jacobson Transport Drivers from T. D. Van Wetter. The subject of the memorandum is Vehicle Inspection.

   b. Use the current date; include your reference initials.

When delivering vehicles, it is important to inspect each vehicle thoroughly. The following are items to assist you with delivery inspections.

The floor mats will be coded. Codes are located in the trunk on a sticker, under the mat, or on the trunk lid. The codes begin with a "B." For example, B-36, B-37, etc.

Remember to submit the inspection checklists to your immediate supervisor. If you have any questions, please contact me by the end of next week at 555-6880.

3. Save the file; use the filename **2skill1** (Chapter 2, skill 1).

4. Use the following information to edit the memorandum:

   a. Change the T. in the From line to Theresa and add her title, Manager.

   b. Delete the last sentence in the second paragraph that begins "For example, . . ."

   c. Insert the following new paragraph between the last two paragraphs: The vans have fog lights. Check the fog light switch that is located on the left side of the dashboard.

   d. Change the phone number in the last paragraph to (408) 555-6999.

5. Proofread and correct any errors.

6. Use the new filename **2skill1r** (Chapter 2, skill 1, revised) and save the file.

7. Print one copy of the memo.

8. Close the document.

1. If necessary, load the WordPerfect program, display the Button Bar and Ribbon, and select the graphics view mode.

2. Use Memorandum—Style 2 (see Chapter 1, Figure 1.8) and the following information.

   a. Send the memorandum to Manuel Espinosa from J. C. Kornhaus. The subject of the memorandum is PLD Briefing.

   b. Use the current date; include your reference initials.

Thank you for your help in preparing the materials for the Jefferson County Board of Supervisors last week.

As a result of your work, our laboratory team was able to provide a well-documented presentation that responded to our critics and answered the questions posed by the Supervisors. We hope to have results of the briefing before the next board meeting.

In the future, if I can be of any assistance to you, please contact me at (314) 555-6767.

---

3. Save the file; use the filename **2skill2** (Chapter 2, skill 2).

4. Use the following information to edit the memorandum:

   a. Change the subject of the memo to Preliminary Lab Data Briefing.

   b. In the first paragraph insert the words PLD Briefing before the word materials.

   c. Insert the following paragraph between the last two paragraphs:
      I deeply appreciate the extra effort you put forth to meet the many deadlines required in putting together this briefing package.

   d. Two returns after your reference initials, use the following format to indicate that a copy of the memo will be sent to another person.
      c: Jaimi Callegari, Lab Director

5. Proofread and correct any errors.

6. Use the new filename **2skill2r** (Chapter 2, skill 2, revised) and save the file.

7. Print one copy of the memo.

8. Close the document.

•• Skill 2.3—Create and Edit a Memorandum; Language Art Skills

1. If necessary, load the WordPerfect program, display the Button Bar and Ribbon, and select the graphics view mode.

2. Use Memorandum—Style 2 (Chapter 1, Figure 1.8) and the following information.

   a. Send the memorandum to Local 70 Shop Stewards from Jane Avery. The subject of the memo is Contract Negotiations.

   b. Use the current date; include your reference initials.

   c. The memo is to be distributed to the following persons (alphabetize by last name): Tamis, D.; Kerdasha, P.; Metzger, A.; DuBoce, R.; Pham, N.; Giovanette, M.; and Taslim, E.

   d. Correct three spelling words and two punctuation errors. Remember to check for the spelling words and grammar rules discussed in both Chapters 1 and 2.

Negotations on a new contract are set to begin next month. In order to avoid any pitfalls we need to have a well-prepared bargaining team. Last year's bargaining team did a comendable job and worked hard to negotiate a strong, well-written contract.

A new bargaining team will be selected by secret ballot at the membership meeting next week. A list of members who have been nomminated to serve on the bargaining team is available at the Union Hall.

Also a form requesting ideas on the contract issues to be negotiated can be picked up at the Union Hall. Some of the areas open for negotiation are: wages, eligibility for retirement benefits, medical benefits, conference reimbursements, and working conditions.

---

3. Save the file; use the filename **2skill3** (Chapter 2, skill 3).

4. Use the following information to edit the memorandum:

   a. Delete the second sentence of the first paragraph.

   b. Insert the following sentence at the end of the second paragraph:

      If desired, members can drop by and pick up the list before the meeting.

   c. Insert the following new paragraph after the last paragraph:

      Please remind union members at your location of the upcoming membership meeting. If a union member cannot be present, contact George Nazzaro for proxy forms. Let me know if I can be of further assistance.

5. Proofread and correct any errors.

6. Use the new filename **2skill3r** (Chapter 2, skill 3, revised) and save the file.

7. Print one copy and Close the document.

8. If you have completed your work, exit WordPerfect (select **File, Exit WP**).

Create Business Letters

Features Covered

- Automatic date feature
- Change vertical line spacing
- Change justification
- Bold, italic, and underline text attributes
- Help

Objectives

After successfully completing this chapter, you will be able to use the automatic date feature, change justification, change the vertical line spacing, and use text attributes such as bold, italic, and underline to create business letters. You will also be able to access the Help function in order to obtain information about WordPerfect commands and features.

Chapter Introduction

Business letters are one of the most important types of written communications. Preparing the business letter often involves creating a draft letter as well as using convenient WordPerfect features such as automatic date, vertical line spacing, justification, and text attributes. In Chapter 4, the business letter will be refined and prepared in final form.

Business Letters

A letter is formal written communication used to convey information from one business to another or from one individual to another. A draft is the initial writing of a letter that will be revised at a later time. A draft of a letter is usually printed with line spacing of two (double-spacing).

The initial letter is typed with vertical line spacing of one (single-spacing), since line spacing of one will be used to print the document in final form (see Figure 3.1). Before printing a draft of a letter, change the vertical line spacing to two (see Figure 3.3). The extra space between lines provides an area for handwritten revisions to be noted on the printout. A letter with line spacing set for two will often print on two pages.

Traditionally, letters have followed one of two styles—a modified block or block style. With the development of word processing machines and programs, the block style has become the most frequently used letter style. With the block style, all lines of the letter begin at the left margin (see Figure 3.1).

Another style of letter that is now being used is the AMS simplified style (Administrative Management Society) letter. The AMS simplified style omits the salutation and complimentary closing. A subject line and the typewritten signature are typed in uppercase letters. Like the traditional block style, all lines of the letter begin at the left margin (blocked). See Figure 3.2.

At the bottom of a letter the following information may be included:

- ☐ The author's initials in capital letters and the typist's initials in lowercase letters.

- ☐ A document identification notation showing the filename and location of the document.

- ☐ If a photocopy of the letter is to be sent to another person(s), a copy notation is typed. Generally a photocopy is indicated by a lowercase "c" followed by a colon (c:). Press the **Tab** key once and type the name; press **Enter**.

  *Note: Always use the **Tab** key before each listed name, otherwise the names may not align when fonts are changed (see Chapter 4 for font change information).*

- ☐ If the letter contains a statement that an item(s) is being enclosed, type an enclosure notation two **Enters** below the document identification notation. For example, type **Enc**.

Automatic Date Feature

WordPerfect provides two methods for inserting the current date into a document automatically—**Date Text** and **Date Code**. In order for the date to be inserted by WordPerfect, the current date must be stored in the computer's memory.

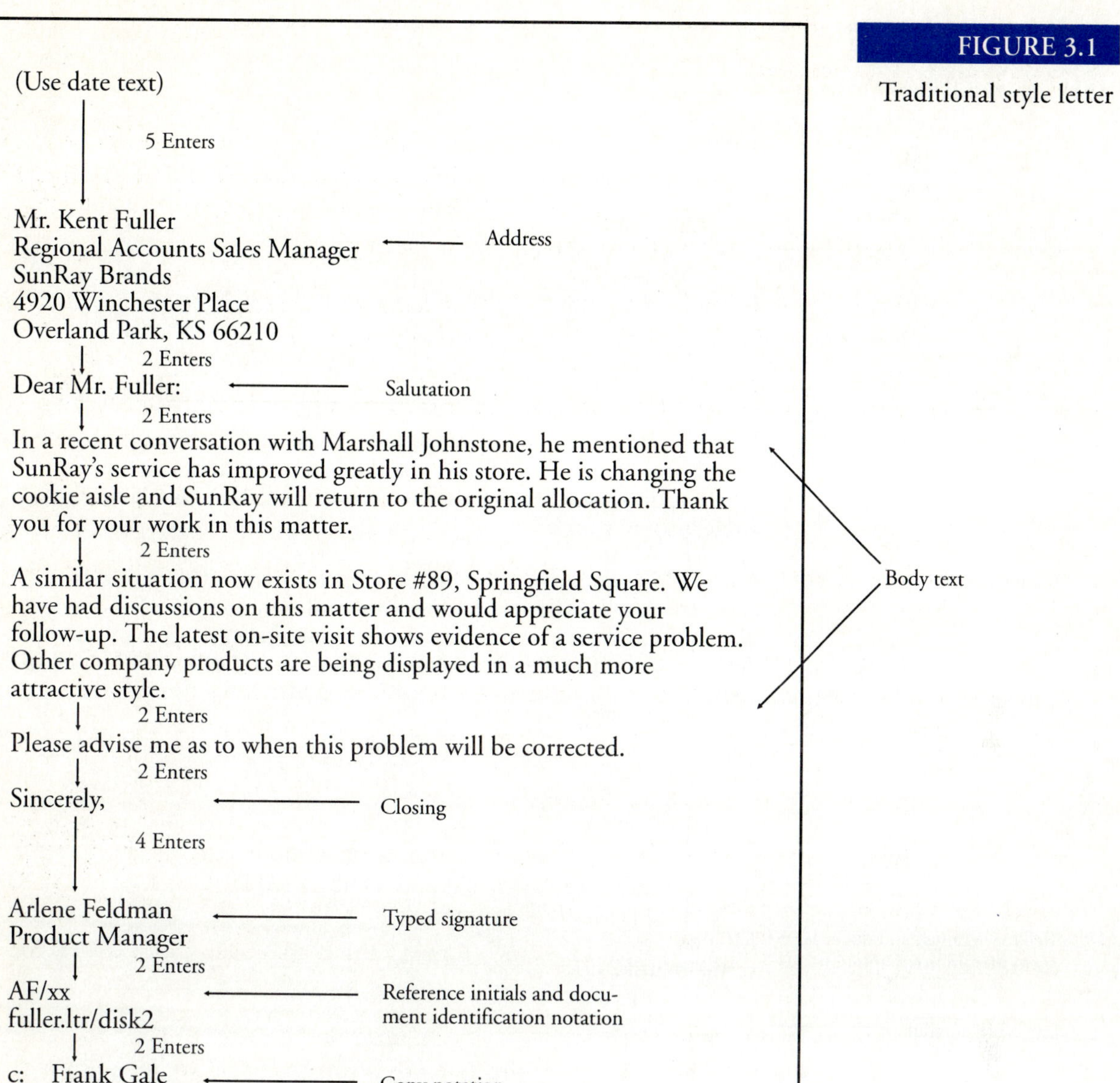

Traditional style letter

When **Tools**, **Date**, **Text** is selected, the current date is placed in the document by WordPerfect. If the document is opened on a different day, the date will not change unless edited manually.

When **Tools**, **Date**, **Code** is selected, a special code is inserted by WordPerfect. If the document is opened on a later date, the date is automatically changed to the current date (see Chapter 12).

Different formats for the current date can be inserted by selecting **Tools**, **Date**, **Format** and choosing the desired date format in the Date Format dialog box.

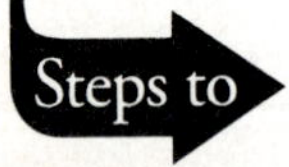

Steps to > Use the Date Text Feature

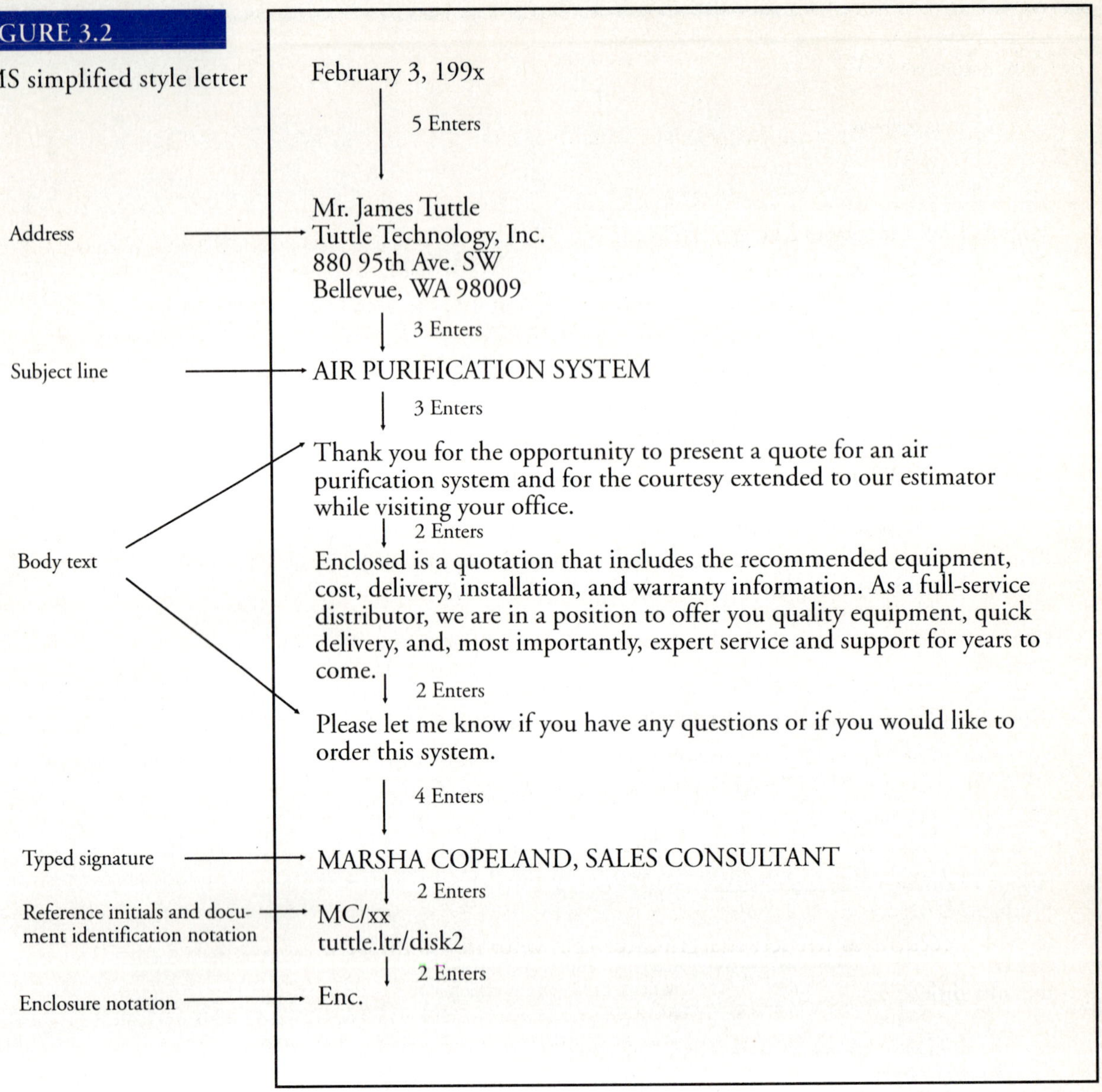

1. Select **Tools, Date, Text** {Shift and F5, t}.

   Note: *The current date is inserted at the location of the cursor/insertion point. If necessary, the date can be changed by the user on a later date.*

Finish-Up Instructions

- ❖ Type the traditional block style letter shown in Figure 3.1 on page 59 using the spacing shown. Use wordwrap to type the body text paragraphs of the letter.

- ❖ After typing the letter, use the filename **3drill1** and save the file (select the **Save As** button on the Button Bar, type the drive letter where the file disk is located followed by a colon and the filename, select **OK**).

Justification

The term *justification* in WordPerfect is used to describe the alignment of text in relation to the left and right margins. The five different types of justification are Left, Right, Center, Full, and Full, All Lines. With Left justification, text is aligned at the left margin and is not aligned at the right margin (ragged right). Left justification is the default setting for WordPerfect 6.0. Right justification is the opposite of Left justification, i.e., text is aligned at the right margin and not at the left margin (ragged left). Center justification aligns text so that an equal amount of blank space displays on the left and right of the centered text. Full justification adjusts lines to begin and end exactly at the left and right margins. The Full, All Lines options is used to evenly space letters of a title or heading between the left and right margins.

When justification is changed, a code is inserted at the beginning of the paragraph where the cursor/insertion point is located. The selected justification remains in effect from that location forward in the document or until a different justification is chosen.

In addition to the Right justification type, WordPerfect provides a Flush Right alignment feature for aligning text at the right margin. The Flush Right alignment feature is used to right align a single line or a portion of a line. The Right justification type is used in WordPerfect to right align multiple lines.

The Center alignment (Chapter 1) and the Center justification are the two types of horizontal centering provided by WordPerfect. When the Center alignment command is used before text is typed, the line is centered and the cursor/insertion point returns to the left margin after the Enter key is pressed. However, if a group of lines is blocked (and no codes or text follow) and the Center alignment command is used, the cursor/insertion point remains in the center of the document window. The code displayed in Reveal codes for Center alignment is [Cntr on Mar].

When the Center justification command is used before text is typed, the line(s) is centered and after the Enter key is pressed the cursor/insertion point remains in the center of the document screen. However, if text is blocked, only the blocked lines are centered. The expanded code [Just:Cntr] displays in Reveal Codes.

With Full justification, additional spaces are placed between words in order to align the text at both the left and right margins. The extra spaces between words may make the text difficult to read and may be visually unattractive. Therefore, after a document is printed, a decision may be made to use Left justification.

Start-Up Instructions

❖ The file named **3drill1** should be displayed on the screen.

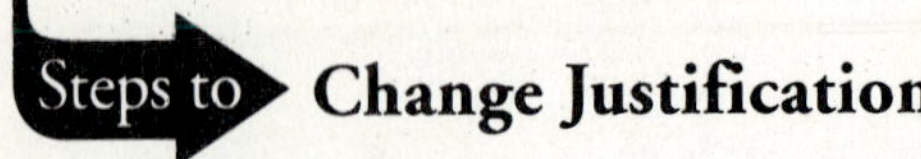

Change Justification

1. The insertion point should be located where the justification is to be changed.

   For example, place the insertion point at the beginning of the document (**Home, Home,** up arrow).

2. Move the mouse pointer to the **Justification** button on the Ribbon and click once.

   Note: A drop-down list of justification choices displays.

3. Move the mouse pointer to highlight the desired justification type.

   For example, highlight **Full**.

4. Release the mouse button {Alt and L, j, f}.

Finish-Up Instructions

❖ Save the file on your file disk; use the filename **3drill1f** (select the **Save As** button on the Button Bar, type the drive letter where the file disk is located followed by a colon and the filename, select **OK**).

❖ Print one copy (select the **Print** button on the Button Bar, choose **Print**).

Text Attributes

Emphasis can be added to text by using text attributes such as bold, underline, and italic. Text attributes can be set in the Font dialog box by selecting the desired attribute(s) in the Appearance box. In addition, text attributes can be set by using the **Bold, Underline,** and **Italic** options in the **Font** menu. More than one text attribute can be applied to the same text characters, e.g., **<u>bold and underline</u>**.

The bold text attribute prints words darker on the page as compared to other printed words. Text to be printed in bold will be displayed highlighted or darker than the other characters on the screen. When bold is selected, WordPerfect inserts a bold code on each side of the text. Display Reveal Codes to view the bold codes, [Bold On] and [Bold Off].

Words are underlined in printed text to show emphasis. Once the text to be underlined is blocked (selected) and the underline feature is used, the text displays underlined or highlighted on the screen.

The italic text attribute prints text somewhat slanted to the right. However, there are some dot matrix printers that do not print italicized text. Once the text to be italicized is selected and the italic attribute is applied, the text displays in a different color or slightly slanted on the screen.

❖ The file named **3drill1f** should be displayed on the screen.

Bold Text

1. Block the text to be printed in bold (see Chapter 2, page 39 for information on blocking text).

   For example, block **SunRay's** in the first sentence of the letter.

2. Select **Font** from the Menu bar, select **Bold** {F6}.

   *Note: If the **Font** menu is selected, a check mark displays beside the word **Bold** to indicate that the text is bolded.*

Underline Text

1. Block the text to be underlined (see Chapter 2, page 39 for information on blocking text).

   For example, block #89, Springfield Square in the first sentence of the second paragraph.

2. Select **Font** on the Menu bar; select **Underline** {F8}.

   *Note: If the **Font** menu is selected, a check mark displays beside the word **Underline** to indicate that the text is underlined.*

Italicize Text

1. Block the text to be italicized (see Chapter 2, page 39) for information on blocking text).

   For example, block the final sentence of the first paragraph.

2. Select **Font** on the Menu bar; select **Italic** {Ctrl and i}.

   *Note: If the **Font** menu is selected, a check mark displays beside the word **Italic** to indicate that the text is italicized.*

Finish-Up Instructions

❖ Block the word SunRay in the second sentence of the first paragraph and bold the text.

❖ Block the final sentence in the first paragraph and bold the text. This sentence will be both bold and italic.

❖ Use the filename **3drill1t** and save the file (select the **Save As** button on the Button Bar, type the drive letter where the file disk is located followed by a colon and the filename, select **OK**).

Note: *The following Steps to Remove Bold, Steps to Remove Underline, Steps to Remove Italic, and Steps to Remove All Text Attributes are for your information.*

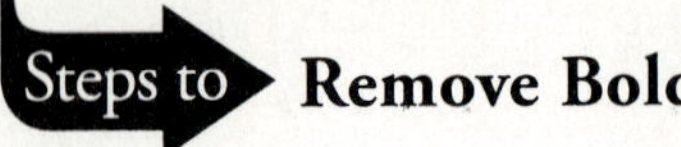

Remove Bold

1. Block the bolded text.
2. Select **Font** from the Menu bar, select **Bold** {F6}.

Remove Underline

1. Block the underlined text.
2. Select **Font** on the Menu bar, select **Underline** {F8}.

Remove Italic

1. Block the italicized text.
2. Select **Font** on the Menu bar, select **Italic** {Ctrl and i}.

Remove All Text Attributes

1. Block the text for which all text attributes are to be removed.
2. Select **Font** on the Menu bar, select **Normal** {Ctrl and n}.

Change Vertical Line Spacing

Additional space can be created between lines of text by changing the vertical line spacing. This added space can be used to accommodate handwritten changes to draft letters and reports. Generally the vertical line spacing is set for two in a draft letter (double-spacing). After a letter is finalized, the line spacing is returned to one (single-spacing). (See Chapter 4.)

When the line spacing is changed, a line spacing code is inserted in the document. In Reveal Codes, the line spacing code is shown as [Ln Spacing]. When the cursor is located on the line spacing code and the code is highlighted, the code expands to show the amount of line spacing selected, e.g., [Ln Spacing:2.0].

Start-Up Instructions

❖ The file named **3drill1t** should be displayed on the screen.

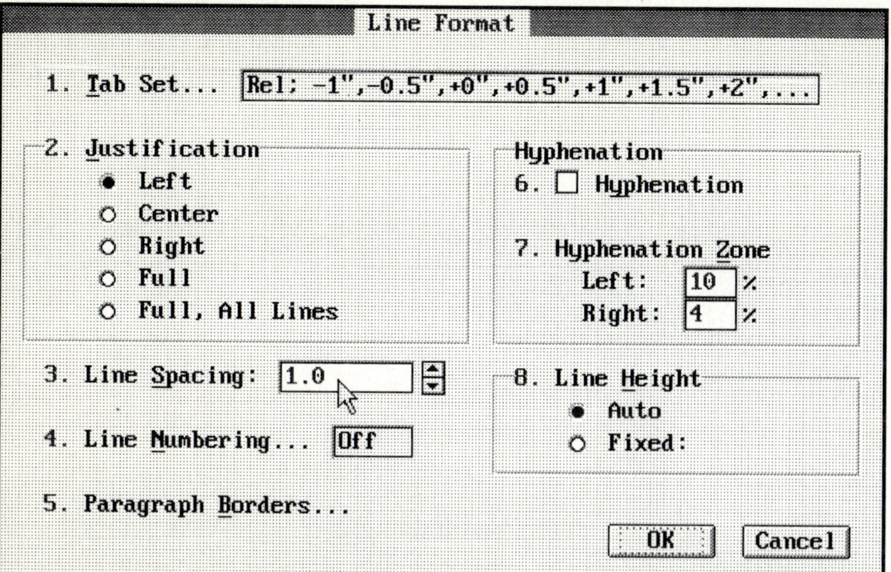

Line Format dialog box

Steps to ▶ Change the Vertical Line Spacing

1. Place the insertion point at the beginning of the text where the vertical line spacing is to be changed (**Home, Home,** up arrow).

2. Select **Layout, Line** {Shift and F8, 1}

   Note: The Line Format dialog box displays (see Figure 3.3).

3. Move the mouse pointer to the box located beside the words **Line Spacing** and click once {s}.

4. Type the desired vertical line spacing.

   For example, type **2.**

5. Select **OK** {press Enter three times}.

   Note: Your document should look similar to Figure 3.4. To view the entire letter, use the horizontal scroll bar or the Page Down key.

Finish-Up Instructions

❖ Save the file on your file disk; use the filename **3drill1d** (Chapter 3, drill 1, draft). (Select the **Save As** button on the Button Bar, type the drive letter where the file disk is located followed by a colon and the filename, select **OK**.)

❖ Print one copy (select the **Print** button on the Button Bar, choose **Print**). The letter will print on two pages.

❖ Close the document (select **File, Close**).

Start-Up Instructions

❖ Optional. Type the AMS simplified letter shown in Figure 3.2. Change the vertical line spacing to two. Use the filename **3drill2** and save the file.

FIGURE 3.4

Traditional style letter draft with vertical line spacing of two and bold, underline, and italic text attributes

(Use date text)

Mr. Kent Fuller

Regional Accounts Sales Manager

SunRay Brands

4920 Winchester Place

Overland Park, KS 66210

Dear Mr. Fuller:

In a recent conversation with Marshall Johnstone, he mentioned that **SunRay's** service has improved greatly in his store. He is changing the cookie aisle and **SunRay** will return to the original allocation. ***Thank you for your work in this matter.***

A similar situation now exists in Store <u>#89, Springfield Square</u>. We have had discussions on this matter and would appreciate your follow-up. The latest on-site visit shows evidence of a service problem. Other company products are being displayed in a much more attractive style.

Please advise me as to when this problem will be corrected.

Sincerely,

Arlene Feldman

Product Manager

AF/xx

fuller.ltr/disk2

c: Frank Gale

Patricia Nielson

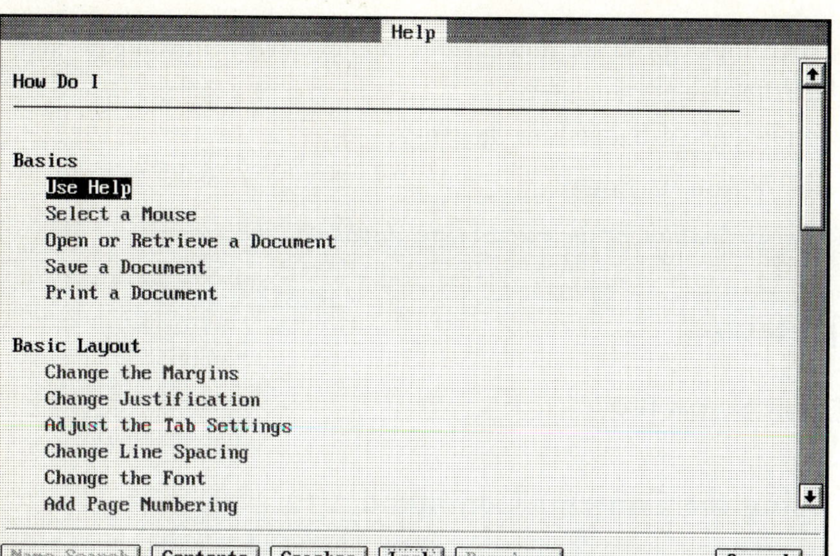

❖ Print one copy (select the **Print** button on the Button Bar).

❖ Close the document (select **File**, **Close**).

Using Help

WordPerfect has an online Help feature that provides detailed information regarding program topics and specific instructions for performing commands. The Help feature can be accessed at any time through the **Help** menu or from any dialog box or menu.

The Help feature can be accessed in several ways. One method is to select the **Help** menu and choose the **How Do I** option. A list of of topics displays (see Figure 3.5). The desired topic is selected in order to display the Help information for the chosen topic.

A second method of accessing the Help feature is to select a menu command or display a dialog box and press **F1**. Help information displays for the menu command or for each option shown in the dialog box.

WordPerfect also provides a Coach option that walks you through the steps necessary to complete a task. With the Coach option, WordPerfect will prompt each step and if desired, hints can be viewed to assist you in completing a task.

Steps to **Access Help Using the How Do I Command**

1. Select the **Help** menu {Alt and h}.

2. Select **How Do I** {h}.

3. Select the desired topic {press the down arrow key repeatedly until the desired topic is highlighted}.

> For example, select **Change Line Spacing**.

4. Select the **Look** button {L, Enter}.

Note: The Help information for the selected topic displays on the screen.

Exit the Help Feature

1. Select the **Cancel** button {Esc}.

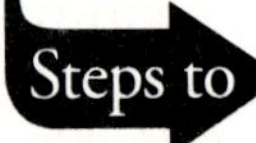

Access Help Using the Contents Command

1. Select **Help, Contents** {F1}.

2. Select the desired topic {press the down arrow key repeatedly to highlight the desired topic}.

> For example, select **Template**.

3. Select **Look** {L, Enter}.

*Note: A Help screen can be printed to a dot-matrix or non-PostScript printer by pressing the **Print Scrn** button on the keyboard. If desired, print the template Help screen.*

4. Select **Cancel** to exit the Help screen {Esc}.

Access the Help Feature for a Menu Command or Dialog Box

1. Highlight the menu command desired or display the desired dialog box.

> For example, select **Tools, Date, Format** {Shift and F5, f}.

Note: The Date Formats dialog box displays on the screen.

2. Press **F1**.

*Note: The Help screen explaining Date Formats displays. Additional information can be obtained for topics that are bolded. Also, in some Help screens a list of related topics displays at the bottom of the Help information. The additional Help information can be accessed by selecting the bolded word or related topic and choosing the **Look** button.*

3. Select **Cancel** {Esc}.

Note: The dialog box for the option selected displays again on the screen.

4. If desired, complete any actions necessary using the options in the dialog box or select **Cancel** {Esc twice} to return to the WordPerfect screen.

Start-Up Instructions

❖ The filename **3drill1d** should be displayed on the screen.

1. Select **Help, Coaches** {Alt and h, o}.

   Note: A list of topics displays.

2. Select the desired Coach topic.

   For example, **Bold, Underline, and Italics** is highlighted.

3. Press **Enter** {s}.

   Note: Wait momentarily until the Coach dialog box displays.

4. Respond to the prompts that display on the screen.

   a. Select **Continue** {Enter}.

   b. When the message displays, "Do you want to change the appearance of some text that you have already typed?", select **Yes** {y}.

   c. Block the company name in the address of the letter.

      *Note: If you would like more information about blocking text, select the **Hint** button {F1}.*

   d. Continue to follow the prompts displayed in the Coach section of the screen.

   e. When the message displays, "The Bold font attribute is still active. Would you like Coach to help you change back to Normal text?", select **Yes** {y} and follow the prompts on the screen.

   f. When the message displays, "You have now applied the Bold attribute in your document.", select **Quit** {Esc}.

   g. Select **Yes** {y} to Quit Coach.

Finish-Up Instructions

❖ Close the document. Do not save the changes to the letter.

The Next Step

Chapter Review and Activities

FEATURES SUMMARY

FEATURES	ACTIONS	PAGE
Date Text feature	Select **Tools**, **Date**, **Text**.	60
Change justification	Move the mouse pointer to the **Justification** button on the Ribbon and click once, move the mouse pointer to the desired justification type and double-click.	62
Bold text	Block text to be bolded, select **Font**, **Bold** (F6). *Remove bold*—Block the bolded text, select **Font**, **Bold** (F6).	63
Underline text	Block the text to be underlined, select **Font**, **Underline** (F8). *Remove underline*—Block the underlined text, select **Font**, **Underline** (F8).	63
Italicize text	Block the text to be italicized, select **Font**, **Italic**. *Remove italic*—Block the italicized text, select **Font**, **Italic**.	63
Remove all text attributes	Block the text for which all text attributes are to be removed, select **Font**, **Normal**.	64

FEATURES *(cont'd.)*	ACTIONS *(cont'd.)*	PAGE
Change vertical line spacing	Select **Layout, Line**, move the mouse pointer to the box beside the words **Line Spacing** and click once, type the desired line spacing, select **OK**.	65
Access Help using the How Do I command	Select **Help, How Do I,** choose the desired topic, select **Look**.	67
Exit Help	Select the **Cancel** button or press **Esc**.	68
Access Help using the Contents command	Select **Help, Contents**, choose the desired topic, select **Look**.	68
Access Help from a menu command or dialog box	Highlight the desired menu command or display the desired dialog box, press **F1**.	68
Use Coach	Select **Help, Coaches**, choose the desired topic, press Enter, respond to prompts that display on the screen.	69

Self-Check Questions

True/False—Circle One

T F 1. A letter typed in single spacing can be changed to line spacing of two before printing.

T F 2. A draft letter with line spacing of two is used by an author to make handwritten revisions on the printed copy.

T F 3. The document identification notation is typed above the reference initials.

T F 4. In the traditional letter style, the **Enter** key is pressed four times after typing the last paragraph.

T F 5. When the body text of a letter is single-spaced, the **Enter** key is pressed twice between paragraphs.

Short Answer

1. What is the purpose of a draft letter? What line spacing is used for a draft letter?

2. List the five different types of justification.

3. Explain the difference between Right justification and the Flush Right alignment feature.

4. Explain the difference between Full justification and Full, All Lines justification.

5. List the steps to remove the bold attribute from blocked text.

Enriching Language Arts Skills

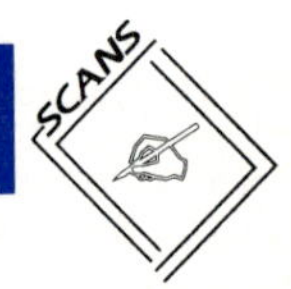

Spelling/Vocabulary Words

telecommunications   electronic transfer of information between two locations.
tailored   made to fit a specific need.
existence   having presence; being; having life.
description   a verbal or written explanation.

Appositives

Appositives are words that immediately follow a noun and further identify the noun but usually are not necessary to the meaning of the sentence. Appositives are set off by commas.

Example:

Ester Tam, a copyeditor for eight years, will be our new senior editor.

Activities

Activity 3.1—Create a Traditional Style Letter with Bold Text Attribute

1. If necessary, load the WordPerfect program, and display the Button Bar and Ribbon, and select the graphics view mode.

2. Type the following letter using the traditional letter style (page 59).

Chapter 3—Create Business Letters

(Use date text)

Hugh and Mary Ellis
752 Cherry Rd.
Newport News, VA 23602

Dear Mr. and Mrs. Ellis:

During the last six months, you have visited Horizon Estates on the Chesapeake Bay.
You have experienced the panoramic views and the quiet country setting. And you have
seen the large, family-oriented floor plans.

Now we have some exciting news! Horizon Estates is releasing seven new homes for
sale. We invite you to revisit our sales office to choose from the home sites now
available.

The moment you have been waiting for is NOW! It is time to own your own home at
Horizon Estates.

Cordially,

Angela H. Santos
Sales Manager

AHS/xx
ellis.ltr/d1

---

3. Bold each occurrence of the words "Horizon Estates" (block the text, press
    F6).

4. Place the cursor/insertion point at the beginning of the document (**Home,
    Home,** up arrow); change the line spacing to two (select **Layout, Line,**
    type **2** in the Line Spacing box, select **OK**).

5. Save the file on your file disk; use the filename **3act1** (Chapter 3, activity
    1). (Select the **Save As** button on the Button Bar, type the drive letter
    where the file disk is located followed by a colon and the filename, select
    OK.)

6. Print one copy (select the **Print** button on the Button Bar, choose **Print**).

7. Close the document (select **File, Close**).

1. Type the following letter using the traditional letter style (see page 59).

(Use date text)

Ms. Marcy Flores
Manager, Systems and Processing
Turtle Markets
850 W. Natanes Rd.
Phoenix, AZ 85017-4168

Dear Marcy:

Thank you for taking the time to speak with me yesterday. Please find enclosed a copy of our 8.1 Migration Seminar brochure.

As we discussed, Syncon Business Consulting will be holding Migration Seminars at the end of next month. I highly recommend that one of your team members plan to attend the Los Angeles seminar.

If SBC can be of any other service to Turtle Markets, please do not hesitate to give us a call.

Regards,

Louis Noble
Operations Manager

LN/xx
flores.ltr/d2

c: M. T. Silverman

Enc.

---

2. Place the insertion point at the beginning of the document (**Home, Home,** up arrow); change the line spacing to two (select **Layout, Line,** type **2** in the Line Spacing box, select **OK**).

3. Change to **Full** justification (move the mouse pointer to the **Justification** button on the Ribbon and click once, move the mouse pointer to **Full** and double-click).

4. Save the file on your file disk; use the filename **3act2** (Chapter 3, activity 2). (Select the **Save As** button on the Button Bar, type the drive letter where the file disk is located followed by a colon and the filename, select **OK**.)

5. Print one copy (select the **Print** button on the Button Bar, choose **Print**).

6. Close the document (select **File**, **Close**).

Activity 3.3—Create an AMS Simplified Style Letter with Bold and Italic Text

1. Type the following letter using the AMS simplified letter style (see page 60). Use the bold and italic text attributes as shown.

(Use date text)

Mr. Dennis Eaton
2295 Miranda Place
Alamo, CA 94507

SPRING MEMBERSHIP PROMOTION

As you are well aware, in the past year *Diablo Fitness Center* has made a great deal of progress in managing, rebuilding, and improving its facility and equipment.

With our spring membership promotion, you will receive **FREE** a beautiful, deluxe bathrobe and three months added to your present membership, compliments of *Diablo Fitness Center.* All you have to do is introduce two new members to the club during the next two months.

We are looking forward to your participation in this program!

MARIZE LOCKE, PRESIDENT

ML/xx
eaton.ltr/disk3

---

2. Place the insertion point at the beginning of the document; (**Home**, **Home**, up arrow); change the line spacing to two (select **Layout**, **Line**, type **2** in the Line Spacing box, select **OK**).

3. Save the file on your file disk; use the filename **3act3** (Chapter 3, activity 3). (Select the **Save As** button on the Button Bar, type the drive letter where the file disk is located followed by a colon and the filename, select **OK**.)

4. Print one copy (select the **Print** button on the Button Bar, choose **Print**).

5. Close the document (select **File**, **Close**).

Challenge Your Skills

Skill 3.1—Create and Edit a Traditional Style Letter

1. Use the traditional letter style and the following information.

   a. Use the current date.

   b. Send the letter to Mrs. Consuelo Sundheimer, 80 Patriot Place, Apt. #5, Downers Grove, IL 60515.

   c. Use Dear Mrs. Sundheimer for the salutation.

   d. Use an appropriate complimentary closing.

   e. The letter is from Debby Reiter, M.D.

   f. Include your reference initials and document identification notation.

   g. Make decisions regarding justification and the use of bold, italic, and underline text attributes.

   h. The letter body text follows:

   At the end of the month, I will be leaving the Lincoln Medical Group in order to enter private practice in Des Plaines, Illinois.

   Our records indicate that you or a member of your family have been seen by me during the past year. Hopefully, you will not be inconvenienced by a change in physicians. I would like to assist you with the transition to a new health-care provider.

   Your health is important to me, and Lincoln Medical is committed to assuring you continuity of care. My entire staff and I will be available to assist you with this transition. Please call if you have any questions or concerns.

2. Save the file on your file disk; use the filename **3skill1** and print one copy.

3. Use the following information to change the letter:

   a. Insert the following paragraph between the second and last paragraphs:

   If you have specific concerns regarding a medical condition or are undergoing prenatal care, please give me a call directly at (708) 555-8900. Otherwise, you may call Celeste Renshaw or Bertha Lenhardt at (708) 555-6303 and they will be happy to help you select another physician.

   b. Change the line spacing to two.

4. Save the file on your file disk; use the filename **3skill1r** (Chapter 3, skill 1, revised).

5. Print one copy and close the document.

Skill 3.2—Create and Edit an AMS Simplified Style Letter

1. Use the AMS simplified letter style and the following information.

   a. Use the current date.

   b. Send the letter to Mrs. Sabrina Alvares, 77 Hazelwood Ln., Menomonee Falls, WI 53051.

   c. The subject of the letter is TAX PLANNING.

   d. The letter is from Tami Nguyen, C.P.A.

   e. Include your reference initials, document identification notation, and enclosure notation.

   f. Make decisions regarding justification and the use of bold, italic, and underline text attributes.

   g. The letter body text follows:

   Enclosed is your new tax organizer. Although it may seem like you just finished last year's taxes, it is not too early to begin thinking about the preparation of this year's taxes.

   As for new law changes, the new 31 percent bracket kicks in, as well as the new "haircut" for itemized deductions. Remember that for federal tax purposes, capital gains are still taxed at 28 percent.

   As you thumb through your tax organizer, you will see that it contains the prior year's figures. Knowing your information from the prior year will help you to verify the accuracy and completeness of the current year information. Please include cost and purchase date of all assets sold.

   If you feel that your tax situation merits an appointment or you need to discuss any matters with me, please call Bob to schedule an appointment.

2. Save the file on your file disk; use the filename **3skill2**.

3. Use the following information to change the letter:

   a. Insert the following paragraph above the last paragraph.

      Forward your estimated tax partnership papers to me as soon as possible. We do not need to delay the filing of your partnership taxes while you gather your individual information.

   b. Change the line spacing to two.

4. Save the file on your file disk; use the filename **3skill2r** (Chapter 3, skill 2, revised).

5. Print one copy and close the document.

⚬ Skill 3.3—Create and Edit an AMS Simplified Style Letter; Language Arts

1. Use the AMS simplified letter style and the following information.

   a. Use the current date.

   b. Send the letter to Mr. Clinton Nomura, Engineering Productivity Division, 18023 Shawsheen St., Andover, MA 01810-1086.

   c. The subject of the letter is NORAM TELECOMMUNICATIONS ASSOCIATION.

   d. The letter is from Josephine Reyes, Membership Chairperson.

   e. Include your reference initials, document identification, and enclosure notation.

   f. Make decisions regarding justification and the use of bold, italic, and underline text attributes.

   g. Correct three spelling and two punctuation errors.

   h. The letter body text follows:

      The enclosed brochure is provided to inform you of the existence of a professional organization taylored to meet the specific needs of telecommuncation professionals.

      The NORAM Telecommunications Association is more than 15 years old and has more than 600 members. There are members from all 50 states and Canada.

      The membership brochure will provide you with a describtion of our programs and information on next month's conference. Our conference will be held in Chicago, Illinois. Hurry now to register and take advantage of the early registration reduced fee.

If you have any questions feel free to contact me or my assistant Billie Detweiler, at (215) 555-8303. Thank you for taking time to consider becoming a member of the NORAM Telecommunications Association.

2. Use the following information to change the letter:

   a. Change the line spacing to two.

   b. Delete the last sentence.

3. Save the file on your file disk; use the filename **3skill3**.

4. Print one copy.

5. If you have completed your work, exit WordPerfect (select **File, Exit WP**).

Refine a Letter and Print Final Copy

Features Covered

- Change margins
- Delete codes in Reveal Codes screen
- Change fonts
- Use Print Preview
- Use Speller

Objectives

After successfully completing this chapter, you will be able to change the top, bottom, left, and right margins; use different font and point sizes; check the placement of text on a page before printing; and use spell check in order to produce a mailable business letter.

Chapter Introduction

After the content of a letter is reviewed and revised, decisions are made for the final document printing. Before the document is printed, the document is proofread for spelling, grammar, and typographical errors; the vertical line spacing is changed to one; and decisions are made to determine the final placement of a letter on a page.

A final letter is customarily printed on letterhead stationery. The letterhead information usually includes the company name, address, phone number, and fax number. Typically, the letterhead information is preprinted on company stationery. Today, however, many individuals who use word processing and desktop publishing programs create their own let-

Traditional style letter printed on letterhead stationery

SunRay Industries
580 Deharo Street, San Francisco, CA 94107
(415) 555-8303   FAX (415) 555-8318

April 2, 199x

Mr. Kent Fuller
Regional Accounts Sales Manager
SunRay Brands Division
4920 Winchester Place
Overland Park, KS 66210

Dear Mr. Fuller:

In a recent conversation with Marshall Johnstone, he mentioned that **SunRay** service has improved greatly in his store. He is changing the cookie aisle and **SunRay** will return to the original allocation. ***Thank you for your work in this matter.***

A similar situation now exists in <u>Store #89, Springfield Square</u>. We have had discussions on this matter and would appreciate your follow-up. The latest on-site visit shows evidence of a service problem. Other company products are being displayed in a much more attractive style.

Please advise me as to when this problem will be corrected.

Sincerely,

Arlene Feldman
National Product Manager

AF/xx
fuller.ltr/disk2

c: Frank Gale
      Patricia Nielson

terheads. In Chapter 14, a letterhead will be created. A letter printed on company letterhead stationery in final form will look similar to Figure 4.1.

                                          Chapter 4—Refine a Letter and Print Final Copy

Change Margins

Generally, WordPerfect's default (preset) margins are used to print the final letter. If a letter is unusually short or long, however, it may be desirable to change the document margins.

The top and bottom margins are preset to 1 inch. Using a standard size 8½ x 11-inch paper and a combined top and bottom margin of 2 inches, 9 inches remain for typed lines on a page. Depending on the information preprinted in a letterhead, the top margin can vary between 2 and 2½ inches. The bottom margin on an average-length letter generally remains unchanged. The left and right document margins are preset for 1 inch. With these settings, 6.5 inches are available across the page. (See Figure 4.2.)

When the margins are changed, codes display in the Reveal Codes screen for each changed margin, for example, [Lft Mar], [Rgt Mar], [Top Mar]. When a margin code is highlighted in Reveal Codes, the code is expanded to show the margin measurement, e.g., [Lft Mar:1.5"].

Once the margins have been changed, the new margins remain effective from that location forward in the document or until different margins are selected. Therefore, if the margins are to be effective for the entire document, the cursor/insertion point should be located at the beginning of the document before the margins are changed.

The margins can be changed in the document at any time, i.e., before or after the document is typed. Changing the margins is best accomplished after the document is completed, because a decision can more easily be made as to whether margins should be changed depending on the length of the document. After printing a document, estimate the desired placement of the document. A letter should be printed on the page with the space around the edges of the letter evenly balanced.

The number of words in the letter body text and the depth of the letterhead are used to make decisions regarding margin changes. The following are some suggested margin settings for letters:

	Top Margin	Left & Right Margins
Short letter (under 100 words*)	2.5"	2.0"
Average letter (100–200 words)	2.0"	1.5"
Long letter (over 200 words)	1.75"	1.0"

*See Document Information in Chapter 9.

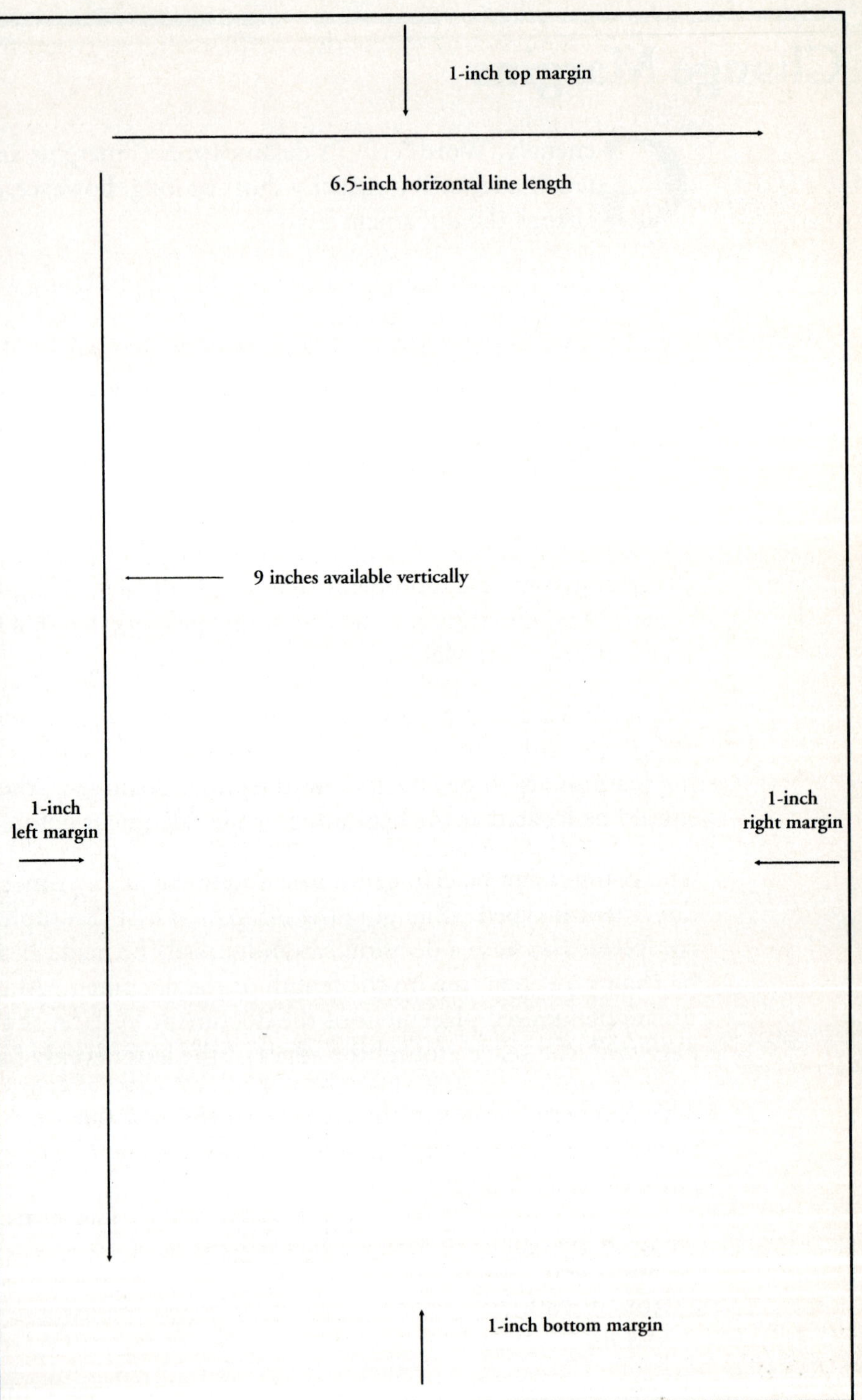

Before printing the final letter, preview the entire document on the screen by selecting **File, Print Preview, Full Page** (see Print Preview later in this chapter).

Start-Up Instructions

❖ Open the document **3drill1d** typed in Chapter 3, page 66 (select **File, Open,** press **F5,** type the drive letter where your disk is located followed by a colon,

                                          Chapter 4—Refine a Letter and Print Final Copy

OK, double-click on the desired filename) or type the letter shown in Figure 4.1.

❖ The cursor/insertion point must be located at the top of the document.

Change Margins

1. Select **Layout, Margins** {press Alt and L, m or Shift and F8, 2}.

   Note: The Margin Format dialog box displays.

2. *To change the left margin,* move the mouse pointer to the box located beside the words **Left Margin**, click once to highlight the measurement and type the desired margin in inches {L, type desired margin, press Enter}.

   For example, type **1.5**. (Do not type the last period.)

   To change the right margin, move the mouse pointer to the box located beside the words **Right Margin**, click once to highlight the measurement and type the desired margin in inches {r, type desired margin, press Enter}.

   For example, type **1.5**. (Do not type the last period.)

   To change the top margin, move the mouse pointer to the box located beside the words **Top Margin**, click once to highlight the measurement and type the desired margin in inches {t, type desired margin, press Enter}. (See Figure 4.3.)

   For example, type **1.5**. (Do not type the last period.)

   To change the bottom margin, move the mouse pointer to the box located beside the words **Bottom Margin**, click once to highlight the measurement and type the desired margin in inches {b, type desired margin, press Enter}.

   For example, check that the default margin of 1" displays.

   Note: When the margin amount displayed in the measurement box is highlighted, the new amount is typed, automatically replacing the existing figure(s). If the cursor displays in the measurement amount box and the amount is not highlighted, the original amount must be deleted and the new amount typed. Typing the quotation mark is not necessary.

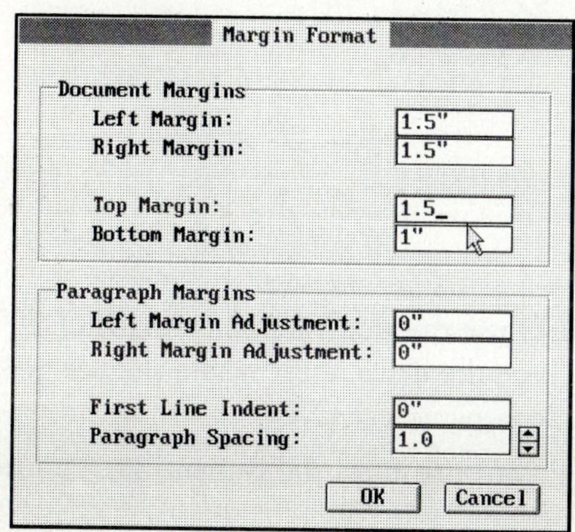

FIGURE 4.3

Margin Format dialog box with changed margins

3. Select **OK** to accept the new margin settings {press Enter twice}.

Finish-Up Instructions

❖   Save the file on your file disk; use the filename **4drill1r** (Chapter 4, drill 1, revised). (Select the **Save As** button on the Button Bar, type the drive letter where the file disk is located followed by a colon and the filename, select **OK**.)

❖   Print one copy (select the **Print** button on the Button Bar, choose **Print**).

Return the Vertical Line Spacing to the Default

In order to print the letter with the original line spacing of one, the vertical line spacing code of two is deleted. The Reveal Codes screen is accessed in order to select and delete the line spacing code. Deleting the line spacing code is often referred to as "returning the line spacing to the default." The default for line spacing is one.

Start-Up Instructions

❖   The file named **4drill1r** that was used for changing margins should be displayed on the screen, and the cursor/insertion point should be located at the top of the document (**Home**, **Home**, up arrow).

Delete the Vertical Line Spacing Code

1. Turn on Reveal Codes (**Alt** and **F3**).

2. Move the mouse pointer to the [Ln Spacing] code and click to select the code {use the arrow keys and move the shaded/black block in the Reveal Codes screen to the line spacing code}. (See Figure 4.4.)

    Note: When the line spacing code is selected, the code expands to show the amount of line spacing defined, e.g., [Ln Spacing:2.0].

3. Press the **Delete** key.

4. Turn off Reveal Codes (**Alt** and **F3**).

Finish-Up Instructions

❖   Save the file on your file disk; use the new filename **4drill1s** (select the **Save As** button on the Button Bar, type the drive letter where the file disk is located followed by a colon and the filename, select **OK**).

❖   Print one copy (select the **Print** button on the Button Bar, choose **Print**).

                                    Chapter 4—Refine a Letter and Print Final Copy

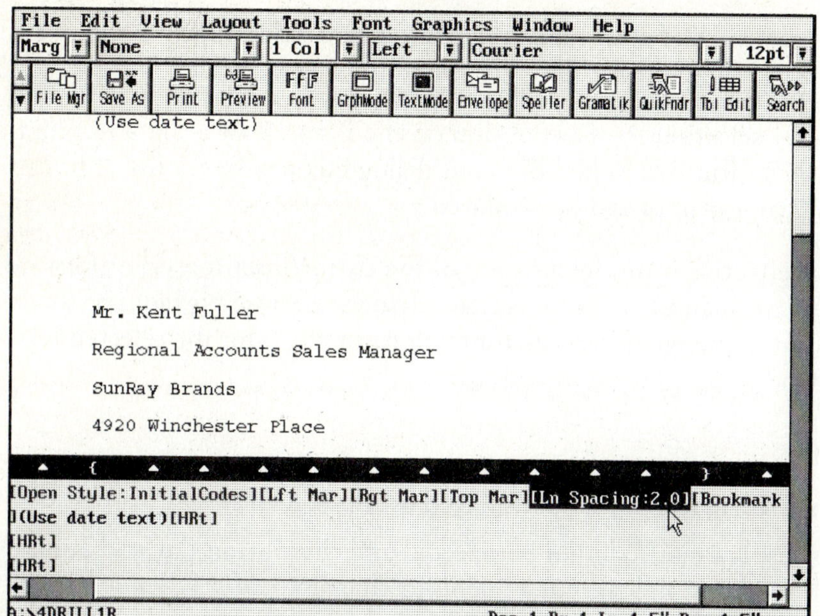

FIGURE 4.4

Reveal Codes screen with
line spacing code

Font Changes

By using a variety of typefaces (fonts) and sizes, the appearance of letters, reports, résumés, or other business documents can be enhanced. A typeface is a specific design of type (shape), such as Helvetica, Roman, or Dutch. A font includes all the letters, numbers, symbols, and punctuation marks for a given typeface in one size and style. For example, Helvetica 14-point bold is one font and Roman 10-point italic is another font.

Each printer has one or more built-in fonts. Many built-in fonts, such as Courier, are monospaced and fixed pitch—each character is allocated the same amount of horizontal space and only one size of type is available per font.

WordPerfect provides additional fonts that can be used with any printer that can print graphics (if necessary, see your instructor). The fonts provided by WordPerfect, such as Bodoni-WP Bold (Type 1) and Dutch 801 Bold (Speedo), are proportional and scalable—the horizontal space allocated for each character varies based on the width of the character and the characters can be printed in almost any size.

These scalable/proportional fonts are measured in points. There are approximately 72 points in an inch. A 24-point character is approximately ¼ of an inch tall. A ruler at the back of this book shows the letter "E" in various point sizes and can be used to assist you in determining appropriate point sizes to use in different documents. Generally, a 10- to 12-point font is used for the text of business letters, memorandums, and reports.

The font names and sizes available will depend on the printer that is currently selected. To determine which printer is selected, choose **File**, **Print/Fax**. If a different printer is desired, choose the **Select** button in the Current Printer area. A list of available printers displays. Highlight the desired printer and choose **Select.**

Fonts are changed by selecting the **Font** option on the Font menu or by selecting the **Font** button on the Button Bar. When the Font dialog box displays, a list of fonts and sizes for the current printer can be displayed.

The font change is effective from the location of the cursor/insertion point forward in the document or until another font is selected. However, if text is blocked (highlighted) and the font is changed, the new font will be in effect for the selected text only. Use Reveal Codes to display font codes.

Start-Up Instructions

❖ The file named **4drill1s** should be displayed on the screen.

❖ The graphics display mode should be selected and the Button Bar and Ribbon displayed. If necessary, use the **View** menu to change the display mode or to display the Button Bar and/or Ribbon.

Steps to ➤ Change Font Name and/or Size

1. Place the cursor/insertion point at the location where the font change is to begin.

    For example, place the cursor/insertion point at the top of the document.

2. Select the **Font** button on the Button Bar {Ctrl and F8}.

    Note: The Font dialog box displays (see Figure 4.5). The current font displays in the Font box.

3. To view a list of available fonts, move the mouse pointer to the Font box and click {f}.

4. Scroll through the list of available fonts and select the desired font name {press the down arrow key until the desired font name is highlighted}.

    For example, select **Dutch 801 Roman (Speedo)** or **make a decision of your own.**

    Note: WordPerfect displays a sample of the chosen font name and size in the Resulting Font box located below the font list. The displayed sample is only an approximate size and style.

5. Select **OK** {press Enter}.

    Note: The text has been changed to display the new font. Use Reveal Codes (Alt and F3) to view the font code.

To Change the Font for Blocked Text Only

6. Block the text for which the font is to be changed.

    For example, block the document notation (fuller.ltr/disk2).

    Chapter 4—Refine a Letter and Print Final Copy

Font dialog box

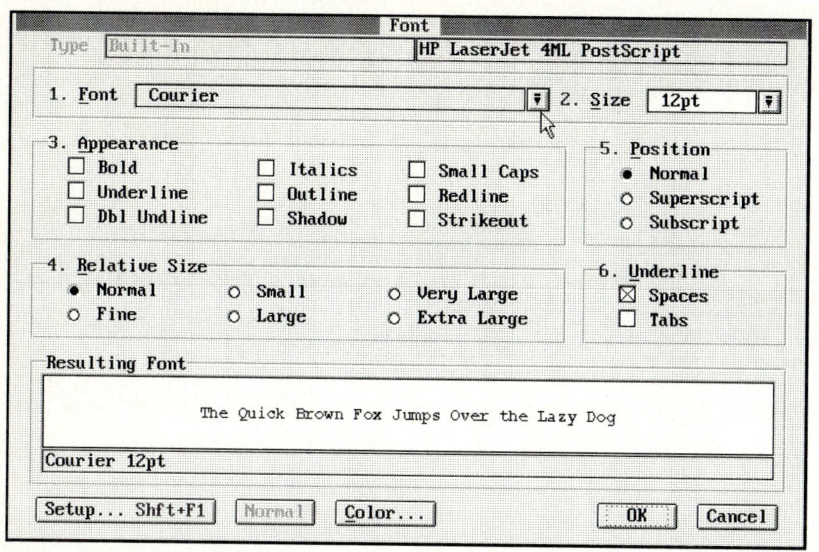

7. Select the **Font** button on the Button Bar {F9}.

8. Move the mouse pointer to the down arrow button beside the Font box and click. Scroll through the list of available fonts and select the desired font name {press the down arrow key until the desired font name displays}.

   For example, select **Dutch 801 Italic (Speedo)** or **make a decision of your own.**

9. Move the mouse pointer to the down arrow button located beside the **Size** box and click.

   Note: A list of point sizes displays.

10. Select the desired point size {press the up or down arrow key to highlight the desired size}.

    For example, select **10.**

11. Select **OK** {press Enter}.

Finish-Up Instructions

❖ Use the new filename **4drill1L** and save the file on your file disk (select the **Save As** button on the Button Bar, type the drive letter where the file disk is located followed by a colon and the filename, select **OK**).

Print Preview

A document is viewed on the screen by using the Print Preview feature. Displaying a document in Print Preview assists in making decisions concerning the alignment of text and the amount of blank space in the margins.

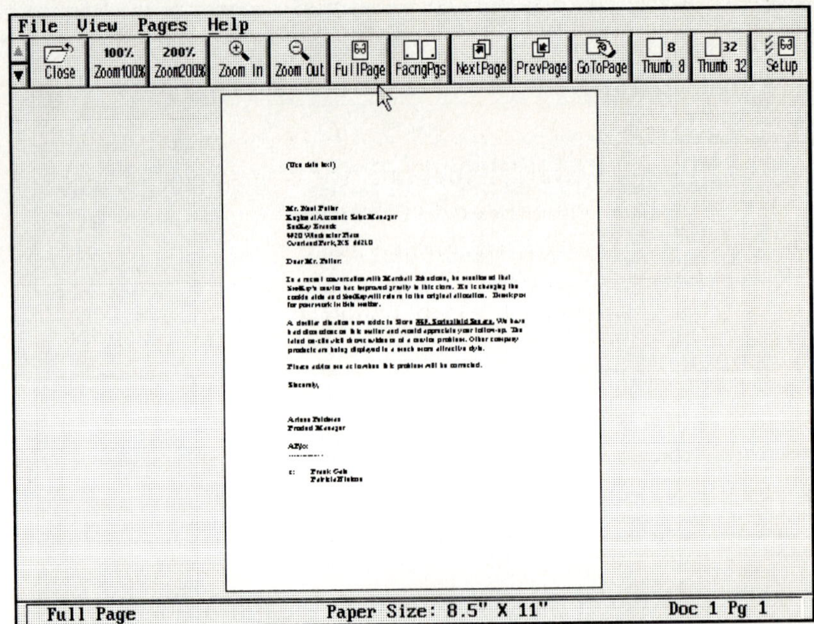

FIGURE 4.6

Print Preview screen with Full Page view

To display a document in Print Preview, select **File, Print Preview**. When Print Preview is selected, the document can be displayed in Full Page, 100%, 200%, or Zoom views. When the Full Page option is used, the text is shown by lines, i.e., the individual characters are not shown. In the 100% view, the top part of the page displays. The 200% and Zoom views display portions of the document with enlarged letters. In 100%, 200% or Zoom views, the vertical and horizontal scroll bar can be used to view different portions of the document.

Start-Up Instructions

❖ The file named **4drill1L** should be displayed on the screen.

 **Use Print Preview**

1. Select the **Preview** button on the Button Bar {Shift and F7, 7}.

   Note: The Print Preview screen displays. Your screen will look similar to Figure 4.6; however, a different view may be selected.

2. Select the **100%** button {Alt and v, 1}.

3. Select the **200%** button {Alt and v, 2}.

4. Select the **Full Page** button {Alt and v, f}.

5. To exit the Print Preview window, select the **Close** button {F7}.

Finish-Up Instructions

❖ If any changes were made, save the file again using the same filename, **4drill1L** (select **File, Save**).

❖ Optional. Print one copy.

The Speller

The Speller is a WordPerfect feature that checks the spelling of each word and identifies duplicate words in a document. When a word is found that is not in one of WordPerfect's dictionaries, a list of words similar to the unrecognized word is displayed on the screen. If the correctly spelled word is displayed in the list of words, it can be selected. If the correctly spelled word is not displayed in the list, the word can be added to one of the WordPerfect dictionaries.

WordPerfect has two types of dictionaries: a main dictionary and supplemental dictionaries. The main dictionary is used to check the spelling of words for all documents. Supplemental dictionaries are created by individual users of WordPerfect and contain terms that an individual uses frequently. For example, a medical secretary might create a supplemental dictionary that contains medical terms. An unlimited number of supplemental dictionaries can be created.

If an entire document is to be checked for spelling accuracy, the cursor/insertion point can be located anywhere in the document. If only part of the document or a single word is to be checked, the desired portion of the document or the individual word is selected.

If the same word is typed twice, the Speller will identify the duplicated word. The duplicated word can be removed by selecting **Delete Duplicate Word**. To leave both occurrences of the word, **Continue** is selected.

Not all errors in a document are discovered by the spelling command. For example, words easily misspelled or mistyped, such as there/their, form/from, she/he, are not identified as incorrect words. Therefore, once the document is checked for spelling, it should also be carefully proofread for accurate meaning.

Start-Up Instructions

❖ The file named **4drill1L** should be displayed on the screen.

❖ Use the following steps and spell check the file named **4drill1L**. After using the Speller, be sure to proofread the document.

Use the Speller

1. Select the Speller button on the Button Bar {Ctrl and F2}.

   Note: The Speller dialog box displays. A dotted rectangle appears around the word Document to indicate that the entire document will be reviewed for spelling accuracy. If the dotted rectangle is not displayed around the word Document, press the up or down arrow key to move the rectangle.

2. Press Enter to begin the spell check.

   Note: The first unrecognized word is highlighted in the document and a list of suggested words displays in the Word Not Found box (see Figure 4.7). WordPerfect displays the

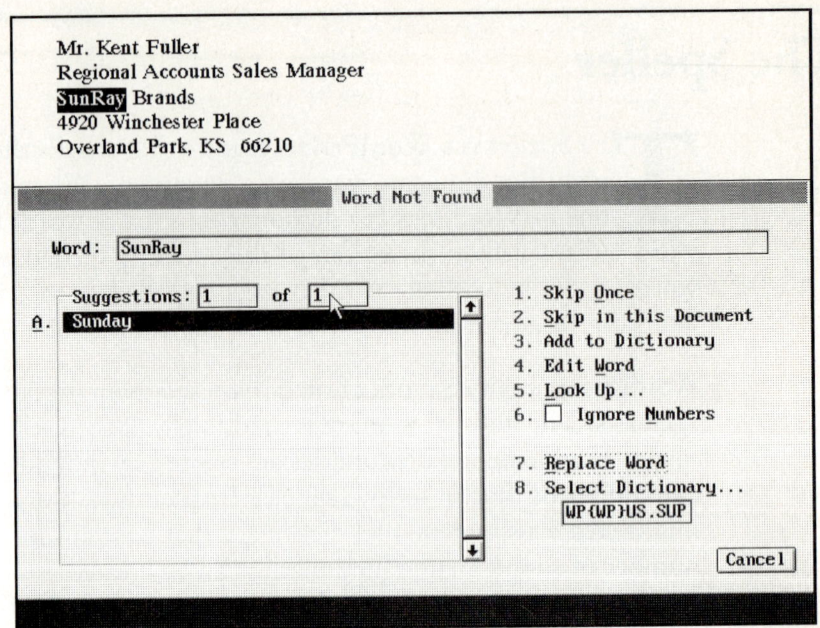

*word that most closely matches the spelling of the unrecognized word in the **Suggestions** box and the word is highlighted at the top of the list of suggested words.*

3. *To accept the highlighted word,* select **Replace Word** {r}. If desired, another word in the list of suggestions can be highlighted.

   If the correctly spelled word is shown in the list of suggestions, select the suggested word and select **Replace Word** {press the down arrow key to highlight the word, r}. The identified word is corrected on the screen and the spell check continues.

4. If the correct spelling of a word is not on the list, other options can be selected.

   a. Select **Skip Once** to skip the current instance of the word {o}.

   b. Select **Skip in this Document** to ignore the word throughout the remainder of the document {s}.

   c. Select **Add to Dictionary** to add the word to a WordPerfect supplemental dictionary {a}. The word will be added to the default supplemental directory. *To choose a different supplemental dictionary,* choose **Select Dictionary** and select the desired dictionary {y}.

   d. Select **Edit word**; type the correct word in the document. After the correction has been typed, press **F7** {w, type the correction, F7}.

   Note: *To discontinue the Speller before completion, select **Cancel** {Esc}.*

5. When the entire document has been checked, "Spell Check Completed." displays. Select **OK** {press Enter}.

Finish-Up Instructions

❖ Save the file on your file disk; use the new filename **4drill2** (select the **Save As** button, type the drive letter where the file disk is located followed a colon and the filename, select **OK**).

❖ Print one copy (select the **Print** button on the Button Bar, choose **Print**).

❖ Close the document (select **File, Close**).

Print Documents Using the File Manager

The WordPerfect File Manager can be used to print the contents of a file without displaying the document on the screen. The ability to print a file without opening it is useful if there are no changes to the document or if more than one document is to be printed.

Print Multiple Files Using the File Manager

1. Select the File Mgr button on the Button Bar {F5}.

2. Type the letter of the drive where the file disk is located followed by a colon and press Enter.

3. In the Sort by box, move the mouse pointer to the filename of the document to be printed and click once {use the arrow keys to highlight the desired filename}.

   For example, move the mouse pointer to 1drill1 and click.

4. Press the Spacebar to mark (place an asterisk beside) the selected filename.

5. To select another document to be printed, repeat Steps 3 and 4.

   For example, move the mouse pointer to 2drill1r and click. Press the Spacebar.

6. Select Print {p}.

   Note: A message displays, "Print marked files?".

7. Select Yes {y}.

   Note: The Print Multiple Pages dialog box displays.

8. Select OK to print all pages of the selected files {Enter}.

9. Select Close to exit the File Manager dialog box {Esc}.

Cancel the Printing of a Document

If a document is sent to be printed, the document usually prints within a few moments. However, if the document does not print, the Control Printer dialog box can be accessed to assist in determining the possible printer problem(s). A message in the Action area of the Control Printer dialog box may display "Check the ca-

ble, make sure printer is turned on" (see Figure 4.8). Check that the printer is turned on and that the printer cable is securely connected. Also, if the printer is shared, check the switch box or local area network (LAN) connection (see your instructor if necessary).

The Control Printer dialog box can also be used to display a list of the document filenames and the order in which the documents were sent to be printed. One or more of the listed filenames can be selected and cancelled from printing. In addition, if a document is the second or higher listed filename, the document can be marked and "rushed" to be the next document printed.

Steps to ▶ Display the Control Printer Dialog Box

1. Select the **Print** button on the Button Bar {Shift and F7}.

2. Select the **Control Printer** option {c}.

   Note: *Information about the document currently being printed displays in the Current Job area of the Control Printer dialog box. A list of all jobs waiting to print displays in the lower section of the dialog box. The program automatically numbers each document waiting to be printed. (See Figure 4.8.)*

3. *To mark and cancel the printing of one document,* highlight the document, select * **(Un)mark** {3}. Select **Cancel Job** {c}.

4. *To mark and cancel the printing of all documents,* select **(Un)mark All** {4}; select **Cancel Job** {c}. Select **Yes** to cancel all print jobs {y}.

5. Select **Close** {Esc}.

The Next Step

Chapter Review and Activities

FEATURES SUMMARY

FEATURES	ACTIONS	PAGE
Change margins	Select **Layout**, **Margins**, click once in the box located beside the margin to be changed, type the desired margin in inches. When desired margins have been changed, select **OK**.	85
Delete the vertical line spacing code	Turn on Reveal Codes (**Alt** and **F3**), move the mouse pointer to the line spacing code and click to select the code, press **Delete**. Turn off Reveal Codes.	86
Change font name and/or size	Select the **Font** button, move the mouse pointer to the down arrow beside the Font box and click to display a list of fonts, choose the desired font name. If desired, move the mouse pointer to the down arrow beside the Size box and click to display a list of sizes; click on the desired size. Select **OK**.	88
Use Print Preview	Select the **Preview** button. If desired, select the **100%**, **200%**, or **Full Page** buttons. Select **Close** to exit the Print Preview window.	90
Use the Speller	Select the **Speller** button, press **Enter**.	91
Print multiple files using the File Manager	Select the **File Manager** button, type the drive letter, press **Enter**. Select each file to be printed by highlight the filename and pressing the **Spacebar**, select **Print**, **Yes**, **OK**.	93

Self-Check Questions

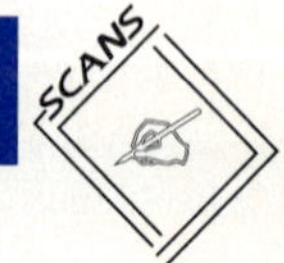

True/False—Circle One

T F 1. WordPerfect's default (preset) margins are each 1 inch.

T F 2. Margins are changed by using the **Layout**, **Margins** command, typing the desired margin in each box, and selecting **OK**.

T F 3. When using the Speller, the user can correct a word that is not found in any of the dictionaries.

T F 4. Once a font change is made for blocked text, the changed font is effective from the cursor/insertion point forward in the document or until another font is selected.

T F 5. The WordPerfect File Manager can be used to print a document without displaying the document on the screen.

Short Answer

1. Explain the difference between the main WordPerfect dictionary and the supplemental dictionaries.

2. List the four steps to delete the line spacing code.

3. List the nine steps to print multiple files using the File Manager.

4. List the top, left, and right margins that are suggested for an average letter (100–200 words).

5. What is one purpose for using Print Preview?

Enriching Language Arts Skills

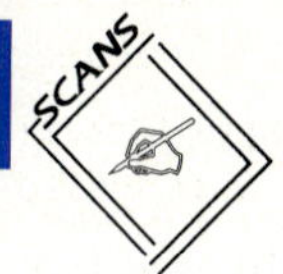

Spelling/Vocabulary Words

compliance   to conform to the rules.
mandatory   required.
regulation   rule or order.

Coordinating Conjunctions

A comma is placed before a coordinating conjunction (*and, or, because*) that joins
two independent clauses, i.e., clauses that are complete sentences.

> *Example:*
>
> *We will respond promptly to the questionnaire, because our company would like to
> maintain a good working relationship with our clients.*

No comma is placed before a conjunction if one or both clauses are dependent.

> *Example:*
>
> *We mailed 400 surveys yesterday and expect to obtain a 3 percent response by the end of May.*

Activities

Activity 4.1—Create a Traditional Style Letter, Change Margins, and Use Speller

1. If necessary, select the graphics mode and display the Button Bar and Ribbon.

2. Open the file named **3act1** that was typed in Chapter 3, page 73 (select
    File, Open, press **F5**, type the drive letter where the file disk is located fol-
    lowed by a colon, select **OK**, double-click on the filename).

3. Delete the line spacing code (**Alt** and **F3** to turn on Reveal Codes, move
    shaded/black block to the code, press **Delete**). Hint: The nonexpanded
    code displays [Ln Spacing].

4. Change the top margin to **2** inches; change the left and right margins to
    1.5 inches (select **Layout, Margins**, type the desired margins, select **OK**).

5. Use Speller to find and correct any misspelled words (select the **Speller**
    button on the Button Bar); also proofread carefully for accurate meaning.

6. Save the file on your file disk; use the filename **4act1** (select the **Save As**
    button, type the drive letter where the file disk is located followed by a co-
    lon and the filename, **OK**).

7. Print one copy (select the **Print** button on the Button Bar, choose **Print**).

8. Close the document (select **File, Close**).

Activity 4.2—Create a Traditional Style Letter, Change Margins, and Use Speller

1. Use the traditional letter style (page 59) and italic and bold text attributes as shown to type the following letter.

(Use current date)

Ms. Francine Meneze
1025 Deep Creek Dr.
St. Peters, MO 63376

Dear Ms. Meneze:

Just a quick note to introduce you to *Minute Express Copy Shop.*

We produce high-quality, low-cost copies quickly. When you figure the cost of maintenance and supplies for your office copier plus the operator's time, we are confident you will find that we can save you money as well as time. Also, our large inventory and complete bindery enable us to provide you with quality manuals, portfolios, and business forms that reflect a polished, professional image.

We have convenient hours to fit your busy schedule. We also offer *free* pick-up and delivery with a minimum order. Give us a chance to serve you; you'll see just how easy those routine copy jobs can be.

Sincerely,

Trung Huang
Manager

TH/xx
meneze.ltr/d5

---

2. Change the left, right, and top margins to **1.75** inches (select **Layout, Margins**, type desired margins, **OK**).

3. Change the font for the entire document to **Dutch 801 Roman, 12-point** or **make a choice of your own** (select the **Font** button, choose the desired font and size, select **OK**).

4. Change the justification to **Full** (select the **Justification** button on the Ribbon, select **Full**).

5. Use the Speller to find and correct any misspelled words (select the **Speller** button on the Button Bar); also proofread carefully for word and sentence meaning.

6. Save the file on your file disk; use the filename **4act2** (select the **Save As** button, type the drive letter where the file disk is located followed by a colon and the filename, **OK**).

7. Print one copy (select the **Print** button on the Button Bar, choose **Print**).

8. Close the document (select the **Close** button on the Button Bar).

Activity 4.3—Create an AMS Simplified Style Letter, Change Margins, and Use Speller

1. Type the following letter using the AMS simplified style (page 60). Bold text as shown.

(Use current date)

Mr. Victor Zelaya
3120 Kahala Ave.
Honolulu, HI 96816

WE APPRECIATE YOUR BUSINESS

Just a short note to thank you for your last purchase. Your business is very much appreciated, and sometimes in our haste to take care of your needs, we forget to say "**Thanks.**"

If I can be of further assistance, please feel free to contact me. Again, thank you for your business, and I hope to see you again soon.

W. R. FLETCHER, PRESIDENT/MANAGER

WRF/xx
zelaya.ltr/d4

---

2. Change the left and right margins to **2** inches and the top margin to **2.5** inches (select **Layout**, **Margins**, type the desired margins, select **OK**).

3. Change the **Font** for the entire document to **Dutch 801 Roman, 12-point** or **make a choice of your own** (select the **Font** button, choose the desired font and size, select **OK**).

4. Change the justification to **Full** (select the **Justification** button in the Ribbon, select **Full**).

5. Use the Speller to find and correct any misspelled words (select the **Speller** button); also proofread carefully for word and sentence meaning.

6. Save the file on your file disk; use the filename **4act3** (select the **Save As** button, type the drive letter where the file disk is located followed by a colon and the filename, **OK**).

7. Print one copy (select the **Print** button on the Button Bar, choose **Print**).

8. Close the document (select **File**, **Close**).

Challenge Your Skills

Skill 4.1—Create a Traditional Style Letter, Change Margins, and Use Speller

1. Use the traditional letter style and the following information.

   a. Use the current date.

   b. Send the letter to Mr. Gilbert Vogtlin, 92 Winston St., Blacksburg, VA 24060.

   c. Use Dear Gil as the salutation.

   d. Use an appropriate complimentary closing.

   e. Select a font of your own choice in a point size of 12.

   f. Use bold, underline, and italic text attributes as appropriate.

   g. The letter is from Carol E. Riggenbach.

   h. Carol's title is Training and Development Manager.

   i. Include your reference initials and document identification.

   j. A copy will be sent to B. G. Waziri.

   k. The letter body text follows:

   Congratulations. You have been selected to participate in the Account Management Selection and Development Seminar. This seminar will be held at the Radisson Hotel, Roanoke, Virginia beginning on the last

Chapter 4—Refine a Letter and Print Final Copy

Monday of next month. Reservations have been made in your name, but you will be responsible for all expenses. You must also make your own travel plans.

Arrive at the hotel by 4:30 p.m. to attend the seminar orientation meeting at 6:30 p.m. When you arrive at the hotel, check in first. The desk clerk will tell you the room number where the orientation meeting will be held.

There will be important materials to review Monday night, so plan to arrive rested and ready to work. Please bring a calculator with you. Attire throughout the seminar will be business dress, e.g., suits and ties. The seminar will end by 6:00 p.m. on Tuesday.

Again, congratulations. You have been recognized for your current performance and future potential and are joining a select group of management people.

2. Change margins to print the letter attractively on the page.

3. Use the Speller and proofread the letter.

4. Save the file on your file disk; use the filename **4skill1**.

5. Print one copy in final form.

6. Close the document.

Skill 4.2—Create an AMS Simplified Style Letter, Change Margins, and Use Speller

1. Use the AMS simplified letter style and the following information.

   a. Use the current date.

   b. Send the letter to Accounts Receivable, Abbey Mobile Services, 1297 Allegheny Ave., Philadelphia, PA 19106.

   c. The subject of the letter is INVOICE NO. 33-4893.

   d. The letter is from NINA SHERROD, ROYAL PRODUCTS.

   e. Select a font of your own choice in a point size of 12.

   f. Use bold, underline, and italic text attributes as appropriate.

   g. Include your reference initials, document identification, and enclosure notation.

   h. The letter body text follows:

   After my car was stolen last month, I immediately contacted your firm to have my mobile phone number disconnected. Apparently, the service was not disconnected, as my mobile car phone bill increased approximately $700.

I am responsible for the calls made prior to the date my car was stolen. These charges totaled $738.52. However, I am not responsible for any calls made after the date my car was stolen or for any of the roaming charges that were incurred from outside the 215 area code. Please credit my account for $694.38.

I have enclosed a check in the amount of $138.52 and would like to pay $100 per month until the total amount is paid. Please advise me if this arrangement is acceptable.

Your consideration in this matter will be very much appreciated.

2.   Change margins to print the letter attractively on the page.

3.   Use Full justification.

4.   Use the Speller and proofread the letter.

5.   Save the file on your file disk; use the filename **4skill2**.

6.   Print one copy in final form.

7.   Close the document.

➥ Skill 4.3—Create a Traditional Style Letter, Change Margins, and Use Speller; Language Arts

1.   Use the traditional letter style and the following information.

   a. Use the current date.

   b. Select a font of your own choice in a point size of 12.

   c. Use bold, underline, and italic text attributes as appropriate.

   d. Send the letter to Hector and Lenora Achtenberg, 209 Stevens Drive, Richland, WA 99342.

   e. Use Dear Mr. and Mrs. Achtenberg as the salutation.

   f. Use an appropriate complimentary closing.

   g. The letter is from Mildred Kosowski.

   h. Mildred's title is Medical Group Director.

   i. Include your reference initials and document identification.

   j. Copies of the letter will be sent to T. Richardson and N. Hyden.

   k. Correct three spelling and two punctuation errors.

   l. The letter body text follows:

This is to update you on changing regulasions in the health care field and how Benton Medical Group fees and billing practices will be affected.

Last year, the federal government changed the way Medicare health care services are defined and charged. Consequently doctors must use new codes and follow new rules to determine the type of service, which then dictates the charge for the office visit.

On June 1, Benton Medical Group will begin to use the new codes for all reporting. Some of our fees have been raised and some lowered, based on the federal schedule, which emphasizes the value of primary care. This is the care given in a doctor's office or in a clinic such as Benton Medical.

We understand that these changes may be inconvenient or confusing. Complience with the new regulations is mandotary, and we wanted you to know why the exact cost of your visit cannot be quoted in advance.

If you have any questions please feel free to call Patient Assistance at (509) 555-6006.

2. Change margins to print the letter attractively on the page.

3. Use full justification.

4. Print one copy with line spacing of two.

5. Save the file on your file disk; use the filename **4skill3**.

6. Use the following information to change the letter.

    a. Delete the fourth paragraph.

    b. Insert the following paragraph above the last paragraph:

    One important factor in determining the proper code is referred to as "the complexity of medical decision-making." This can only be decided by the physician after he or she has interacted with the patient. Because this is not known before the visit, we cannot tell you exactly what the office charge will be in advance.

    c. Return the document to line spacing of one.

7. Use the Speller and proofread the letter.

8. Save the file again using the new filename **4skill3r**.

9. Print one copy and close the document.

10. If you have completed your work, exit WordPerfect (select **File**, **Exit WP**).

Part 1
Checking Your Step

Production Skill Builder Activities
Chapters 1-4

Production Activity 1.1—Create and Edit a Memorandum—Style 1

1. Use Memorandum—Style 1 and the following information to create a memorandum.

   a. Make decisions regarding:

      Margins
      Justification
      Memo date
      Use of Speller
      Reference initials

   b. Send the memorandum to All Administrative Support Staff from Chris Fosdahl.

   c. The subject of the memorandum is Alternative Work Schedules.

   d. Memorandum body text follows:

   For the past three years, we have been researching alternative work schedules such as flex time, shared time, and the four-day week. We appreciate your opinions and ideas concerning this matter.

   At its last meeting, the board of directors granted approval for a flex-time schedule in two departments and a shortened work week in a third department. Both of these plans will operate for a six-month trial period. Accounting, Marketing, and Quality Assurance are the three departments involved in this experiment. All other departments will remain on their normal schedules.

At the end of the trial period, wc will assess the results and determine whether we should stay with the old schedules or convert all departments to alternative work plans.

2. Save the file; use the filename **1pact1**.

3. Revise the memorandum as shown:

For the past three years, we have been researching alternative work schedules such as flex time, shared time, and the four-day week. ~~We appreciate~~ your opinions and ideas ~~concerning this matter~~ *a* *have been very much appreciated.*

At its last meeting, the board of directors granted approval for a flex-time schedule in ~~two~~ *the* departments and a shortened work week in a ~~third~~ *fourth* department. ~~Both~~ *All* of these plans will operate for a ~~six~~ *four*-month trial period. Accounting, Marketing, and Quality *Personnel,* Assurance are the ~~three~~ *four* departments involved in this experiment. All other departments will remain on their normal schedules.

¶ Personnel in the affected departments should discuss their new work schedules with their respective managers. A survey will be sent out to all employees to obtain each individual's opinion concerning the new work schedules.

At the end of the trial period, ~~we will assess~~ *will be assessed* the results and determine whether we *a decision will be made to* should stay with the old schedules or convert all departments to alternative work plans.

---

4. Save the file again.

5. Print one copy and close the document.

Production Activity 1.2—Create and Edit a Memorandum—Style 2

1. Use Memorandum—Style 2 and the following information to create a memorandum.

   a. Make decisions regarding:

      Margins
      Justification
      Memo date
      Use of Speller
      Reference initials
      Enclosure notation

b. The memorandum should be sent to All Engineering Departments.

c. The memorandum is from G. L. Fetter.

d. The subject of the memorandum is Engineering Change Notice Audit.

e. The memorandum will be distributed to R. Hightower, O. Crockett, V. Brauer, S. Vaughn, B. Ziegler, T. Wong, and K. Milani.

f. The memorandum body text follows:

In response to your request to audit Engineering Change Notices, the following plan will be implemented in the Design and Configuration Control department starting with the fiscal year in July.

On a monthly basis, the Design and Configuration Control department will provide a package of ECNs and associated documents gathered from a 25 percent random sample of all ECNs processed through Unit 168. A weekly tally sheet (see enclosed) will be used to indicate the reason for changing every tenth ECN collected.

Unit 168 will not make prints of any associated documents to ECNs as they are processed, since the process is quite costly. We will wait approximately two weeks to request additional documents for DRC.

I hope these procedures will alleviate our current mutual problems.

2. Save the file; use the filename **1pact2**.

3. Use the following information to revise the memorandum.

   a. In the first sentence after Engineering Change Notices, type (ECNs).

   b. Delete the last sentence of the second paragraph.

   c. Insert the following paragraph above the last paragraph:

   Unit 168 will schedule regular monthly meetings with you and your staff to review the ECN package. In addition, Unit 168 will publish a report for Terry Woolcock based on the results of each monthly meeting.

4. Save the file again.

5. Print one copy and close the document.

Production Activity 1.3—Create and Edit a Traditional Style Letter

1. Use the traditional style letter and the following information to create a letter.

   a. Make decisions regarding:
      Margins
      Justification

Fonts
Salutation
Closing
Use of Speller
Reference initials
Documentation identification
Enclosure notation

b. The letter should be sent to Mrs. Cecelia Janowsky, 1415 Brevard West, Tallahassee, FL 32304.

c. The letter is from Mr. Lester Briegleb, District Manager.

d. The letter body text follows:

Here is your new **Allied Banking Check Guarantee Card**. It replaces your current check guarantee card. This new card is effective immediately. Destroy your old check guarantee card immediately.

This card guarantees your personal check for up to $200 <u>at more than 300 Allied Banking offices</u> statewide and at thousands of merchant locations throughout Florida as well. Our check guarantee program is still relatively new, and more merchants are being added daily.

Please sign your new card right away, carry it with you for convenience, and let us know promptly if it is lost or stolen.

Your **Allied Banking Card** assures everyone that the reputation and resources of Florida's newest bank stand firmly behind the checks you write. We hope you find it a useful financial aid.

It is a pleasure to be of service to you.

2. Save the file; use the filename **1pact3**.

3. Revise the letter as shown:

Enclosed

~~Here~~ is your new **Allied Banking Check Guarantee Card**. It replaces your current *at the end of the month.* check guarantee card. This new card is effective/~~immediately~~./~~Destroy~~ your old check *In order To protect yourself, cut up* guarantee card immediately. *The new Check Guarantee Card is designed with a hologram to assure the authenticity of the card.*

This card guarantees your personal check for up to $~~200~~ *300* at more than ~~300~~ *350* Allied Banking offices statewide and at thousands of merchant locations throughout Florida as well. Our check guarantee program is still relatively new, and more merchants are being added daily./ *This means that every day your Allied Banking Check Guarantee Card becomes more useful.*

Please sign your new card right away, carry it with you for convenience, and let us know promptly if it is lost or stolen. *To report a lost or stolen card, call our 24-hour customer service hotline at 1-800-555-3033.*

Your **Allied Banking Card** assures everyone that the reputation and resources of Florida's newest bank stand firmly behind the checks you write. We hope you find it a useful financial aid.

We are glad ~~It is a pleasure~~ to be of service to you.

4. Save the file again.

5. Print one copy and close the document.

❧ Production Activity 1.4—Create and Edit an AMS Simplified Style Letter; Language Arts

1. Use the AMS simplified style letter and the following information to create a letter.

   a. Make decisions regarding:

   Margins
   Justification
   Fonts
   Subject line
   Text attributes (bold, underline, italic)
   Use of Speller
   Reference initials
   Documentation identification
   Enclosure notation
   Correct three spelling and two punctuation errors

   b. The letter should be sent to Leland and Nelly Kroff, 2403 Mill Glenn Court, Atlanta, GA 30338.

   c. The letter is from Shane Treakle, Vice President.

   d. The letter body text follows:

   You have undoubtedly read and heard a lot recently about the problems of the nation's financial institutions, including some insurance companies. Therefore we are pleased to send you a copy of last year's annual report for Global Consolidated Life Insurance (GCL).

We have just experienced one of the most comendable years in the company's 93-year history. We had a record net income of $30 million on total revenue of almost $890 million. We actually held operating expenses below the previous year's level, and the company reached a new milestone last month--$5 billion in assets.

More than 95 percent of the company's assets are invested in bonds, short-term debt instruments, and first mortgage loans. At year end, not a single bond issues was in payment default, and not a single mortgage was in foreclosure.

When you need additional insurance or seek a high return on an individual anuity, we hope you will contact your GCL agent. Our company has been in existance for more than 90 years, and you can count on GCL being there when you need us.

2.   Save the file; use the filename **1pact4**.

3.   Use the following information to revise the letter.

   a. In the second paragraph change the word "company's" to GCL's.

   b. Change the net income to $32.5 million and total revenues to $900 million.

   c. Delete the last sentence of the third paragraph and insert the following sentences:

     Based on the company's financial condition and operating performance, GCL continues to earn a superior rating. We have had a top rating recommendation since 1955.

   d. Insert the following paragraph above the third paragraph:

     Of course, the financial strength of the company really rests on the quality of our invested assets, and we believe that our invested assets are first rate.

4.   Use the new filename **1pact4r** and save the file again.

5.   Print one copy and close the document.

Use Automatic Functions

Features Covered

- Move
- Copy
- Search
- Replace
- Indent
- Double indent
- Print selected text

Objectives

After successfully completing this chapter, you will be able to rearrange text using the Move and Copy features, search for specified text, and replace the text automatically. You will also create enumerated lists using the Indent feature and you will be able to indent paragraphs from both the left and right margins.

Chapter Introduction

Automatic functions are special WordPerfect features designed to efficiently replace text and/or rearrange text. Text can be moved, copied, searched for, and replaced automatically. In addition, text can be rearranged by indenting lines of a paragraph from the left margin or from the left and right margins. Also, once a document has been arranged, a portion can be printed.

Move Text

Moving text is the process of relocating text. For example, a paragraph in the middle of a letter can be moved to the end of the letter. Paragraphs, sentences, or lines can be moved. Generally, once text has been typed, retyping should be unnecessary.

The text to be moved must first be blocked (selected). Once the text is blocked, WordPerfect provides several methods for moving text. Three methods for moving text are described in the Steps to Move Text Using the Edit, Cut and Paste Command; the Steps to Move Text Using Edit, Cut and Edit, Paste Commands; and the Steps to Move Text Using the Drop and Drag Text Feature.

Start-Up Instructions

- ❖ Type the letter shown in Figure 5.1.

- ❖ Save the file on your file disk; use the filename **5drill1** (select the **Save As** button, type the drive letter where the file disk is located followed by a colon and the filename, select **OK**).

Move Text Using the Edit, Cut and Paste Command

Note: With this method, the text must be pasted (retrieved) into the document before performing any other actions.

1. Block the desired text.

    For example, place the cursor/insertion point in the second paragraph and block the paragraph and following line by choosing **Edit, Select, Paragraph** {Alt and e, s, p}.

2. Select **Edit, Cut and Paste** {press **Ctrl** and **Delete**}.

    Note: The text is deleted from the original location and placed in the temporary memory.

3. Place the insertion point to the left of (or the cursor under) the first character or space that will follow the moved text.

    For example, move the cursor under or insertion point to the left of the first character of the first paragraph.

4. Press **Enter** to insert the text at the new location. Notice that the second paragraph is now the first paragraph.

    Note: A copy of the moved text remains in temporary memory until replaced by other deleted or copied text or WordPerfect is exited.

Finish-Up Instructions

- ❖ Save the file on your file disk; use the new filename, **5drill1r** (select the **Save As** button, type the drive letter where the file disk is located followed by a colon and the filename, select **OK**).

(Use current date)

Ms. Candace Boardman
Newcastle, Inc.
6300 Marina Ave., Suite 40
Emeryville, CA 94608

Dear Ms. Boardman:

Per our conversation of last Tuesday, enclosed is a remittance check for $300 on the disputed amount owed on my bill.

It is understood that my line of credit will be reestablished. In the spirit of cooperation, $75 will be waived by Newcastle as agreed by your collection manager, Samuel Alexander.

Sincerely,

Fred Thompson

FT/xx
bdman.ltr/disk4

Enc.

Document used to practice
moving text

❖   Print one copy (select the **Print** button on the Button Bar).

❖   Close the document (select **File, Close**).

Start-Up Instructions

❖   Open the file named **5drill1** or type the letter shown in Figure 5.1.

Move Text Using the Edit, Cut and Edit, Paste Commands

Note: With this method, text can be pasted (retrieved) into the current document or into other documents as many times as needed. Other actions can be accomplished between the cut step and the paste step.

1. Block the desired text.

    For example, place the cursor/insertion point in the second paragraph and block the paragraph and following blank line by choosing **Edit, Select, Paragraph** {Alt and e, s, p}.

2. Select **Edit, Cut** {press Ctrl and x}.

    Note: The text is deleted from the original location and placed in the temporary memory.

3. Place the insertion point to the left of (or the cursor under) the first character or space that will follow the moved text.

For example, move the insertion point to the left of (or the cursor under) the first character in the first paragraph.

4. Select **Edit, Paste** to insert the text at the new location {press Ctrl and v}. Notice that the second paragraph is now the first paragraph.

Note: A copy of the moved text remains in temporary memory until replaced by other cut or copied text or until WordPerfect is exited.

Finish-Up Instructions

❖ Use the new filename **5drill2** and save the file on your file disk (select the **Save As** button, type the drive letter where the file disk is located followed by a colon and the filename, select **OK**).

❖ Print one copy (select the **Print** button on the Button Bar).

❖ Close the document (select **File, Close**).

Start-Up Instructions

❖ Open the file named **5drill1** or type the letter shown in Figure 5.1.

Move Text Using the Drop and Drag Text Feature

Note: A mouse must be used to drop and drag text.

1. Block the desired text.

   For example, place the cursor/insertion point in the second paragraph and block the paragraph and following blank line by choosing **Edit, Select, Paragraph**.

2. Move the mouse pointer into the blocked (highlighted) text.

3. Press and hold the left mouse button and drag the mouse pointer to the new location.

   For example, while holding the mouse button, drag the mouse pointer to the left of the first character of the first paragraph.

   Note: A small square and an outline of a square display at the bottom of the mouse pointer.

4. Release the mouse button.

   Note: The paragraph is moved to the new location.

Finish-Up Instructions

❖ Use the new filename **5drill3** and save the file on your file disk (select the **Save As** button, type the drive letter where the file disk is located followed by a colon and the filename, select **OK**).

❖ Print one copy (select the **Print** button on the Button Bar).

❖ Close the document (select **File, Close**).

Chapter 5—Use Automatic Functions

Copy Text

Copying text is the process of duplicating text. For example, a document, sentence, name, or paragraph may need to appear again on the page, in another part of the current document or in a different document. Text can be copied from the original location and repeated in a second location. The text to be copied must first be blocked (selected). Once the text has been blocked, WordPerfect provides several methods for copying text. Three methods for copying text are described in the Steps to Copy Text Using the Edit, Copy and Paste Command; the Steps to Copy Text Using Edit, Copy and Edit, Paste Commands; and the Steps to Copy Text Using the Drop and Drag Text Feature.

Start-Up Instructions

❖ Open the file named **1drill2** typed in Chapter 1, page 23.

❖ Move the insertion point to the bottom of the document (**Home**, **Home**, down arrow key) and press **Enter** twice.

❖ The following steps will be used to make a copy of the entire document. Both copies will appear on the same page.

Copy Text Using the Edit, Copy and Paste Command

Note: With this method, the text must be pasted (retrieved) into the document before performing any other actions. Other actions can not be accomplished between the copy step and the paste step.

1. Block the text to be copied.

   For example, block the entire document by choosing **Edit, Select, Page** {Alt and e, s, a}.

2. Select **Edit, Copy and Paste** to copy the blocked text {press Ctrl and Insert}.

3. Place the insertion point to the left of (or the cursor under) the first character or space that will follow the copied text.

   For example, move the cursor/insertion point to the blank line below the last name in the distribution list.

4. Press **Enter** to insert the copied text into the document.

   Note: When the copied text is inserted, the insertion point is located to the left of (or the cursor is under) the first character of the copied text. Use the arrow keys to move down through the document to see the copied text. The copied text remains in the original location and is displayed in the new location.

Finish-Up Instructions

❖ Use the new filename **5drill4** and save the file on your file disk (select the **Save As** button, type the drive letter where the file disk is located followed by a colon and the filename, select **OK**).

❖ Print one copy (select the **Print** button on the Button Bar).

❖ Close the document (select **File, Close**).

Start-Up Instructions

❖ Open the file named **1drill2** typed in Chapter 1, page 23.

❖ The following steps will be used to make a copy of the entire document. Both copies will appear on the same page.

Copy Text Using the Edit, Copy and Edit, Paste Commands

Note: With this method, text can be copied into the current document or other documents as many times as needed.

1. Block the text to be copied.

   For example, block the entire document by choosing **Edit, Select, Page** {Alt and e, s, a}.

2. Select **Edit, Copy** to copy the blocked text {Ctrl and c}.

3. Place the insertion point to the left of (or the cursor under) the first character or space that will follow the copied text.

   For example, move the cursor/insertion point to the blank line below the last name in the distribution list and press the **Enter** key three times.

4. Select **Edit, Paste** to insert the copied text into the document {Ctrl and v}.

   Note: When the copied text is inserted, the insertion point is located to the left of (or the cursor is under) the first character of the copied text. Use the arrow keys to move down through the document to see the copied text. The copied text remains in the original location and is displayed in the new location. A copy of the copied (or deleted) text also remains in temporary memory until replaced by other copied (or deleted) text or WordPerfect is exited.

Finish-Up Instructions

❖ Use the new filename **5drill4c** and save the file on your file disk (select the **Save As** button, type the drive letter where the file disk is located followed by a colon and the filename, select **OK**).

❖ Print one copy (select the **Print** button on the Button Bar).

❖ Close the document (select **File, Close**).

- ❖ Open the file named **1drill2** typed in Chapter 1, page 23.

- ❖ Move the insertion point to the bottom of the document (**Home**, **Home**, down arrow key) and press **Enter** twice.

- ❖ The following steps will be used to make a copy of the entire document. Both copies will appear on the same page.

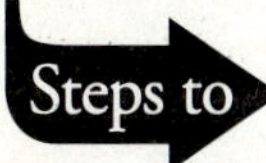

Copy Text Using the Drop and Drag Text Feature

Note: A mouse must be used to drop and drag text.

1. Block the desired text.

   For example, place the cursor/insertion point in the second paragraph and block the paragraph and following blank line by choosing **Edit**, **Select**, **Paragraph** {Alt and e, s, p}.

2. Move the mouse pointer into the blocked (highlighted) text.

3. Press and hold and the left mouse button and drag the mouse pointer to the new location.

   For example, while holding the mouse button, drag the mouse pointer to the second blank line below the last name in the distribution list.

   Note: A small square and an outline of a square display at the bottom of the mouse pointer.

4. Press and hold the **Ctrl** key as the mouse button is released.

   Note: The copied paragraph displays in the original location and the new location.

Finish-Up Instructions

- ❖ Use the new filename **5drill4d** and save the file on your file disk (select the **Save As** button, type the drive letter where the file disk is located followed by a colon and the filename, select **OK**).

- ❖ Print one copy (select the **Print** button on the Button Bar).

- ❖ Close the document (select **File**, **Close**).

Search for Text

Searching is the process of locating a word or group of words in a document. With the Search command, text can be easily located in a document. Once the text is located, changes can be made in a document. The Search command is accessed by selecting **Edit**, **Search** or by selecting the **Search** button on the Button Bar. When the Search dialog box displays, the text to be located is typed in the Search For box. The Search dialog box also contains the Backward Search, Case Sensitive

Search, Find Whole Words Only, and Extended Search options that are used to fine-tune the search process.

WordPerfect can also search a document for codes such as margin, justification, and line spacing codes. The Codes and Specific Codes buttons are used to instruct Word-Perfect to look for codes in a document. See Chapter 10 for additional information on searching for codes.

Start-Up Instructions

- ❖ Type the paragraphs shown in Figure 5.2. (Your typed paragraph lines may not end with the same words as shown; that's OK.)
- ❖ Save the file on your file disk; use the filename **5drill5** (select the **Save As** button, type the drive letter where the file disk is located followed by a colon and the filename, select **OK**).
- ❖ Print one copy (select the Print button on the Button Bar).

Search for Text

1. Place the cursor/insertion point at the beginning of the text to be searched (**Home**, **Home**, up arrow key).

2. Select the **Search** button on the Button Bar {F2}.

   Note: The Search dialog box is displayed at the bottom of the screen. The cursor is located in the Search For box (see Figure 5.3).

3. Type the word or words to be found in the Search For box.

   For example, type **LFS** in the Search For box.

   Note: The Search dialog box contains the following options.

   Backward Search—When the Backward Search option is selected, WordPerfect will look for the specified text from the location of the cursor/insertion point back to the beginning of the document. An "X" in the box next to the words "Backward Search" indicates that the option is turned on.

<table>
<tr><td>

Document used to practice searching for text

</td><td>

The loan processing computer system at LFS has recently been upgraded in order to better serve our customers. New loan numbers have been assigned to all LFS mortgage accounts. Your new loan number is shown on your monthly loan statement.

At LFS we are continually looking for ways to improve service to our customers. A newly instituted service--LFS Automatic Transfer--provides for the payment of mortgage loans via an automatic monthly transfer of funds from a checking or savings account.

</td></tr>
</table>

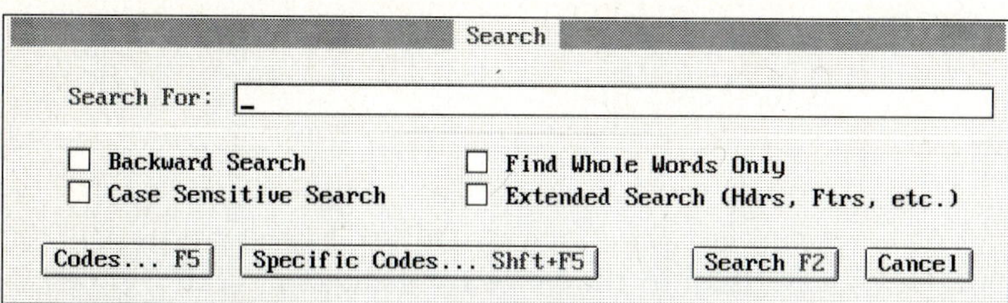

Search dialog box

Case Sensitive Search—When the Case Sensitive Search option is selected, WordPerfect will search for text that exactly matches the case of the text typed in the Search For box. An "X" in the box next to the words "Case Sensitive Search" indicates that the option is turned on.

Find Whole Words Only—When the Find Whole Words Only option is selected, WordPerfect will locate the next occurrence of matching text that is a word by itself. An "X" in the box next to the words "Find Whole Words Only" indicates that the option is turned on.

Extended Search—When Extended Search is turned on, WordPerfect will search the document text and any headers, footers, footnotes, etc. An "X" in the box next to the words "Extended Search (Hdrs, Ftrs, etc.)" indicates that the option is turned on.

4. Select **Search** {F2}. Notice that the insertion point moves to the right of the found text.

5. The text can be edited and the Search procedure continued.

   a. Edit by deleting, inserting, or replacing.

      For example, press **Ctrl** and **Backspace** to delete the letters LFS and type **LaGrande Federal Savings** and press the **Spacebar** once.

   b. To continue to search for the next occurrence of the same text, select the **Search** button, choose **Search** in the Search dialog box {press F2 twice}.

      For example, continue the search process and change all occurrences of **LFS** to **LaGrande Federal Savings**.

   c. When the message "Not Found" displays, no additional occurrences of the searched text can be located.

   d. Select **OK** {Enter}.

Finish-Up Instructions

   ❖ When the entire text has been searched, use the new filename **5drill5s** and save the file on your file disk (select the **Save As** button, type the drive letter where the file disk is located followed by a colon and the filename, select **OK**).

   ❖ Print one copy (select the **Print** button on the Button Bar).

   ❖ Close the document (select **File, Close**).

Mouse and Menu Method

1. Place the insertion point at the beginning of the text to be searched (**Home, Home,** up arrow).

2. Select **Edit, Search** {F2}.

3. Continue with Steps 3-5 described in the Steps to Search for Text.

Replace Text Automatically

Replacing text automatically is the process of locating and deleting specific text and inserting new text. The document is searched for a specific word or group of words. Each occurrence of the specified text can be replaced automatically with new text.

Start-Up Instructions

❖ Open the file named **5drill5**.

❖ All occurrences of **LFS** are to be replaced with the text **Landmark Financial Services**.

Replace Text Automatically

1. Place the cursor/insertion point at the beginning of the text to be searched (**Home, Home,** up arrow key).

2. Select **Edit, Replace** {Alt and F2}.

   Note: The Search and Replace dialog box is displayed at the bottom of the screen. The cursor is located in the Search For box (see Figure 5.4). The code <Nothing> may display in the Replace With box.

3. Type the text to be replaced in the Search For box.

   For example, type **LFS** in the Search For box.

   Note: The Search and Replace dialog box contains several options including the Backward Search, Case Sensitive Search, Find Whole Words only, and Extended Search options (see Step 3 on pages 120 and 121 for information on these options). The Search and Replace dialog box also contains the Confirm Replacement and Limit Number of Matches options.

   Confirm Replacement—When the Confirm Replacement option is selected, WordPerfect will stop at each occurrence of the specified text and ask whether the text should be replaced.

   Limit Number of Matches—When Limit Number of Matches is selected, you can specify the number of times the Search For text should be replaced.

4. Click in the **Replace With** box {Tab}.

FIGURE 5.4

Search and Replace dialog box

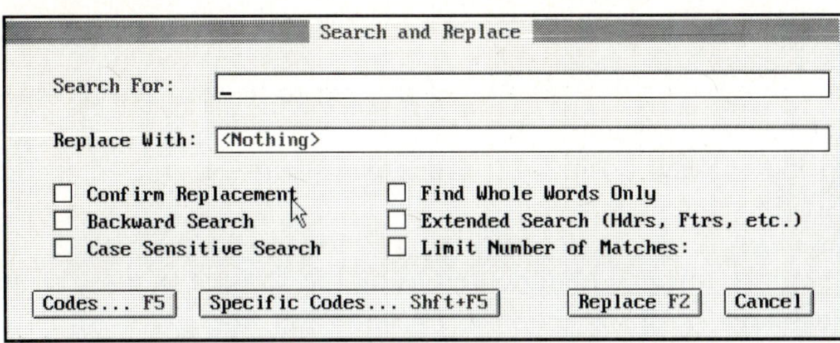

Note: The code <Nothing> is removed from the Replace With box.

5. Type the new text in the Replace With box.

   For example, type **Landmark Financial Services**. (Do not type the period.)

6. Select **Replace** {F2}. WordPerfect instantly changes the specified text.

7. When all occurrences of the specified text are replaced, the message displays, *Search and Replace Complete* and the number of occurrences of the specified text and the number of replacements made are indicated. Select **OK** {Enter}.

   Note: The cursor/insertion point displays at the location where text was last replaced.

Finish-Up Instructions

❖ Use the new filename **5drill5r** and save the file on your file disk (select the **Save As** button, type the drive letter where the file disk is located followed by a colon and the filename, select **Save**).

❖ Print one copy (select the **Print** button on the Button Bar).

❖ Close the document (select **File**, **Close**).

Undo Replaced Text

Since WordPerfect replaces all occurrences of specified text rapidly, it may be necessary to undo the replaced text if word(s) are found that should not have been changed. To undo the replaced text, select **Edit**, **Undo** {Alt and e, u} before performing any other actions.

Create Lists and Paragraphs Using the Indent Feature

Text can be indented to improve readability and enhance the document's appearance. Indenting all lines temporarily from the left margin is accomplished by pressing the **F4** key or by selecting **Layout**, **Alignment**, **Indent**. If the Indent feature is used, all lines of a paragraph are indented until the **Enter** key is pressed. Frequently, text is indented to align the lines that follow the first line of an enumerated item (see Figure 5.5).

The first time the Indent feature is used, the insertion point moves to the first preset tab and all text is indented at that position. If the Indent feature is utilized again, the second preset tab is used to indent the text.

Both sides of a paragraph or line can be indented using the Double Indent feature. To indent text an equal amount of space on the left and right sides, press **Shift** and **F4** or select **Layout**, **Alignment**, **Indent** → ←. Often a paragraph is double-indented in a letter to show emphasis.

Start-Up Instructions

❖ In a clear document window, type and center the title of the document shown in Figure 5.5. Press **Enter** three times.

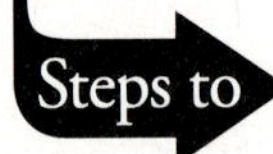

Create a Numbered List

1. Type the number for the enumerated item followed by a period.

   For example, type a **1** followed by a period.

2. Select **Layout**, **Alignment**, **Indent** or press **F4**.

3. Type the text to be indented.

   For example, type: **Any combination equivalent to completion of high school and three years of increasingly responsible experience in the operation, repair, and maintenance of heating, ventilation, and cooling systems.**

   Note: WordPerfect will automatically indent all the lines of the paragraph to align with the indent of the first line.

4. Press the **Enter** key twice after each enumerated paragraph.

   *Note: Once the **Enter** key is pressed, the cursor/insertion point returns to the left margin and the Indent feature is turned off.*

Finish-Up Instructions

❖ Use the Steps to Create a Numbered List and complete the document shown in Figure 5.5.

❖ Save the file on your file disk; use the filename **5drill6** (select the **Save As** button, type the drive letter where the file disk is located followed by a colon and the filename, select **OK**).

❖ Print one copy (select the **Print** button on the Button Bar).

❖ Close the document (select **File**, **Close**).

Applicant Requirements--Air Conditioning Mechanic

1. Any combination equivalent to completion of high school and three
    years of increasingly responsible experience in the operation,
    repair, and maintenance of heating, ventilation, and cooling
    systems.

2. Hold a valid driver's license authorizing operation of motor
    vehicles.

3. Successful compliance with job-related medical standards as
    determined by a medical examination conducted by a
    company-approved physician.

4. Proof of U.S. citizenship or proof of legal authorization to work in
    the United States.

Start-Up Instructions

❖ In a clear document window, type the salutation and the first paragraph of the
   letter shown in Figure 5.6. Press **Enter** twice after the first paragraph.

Steps to ▶ Create Paragraphs Using the Double Indent Feature

1. Select **Layout, Alignment, Indent** → ← to turn on the Double Indent feature
    {Shift and F4}.

2. Type the paragraph to be indented from both the left and right margins. Press
    Enter twice at the end of the paragraph.

    > For example, type: **If you were to die as a result of an accident,
    > the All-in-One Plan would cancel your mortgage debt and leave
    > your family secure in a mortgage-free home.**

    *Note: When **Enter** is pressed, the insertion point returns to the left margin and the
    Double Indent feature is turned off.*

Finish-Up Instructions

❖ Use the Steps to Create Paragraphs Using the Double Indent Feature and complete the document shown in Figure 5.6.

❖ Save the file on your file disk; use the filename **5drill7** (select the **Save As** button, type the drive letter where the file disk is located followed by a colon and
   the filename, select **OK**).

❖ Print one copy (select the **Print** button on the Button Bar).

❖ Close the document (select **File, Close**).

Dear Mortgage Customer:

Recently we wrote to you about a unique plan of insurance that would provide flexible protection for your family.

    If you were to die as a result of an accident, the All-in-One Plan would cancel your mortgage debt and leave your family secure in a mortgage-free home.

This insurance plan would also provide your family with an important financial cushion when they would need it most. After the plan pays off the mortgage balance, any remaining benefit goes to the beneficiary of your choice.

    You simply cannot be turned down, regardless of your health or occupation. No medical exam or answers to health questions are required.

Take action today. Send for your application form by filling out the enclosed, postage-paid card.

Sincerely,

Jean Silverburg
Vice President

Print Blocked Text

Once a document has been typed, only a portion of the text can be printed if desired. The text to be printed is blocked. The **Print** button is chosen. Blocked text prints at the location on the page where the text would have printed if the entire document were to be printed. For example, if the blocked text is located in the middle of the page, the text will print in the middle of the page.

Start-Up Instructions

❖ Open the file named **5drill6**.

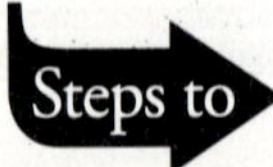

Steps to ▶ Print Blocked Text

1. Block the text to be printed.

   For example, block the entire number 3 paragraph.

2. Select the **Print** button on the Button Bar {Alt and f, p}.

   Note: When the Print dialog box displays, a black dot appears to the left of the Blocked Text option in the Print box.

Chapter 5—Use Automatic Functions

3. Select **Print** to print the blocked text {Enter}.

Finish-Up Instructions

❖ Close the document (select **File, Close**).

The Next Step

Chapter Review and Activities

FEATURES SUMMARY

FEATURES	ACTIONS	PAGE
Move text:		
Edit, Cut and Paste	Block the text to be moved, select **Edit, Cut and Paste**, move the insertion point to the new location, press **Enter**.	114
Edit, Cut and Edit, Paste	Block the text to be moved, select **Edit, Cut**, move the insertion point to the new location, select **Edit, Paste**.	115
Drop and drag	Block the text to be moved, move the insertion point into the highlighted text, press and hold the left mouse button and drag the mouse pointer to the desired location, release the mouse button.	116
Copy text:		
Edit, Copy and Paste	Block the text to be copied, select **Edit, Copy and Paste**, move the insertion point to the desired location, press **Enter**.	117
Edit, Copy and Edit, Paste	Block the text to be copied, select **Edit, Copy**, move the insertion point to the desired location, select **Edit, Paste**.	118
Drop and drag	Block the text to be copied, move the mouse pointer into the highlighted text, press and hold the mouse button and drag the mouse pointer to the desired location, press the **Ctrl** button as the mouse button is released.	119

FEATURES *(cont'd.)*	ACTIONS *(cont'd.)*	PAGE
Search for text	Select the **Search** button, type the word(s) to be found in the Search For box, select desired options, select **Search**.	120
Replace text automatically	Select **Edit**, **Replace**, type the word(s) to be replaced in the Search For box, click in the **Replace With** box, type the new text, select desired options, select **Replace**.	122
Create numbered list	Type the number for the enumerated item followed by a period, select **Layout**, **Alignment**, **Indent** (F4), type the text to be indented, press **Enter** after the enumerated paragraph.	124
Double indent	Select **Layout**, **Alignment**, **Indent** → ← to turn on the Double Indent feature.	125
Print blocked text	Block the text to be printed, select the **Print** button, select **Print**.	126

Self-Check Questions

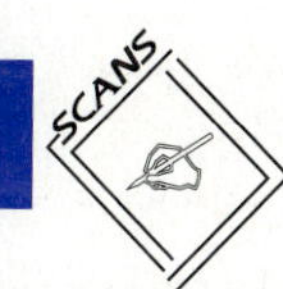

True/False—Circle One

T F 1. Select the **Search** button on the Button Bar to begin the function to find specified text.

T F 2. Moving text is the process of duplicating text.

T F 3. Before text can be copied or moved, the text is blocked.

T F 4. To begin the Replace function, select **Edit**, **Replace**.

T F 5. A single paragraph cannot be blocked and printed.

Short Answer

1. Which option in the Search and Replace dialog box should be selected in order to instruct WordPerfect to find only the word(s) typed in the Search For box?

2. List the four steps to *move* text using the Drop and Drag text feature.

3. What is the difference between the Indent feature and the Double Indent feature?

4. Describe one of the three methods for moving text.

5. Describe the difference between the move feature and the copy feature.

Enriching Language Arts Skills

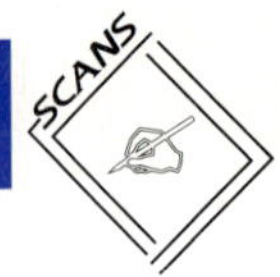

Spelling/Vocabulary Words

dues   fees paid by members to an organization at regular intervals.
affiliation   act of belonging or being connected to a specific group.
outweigh   to be of more importance or value.
distinguished   worthy of notice; excellent; outstanding.

Compound Adjectives

Hyphenate two words that precede and describe a noun and function as a single adjective.

Example:

The designer sent a well-defined sample of the proposed meeting area.

Activities

Activity 5.1—Indent and Move Text

1. Type the following paragraphs using the Indent feature to align each paragraph with the text in the first line (type the number followed by a period, press **F4**).

New Features of WordPerfect 6.0

1. Ribbon and Button Bar--The Ribbon and Button Bar provide a quick and easy way to format, edit, save, and print documents. Commonly used features are represented by icons (pictures). When an icon is selected, the associated command is performed immediately.

2. Multiple documents--With WordPerfect 6.0, a user can have up to nine documents open at one time. Each document is placed in a separate window. Information can be copied or moved from one window to another as desired.

3. WordPerfect Characters--Over 1,500 special characters can be displayed on the screen and inserted easily into any document.

4. Graphics--With WordPerfect 6.0, both text and graphics are displayed on the screen. With the use of the mouse, graphics can be positioned and sized interactively.

---

2. Save the file on your file disk; use the filename **5act1** (select the **Save As** button, type the drive letter where the file disk is located followed by a colon and the filename, select **OK**).

3. Print one copy (select the **Print** button on the Button Bar).

4. Move the items as shown and renumber the paragraphs.

New Features of WordPerfect 6.0

1. Ribbon and Button Bar--The Ribbon and Button Bar provide a quick and easy way to format, edit, save, and print documents. Commonly used features are represented by icons (pictures). When an icon is selected, the associated command is performed immediately.

2. Multiple documents--With WordPerfect 6.0, a user can have up to nine documents open at one time. Each document is placed in a separate window. Information can be copied or moved from one window to another as desired.

3. WordPerfect Characters--Over 1,500 special characters can be displayed on the screen and inserted easily into any document.

4. Graphics--With WordPerfect 6.0, both text and graphics are displayed on the screen. With the use of the mouse, graphics can be positioned and sized interactively.

---

5. Save the file on your file disk; use the filename **5act1r** (select the **Save As** button, type the drive letter where the file disk is located followed by a colon and the filename, select **OK**).

6. Print one copy (select the **Print** button on the Button Bar).

7. Close the document (select **File**, **Close**).

Activity 5.2—Indent and Replace Text Automatically

1. Use the traditional block style and type the following letter. Use the Indent feature to create the numbered list (type the number followed by a period; press **F4**).

(Use current date)

Mr. Austin Estes
55 Johnston Rd., #8
Albany, NY 12203

Dear Mr. Estes:

Enclosed is a copy of the DWA Constant Traveler newsletter highlighting our expanded world of service and membership benefits.

Our latest expansion opens new corners of the globe to you for mileage building and award opportunities. Wherever you fly on DWA, you will earn our minimum of 1,500 miles per flight segment. No airline offers more.

In addition to our expanded service, the newsletter highlights:

1.   DWA's new fares for business-class flyers.

2.   DWA's triple mileage for selected intercontinental routes.

3.   DWA's special "Partners Program" holiday promotion.

To increase your flexibility when traveling within North America, DWA has introduced upgrade awards for our business flyers. Also, members may continue to purchase a DWA First Class seat at reduced rates anytime before departure through our paid upgrade program.

We at DWA thank you for flying with us and look forward to serving your air travel needs.

Sincerely,

Anna R. Ingram
Senior Vice President

ARI/xx
estes.ltr/disk4

Enc.

---

2.   Save the file on your file disk; use the filename **5act2** (select the **Save As** button, type the drive letter where the file disk is located followed by a colon and the filename, select **OK**).

3. Print one copy (select the **Print** button on the Button Bar).

4. Replace all occurrences of DWA with Diamond West Airlines (**Ctrl** and **Home**; select **Edit**, **Replace**; type **DWA** in the Search For box; type **Diamond West Airlines** in the Replace With box; select **Replace All**).

5. Save the file on your file disk; use the filename **5act2r** (select the **Save As** button, type the drive letter where the file disk is located followed by a colon and the filename, select **OK**).

6. Print one copy (select the **Print** button on the Button Bar).

7. Close the document (select **File**, **Close**).

Activity 5.3—Copy, Edit; Block and Print Selected Text

1. Open the file named **5drill6** or type the document shown on page 125 (Figure 5.5).

2. Add three **Enters** at the bottom of the document.

3. Block the entire document.

4. Copy the entire document by selecting **Edit**, **Copy**.

5. Move the insertion point to the blank line at the bottom of the document and select **Edit**, **Paste** to insert a copy of the document.

6. Make the changes shown to the pasted copy. (Do not change the line spacing.)

Applicant Requirements--~~Air Conditioning Mechanic~~ *Maintenance Supervisor*

1. Any combination equivalent to completion of high school and ~~three~~ *five* years of increasingly responsible experience in the operation, ~~repair, and maintenance of~~ *janitorial services* *as well as supervising a staff* ~~heating, ventilation, and cooling systems.~~ *of ten or more persons.*

2. Hold a valid driver's license authorizing operation of motor vehicles.

3. Successful compliance with job-related medical standards, as determined by a medical examination conducted by a company-approved physician.

4. Proof of U.S. citizenship or proof of legal authorization to work in the United States.

7. Save the file on your file disk; use the filename **5act3** (select the **Save As** button, type the drive letter where the file disk is located followed by a colon and the filename, select **OK**).

8. Block the edited copy and print one copy of the blocked text (select the **Print** button on the Button Bar, choose **Print**).

9. Close the document (select **File**, **Close**).

Activity 5.4—Create Paragraphs Using the Double Indent Feature

1. Use the traditional block style and type the following letter. Use the Double Indent feature to indent the second and third paragraphs from both the left and right margins (select **Layout**, **Alignment**, **Indent** →←).

(Use current date)

Mr. Phil Emerson
P. O. Box 7526
London, KY 40741-9945

Dear Mr. Emerson:

We have great news for you! Your application for a ValueCard account has been preliminarily approved. However, before we can send you your new card, we need your assistance in verifying all income.

Please send us a copy of your last two paycheck stubs issued within the last thirty (30) days. If you have listed other income, please provide verification.

If we receive the requested information within thirty (30) days, we will be able to complete your evaluation.

We certainly hope to hear from you so that we can complete our approval process and you can begin to enjoy the many advantages that a ValueCard has to offer.

Sincerely,

Carol Shaw
Credit Card Director

CS/xx
emerson.ltr/d2

---

2. Save the file on your file disk; use the filename **5act4** (select the **Save As** button, type the drive letter where the file disk is located followed by a colon and the filename, select **OK**).

3. Print one copy (select the **Print** button on the Button Bar).

4. Close the document (select **File, Close**).

Challenge Your Skills

Skill 5.1—Indent, Move, and Edit Text

1. Use the Memorandum—Style 1 and the following information:

   a. Send the memo to Sales Associates from Suzanne Boscacci, Division Manager.

   b. Use the current date; include your reference initials.

   c. The subject of the memo is Current Sales Promotion.

   d. Send copies to J. Matarazzo and G. Higgins.

   e. Use the Indent feature for the enumerated items.

   f. The unformatted memorandum body text follows:

   Enclosed are photographs to assist in building your current sales promotion displays.

   Please note the following:

   1. Wingits have been discontinued and Chocwiz quantities reduced in order to incorporate Ultimate Almonds and expand on the successful Cheesecake Minis. Chocwiz should be placed next to snack crackers for a common price point. Ultimate Almonds should be placed in the space previously occupied by Chocwiz.

   2. Order quantities will be communicated through the central ordering office and will be processed automatically. Sales associates will not key in any orders.

   3. Orders reflect only the quantities necessary to build displays. Make plans to order refill quantities when necessary.

   4. Stores will require extra service calls during this promotion. Let your stores know when you will be visiting their sites.

Announcement to the stores of this promotion has already been distributed. Orders will now be processed electronically. The new electronic order processing will ensure accurate and timely delivery of products.

Remember—proper point of sale, displays, and shelf!

2. Move items 3 and 4 above item number 2 and renumber paragraphs.

3. Delete the last paragraph and insert the following two paragraphs:

Advise stores now of their upcoming shipment and make plans to build displays. Stores resisting this promotion should be advised to call Leonard Koenig or Laura Gonzales (department buyers) at 555-3422.

LET'S SELL SOME PRODUCTS!

4. Save the file on your file disk; use the filename **5skill1**.

5. Print one copy and close the document.

Skill 5.2—Copy and Edit Text

1. Create the following form using the format and spacing shown.

    *Hint: Change to line spacing of two; use Flush Right justification to align items at the right margin; press **Enter** three times after the last line of the form.*

SALES INVENTORY SUMMARY

SALES ASSOCIATE: JACQUELINE VILLEGAS

STORE #: 286

Item Name	Amount Purchased
Cheesecake Minis	12 gross
Chocwiz	10 gross
Ultimate Almonds	20 gross

---

2. Copy the form below the original form. Change the data in the copied form as follows:

    Sales Associate: David Novak
    Store #: 235
    Cheesecake Minis: 10 gross

Chocwiz: 5 gross
Ultimate Almonds: 22 gross

3. Copy the original form again and place below the second form. Change the data in the copied form as follows:

   Sales Associate: Monie Lucero
   Store #: 182
   Cheesecake Minis: 15 gross
   Chocwiz: 8 gross
   Ultimate Almonds: 18 gross

4. Save the file on your file disk; use the filename **5skill2**.

5. Print one copy and close the document.

◦• Skill 5.3—Replace Text Automatically; Language Arts

1. Use the Memorandum—Style 1 and the following information:

   a. Change both the left and right margins to **1.25"** and the top margin to **1.5"**.

   b. Send the memo to Consolidated Life Insurance Field Force from Juan Valdivia, Vice President.

   c. Use the current date; include your reference initials.

   d. The subject of the memo is IUA Membership.

   e. Correct three spelling and four punctuation errors.

To qualify for the National Quality, National Sales Achievement, Health Insurance, or the Million Dollar Roundtable Awards, your IUA membership dues must be current.

If you are a recent member of the Consolidated Life Insurance field force and were previously a member of IUA under another company's name, please write a letter to IUA National Headquarters and ask that your afilliation be changed to Consolidated Life Insurance.

Your IUA membership is important because of the awards or honors it can bring you personally. Additionally IUA has a long and distinguished history in representing professional agents in the Life, Health, and Financial Services industry. The benefits far outweight the membership dues. IUA provides information for agents to learn from each other and share sales ideas, and it serves as a platform for defending your interests in relation to state and federal legislation.

In order to help us fight legislative efforts to control the insurance industry we need your help by renewing or beginning your membership with IUA.

Consolidated Life Insurance takes great pride in the number of agents who are members of the IUA and the dissinguished service rendered by members of our field force. We here at Consolidated Life Insurance appreciate your services and applaud you for a well done job. If you are not a member of IUA please give this serious consideration.

2. Automatically replace all occurrences of IUA with Insurance Underwriters Association.

3. Automatically replace all occurrences of Consolidated Life Insurance with CLI.

4. Save the file on your file disk; use the filename **5skill3**.

5. Print one copy.

6. If you have completed your work, exit WordPerfect (select **File**, **Exit WP**).

Create a Table

Features Covered

Features Covered

- Use the Tables Button Bar
- Use Decimal Alignment
- Change column widths
- Insert a row
- Join cells
- Insert a column
- Set row height
- Horizontally and vertically center a table
- Convert text to a table
- Shade cells
- Change table lines

Objectives

After successfully completing this chapter, you will be able to create a table, increase and decrease column widths, insert columns and rows, join table cells, and align figures at the decimal point. In addition, you will be able to change row height, center a table horizontally, display and use the Tables Button Bar, and create a table using existing text.

Chapter Introduction

Traditionally, a table has been created by calculating the location of column tabs so that when the table is printed it will be centered horizontally on the page. Tables in this book will be created using the Tables feature which will determine the column tabs automatically and display lines around each column and row.

Note: In order to view these buttons, select the down triangle located at the left end of the Tables Button Bar.

Display the Tables Button Bar

The Tables Button Bar can be selected to replace the WordPerfect default Button Bar (WPMAIN) which is normally displayed on the screen. The Tables Button Bar provides buttons for quickly accessing the WordPerfect table features (see Figure 6.1). Selecting options from the Tables Button Bar is much quicker than selecting the drop-down menus and submenus for obtaining the various table dialog boxes. The Tables Button Bar options can be accessed only by using a mouse (keyboard keys cannot be used to access the Tables Button Bar).

Display a Different Button Bar

Note: A mouse is required to select and access the buttons on the Tables Button Bar.

1. Select **View, Button Bar Setup** {Alt and v, s}.

2. Choose **Select** {s}.

3. Move the mouse pointer to the desired Button Bar name and double-click with the left mouse button {press the up or down arrow key to highlight the Button Bar name and press s}.

   For example, move the mouse pointer to **TABLES** and double-click.

   Note: The original Button Bar (WPMAIN) is replaced by the Tables Button Bar (see Figure 6.1).

Create, Format, and Modify a Table

A table can be easily created using the **Tbl Crt** button on the Tables Button Bar. Also, text typed in columns can be converted to a table using the Create Table from Block feature. When a table is created, the number of columns and rows are specified. Once the table columns and rows are specified, lines (a grid) for the columns and rows display in the Table Edit window (see Figure 6.3). The table lines are set by default to print but can be omitted if desired (see Chapter 7).

Chapter 6—Create a Table

The table lines form columns and rows. The columns are identified by letters A, B, C, etc., and the rows are numbered 1, 2, 3, etc. The intersection of each column and row is called a cell. Each cell is identified by an address. When the cursor/insertion point is located in the third column (column C) and row 2, the cell address is C2.

The Table Edit window must be exited before text can be typed in to the table cells. Text typed in each cell wraps around in the cell. If the **Enter** key is pressed in a cell, the cell automatically increases in height.

The **Tab** key and **Shift** and **Tab** keys or the arrow keys are used to move the cursor/insertion point from cell to cell. After text is typed in one cell, the **Tab** key or an arrow key is used to move the cursor/insertion point to the next cell. To return to the previous cell, press **Shift** and **Tab**. If text within a cell is to be indented, press the **Home** and **Tab** keys to activate the tab.

Formatting a table is the process of completing such tasks as aligning figures at the decimal point, centering text in the cell, increasing or decreasing the column width, and centering the table horizontally on the page. The primary goals of formatting a table are to present a pleasing appearance and to make reading easier. To produce a table that is formatted for an appealing appearance, *visually* adjust the width and height of cells and the alignment of text within the cells. (If desired, the ruler provided in the back of this book can be used to assist in estimating column width.) Formatting a table can be accomplished using the Table Edit window and/or the Tables Button Bar.

Modifying a table is the process of restructuring a table to include new columns or rows or to join cells. If **Ins** is selected in the Table Edit window, a new column or row can be inserted into an existing table before or after the cell that contains the cursor. If the **Ins Row** button is selected on the Button Bar, the new row is inserted above the row that contains the cursor/insertion point.

Modifying a table can also include changing row height. Row height is the amount of space between the top and bottom cell lines. When row height is increased, the cell text will be placed at the top of the cell and the additional space will be added between the text and the bottom cell line. Two row height options are available: Auto and Fixed. Auto is the default row height setting. With the Auto setting selected, WordPerfect will increase or decrease the row height to accommodate any amount of text typed in the cells. The height for the row will be adjusted to the maximum height needed for any cell in the row. When the Fixed setting is selected, an exact amount of space can be specified for each row. The row height amount must be changed if text is added or deleted by entering a new Fixed row height amount.

Two or more cells in a row can be joined in order to provide space for information that relates to more than one cell or column. Also, some or all of the cells in the column can be joined.

FIGURE 6.2

Create Table dialog box

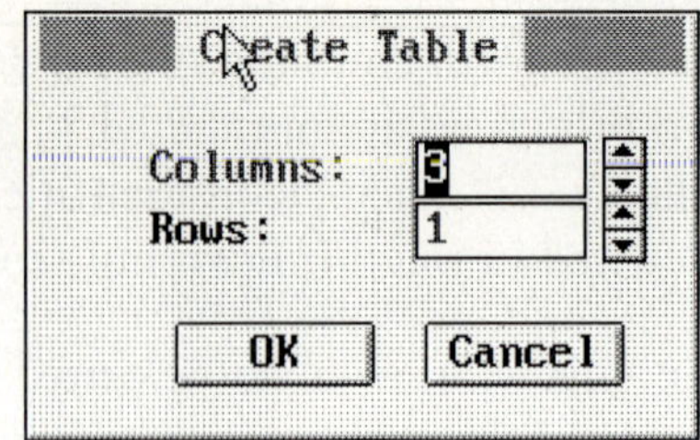

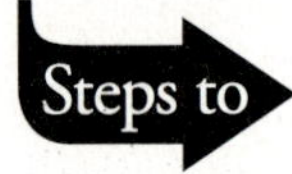

Steps to ▶ Create a Table

1. Select the **Tbl Crt** button on the Tables Button Bar {Alt and F7, t, c}.

   Note: The Create Table dialog box displays (see Figure 6.2). The Columns box with the default setting of 3 is highlighted.

2. Type the number of columns desired or click the up or down triangles to increase or decrease the number of columns

   For example, no change is made to accept the default setting of 3.

3. Move the mouse pointer to the **Rows** box; click once to highlight the current number {press Tab}.

4. Type the desired number of rows

   For example, type **3**.

5. Select **OK** {press Enter twice}.

   Note: The empty columns and rows for the table display in the Table Edit window (see Figure 6.3).

6. Select **Close** to exit the Table Edit window and return to the document window {F7}.

   Note: Typing information into cells can be accomplished only in the document window.

FIGURE 6.3

Table Edit window

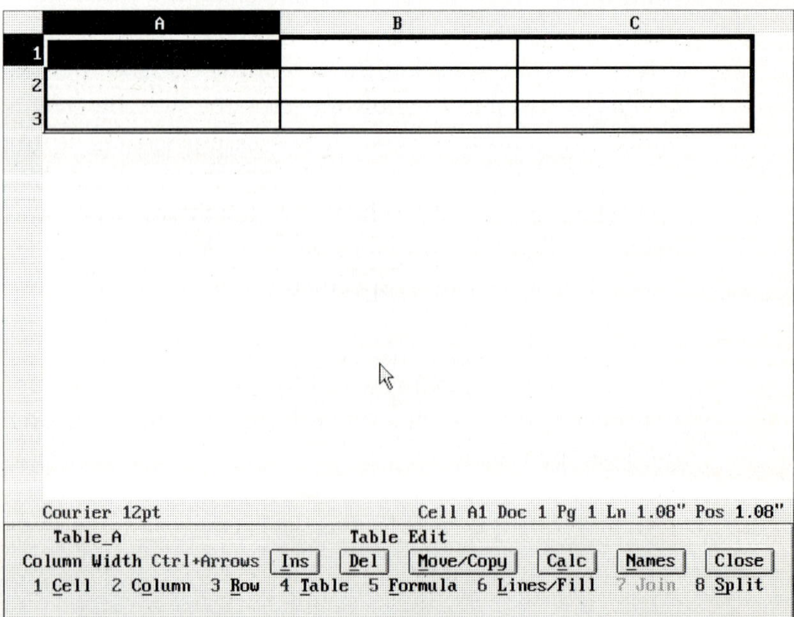

Chapter 6—Create a Table

Emma Croft	Western	$155,575.25
Tan Nguyen	Central	155,295.95
Lloyd Guevara	Southern	155,333.75

FIGURE 6.4
Unformatted table

Finish-Up Instructions

❖ To type the unformatted information in each cell, press the **Tab** key or the arrow keys to move from cell to cell and row to row. Type the unformatted information shown in Figure 6.4.

*Note: If the **Enter** key is mistakenly pressed while typing information into the table cells, press the **Backspace** key to delete the unwanted return. If the **Tab** key is pressed after the last cell entry, select the **Del Row** button on the Button Bar to delete the extra row.*

❖ Use the filename **6drill1** and save the file (select **File**, **Save**, type the drive letter where the file disk is located followed by a colon and the filename, select **OK**).

❖ Optional. Print one unformatted copy.

Start-Up Instructions

❖ The file named **6drill1** should be displayed on the screen.

❖ The Tables Button Bar should be displayed on the screen (if necessary, select **View**, **Button Bar Setup**, **Tables**, **Select**).

Align Figures at the Decimal Point

1. Place the cursor/insertion point in any cell of the column where the decimals are to align.

   For example, place the cursor/insertion point in any cell in column 3.

2. Select the **TColFmt** button on the Tables Button Bar {Alt and F7, t, e, o, or Alt and F11, o}.

   Note: The Column Format dialog box displays (see Figure 6.5).

3. Select **Decimal Align** justification in the Alignment box {j, d}.

4. Select **OK** {Enter, F7}.

   Note: The dollar amounts in column 3 are aligned at the decimal point and are moved to the right side of the column cells.

Finish-Up Instructions

❖ Use the new filename **6drill1r** and save the table on the file disk (select **File**, **Save As**, if necessary, type the drive letter where the file disk is located followed by a colon and the filename, select **OK**).

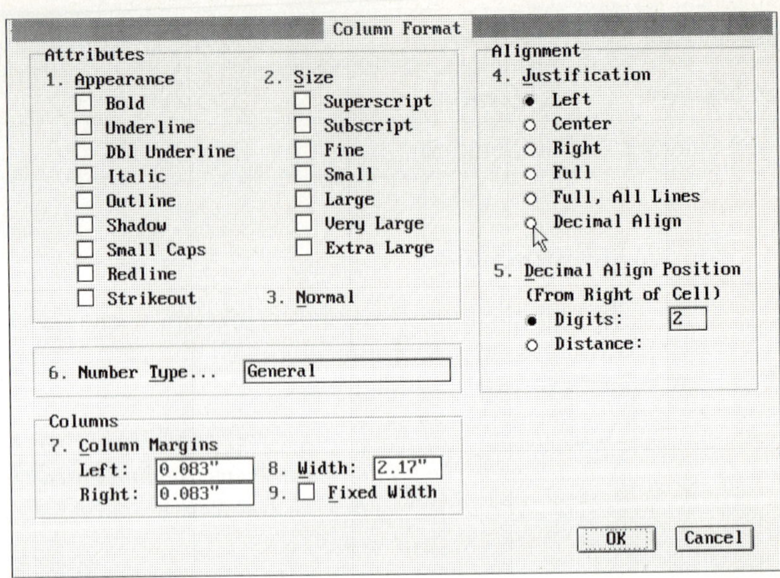

* Print one copy (select **File**, **Print/Fax**).

Start-Up Instructions

* The file named **6drill1r** should be displayed on the screen.

* The Tables Button Bar should be displayed on the screen (if necessary, select **View**, **Button Bar Setup**, **Tables**, **Select**).

* A mouse is required to complete the Steps to Change Column Widths Using the Tables Button Bar. To change column widths without a mouse, see Steps to Change Column Widths Using the Table Edit Window.

 **Change Column Widths Using the Tables Button Bar**

Note: A mouse is required to complete the following steps.

1. Place the cursor/insertion point in any cell in the column where the width is to be changed.

   For example, place the cursor/insertion point in the first cell in column 1.

2. *To decrease the column width,* select the **TColNarr** button on the Tables Button Bar.

3. *To increase the column width,* select the **TColWide** button on the Tables Button Bar

Finish-Up Instructions

* Move the mouse pointer to the **TColNarr** button on the Tables Button Bar and press the left mouse button repeatedly until the desired column width is displayed, e.g., press the mouse button three times to visually estimate that ap-

Emma Croft	Western	$155,575.25
Tan Nguyen	Central	155,295.95
Lloyd Guevara	Southern	155,333.75

Table with decimal alignment and changed column widths

proximately 0.75" displays between the longest line in column 1 and the beginning of the text in column 2.

Note: If desired, use the ruler provided in the back of this book.

❖ Repeat Steps 1-2 to decrease the widths in columns 2 and 3. Visually estimate that approximately 0.75" displays between the longest line in column 2 and the beginning of the text in column 3. Also, notice that the column widths are approximately the same.

Note: Your table should look similar to Figure 6.6.

❖ Save the file again using the new filename **6drill1d** (select **File, Save As**, delete the r and type **d**, select **OK**).

Start-Up Instructions

❖ The file named **6drill1r** should be displayed on the screen.

Steps to ▶ **Change Column Widths Using the Table Edit Window**

1. With the cursor/insertion point located in any cell in the table, select the **Tbl Edit** button or select **Layout, Tables, Edit** {Alt and F7, t, e}.

2. Place the cursor/insertion point in any cell in the column to be changed.

   For example, place the cursor in column A.

3. Press and hold the **Ctrl** key while tapping the left arrow key to decrease the width of the column.

   For example, tap the left arrow key approximately four times. Visually estimate that approximately 0.75" displays between the longest line in column A and the beginning of the text in column B.

*Note: To increase the column width, press and hold the **Ctrl** key while tapping the right arrow key.*

Finish-Up Instructions

❖ Repeat Steps 1-2 to decrease the widths in column B and C. Visually estimate that approximately 0.75" displays between the longest line in column B and the beginning of the text in column C. Notice that the column widths are approximately the same. Your table should look similar to Figure 6.6.

❖ Select **Close** {F7} to exit the Table Edit window.

❖   Use the new filename **6drill1d** and save the file again (select **File**, **Save As**, type the drive letter where the file disk is located followed by a colon and the file-name, select **OK**).

Start-Up Instructions

❖   The file named **6drill1d** should be displayed on the screen.

❖   A mouse is required to complete the Steps to Insert a Table Row Using the Button Bar. If you do not have a mouse available, use the Steps to Insert a Table Row using the Table Edit Window.

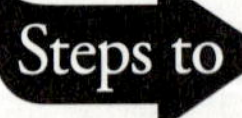

Steps to ▶ Insert a Table Row Using the Tables Button Bar

Note: A mouse is required to complete the following steps.

1. Place the cursor/insertion point in the row that will be located below the inserted row.

   For example, place the cursor/insertion point in any cell in the first row.

2. Select the **Ins Row** button on the Tables Button Bar repeatedly to insert the desired number of rows.

   For example, select the **Ins Row** button twice to insert two new rows.

Note: Skip the following steps and proceed to the Finish-Up Instructions.

Steps to ▶ Insert a Table Row Using the Table Edit Window

Note: A mouse or keystrokes can be used to complete the following steps.

1. With the cursor/insertion point located in any table cell, select the **Tbl Edit** button or select **Layout, Tables, Edit** to display the Table Edit window {Alt and F7, t, e}.

2. Place the cursor in the row that will be located before or after the inserted row.

   For example, place the cursor in any cell in the first row.

3. Select **Ins** {press the Insert key}.

4. Select **Rows** {r}.

5. Click once in the box located beside the words **How many?** and type the number of rows to be inserted {h, type desired number of rows}.

   For example, type **2** {h, 2}.

6. Select the desired Cursor Position option.

   For example, check that the **Before Cursor Position** option is selected {b}.

7. Select **OK** {press Enter twice}.

Finish-Up Instructions

- ❖ If necessary, exit the Table Edit window by selecting **Close** {F7}.
- ❖ If necessary, press **Shift** and **Tab** to move the cursor/insertion point to the first cell in the table.
- ❖ Type the following text into the new cells as shown. (Remember: Text may wrap around in the cells; press the **Tab** key to move from cells to cell and row to row.)

SEMIANNUAL SALES		
NAMES	DIVISIONS	SALES

- ❖ Save the file again using the new filename **6drill1n** (select **File, Save As**, if necessary, type the disk drive where the file disk is located followed by a colon; type the new filename, select **OK**).

Start-Up Instructions

- ❖ The file named **6drill1n** should be displayed on the screen.

Join Table Cells

1. With the cursor/insertion point located in any cell of the table, select the **Tbl Edit** button on the Tables Button Bar or select **Layout, Tables, Edit** {Alt and F7, t, e or Alt and F11}.

2. Block the cells to be joined {press Alt and F4 and press the right arrow key repeatedly to highlight desired row cells}.

   For example, block the cells in the first row by placing the cursor in cell A1; press and hold the left mouse button while dragging the mouse to highlight row 1.

3. Select **Join** {j}.

4. Select **Yes** {y}.

   Note: All cells in row 1 are now one cell.

Center Text in Multiple Cells

*Note: The Table Edit window should be displayed on the screen. (If necessary, select **Layout, Tables, Edit**.)*

1. Block the cells in which text is to be centered. (If necessary, see Step 2 of the Steps to Join Table Cells).

   For example, block rows 1 and 2.

2. Select **Cell** {c}.

3. Select **Center Justification** in the Alignment box {j, c}.

4. Select **OK** {Enter}.

Finish-Up Instructions

❖ Select **Close** to exit the Table Edit window.

❖ Save the file again using the same filename, **6drill1n** (select **File, Save**).

Start-Up Instructions

❖ The file named **6drill1n** should be displayed on the screen.

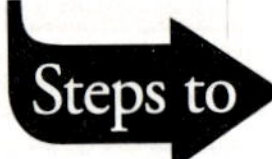

Insert a Table Column

1. Select the **Tbl Edit** button on the Tables Button Bar {Alt and F7, t, e or Alt and F11}.

2. Place the cursor in the column that will be located before or after the inserted column.

   For example, place the cursor in any cell in column C.

3. Select **Ins** {press the Insert key}.

4. If necessary, select the **Columns** option {c}.

5. If necessary, click once in the box located beside the words **How many** and type the number of columns to be inserted {h, type desired number of columns}.

   Note: One column is to be inserted. The default of 1 should be displayed. If necessary, type 1.

6. Select the **Before Cursor Position** or the **After Cursor Position** option.

   For example, select **Before Cursor Position** {b}.

7. Select **OK** to return to the Table Edit window {press Enter once or twice}.

   Note: The new column is inserted between the original columns B and C.

Left Align a Partial Table Column

Note: The table should be displayed in the Table Edit window.

1. Place the cursor/insertion point in the desired column cell.

   For example, place the cursor in cell C3.

2. Block the cells where justification will be changed. (If necessary, see Step 2 of the Steps to Join Table Cells.)

   For example, block C3-C5.

3. Select **Cell** {c}.

4. Select **Left Justification** in the Alignment box {j, L}.

5. Select **OK** {Enter}.

Note: Since no text is displayed in the empty cell, no change is seen on the screen.

Finish-Up Instructions

❖ Select **Close** to exit the Table Edit window and return to the document window {F7}.

❖ Type the following information into the new column cells.

OFFICE
Los Angeles
Kansas City
Atlanta

Note: The original Center justification is in effect in the cell containing the column heading, while the remaining column cells are left aligned.

❖ Save the file again using the same filename **6drill1n** (select **File, Save**).

Start-Up Instructions

❖ The file named **6drill1n** should be displayed on the screen.

Change Table Row Height

1. With the cursor/insertion point located in any table cell, select the **Tbl Edit** button on the Tables Button Bar {Alt and F7, t, e or Alt and F11}.

2. Block and highlight the rows where the row height is to be changed. (If necessary, see Step 2 of the Steps to Join Table Cells.)

   For example, block the first two table rows.

3. Select **Row** {r}.

   Note: The Row Format dialog box displays (see Figure 6.7).

4. Select the **Row Height Fixed** option {f}.

5. Type the desired row height.

   For example, type .4.

6. Select **OK** {press Enter twice}.

   Note: Rows 1 and 2 are increased in height.

7. Select **Close** to exit the Table Edit window {F7}.

Finish-Up Instructions

❖ Save the file again using the same filename **6drilln** (select **File, Save**).

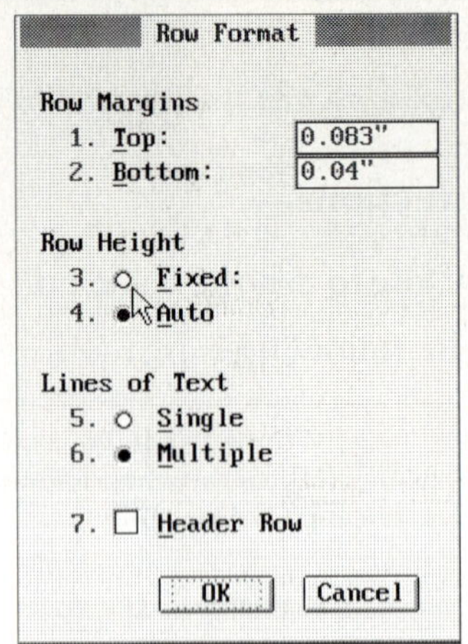

Start-Up Instructions

❖ The file named **6drill1n** should be displayed on the screen.

Center a Table Horizontally

1. Place the cursor/insertion point in any cell in the table.

2. Select the **Tbl Edit** button on the Tables Button Bar {Alt and F7, t, e or Alt and F11}.

3. Select **Table** {t}.

4. Move the mouse pointer to **Left** in the Table Position option, press and hold the left mouse button and drag the mouse pointer to **Center,** release the mouse button {p, c}.

5. Select **OK** {press Enter}.

6. Select **Close** {F7}.

   Note: The table displays centered horizontally on the screen.

Shortcut:

1. Select the **Tbl Fmt** button on the Tables Button Bar.

2. Move the mouse pointer to the word **Position** in the Table Position box and click once.

3. Move the mouse pointer to the desired position option and click once.

   For example, move the mouse pointer to **Center** and click.

4. Select **OK.**

Finish-Up Instructions

❖ Save the file again (select **File, Save**).

- ❖ Print one copy (select **File**, **Print/Fax**).
- ❖ Close the document (select **File**, **Close**).

Convert Existing Text to a Table

Text that is separated by tabs and hard returns can be converted easily to a table. Once the text is typed, block the columns. The Create Table from Block dialog box displays after selecting the **Table Crt** button on the Tables Button Bar, or after choosing **Layout**, **Tables**, **Create**.

Once the text is converted to a table, the information that was once horizontally separated by tabs is now contained in individual cells and surrounded by table lines. The information in the cells can be formatted and the structure of the table modified by using the buttons on the Tables Button Bar or by selecting the desired options from the **Layout**, **Tables** drop-down menus.

Start-Up Instructions

- ❖ Type the text to be converted to a table. Press the **Tab** key once between each item and press the **Enter** key at the end of each line.
- ❖ Type the information shown in Figure 6.8 using the default tabs.
- ❖ If a mouse is available, the Tables Button Bar should be displayed and used to accomplish the following steps.

Convert Existing Text to a Table Using the Tables Button Bar

1. Block the entire text to be converted to a table.

   For example, block all three lines of text.

2. Select the **Tbl Crt** button on the Tables Button Bar {Alt and F7, t, c or Alt and F11}.

   Note: The Create Table from Block dialog box displays.

3. The Tabular Text option should display selected. If necessary, select Tabular Text {t}.

4. Select OK {Enter}.

<table>
<tr><td>Telecommunications → TTH → 108 (press Enter)
Word Processing → MW → 110 (press Enter)
Local Area Networks → MWF → 145 (press Enter)</td></tr>
</table>

Text to be converted to a table

- ❖ Change the column widths. (If necessary, see the Steps to Change Column Widths Using the Tables Button Bar on page 144 for additional information on changing column widths.)

  a. Decrease column C to approximately 1" in width.

     *Hint: Press and hold the **Ctrl** key and tap the left arrow key approximately 23 times or select **Column**, type **1** in the Width box, and select **OK**.*

  b. Increase the width of column B so that there is approximately ½" between the longest line in column B and the beginning of column C.

- ❖ Center the table horizontally (select **Table**, **Table Position Center**, **OK**).

- ❖ Select **Close** to exit the Table Edit window {F7}.

- ❖ Save the file on your file disk; use the filename **6drill2** (select **File**, **Save**, type the drive letter where the file disk is located followed by a colon and the filename, select **OK**).

Center a Table or Text Vertically

Table rows or lines of text can be centered vertically on a page between the top and bottom margins. On an 8½ by 11-inch sheet of paper, approximately 66 lines (6 lines per inch) or approximately 33 table rows (3 lines per inch) can be printed. Text that occupies fewer than 54 lines (66 - 12 = 2" top/bottom margins) and tables that occupy fewer than 27 rows will usually display more attractively on a page if the lines/rows are centered between the top and bottom margins. The tables typed in this book will be fewer than 20 rows; therefore, vertical centering will be useful.

- ❖ If a mouse is available, the Tables Button Bar should be displayed. (If necessary, see page 140.)

- ❖ Create a table with 3 columns and 7 rows. Select **Close** or press **F7** to return to the document window.

- ❖ Type the unformatted information shown in Figure 6.9 into the table cells.

  *Note: Remember to press the **Tab** key to move from one cell to another and from one row to another. (Do not press the Enter key.)*

- ❖ Select the **Tbl Edit** button and use the Table Edit window to format the table as follows:

  a. Block and join the cells in row 1.

  b. Block and center the title and column headings in rows 1 and 2.

CURRENT ASSETS		
Account Name	1992	1993
Cash	$12,556	$15,660
Petty cash fund	1,250	1,500
Change fund	975	1,000
Accounts receivable	10,920	12,863
Notes receivable	5,800	4,000

Table to be centered
vertically

    c. In columns B and C, select only the cells that contain dollar amounts; choose **Decimal** justification.

    d. Block the entire table by moving the mouse pointer to cell A1 and drag the mouse to highlight all cells. Change the row height to 0.4.

    e. Decrease columns B and C. Visually estimate that approximately 1" displays between the longest line in each column.

    f. Center the table horizontally (see page 150).

    g. Select **Close** {F7}.

❖ Use the filename **6drill3** and save the table on your file disk (select **File**, **Save**, type the drive letter where the file disk is located followed by a colon and the filename, select **OK**).

Steps to ▶ Center a Table or Text Vertically

1. Select **Layout, Page** {Alt and L, p}.

2. Select the **Center Current Page** option in the Center Page (Top to Bottom) box {c}.

3. Select **OK** {Enter}.

   *Note: The table's position on the screen may not change. Select **View**, **Page mode** {Alt and v, s} or **File**, **Print Preview**, **Full Page** to view the table centered vertically on the page.*

Finish-Up Instructions

❖ Save the file again using the same filename {select **File**, **Save**}.

❖ Print one copy {select **File**, **Print/Fax**}.

Change Table Border Lines and Shade Cells

The lines and borders that display around the table cells can be changed by choosing a line style or a fill style. Lines can also be omitted (see Chapter 7). There are various types of line styles, such as dashed, dotted, thick, thin-thick, etc. (see Figure 6.10). The line styles can be designated to print around all table cells or only specific cells. The default (preset) line style for the entire table and the left, right, top, bottom, inside, and outside cell lines is "single line." The default border line style is "double border."

The fill style is a pattern (or gradient) that includes foreground and background colors. The foreground or background colors are shaded percentages of a color. For example, the 10% Shaded Fill appears light gray similar to a checkerboard pattern. Background colors display in the graphics mode. Use **Preview** to display a gradient fill on the screen. If a color monitor is used, various colors or shades can also be chosen and displayed on the screen. Use the Table Edit window and the Lines/Fill option to change table line styles and fill styles.

Start-Up Instructions

❖ The file named **6drill3** should be displayed.

Steps to ▶ Change Table Border

Note: When changing the table border, the cursor/insertion point can be located in any cell of the table.

1. Select the **Tbl Edit** button on the Tables Button Bar {Alt and F7, t, e or Alt and F11}.

                                Chapter 6—Create a Table

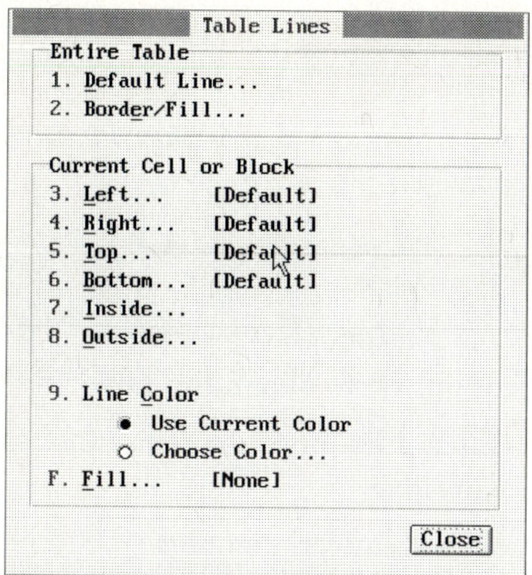

Table Lines dialog box

2. Select **Lines/Fill** {L}.

    Note: The Table Lines dialog box displays (see Fig. 6.11).

3. Select the desired option in the Entire Table box.

    For example, select **Border/Fill** {e}.

    Note: The Table Border/Fill dialog box displays.

4. Select the desired style option.

    For example, select **Border Style** {b}.

5. Double-click on the desired border style {press the down arrow key and highlight desired option, Enter}.

    For example, double-click **Dashed Border**.

6. Select **OK** {Enter}.

7. Select **Close** to return to the Table Edit window {F7}.

Change Table Lines

1. If necessary, select the **Tbl Edit** button to obtain the Table Edit window.

2. Block the cell(s) where the line(s) is to be changed. (If necessary, see Step 2 of the Steps to Join Table Cells for blocking cells.)

    For example, block all cells in row 2.

3. Select **Lines/Fill** {L}.

4. Select the desired option in the Current Cell or Block box.

    For example, select **Bottom** {b}.

5. Double-click on the desired Line Style {press the down arrow key to highlight the desired option, Enter}.

For example, double-click on **Double Line.**

6. Select **Close** twice {F7 twice}.

   Note: The bottom border may not display as a double line on the screen. If desired, use Print Preview to display the double lines.

Shade (Fill) Table Cells

1. If necessary, select the **Tbl Edit** button to obtain the Table Edit window.

2. Block the cells to be shaded {Alt and F4, press the right arrow key and the down arrow key the desired number of times}.

   For example, block all cells with money amounts.

3. Select **Lines/Fill** {L}.

4. Select **Fill** in the Current Cell or Block box {f}. See Figure 6.11.

5. Select **Fill Style** {y}.

6. Double-click on the desired Shaded Fill {press the down arrow key to highlight the desired option, Enter}.

   For example, double-click on **10% Shaded Fill.**

   Note: The Fill Style and Color dialog box displays with a sample of the current Fill Style.

7. Select **OK** {Enter}.

8. Select **Close** {F7} to return to the Table Edit window.

   Note: The blocked cells display with the 10% Shaded Fill.

9. Select **Close** to return to the document window {F7}.

Finish-Up Instructions

* Block the title and column headings in rows 1 and 2 and change the font to Bodoni-WP Bold, 18-point.

* Block the text and figures in rows 3 through 7 and change the font to Helve-WP, 12-point.

* Save the file; use the filename **6drill4** (select **File**, **Save As**, type the drive letter where the file disk is located followed by a colon and the filename; select **OK**).

* Print one copy (select **File**, **Print**).

* Close the document (select **File**, **Close**).

The Next Step

Chapter Review and Activities

FEATURES SUMMARY

FEATURES	ACTIONS	PAGE
Display Tables Button Bar	Select **View**, **Button Bar Setup**, **Select**, double-click on **TABLES**.	140
Create a table	Select the **Tbl Crt** button on the Tables Button Bar, type the desired number of columns and rows, select **OK**.	142
Display the Table Edit window	Select the **Tbl Edit** button on the Tables Button Bar.	142
Move cursor/insertion point from cell to cell	Press the **Tab** key, the **Shift** and **Tab** keys, or arrow keys.	142
Decimal align figures in a table	Select the **Tbl Edit** button on the Tables Button Bar, block the cell(s) desired, select **Cell**, **Decimal Align** justification.	143
Increase column width	Place the cursor/insertion point in any cell in the column. Select the **TColWide** button on the Tables Button Bar or press the **Ctrl** and right arrow key in the Table Edit window.	144
Decrease column width	Place the cursor/insertion point in any cell in the column. Select the **TColNarr** button on the Tables Button Bar or press the **Ctrl** and left arrow key in the Table Edit window.	144

FEATURES *(cont'd.)*	ACTIONS *(cont'd.)*	PAGE
Insert a table row	Select the **Ins Row** button on the Tables Button Bar.	146
Join table cells	Select the **Tbl Edit** button on the Tables Button Bar, block cells to be joined, select **Join**, **Yes**.	147
Center text in multiple cells	Select the **Tbl Edit** button on the Tables Button Bar, block desired cells, select **Cell**, **Center** Justification, **OK**.	147
Insert table column(s)	Select the **Tbl Edit** button on the Tables Button Bar, select **Ins**, select **Columns**, type desired number of columns to be inserted, select **Before** or **After Cursor Postion**, select **OK**.	148
Change row height	Select the **Tbl Edit** button on the Tables Button Bar, block the row(s) desired, select **Row**, **Fixed**, type desired height in inches, select **OK**.	149
Center table horizontally	Select the **Tbl Fmt** button on the Tables Button Bar, select **Position**, **Center**, select **OK**.	150
Convert existing tabbed text to a table	Block desired text, select **Tbl Crt** button on the Tables Button Bar, select **Tabular Text**, **OK**.	151
Center table vertically	Select **Layout**, **Page**, **Center Current Page**, **OK**.	153
Change table border	Select the **Tbl Edit** button on the Tables Button Bar, select **Lines/Fill**, select **Border/Fill**, **Border Style**, double-click on desired border style, **OK**.	154
Change table lines	Select the **Tbl Edit** button on the Tables Button Bar, block the desired cell(s), select **Lines/Fill**, select desired option, double-click on the desired line style, select **Close** twice.	155
Shade table cells	Select the **Tbl Edit** button on the Tables Button Bar, block cell(s) to be shaded, select **Lines/Fill**, **Fill**, **Fill Style**, double-click on desired shaded fill, select **OK**, **Close**.	156

Self-Check Questions

True/False—Circle One

T F 1. A table can be created using the **Tools** menu or using the **Tables** button on the default WordPerfect Button Bar.

T F 2. The intersection of each column and row is called a cell.

T F 3. The **Enter** key is pressed in a cell in order to insert a new row.

T F 4. When the **Decimal** justification option is selected, figures are aligned at the left digit.

T F 5. Formatting a table can include increasing or decreasing the table column width.

T F 6. Text that is separated by tabs and hard returns can be converted to a table.

Short Answer

1. List three tasks that can be accomplished when formatting a table.

2. State the primary purpose for formatting a table.

3. List the keystrokes used to tab text *within* a table cell.

4. List two advantages to using the Tables Button Bar.

Enriching Language Arts Skills

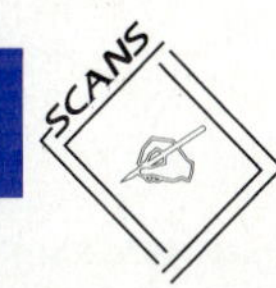

Spelling/Vocabulary Words

initiative   readiness to begin action.
strategic   pertaining to the importance of accomplishing a plan.
alliances   a joining together to meet a common goal.

Dollar Amounts Formats

Use a comma to separate the number digits into groups of thousands. No space is placed between a number and dollar sign unless the dollar signs are aligned in a column (see Chapter 7).

If a column of numbers has even dollar amounts, the zeros are omitted. Even dollar amounts can either be right justified or decimal justified in a column in order to align the numbers on the right.

Example:

$28,655,342
1,389
10,843

Activity 6.1—Create and Format a Table

1. If necessary, load the WordPerfect program and display the Tables Button Bar (select **View**, **Button Bar Setup**, **Select**, double-click on **TABLES**).

2. Create a table with 3 columns and 3 rows (select the **Tbl Crt** button, type the desired number of columns and rows, select **OK**).

3. Select **Close** {F7} to exit the Table Edit window.

4. Type the unformatted text as shown. (Remember: Text wraps around in the cells; do not press Enter when typing text into column cells.)

Federated Growth Trust	4.1%	$33.60
Colonial Growth Shares	7.1%	45.75
Fidelity Set Energy	0.2%	10.00

5. Use the filename **6act1** and save the file.

6. Use the following instructions to format the table:

   a. Use the **TColNarr** button on the Tables Button Bar and decrease the width of columns 2 and 3 to approximately **1.5"** each {Alt and F7, t, e, move cursor to desired column and press Ctrl and the left arrow key repeatedly to decrease column width}.

   b. Use the **TColWide** button on the Tables Button Bar and increase the width of column 1 so that the words display on one line {Alt and F7, t, e, move cursor to desired column and press Ctrl and the right arrow key repeatedly to increase column width}.

   c. If necessary, select the **Tbl Edit** button {Alt and F7, t, e or Alt and F11} to display the table in the Table Edit window.

   d. Block all cells in columns B and C and align the figures on the decimal point (select **Cell**, **Decimal Align** justification, **OK**).

   e. Position the table centered horizontally on the page (select **Table**, **Table Position**, **Center**, **OK**).

7. Select **Close** {F7}.

   Note: Your table should look similar to the following:

Federated Growth Trust	4.1%	$33.60
Colonial Growth Shares	7.1%	45.75
Fidelity Set Energy	0.2%	10.00

8. Use the same filename, **6act1**, and save the file again (select **File**, **Save**).

9. Return the default WPMAIN Button Bar to the screen (select **View**, **Button Bar Setup**, choose **Select**, double-click on **WPMAIN**).

10. Print one copy (select the **Print** button on the Button Bar, choose **Print**).

11. Close the document (select **File**, **Close**).

Activity 6.2—Create and Format a Table, Insert Rows, Join Cells, and Change Row Height

1. If necessary, load the WordPerfect program and display the Tables Button Bar (select **View**, **Button Bar Setup**, **Select**, double-click on **TABLES**).

2. Create a table with 2 columns and 5 rows (select the **Tbl Crt** button, type the desired number of columns and rows, select **OK**).

3. Select **Close** {F7} to exit the Table Edit window.

4. Type the unformatted text as shown.

Alaska	402,000
Iowa	2,993,000
New York	18,000,000
Oklahoma	3,100,000
Texas	14,500,000

5. Select the **Tbl Edit** button to display the table in the Table Edit window.

6. Right justify column B (place the cursor in column B, select **Column**, **Right** justification, **OK**).

7. Insert three rows (place the cursor in any cell in row 1, select **Ins**, **Rows**, select **How many?** and type **3**, select **OK**).

8. Join the top row cells (block the cells in row 1; select **Join**, **Yes**).

9. Join the second row cells.

10. Block all cells in rows 1, 2, and 3 and set **Center** justification (select **Cell**, **Center** justification, **OK**).

    Note: No change displays on the screen.

11. Change the row height for the first row and subtitle to .5 (block the first two rows; select **Row**; select **Fixed**; type .5; **OK**).

12. Select **Close** to exit the Table Edit window {F7}.

13. In row 1, type the title **State Populations** in the top row. Notice that the text is centered.

14. In row 2, type the subtitle (**Approximately**).

15. Type the column headings **State** and **Population** in the third row cells.

16. Decrease the width of columns 1 and 2 (use the **TColNarr** button). Visually estimate that approximately two inches display between the column headings in columns one and two.

   Note: Your table should look similar to the following table:

State Populations	
(Approximately)	
State	Population
Alaska	402,000
Iowa	2,993,000
New York	18,000,000
Oklahoma	3,100,000
Texas	14,500,000

17. Center the table horizontally on the page (select the **Tbl Fmt** button; in the Table Position box, select **Position, Center, OK**).

18. Use the filename **6act2** and save the file (select **File, Save**).

19. Return the default WPMAIN Button Bar to the screen (select **View, Button Bar Setup, Select**, double-click on **WPMAIN**).

20. Print one copy (select the **Print** button, **Print**).

21. Close the document (select **File, Close**).

Activity 6.3—Create and Format a Table, Insert a Column, Shade Cells

1. If necessary, load the WordPerfect program and display the Tables Button Bar (select **View, Button Bar Setup, Select**, double-click on **TABLES**).

2. Create a table with 2 columns and 5 rows (select the **Tbl Crt** button, type the desired number of columns and rows, select **OK**).

3. Select **Close** to exit the Table Edit window {F7}.

4. Type the unformatted text as shown.

Mortgage Affordability	
Annual Income	Mortgage
$20,000	$55,000
40,000	110,000
60,000	164,000

5. Select the **Tbl Edit** button to display the table in the Table Edit window.

6. Use the following information to format the table shown:

    a. Block and join the cells in row 1 (select **Join, Yes**).

    b. Block and center the title and column heading cells in rows 1 and 2 (select **Cell, Center** justification, **OK**).

    c. Block all cells in rows 1 and 2 and use 10% shading (select **Lines/Fill**, choose **Fill, Fill Style**, double-click on **10% Shaded Fill, OK, Close**).

    d. Block and decimal align all cells that contain dollar amounts (select **Cell, Decimal Align** justification, select **OK**).

    e. Insert one new table column between columns A and B (place cursor in column B, select the **Ins** button, **OK**) .

    f. Select **Close** {F7}.

    g. Type the information shown into the new column cells:

Home Price
$68,500
136,700
205,200

    h. Use the **TColNarr** and **TColWide** buttons to adjust each table column to approximately 2" wide.

    i. Center the table horizontally (select the **Tbl Fmt** button on the Tables Button Bar, choose **Center** in the Table Position box, **OK**).

    Note: Your table should look similar to the following:

Mortgage Affordability		
Annual Income	Home Price	Mortgage
$20,000	$68,500	$55,000
40,000	136,700	110,000
60,000	205,200	164,000

7. Use the filename **6act3** and save the file (select **File**, **Save**).

8. Print one copy (select **File**, **Print/Fax**).

9. Return the WPMAIN Button Bar to the screen (select **View**, **Button Bar Setup**, **Select**, double-click on **WPMAIN**).

10. Close the document (select **File**, **Close**).

Activity 6.4—Create and Format a Table, Change Table Lines

1. If necessary, load the WordPerfect program and display the Tables Button Bar (select **View**, **Button Bar Setup**, **Select**, double-click on **TABLES**).

2. Create a table with 4 columns and 6 rows (select the **Tbl Crt** button, type the desired number of columns and rows, select **OK**).

3. Select **Close** to exit the Table Edit window {F7}.

4. Type the unformatted text as shown.

Daily Summary of Sales Calls			
July 21	General	Agency	Total
Calls offered	5,393	971	6,364
Calls lost	121	10	131
Inquiries	1,877	896	2,773
Bookings	650	251	901

5. Select the **Tbl Edit** button to display the table in the Table Edit window.

6. Use the following information to format the table:

   a. Block and join the cells in row 1 (select **Join**, **Yes**).

   b. Center the title in row 1 (select **Cell**, **Center** justification, **OK**).

   c. Block cells B2 through D6 and use Right justification (select **Cell**, **Right** justification, **OK**).

d. Decrease the column width of columns B, C and D to approximately 1.5" (place the cursor in the desired column, press **Ctrl** and the left arrow key).

e. Block all table cells and set the row height to .5" (select **Row, Fixed**, type **.5**, select **OK**).

f. Center the table horizontally (select **Table, Table Position, Center, OK**).

g. Block all cells in row 2 and choose double lines for the top and bottom (select **Lines/Fill, Top**, double-click on **Double Line**, select **Bottom**, double-click on **Double Line**, select **Close**).

h. Select **Close** to exit and return the cursor to the Table Edit window {F7}.

i. Center the table vertically (select **Layout, Page, Center Current Page, OK**).

*Note: If desired, select **File, Print Preview, Full Page** to view the centered table. Your table should look similar to the following:*

Daily Summary of Sales Calls			
July 21	General	Agency	Total
Calls offered	5,393	971	6,364
Calls lost	121	10	131
Inquiries	1,877	896	2,773
Bookings	650	251	901

7. Use the filename **6act4** and save the file (select **File, Save**).

8. Print one copy (select **File, Print/Fax**).

9. Return the WPMAIN Button Bar to the screen (select **View, Button Bar Setup, Select**, double-click on **WPMAIN**).

10. Close the document (select **File, Close**).

Skill 6.1—Create and Format a Table; Insert a Column, Change Row Height, and Shade Cells

1. If necessary, load the WordPerfect program and display the Tables Button Bar.

2. Create a table with 3 columns and 12 rows

3. Exit the Table Edit window.

4. Type the unformatted text as shown.

PARTS LIST		
ITEM	DESCRIPTION	PART NO.
A	Left upright	3307-6
B	Right upright	3308-4
C	Top shelf	3310-5
D	Rail	3311-7
E	Bottom shelf	3314-2
F	Adjustable shelf	4400-1
G	Kick panel	4415-8
H	Back panel	4418-2
I	Screw	4420-2
J	Dowel	4422-6

5. Use the following information to format the table:

   a. Join the cells in row 1.

   b. Block and center the title and column heading cells in rows 1 and 2.

   c. Use **Center** justification in all cells of column A except the title and column heading. Use **Right** justification in all the cells of column C except the column heading.

   d. Insert a column between columns B and C.

   e. Set **Center** justification for all cells of the new column C, including the column heading.

   f. Use **10% shading** in rows 1 and 2.

   g. Set the row height for rows 1 and 2 to .4".

h. Type the text as shown into the new column.

Quantity
1
1
1
3
1
2
1
1
8
12

i. Change the font to **Roman-WP (Type 1), 14-point**.

j. Adjust the widths of the columns so that the table information is appealing and easy to read.

k. Center the table horizontally and vertically.

6. Use the filename **6skill1** and save the file.

7. Print one copy.

8. Return the WPMAIN Button Bar to the screen.

9. Close the document.

Skill 6.2—Create and Format a Table; Insert Rows and a Column

1. If necessary, load the WordPerfect program and display the Tables Button Bar.

2. Create a table with 2 columns and 8 rows and type the unformatted text as shown.

Cost/Expense Items	Amount Budgeted
Salaries, Programmers	$ 96,000
Salaries, System designers	106,000
Salaries, Computer operators	120,000
Salary, Manager	68,000
Computer supplies	35,000
Miscellaneous expenses	5,500
Insurance	12,500

3. Use the following information to format the table:

   a. Insert a row at the top of the table. Join the cells in row 1. Set the row height for row 1 to .5".

   b. Use **Decimal Align** justification in cells B2 through B8 (including the column heading cell).

   c. Set **Center** justification for the new top row.

   d. Insert a row above *Miscellaneous expenses.*

   e. Insert a column between columns A and B.

   f. Type the title **R & A Consulting Services**.

   g. Type the following information into the new row:
      Depreciation, furniture; 6,500.00; 6,500

   h. Type the following information into the new column cells:
      Actual Amount Spent; $ 95,060.25; 85,081.16; 129,882.43;
      73,247.20; 43,463.50; 6,500.00; 6,500.00; 13,240.00

4. Make decisions regarding shading cells, font changes, table lines, and column widths so that the table information appears pleasing and easy to read.

5. Use the filename **6skill2** and save the file.

6. Print one copy.

7. Return the WPMAIN Button Bar to the screen.

8. Close the document.

➥ Skill 6.3—Create and Format a Memorandum with a Table; Language Arts

1. If necessary, load the WordPerfect program.

2. Use Memorandum—Style 1 and the following information:

   a. The memo should be sent to Abby Foods Group from Helen Millard.

b. The subject of the memo is New Vice President.

c. Use the current date; include your reference initials.

d. Correct three spelling and three punctuation errors.

e. After creating the table, format cells as desired, e.g., increase or decrease column widths, change the alignment of column headings, shade cells, change table lines, and decimal align dollar amounts.

f. The memorandum body text follows:

Douglas Bartlett has been appointed to the position of Vice President, Business Development and National Accounts--Grocery, Sales & Integrated Logistics Division.

The role of Business Development continues to grow in importance as the cornerstone of Sales & Integrated Logistics' intiative to pursue strategic customer aliances. In this new position Douglas will be responsible for developing and directing startegic programs and partnership alliances with national and regional account grocery customers. He will report to Gayleen Kirkland, Senior Vice President, Sales & Integrated Logistics Division, Abby Foods Group.

Reporting to Douglas are:

Name	Accounts	Account Value
Santiago Cruz	Business Development & National Accounts	$ 390,000
Veronica Johnson	Business Development & Eastern Region	135000
Richard Epstein	Business Development & Midwestern Region	96,000
Connie Jimenez	Business Development & Southern Region	78,000.00

Douglas assumes his new responsibilities from the position of Regional Vice President, Broker Sales, Central Region. His office is located at 2022 Oakton Street, Des Plaines, IL 60018, and the telephone number is (708) 555-9009.

---

3. Use the filename **6skill3** and save the file.

4. Print one copy.

5. If necessary, return the WPMAIN Button Bar to the screen.

6. Close the document.

7. If you have completed your work, exit WordPerfect.

Edit a Table

Features Covered

- Move a row and column
- Delete a row and column
- Change table row margins
- Copy a table
- Delete a table
- Calculate column and row totals
- Copy a formula
- Omit table lines and borders
- Double underlines

Objectives

After successfully completing this chapter, you will be able to move and delete a table row and column, change table row margins, and copy and delete a table. You will also be able to calculate a column or row total, set the number type and digits after the decimal, omit table lines, and use double underlines.

Chapter Introduction

Once a table has been typed and printed, the table information can be edited. Changes can include moving or deleting table columns and rows, changing row margins, and omitting table lines. A formula can be used to total a column or row and the formula can be copied to other cells. An entire table can also be copied or deleted.

Move a Table Column or Row

A table column or row can be moved to another column or row location in a table. When a column or row is moved, the column/row is deleted from the original location and displays in the new location. When a column/row is copied, the column/row displays in the original location *and* the new location. Reposition a column or row by using the **Move/Copy** option in the Table Edit window.

The cursor is placed in any cell of the column or row to be moved. After selecting the **Move/Copy** option, the column or row is deleted from the screen and placed in the temporary memory. Before a moved (deleted) column or row is retrieved to the screen, the cursor is positioned where the moved column or row is to be inserted. For a moved column, the cursor is placed in the column that will be located to the right of the moved column. For a moved row, the cursor is placed in the row that will be located below the moved row. After placing the cursor in the desired column or row, the **Enter** key is pressed and the deleted (moved) column or row displays in the new location.

Start-Up Instructions

❖ If a mouse is available, the Tables Button Bar should be displayed. (If necessary, see Steps to Display a Different Button Bar in Chapter 6, page 140.)

❖ Create a table with 5 columns and 5 rows.

❖ Type the unformatted information shown in Figure 7.1 into the table cells.

❖ Format the table as follows:

   a. Select the **Tbl Edit** button to obtain the Table Edit window.

   b. Join the cells in row 1 (block row 1, select **Join, Yes**).

   c. Center the title and column headings in rows 1 and 2 (block the rows, select **Cell, Center** justification, **OK**).

   d. Block the cells in columns B, C, D, and E that contain numbers and dollar amounts; use **Right** justification (block the cells, select **Cell, Right** justification, **OK**).

FIGURE 7.1

Unformatted table

PRODUCT DATA				
Product Name	Disk Size	Part No.	List Price	Discount Price
WinPro 3.5	5.25" or 3.5"	1269	$150	$85
Matrix 1.0	3.5"	1270	$175	$95
ArtFree Design 2.0	3.5"	4688	$495	$299

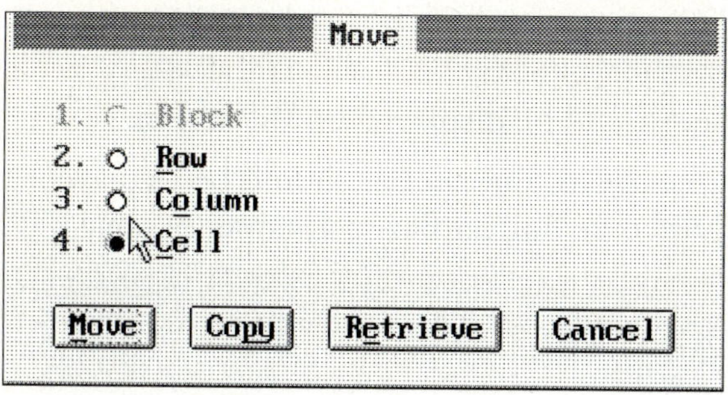

    e. Select **Close** {F7}.

❖ Save the file on the file disk; use the filename **7drill1** (select **File**, **Save**, type the drive letter where the file disk is located followed by a colon and the filename, select **OK**).

Move a Table Column

*Note: The Table Edit window should be displayed. (If necessary, select the **Tbl Edit** button.)*

1. Place the cursor in any cell of the column to be moved.

    For example, place the cursor in any cell in column C.

2. Select **Move/Copy** {m}.

   Note: The Move dialog box displays (see Figure 7.2).

3. Select the **Column** option {o}.

4. Select **Move** {m}.

   Note: The selected column is removed temporarily from the Table Edit window.

5. Move the cursor to any cell in the column that will be located to the right of the moved column.

    For example, place the cursor in any cell in column B.

6. Press **Enter**.

   Note: When the deleted column is inserted at the new location, the cells in row 1 are no longer joined.

Finish-Up Instructions

❖ Rejoin the cells in row 1 (block row 1 and select **Join**, **Yes**).

❖ Select **Close** {F7}.

❖ Use the new filename **7drill1m** and save the file on the file disk (select **File**, **Save As**, type the drive letter where the file disk is located followed by a colon and the filename, select **OK**).

❖ Print one copy (select **File**, **Print/Fax**).

❖ The file named **7drill1m** should be displayed on the screen.

❖ If a mouse is available, the Tables Button Bar should be displayed. (If necessary, see Steps to Display a Different Button Bar in Chapter 6, page 140.)

Move a Table Row

*Note: The Table Edit window should be displayed. (If necessary, select the **Tbl Edit** button.)*

1. Place the cursor in any cell in the row to be moved.

   For example, place the cursor in any cell in row 4.

2. Select **Move/Copy** {m}.

3. Select the **Row** option {r}.

4. Select **Move** {m}.

   Note: The selected row is temporarily removed from the Table Edit window.

5. Move the cursor to any cell in the row that will be located below the moved row.

   For example, place the cursor in any cell in row 3.

6. Press **Enter**.

Finish-Up Instructions

❖ Select **Close** {F7}.

❖ Use the new filename **7drill2** and save the file on the file disk (select **File, Save As**, type the drive letter where the file disk is located followed by a colon and the filename, select **OK**).

❖ Print one copy (select **File, Print/Fax**).

Delete a Table Column or Row

When editing a table, a table column or row can be deleted. A column or row is deleted by first placing the cursor/insertion point in the column or row to be deleted. A row can be deleted by using the **Del Row** button on the Tables Button Bar or by choosing **Del** in the Table Edit window. A column can only be deleted by selecting **Del** in the Table Edit window.

If a column or row is deleted by mistake, **Edit, Undo** can be selected to retrieve and display the deleted column or row. However, **Edit, Undo** must be selected immediately after a column or row is deleted and before another action is performed.

- ❖ The file named **7drill2** should be displayed on the screen.
- ❖ If a mouse is available, the Tables Button Bar should be displayed. (If necessary, see Steps to Display a Different Button Bar in Chapter 6, page 140.)

Delete a Table Column

1. Select the **Tbl Edit** button {Alt and F7, t, e or Alt and F11}.

2. Place the cursor in any cell in the column to be deleted.

   For example, place the cursor in any cell in column B.

3. Select **Del** {d}.

   Note: The Delete dialog box displays. The Columns option is already selected. (If necessary, select the Columns option button.)

4. Select **OK** to accept the default of deleting one column {Enter}.

   *Note: If a table column is deleted by mistake, select **Close**, then choose **Edit**, **Undo** to retrieve the deleted column.*

Finish-Up Instructions

- ❖ Select **Close** {F7}.
- ❖ Save the file on the file disk; use the new filename **7drill2d** (select **File**, **Save As**, type the drive letter where the file disk is located followed by a colon and the filename, select **OK**).
- ❖ Print one copy (select **File**, **Print/Fax**).

Start-Up Instructions

- ❖ The file named **7drill2d** should be displayed on the screen.
- ❖ If a mouse is available, the Tables Button Bar should be displayed. (If necessary, see Steps to Display a Different Button Bar in Chapter 6, page 140.) If a mouse is not available, skip to the Steps to Delete a Table Row Using the Table Edit Window.

Delete a Table Row Using the Tables Button Bar

1. Place the cursor/insertion point in any cell in the row to be deleted.

   For example, place the insertion point in any cell in row 3.

2. Select the **Del Row** button on the Tables Button Bar.

   *Note: If a table row is deleted by mistake, select **Edit**, **Undo** to retrieve the deleted row.*

   Note: Skip to the following steps and proceed to the Finish-Up Instructions.

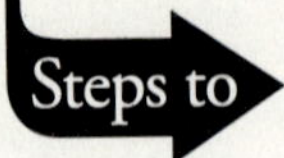

Delete a Table Row Using the Table Edit Window

1. Select the **Tbl Edit** button {Alt and F7, t, e or Alt and F11}.

2. Place the cursor in any cell in the row to be deleted.

   For example, place the cursor in any cell in row 3.

3. Select **Del** {d}.

4. Select the **Rows** option {r}.

5. Select **OK** {Enter}.

   *Note: If a table row is deleted by mistake, select **Close**, then choose **Edit**, **Undo** to retrieve the deleted row.*

6. Select **Close** {F7}.

Finish-Up Instructions

❖ Save the file on the file disk; use the new filename **7drill2w** (select **File**, **Save As**, type the drive letter where the file disk is located followed by a colon and the filename, select **OK**).

❖ Print one copy (select **File**, **Print/Fax**).

Change Table Row Margins

Another WordPerfect editing feature is the capability to change any or all table row margins. The row margins are the spaces that are placed between the cell text and the top and bottom table cell lines. For example, the space placed between the top table line and the cell text is the top row margin. The cell margins are measured in fractions of inches. A suggested top row margin is .2 inches.

Row margins are changed in the Table Edit window. Before setting row margins, block the cell or cells where margins are to be changed. The **Row** option is chosen to display the Row Format dialog box. Both the top and bottom row margin options can also be changed in the Row format dialog box.

Start-Up Instructions

❖ The file named **7drill2w** should be displayed on the screen.

❖ If a mouse is available, the Tables Button Bar should be displayed. (If necessary, see Steps to Display a Different Button Bar in Chapter 6, page 140.)

   Chapter 7—Edit a Table

 **Change Table Row Margins**

1. Place the insertion point in any table cell.

2. Select the **Tbl Edit** button on the Tables Button Bar {Alt and F7, t, e or Alt and F11}.

3. Block the row(s) where the row margin is to be changed.

   For example, block all rows.

4. Select **Row** {r}.

   Note: The Row Format dialog box displays.

5. Click in the desired Row Margins box.

   For example, click in the **Top** option box {t}.

6. Type the desired margin for the table rows.

   For example, type .2.

7. Click in the desired Row Margins box.

   For example, click in the **Bottom** option box {b}.

8. Type the desired margin for the table rows.

   For example, type .2.

   *Note: Check that the **Auto** option is selected in the Row Height box.*

9. Select **OK** {press Enter twice}.

Finish-Up Instructions

❖ Select **Close** {F7}.

❖ Save the file on the file disk; use the filename **7drill2g** (select **File**, **Save As**, type the drive letter where the file disk is located followed by a colon and the filename, select **OK**).

❖ Print one copy (select **File**, **Print/Fax**).

❖ Close the document (select **File**, **Close**).

Copy a Table

An entire table can be copied to another window or to another location within the current window. A table is often copied for the purpose of making changes to the copied table without changing the original table or for the purpose of using the table information in another letter, memorandum, or report.

Before a table is copied, the table is blocked, including the table definition and table off codes. In Reveal Codes, the table definition code is enclosed by left and right brackets, e.g., [Tbl Def]. The table definition code is expanded when the code is highlighted, e.g., [Tbl Def:Table A;...]. When using a mouse, you may find it easier to block the table by placing a hard return above the table definition code. The arrow keys can be used to locate the cursor/insertion point on the table definition code (e.g., if the table is the first item on the page, press **Home**, **Home**, **Home**, and the **up** arrow key).

Start-Up Instructions

* The file named **7drill2g** should be displayed on the screen.
* If a mouse is available, the Tables Button Bar should be displayed. (If necessary, see Steps to Display a Different Button Bar in Chapter 6, page 140.)

Copy a Table

1. Select **View, Reveal Codes** {Alt and F3}.

2. Press the arrow keys to locate the cursor/insertion point on the table definition code [Tbl Def:...].

   For example, press **Home, Home, Home,** and the up arrow key to highlight the table definition code.

3. Press the **Enter** key once to place a hard return before the table definition code.

4. Block the entire table (including the table definition code) by moving the mouse pointer to the blank line above the table and dragging the mouse down until the entire table is highlighted {Alt and F4; press the down arrow key to highlight all cells in the table}.

5. Select **Edit, Copy** {Ctrl and c}.

   Note: A copy of the table is placed in a buffer (temporary memory). The original table remains on the screen with the cursor/insertion point located below the table.

6. Locate the cursor/insertion point at the desired position.

   For example, press the **Enter** key once to place a hard return after the table.

7. Select **Edit, Paste** {Ctrl and v}.

   Note: A copy of the table is inserted at the location of the cursor/insertion point. If necessary, press the down arrow key a few times to display the copied table.

Finish-Up Instructions

* Save the file on the file disk; use the new filename **7drill3** (select **File, Save As**, type the drive letter where the file disk is located followed by a colon and the filename, select **OK**).
* Optional. Print one copy (select **File, Print/Fax**).

                                                    Chapter 7—Edit a Table

Delete a Table

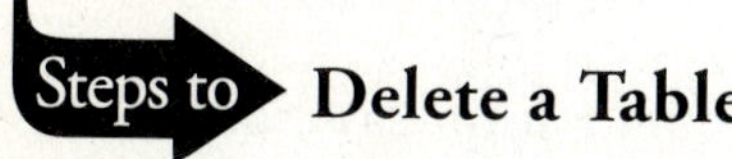 table can be deleted by blocking the entire table, including the table definition and table off codes (see Steps to Copy a Table presented earlier). If a table is deleted by mistake, select **Edit, Undo** to retrieve and display the table on the screen again. **Edit, Undo** must be selected immediately before any other operation is completed.

Start-Up Instructions

❖ The file named **7drill3** should be displayed on the screen.

Steps to ▶ **Delete a Table**

1. Turn on Reveal Codes {Alt and F3}.

2. Move the mouse pointer to the hard return code [Hrt] above the table definition code. Press and hold the mouse button and drag the mouse to block the entire table {Alt and F4, press the down arrow key to block the entire table}.

     For example, block the second table.

3. Press the **Delete** key.

   Note: The entire table is deleted.

Finish-Up Instructions

❖ Close the document and do not save the file.

Calculate a Column Total

Table cells containing numbers (values) can be calculated by using formulas to add, subtract, multiply, or divide. A value number is a number used to obtain a mathematical result. A text number is a number that will not be used to compute a result. Examples of text numbers are a social security number or a year, e.g., 1994.

Columns are totaled by using a table formula. Table formulas are created in the Table Edit window. The cursor is placed in the cell that will contain the column total and **Formula** is selected. The cell addresses to be totaled are typed followed by a plus in the Table Formula dialog box. For example, if rows 3, 4, and 5 in column C are to be totaled, the cursor is placed in the cell where the results will be located (C6), and the formula is C3+C4+C5 is typed in the Table Formula dialog box. The shortcut formula for adding a column is to type only a plus (+) in the Table Formula dialog box.

Table numbers can be formatted by selecting from a list of standard formats, such as Currency and Commas. When the Currency format is selected, WordPerfect automatically inserts a dollar sign in front of table numbers as well as inserts commas to separate thousands within the table numbers ($12,652.00). With the Commas format, the table numbers are formatted with commas to separate thousands (12,652.00). The default number of digits after the decimal for both the Currency format and Commas format is two. The number of digits after the decimal can be changed. For example, to eliminate the decimal point and zeros in the number 12,652.00, the number of digits after the decimal can be changed to zero.

In the Table Edit window, a formula is deleted from a cell by placing the cursor in the cell and selecting **Del** and choosing **Cell Contents**. Also, a formula can be deleted in the document window by selecting the number and choosing **Edit, Cut**.

If numbers are changed in the table cells, the cells that contain formula results will need to be recalculated. The formula results can be updated in one of three ways: select the **Tbl Calc** or **Calc All** buttons on the Tables Button Bar; choose **Layout, Tables, Calculate**; or choose **Calc** in the Table Edit window. When any one of these methods is used, all formula results in the table are recalculated.

Start-Up Instructions

❖ If a mouse is available, the Tables Button Bar should be displayed. (If necessary, see Steps to Display a Different Button Bar in Chapter 6, page 140.)

❖ Create a table with 3 columns and 8 rows. Select **Close** {F7}.

❖ Type the unformatted information shown in Figure 7.3 into the table cells. (Do not type column totals; column totals will be calculated later.)

❖ Select the **Tbl Edit** button and format the table as follows:

    a. Block and join the cells in row 1 (select **Join, Yes**).

    b. Block rows 1 and 2 and center the title and column headings (select **Cell, Center** justification, **OK**).

Division Expenses		
Expense Category	Eastern Division	Western Division
Indirect labor	34500	38600
Materials	14800	15200
Supplies	15800	16200
Utilities	17400	18200
Insurance	12500	13700
TOTALS		

Chapter 7—Edit a Table

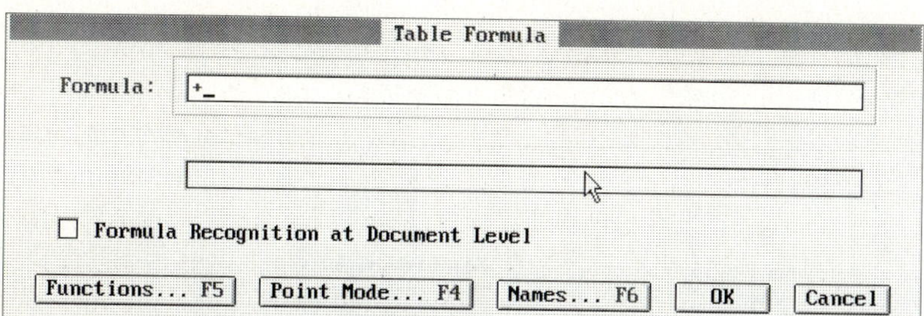

Table Formula dialog box

> c. Block the cells in columns B and C that contain figures (include the empty cells at the bottom of the columns) and choose **Cell, Decimal Align** justification, **OK**.
>
> d. Select **Close** {F7}.

❖ Save the file on the file disk; use the filename **7drill4** {select **File, Save**, type the drive letter where the file disk is located followed by a colon and the filename, select **OK**).

Steps to Use a Formula and Calculate a Column Total

1. If necessary, select the **Tbl Edit** button {Alt and F7, t, e or Alt and F11}.

2. Place the cursor in the cell where the calculated amount will be placed.

   For example, place the cursor in cell B8.

3. Select **Formula** {f}.

   Note: The Table Formula dialog box displays.

4. Type the desired formula in the Formula box

   For example, type a + (plus). See Figure 7.4.

5. Select **OK** {Enter twice}.

   Note: WordPerfect automatically adds the values in the cells above the cursor and displays the total at the location of the cursor.

Finish-Up Instructions

❖ Place the cursor in cell C8 and repeat steps 3-5 to total column C.

❖ Select **Close** {F7}.

❖ Save the file on the file disk; use the filename **7drill4c** (select **File, Save As**, type the drive letter where the file disk is located followed by a colon and the filename, select **OK**).

Steps to Set the Number Type and Digits After the Decimal

1. If necessary, select the **Tbl Edit** button {Alt and F7, t, e or Alt and F11}.

Number Type Formats
dialog box

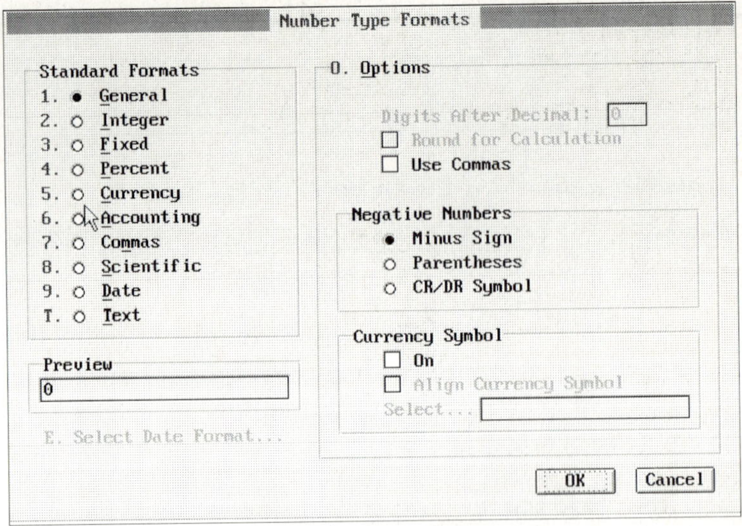

2. Block the cell or cells for which the number type and digits after the decimal are to be set.

> For example, block cells B3 and C3.

3. Select **Cell** {c}.

   Note: The Cell Format dialog box displays.

4. Select **Number Type** in the middle box (option #6) {t}.

   Note: The Number Type Formats dialog box displays (see Figure 7.5).

5. Select the desired standard format.

   > For example, select **Currency** {c}.

6. Click in the **Digits After Decimal** box to highlight the number displayed {o, d}.

7. Type the desired number of digits to be placed to the right of the decimal point.

   > For example, type **0** (zero).

8. Select **OK** twice {press Enter three times}.

Finish-Up Instructions

❖ Block cells B8 and C8 and repeat Steps 3-8 to set the number type to the Currency format and set the Digits After Decimal to zero.

❖ Block cells B4 through C7 and repeat Steps 3-8 to set the number type to the Commas format and set the Digits After Decimal to zero.

❖ Select **Close** {F7}.

❖ Use the new filename **7drill4t** and save the file (select **File, Save As**, type the drive letter where the file disk is located followed by a colon and the filename, select **OK**).

Start-Up Instructions

❖ The file named **7drill4t** should be displayed on the screen.

    Chapter 7—Edit a Table

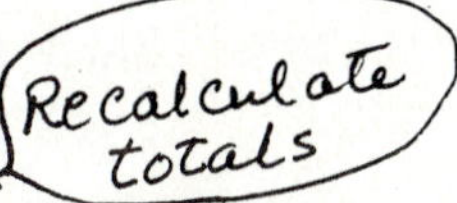

Division Expenses		
Expense Category	Eastern Division	Western Division
Indirect labor	$34,500	$38,600
Materials	*16, 300* ~~14,800~~	15,200
Supplies	15,800	*17, 890* ~~16,200~~
Utilities	*19, 610* ~~17,400~~	18,200
Insurance	12,500	13,700
TOTALS	$95,000	$101,900

Recalculate totals

- ❖ If a mouse is available, the Tables Button Bar should be displayed. (If necessary, see Steps to Display a Different Button Bar in Chapter 6, page 140.)
- ❖ Edit the table as shown in Figure 7.6.

Steps to ▶ Edit Table Figures and Recalculate

1. After the table figures have been changed, place the cursor/insertion point in any table cell.

2. Move the mouse pointer to the **Down** triangle button located at the left of the Tables Button Bar; click the left mouse button once to display the **Calc All** button. Select the **Calc All** button on the Tables Button Bar {Alt and F7, t, a}.

   *Note: Calc All updates all tables in the document. When the **Tbl Calc** button is selected, WordPerfect automatically updates all table column totals in the current table.*

3. Select the **Up** arrow button located at the left of the Tables Button Bar to return the Tables Button Bar to its original position.

Finish-Up Instructions

- ❖ Use the new filename **7drill5** and save the file on the file disk (select **File**, **Save As**, type the drive letter where the file disk is located followed by a colon and the filename, select **OK**).
- ❖ Print one copy (select **File**, **Print/Fax**).

Total a Table Row

A row is totaled by placing a formula in the cell where the result is desired. For example, type B2+C2+D2 in the Table Formula dialog box to add the values in row 2. An abbreviated formula cannot be used. If a value in the row is changed, the row total should be recalculated by placing the cursor/insertion point in any cell in the table and selecting the **Tbl Calc** or **Calc All** button on the Tables Button Bar.

- ❖ The file named **7drill5** should be displayed on the screen.

- ❖ If a mouse is available, the Tables Button Bar should be displayed. (If necessary, see Steps to Display a Different Button Bar in Chapter 6, page 140.)

- ❖ Insert a table column after column C (3) (select the **Tbl Edit** button, place the cursor in column C, select **Ins, Columns, After Cursor Position, OK**).

- ❖ Block and join the cells in row 1 (select **Join, Yes**).

- ❖ Select **Close** {F7}.

- ❖ Type the column heading **Total Expenses** in column 4, row 2. The column amounts will be totaled in the following Steps to Total a Row.

Steps to ▶ Total a Row

1. If necessary, select the **Tbl Edit** button {Alt and F7, t, e or Alt and F11}.

2. Place the cursor in the cell where the row total is to be located.

   For example, place the cursor in cell D3.

3. Select **Formula** {f}.

   Note: The Table Formula dialog box displays.

4. In the Formula box, type the desired formula.

   For example, type **B3+C3**.

5. Select **OK** {Enter}.

   Note: The results of the formula display in the cell where the cursor is located. The remaining row totals will be totaled in the following Steps to Copy a Formula.

Finish-Up Instructions

- ❖ Select **Close** {F7}.

- ❖ Use the new filename **7drill6** and save the file on the file disk (select **File, Save As**, type the drive letter where the file disk is located followed by a colon and the filename, select **OK**).

Copy a Formula

After a formula is placed in a table cell the formula can be copied to one or more cells. A cell formula is either copied down to other column cells or right to other row cells. A formula can be copied to multiple cells by typing the desired number of cells in which the formula should appear in the How Many option of the Table Formula dialog box.

After the formula is copied, the results are displayed immediately in the cells where the formula was copied. When a formula is copied, the row and column cell addresses in the formula are automatically changed to reflect the cell addresses where the formula was copied.

Start-Up Instructions

- ❖ The file named **7drill6** should be displayed on the screen.
- ❖ If a mouse is available, the Tables Button Bar should be displayed. (If necessary, see Steps to Display a Different Button Bar in Chapter 6, page 140.)

Copy a Formula

1. If necessary, select the **Tbl Edit** button {Alt and F7, t, e or Alt and F11}.

2. Place the cursor in the cell that contains the formula to be copied.

    For example, place the cursor in cell D3.

3. Select **Move/Copy** {m}.

    Note: The Move dialog box displays.

4. If necessary, select **Cell** {c}.

5. Select **Copy** {p}.

    Note: The Copy Cell dialog box displays.

6. Select **Down** {d}.

7. In the *How Many?* box, type the number of cells where the formula should be copied.

    For example, type **5**. (Do not type the period.)

8. Select **OK** {Enter twice}.

    Note: WordPerfect immediately copies the formula and cell format (currency) into each cell in Column D and displays the total results for each row.

Finish-Up Instructions

- ❖ Select **Close** {F7}.
- ❖ Use the **TColNarr** button to reduce the width of columns 1 and 2 so that the column headings display on two lines. Use the TColWide button and increase the widths of columns 3 and 4 so that all the columns containing dollar amounts are approximately the same width.
- ❖ Use the new filename **7drill6f** and save the file again (select **File**, **Save As**).
- ❖ Print one copy (select **File**, **Print/Fax**).

Omit Table Lines and Table Border

The double border lines that display around the table and the single lines that display around each cell are defaulted (preset) to print. The table lines and/or border can be omitted from table rows and cells. After the table lines or border are omitted, the table's row and column structure remains in effect.

The table lines and border are two separate elements and are selected, created, and edited separately. The single line that displays around the outside of each cell is concealed when the double border is displayed. Therefore, if the table border is omitted, the single outside line will remain. The single outside line can be omitted also.

Start-Up Instructions

❖ The file named **7drill6f** should be displayed on the screen.

❖ If a mouse is available, the Tables Button Bar should be displayed. (If necessary, see Steps to Display a Different Button Bar in Chapter 6, page 140.)

Omit All Table Lines and Table Borders

1. If necessary, select the **Tbl Edit** button {Alt and F7, t, e or Alt and F11}.

2. Block the cell or cells for which table lines are to be omitted.

   For example, block all table cells.

3. Select the **Lines/Fill** {L}.

4. Select the **Default Line** option in the Entire Table box {d}.

   Note: The Default Table Lines dialog box displays.

5. Select **Line Style** {L}.

6. Double-click on **None** {press the up arrow key until None is highlighted, press Enter}.

7. Select **Close** {Enter} to exit the Default Table Lines dialog box.

   Note: The Table Lines dialog box displays.

8. Select **Border/Fill** {e}.

   Note: The Table Border/Fill dialog box displays.

9. Select **Border Style** {b}.

10. Double-click on **None** {press the up arrow key until None is highlighted, press Enter}.

11. Select **OK** to exit the Table Border/Fill dialog box {Enter}.

12. Select **Close** to exit the Table Lines dialog box {Enter}.

Note: The table lines no longer display on the screen; however, the table's column and row structure remains in effect.

Finish-Up Instructions

- ❖ Select **Close** {F7}.
- ❖ Save the file again using the same filename, **7drill6f** (select **File**, **Save**).
- ❖ Optional. Print one copy (select **File**, **Print/Fax**).

Print Double Underlines Below the Total Amount

Double underlines are placed under a column total amount in order to emphasize the total. Generally, if double underlines are used, table lines are not printed. When a column is totaled, a single underline is used to separate the last column amount from the total amount. When a table is located in the Table Edit window, the last column number is underlined by selecting the cell(s) and choosing **Cell**, **Underline**. When a table is located in the document window, the last column number is underlined by selecting the cell(s) and choosing **Font**, **Underline** or by selecting the **TCellFmt** button and choosing **Underline**.

The single underline traditionally has been formatted to extend the width of the following total amount. Therefore, one or more spaces were placed to the left of the last column number in order to extend the underline. Since WordPerfect's number type format feature does not allow a space(s) to be used to extend the underline, the additional space(s) will not be effective (unless the General number format is used).

Traditionally, the dollar sign ($) in the first figure and the last figure of a column have been formatted to align. Since there is often an additional digit(s) in the total amount, an extra space(s) is placed between the dollar sign and the first digit in the first column entry. However, WordPerfect's number type format feature does not allow a space to be placed between a dollar sign and total amount when the Currency format is selected.

Once the column total has been calculated, the amount is selected and the **Double Underline** attribute is selected in the Cell Format dialog box. The double underlines display immediately below the selected cell amount.

Start-Up Instructions

- ❖ The file named **7drill6f** should be displayed on the screen.
- ❖ Select the column heading cells in row 2; select **Font**, **Underline** {F8}.
- ❖ Select the cells in the row above the row containing the total amounts. Select **Font**, **Underline**.

 Print Double Underlines

1. If necessary, select the **Tbl Edit** button {Alt and F7, t, e or Alt and F11}.

2. Block the cells that contain the total amounts.

   For example, block cells B8, C8, and D8.

3. Select **Cell** {c}.

4. Select the **Dbl Underline** option in the Attributes box {d}.

5. Select **OK** {Enter}.

Finish-Up Instructions

❖ Select **Close** {F7}.

❖ Use the new filename **7drill6u** and save the file on the file disk (select **File, Save As**, type the drive letter where the file disk is located followed by a colon and the filename, select **OK**).

❖ Print one copy (select **File, Print/Fax**).

❖ Close the document (select **File, Close**).

The Next Step

Chapter Review and Activities

FEATURES SUMMARY

FEATURES	ACTIONS	PAGE
Move a table colum	Select the **Tbl Edit** button, place the cursor in any cell in the column to be moved, select **Move/Copy**, select **Column, Move.** Place the cursor to any cell in the column that will be located to the right of the moved column, press **Enter.**	173
Move a table row	Select the **Tbl Edit** button, place the cursor in any cell in the row to be moved, select **Move/Copy**, select **Row, Move.** Place the cursor to any cell in the row that will be located below the moved row, press **Enter.**	174
Delete a table column	Select the **Tbl Edit** button, place the cursor in the column to be deleted, select **Del**, select **OK.**	175
Delete a table row	Place the cursor/insertion point in any cell of the row to be deleted, select the **Del Row** button on the Tables Button Bar.	175
Change table row margins	Select the **Tbl Edit** button, block the row(s) where margins are to be changed, select **Row**, type the desired margins in the option boxes, select **OK.**	177

FEATURES *(cont'd.)*	ACTIONS *(cont'd.)*	PAGE
Copy a table	Turn on Reveal Codes, press the arrow keys to locate the cursor/insertion point on the [Tbl Def:...] code, press **Enter** to place a hard return code before the table definition code, block the entire table (including the table definition code). Select **Edit, Copy,** locate the cursor/insertion point at the desired position, select **Edit, Paste.**	178
Delete a table	Turn on Reveal Codes, place the cursor/insertion point on or before the table definition code, block the entire table (including the table definition code), press **Delete.**	179
Calculate a column total (using a formula)	Select the **Tbl Edit** button, locate the cursor in the cell where the formula and calculated total will be placed, select **Formula,** type the desired formula (type a +), select **OK.**	181
Set number type and digits after the decimal	Select the **Tbl Edit** button, block the cell(s), select **Cell, Number Type** (option #6), select the desired format, click in the **Digits After Decimal** option, type the desired number of digits, select **OK.**	181
Recalculate	Click on the **Down** triangle button located beside the Tables Button Bar, select the **Calc All** button.	183
Total a table row	Select the **Tbl Edit** button, locate the cursor in the cell where the formula and total amount will be placed, select **Formula,** type the desired formula (cell address + cell address, e.g., B3+C3), select **OK.**	184
Copy a formula	Select the **Tbl Edit** button, locate the cursor in the cell that contains the formula, select **Move/Copy, Cell, Copy, Down** or **Right,** type the number of cells the formula should be copied to, select **OK.**	185
Omit table lines and table border	Select the **Tbl Edit** button, block the desired cell(s), select **Lines/Fill,** select **Default Line** option, select **Line Style,** double click on **None, Close.** Select **Border/Fill,** select **Border Style,** double-click on **None, Close.**	186
Underline or double underline	Select the **Tbl Edit** button, block desired cell(s), select **Cell,** choose **Underline** or **Dbl Underline, OK.**	188

Chapter 7—Edit a Table

True/False—Circle One

T F 1. A table column can be moved; a table row cannot be moved.

T F 2. Before deleting a table column, place the cursor/insertion point in any cell in the column to be deleted.

T F 3. Before a table column is moved, the table must be displayed in the Table Edit window.

T F 4. The **Tbl Form** button is selected in order to insert a formula to calculate column or row totals.

T F 5. If table cell values or formulas are changed, the column or row totals can be re-calculated and updated by selecting the **Calc All** button.

Short Answer

1. State the main difference between copying a column and moving a column.

2. What is the shortcut formula for adding (calculating) a column?

3. Write down the formula for adding two cells in row 4. The cells are located in columns D and E.

4. When the **Calc All** button is selected on the Tables Button Bar, are the results for one or all formulas updated?

5. Describe a table row margin.

Enriching Language Arts Skills

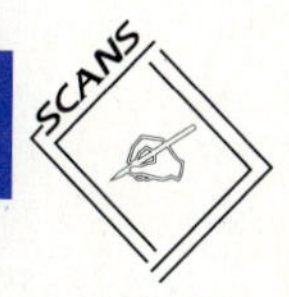

Spelling/Vocabulary Words

adversely   having an unfavorable effect.
per diem   an amount allowed for daily expenses.
reimbursement   money repaid for expenses incurred.

Single and Double Underlines for Dollar Amounts

Place a single underline below the last column amount and before the total amount. The single underline should extend the width of the amount that has the most characters, including the dollar sign. However, if any one of WordPerfect's number type options (other than General) is used, the spaces cannot be added to extend the single underline. In a table without lines or borders, a total amount is usually emphasized by placing double underlines beneath the total amount. Both of the following examples are acceptable.

Examples:

Formatted using the General number type	Formatted using the Currency and Commas number types
$110,550	$110,550
3,600	3,600
2,820	2,820
$116,970	$116,970

Activities

Activity 7.1—Calculate a Column Total Using a Formula, Set Number Type and Digits after the Decimal

1. If necessary, display the Tables Button Bar.

2. Create a table with 3 columns and 7 rows. Select **Close** {F7}.

3. Type the following unformatted information into the table cells:

GENERAL FUND EXPENDITURES		
Fund	June	July
Remodeling	55000	30500
Equipment	50000	25000
Interfund transfers	48000	12460
Capital outlays	95000	72680
TOTALS		

4. Use the following instructions to format the table:

   a. Select the **Tbl Edit** button on the Tables Button Bar.

   b. Block and join the cells in row 1 and center the title (select **Join, Yes**).

c. Block and center the title and column headings in rows 1 and 2 (select **Cell**, **Center** justification, **OK**).

d. Calculate the column totals for columns B and C (place the cursor in cell B7, select **Formula**, type a **+**, select **OK**). Move the cursor to cell C7 and repeat the instructions.

e. Block cells B3 and C3 and set **Decimal Align** justification, choose the **Currency** number type, and set the number of digits after decimal to zero (select **Cell**, **Decimal Align**, select **Number Type** [option #6], select **Currency**, select the **Digits After Decimal** option box and type **0** [zero], select **OK** twice).

f. Block the figures in cells B4 through C6 and set **Decimal Align** justification, choose the **Commas** number type, and set the Digits After Decimal to zero (select **Cell**, **Decimal Align**, select **Number Type** [option 6], select **Commas**, select the **Digits After Decimal** option box and type **0** [zero], select **OK** twice).

g. Block cells B7 and C7and set the justification to **Decimal Align** justification, set the number type to **Currency**, and set the Digits After Decimal to zero (if necessary, see Step 4e).

h. Select **Close** {F7}.

5. Change the column widths so that all the columns containing dollar amounts are approximately the same width.

6. Center the table horizontally (select the **Tbl Fmt**, **Position**, **Center**, **OK**).

   Note: Your table should look similar to the following table:

GENERAL FUND EXPENDITURES		
Fund	June	July
Remodeling	$55,000	$30,500
Equipment	50,000	25,000
Interfund transfers	48,000	12,460
Capital outlays	95,000	72,680
TOTALS	$248,000	$140,640

7. Save the file on the file disk; use the filename **7act1**.

8. Print one copy.

9. If necessary, return the WPMAIN Button Bar to the screen (select **View**, **Button Bar Setup**, **Select**, double-click on **WPMAIN**).

10. Close the document.

1. If necessary, display the Tables Button Bar.

2. Create a table with 4 columns and 8 rows. Select **Close** {F7}.

3. Type the following unformatted information into the table cells as shown. (Remember: Text will automatically wrap around in cells.)

NORTON PRODUCTS			
Annual Conference Costs			
Item	1991	1992	1993
Conference facilities	3600	4000	5000
Demonstration materials	2500	3400	4000
Accommodations	35500	36800	37600
Meals	25000	26000	26700
Travel	31900	32300	35400

4. Use the following instructions to format the table:

   a. Select the **Tbl Edit** button on the Tables Button Bar.

   b. Move column D (1993 information) between columns A and B (place the cursor in any cells in column D, choose **Move/Copy**, **Column**, **Move**; place the cursor to any cell in column B, press **Enter**).

   c. Move the now column D (1992 information) between columns B and C (see Step 4b, if necessary).

   d. Block and join the cells in row 1.

   e. Block and join the cells in row 2.

   f. Block and center the title and subtitle.

   g. Block all cells in columns B, C, and D and choose **Decimal Align** justification.

   h. Block cells B4 through D4 and set the number type to **Currency** and set the Digits After Decimal to zero (select **Cells**, select **Number Type** [option #6], select **Currency**, select the **Digits After Decimal** option box and type **0** [zero], select **OK** twice).

   i. Block cells B5 through D8 and set the number type to **Commas** and set the Digits After Decimal to zero.

   j. Increase the width of column A so the words display on one line.

k. Block the entire table and change the top and bottom row margins to .15 (select **Row**, choose the **Top** Row Margins option box, type **.15**; select the **Bottom** Row Margins option box, type **.15**, select **OK**).

l. Select **Close** {F7}.

Note: Your table should look similar to the following table:

NORTON PRODUCTS			
Annual Conference Costs			
Item	1993	1992	1991
Conference facilities	$5,000	$4,000	$3,600
Demonstration materials	4,000	3,400	2,500
Accommodations	37,600	36,800	35,500
Meals	26,700	26,000	25,000
Travel	35,400	32,300	31,900

5. Copy the table.

   a. Turn on Reveal Codes (**Alt** and **F3**).

   b. Press **Home, Home, Home**, and the up arrow key.

   c. Press **Enter** once.

   d. Block the entire table including the table definition and table off codes.

   e. Select **Edit, Copy** {Ctrl and c}.

   f. With the cursor/insertion point located at the bottom of the table, press **Enter** twice.

   g. Select **Edit, Paste** {Ctrl and v}.

   *Note: To view the both tables on the screen, select **File**, **Print Preview**, **Full Page**. Select **Close** to return to the document window.*

6. Save the file on the file disk; use the filename 7**act2**.

7. Print one copy.

8. Delete the first table.

a. Repeat steps 5a, 5b and 5d to block the entire table.

b. Press **Delete**.

> *Note: Select **File, Print Preview** to view the single remaining table.*

c. Press **Alt** and **F3** to turn off Reveal Codes.

9. Optional. Print the single table.

10. If necessary, return the WPMAIN Button Bar to the screen.

11. Close the document (do not save the modified file).

Activity 7.3—Copy a Formula, Delete a Row and Column, and Recalculate

1. If necessary, display the Tables Button Bar.

2. Create a table with 4 columns and 10 rows. Select **Close** {F7}.

3. Type the following unformatted information into the table cells. (Remember: Text will automatically wrap around in cells.)

MAINTENANCE COSTS			
Ardenwood Condominiums			
Job	April	May	June
Landscaping	$1,500	$1,500	$1,500
Pool cleaning	300	450	700
Roof repairs	8,670	4,200	3,700
Light fixtures	50	50	50
Deck repairs	5,000	4,600	4,950
Tennis courts	175	225	380
TOTALS			

4. Use the following instructions to format the table:

a. Select the **Tbl Edit** button on the Tables Button Bar.

b. Block and join the cells in row 1.

c. Block and join the cells in row 2.

d. Block rows 1, 2, and 3 and center the title, subtitle, and column headings (select **Cell, Center** justification, **OK**).

e. Block cells B4-D10 and use **Decimal Align** justification.

f. Calculate the total of column B (place the cursor in cell B10, select **Formula**, type a **+**, select **OK**).

g. Copy the formula in cell B10 to C10 and D10 (place the cursor in cell B10, Select **Move/Copy**, **Cell**, **Copy**, **Right**, type **2** in the How Many option box, select **OK**).

h. Block cells B10-D10 and set the number type to **Currency** and set the Digits After Decimal to zero (select **Cell**, **Number Type** [option #6], **Currency**, select the **Digits After Decimal** option box and type **0** [zero], select **OK** twice).

i. Block cells B4 through D4 and set the number type to **Currency** and set the Digits After Decimal to zero.

j. Select **Close** {F7}.

Note: Your table should look similar to the following table:

MAINTENANCE COSTS			
Ardenwood Condominiums			
Job	April	May	June
Landscaping	$1,500	$1,500	$1,500
Pool cleaning	300	450	700
Roof repairs	8,670	4,200	3,700
Light fixtures	50	50	50
Deck repairs	5,000	4,600	4,950
Tennis courts	175	225	380
TOTALS	$15,695	$11,025	$11,280

5. Save the file on the file disk; use the filename **7act3**.

6. Print one copy.

7. Edit the table as follows:

a. Select the **Tbl Edit** button.

b. Delete row 9 (place the cursor in any cell in row 9, select **Del**, **Rows**, **OK**).

c. Delete column D (place the cursor in any cell in column D, select **Del**, **OK**).

d. Select **Calc** to recalculate the column totals.

e. Block the entire table and remove table border and lines (select **Lines/Fill**, **Default Line**, **Lines Style**, double-click on **None**; select **Border/Fill**, **Border Style**, double-click on **None**; select **OK**, **Close**).

    f. Block row 3 and underline the column headings (select **Cell**, **Underline**, **OK**).

    g. Underline the figures in row 8.

    h. Block and double underline the total amounts in row 9 (select **Cell**, **Dbl Underline**, **OK**).

    i. Center the table horizontally on the page (select **Table**, **Position**, **Center**, **OK**).

    j. Select **Close** {F7}.

8. Use the new filename **7act3r** and save the file on the file disk.

9. Print one copy.

10. If necessary, return the default WPMAIN Button Bar to the screen.

11. Close the document.

Challenge Your Skills

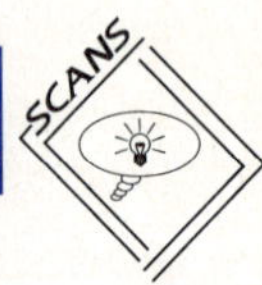

Skill 7.1—Create a Table and a Formula

1. If necessary, display the Tables Button Bar.

2. Create a two-column table using the following information:

    a. The title of the table is TOTAL PRINTER STAND COST.

    b. The price of the Premium Printer Stand is $99.99.

    c. Shipping and Handling will be $5.50.

    d. The charge for Express Delivery is $15.00.

    e. Calculate the total amount due.

3. Make decisions regarding:

    Justification for table columns
    Row margins
    Column widths
    Placement of the table on the page (vertically and horizontally)
    Table lines and border
    Shading cells
    Single and double underlines

4. Use the filename **7skill1** and save the file.

5. Print one copy.

6. If necessary, return the WPMAIN Button Bar to the screen.

7. Close the document.

1. If necessary, display the Tables Button Bar.

2. Use the traditional style letter and the following information:

   a. The letter should be addressed to Mr. N. G. Specht, Branch Manager, Tucker-Haynes Corporation, 206 Midvale Blvd., Madison, WI 53705.

   b. The letter is from Loreen K. Faulkner, District Manager.

   c. Make decisions regarding:

      Margins
      Justification
      Salutation
      Closing
      Displaying the WPMAIN or TABLES Button Bar
      Justification for table columns
      Formulas
      Table lines and border
      Shading cells
      Reference initials
      Document identification

   d. Correct three spelling, two punctuation, and two dollar amount format errors.

   e. Letter body text follows:

   Changes in our corporate travel reimbursement rates are necessary because of increased capital expenditures. The current travel rates remain in effect until the first of next month.

   The following table shows the current and new rates.

Per Diem Amounts		
Item	Current Rate	New Rate
Lodging	$ 95.00	$ 105.00
Breakfast	9.00	6.00
Lunch	10.50	8.75
Dinner	28.00	23.00
Car rental	36.00	28.00
Total Per Deim		

   As you will note while the amount allowed for lodging has been increased, the amount allowed for meals and car rental has decreased.

Please let me know by the first of the month if you feel that these changes will adverseily affect your personnel.

Please remind all employees that receipts for every item must be submitted before a reinbursement check can be written. As of the first of the month, no out-of-pocket expenses will be reimbursed unless preapproved by a branch manager.

If you have any questions regarding these rate changes please call me.

3.   Use the filename **7skill2** and save the file.

4.   Print one copy.

5.   If necessary, return the WPMAIN Button Bar to the screen.

6.   If you have completed your work in WordPerfect, exit the program.

Part 2
Checking Your Step

Production Skill Builder Activities
Chapters 5-7

Production Activity 2.1—Indent and Copy

1. Type the following information unformatted.

2. Press **Enter** three times after the last item.

3. Center and bold as shown.

Golden Plan Realty Marketing Strategy

1. Enter the information about your home in the MLS computer.

2. Inform all GPR sales representatives about your home.

3. Develop a list of features and benefits of your home to be given to company sales agents and area brokers.

4. Develop a list of items to give your home more **curb appeal**.

5. Contact twenty homeowners in the surrounding area and ask if they know anyone who would like to purchase your home.

6. Hold **open houses** as needed.

7. Prepare and distribute **advertising** for your home.

---

4. Select a font of your choice with a point size of 12 to 14 for the entire document.

5. Save the file; use the filename **2pact1**.

6. Print one copy.

7. Select and copy the entire document.

8. Place the copied text three **Enters** below the original copy.

    Note: Both the copy and the original will be on the same page. It may be necessary to center and bold the title of the copied list.

9. Save the file again using the same filename, **2pact1**.

10. Print one copy.

11. Close the document.

Production Activity 2.2—Indent, Move, and Replace Text

1. Use Memorandum—Style 1 and the following information to create a memorandum.

    a. Make decisions regarding:

    > Margins
    > Justification
    > Fonts
    > Memo date
    > Reference initials
    > Indention

    b. Send the memorandum to Kirsten R. Muller, Regional Vice President.

    c. The memorandum is from P. W. Cooper, Sales Manager.

    d. The subject of the memorandum is Promotion of Jeanine Castello.

    e. Memorandum body text follows:

    As part of the Sales Compensation Program, the company will be setting up new job titles for all secretarial and clerical employees. The new job titles will be: Division Administrative Assistant, Division Secretary, and Sales Clerk.

    Under the previous system, I am budgeted for three (3) clerical support people, but have utilized two (2) clerical people (Meagan O'Hara and Jeanine Castello).

    I would like to recommend that J. M. Castello be upgraded from a Division Secretary, Grade 5, to a Division Administrative Assistant, Grade 7. The following are my reasons for requesting this promotion:

    1. J. M. Castello has been a Division Secretary for over two and one-half (2.5) years. In addition, she has provided secretarial support for the District Account Managers.

2. J. M. Castello filled in for Meagan O'Hara when Meagan was on maternity leave. J. M. Castello displayed her ability to perform the duties of a Division Administrative Assistant during that time.

3. When our new facility is ready for our account managers to occupy, J. M. Castello will be the secretary for three (3) sales managers and five (5) account managers. She will also have a part-time clerk reporting to her.

4. J. M. Castello has proven her skills by preparing the current sales manual and annual budget, as well as handling telephones and greeting visitors.

Your consideration of J. M. Castello's promotion is very much appreciated.

2. Move the listed item number four above listed item number two and renumber the list.

3. Replace J. M. Castello with Jeanine.

4. Save the file; use the filename **2pact2**.

5. Print one copy.

6. Close the document.

Production Activity 2.3—Create and Copy Table Formulas, Insert a Row, Recalculate

1. If necessary, display the Tables Button Bar.

2. Create the table shown. Type the following unformatted information into the table cells.

   Note: The text may wrap around in the cells differently than shown because of the fonts and point sizes selected on your computer.

PROPERTY SALES			
1st Quarter			
Location	Original Purchase Price	Appraised Value	Price Realized
30661 W. Elliot Ave.	145000	185000	182950
895 Garden Rd.	108000	191000	193450
309 Talco Ave.	220000	259000	256500
73 Walnut St.	179000	299000	293750
Totals			

3. Block and join the cells in rows 1. Also join the cells in row 2.

4. Make decisions regarding:

   Justification for title, subtitle, and column heading cells
   Justification for columns containing dollar amounts
   Table lines
   Shading cells
   Column widths

5. Insert a formula into cell B8 to calculate the column total.

6. Copy the formula in cell B8 to cells C8 and D8.

7. Set the number type format for cells B4 through D4 to **Currency**. Set the number of digits after the decimal to zero.

8. Set the number type format for cells B5 through D7 to **Commas**. Set the number of digits after the decimal to zero.

9. Set the number type format for cells B8 through D8 to **Currency**. Set the number of digits after the decimal to zero.

10. Insert a row between row 6 and 7. Type the following information into the new row table cells: 652 Parkland; 89000; 169000; 168200. Recalculate the table column totals.

11. Save the file; use the filename **2pact3**.

12. Print one copy.

13. Close the document.

➠ Production Activity 2.4—Create a Table, Replace Text and Print Selected Text; Language Arts

1. Use the Memorandum—Style 2 and the following information.

a. Make decisions regarding:
   Margins
   Justification
   Memo date
   Reference initials
   Table format including justification of text in table cells, number
      type format, table border and lines, shading
   Bold, underlines, and font selections

b. Correct four spelling and three punctuation and two dollar sign errors.

c. Send the memorandum to All Agents and Regional Managers.

d. The memorandum is from Jill Kuhn.

e. The subject of the memorandum is Financial Results.

f. The memorandum body text follows:

For CBL last year was a time of tremendous growth with new sales records set in a number of areas and establishment of many aliances with
prosperous and progressive companies and individuals.

The following table shows CBL's financial highlights from the past two
years.

Financial Highlights		
(In Millions)		
Desscription	Actual 1993	Actual 1992
Premium income	$ 563.3	$ 451.3
Net investment income	293.3	261.5
Total income	856.6	712.8
Benefit payments to policyholders	340.1	279.0
Expenses	55.5	46.5
Commissions	42.3	32.0
Taxes	7.6	10.4
Net gain from operations	9.9	18.1
Realized capital gains	5.8	3.4
Total net income	15.7	21.5

Total income was a record $856.6 million--up more than 20 percent over
CBL's previous high. Net investment income was $293.3 million--up 12

percent and premium income was $563.3 million--up 24.8 percent--the biggest one year increase ever for CBL.

Some of the satisfaction that should have come from our life insurance sales achievements was adverseley affected by concern over our losses in group health insurance. However our net gain from operations of $9.9 million allowed us again to add to the CBL's financial reserves.

You helped make all of this happen, and for that you are comended. The CBL field force did an outstanding job!

2. Replace CBL with Crocker Benefit Life.

3. Save the file; use the filename **2pact4**.

4. Select and print the table only.

5. Print one copy of the entire memorandum.

6. Close the document.

Part 3
A Step Up

Format Columns and Reports

Chapters 8-10

- Newspaper columns
- Border line between columns
- Balanced newspaper columns
- Hyphenation
- Parallel columns
- Document information
- Thesaurus
- Grammatik
- Assemble personalized documents using standard paragraphs

- Copy text between windows
- Page numbers
- Headers and footers
- Widow/Orphan Protect
- Footnotes and endnotes
- Search for codes
- Print specific pages

Create Newspaper and Parallel Text Columns

Features Covered

- Newspaper-style columns
- The Columns Button
- Change column definitions
- Balanced newspaper columns
- Column breaks
- Hyphenation
- Parallel columns
- Convert text in parallel columns to a table

Objectives

After successfully completing this chapter, you will be able to use the Columns button to format text in newspaper-style columns and use the Columns feature or the Tables feature to create parallel columns. In addition, you will also learn how to control the flow of text in newspaper columns using the balanced newspaper column feature and column breaks and how to use the hyphenation feature to improve the look and readability of columnar text.

Chapter Introduction

Columns of text can be arranged in newspaper style or parallel style. Text in newspaper columns wraps around from line to line, column to column, and page to page (see Figure 8.3). Paragraphs of related text can be arranged in parallel columns so that information can be read from left to right (see Figure 8.6). The Hyphenation feature can be used to improve the readability of columnar text by reducing the amount of space at the end of lines.

Newspaper Columns

Newspaper columns are created by placing a column definition code at the beginning of the text that will be arranged in columns. Newspaper columns can be created by placing the column code in a document either before or after the text is typed. However, the simplest method for creating columns is to place the code in the document *after* the text is typed. When the column code is inserted, the column arrangement displays instantly on the screen (see Figure 8.3).

Once text has been typed, the column code can be placed at the beginning of the text using one of two methods. The first method is to select the **Columns** button on the Ribbon and then choose the desired number of columns. WordPerfect automatically calculates even column widths based on the page margins, inserts a .5-inch gutter (blank space between columns), and displays the text in columns on the screen. (The **Columns** button creates newspaper-style columns only.)

The second method of inserting column codes is to select **Layout, Columns**. The Text Columns dialog box displays showing the default column settings (see Figure 8.2). The *Column Type* section is used to specify newspaper, balanced newspaper, or parallel columns (the default is newspaper). The *Number of Columns* box is used to specify the number of desired columns (the default is 2). Parallel columns are discussed later in this chapter.

The *Distance Between Columns* box in the Text Columns dialog box is used to specify the amount of space (in inches) to be placed between the columns. The default setting is .5 inch and can be changed. The distance between columns is often referred to as the gutter space.

Once the number of columns is specified, WordPerfect automatically calculates even widths for each column and determines the left and right margins for each column. The width of each column and the distance between each column can be displayed and changed by selecting the **Custom Widths** option. If the number of columns or distance between columns is changed, the column margins are automatically recalculated.

The Column Borders option can be used to place either a vertical line between columns or a border around the text. WordPerfect provides several types of lines/borders including single, double, dotted, dashed, thick, and extra thick. In this chapter, we will work with the default setting of a single line between columns. Borders are also discussed in chapters 6 and 14.

Once all the column settings are confirmed or changed, **OK** is chosen and the text displays in columns on the screen. Turn on Reveal Codes to view the column definition code ([Col Def]). When the column definition code is selected, the code ex-

Chapter 8—Create Newspaper and Parallel Text Columns

pands to show the column type and number of columns, e.g., [Col Def:Newspaper;2].

When newspaper columns have been defined and turned on, the text flow can be controlled by inserting a column break to force text to the next column or page. A column break is inserted by pressing **Ctrl** and **Enter**. After newspaper columns are turned on and **Ctrl** and **Enter** are pressed, the cursor/insertion point and any text that follows the cursor/insertion point moves to the top of the next column. If the cursor/insertion point is located in the final column of the page when **Ctrl** and **Enter** are pressed, the text is forced to the top left column of the next page.

Text in newspaper and balanced newspaper columns automatically flows from the bottom of one column to the top of the next column as well as flows from the bottom of one page to the top left column of the next page. The term *snaking* is often used to describe columnar text that wraps from column to column and page to page.

When the **Balanced Newspaper** option is selected, the flow of text is adjusted so that each column is approximately the same length. This method provides a more balanced appearance on the page.

After newspaper columns are typed, extra space may display at the end of lines, making the columnar information difficult to read. Hyphenation can be used to align words more evenly at the margin and improve the appearance and readability of the columnar text.

A column off code can be placed at the end of the columnar text in order to change the number of columns, e.g., to return to a single-column layout. To end a multi-column layout, a column off code should always be inserted by selecting **Layout**, **Columns**, **Off**.

Start-Up Instructions

❖ Type the unformatted information shown in Figure 8.1.

❖ Center the title of the document.

❖ Save the file on your file disk; use the filename **8drill1**.

Create Newspaper Columns Using the Columns Button on the Ribbon

1. Place the cursor/insertion point to the left of the first character in the text to be placed in columns.

   *For example, place the cursor/insertion point to the left of **T** in the word "The" (first word of the first paragraph).*

2. Move the mouse pointer to the **Columns** button on the Ribbon and click once {Alt and F7, c}.

SAVING AND INVESTING TRENDS

The pattern for saving and investing money during the next ten years will be drastically different than in years past. Several distinct areas are the driving forces of the changes predicted for the next decade.

Healthy Savings Attitudes

Americans' attitudes towards saving and investing are improving. During the past few years, the average savings rate for Americans was 5% of after-tax income, far less than the previous decade. However, last year Americans had a healthy increase in savings to 6.5%.

Demographics

The baby boomer generation is fast approaching middle age. They are planning for their children's education, their own retirement, and their own leisure activities. In addition, Americans have increased their wealth dramatically and are recognizing the need to save and invest wisely.

Products

During the past decade, Americans began to achieve their savings goals by investing in nontraditional products. For example, mutual funds, money market funds, and annuities have been selected for investments because they provide an opportunity for higher returns with limited risks. In the next decade, demand for unconventional investments will be even more noticeable.

Demand for Change

The American people are telling the financial institutions that they want more products, more security, and honest advisors. Such requests are driving financial institutions to look inward and re-evaluate their philosophies in order to make primary changes in the way they conduct business.

Financial Institutions

Traditionally, individuals have used savings and loan associations for many of their savings needs and turned to brokerage firms for investments. Since the savings and loan industry has experienced great difficulties, many people have lost confidence and are seeking a more secure place for their savings.

3. Move the mouse pointer to the desired number of columns and double-click {n, type desired number of columns, Enter twice}.

    For example, double-click on **2 Cols** {press Enter once to accept the default of 2 columns}.

Note: The text is displayed in columns on the screen.

Finish-Up Instructions

❖ Press **Home, Home,** up arrow key to return the cursor/insertion point to the top of the document. Turn on Reveal Codes (**Alt** and **F3**). Place the cursor on

                                    Chapter 8—Create Newspaper and Parallel Text Columns

the column definition code, [Col Def], to display the expanded code [Col Def:Newspaper;2].

❖ Press **Home, Home,** down arrow key to go to the end of the document. Place the cursor on the column off code [Col Off] to display the expanded code [Col Def:Off]. Turn off Reveal Codes (**Alt** and **F3**).

❖ Use the new filename **8newsp** and save the file on your file disk.

Start-Up Instructions

❖ The file named **8newsp** should be displayed on the screen.

Place a Border Line Between Newspaper Columns

1. With the cursor/insertion point located anywhere in the newspaper columns, select **Layout, Columns** {Alt and F7, c}.

   Note: The Text Columns dialog box displays (see Figure 8.2).

2. Select the **Column Borders** option {b}.

   Note: The Create Column Borders dialog box displays. The default border style is Column Border (Between Only). This setting places a single vertical line between the columns.

3. Select **OK** to accept the default Column Border (Between Only) setting {Enter}.

4. Select **OK** {Enter} to exit the Text Columns Dialog box.

   *Note: Your document should look similar to Figure 8.3. Select the **Preview** button on the Button Bar, if desired; select Close to return to the document window.*

Finish-Up Instructions

❖ Save the file again using the same filename, **8newsp**.

❖ Print one copy.

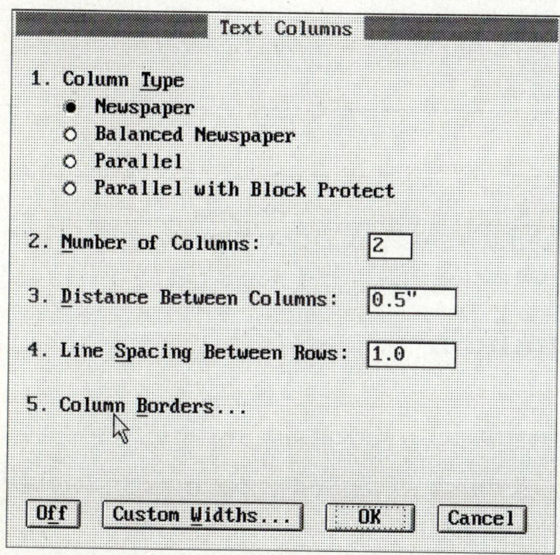

FIGURE 8.2

Text Columns dialog box

SAVING AND INVESTING TRENDS

The pattern for saving and investing money during the next ten years will be drastically different than in years past. Several distinct areas are the driving forces of the changes predicted for the next decade.

Healthy Savings Attitudes

Americans' attitudes towards saving and investing are improving. During the past few years, the average savings rate for Americans was 5% of after-tax income, far less than the previous decade. However, last year Americans had a healthy increase in savings to 6.5%.

Demographics

The baby boomer generation is fast approaching middle age. They are planning for their children's education, their own retirement, and their own leisure activities. In addition, Americans have increased their wealth dramatically and are recognizing the need to save and invest wisely.

Products

During the past decade, Americans began to achieve their savings goals by investing in nontraditional products. For example, mutual funds, money market funds, and annuities have been selected for investments because they provide an opportunity for higher returns with limited risks. In the next decade, demand for unconventional investments will be even more noticeable.

Demand for Change

The American people are telling the financial institutions that they want more products, more security, and honest advisors. Such requests are driving financial institutions to look inward and re-evaluate their philosophies in order to make primary changes in the way they conduct business.

Financial Institutions

Traditionally, individuals have used savings and loan associations for many of their savings needs and turned to brokerage firms for investments. Since the savings and loan industry has experienced great difficulties, many people have lost confidence and are seeking a more secure place for their savings.

Start-Up Instructions

❖ The file named **8newsp** should be displayed on the screen.

Change the Column Definition

1. Place the cursor/insertion point at any location in the newspaper columns.

    Note: The cursor/insertion point must be located to the right of the [Col Border] and [Col Def] codes. If necessary, turn on Reveal Codes

2. Select **Layout, Columns** {Alt and F7, c}.

3. Make the desired changes to the type of columns, number of columns, distance between columns, etc.

> For example, move the mouse pointer to the **Number of Columns box** and click. Type **3** {n, type 3, Enter}.

> Also, click in the **Distance Between Columns** box {d}. Type .25.

4. Select **OK** {Enter twice}.

Move the Cursor/Insertion Point in Newspaper Columns or Parallel Columns

Note: The text must first be typed and arranged in either newspaper or parallel columns.

1. To move the cursor/insertion point quickly from one column to another, place the mouse pointer in the desired column and press the left mouse button once {press Alt and the left or right arrow key or press Ctrl and Home and the left or right arrow keys}.

Finish-Up Instructions

❖ Use the new filename **8newsp3** and save the file on your file disk.

❖ Print one copy.

❖ Close the document.

Start-Up Instructions

❖ Open the file named **8drill1** typed earlier in this chapter.

Create Balanced Newspaper Columns

1. Place the cursor/insertion point to the left of the first character in the text to be placed in columns.

> For example, place the cursor/insertion point to the left of the **T** in the word "The" (first word of the first paragraph).

2. Select **Layout, Columns** {Alt and F7, c}.

   Note: The Text Columns dialog box displays.

3. Select the **Balanced Newspaper** option listed under Column Type {t, e}.

4. Type the number of columns desired in the Number of Columns box {n, type desired number of columns, Enter}.

> For example, if necessary, type **2**.

5. To change the amount of space between columns, click in the **Distance Between Columns** box and type the desired amount {d, type desired amount, Enter}.

For example, type .35. (Do not type the final period.)

6. Select **OK** {press Enter twice}.

   Note: The text is displayed in columns on the screen and the text columns are balanced on the page.

Insert a Column Off Code

1. Press **Home, Home,** and **down arrow key** to move the cursor/insertion point to the end of the columns after the last column entry.

2. Select **Layout, Columns, Off** {Alt and F7, c, f, Enter}.

Finish-Up Instructions

❖ Press **Enter** twice. Type and center the following sentence:

   START YOUR SAVINGS PLAN TODAY!

   Note: The one-column format is in effect.

❖ Use the new filename **8newsp.bal** and save the file on your file disk.

❖ Print one copy.

❖ Close the document.

Start-Up Instructions

❖ Type the unformatted text shown in Figure 8.4.

❖ Center and bold the title and subtitle.

❖ Place the cursor/insertion point below the subtitle to the left of the **G** in the word *Gerald* in the first paragraph. Create two newspaper columns (select the **Column** button on the Ribbon and choose the **2 Cols** option).

FIGURE 8.4

Document for practicing controlling the flow of column text

GERALD M. FREEDMAN
CHIEF ANALYST

Gerald M. Freedman became involved with U.S. Realty when the well-known real estate investment firm of Wilson, Mason and Associates was engaged to analyze and evaluate U.S. Realty's real estate holdings. Mr. Freedman served as the principal analyst.

With the analysis complete, Mr. Freedman has accepted the position of Chief Analyst with U.S. Realty. His vast background in real estate analysis and management as well as his exceptional organizational skills will greatly enhance our management team.

Before joining Wilson, Mason and Associates, Mr. Freedman was the Director of Facilities and Construction with Speedway Construction Company. In this position, he managed over 300 people and administered over $50 million in new construction contracts. Mr. Freedman was actively involved in the research and planning of new construction projects as well as managing the over 100 facilities owned and operated by Speedway Construction.

❖ Press **Home, Home, Home** and the **down** arrow key and insert a column off code (select **Layout, Columns, Off**).

❖ Save the file on your file disk; use the filename **8drill2**.

Insert a Column Break to Control the Flow of Columnar Text

1. Locate the cursor/insertion point to the left of the first character of the text to be placed in another column.

   For example, place the cursor/insertion point at the beginning of the third paragraph to the left of the **B** in the word *Before*.

2. Press **Ctrl** and **Enter**.

   Note: The text following the cursor/insertion point is immediately moved to the second column.

Finish-Up Instructions

❖ Center the document vertically on the page (place the cursor/insertion point at the beginning of the document, select **Layout, Page, Center Current Page, OK**).

❖ Save the file on your file disk using the same filename.

❖ Print one copy.

❖ Close the document.

Hyphenation

Hyphenation is the process of dividing a word at the right margin so that the first part of the word prints at the end of the line and the remainder of the word prints at the beginning of the next line. Hyphenating words is used to make left-justified line endings at the right margin look more even (less ragged) or to avoid large gaps between words in a line with full justification. Hyphenation can be controlled by using the Prompt for Hyphenation *When Required* or Prompt for Hyphenation *Always* options.

When text is typed, regular, soft, and hard hyphens and hyphenation soft returns can be inserted. Regular hyphens break compound words at the right margin when necessary. For example, the hyphenated word *well-qualified* will split after the hyphen if the hyphen is at the right margin.

A hard hyphen, such as the hyphen in the compound name *Jones-Meyer*, is inserted between words that should always appear on the same line of text. A hard hyphen is inserted by pressing the **Home** and hyphen (-) keys (**Home** and -). The hard hyphen is also referred to as a required hyphen.

A soft hyphen can be typed by pressing the **Ctrl** and the hyphen (-) key once. When soft hyphens are inserted manually, the cursor/insertion point is placed in front of the character that will follow the hyphen. However, if text with a hyphen is edited and the hyphenated word does not break at the end of the line, the hyphen will be made invisible. A soft hyphen will display only if the hyphenated word needs to break at the end of the line. The soft hyphen code will always display in Reveal Codes.

A hyphenation soft return is used for words that are separated by slashes, e.g., administrator/director. If the words separated by a slash reach the right margin, WordPerfect separates the words after the slash only if a hyphenation soft return has been inserted after the slash. The hyphenation soft return is actually a code [Hyph Srt] and, similar to a soft hyphen, affects the document only when words separated by slashes need to be broken at the right margin.

WordPerfect uses a hyphenation zone to determine which words need to be hyphenated. The hyphenation zone includes an area to the left of the right margin and also an area to the right of the right margin. If a word begins before the left area and extends beyond the right area, hyphenation of the word is desirable. The default hyphenation zone is 10 percent left and 4 percent right. This means that WordPerfect will determine an area that is 10 percent of the line length as the left area and 4 percent of the line length as the right area. A small hyphenation zone will produce more hyphenated words; a larger hyphenation zone will reduce the number of hyphenated words. Generally, the default hyphenation zone will produce acceptable hyphenation points.

There are three options for controlling the hyphenation process. The hyphenation options are found in the Prompt for Hyphenation section of the **File**, **Setup**, **Environment** dialog box (see Figure 8.5).

The three hyphenation options, *Never, When Required,* and *Always,* are used to control how and when WordPerfect will hyphenate words. The default setting is Prompt

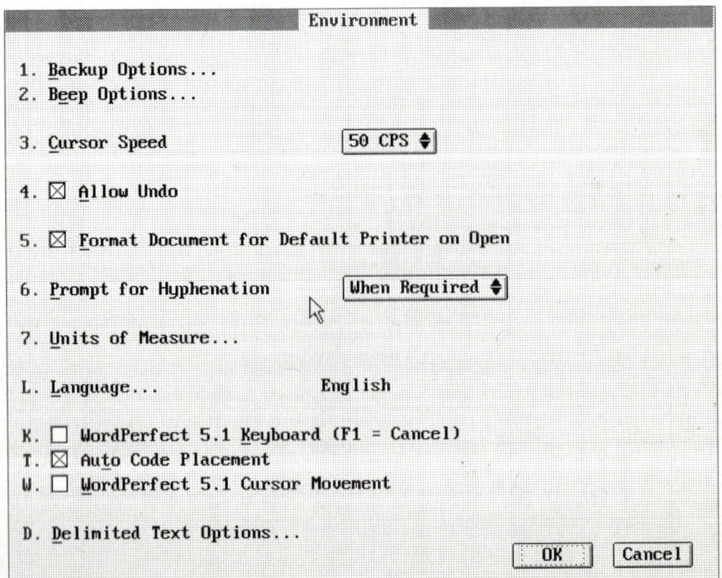

FIGURE 8.5

Environment dialog box

Chapter 8—Create Newspaper and Parallel Text Columns

for Hyphenation When Required. With When Required in effect, words found in the WordPerfect main dictionary are automatically hyphenated. However, if a word is not found in the dictionary, the program will pause and ask the user to select the appropriate hyphenation point.

When Prompt for Hyphenation *Never* is selected, WordPerfect hyphenates words found in the main dictionary without pausing. However, if a word is not found in the dictionary, WordPerfect does not pause and allow the user to make a hyphenation decision. The Prompt for Hyphenation *Never* and *When Required* settings are not recommended because the main dictionary words may not include all the words that need to be hyphenated and the hyphenation decisions made by WordPerfect may not follow basic word division guidelines (see page 220).

If Prompt for Hyphenation *Always* is selected, WordPerfect will pause at each word to be hyphenated and ask the user to confirm the displayed hyphenation suggestion. The user can also move the hyphenation point if desired.

Turn on hyphenation only after a document has been proofread, edited, and is being prepared for final form. Use one of the hyphenation procedures only if there are gaps between words or large spaces at the right margins. If the gaps or spaces are small, hyphenation may be unnecessary.

Once hyphenation has been turned on, WordPerfect begins looking for words that can be hyphenated. Typically, WordPerfect decides where to divide a word, then separates the word and places the hyphen at the end of the line. Depending on the Prompt for Hyphenation setting selected, WordPerfect may or may not pause for hyphenation confirmation.

Start-Up Instructions

- ❖ Open the filename **8newsp** created earlier in this chapter.
- ❖ Check that the Prompt for Hyphenation, When Required setting is selected. Select **File, Setup, Environment, Prompt for Hyphenation, When Required, OK** {Shift and F1, t, e, p, w, Enter until cursor/insertion point returns to the document window}.

Hyphenate Text Using the Prompt for Hyphenation When Required Option

1. Place the cursor/insertion point at the beginning of the document (**Home, Home,** up arrow key).

2. Select **Layout, Line** {Shift and F8, L}.

   Note: The Line Format dialog box displays.

3. Click in the box located beside the word *Hyphenation* {6 or y}.

   Note: An X should display in the Hyphenation box.

4. Select **OK** {Enter once or twice}.

Note: If WordPerfect does not recognize a word that needs to be hyphenated, a Position Hyphen dialog box displays. If necessary, press the left or right arrow keys to position the hyphen at the appropriate location. Select **Insert Hyphen** *{1}. If a word should not be hyphenated, select* **Ignore Word** *{5}.*

5. When the entire document has been reviewed for possible words to be hyphenated, any words that were hyphenated display with a hyphen at the end of the text line(s).

   Note: Depending on the selected font and point size (see Chapter 4), the hyphenation zone settings, and the words in the document, there may not be any words hyphenated.

Finish-Up Instructions

❖ Use the new filename **8newsp.hyp** and save the file on your file disk.

❖ Print one copy.

❖ Close the document.

Start-Up Instructions

❖ Open the file named **8drill2** created earlier in this chapter.

Hyphenate Text Using the Prompt for Hyphenation Always Option

1. Read the following guidelines for correct word division before proceeding to Step 2.

   a. Hyphenate only between syllables. Use a dictionary, if necessary.

   b. Avoid hyphenating words of five characters or less, e.g., *often.*

   c. Hyphenate a word so that at least three characters remain on the line, e.g., *in-* or *ly.,* but not *i-* or *ly* without the period.

   d. Place a hyphen after a vowel, e.g., *initi-ate.*

   e. Place a hyphen between double consonants, e.g., *accom-modate.*

   f. Do not hyphenate the last word of a paragraph; do not hyphenate the last word in the first line of a document.

   g. Avoid hyphenating words at the end of two consecutive lines.

   h. Do not hyphenate proper nouns, e.g., Apprenticeship Council.

   Note: Once a document has been checked for possible words to be hyphenated, there may not be any words hyphenated.

2. Select **File, Setup, Environment** {Shift and F1, t, e}.

3. Move the mouse pointer to the Prompt for Hyphenation option and click once to display the available choices {6 or p}.

4. Select the **Always** option {a}.

5. Select **OK** {press Enter once or twice}.

6. Select **Layout, Line** {Shift and F8, L}.

7. Click in the box to the left of the word **Hyphenation** {6 or y}.

   Note: An X should display in the Hyphenation box.

8. Select **OK** {Enter twice}.

9. When the Position Hyphen dialog box displays, make appropriate hyphenation decisions.

   Note: The following hyphenation decisions are based on your text being set for Courier font, 12-point, or Roman 10 cpi. If a different font is used, the words to be hyphenated may be different.

   a. The word evaluate displays in the Position Hyphen dialog box. The hyphen displays after the u. This is a correct and desirable hyphenation point; select **Insert Hyphen** {1}.

   b. The word background displays with a correct hyphenation point; select **Insert Hyphen** {1}.

   c. The word construction displays with a correct hyphenation point; select **Insert Hyphen** {1}.

   Note: When the hyphenation process is completed, the Position Hyphen dialog box no longer displays.

Finish-Up Instructions

❖ Use the new filename **8drill2.hyp** and save the file on your file disk.

❖ Print one copy and close the document.

Parallel Columns

Parallel columns are blocks of related information that are placed next to each other in rows so that the information can be read across the page from left to right. Text in parallel columns, also referred to as side-by-side columns, wraps around within each column similar to newspaper columns. However, the main difference between newspaper and parallel columns is that the information in the first column and the related information in the second column may vary in length. For example, the information in the first column might include only one or two lines of text while the related information in the second column might include three or more lines of text. (See Figures 8.6 and 8.7.) Either the Columns or Tables feature can be used to create parallel columns.

When using the Columns feature, **Layout, Columns** is selected. The **Parallel** or **Parallel with Block Protect** option is chosen for the type of columns desired. Either of these options creates parallel columns; however, the Parallel with Block Protect option will keep all lines of related information (one block) together on the same page. The default number of columns is two. Select **OK** to accept the chosen settings.

When typing text in parallel columns, press **Ctrl** and **Enter** to move the cursor/insertion point from column to column. When the cursor/insertion point is located in the right column and **Ctrl** and **Enter** are pressed, the cursor/insertion point moves back to the left column and inserts a vertical blank line space above the cursor/insertion point.

Parallel columns can also be created using the Tables feature. A table is often the most efficient way to set up parallel columns because it is easier to move, insert, and change column widths and the **Tab** key is used to move between columns and rows. To create a table with the desired number of columns and rows, see Chapter 6. When typing, text automatically wraps around in each cell. The table lines can be omitted if desired (see Chapter 7).

Parallel columns that have been created using the Columns feature can be converted to a table. This is useful if additional columns or rows are needed or if lines around or between columns are desired.

Start-Up Instructions

❖   Type and center the title of the document shown in Figure 8.6 and press **Enter** three times. Use the following steps to type the remainder of the document.

Steps to ▶ Create Parallel Columns Using the Columns Feature

1. Select **Layout, Columns** {Alt and F7, c}.

    Note: The Text Columns dialog box displays.

2. Select the **Parallel with Block Protect** option in the Column Type box {t, b}.

3. Select **OK** {press Enter}.

    Note: The column code has been inserted into the document, e.g., [Col Def:Parallel with Protect;2]. If you wish to view the expanded code, turn on Reveal Codes and select the [Col Def] code.

4. Type the information for the first entry in the left column.

    For example, type **ASCII**.

5. Press **Ctrl** and **Enter** to move the cursor/insertion point to the right column.

    Note: A hard column break code [Hcol] is inserted into the document. The code can be viewed by turning on Reveal Codes.

6. Type the information for the first entry in the right column.

    For example, type **The acronym ASCII....**

7. Press **Ctrl** and **Enter** to move the cursor/insertion point back to the left column.

    Note: A vertical blank line space is inserted automatically above the cursor/insertion point.

The following is a bordered figure box:

FIGURE 8.6

Parallel text columns

Finish-Up Instructions

- ❖ Continue to type each block of information shown in Figure 8.6 using Steps 5–7.
- ❖ Save the file on your file disk; use the filename **8drill3**.
- ❖ Print one copy.
- ❖ Close the document.

Start-Up Instructions

- ❖ The text shown in Figure 8.7 will be used to create parallel columns using the Tables feature.

Create Parallel Columns Using the Tables Feature

1. Select **Layout, Tables, Create** and type the desired number of columns and rows.

Parallel columns created using the Table feature

Performance Expectations: Achieves total business objective within division for the most recent 12 periods	Distinguished Rating	102.0 and higher
Achieves division annual management objective	Distinguished Rating	101.0 and higher
Maintains or increases total dollar market share	Distinguished Rating	+1.5 and greater

For example, 3 columns and 3 rows. Select **OK** to exit the Create Table dialog box and select **Close** to exit the Table Edit window.

2. Type the text for Column 1.

   For example, type **Performance Expectations: Achieves...**

   Note: The text wraps around within each cell; do not press Enter.

3. Press the **Tab** key to move the cursor/insertion point to Column 2.

4. Type the text for the first paragraph in Column 2.

   For example, type **Distinguished Rating**.

5. Press the **Tab** key to move the cursor/insertion point to Column 3.

6. Type the text for the first paragraph in Column 3.

   For example, type **102.0 and higher**.

7. Press the **Tab** key to move the cursor/insertion point to Column 1.

Finish-Up Instructions

* Repeat Steps 2–7 to type the remaining information in Figure 8.7.
* If desired, omit all table lines (see Steps to Omit Table Lines, Chapter 7, page 186).
* Save the file on your file disk; use the filename **8drill4**.
* Print one copy (select the **Print** button on the Button Bar).
* Close the document.

❖   Open the file named **8drill3**.

Steps to ▶ Convert Parallel Columns to a Table

1. Block all the text typed in parallel columns. (Do not block the title.)

2. Select the **Layout, Tables, Create** {Alt and F7, t, c}.

   Note: The Create Table from Block dialog box displays.

3. Check that the **Parallel Columns** option button is selected in the Create Table from Block dialog box {p}.

4. Select **OK** {press Enter}.

   Note: The Table Edit window displays showing the parallel columnar text in a table format. The table format can be edited using standard steps to edit a table.

Finish-Up Instructions

❖   In the Table Edit window, decrease the width of Column A by highlighting any cell in Column A and press the **Ctrl** and left arrow key 9-10 times.

❖   Insert a new column after Column B by highlighting any cell in Column B and selecting **Ins, Columns, 1, After Cursor Position, OK**.

❖   Increase the width of Column B by highlighting any cell in Column B and pressing **Ctrl** and right arrow key 16-17 times.

❖   Exit the Table Edit window by selecting **Close**.

❖   Type the following information into the empty cells in Column C (3):

| See page 20 |
| See page 34 |
| See page 18 |
| See page 25 |

❖   Save the file on your file disk; use the new filename **8drill5**.

❖   Print one copy.

❖   Close the document.

The Next Step

Chapter Review and Activities

FEATURES SUMMARY

FEATURES	ACTION	PAGE
Create newspaper columns	Select the **Columns** button on the Ribbon, point to the number of columns desired and double-click.	211
Place a border between newspaper columns	Select **Layout**, **Columns**, **Column Border**, **OK**.	213
Change the column definition	Select **Layout**, **Columns**, make desired changes, **OK**.	214
Move the cursor/insertion point in newspaper columns or parallel columns	Place the mouse pointer in the desired column and click once.	215
Create balanced newspaper columns	Select **Layout**, **Columns**, **Balanced Newspaper**, type the desired number of columns and desired amount of space between columns, select **OK**.	215
Insert a column off code	Select **Layout**, **Columns**, **Off**.	216
Insert a column break	Press **Ctrl** and **Enter**.	217
Change the Prompt for Hyphenation option	Select **File**, **Setup**, **Environment**, move the mouse pointer to the **Prompt for Hyphenation** option, click once, select desired option, select **OK**.	219

Self-Check Questions

True/False—Circle One

T F 1. When typing parallel columns that have been created using the Column feature, press **Ctrl** and **Enter** to move the cursor/insertion point to the next column.

T F 2. Parallel columns require that the number of lines in the left column equal the number of lines in the right column.

T F 3. Newspaper-style columns can be defined before *or* after text is typed.

T F 4. The amount of blank space between newspaper columns cannot be changed.

T F 5. The Tables feature can be used to create parallel columns.

Short Answer

1. List three reasons why it may be more efficient to create parallel columns using the Tables feature instead of the Columns feature.

2. List the steps to create two balanced newspaper columns.

3. Show the correct hyphenation points for the following words.

    attitude   unkempt   offensive

4. What are the keystrokes used to move the cursor/insertion point between newspaper columns?

5. When and why should hyphenation be used?

Enriching Language Arts Skills

Spelling/Vocabulary Words

prompt   done at once without delay; on time.

unkempt   in a messy or untidy condition.

offensive   undesirable; highly annoying.

antagonistic   behaving in a hostile or unfriendly manner.

attitude   a manner toward or feeling about something or someone.

Using the Abbreviations *e.g.* and *i.e.*

The abbreviation *e.g.* is used in place of "for example" and is often used when one or more of many examples are listed. The abbreviation *i.e.* is used in place of "that is" and is used when all potential conditions are listed. A period follows each initial with no space between the period and the initials. The final period is followed by a comma.

> *Examples:*
>
> *There are many word processing programs that include desktop publishing features, e.g., WordPerfect, Microsoft Word, and AmiPro.*
>
> *When the president's name is typed in the signature line, use the first name initial and include Sr., i.e., J. Thomas-Meyers, Sr.*

Activities

Activity 8.1—Create Balanced Newspaper Columns

1. Type the following unformatted information with the spacing and bolding as shown:

UPDATES FOR THE EMPLOYER

Report Corporate Changes

Any changes in corporate status (e.g., mailing addresses, corporate name, and organizational form) should be reported on the new corporate change form. The form should be attached to your quarterly reports return envelope. There are four parts to the corporate change form.

I.   Part I is for a mailing address change.
II.   Part II is used for reporting changes in the corporation name.
III. Part III is used to report the dissolution of the corporation. If Part III is filed, you may also need to complete Part IV.
IV.   Part IV requires specific information on all parties involved in the changes.

If you have questions about the corporate change form, call the Corporate Employer department.

New Wage Reporting (Public Works)

As of the last quarter, all contractors and subcontractors performing public works construction projects must use the new payroll reporting guidelines. In accordance with the new guidelines, certified payroll records must be submitted within 15 days of the payment of the wages.

Contractors and subcontractors can be assessed a penalty of up to $250 per day for failure to provide the required payroll records.

Quarterly Wage Reports

Over half of all employers submit quarterly wage reports on magnetic tape. For smaller operations or where magnetic tape is not available, employers can use personal computers to submit their wage reports on disks. An IBM-compatible program, WageReps, can be used to generate the wage information in the format necessary for submission to the Corporate Employer department. Two versions of WageReps are available: 1.1 for employers with fewer than 250 employees and 2.0 for employers with 250 or more employees.

Employer Seminars

A series of seminars for employers will be held to introduce new programs and services of the Corporate Employer department. One-day seminars are offered at convenient locations, and a small registration fee is required. For more information about these seminars, call (619) 555-3030.

---

2. Center the title.

3. Create balanced newspaper columns:

a. Place the cursor/insertion point at the left of (or under) the **R** in the first word of the first sideheading, Report.

b. Select **Layout, Columns.**

c. Select **Balanced Newspaper** in the Column Type box.

d. Select **Column Borders, OK** to insert a vertical line (border) between the columns.

e. Select **OK.**

f. Place the cursor/insertion point after the last character in the second column; select **Layout, Columns, Off.**

4. Use the filename **8act1** and save the file.

5. Print one copy.

6. Close the document.

Activity 8.2—Create Parallel Columns Using the Columns Feature

1. Type, center, and bold the title, **PEOPLE IN THE NEWS.** Press **Enter** three times.

2. Create and keyboard parallel columns:

    a. Select **Layout, Columns.**

    b. Select the **Parallel with Block Protect** option in the Column Type box.

    c. Check that **2** displays in the Number of Columns box.

    d. Select **OK.**

    e. Continue typing each entry from left to right.

PEOPLE IN THE NEWS

Sherry Osborne   Enter   Sherry received the 1992 Woman of
Branch Manager   Enter   Achievement Award. North Bay
Astoria, Oregon   Ctrl and Enter   United Bank nominated her for the
                                     award because of her exceptional
                                     leadership and community activities. Ctrl and Enter

David Mathiesen   Enter   David raised $1,340 selling T-shirts at
Customer Service Representative   Enter   the Jet Fan Fly Air Show. The
Eugene, Oregon   Ctrl and Enter   proceeds from the sale were used to
                                               provide grocery gift certificates for
                                               homeless families in the Eugene area. Ctrl and Enter

Bennett Dobson   Enter
Director of Foreign Currency   Enter
Portland, Oregon   Ctrl and Enter

Bennett's department handles wholesale trading of foreign currency for corporations, hotels, and travel agencies. Bennett's time is divided between currency trading and business development.   Ctrl and Enter

---

3. After the final character in the last column is typed, select **Layout, Columns, Off**.

4. Use the filename **8act2** and save the file.

5. Print one copy.

6. Close the document.

Activity 8.3—Create Parallel Columns Using the Tables Feature

1. Change the left and right margins to .75".

2. Center and type the title, **DAILY SCHEDULE**, in all capital letters.

3. Create a table with 3 columns and 5 rows. (If necessary, see Chapter 6, Steps to Create a Table.)

4. Type the following information into the table cells as shown. Remember to use the **Tab** key to move from column to column and row to row.

Times	Names	Tasks
8:30 a.m.-10:30 a.m.	Clyde Rice Caroline Pyle	Call title companies to request open deeds of trust information. Follow up on calls made to title companies the previous day.
10:30 a.m.-12:00 noon	Cary Fong Clyde Rice	Update property information on the computer using the Daily Sales report, Lender Field Representative report, and information received from the title companies.

Cont'd.

1:00 p.m.-3:30 p.m.	Gus Lynch Caroline Pyle Cary Fong	As newspapers are delivered, record the date of the newspaper in the Newspaper Log. Cut out all Notice of Trustee Sales. Enter information on new notices into the computer database. Print the Fresh Cut report and deliver it to the department manager.
3:30 p.m.-5:00 p.m.	Caroline Pyle Clyde Rice	Generate a daily sales report for the next day. Contact trustees and verify status of all scheduled sales. Record this information on the Daily Sales report.

5. Use the filename **8act3** and save the file.

6. Print one copy.

7. Close the document.

Challenge Your Skills

Skill 8.1—Create Newspaper Columns

1. Type the following unformatted text.

LOAN PROGRAM INFORMATION

INTRODUCTION

This document describes some of the features of the fixed-rate home loans offered by Golden Trust Bank. The following information is a summary concerning the differences between this mortgage loan and other mortgage loans.

This information is intended to provide an individual with a general description of our loan program and is not a contract or commitment to grant a loan.

Chapter 8—Create Newspaper and Parallel Text Columns

INTEREST RATE

The loan interest rate will be determined at the time of the loan commitment and will be based on the current market conditions.

MONTHLY PAYMENT AMOUNTS

<u>A conventional fully amortized loan</u>. When your loan is granted, the amount of the monthly payment is determined. The monthly payments will be an amount adequate to fully amortize the loan in equal installments over the term of the loan at a fixed interest rate.

<u>A balloon loan with partially amortizing payment</u>. Balloon loans are offered with terms of five (5), seven (7), ten (10), or fifteen (15) years. Monthly payment will be an amount large enough to fully amortize the loan in equal installments at the fixed interest rate over a thirty (30) year loan term.

However, since the actual loan term is less than thirty (30) years, a balloon payment of all remaining amounts owed will be due once the loan term has been reached. Unless the loan is convertible to a longer maturity, Golden Trust is not obligated to refinance or extend the terms of the loan.

<u>A temporary payment buydown loan</u>. A buydown loan provides for a fixed-rate loan with a special payment feature that permits the monthly payments to start at a lower level and increase gradually during the first three years of the loan. After the third year, the payment will level off at a constant amount for the duration of the loan.

TIMELINESS OF PAYMENTS

Loan documents require monthly payments to be made in a timely manner. For example, payment will be due on the first day of each month until the loan is paid in full. Failure to make loan payments promptly will result in the loan going into default. When a loan is in default, all sums declared under the loan may be due and payable immediately.

LATE PAYMENT CHARGES

Late charges in the amount equal to the maximum permitted by applicable law and regulations will be added to a late payment. The late charge will be added if the loan payment is not received with 15 days of the due date.

---

2.   Change the text to a two-column newspaper format and make decisions regarding:

        Newspaper or balanced newspaper type
        Distance between columns
        Column border between columns
        Justification
        Appropriate use of bold, underline, and spacing for title
          and sideheadings

Fonts

Hyphenation

3. Save the file as **8skill1**.

4. Print one copy.

5. Close the document.

Skill 8.2—Create Parallel Columns

1. Create parallel columns for the following information and make decisions regarding:

   Method to use to create the parallel columns (i.e., Columns feature or Tables feature)

   Fonts

   Hyphenation

   Justification

WATER WASTE PREVENTION

KITCHEN AND LAUNDRY	Use the automatic dishwasher and washing machine only when fully loaded.	
	When washing dishes by hand, don't leave the water running.	Use two different containers: one for washing the dishes and one for rinsing the dishes.
	Check faucets and pipes for leaks.	Leaks waste water 24 hours a day, 7 days a week.
OUTSIDE WATER USE	Water lawns and plants during the cool part of the day.	Early morning watering is generally better than watering at dusk since it helps prevent the growth of fungus.
	Don't water the street.	Position sprinklers to water the lawn or garden and not the paved areas.
	Use a broom instead of a hose to clean the driveway and decks.	

Cont'd.

| Don't have the water hose on while washing a vehicle. | Clean the car with a pail of soapy water and use the hose only for rinsing. |

2. Save the file as **8skill2** and print one copy.

❧ Skill 8.3—Create Parallel Columns; Language Arts

1. Type and center the title. Press **Enter** three times.

2. Create parallel columns and make decisions regarding:

> Method to use to create the parallel columns (i.e., Columns feature or Tables feature)
> Margins
> Justification
> Amount of space between parallel columns
> Fonts
> Bold
> Correct five spelling errors and two punctuation errors.

INTERVIEW TIPS

DO'S	DON'TS
Inquire prior to the interview whether any tests will be given.	Don't drink alcoholic beverages before the interview.
Learn about the company before the interview.	Don't show up in unkept attire.
Travel to the interview location a day before the interview in order to determine travel times, bus schedules, parking availability, etc.	Don't be late.
Take a copy of your résumé and the names, addresses, and phone numbers of personal and business references.	Don't sit down before the interviewer sits down.
Dress appropriately, e.g. business attire--skirts or suits for women and sports coats or suits for men.	Don't chew gum.

Cont'd.

Be prommpt; leave an extra half hour for unexpected delays.

Be well groomed.

Use good eye contact.

Answer interviewer's questions briefly and concisely.

Be honest about your past experience and education.

If you can't make your appointment, call to cancel and reschedule.

Maintain a positive atitude during the interview.

Don't smoke even if a cigarette is offered to you.

Don't be antegonistic to the interviewer.

Don't discuss unnecessary personal issues or views.

Don't give lengthy answers to the interviewer's questions.

Don't exaggerate your past job experiences.

Don't go to an interview with ofensive odors, ie., bad breath, body odor, heavy perfumes/colognes, smoky clothing or breath.

---

3. Use the filename **8skill3** and save the document. Print one copy.

4. If you have completed your work, exit WordPerfect.

Chapter 8—Create Newspaper and Parallel Text Columns

Create a One-Page Document

- Document information
- Thesaurus
- Grammatik
- Standard paragraphs
- Copy text between windows

Objectives

After successfully completing this chapter, you will be able to create a one-page document with vertical line spacing of one and left justification and to use Document Information to determine the word count. You will also be able to create a one-page document with vertical line spacing of two and full justification and to use the Thesaurus to find alternative synomyns. In addition, you will learn to assemble personalized documents using standard paragraphs, to copy text between document windows and to use the Grammatik program to check a document for correct grammar.

Chapter Introduction

A one-page document can be an article, essay, minutes, agenda, report, or any type of document that describes an event or provides information. Investment, insurance, sales, real estate, and medical documents are examples of one-page business documents.

Create a One-Page Document

A document can be created with vertical line spacing of one (single-spacing) or vertical line spacing of two (double-spacing). If a document is typed with vertical line spacing of one, the paragraphs begin at the left margin with one blank line space between paragraphs (see Figure 9.1). If a document is typed with vertical line spacing of two, the first line of each paragraph is indented approximately one-half inch from the left margin (see Figure 9.3). Either left justification or full justification can be used in a one-page document, depending on the writer's preference and the appearance of the document.

Format a Document

A standard 8½ by 11-inch sheet of paper using the default 1" top and bottom margins has 9 vertical inches available for printed text (see Chapter 4, Figure 4.2). Normally the default margins will be used when creating a one-page document; however, if desired, the margins can be changed.

The document title is centered and usually typed in uppercase letters. If a subtitle is used, one blank line follows the title. A subtitle is typed in lowercase letters with the first letter of each main word capitalized. Initial caps is the phrase used to indicate words/phrases typed with the first letter of each main word capitalized.

If the document is typed with vertical line spacing of one, two blank lines precede the first paragraph of the document (press **Enter** three times). If a document is typed with vertical line spacing of two, one or three *blank* lines precede the first paragraph of the document (press **Enter** once or twice).

When a document is typed with line spacing of one, one or two blank lines precede a sideheading (press **Enter** two or three times). (See Figure 9.1.) When a document is typed with line spacing of two, one or three *blank* lines precede a sideheading (press **Enter** one or two times). One blank line follows a sideheading (press **Enter** twice when line spacing of one is used and press **Enter** once when line spacing of two is used). Also with line spacing of two, the **Tab** key is pressed once before typing the first line of a paragraph (see Figure 9.3).

Start-Up Instructions

- ❖ Use the default left, right, top, and bottom margins and the default left justification.
- ❖ After reviewing the Steps to Create a One-Page Document with Vertical Line Spacing of One and Left Justification, type the information in Figure 9.1.

Create a One-Page Document with Vertical Line Spacing of One and Left Justification

1. Bold and center the title. The title should be typed in all uppercase letters.

2. Press **Enter** three times after the title.

3. Press **Enter** twice after typing each sideheading.

4. Press **Enter** two or three times after each body text paragraph.

   For example, **Enter** is pressed twice after each body text paragraph in Figure 9.1.

5. Type the body text paragraphs in line spacing of one.

6. If desired, the sideheadings can be bolded.

Finish-Up Instructions

❖ Use the filename **9drill1** and save the file.

❖ Print one copy.

Document Information

WordPerfect provides various statistics for a document or partial document. The statistics include the number of characters, words, lines, and sentences and are listed in the Document Information dialog box (see Figure 9.2).

When a portion of a document is blocked and the statistics are listed, the dialog box displays as Block Information. All statistics displayed indicate the blocked text statistics except for the Size option that lists the approximate size for the entire document.

A total word, character, or line count is useful when preparing a document that must meet specific guidelines, e.g., a school research paper or an article submitted for publication.

Start-Up Instructions

❖ The file named **9drill1** should be displayed on the screen.

Use Document Information

1. Select **Tools, Writing Tools** {Alt and F1, d}.

   Note: The Writing Tools dialog box displays.

2. Select **Document Information** {d}.

TSM STAFF PROFILES ← Report title

3 Enters

Cynthia Runyan, President ← Sideheading

2 Enters

Cynthia initiates and manages the textbook and trade series books. Prior to establishing TSM, she founded and managed Hegstrom Press and Bay Publishing. Her previous experience includes acting as Editor-in-Chief of Engineering and Computer Books for Stanton Hill and Marketing Director and Vice President for Ross & Collins Publishers. Cynthia has developed and published hundreds of technical, reference, and trade books.

2 Enters

William Donovan, Director of Production

2 Enters

Bill supervises book production for TSM, organizes projects, sets and maintains schedules, and manages the internal and freelance staff. His 25 years in publishing include Regional Editor, Production Editor, Production Manager, and Director of Marketing Operations for Ross & Collins, Los Angeles, and most recently, Director of Composition and Graphic Services and Publisher, Hartman Publications. His experience covers text, trade, reference, and professional books, as well as magazine and journal publishing.

2 Enters

Samuel Clayworth, Marketing Services Director

2 Enters

Sam creates and administers marketing programs, including implementing and analyzing direct mail and advertising campaigns. His prior positions at TSM include Account Executive, Production Manager, and Operations Manager. At Jay Marketing Services, Colonial Publications, and the Crown Institute, Sam developed expertise in sales promotion, advertising, book and print production, financial management, budget control, and telemarketing.

2 Enters

Becky Rodriguez, Senior Account Manager

2 Enters

Becky manages books and media projects in computer applications, health sciences and vocational/technical curricula. Previously Vice President for Winston House, she was responsible for all operations of the Health Sciences division, including their best-selling nursing list. She has developed and marketed texts in the health sciences, biology, mathematics, and more.

2 Enters

Leo Sandoval, Account Manager

2 Enters

Leo manages book and media projects in business education and other vocational areas. Before joining TSM, he was with Mills Corporation managing the development and production of unauthored, heavily illustrated, complex books. At Appleby, Leo was Director of Sales and Marketing, Executive Editor for Business Education, and Senior Editor for Business and Economics. In addition, he published "how-to" books at Sullivan.

Note: A Document Information dialog box similar to Figure 9.2 displays.

3. Select **OK** {Enter}.

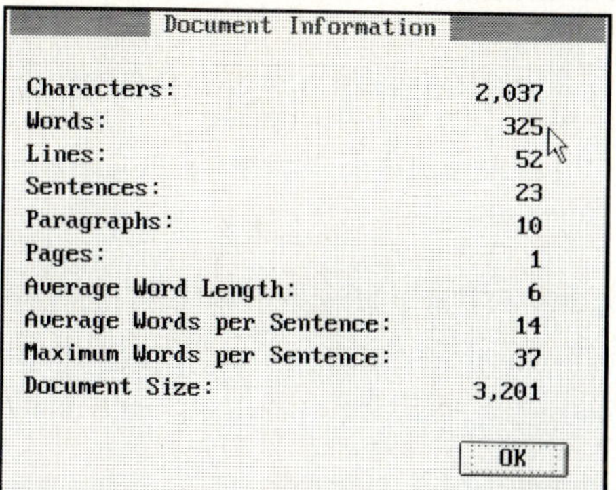

FIGURE 9.2

Document Information
dialog box

Finish-Up Instructions

❖ Optional. At the top of the printed document, handwrite the total number of words.

❖ Optional. If any changes are made to the document, save the file again using the same filename, **9drill1**.

❖ Close the document.

Start-Up Instructions

❖ Use the default left, right, top, and bottom margins.

❖ After reviewing the Steps to Create a One-Page Document with Vertical Line Spacing of Two and Full Justification, type the information in Figure 9.3.

 Steps to ▶ **Create a One-Page Document with Vertical Line Spacing of Two and Full Justification**

1. Use vertical line spacing of two (double-spacing).

2. Center and bold the report title. The title should be typed in all uppercase letters.

3. Press **Enter** once after the report title.

4. Type the subtitle in bold, lowercase letters with the first letter of each main word capitalized.

5. Press **Enter** once or twice after the subtitle.

   For example, **Enter** is pressed twice after the subtitle in Figure 9.3.

   *Note: When using line spacing of two, pressing **Enter** twice creates three blank lines between the subtitle and the first paragraph.*

6. Use Full justification (select the **Justification** button on the Ribbon, double-click on **Full**).

7. Press the **Tab** key once to indent the first line of the body text paragraphs; press the **Enter** key once between body text paragraphs.

ANNUAL REPORT SUMMARY ⟶ Report title
1 Enter

Employee Stock Ownership Program ⟶ Subtitle

2 Enters

The following is an annual report summary for the Canon & Cambridge Employee Stock Ownership Program for the period of January 1, 199x to December 31, 199x. The full annual report has been filed with the IRS as required under the Employee Retirement Income Security Act of 1974 (ERISA).

2 Enters

PRIMARY FINANCIAL STATEMENT ⟵ Sideheading
1 Enter

A trust maintained by Merritt Banking Corporation provides the benefits under this program. For the program year, benefit payments to participants and beneficiaries totaled $4.4 million. The cost of administering the program totaled $58,000. At the end of the program year, there was a total of 9,409 individuals who were participants or beneficiaries of the program.
1 Enter
After subtracting liabilities, the program assets are valued at $35.5 million. This is a net increase of $2.6 million over the previous program year. The program had a net income of $6.6 million, including employer contributions of $5.2 million and investment profits of $1.2 million.

2 Enters

REQUEST FOR ADDITIONAL INFORMATION
1 Enter
As a member of the Employee Stock Ownership program, you have the right to receive a copy of the annual report upon request. A copy of the full annual report can be received by writing to Lukito Press, P.O. Box 3062, Los Angeles, CA 90010.

8. Press **Enter** twice before each sideheading. Type sideheadings in bold, uppercase letters.

Finish-Up Instructions

❖ Use the filename **9drill2** and save the file.

❖ Print one copy.

Use the Thesaurus

A list of words that have the same or similar meaning (synonyms) are stored in the WordPerfect Thesaurus. An author writing a letter or other information attempts to use words that will effectively communicate ideas. A thesaurus assists a writer by providing synonyms that may more clearly convey his/her message. The WordPerfect Thesaurus can be used during the writing process or after a document is written.

When the Thesaurus command is selected, a dialog box displays containing a list of synonyms with subgroups of nouns, verbs, and/or adjectives. Words marked with a bullet character are called "headwords." By double-clicking on a headword, additional synonyms can be displayed. Also a list of *antonyms* (words with opposite meanings) may display at the bottom of the synonyms list.

In the Thesaurus, the author can replace the word, look up a listed word, view the text in the document window, clear a thesaurus column, or cancel. (If the selected word cannot be found, the message "Word not found..." displays.) The author can choose a word from the displayed list, key in a different word to be looked up, or double-click on a listed word that is marked with a bullet. After double-clicking on a marked word, a list of related synonyms and antonyms displays in the next column in the Thesaurus dialog box. Words that are not marked with a bullet are not included in the WordPerfect Thesaurus in the form requested, e.g., the word *inventory* displayed for the requested verb *list* is not marked because the requested word is for a verb, not a noun. However, if you double-click on an unmarked word, another form of the word may display, e.g., *face* will display after double-clicking on the unmarked word *facing*.

Start-Up Instructions

❖ The filename **9drill2** should be displayed on the screen.

Select Synonyms From the Thesaurus

1. Place the cursor/insertion point to the left or right of any character in the word to be looked up in the Thesaurus.

   For example, place the cursor/insertion point in the word *full* in the second sentence of the first paragraph.

2. Select **Tools, Writing Tools, Thesaurus** {Alt and F1, t}.

   Note: The Thesaurus dialog box displays (see Figure 9.4).

3. Place the mouse pointer directly above the down arrow in the scroll bar to the right of the listed words. Press the left mouse button repeatedly to scan through the listed words until the desired word displays {press the down arrow key repeatedly until the desired word displays}.

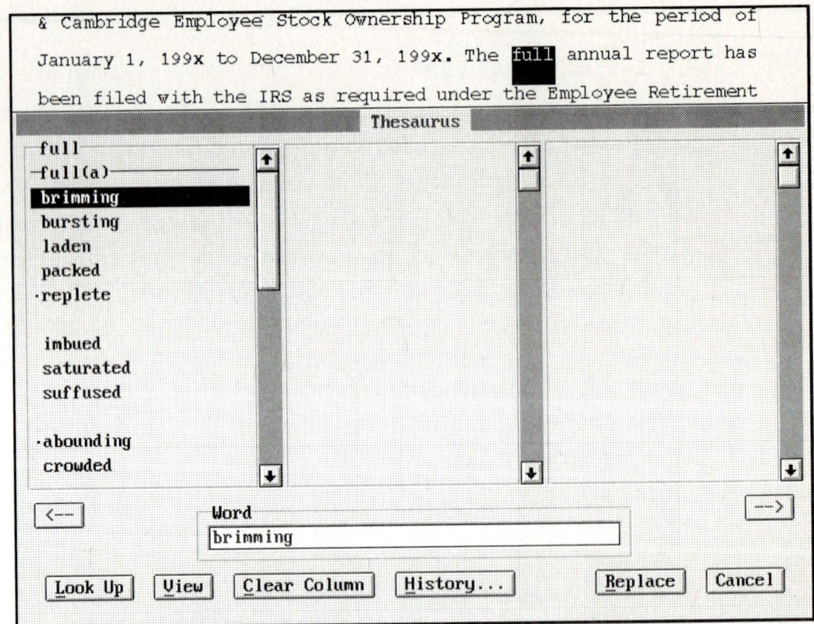

> For example, press the left mouse button two or three times to display the word **complete.**

4. Move the mouse pointer to the desired replacement word and click once {press the up or down arrow key to highlight the desired word}.

5. Select **Replace** {r}.

6. Place the cursor/insertion point to the left or right of any character in the next word to be looked up.

> For example, place the cursor/insertion point in the word *benefit* in the second sentence of the second paragraph.

7. Select **Tools, Writing Tools, Thesaurus** {Alt and F1, t}.

8. Scan through the words listed on the screen and determine if there is a suitable replacement. If no suitable replacement word displays, select **Cancel** {press Esc twice}.

> For example, because there is no suitable replacement for the word *benefit,* select **Cancel.**

9. Place the cursor/insertion point in the next word to be looked up.

> For example, place the cursor/insertion point in the word *administering* in the third sentence of the second paragraph.

10. Select **Tools, Writing Tools, Thesaurus** and scan the words. If a suitable replacement word exists, select the word and choose **Replace.**

> For example, choose the word **manage.** Select **Replace.**

Note: The Thesaurus does not replace the word with the original "ing" ending. Continue with the Finish-Up Instructions.

- ❖ Delete the **e** in *manage* and type **ing**.

- ❖ Place the cursor/insertion point in the word *assets* in the first sentence of the third paragraph; select **Tools, Writing Tools, Thesaurus** and scroll down the list until the word *holdings* displays; select **holdings**; select **Replace**.

- ❖ Place the cursor/insertion point in the word *receive* in the first sentence of the fourth paragraph; select **Tools, Writing Tools, Thesaurus** and scan the words. Select **obtain**; choose **Replace**.

  Note: Normally the file with the new synonyms is saved and, if desired, renamed.

- ❖ Use the new filename **9drill2r** and save the file.

- ❖ Print one copy.

- ❖ Close the document.

Use the Grammatik Program

Grammatik 5 is a grammar-checking program that accompanies WordPerfect 6.0. Grammatik 5 checks a document for grammatical, spelling, and writing-style errors. When the **Gramatik** button is selected, the text is checked against a list of grammar rules, such as passive voice, subject-verb agreement, double negatives, repetitive expressions, and capitalization.

The grammar rules used to check text can be viewed or changed by selecting **Preferences, Writing style** in the Grammatik program. Select a writing style option such as Business Letter, Memo, or Advertising. The default setting for the General writing style is used in this book.

When Grammatik checks a document, the suggested change is often displayed. The suggested grammar change can be accepted, ignored, or rewritten. The grammar suggestions provided should be used only as a guide, because the grammar information may or may not be correct according to other grammatical sources.

Start-Up Instructions

- ❖ The WPMAIN Button Bar should be displayed.

- ❖ The file named **9drill2r** should be displayed on the screen.

Use the Grammatik Program

1. The document to be grammar checked must be saved and displayed on the screen.

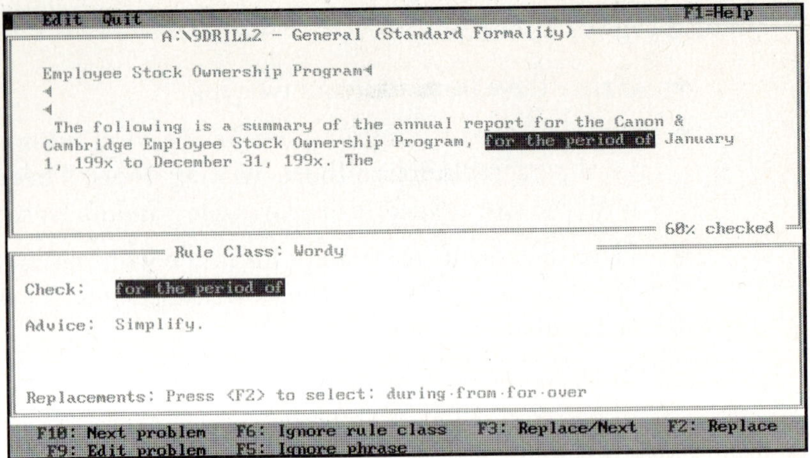

2. Select the **Gramatik** button on the WPMAIN Button Bar {Alt and F1, g}. (If text mode is active, select the down triangle at the left of the Button Bar to display the Gramatik button.)

   Note: The Grammatik 5 program is loaded, the copyright screen displays briefly, and the opening screen displays.

3. Select **Interactive check** {i}.

   *Note: The first occurrence of a word, phrase, or sentence to be checked is displayed. The item to be checked is highlighted in both the editing and Rule Class (advice) windows, e.g., **for the period of** and the advice, e.g., **Simplify** displays in the Rule Class window (see Figure 9.5).*

4. View the advice and suggested Replacements in the Rule Class window by pressing **F2**. Double-click on the desired replacement option {press F2, press the down arrow key to highlight option; press Enter}.

   For example, press **F2** and double-click on **from**.

5. Select **Ignore rule classe** to ignore rule class for this occurrence and any other in the same rule class (until Grammatik is exited) {F6}.

   Note: If Next Problem is selected, the rule class is skipped for this occurrence only. Notice that the next item to be checked (ERISA) is highlighted.

6. Select **Ignore word** because the acronym (ERISA) is spelled correctly {F5}.

   *Note: The next item to be checked is highlighted, e.g., **has been filed**.*

7. Select **Ignore rule class** because "has been filed" is grammatically correct {F6}.

   *Note: The next item to be checked is highlighted, e.g., **with the IRS...***

8. Select **Edit Problem** to change one of the prepositional phrases {F9}.

   For example, place the cursor in front of *Employee*, press the Spacebar once, and type **1974**. Delete the prepositional phrase "of 1974" at the end of the sentence.

9. Select **Next Problem** {F10}.

   *Note: The next item to be checked is highlighted, e.g., **total of 9,409...***

                                                      Chapter 9—Create a One-Page Document

10. Select **Edit Problem** to rewrite the sentence {F9}.

    For example, delete the sentence and rewrite as follows: **At the end of the year, 9,409 individuals were participants in or beneficiaries of the Employee Stock Ownership Program.**

11. Select **Next Problem** {F10}.

    *Note: The next item to be checked is highlighted, e.g., the word **The**.*

12. Select **Ignore rule class** because the sentences beginning with the word *The* are not consecutive {F6}.

    *Note: The next item to be checked is highlighted, e.g., **Lukito**.*

13. Select **Ignore word** because *Lukito* is a proper name and is spelled correctly {F5}.

    Note: A box displays asking if you want to save the "turned off" rule class.

14. Select **No** {n}.

15. Select **Quit Grammatik** to return to the WordPerfect document window {q}.

    Note: Wait momentarily and the document window displays with the changed document.

Finish-Up Instructions

❖ Use the new filename **9gram** and save the file.

❖ Print one copy.

❖ Close the document.

Use Standard Paragraphs to Assemble Individualized Documents

Text that is used repeatedly to create personalized documents can be saved and retrieved when needed. For example, a will created by a lawyer contains many standard paragraphs that are common to all wills. The standard paragraphs are saved in a separate document, and the desired paragraph(s) is retrieved to assemble a document created for a specific individual.

The first part of the process to assemble documents using standard paragraphs is to create and save a document that contains the standard paragraphs. The second part of the process is to open a new document file and type the information that is specific to the personalized document, e.g., date, name, address, and nonstandard paragraphs.

The final process to assemble documents using standard paragraphs is to copy text from the standard paragraphs document to the personalized document. WordPerfect has the capability of having more than one document window open (in memory) at a time. Each document is placed in a separate document window. For example, the

Standard paragraphs document

Standard Seminar Information

Seminar Locations and Dates

March 5-6, 199x--Park Plaza, Boston, Massachusetts
March 14-15, 199x--Four Ambassadors, Miami, Florida
March 19-20, 199x--Hyatt Regency, Phoenix, Arizona
March 21-22, 199x--Seattle Hilton, Seattle, Washington

Session Descriptions

New Technologies--This session provides a preview of new technologies, including wireless communications and interactive television. Hand-held pen devices and voice user interfaces will be demonstrated.

Electronic Distribution--This session discusses the best way to distribute sophisticated print documents in electronic form that can be viewed on a screen and printed out when needed.

The Future of Electronic Delivery--This session includes the impact of developments that are predicted to take place over the next decade: on-line delivery using telephone, cable, and satellite services.

Telecommunications for Print Production--This session begins with a summary of the status of high-speed digital communications around the world. Specific user examples illustrating methods in which print publishers are using the technology will be discussed.

Advertising in a Digital World--This session will be a panel discussion on the impact of online interactive services and the effect the digital world will have on advertising.

standard paragraphs document and the personalized document are both open and each is in a separate window. With the standard paragraphs document displayed, the desired standard paragraph(s) is copied to temporary memory. After switching to the personalized document window, the text is pasted in the personalized document at the location of the cursor/insertion point.

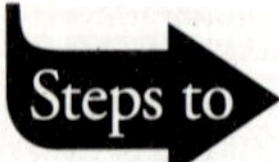

Create the Standard Paragraphs Document

1. Type the standard paragraphs.

   For example, type the information shown in Figure 9.6.

2. Save the file that contains the standard paragraphs.

   For example, save the file on your file disk; use the filename **9drill3.stn**.

Chapter 9—Create a One-Page Document

(Use current date)

Mr. Theodore Nunes
4808 Cameron Creek, Apt. 8
Fort Worth, TX 76132

Dear Mr. Nunes:

Your registration has been received to attend the upcoming Communications Conference.

The conference date, location, and description of your selected session(s) is as follows:

> Copy the following paragraphs from the list of standard seminar information (9drill3.stn).
>
> March 19-20 conference date and location information
>
> New Technologies
>
> Telecommunications for Print Production

If you need additional information about the seminar or hotel accommodations, please call 1-800-555-1800.

Sincerely,

Howard Walsh
Seminar Coordinator

HW/xx
nunes.ltr/disk1

FIGURE 9.7

Personalized document assembled using standard paragraphs

Steps to Create the Personalized Document

3. Open a new document by selecting **File, New** {Alt and f, n}.

   Note: *An empty document window displays on the screen. The file named* ***9drill3.stn*** *is still in memory but is currently hidden.*

4. Type the information that is specific to the personalized document.

   For example, type the current date, inside address, salutation, and first two paragraphs of the letter shown in Figure 9.7. Press **Enter** twice after the second paragraph.

5. Save the personalized document.

   For example, save the file on your file disk; use the filename **9nunes.ltr**.

FIGURE 9.8

Switch to Document
dialog box with list of
open document files

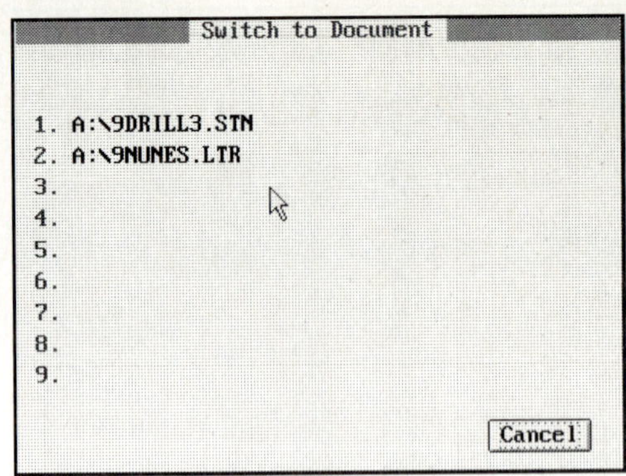

Steps to ▶ Copy Text Between Windows

6. Select **Window, Switch to** {F3}.

   Note: The Switch to Document dialog box displays showing a list of open document files (see Figure 9.8).

7. Select the name of the document that contains the standard paragraphs {press the down arrow key as many times as needed to highlight the desired filename, press Enter}.

   For example, select **9drill3.stn**.

   Note: The file containing the standard paragraphs displays on the screen. The file containing the new document is still open in memory but is currently hidden.

8. Block the desired text to be copied to the personalized document.

   For example, block **March 19-20, 199x--Hyatt Regency, Phoenix, Arizona**.

9. Select **Edit, Copy** {Ctrl and c}.

   Note: A copy of the selected text has been placed in temporary memory.

10. Select **Window, Switch to** {F3}.

11. Choose the filename of the personalized document.

    For example, select **9nunes.ltr**.

    Note: In the personalized letter, the cursor/insertion point should be located at the left margin one blank line space below the second paragraph.

12. Select **Edit, Paste** {Ctrl and v}.

    Note: The copied text is retrieved from temporary memory and displays on the screen.

13. If necessary, press the **End** key to locate the cursor/insertion point at the end of the line and press **Enter** one or two times in order to locate the cursor/insertion point one blank line space below the copied text.

14. Select **Window, Switch to**; choose the filename of the document that contains the standard paragraphs.

    For example, switch to the **9drill3.stn**.

Chapter 9—Create a One-Page Document

15. Select the text to be copied to the personalized document.

> For example, select the paragraph that begins **New Technologies--**.

16. Select **Edit, Copy** {Ctrl and c}.

17. Select **Window, Switch to** {F3}. Choose the filename of the personalized document.

> For example, choose **9nunes.ltr**.

Note: The cursor/insertion point should be located at the left margin one blank line below the conference date information.

18. Select **Edit, Paste** {Ctrl and v}.

19. If necessary, place the cursor/insertion point at the end of the paragraph and press **Enter** one or two times to locate the cursor/insertion point one blank line space below the copied paragraph.

Finish-Up Instructions

- ❖ Repeat Steps 14-18 and copy the paragraph that begins **Telecommunications for Print Production--**.

- ❖ Type the final paragraph, complimentary closing, typed signature, title, reference initials, and document identification as shown in Figure 9.7.

- ❖ Save the personalized document file using the same filename, **9nunes.ltr**.

- ❖ Print one copy.

The Next Step

Chapter Review and Activities

FEATURES SUMMARY

FEATURES	ACTIONS	PAGE
Use Document Information	Select **Tools**, **Writing Tools**, select **Document Information**.	239
Use the Thesaurus	Select **Tools**, **Writing Tools**, **Thesaurus**, select the desired replacement word, select **Replace**.	243
Use Grammatik	Select the **Gramatik** button on the WPMAIN Button Bar, select **Interactive Check**, select the desired option(s), select **Quit Grammatik** to exit and return the cursor/insertion point to the WordPerfect document window. Save the changed file.	245
Copy text between windows	Select **Window**, **Switch to**; select the desired document; block the desired text, select **Edit**, **Copy**; select **Window**, **Switch to**; select the desired document; place the cursor/insertion point at the chosen location in the document, select **Edit**, **Paste**.	250

True/False—Circle One

T F 1. The title of a report is typed in uppercase and lowercase letters.

T F 2. The first line of a paragraph for a document with vertical line spacing of one is indented approximately five spaces from the left margin.

T F 3. A thesaurus contains synonyms that assist a writer in communicating clearly.

T F 4. A document typed with vertical line spacing of two is always printed with full justification.

T F 5. The standard paragraphs file must be open before copying text to an individualized document.

T F 6. The advice presented by the Grammatik program should always be used to correct the grammar in a document.

Short Answer

1. List the number of inch(es) used for the top, bottom, left, and right margins when creating a one-page document.

2. A subtitle is typed in ____________ letters with the first ____________ of each main word capitalized.

3. List the steps to obtain the Document Information.

4. State one purpose for using standard paragraphs to assemble individualized documents.

Enriching Language Arts Skills

Spelling/Vocabulary Words

partnership   a legal association of individuals joined together, often for business purposes.

accrual method   an accounting technique that reports income when earned. In contrast, the cash accounting method records income when payment is received.

maturity   the date when a financial exchange is due, e.g., the day a promissory note or bond is to be paid.

depreciation   reduction in the value of an asset; decrease in price.

liability   a debt owed; a disadvantage.

amortized   the method of distributing the cost of an asset over the life of the debt.

Speller Hint

The speller approves words that are correctly spelled; however, a correctly spelled word can be incorrectly used in a sentence. After using the speller, proofread the document for words used incorrectly.

Examples:

of, off	*you, your, you're*	*is, it, in, if*	*to, too, two*	*its, it's*
no, not	*for, from, form*	*a, as, an*	*there, their*	*used, sued*

Activities

Activity 9.1—Create a One-Page Document

1. Type the following document with vertical line spacing of one and left justification.

2. Use the default left, right, top, and bottom margins.

TELEPHONE SYSTEM

Enhanced Phone System

Flextex Health Care has improved its telephone system. The phone changes enhance previous improvements made to the system and, as a result, have increased ease of use for our customers' convenience.

The new system features direct dial access to the Client Services Department for all client inquiries. Client representatives are available to provide information and assistance Monday through Friday from 9:00 a.m. to 4:00 p.m. and on Saturday from 9:00 a.m. to 3:00 p.m.

Who to Call

All questions should be directed to the Client Services Department. If the staff is unable to answer your particular question at the time of your call, they will research the answer and call you with a response.

Where to Call

Next week you will be provided with a list of numbers to call for specific inquiries. One set of numbers is for claims and referral information; the other is for benefits information. It is important that you use the new department extension numbers since the new phone system replaces all previous telephone extension numbers. All calls to Client Services will be answered in the order that the calls are received.

Clients calling Flextex's main phone number, (505) 555-2310, will reach the automated phone system with a current list of options. Callers can access the list by using a touch-tone telephone. Clients with rotary telephones can remain on the line for an operator's assistance.

Current and New Phone Numbers

Please use the following information for the current telephone numbers.

Call 1 + (800) 555-4554 or (505) 555-7878 for information concerning bills, medical referrals, reimbursements, and third-party liability.

Call 1 + (800) 555-8322 or (505) 555-4849 for information concerning copayments, benefits, changing a primary care physician, replacing identification cards, enrollment eligibility information, group coverage, and notification of address or telephone changes.

---

3. Use the filename **9act1** and save the file.

4. Print one copy.

5. Select **Tools, Writing Tools, Document Information** to determine the total number of words in the document {Alt and F1, d}. Note the number of words and handwrite the number of words at the top of your printed copy. Select **OK** {Enter}.

6. Close the document.

Activity 9.2—Create Personalized Letters Using Standard Paragraphs

1. Open the file named **9drill3.stn** that was created previously in this chapter or create the standard paragraphs document shown in Figure 9.6.

2. Open a new file and type a personalized letter to the following individual:

(Use current date)

Ms. Mary Sinclair
951 David Ross Road
W. Lafayette, IN 47906

Dear Ms. Sinclair:

Thank you for your interest in attending our Communications Conferences. Below is a listing of the upcoming conference dates and a description of the two seminars in which you have expressed an interest.

Copy the following paragraphs from the list of standard seminar information in the file named **9drill3.stn.**

Copy all four seminar locations and dates.

Copy the paragraph that begins "Advertising in a Digital World."

Copy the paragraph that begins "The Future of Electronic Delivery."

If you need additional information about the seminars or hotel accommodations, please call 1-800-555-1800.

Sincerely,

Howard Walsh
Seminar Coordinator

HW/xx
sinclair.ltr/disk3

---

3.   Save the file as **9sincl.ltr.**

4.   Print one copy.

5.   Open a new file and type a personalized letter to the following individual:

(Use current date)

Ms. Pamela R. Parkins
Professional Technologies
3007 College Oak St.
Sacramento, CA 95841

Dear Ms. Parkins:

We appreciate your request for information regarding our upcoming West Coast
seminars. Currently, the following two seminars are scheduled for the Western Region:

> Copy the seminar location and date information for the Phoenix, Arizona, and Seattle,
> Washington, seminars from the list of standard seminar information in the file named
> **9drill3.stn**.

With regard to your interest in future electronic distribution systems, the following
seminar is recommended:

> Copy the paragraph that begins "The Future of Electronic Delivery" from the list of stand-
> ard seminar information in the file named **9drill3.stn**.

I hope to see you at one of our Western Region seminars.

Sincerely,

Howard Walsh
Seminar Coordinator

HW/xx
parkins.ltr/disk2

---

6. Save the file as **9parkin.ltr**.

7. Print one copy and close the documents (close both the personalized letter
    files and the standard paragraphs file).

■ Activity 9.3—Format a One-Page Document and Use the Thesaurus

1. Open the file named **9act3**.

2. Set the vertical line spacing to two and use left justification; use the de-
    fault left, right, top, and bottom margins.

---

3. Use the Thesaurus to find synonyms for the underlined words (select **Tools, Writing Tools, Thesaurus**). Boldface the replaced synonyms.

   Note: There may not be appropriate synonyms for all underlined words.

4. Use the new filename **9act3r** and save the file.

5. Print one copy and close the document.

Activity 9.4—Create a One-Page Document and Use Grammatik

1. Type the following document using the default margins, vertical line spacing of two, and full justification.

One solution is to ensure that the system increases the user's capability by delivering professional results and functions needed for the job. For example, voice has been overlooked in many systems; telephone integration and voice mail are being added to some office systems.

A second solution is to give the user more control over the system resources by providing personal tools. Personal computers are turning out to be a most powerful motivator for office personnel.

Individual satisfaction and motivation are the critical components of working life quality and productivity improvement. Designs that address users' personal concerns by providing intuitive and efficient interfaces, needed functions, and resource control can improve job satisfaction and motivation.

---

2. Save the file; use the filename **9act4**.

3. Use Grammatik to check the document using the following information:

   a. Select the **Gramatik** button on the WPMAIN Button Bar.

   b. The first highlighted words "has been overlooked" are grammatically correct; select **Ignore rule class**.

   c. The word "Personal" is highlighted and is correctly used; select **Ignore rule class**.

   d. The advice for the highlighted words "computers are turning out..." is helpful. Change the subject to a singular subject by locating the cursor/insertion point at the beginning of the sentence and then changing "Personal computers are" to **A personal computer is** (select **F9** to Edit Problem, type the correction, press **F10** for Next Problem).

   e. The message to allow you to save changes to the Rule classes displays, select **No**.

   f. Select **Quit Grammatik** to return the cursor/insertion point to the document window.

　　　　Chapter 9—Create a One-Page Document

4. Use the new filename **9act4g** and save the corrected file.

5. Print one copy and close the document.

Challenge Your Skills

■ Skill 9.1—Create and Edit a One-Page Document

1. Open the file named **9skill1**.

2. Make decisions regarding:

   Margins
   Justification
   Bold

3. Edit the document as follows:

   a. Delete the last sentence of paragraph two; combine paragraphs one and two into a single paragraph.

   b. Add the sideheadings:

   Add TECHNICAL TRAINING PROGRAM above the now paragraph two.

   Add MANAGEMENT TRAINEE PROGRAM above the now paragraph three.

   Add EMPLOYEE SUPPORT PROGRAM above the now paragraph five.

   c. Make decisions regarding spacing and bolding for the subheadings.

4. Use the filename **9skill1.fin** and save the file.

5. Print one copy and close the document.

Skill 9.2—Create a One-Page Document and Use the Thesaurus

1. Create the following document using vertical line spacing of two. Do not underline the underlined words. Make decisions regarding:

   Indents
   Margins
   Justification
   Title alignment and capitalization
   Bold
   Subhead spacing and capitalization

2. Use the Thesaurus to make decisions for replacing (or not replacing) the underlined words. Bold (do not underline) the substituted words.

Transfer and Servicing Disclosure

When applying for a mortgage loan, the Real Estate Settlement Procedures Act (RESPA) specifies certain rights that are granted under federal law. This statement indicates that the servicing for this loan may be transferred to a different loan servicer. "Servicing" refers to collection of the principal, interest, and escrow account payments. If the loan servicer changes, there are certain <u>procedures</u> that must be followed.

Transfer practices and requirements

If the loan servicing is assigned, sold or transferred to a new servicer, written notice must be given describing the transaction. The <u>present</u> loan servicer must send a written notice of the transfer not fewer than 15 days before the date of transfer.

Complaint resolution

Section 6 of RESPA <u>gives</u> certain consumer rights. If a qualified written request is sent to the loan servicer regarding the loan servicing, the servicer must <u>provide</u> a written acknowledgment within twenty (20) business days of receipt of the request. A "qualified written request" is a written correspondence other than notice on a payment coupon, which includes the mortgagee's name, account number, and <u>reasons</u> for the request. The loan servicer must take action on the qualified written request within sixty (60) days after receiving the request.

3. Save the file; use the filename **9skill2**.

4. Print one copy and close the document.

⊷ Skill 9.3—Create Standard Paragraphs and Assemble Individual Documents; Language Arts

Part I

1. Type the standard list of accounting policies as shown.

2. Correct three spelling errors, three misused words, and four punctuation errors.

Standard List of Accounting Policies

Accounting Method

The partnership maintains its records on the accural method of accounting for financial reporting and Federal and State income tax purposes.

Cash Equivalents

For purposes of the statements of cash flows the partership considers all highly liquid debt instruments purchased with an original maturity of three months or less to be cash equivalents.

Depreciation

The partnership records depreciation on the building and improvements using the straight-line method over an estimated useful life of 30 years.

Income Taxes

The entity is treated as a partnership for income tax purposes and any taxable income or loss realized is that of the individual partners. Therefore there is not libility for income taxes. There can be no assurance that the partnership and its partners will receive the benefits of being taxed as a partnership rather than as a corporation.

Loan Restructuring Fees

Loan restructuring fees are amortized on a straight-line basis over the term off the respective trust deed note payable.

Net Income (Loss) Per Limited Partnership Unit

Net income (loss) per limited partnership unit was based on the weighted average number of limited partnership units outstanding of 2,000 during 1990 1991, and 1992.

Reclassification

Certain amounts in the 1990 and 1991 financial statements have been reclassified two conform with the 1992 presentation.

Revenue Recognition

Sales of golf course club memberships were recorded upon acceptance of membership applications and receipt of corresponding membership fees. Membership dues were recorded as earned on a monthly basis.

---

3. Save the standard list as **9skill3.stn**.

4. Print one copy.

Part II

1. If necessary, open the file named **9skill3.stn**.

2. The standard list of accounting policies will be used to construct two one-page documents reporting the accounting policy for the two limited partnerships.

3. For each document, make decisions regarding:

    Line spacing (one or two)
    Justification
    Margins

Bold
Fonts

4. Open a new file and type the following individualized document:

CORONADO RANCH, LTD.
A Limited Partnership
Accounting Policy Notes

Copy the following paragraphs in the order listed below from the standard list of accounting policies (**9skill3.stn**).

Accounting Method
Cash Equivalents
Depreciation
Income Taxes
Net Income (Loss) Per Limited Partnership Unit
Reclassification

---

5. Save the personalized document as **9skill3a**.

6. Print one copy.

7. Open a new file and type the following individualized document:

YUMA FIELD BUSINESS PARK, LTD.
A Limited Partnership
Accounting Policy Notes

Copy the following paragraphs in the order listed below from the standard list of accounting policies (**9skill3.stn**).

Accounting Method
Cash Equivalents
Income Taxes
Net Income (Loss) Per Limited Partnership Unit
Revenue Recognition
Loan Restructuring Fees

---

8. Save the personalized document as **9skill3b**. and print one copy.

9. If you have completed your work, exit WordPerfect.

Create a Multiple-Page Document

- Page numbering
- Headers and footers
- Widow and orphan lines
- Footnotes and endnotes
- Search for codes
- Print specific pages

Objectives

After successfully completing this chapter, you will be able to create a multiple-page document, print page numbers on each page, and use widow/orphan protect. Also you will be able to create and edit headers, footers, footnotes, and endnotes; print a specific page(s); and search for codes.

Chapter Introduction

A multiple-page document is comparable to a one-page report and can be an article, essay, minutes, agenda, or any type of document that describes an event or provides information. A multiple-page document contains two or more pages. Examples of multiple-page business documents are investment, insurance, legal, medical, and sales documents.

Create a Multiple-Page Document

Like a one-page document, a multiple-page document can be created with vertical line spacing of one (single-spacing) or two (double-spacing). The pages of a
multiple-page document are formatted in the same way as a one-page document
with 1-inch top, bottom, left, and right default margins (see Figures 9.1 and 9.2).

Each page of a multiple-page document is separated by a page break. A page break is
a single horizontal line placed on the screen to indicate that the number of vertical
lines on the page has reached 9 inches. As text is typed, the text automatically wraps
to the next page, and WordPerfect inserts a page break between the pages. The page
break is also referred to as an automatic page break or a soft page break. In Reveal
Codes, a soft page break is identified with an [SPg] code.

If a new page is desired before the lines on the screen reach 9 inches, a hard page
break is used to create the new page. A hard page break is placed in a document by
pressing the **Ctrl** and **Enter** keys. A hard page break displays as a double horizontal
line across the screen. The hard page break is also known as a required page break. In
Reveal Codes, a hard page break is identified with an [HPg] code.

The pages of a multiple-page document can be viewed on the screen to see the placement of the lines and page numbers. The current page is viewed by using the Page
Mode view or Print Preview. In the page mode view, additional pages can be viewed
by pressing the **Page Up** and **Page Down** keys. Also, in Print Preview, additional
pages can be viewed by selecting the **Prev Page** and **Next Page** buttons. If desired,
two pages can be displayed on the screen at one time by selecting the **Facing Pgs** button.

Start-Up Instructions

❖ Use the default top, bottom, left, and right margins.

❖ Use vertical line spacing of two. If desired, vertical line spacing of one can be
used (follow the instructions in parentheses).

❖ After reviewing the Steps to Create a Multiple-Page Document, type the multiple-
page document shown in Figure 10.1.

Create a Multiple-Page Document

1. Center and type the title in uppercase letters; press **Enter** once. (If line spacing
of one is used, press the **Enter** key twice.)

2. Type the subtitle in lowercase letters with the first letter of each main word capitalized and then press **Enter** twice. (If line spacing of one is used, press **Enter**
three times.)

COORDINATOR FOR SUPPORT SERVICES
Job Description

General Description
Provide support for the training and distribution of software documentation; interact with consultants and administrative personnel. Includes general administrative duties.

Reporting Structure
The incumbent for this position reports directly to the manager of Support Services.

Experience Level
Required skills are knowledge of computer software (e.g., Ventura Publisher, WordPerfect, and Corel Draw) and typing. Communications and writing skills are also essential.

Duties and Responsibilities
1. Create and implement documentation for training courses using various company software packages.
2. Maintain a master copy of all developed documentation. Maintain transparencies for all training courses.
3. Receive and incorporate upgrades to courses and modules and distribute as necessary. Copy and distribute documentation to all office sites.
4. Coordinate timely delivery of training materials to client sites including verification of number of enrollees, shipping information, shipping materials, and transparencies.
5. Analyze bids requested from vendors and negotiate for special supplies. Maintain supplies of binders, paper, tabs, covers, spines, and backs to ensure availability.
6. Assist with the development, production, and distribution for training courses and modules.
7. Provide software training, support, and troubleshooting via phone for all administrative office personnel.
8. Develop and maintain consultant orientation/training programs, quick WordPerfect training materials, and style sheets for Ventura.
9. Assist with evaluation of new and upgraded software and new office machines prior to purchase.
   Duties and responsibilities may be added, deleted, or changed at any time at the discretion of management, formally or informally, either verbally or in writing.

Text for a multiple-page
document

3. Press the **Tab** key once before typing the first line of each paragraph. (If the vertical line spacing is set for one, the first line of each paragraph begins at the left margin and is not indented).

4. Press the **Enter** key once between body text paragraphs. Press the **Enter** key twice before sideheadings. (If the vertical line spacing is set for one, press the **Enter** key twice between body text paragraphs and three time before sideheadings.)

5. Bold and number paragraphs as shown.

❖ Use the filename **10drill1** and save the file.

Print Page Numbers

Each page of a multiple-page document should be numbered. If the pages are numbered at the bottom, the page number 1 is printed at the bottom of the first page. If pages are numbered at the top, the first page may or may not be numbered. WordPerfect's default is to print without page numbers.

The page number can be instructed to print at the top or bottom left, center, or right margin as well as alternating on the top or bottom of pages. The default position for page numbers is 1" from the top of the page or 1" from the bottom of the page. The Page Numbering dialog box is used to indicate the location and format of the page numbers (see Figure 10.2). If desired, text can also be included with the page number. For example, the word *Page* can be printed along with the page number (Page 1). Type the desired text in the Page Number Format option before or after the page number code ([page#]).

The Set Page Number dialog box is used to select the numbering method and/or set a new (different) page number. Using the Numbering Method option, numbers can be set to print as lowercase letters (a, b, c) or uppercase letters (A, B, C), lowercase Roman numerals (i, ii, iii), uppercase Roman numerals (I, II, III), or Arabic numbers (1, 2, 3). Using the New Number option, a different beginning page number can be set. For example, to begin numbering pages with page 4, type 4 in the New Number option box.

A header or footer can also be used to print page numbers. (See Headers and Footers later in this chapter.)

❖ The file named **10drill1** should be displayed on the screen.

Number Pages

1. Place the cursor/insertion point at the beginning of the document (press **Home** three times and the up arrow key once to locate the cursor/insertion point after the [Open Style:Initial Codes] code).

2. Select **Layout, Page** {Shift and F8, p}.

   Note: The Page Format dialog box displays.

3. Select **Page Numbering** {n}.

   Note: The Page Numbering dialog box displays.

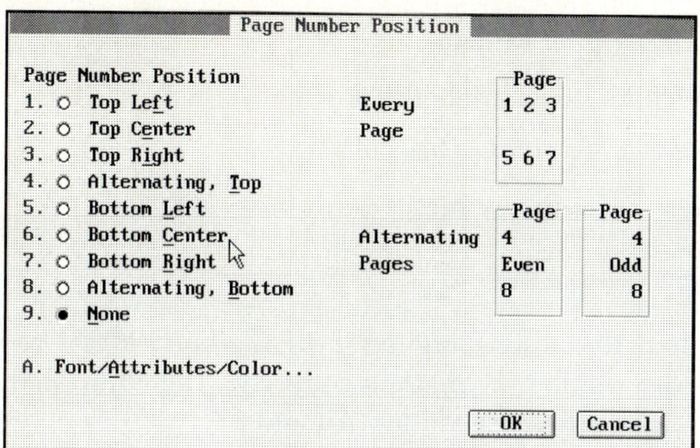

Page Number Position
dialog box

4. Move the mouse pointer to the words **Page Number Position** and click once {p}.

   Note: The Page Number Position dialog box displays (see Figure 10.2).

5. Select the desired position for the page numbers.

   For example, select **Bottom Center** {c}.

6. Select **OK** three times {press Enter four times}.

Finish-Up Instructions

❖ Turn on Reveal Codes (**Alt** and **F3**). Highlight the [Pg Num Pos] code and view the expanded page numbering code, e.g., [Pg Num Pos:BotCntr]. Turn off Reveal Codes (**Alt** and **F3**).

❖ Use the page mode view and scroll to the bottom of the pages to view the page numbers (select **View**, **Page Mode**).

❖ Use the new filename **10drill1.num** and save the file.

❖ Print one copy.

Start-Up Instructions

❖ The file named **10drill1.num** should be displayed on the screen.

Steps to ▶ **Change Page Number Method**

1. Place the cursor/insertion point at the beginning of the document (press **Home** three times and the up arrow key once).

2. Select **Layout, Page, Page Numbering** {Shift and F8, p, n}.

3. Select **Page Number** {n}.

4. Select **Numbering Method** {m}.

   Note: The number types display in a drop-down list.

5. Select the desired numbering method {press the down arrow key to highlight the desired option, press Enter}.

For example, select Upper Roman.

6. Select **OK** to return to the Page Number dialog box {Enter}.

   Note: Roman numeral I displays in the Page Number box.

7. Select **OK** twice {press Enter three times}.

Finish-Up Instructions

❖ Turn on Reveal Codes (**Alt** and **F3**), highlight the [Pg Num Meth] code, and view the expanded page numbering method code, e.g., [Pg Num Meth:Lev 1; Uppercase Roman]. Turn off Reveal Codes (**Alt** and **F3**).

❖ Use the filename **10drill1.II** and save the file.

❖ Print one copy.

Start-Up Instructions

❖ The file named **10drill1.II** should be displayed on the screen.

Delete Page Numbers

1. If necessary, turn on Reveal Codes (**Alt** and **F3**).

2. Locate and highlight the page numbering code.

   For example, highlight **[Pg Num Pos:BotCntr]**.

3. Press **Delete**.

4. If necessary, highlight and delete the page numbering method code.

   For example, highlight **[Pg Num Meth:Lev 1; Uppercase Roman]** and press **Delete**.

5. Turn off Reveal Codes (**Alt** and **F3**).

Finish-Up Instructions

❖ Use the page mode view and scroll to the bottom of the pages. Notice that the page numbers no longer display at the bottom of the document pages.

❖ Close the document. Do not save the file.

Headers and Footers

Generally, a multiple-page document includes headers or footers. A header is a title or information that prints in the top margin of the second and following pages (see Figure 10.3). A footer is a title or information that prints in the bottom margin of each page (see Figure 10.5). Headers and footers can consist of

Header for two-page
memorandum or report

Right Moves Presentation
Page 2
March 25, 199x

This process will not fail if made a part of the presentation
format discipline. Additionally, remember that no more than
three recommended changes should be presented at one time.
The recommendations should be presented in a concise and
informative manner.

Header for two-page
letter

Ms. Holly Pierce   Page 2   March 25, 199x

Costs included in this invoice are for final preparation by a
Senior Engineer, review by a Principal, geotechnical drafting
and typing, and reproduction of the Distress Investigation
report. Expenses are for film purchase, developing, and
printing.

more than one line of text. Once created, headers and footers can be edited, suppressed for a single page, discontinued, or deleted.

When a header is used, the header information is normally not printed on the first page of a document but prints at the top of the second and following pages. When a footer is used, the title information along with the page number (optional) prints at the bottom of every page. The default position for headers is 1" from the top of the page, and 1" from the bottom of the page for footers. A header or footer can be viewed by selecting **View**, **Page Mode** or by choosing the **Preview** button.

Two different headers or footers can be created. Header A & B and Footer A & B are options available in the Header/Footer/Watermark dialog box. Usually, only Header A or Footer A is used. However, if a document is set up to display different headers/footers on left and right pages, Header/Footer A would be used to create a left-page header or footer and Header/Footer B would be used to create a right-page header or footer. The footers in this textbook are an example of different left- and right-page footers.

If the format of a document is changed, the format of the header or footer must also be altered to match the changed document format. For example, if the margins or fonts are changed for the entire document, the margins or fonts for the header and/or footer must also be changed.

When a one-line header or footer is typed, a one-row table with two or three columns can be created to make formatting and aligning the text easier. For example, in the one-row header displayed in the second sample in Figure 10.3, Page 2 is centered

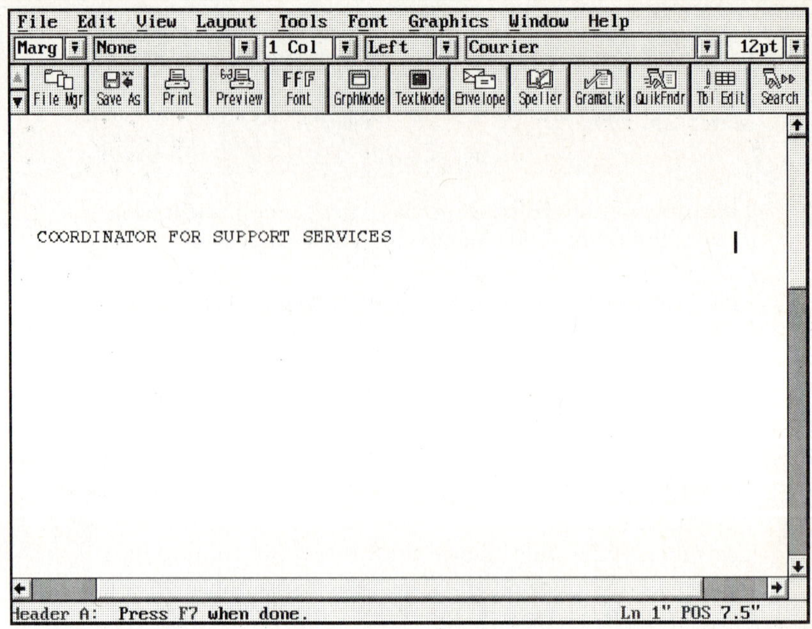

FIGURE 10.4

Header window

in the middle column and the date is right aligned in the right column. The table border and table lines are omitted.

Start-Up Instructions

- ❖ Open the file named **10drill1** created earlier in this chapter.
- ❖ If necessary, select page mode (select **View, Page Mode**).

Steps to > Create a Header and Insert a Page Number

1. Place the cursor/insertion point at the beginning of the document (press **Home** three times and press the up arrow key once).

2. Select **Layout, Header/Footer/Watermark** {Shift and F8, h}.

3. Select **Header A** {h, Enter}.

   Note: The Header A dialog box displays and All Pages is selected (a black dot appears beside the option name).

4. Select **Create** {c}.

   Note: The Header A window displays on the screen. The Status bar displays "Header A: Press F7 when done."

5. Type the header information.

   For example, type **COORDINATOR FOR SUPPORT SERV-ICES**. Press **Alt** and **F6** to move the cursor/insertion point to the right margin (see Figure 10.4).

6. To insert a page number, select **Layout, Page** {Shift and F8, p}.

7. Select **Page Numbering** {n}.

8. Select the **Insert Formatted Page Number** option to insert the page number code into the header automatically {i}.

9. Press **Enter** once to create a blank line.

10. Press **F7** to exit the Header A window.

    Note: Turn on Reveal Codes to display the [Header A] code. Turn off Reveal Codes.

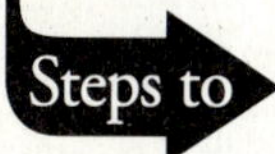 ## Suppress the Header on Page One

11. Select **Layout, Page, Suppress** {Shift and F8, p, u}.

12. Select the box located beside the **Header A** option {h}.

    Note: An X displays in the Header A box.

13. Select **OK** twice {Enter three times}.

Finish-Up Instructions

❖ Press the **Page Down** (PgDn) key to view the header on page 2 of the document.

❖ Use the new filename **10drill1.hdr** and save the file.

❖ Print one copy.

Start-Up Instructions

❖ The file named **10drill1.hdr** should be displayed on the screen.

 ## Edit Headers/Footers

1. Select **Layout, Header/Footer/Watermark** {Shift and F8, h}.

2. Select **Headers** or **Footers** {h or f, Enter}.

    For example, select **Header A.**

3. Select **Edit** {e}.

4. Make the desired changes to the header or footer text using the customary editing methods.

    For example, delete the page number code [Formatted Pg Num] and type **JOB DESCRIPTION**.

    Note: The text JOB DESCRIPTION should be aligned flush right (see Figure 10.5).

5. Press **F7**.

Finish-Up Instructions

❖ In the page mode view, press the **Page Down** or **Page Up** (PgUp) key to view the changed header.

The figure box contains:

COORDINATOR FOR SUPPORT SERVICE   JOB DESCRIPTION

4. Coordinate timely delivery of training materials to client sites including verification of number of enrollees, shipping information, shipping materials, and transparencies.

5. Analyze bids requested from vendors and negotiate for special supplies. Maintain supplies of binders, paper, tabs, covers, spines, and backs to ensure availability.

6. Assist with the development, production, and distribution for training courses and modules.

7. Provide software training, support, and troubleshooting via phone for all administrative office personnel.

8. Develop and maintain consultant orientation/training programs, quick WordPerfect training materials, and style sheets for Ventura.

9. Assist with evaluation of new and upgraded software and new office machines prior to purchase.

Duties and responsibilities may be added, deleted, or changed at any time at the discretion of management, formally or informally, either verbally or in writing.

Revision date: 11/9x   Page 2

❖ Use the new filename **10drill1.edi** and save the file.

Start-Up Instructions

❖ The file named **10drill1.edi** should be displayed on the screen.

Steps to ▶ Create a Footer

1. Place the cursor/insertion point at the beginning of the document (press **Home** three times and the up arrow key once).

2. Select **Layout, Header/Footer/Watermark** {Shift and F8, h}.

   Note: The Header/Footer/Watermark dialog box displays.

3. Select **Footer A** {f, Enter}.

   Note: The Footer A dialog box displays.

4. Select **Create** {c}.

Note: The Footer A window displays on the screen. The footer window is exactly like the header window, except Footer A displays in the Status bar.

5. Type the footer information.

   For example, type **Revision date: 11/9x**. Press **Alt** and **F6** to move the cursor/insertion point to the right margin. Type **Page** and press the **Spacebar** once .

6. To insert the page number into the footer, select **Layout, Page, Page Number** {Shift and F8, p, n} .

7. Select the **Insert Formatted Page Number** option to insert the page number into the footer automatically {i}.

8. Press **F7**.

   *Note: In the page mode view, the footer can be viewed by pressing the **Page Down** key and **Page Up** or by selecting the **Preview** button. Also, if desired, turn on Reveal Codes to display the [Footer A] code.*

Finish-Up Instructions

❖ Use the new filename **10drill1.ftr** and save the file.

❖ Print one copy.

Delete Headers/Footers

Note: The Steps to Delete Headers/Footers are for your information.

1. Turn on Reveal Codes (**Alt** and **F3**).

2. Locate and highlight the header or footer code in the Reveal Codes screen.

3. Press **Delete**.

Widow and Orphan Lines

A widow line is the last line of a paragraph that prints at the top of the next page while the preceding paragraph lines print at the bottom of the previous page. An orphan line is the first line of a paragraph that prints at the bottom of the page while the remaining paragraph lines print at the top of the next page.

A minimum of two lines of a paragraph should be printed at the bottom and top of a page. Using WordPerfect's widow/orphan protect feature is recommended when working with multiple-page or multiple-column documents.

Start-Up Instructions

❖ The file named **10drill1.ftr** should be displayed on the screen.

 **Use Widow/Orphan Protect**

1. Place the cursor/insertion point at the beginning of the document (press **Home** three times and the up arrow key once).

2. Select **Layout, Other** {Shift and F8, o}.

3. Select **Widow/Orphan Protect** {w}.

   Note: An X displays in the box beside Widow/Orphan Protect.

4. Select **OK** {Enter twice}.

Finish-Up Instructions

❖ Turn on Reveal Codes (**Alt** and **F3**) to view the widow/orphan protect code [Wid/Orph]. Turn off Reveal Codes (**Alt** and **F3**).

❖ Save the file again using the same filename.

❖ Print one copy.

❖ Close the document

Create Footnotes and Endnotes

A multiple-page document can include footnotes or endnotes. The footnote or endnote reference information provides the name, date, and page number of the source from which the information being discussed was obtained (see Figure 10.6). Footnotes and endnotes are also referred to as reference notes.

To create footnotes and endnotes, place the cursor/insertion point at the location in the text where the reference is needed, select the **Layout** menu, and choose the option desired, i.e., **Footnote** or **Endnote**. Choose **Create** to display the Footnote or Endnote window. WordPerfect automatically places a footnote or endnote number at the location of the cursor/insertion point in the Footnote/Endnote window. Type the reference information for the footnote or endnote and press F7 to return the cursor/insertion point to the document window. WordPerfect places the footnote or endnote reference number in the document text. The reference number is superscripted (raised slightly above the text line).

Codes for the footnote and endnote references are placed in the document text and are displayed by using Reveal Codes. The footnote and endnote reference information is displayed in the document window by using the Page Mode view. The footnote or endnote information can also be displayed by selecting the **Preview** button.

Footnote reference information is printed at the bottom of the page where the footnote reference number is located. A 2-inch separator line is placed above the footnote reference information. The first line of the footnote reference information is in-four-year scholarships have been established for children of firefighters who have died in the line of duty. Other Lieberman Enterprises scholarship programs have been for graduates of West City Community College, city employees, and Norfolk high school teachers. In response to the need for more qualified science teachers, Lieberman Enterprises offers training in computer science to high school teachers. A Science Seminar Program provides science teachers with updated teaching materials and methods.[2]

[1]J. Russell Mason, The President's Report to the Board of Directors, Spring 1990, p. 2.

[2]Ibid., p. 3.

dented, the footnote reference number is superscripted, and the information is printed with vertical line spacing of one (see Figure 10.6).

Endnotes are automatically placed at the end of the document text. A hard page break (**Ctrl** and **Enter**) is inserted after the last line of text in the document so that endnotes will print on a separate page. A title such as *Notes* is usually placed at the top of the endnote page. The first line of the endnote reference information is indented, and the information is printed with line spacing of one.

The footnote or endnote format can be changed easily by adding or deleting formatting codes in the Footnote/Endnote Style in Note dialog box. For example, if the endnote is to be preceded by a tab, the tab code can be placed in the Endnote Style in Note dialog box. Other formatting changes can include font or number position changes. When a format change is made for a footnote or endnote, the change affects all occurrences throughout the document.

Footnote/endnote reference marks are normally numbers. However, a custom footnote/endnote mark, such as an asterisk, can be defined by selecting **Layout**, **Footnote** or **Endnote**, **New Number**, and choosing **Characters** in the Numbering Method box. The * character is defaulted and displays in the Characters option box.

Start-Up Instructions

❖   🖫 Open the file named **10drill2**.

Create Footnotes

1. Place the cursor/insertion point to the right of the text to be referenced.

2. Select **Layout, Footnote, Create** {Ctrl and F7, f, c}.

   Note: The footnote window displays and the footnote number is shown. Notice that the word "Footnote" displays in the Status bar.

3. Type the footnote information.

   For example, **J. Russell Mason, The President's Report to the Board of Directors, Spring 1990, p. 2.**

4. Press **F7**.

   Note: The footnote number displays at the location of the cursor/insertion point. To display the footnote, use the page mode view or select the **Preview** *button and scroll to the bottom of the page.*

Finish-Up Instructions

❖ Place the cursor/insertion point after the last period in the third paragraph that ends with the word *methods*.

❖ Use Steps 2-4 to create the following footnote:

   Ibid., p. 3.

❖ Place the cursor/insertion point after the last period in the final paragraph that ends with the word *centers*.

❖ Use Steps 2-4 to create the following footnote:

   Lois Hodges, "Contribution to Community Education," *The Times Crier,* **3 May 1991, p. 10.**

❖ Use the new filename **10drill2.fnt** and save the file.

❖ Print one copy.

Start-Up Instructions

❖ The file named **10drill2.fnt** should be displayed on the screen.

Edit a Footnote or Endnote

Note: The same method is used to edit footnotes and endnotes. For information on creating endnotes, see page 277.

1. Select **Layout, Footnote** or **Endnote, Edit** {Ctrl and F7, f or e, e} .

   For example, select **Layout, Footnote, Edit** {Alt and L, f, e}.

   Note: The Footnote Number box displays.

2. Type the number of the footnote/endnote to be edited.

   For example, type **3**.

3. Select **OK** to display the footnote/endnote window {Enter}.

   Note: The Edit Footnote/Endnote window displays showing the complete footnote text.

4. Make corrections using the customary edit methods.

   For example, change p. 10 to **p. 24**.

5. Press **F7**

Finish-Up Instructions

❖ Save the file again using the same filename.

Start-Up Instructions

❖ The file named **10drill2.fnt** should be displayed on the screen.

Delete a Footnote or Endnote

Note: The same method is used to delete footnotes and endnotes. For information on creating endnotes, see Steps to Create Endnotes below.

1. Block the footnote or endnote reference number in the document.

   For example, block the footnote reference number **2**.

2. Press the **Delete** key once. The footnote/endnote number and the footnote/endnote information are both deleted.

   Note: If other footnotes/endnotes follow the deleted footnote or endnote, the remaining footnotes/endnotes are automatically renumbered.

Finish-Up Instructions

❖ Use the new filename **10drill2.fin** and save the file.

❖ Print one copy.

❖ Close the document.

Start-Up Instructions

❖ Open the file named **10drill2**.

Create Endnotes

1. Locate the cursor/insertion point at the end of the document by pressing **Home** twice and the down arrow key once.

2. Press **Ctrl** and **Enter** to insert a hard page break.

3. With the cursor/insertion point located below the hard page break, set the vertical line spacing to one (select **Layout**, **Line**, type **1** in the Line Spacing option box, **OK**).

4. Type and center the endnote page title.

   For example, type **Notes**. Press **Enter** three times.

5. Select **Layout, Endnote, Edit Style in Notes** {Ctrl and F7, e, s}.

6. Press the **Tab** key once.

   Note: The tab code [Lft Tab] should be located before the endnote number display code [Endnote Num Disp].

7. Press **F7** (if Ctrl and F7 was used in Step 5, press **F7** twice).

   Note: No changes are shown on the screen; however, when an endnote is created, the first line of the endnote text will be indented when viewed and/or printed.

8. Place the cursor/insertion point to the right of the text to be referenced.

   For example, place the cursor/insertion point to the right of the period after the last sentence in the first paragraph that ends with the word *annually*.

9. Select **Layout, Endnote, Create** {Ctrl and F7, e, c}.

   Note: The endnote window displays and the endnote number is shown. Notice that the word "Endnote" displays in the Status bar.

10. Press the **Tab** key once; type the endnote information.

    For example, **J. Russell Mason, The President's Report to the Board of Directors, Spring 1990, p. 2.**

11. Press **F7**.

    Note: The number 1 displays at the end of the paragraph. To view the endnote text in the page mode view, scroll down to display the last page of the document.

Finish-Up Instructions

❖ Place the cursor/insertion point after the last period in the third paragraph that ends with the word *methods*.

❖ Use Steps 9-11 to create the second endnote:

   Ibid., p. 3.

❖ Place the cursor/insertion point after the last period in the final paragraph that ends with the word *centers*.

❖ Use Steps 9-11 to create the third endnote:

   Lois Hodges, "Contribution to Community Education," *The Times Crier*, **3 May 1991, p. 24.**

❖ Use the new filename **10drill2.end** and save the file.

❖ To view the endnote text in the Page Mode view, scroll down the document to display the last page of the document. If desired, select the **Preview** button to use the Print Preview feature.

❖ Print one copy.

Search for Codes

To quickly locate a specific place in a document, the user can search for text or codes. Searching for codes is quite similar to searching for specific document text (see Chapter 5). Locating a code is useful for deleting or moving a code or for finding a specific area of the document. Search for a code by selecting the **Search** button on the Button Bar and choosing **Codes**. A list of WordPerfect codes displays. Double-click on the desired code and select **Search**.

Start-Up Instructions

❖ The file named **10drill2.end** should be displayed on the screen.

❖ The WPMAIN Button Bar should be displayed.

❖ Turn on Reveal Codes (**Alt** and **F3**).

Search for a Code

1. Locate the cursor/insertion point at the top of the document to be searched (press **Home** three times and the up arrow key once).

2. Select the **Search** button on the Button Bar {F2}.

   *Note: If the text mode is active, select the down triangle at the left of the Button Bar to display the **Search** button.*

3. Select the **Codes** button {F5}.

   Note: The Search Codes dialog box displays (see Figure 10.7).

4. Place the mouse pointer on the down scroll arrow in the Search Codes dialog box, and press the left mouse button repeatedly until the desired code displays {press the down arrow key until the desired code is highlighted}.

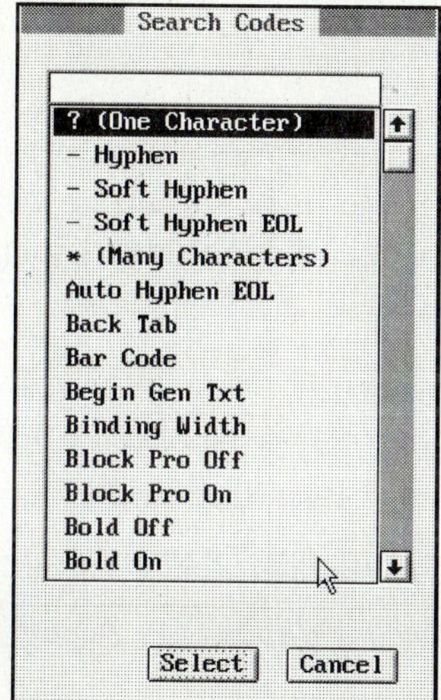

FIGURE 10.7

Search Codes dialog box

For example, scroll down until **Endnote** is highlighted.

5. Double-click on the desired code {press Enter}.

   For example, double-click on the endnote code.

   Note: The code [Endnote] is placed in the Search For box in the Search dialog box.

6. Select Search in the Search dialog box {F2}.

   Note: The cursor/insertion point is located to the right of the endnote code.

Finish-Up Instructions

v   Press the **Backspace** key to delete the endnote code in the document.

v   Save the file again using the same filename, **10drill2.end**.

Print Specific Pages

After printing a multiple-page document, one or more of the pages may be edited and only the changed pages will need to be reprinted. To specify the exact pages to print, the Multiple Pages option is selected in the Print dialog box, and the desired pages are entered as follows:

- Place a comma or space between nonconsecutive pages, e.g., 1,3 or 2 4 6.

- Place a dash between the beginning and ending page numbers to print a consecutive range of pages, e.g., 5-9.

- Place a dash after the beginning page number to print from a specific page to the end of the document, e.g. 5-.

- Place a dash before the page number to print from the beginning of a document up to a specific page, e.g., -6.

Also, a single page can be printed by placing the cursor/insertion point anywhere in the page, selecting the **Print** button on the Button Bar, choosing the **Page** option, and selecting **Print**. Only the page where the insertion point is located will print.

Start-Up Instructions

v   The document containing the pages to print should be displayed on the screen. For example, the file named **10drill2.end** should be displayed on the screen.

Print Specific Pages

1. Select the Print button on the Button Bar {Shift and F7}.

2. Select the **Multiple Pages** option in the Print dialog box {m}.

   Note: The Print Multiple Pages dialog box displays (see Figure 10.8).

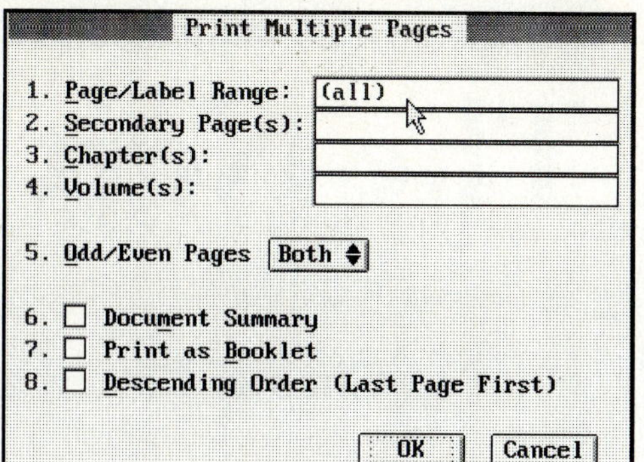

FIGURE 10.8

Print Multiple Pages dialog box

3. Select **Page/Label Range** {p}.

4. Type the page numbers to be printed.

> For example, type **1,3** to print pages 1 and 3 only.

5. Select **OK** {press Enter twice}.

6. Select **Print** in the Print/Fax dialog box {Enter}.

Finish-Up Instructions

❖ Close the document.

The Next Step

Chapter Review and Activities

FEATURES SUMMARY

FEATURES	ACTIONS	PAGE
Number pages	Place the cursor/insertion point at the beginning of the document, select **Layout**, **Page**, choose **Page Numbering**, select **Page Number Position**, choose the desired position, select **OK** until the document window displays.	266
Change the page number method	Place the insertion point at the beginning of the document, select **Layout**, **Page**, **Page Number**, select **Numbering Method**, select the desired method, select **OK** three times.	267
Delete page numbers	With Reveal Codes on, highlight the page numbering code, press the **Delete** key.	268
Create a header or footer	Place the cursor/insertion point at the beginning of the document, select **Layout**, **Header/Footer/Watermark**, select **Header A** or **Footer A**, choose **Create**, type and format the header/footer information, press **F7**.	270, 272
Suppress the header on page one	Select **Layout**, **Page**, **Suppress**, select **Header A**, select **OK** until the document window displays.	271
Edit headers or footers	Select **Layout**, **Header/Footer/Watermark**, select **Headers** or **Footers**, select **Edit**, make the desired changes, press **F7**.	271

   Chapter 10—Create a Multiple-Page Document

<table>
<tr><td>FEATURES (cont'd.)</td><td>ACTIONS (cont'd.)</td><td>PAGE</td></tr>
<tr><td>Delete headers or footers</td><td>With Reveal Codes on, highlight the header or footer code, press Delete.</td><td>273</td></tr>
<tr><td>Widow/Orphan Protect</td><td>Place the cursor/insertion point at the beginning of the document, select Layout, Other, Widow/Orphan Protect, OK.</td><td>274</td></tr>
<tr><td>Create footnotes</td><td>Place the cursor/insertion point to the right of the text to be referenced, select Layout, Footnote, Create, type the footnote information, press F7.</td><td>275</td></tr>
<tr><td>Create endnotes</td><td>Place the cursor/insertion point at the end of the document, press Ctrl and Enter to create a new page. If necessary, set line spacing to one. Type and center the endnote page title and press Enter three times.

To set the endnote format, select Layout, Endnote, Edit Style in Notes, press the Tab key, press F7.

Place the cursor/insertion point at the right of the text to be referenced, select Layout, Endnote, Create, press the Tab key, type the endnote information, press F7.</td><td>277</td></tr>
<tr><td>Search for codes</td><td>Place the cursor/insertion point at the top of the document, select the Search button, choose Codes, scroll down the list of codes to display the desired code, double-click on the code, select Search.</td><td>279</td></tr>
<tr><td>Print specific pages</td><td>Select the Print button, choose Multiple Pages, select Page/Label Range, type the desired page numbers, select OK, choose Print.</td><td>280</td></tr>
</table>

Self-Check Questions

True/False—Circle One

T F 1. A multiple-page report is printed with vertical line spacing of one or two.

T F 2. A footer is typed once and printed on all pages of a multiple-page document.

T F 3. A header is normally printed on all pages of a document.

T F 4. Endnote information is printed on a separate page at the end of a document.

T F 5. Footnotes are consecutively numbered and printed on the page where the information is referenced.

Short Answer

1. List the four steps to turn on Widow/Orphan Protect.

2. State the difference between a footnote and a footer.

3. Press _____ and **Enter** to place a hard page break in a document.

4. List the six steps to number pages in a document.

5. List two reasons for seaching for a code.

Enriching Language Arts Skills

Spelling/Vocabulary Words

phenomenon   an event perceived and/or felt by one's senses; sensation; spectacle.
biosphere   region of the earth that provides a self-sustaining ecological system.
analysis   the study and inquiry of the nature of something; investigation; evaluation.
profound   intense; extreme; significant.
euphoria   a feeling of well-being, usually not based on reality.

Quotation Marks with Punctuation

Always place a comma or period inside a closing quotation mark.

Example:

"I wonder," said Joan to herself, "how I got myself into this situation."

Place a question or exclamation mark inside a closing quotation mark if the question
or exclamation pertains only to the quoted information. Place a question or exclamation mark outside the closing quotation mark if the question or exclamation pertains
to the entire sentence.

Example:

Jan said, "Help me!" (The exclamation mark pertains only to the quoted information.)

Was the returned check marked "Insufficient Funds"? (The question mark pertains to the entire sentence.)

Semicolons and colons are placed outside the closing quotation mark.

Example:

The following items were in a package marked "Fragile": an antique bowl, four glasses, and a pitcher.

Activities

Activity 10.1—Create a Multiple-Page Document with Page Numbers

1. Type the following report with vertical line spacing of two.

COMPUSOFT MODULAR FOR WINDOWS AND OS/2

Compusoft Modular is a fresh new design of communications software for all categories of users. Modularity and profiling strengths provide the user with the ability to "customize" and "personalize" Compusoft for precise functions.

Compusoft Modular offers more LAN/Gateway connectivity and terminal emulations than any other product in today's market. Uniform support for both Windows and OS/2 platforms is included in every package; the user simply chooses the appropriate installation diskette.

Compusoft's simulated reasoning capability lets users create a mental model compatible with their own thinking process, and it makes expanded and advanced use occur without conscious effort. Once users successfully configure a task, they never need to configure that particular task again. Over time, users achieve a higher level of user interaction.

By the end of the next quarter, Compusoft Modular will support over 50 terminal emulations. By the end of the third quarter, an additional 10 terminal emulations will be available. Another standard Compusoft module will enable the user to utilize Telenet to run multisessions with integrated file transfer protocols. Users can download these new modules at no charge from Corbin's bulletin board service as they are made available.

Compusoft Modular also includes all of the features that users of the Compusoft PC Classic have been accustomed to during the past eight years, such as an extensive number of file transfer protocols, dynamic keyboard remapping, an extensive script language, keyboard macros, multinational keyboard/emulation support, session scrollback, and preconfigured sessions for most online services.

Even though Compusoft has numerous features and functionality, it is extremely easy to manage and run. An excess of features is eliminated by removing functions that are not needed during the installation process, leaving only the desired modules. Compusoft Modular's dynamic graphic user interface displays only the functionality chosen by the user.

Compusoft Modular, version 1.0, costs $315 per user. For more information about Compusoft Modular, call (800) 555-5050.

---

2. Turn on Widow/Orphan Protect (with the cursor/insertion point at the beginning of the document, select **Layout**, **Other**, **Widow/Orphan Protect**, **OK**).

3. Use page numbering to print numbers at the bottom center of each page (select **Layout**, **Page**, **Page Numbering**, choose **Page Number Position**, and select **Bottom Center**, select **OK** until the document window displays).

4. Use the filename **10act1** and save the file. Print one copy.

5. Close the document.

◼ Activity 10.2—Create a Header for a Two-Page Memorandum

1. Open the memorandum with the filename **10act2**.

2. Select **Layout**, **Header/Footer/Watermark**, **Header A**, and create a header that contains the following information:

   Right Move Presentations
   Date
   Page (insert page number code)

3. Suppress the header on the first page (select **Layout**, **Page**, **Suppress**, **Header A**, **OK** twice).

4. Use the new filename **10act2.fin** and save the file. Print one copy.

5. Close the document.

◼ Activity 10.3—Create a Header and Footer for a Multiple-Page Document

1. Open the report with the filename **10act3**.

2. Set vertical line spacing of two.

3. Turn on widow/orphan protect (**Layout**, **Other**, **Widow/Orphan Protect**).

4. Select **Layout**, **Header/Footer/Watermark**, **Header A**, and create a header:

   EVERYDAY MAGIC   **(CURRENT DATE)**

5. Suppress the header on the first page (select **Layout**, **Page**, **Suppress**, **Header A**, **OK** twice).

6. Select **Layout**, **Header/Footer/Watermark**, **Footer A**, and create a footer:

7. Use the new filename **10act3.fin** and save the file. Print one copy.

8. Close the document.

 Activity 10.4—Create a Header and Footnote for a Multiple-Page Document

1. Open the report with the filename **10act4**.

2. Turn on widow/orphan protect (select **Layout**, **Other**, **Widow/Orphan Protect**).

3. Optional. Set the vertical line spacing for two.

4. Select **Layout**, **Header/Footer/Watermark**, **Header A**, and create a header:

    Desktop Publishing and Graphic Design   Page (insert page number code)

5. Suppress the header for the first page (select **Layout**, **Page**, **Suppress**, **Header A**, **OK** twice).

6. Create a footnote:

    a. Place the cursor/insertion point after the last character in the document, select **Layout**, **Footnote**, **Create**, and insert the following footnote:

    LaVaughn Hart and Katie Layman, "Desktop Publishing and Graphic Design," *The California Business Teacher*, Spring 1990, pp. 22-23.

7. Use the filename **10act4.fin** and save the file. Print one copy.

8. Close the document.

Challenge Your Skills

Skill 10.1—Create a Header and Format a Two-Page Memorandum and Table

1. Use Memorandum—Style 1 and the following information to complete the memorandum.

    a. Make decisions regarding:

    Margins
    Justification
    Fonts
    Table format

Widow/Orphan Protect
Reference initials

b. The memo should be sent to Noah Demello, Vice President, Field Sales.

c. The memo is from Joyce S. Greiner, Regional Vice President.

d. The memo should be dated June 22, 199x.

e. The subject of the memo is Weekly Business Conditions Report.

f. Copies of the memo should be sent to:

T. W. Hakinson, Ellen Harrell, Alvin Lai, and Region Staff.

g. The memorandum body text follows:

Regional Sales Performance

Period: 6
Week: 4
Week ending: 6/19/9x

Dollar Sales				
(in thousands)				
	1993 Actual	1993 Objectives	Difference in Dollars	Percent Change
Week Ending	8,244	7,473	771	10.3%
Period Ending	28,695	29,099	(404)	(1.4)%

General Business Conditions

The Northwest Region delivered 26.4% of its Period 6 objective in Week 4, which reduced the deficit by $771,229 to finish the period down ($404,065). This Week 4 push enabled three divisions, Portland, Seattle, and San Francisco, to exceed their objectives.

This week's business was primarily driven by retailers seeking to maximize overlay payout potentials, some sales teams striving to achieve consistency bonuses, and preshipment of Cheesecake Yummies inventory prior to Week 1, Period 7 ad feature activity.

Significant Competitive Activity

<u>Whitehouse</u>

If a customer buys Mom's Tasties, Bite Size Fudge Chips are free!

Whitehouse will introduce their 7 oz. Ponderosa Munch'ems into the Portland Division during Period 7, and the new Deluxe Crispies will arrive Period 8.

The Seattle Division reports coupons being distributed in stores offering a free pound of bananas with the purchase of one package of Heart Wafers.

Lucky Star

The price for Super Snack Cookies 12 oz. or larger is $.45.

In the San Francisco Division, Lucky Star is hosting a "Grocery Giveaway Contest" that customers can enter to win $60 worth of groceries.

Other Information

The current issue of FOOD SNACKS profiles Milano, a Seattle, Washington snack supplier, plotting a course towards retail expansion by emphasizing quality, competitive pricing, innovative products, and dedicated service. Although its roots are in the bulk/industrial snack trade, Milano knows they will have to decide whether to concentrate on being a retail snack supplier or continue to emphasize re-packers' demands. This is an example of a lower-priced, "less fancy" snack variety entering the growing "All Other" cracker category.

2. Create a two-line header:

> **Weekly Business Conditions** June 22, 199x
> **Northwest Region** Page (insert page number code)

Note: Remember to suppress the header on the first page.

3. Use the filename **10skill1.fin** and save the file.

4. Print one copy.

5. Close the document.

◨ Skill 10.2—Create a Header and Footnotes; Format a Multiple-Page Document with Table

1. Open the multiple-page document with the filename **10skill2**.

2. Make decisions regarding:

> Margins
> Line spacing
> Justification
> Fonts
> Table format

Widow/Orphan protect
Header format and placement
Spacing before and after, capitalization, and bold for title and
sideheadings

3. Create the following footnotes in the document.

    a. Place the first footnote reference after the closing quotation mark in
        the first paragraph "...which includes national and international list-
        ing." Footnote text: The Southwest Stock Exchange Bulletin, p. 6.

    b. Place the second footnote reference in the third paragraph after the
        closing quotation mark that ends "...prices and trades on a daily ba-
        sis." Footnote text: EITAK Commodities Annual Report, p. 2.

    c. Place the third footnote reference at the end of item number 3,
        "... inquiries by account executive." Footnote text: Ibid.

4. Create an appropriate header including the page number.

5. Use the new filename **10skill2.fin** and save the file.

6. Print one copy and close the document.

Skill 10.3—Create a Footnote and Page Numbering for a Multiple-Page Document; Language Arts

1. Open the multiple-page document with the filename **10skill3**.

2. Make decisions regarding:

    Margins
    Line spacing
    Justification
    Hyphenation
    Headers and footers
    Correct four spelling and three punctuation errors

3. Create the following footnote in the document.

    a. Place the footnote reference after the period in the last sentence of the
        document. Footnote text: "Book Review--The Overview Effect: Space
        Exploration and Human Evolution," *Spacefaring Gazette*, August
        1988, p. 9.

4. Number the document pages at the top right corner.

5. Use the filename **10skill3.fin** and save the file.

6. Print one copy.

7. If you have completed your work, exit WordPerfect.

Production Skill Builder Activities
Chapters 8-10

Production Activity 3.1—Create Standard Paragraphs and Assemble Personalized Letters

1. Create a document that contains the following standard paragraphs:

Allied Health Plan

Allied Health is an individual practice health maintenance organization (HMO). It provides health care directly to its members through hospitals, physicians, and other health care providers who have entered into agreements with Allied Health and who are located in your community.

Health Care Solutions Plan

Health Care Solutions, a statewide HMO, offers its members access to a comprehensive network of respected medical groups and independent practice associations. It provides a health care delivery system that cares for the individual needs of all members. Chiropractic care and prescription drug coverage are also included.

Martin Health Care Plan

With Martin Health Care's HMO service, your medical care is provided or arranged by the physicians at Martin Health Care medical facilities. Representing virtually all major medical and surgical specialties, these physicians work together in one of the nation's largest medical group partnerships to care for one special group of people--their members.

Ready-Care Health Plan

Ready-Care Health is a fee-for-service plan that contracts with private practice physicians and community hospitals to provide quality care to all members. They work diligently with their doctors to help ensure that members receive consistent, high-quality care. The provider network is currently comprised of over 1,700 highly respected physicians and specialists and 26 community hospitals.

Zion-Care Health Plan

Zion-Care Health is a fee-for-service health plan that allows its members to manage their own health care through the selection of physicians, hospitals, and other specialists. When selecting a physician or hospital provider, Zion-Care provides a higher level of reimbursement when the provider is a member of the Zion-Care physician network. This statewide network includes 270 hospitals, 36,000 physicians, and 30,000 related health professionals.

---

2. Save the standard paragraphs document; use the filename **3pact1.stn**.

3. Use the following information and the standard paragraphs document to create personalized letters for the following individuals:

   a. Ms. Mary Ann Weinstein
      85 Main Street, #4
      University Park, PA 16802
      Ms. Weinstein is interested in HMO plans.

   b. Mr. Irvin H. McCarthy
      P.O. Box 568
      Philadelphia, PA 19104
      Mr. McCarthy is interested in fee-for-service plans.

   c. Kenneth and Judy Chitwood
      2403 State Street
      Philadelphia, PA 19106
      Mr. and Mrs. Chitwood are interested in both HMO and a fee-for-service program that offer statewide health coverage.

   d. The letters are from Virginia A. Velasquez, Health Care Broker.

   e. Make decisions regarding:

      Letter style
      Margins
      Justification
      Fonts
      The health care plan descriptions (2-3) that should be
         copied into each letter
      Reference initials/document identification/enclosure
         notation
      Filename for each letter

   f. The body of the letter follows:

      Thank you for contacting Health Care Referral Network regarding
      health care programs in your area. Based on our conversation, below are

---

brief descriptions of several programs I feel will provide the health care
you desire.

> Copy the desired health care program descriptions from the file named
> **3pact1.stn.**

Please call me after you have reviewed the enclosed brochures on each of
these programs. I will be happy to answer any additional questions you
may have and to enroll you and your family in the program that best
meets your needs.

4. Print one copy of each letter.

5. Close all documents.

◨ Production Activity 3.2—Multiple-Page Report with Footnotes and Page Numbering; Use Thesaurus

1. Open the report with the filename **3pact2**.

2. Use the following information to complete the report.

   a. Make decisions regarding:

      Margins
      Vertical line spacing
      Justification
      Fonts
      Widow/Orphan control
      Spacing before and after sideheadings
      Bold/underline/capitalization of title and sideheadings
      Spacing before, between, and after enumerated items
      Possible replacement words from Thesaurus for underlined
         words
      Page numbering using the page number feature or a header
      Page number position on the page

      *Note: If the page number is placed at the top of the page, the
      page number should be suppressed on the first page.*

3. Create the following footnotes in the document:

   a. Place the first footnote reference after the period in the first sentence
      in the second paragraph. Footnote text: Tony S. Carr, "Five Hundred
      Invest in Credit Union," *The Times*, 8 September 1992, sec. B, p. 1.

   b. Place the second footnote reference after the period in the second sen-
      tence in the second paragraph. Footnote text: Ibid.

   c. Place the third footnote reference after the period at the end of item
      number six. Footnote text: Norma H. Ames, "Historical Perspective of

Credit Unions," presented at the National Association of Credit Unions Annual Conference, February 8, 1991.

4. Use the new filename **3pact2.fin** and save the file.

5. Print one copy.

6. Close the document.

Production Activity 3.3—Multiple-Page Document with Parallel Columns, a Header, and a Footer

1. Create the following document using parallel columns. Make decisions regarding:

> Margins
> Justification
> Fonts
> Width of parallel columns
> Content and format of header and footer
> Bold/underline/capitalization of title, subtitle, and headings

---

Engineer's property inspection report
306 West 98th St.
July 18, 199x

general	The property is known as 306 West 98th Street and is located on the north side of West 98th Street.
construction	The building was built in 1920 under the new building application NB-584. It is constructed of wood floor and roof beams of a masonry bearing wall and is classified as a Class 3, non-fireproof construction under the Indianapolis City Administrative Building Code.
occupancy	The building is classified as a Class "A" multiple dwelling. The occupancy, room, and apartment count have not changed since the building was constructed. The building does not have a Certification of Occupancy (COO) and none was required at the time of construction.
street	The front building abuts West 98th Street, which is a publicly owned and maintained street with a single sidewalk on the north side of the street. The

street is paved with asphalt and is in fairly good condition.

utilities

The water supply, the sewer connection, and house trap are contained and have valves, controls, or cleanouts in a trap below the cellar floor at the entry.

Water is supplied to the building from an Indianapolis City main in the bed of 98th Street from a curb box at the edge of the sidewalk at the south property line.

Gas for domestic cooking ranges is supplied from a main in the bed of 98th Street maintained and supplied by the Consolidated Gas Co. through a curb box and a 2" tap in the street along the curb at the east end of the property. The gas is metered and billed to each apartment occupant with the exception of the one public meter.

Electricity is supplied and individually metered and billed to each apartment occupant from a main line in the bed of 98th Street maintained by Consolidated Gas Co. The power is connected to a junction box under the entry steps at the front of the building.

sub-soil

The foundations are brick masonry and stone and vary in thickness from 2' to 3'. They are even, level, and free of cracks, settlement, or other obvious movement. The exterior walls are stone and brick masonry and have no differential cracks or settling. There are no visible signs of any sub-soil conditions or underground water. There appear to have been no signs of flooding, erosion, mudslides, earthquakes, or other man-made or natural disasters.

---

2. Save the file; use the filename **3pact3**.

3. Print one copy.

4. Close the document.

1. Open the multiple-page document with the filename **3pact4**.

2. Use newspaper columns and the following information to complete the document.

   a. Make decisions regarding:

      Margins
      Number of columns
      Space between columns
      Widow/Orphan control
      Justification
      Fonts
      Spacing before and after sideheadings
      Bold/underline/capitalization of title, subtitle, and
        sideheadings
      Correct three spelling errors, two punctuation errors, and one
        misused word.

3. Use the filename **3pact4.fin** and save the file.

4. Close the document.

Part 4
A Step Ahead

Create Special Documents

Chapters 11-13

- Uppercase/lowercase change
- Hard space
- Insert special characters
- Set tabs
- Create form and data table files

- Fields and records
- Merge files
- Envelope addresses
- Mailing labels
- Sort records in a data table file

Create a Résumé

Features Covered

- Special characters/bullet characters
- Convert case
- Hard space
- Set tabs

Objectives

After successfully completing this chapter, you will be able to insert special Word-Perfect characters, use bullet characters to emphasize text, change the case for characters to all lowercase, all uppercase, or initial capitals, use a hard space to keep words on the same line, and set tabs in order to format an attractive, easy-to-read résumé.

Chapter Introduction

A résumé is a document that summarizes a person's education, work experience, and work skills. A résumé is submitted to a prospective employer when applying for a job. Since a résumé serves as a person's introduction to a prospective employer, it is important that the résumé be attractive and easy to read. A résumé may be formatted by using the Tab and Indent features, or the Tables feature may be used to arrange information in parallel columns.

Tab settings can be changed so that paragraphs can be indented in an attractive manner. Emphasis can be added to text by using text attributes such as bold, underline, and italics. Special characters such as the accent marks in résumé can be inserted into a document. In addition, special emphasis can be given by placing a bullet (symbol) character in front of desired paragraphs. (See Figure 11.1.)

Résumé
Will Swanson
45 Frederick Court
Belmont, CA 94002
(415) 555-8743

EDUCATIONAL BACKGROUND

A.A. Information Processing, DeAnza College 6/93
♦ Studied microcomputer courses—WordPerfect, MS/DOS, Telecommunications, and Desktop Publishing

Certificate, City College of Chicago 9/91
♦ Obtained a Certificate in BASIC programming

Completed U.S. Navy correspondence course 4/90

EMPLOYMENT EXPERIENCE

<u>U.S. Navy--4 years</u>
Have experience as a member of the flight crew for the P3 Orion; also worked as a shipboard navigator and computer operator.

<u>Stanford Linear Accelerator--1 year</u>
Operated a 20-ton forklift, oscilloscope, vacuum systems and was a machine operator.

<u>Kentucky Fried Chicken--1 year</u>
Managed employees, handled inventory, and supervised kitchen operations.

REFERENCES

Available upon request.

Special Characters

Special text characters such as the é's in résumé and bullet symbols such as (♦) can be inserted into a document by accessing WordPerfect's character sets. The WordPerfect character sets contain characters that are not on the keyboard, such as mathematical symbols, foreign letters, and graphics symbols. To insert a character or symbol from a WordPerfect character set, select **Font** from the Menu bar and choose **WP Characters**. There are fourteen character sets available containing over 1,500 characters and symbols.

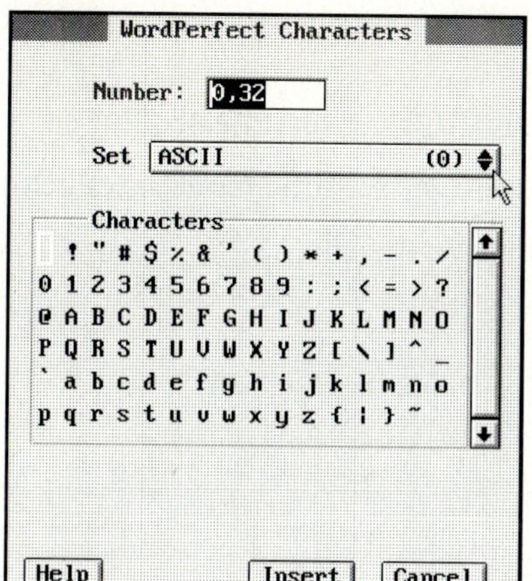

FIGURE 11.2

WordPerfect Characters
dialog box

Start-Up Instructions

❖ Type an **R** (to begin typing the word Résumé).

Insert Text Using WP Characters

1. Place the cursor/insertion point at the location where the special text character should be inserted.

   For example, the cursor/insertion point should be located immediately following the *R*.

2. Select **Font** on the Menu bar, select **WP Characters** {Ctrl and w}.

   Note: The WordPerfect Characters dialog box displays (see Figure 11.2).

3. Move the mouse pointer to the triangles in the Set box. Press and hold the left mouse button to drop down the list of available WP Character sets {Tab, s}.

4. Drag the mouse pointer to the desired WP Character set and release the mouse button {press the down or up arrow key until the desired character set is highlighted, Enter}.

   For example, point to **Multinational** and release the mouse button.

5. Move the mouse pointer to the desired special text character and click to select the character {c; use the arrow keys to locate the outline around the desired character}.

   For example, select the é.

   Note: An outline displays around the selected character.

6. Select **Insert** to copy the selected special text character into the document at the location of the cursor/insertion point {Enter}.

   Note: The WordPerfect Characters dialog box is removed from the screen and the selected special character is placed in the document.

Special Characters

- ❖ Type the letters sum. Use Steps 2-6 to insert the second é.
- ❖ Press the **Enter** key several times to insert some blank lines below the word Résumé.
- ❖ Use the filename **11drill1** and save the file.

Start-Up Instructions

- ❖ Type the following information:
  Technical Writer
  Copyeditor
  Assistant Copyeditor

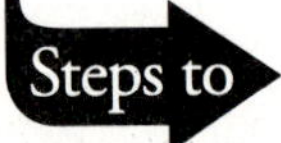

Insert Bullets Using WP Characters

1. Place the cursor/insertion point at the location where the bullet character will be inserted.

   For example, place the cursor/insertion point to the left of the *T* in *Technical.*

2. Select **Font** on the Menu bar, select **WP Characters** {Ctrl and w}.

3. Move the mouse pointer to the triangles in the Set box. Press and hold the left mouse button to drop down the list of available WP Character sets {Tab, s}.

4. Drag the mouse pointer to the desired WP Character set and release the mouse button {press the down or up arrow key until the desired character set is highlighted, Enter}.

   For example, point to **Math/Scientific** and release the mouse button.

5. Select the desired special text character {c, use the arrow keys to locate the outline around the desired character}.

   For example, scroll down and select the ♦.

   Note: It may be necessary to use the scroll bar located at the left of the Characters box to display the desired character.

6. Select **Insert** {Enter}.

Finish-Up Instructions

- ❖ Press the **F4** key to indent the text that follows the bullet character.
- ❖ Select the bullet character and the blank space ([Lft Indent] code) before the letter *T* (see Figure 11.3).
- ❖ Select **Edit, Copy** {Ctrl and c}.

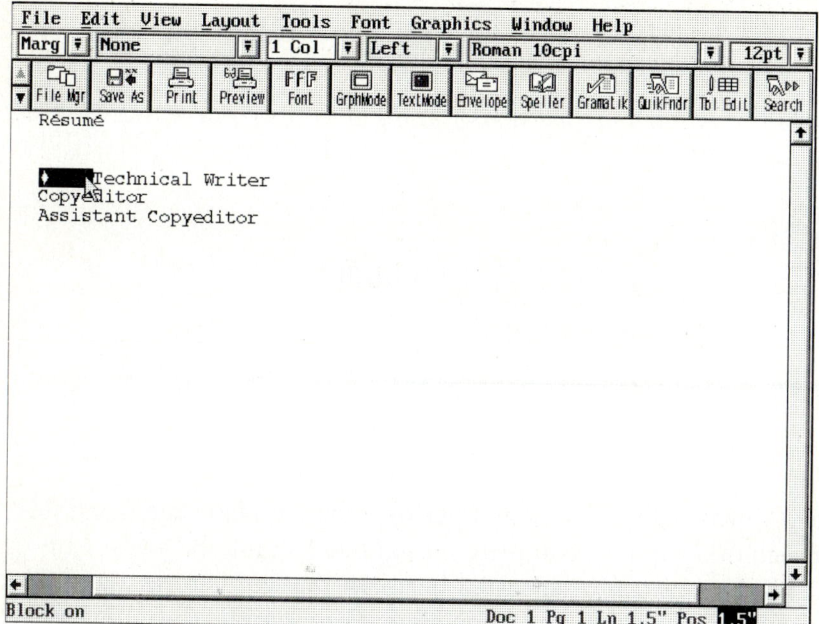

Selecting the bullet
character in the text

❖ Move the cursor/insertion point to the location where the bullet character should be inserted, e.g., place the cursor/insertion point to the left of the *C* in *Copyeditor.*

❖ Select **Edit, Paste** {Ctrl and v}.

❖ Insert the bullet character in front of the text *Assistant Copyeditor.*

❖ Save the file again using the same filename, **11drill1.**

Upper/Lowercase Change

After text has been typed, the WordPerfect program can automatically convert the case of the text to all uppercase characters, all lowercase characters, or initial capitals. First, the text to be converted is blocked, and then the **Edit, Convert Case** option is selected.

Start-Up Instructions

❖ The file named **11drill1** should be displayed on the screen.

Convert the Case of Characters

1. Block the text to be converted to uppercase or lowercase.

   For example, block the word **Résumé.**

2. Select **Edit, Convert Case** {Shift and F3}.

3. Select **Uppercase, Lowercase,** or **Initial Caps.**

For example, select **Uppercase** to convert all blocked text to uppercase characters {u}.

Note: *Although the É may not display as large as the other uppercase letters, the É will print correctly.*

Finish-Up Instructions

❖ Save the file again using the same filename, **11drill1**.

Hard Space

Sometimes two words, such as dates or a person's first and last names, are dependent on each other to be a complete thought and should be printed on the same line. A hard space can be inserted between the words to instruct Word-Perfect to always print the word(s) on the same line. For example, the date September 25, 199x, should print on the same line; therefore, a hard space is placed between September and 25 and between the comma and 199x. A hard space can also be referred to as a nonbreaking space.

Start-Up Instructions

❖ The file named **11drill1** should be displayed on the screen.

❖ Place the cursor/insertion point at the end of the document (**Home, Home, down arrow key**).

❖ Type the following information on a new line:

Assisted with the copyediting of a company newsletter and procedures manual. Was promoted to Assistant Copyeditor on May 1, 1987.

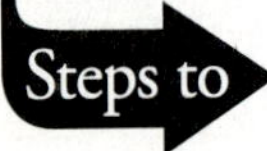

Insert a Hard Space

Note: *If the numeric keypad is used, Num Lock must be turned off in order for a hard space to be inserted. If necessary, press the Num Lock key to turn off Num Lock.*

1. Move the cursor/insertion point to the location where the hard space should be inserted.

   For example, place the cursor/insertion point immediately after the *y* in *May.*

2. Press the **Delete** (Del) key once to delete the space between letters.

3. Press the **Home** key and then press the **Spacebar** once (**Home, Spacebar**) to insert a hard space.

* Place the cursor/insertion point immediately after the comma that follows the number *1*. Repeat Steps 2 and 3 to insert a hard space.

* Turn on Reveal Codes to view the hard space [HSpace] code (**Alt** and **F3**). Turn off Reveal Codes (**Alt** and **F3**).

* Save the document again using the same filename, **11drill1**, and close the document.

Tabs

By default, tabs are set every half inch. If desired, tabs can be changed to indent information at a position other than those preset by the WordPerfect program. Tab locations are changed by selecting **Layout**, **Tab Set** and specifying the desired tab(s) type and locations in the Tab Set dialog box. There are four types of tabs available: left, center, right, and decimal. Dot leaders can be included with a tab if desired. Dot leaders are periods that display between tabbed information.

Tab locations can be measured from the left margin (relative) or from the left edge of the page (absolute). The default is relative tabs. With relative tabs, if the left margin is changed, the location of all tab(s) will also be changed. Therefore, the distance between the left margin and the tab location(s) will always remain the same. With absolute tabs, the location of the tabs does not change when the left margin is changed. Therefore, the distance between the left margin and the tab locations will change if the left margin is changed.

When creating a document, type the text and press the **Tab** key once between each section (column) of information. Once all the text is typed, tab settings can be adjusted using the Tab Set dialog box to create a readable, attractive presentation. Also, the WordPerfect table feature can be used to type and format each column of information (see Chapter 6 for information on converting existing text to a table).

After tabs are changed, the new tab settings can be viewed by turning on Reveal Codes. If necessary, all tab set codes can be deleted to return to the default tab settings.

Start-Up Instructions

* Type the information shown in Figure 11.4. Press the **Tab** key once at the beginning of each line and between each item in the lines. The tabbed text will not align. Press **Enter** twice after the last line of text.

* Use the filename **11drill2** and save the file.

Steps to ▶ Set Tabs

1. If text has been typed, place the cursor/insertion point where tabs are to be set.

NAMES AND PHONE NUMBERS OF REFERENCES

Robert T. Joyner	Coordinator	555-3488	3.5 years
Georgette McCoy	Supervisor	555-8119	2.25 years
Jesse Bridges	Director	206-555-5677	10.5 years
Muoi Tai	Vice-President	555-9006	.5 years

For example, place the cursor/insertion point in the blank line after the title.

2. Select **Layout, Tab Set** {Alt and L, b}.

   Note: The Tab Set dialog box displays (see Figure 11.5). The preset tabs are indicated by an L (left) located every half inch on the ruler at the top of the Tab Set dialog box.

3. Select **Clear All** to delete all the preset tabs {a}.

   Note: All tabs have been cleared from the ruler and the space between columns is temporarily removed.

4. Move the mouse pointer to the Set Tab box and click once. Type the desired tab location {s, type desired tab location}.

   For example, type **.25**. (Do not type the final period.)

   Note: Check that a black dot displays beside the Left option.

5. Double-click on the **Set Tab** box to set the tab location {press Enter}.

   Note: An L is placed on the tab ruler to indicate the position of the new tab.

6. Move the mouse pointer to the **Set Tab** box and click once. Type the desired tab location {s, type desired tab location}.

   For example, type **2.75**. (Do not type the final period.)

7. Select the desired tab alignment

   For example, select the **Center** option {press Enter, c}.

   Note: A C is placed on the tab ruler to indicate the position of the new center tab.

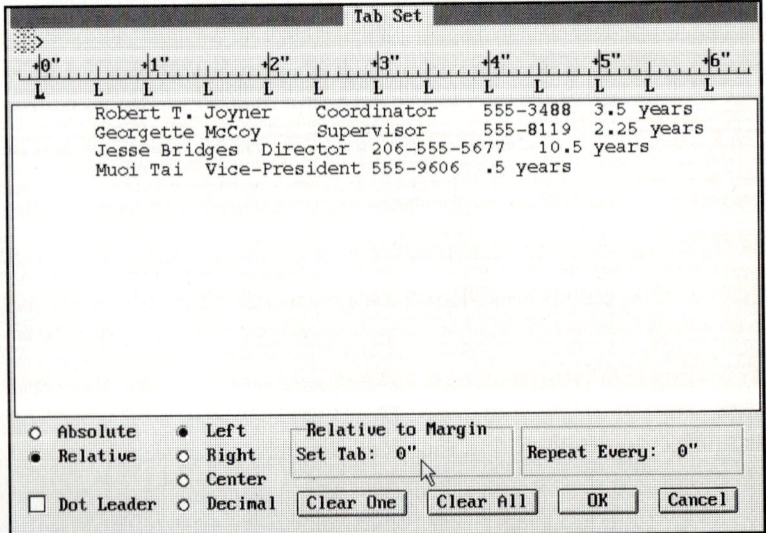

Chapter 11—Create a Résumé

8. Move the mouse pointer to the **Set Tab** box and click once. Type the desired tab location {s, type desired tab location}.

> For example, type **5.5**. (Do not type the final period.)

9. Select the desired tab alignment.

> For example, select the **Decimal** option {press Enter, d}.

Note: The decimals will align after the following tab is set.

Set a Tab Using the Tab Set Ruler

10. Move the mouse pointer to the desired tab location on the tab set ruler and click once {press the left or right arrow keys to move the underline character to the desired location on the ruler}.

> For example, move the mouse pointer to **5"** on the ruler and click.

Note: An underline character is placed below the tab set ruler, and the Set Tab box displays approximately 4.98".

11. Select the desired tab alignment.

> For example, select **Right** {r}.

12. Select **OK** to exit the Tab Set dialog box {F7}.

Note: The columns are aligned at each tab.

Finish-Up Instructions

❖ Save the file; use the filename **11drill2**.

❖ Print one copy and close the document.

Start-Up Instructions

❖ Open the file named **11drill1** created earlier in this chapter.

Set Tabs for a Block of Text

1. Block the text for which tabs are to be set.

> For example, block the three bulleted items.

2. Select **Layout, Tab Set** {Alt and L, b}.

3. Select **Clear All** to delete existing (default) tabs {a}.

4. Move the mouse pointer to the desired tab location on the tab set ruler and click once {press the right arrow key to move the underline character to the desired location}.

> For example, move the mouse pointer to **.4"** on the ruler and click. (The Set Tab box displays approximately .0367".)

5. Select the desired tab alignment.

FIGURE 11.6

Document with dot leader characters

For example, select the **Left** option {L}.

Insert a New Tab with Dot Leaders

6. Move the mouse pointer to the desired tab location on the ruler and click once {press the right arrow key to move the underline character to the desired location}.

   For example, move the mouse pointer to **6"** and click. (The Set Tab box displays approximately 5.98".)

7. Select the **Dot Leader** option {press a . (period)}.

8. Select the desired tab alignment.

   For example, select the **Right** option {r}.

9. Select **OK** {F7}.

   Note: Continue with the following Finish-Up Instructions to complete the typed information.

Finish-Up Instructions

❖ Place the cursor/insertion point to the right of the last character in the word *Writer*. Press the **Tab** key once.

   Note: Dot characters display from the end of the word **Writer** *to the right margin, and the insertion point is located at the right margin.*

❖ Type **June 199x.**

❖ Move the cursor/insertion point to the right of the last character in the next line, *Copyeditor*. Press the **Tab** key and type **February 1992.**

❖ Move the cursor/insertion point to the right of the last character in the final line, *Assistant Copyeditor*. Press the **Tab** key and type **August 1989.**

❖ Your document should look similar to Figure 11.6.

❖ Use the filename **11drill3** and save the file.

❖ Print one copy and close the document.

Steps to ▶ **Create Evenly Spaced Tabs**

Note: The following Steps to Create Evenly Spaced Tabs and Steps to Delete Tab Set Codes are for your information.

1. Place the cursor/insertion point at the location where the evenly spaced tabs are to be in effect.

2. Select **Layout, Tab Set** {Alt and L, b}.

3. Select Clear All to delete all existing tabs {a}.

4. Move the mouse pointer to the Repeat Every box and click once {p}.

5. Type the spacing desired between tabs.

6. Select OK {press Enter}.

Delete Tab Set Code

1. Turn on Reveal Codes (**Alt** and **F3**).

2. Highlight the tab set code [Tab Set...] to be deleted.

3. Press Delete.

Create a Résumé

❖ Use the following information to create the résumé shown in Figure 11.1 on page 300.

❖ Change the font to **Dutch 801 Roman (Speedo)**, **12-point**, or **make a choice of your own**. Use bold, italic, and underline text attributes as shown.

❖ Use the Tab Set dialog box to set a left tab **.25** and a right tab with dot leaders at **6.5**. (Do not type the final period.)

❖ Use special text and bullet characters as shown. The *é* is found in the Multinational character set and the (♦) is found in the Math/Scientific character set.

❖ Remember to use the **F4** key to indent paragraphs.

❖ Save the file on your file disk; use the filename **11drill4**.

❖ Print one copy.

❖ Close the document.

Create a Résumé Using the Tables Feature

A résumé can also be created using the Tables feature to format the information in parallel columns. The sideheadings, such as EMPLOYMENT EXPERIENCE, EDUCATIONAL BACKGROUND, HONORS, and REFERENCES, can be typed in the first column and related information can be placed in the second column. The widths of the table columns can be adjusted to accommodate headings and text. Some of the advantages of using parallel columns to

Résumé created using the Tables feature

RÉSUMÉ
MAXINE WENRICH
45 BLACKSTONE DRIVE
AVENEL, NJ 07001
(201) 555-4828

EMPLOYMENT EXPERIENCE	<u>Berkhard Newsletter</u>, Hillside, New Jersey. Full-time editor/reporter. Responsible for reporting and editing several industry newsletters. March 1991 to present. <u>The Trentonian</u>, Trenton, New Jersey. Part-time reporter. Responsibilities included covering municipal meetings and developing feature articles. November 1988 to March 1991.
EDUCATIONAL BACKGROUND	Camden Community College, Cherry Hill, New Jersey. A.A. Communications; specialized in journalism. Computer courses studied: Microsoft Word for Windows, WordPerfect, PageMaker, and Paradox. High School Diploma, Camden High School, Cherry Hill, New Jersey.
HONORS	Dean's Scholar, 1988. Member Beta Gamma, Honorary Scholastic Society.
REFERENCES	Available upon request.

format a résumé are ease of setup and formatting, ease of reading, and visual attractiveness.

Create a Résumé Using the Tables Feature

- ❖ Use the following information to create the résumé shown in Figure 11.7.
- ❖ Change the font to **Dutch 801 Roman (Speedo), 12-point**, or **make a choice of your own**. Use bold, italic, and underline text attributes as shown.
- ❖ Type and center the heading information.
- ❖ Create a table with two columns and seven rows. Decrease the width of column 1 and increase the width of column 2. Omit all table lines.
- ❖ Save the file on your file disk; use the filename **11drill5**.
- ❖ Print one copy.
- ❖ Close the document.

The Next Step

Chapter Review and Activities

FEATURES SUMMARY

FEATURES	ACTIONS	PAGE
Insert special characters	Select **Font, WP Characters**, choose the desired character set in the Set box, select the desired special character or bullet, choose **Insert**.	301
Convert case	Block text, select **Edit, Convert Case**, select **Uppercase, Lowercase**, or **Initial Caps**.	303
Insert a hard space	Press **Home, Spacebar**.	304
Set tabs	Select **Layout, Tab Set**. Select **Clear All** to delete existing tabs. Click in the **Set Tab** box and type the desired tab location or move the mouse pointer to the tab set ruler and click at the desired location. Select the tab alignment type. If desired, select the **Dot Leader** option. Select **OK** when all tabs have been set.	305
Set evenly spaced tabs	Select **Layout, Tab Set**. Select **Clear All**. Click in the **Repeat Every** box and type the desired spacing between tabs, select **OK**.	308
Delete tab set code	Press **Alt** and **F3** to turn on Reveal Code, highlight the tab set code to be deleted, press **Delete**.	309

True/False—Circle One

T F 1. Tabs are set by default every inch.

T F 2. The four tab types are left, center, decimal, and right.

T F 3. A hard space between words instructs WordPerfect to always print both words on the same line.

T F 4. Changing from uppercase to lowercase letters or vice versa can be accomplished by pressing **F3**.

T F 5. The WordPerfect Characters dialog box is accessed by selecting **Font, WP Characters.**

Short Answer

1. In which WP Character set are the following symbols located?

   é   ♦   ➥   ✎   ©

2. Why is a hard space inserted between words in a document?

3. What is the difference between relative and absolute tabs?

4. List the four steps necessary to set a new tab with dot leader characters.

5. List the six steps you would use to insert the ♦ character into a document.

Enriching Language Arts Skills

Spelling/Vocabulary Words

implement   to carry out; to set in motion.
incentive   that which inspires action; motivation.
promotional   a way of publicizing a product or service.
wholesalers   people who sell in large amounts to retailers.

Commas Used in a Series

Words and/or ideas listed in a series are separated by commas.

Example:

The mailing list was sent to Karen Smith, Georgia Cain, and Perry Arnston.

Activities

Activity 11.1—Create a Résumé, Set Tabs, and Insert Special Characters

1. Use the following information and type the résumé shown.

   a. Change the left and right margins to **1.25"**; change the top margin to **1.5"** (select **Layout**, **Margins**, type desired margins, **OK**).

   b. Clear all existing tabs and set a left tab at .3 and a right tab with dot leaders at 6 (select **Layout**, **Tab Set**, **Clear All**, click in the Set Tab box and type .3, press **Enter**; click in the **Set Tab** box, type 6, select **Right** alignment, select **Dot Leader**, select **OK**) .

   c. Change the font to **Dutch 801 Roman (Speedo), 12-point**, or **make a choice of your own.**

   d. Use bold and underline text attributes as shown.

   e. Use special text characters for the *é*s in *Résumé* (select **Font**, **WP Characters**). The *é* is found in the Multinational character set.

Résumé
Olivia R. Norton
2634 Mississippi Avenue
Ft. Pierce, FL 33451

<u>EDUCATIONAL BACKGROUND</u>

A.A. Business, Indian River Community College 1/92
◆ Major courses: Accounting, Business Law, Office Management, Word Processing, and Telecommunications.

G.E.D., Tampa, Florida 1990

<u>SPECIAL SKILLS</u>

Shorthand: 100 words per minute; typing: 80 words per minute; WordPerfect and Microsoft Word on an IBM PC. Experience with Windows and Microsoft Excel.

<u>EMPLOYMENT EXPERIENCE</u>

Delcon Corporation, Ft. Pierce, Florida
◆ Office Assistant 3/92-Present
General backup support for sales department. Responsibilities include answering phones, typing correspondence using WordPerfect, maintaining files, processing mail, making travel arrangements, and entering expense data into an Excel spreadsheet.

Indian River Community College, Ft. Pierce, Florida

◆ Clerk Typist (part-time) 12/90-1/92
Responsible for keyboarding notices of faculty meetings, board minutes, and special reports. Filed office materials using alpha/numeric system.

<u>REFERENCES</u>

Available upon request.

---

2. Use the filename **11act1** and save the file.

3. Print one copy and close the document.

Activity 11.2—Create and Edit a Résumé Using the Tables Feature

1. Use the Tables feature and the following information to type the résumé shown.

   a. Use bold and underline text attributes as shown.

   b. Select a font of your own choice in a point size of 12.

   c. Use special text characters for the *É*s *in RÉSUMÉ*. The *É* is found in the Multinational character set.

RÉSUMÉ
W. KEVIN KINCAID
172 VINE STREET, APT. 12
ATLANTA, GA 30314

Education	Georgia State, Atlanta, Georgia B.S. Business Administration, Minor in Psychology Studied microcomputer applications: Lotus, dBase IV, Word, and Ventura. Also studied BASIC, PASCAL, and C programming languages. 5/93

Experience   Goldman Research, Hapeville, Georgia (part-time)
Responsible for interviewing prospective panel members for the firm. Handled public relations as a host and supervised numerous focus groups. 9/92-4/93

GTE Service Corporation, Macon, Georgia
Worked with a small group of individuals on a project to develop a computer-based Vertical Services costing model used to develop costs of a new company telephone service. Summer 1992

Southern National Bank, Atlanta, Georgia (part-time)
Worked in the Customer Service Department. Answered phones, distributed mail, and researched microfiche documents to verify answers to customer questions. 10/89-5/92

Activities   Member of Voyagers Club, Newton Math Society, and Tau Sigma Kappa (Computer Honor Society).

References   Available upon request.

---

2. Use the filename **11act2** and save the file.

3. Use the following information and edit the résumé.

    a. Change the sideheadings to all uppercase letters.

    b. Insert and center the phone number (404) 555-2438 beneath the city, state, and zip code.

    c. Delete the words "Available upon request" that follow the References sideheading.

    d. Insert the following two references:

        Cynthia Bates, Office Supervisor
        Goldman Research
        390 Walker St.
        Hapeville, GA 30354
        (404) 555-8901

        Rubin Cortez, Bank Manager
        Southern National Bank
        2012 Spring NW
        Atlanta, GA 30318
        (404) 555-2200

4. Use the filename **11act2r** and save the file.

5. Print one copy and close the document.

1. Create your own résumé using Figure 11.1 or Figure 11. 7 as a guide.

2. If necessary, use margin changes to increase or decrease the amount of text that will fit on a page. For example, if your résumé is short, it may be desirable to increase the left, right, and top margins. If your résumé is long, decrease the top, bottom, left, and right margins.

3. Remember to insert special characters for the word *résumé*.

4. Use font changes to enhance the appearance of your résumé.

5. Use the Speller and proofread carefully.

6. Use the filename **11act3** and save the file.

7. Print one copy and close the document.

Challenge Your Skills

Skill 11.1—Create a Résumé, Set Tabs, and Insert Special Characters

1. Use the following information to type the résumé shown.

   a. Change the top margin to .75" and the bottom margin to .5"; reduce the left and right margins by .25" each.

   b. Clear all tabs. Set left tabs at .25" and .5" and set a right tab with dot leaders at the right margin.

   c. Use the bold and italic text attributes as shown.

   d. Select a symbol from the Math/Scientific character set. Insert the chosen symbol in front of each indented paragraph.

Résumé
Randall McChesney
3845 West 23rd Place
Chicago, IL 60623
(312) 555-3841

EDUCATIONAL BACKGROUND

Northwestern University, Evanston, Illinois 6/92
Candidate for Masters of Management degree. Concentration in marketing and finance. Member of the Finance Club and Black Management Association.

B.A. Economics, Spelman College, Atlanta, Georgia 5/90
Sun Oil Scholar, Avon Scholar, and recipient of four-year Honors Program Scholarship.
President of Economics Club.

EMPLOYMENT EXPERIENCE

Wyle Services, Inc., Chicago, Illinois
Corporate Planning Assistant 8/90-Present
Review and analyze the strategic plans, prepare presentations for senior management,
and evaluate Wyle's presence in Japan with respect to imports, exports, and net income.

Stein Roe & Farnham Mutual Funds, Inc., Chicago, Illinois
Summer Intern 1989
Prepared new account reports and analyzed the flow of dollars into the funds. Utilized
Microsoft Excel and MacDraw microcomputer programs for the Macintosh computer.

Prudential Insurance Co., Chicago, Illinois
Claims Representative 6/85-8/86
Initiated correspondence between the company and municipalities, made arrangements
for outside adjusters to inspect cars and homes, and settled claims over the telephone.

REFERENCES

Mrs. Roberta Anzac, Manager
Prudential Insurance Co.
1290 Michigan Ave.
Chicago, IL 60600
(312) 555-5000 ext, 3423

Mr. Benjamin Harpreet
Corporate Planner
121 Adams West
Chicago, IL 60604
(312) 555-6200

---

2.   Use the filename **11skill1** and save the file.

3.   Print one copy and close the document.

☙ Skill 11.2—Create a Résumé with Special Characters; Language Arts

1.   Create a résumé for Carlene Quevedo using the following information.

  a. Make decisions regarding:

   Résumé format
   Margins

Tab settings and indentions
Fonts
Hard spaces
Uppercase and lowercase headings
Bold and italic text attributes
Special characters
References
Correct four spelling and two punctuation errors

b. Carlene lives at 570 Betner Dr., Mansfield, OH 44907 (419) 555-8387.

c. Carlene graduated in 1988 with a B.A. in Political Science from Ohio State University, Columbus, OH. She is currently a master's degree candidate in Business Administration at Ohio State University, Columbus, OH.

d. Carlene's work experience is as follows:

Hayden Services, Network Services Department, Mansfield, OH
Product Developer
7/90-Present

Job responsibilities include: develop and impliment the insentive program for the Smart Ring product line. Specifically, develop the tracking systems and implementation booklet for the program.

J. M. Smucker Company, Orrville, OH
District Sales Manager
9/88-6/90

Job responsibilities included managing food brokers over a five-state region, including training for office and sales staff. Assisted in sales presentations and customer relations. Responsible for personal selling to large restaurants, hotels and food service chains.

Also at J. M. Smucker Company, Carlene worked as a part-time sales representative in the Columbus district from 6/86-9/88. Her responsibilities were: direct contact with grocery retailers and wholesalors; introduction of new products, presentation of promottional deals, and maintenance of customer relations.

e. Carlene's references are:

Marly Lawson, Hayden Services, 30 Park Ave. West, Mansfield, OH 44902 (419) 555-4550

Norman P. Costello, Jr., J.M. Smucker Company, 689 Main St., Orrville, OH 44667 (216) 555-8799

2. Use the filename **11skill2** and save the file.

3. Print one copy.

4. If you have completed your work, exit WordPerfect.

Create a Form Letter and Mailing List

Features Covered

- Form (primary) file
- Data (secondary) file
- Merging files
- Fields
- Records
- Edit data and form files
- Mark a record(s) by field

Objectives

After successfully completing this chapter, you will be able to create and merge a data table file and form file. You will also understand fields and records and learn how to remove the blank line that results from an empty field. In addition, you will be able to edit data table and form files and mark records by fields.

Chapter Introduction

A form letter is a standard letter that is sent to many individuals or companies. The same letter can be typed once, merged with a list of names and addresses, and printed. A form letter can be used for collecting overdue accounts, requesting donations, presenting product information, etc. The form letter is referred to as the form file. The list of names and addresses is referred to as the data file.

A data table file with field names and data

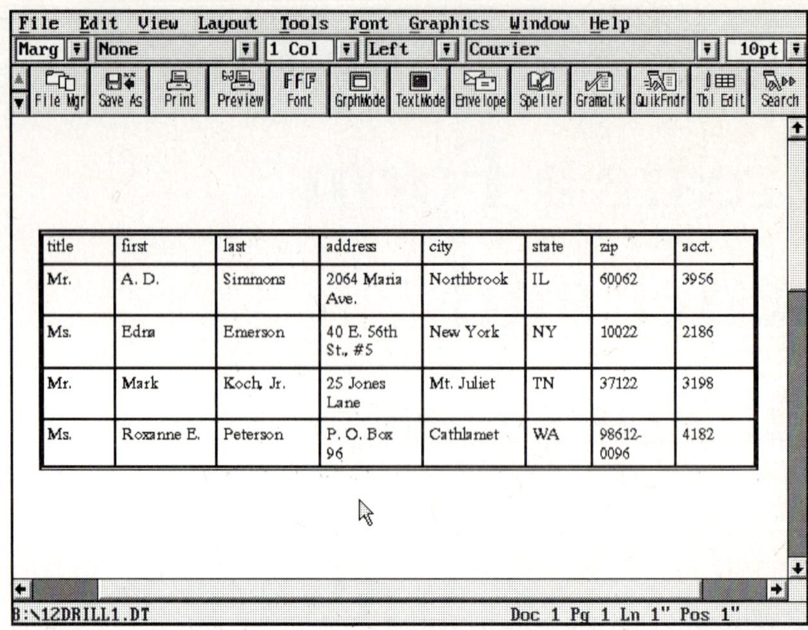

title	first	last	address	city	state	zip	acct.
Mr.	A. D.	Simmons	2064 Maria Ave.	Northbrook	IL	60062	3956
Ms.	Edna	Emerson	40 E. 56th St., #5	New York	NY	10022	2186
Mr.	Mark	Koch, Jr.	25 Jones Lane	Mt. Juliet	TN	37122	3198
Ms.	Roxanne E.	Peterson	P. O. Box 96	Cathlamet	WA	98612-0096	4182

Create a Data File

The *data file* is a group of variables and merge field names. A variable is the information that changes in each form letter and can include names, addresses, dollar amounts, dates, special comments, etc. The variable information is referred to as data. The data file can be either a text or table file. If a text data file is used, each variable displays on a separate line followed by a code. If a table data file is used, the variable information is placed in table cells (see Figure 12.1). A table data file is recommended because it is easier to create, proofread, and edit.

A *field* is the name given to a variable; for example, a dollar amount field can be named "dollar." Field names should be determined before beginning the process to create a data file. The field names in the data file must correlate exactly with the field names in the form file. All the fields that pertain to one individual are referred to as a record. A record is a single "set" of information, e.g., one individual's first name, last name, company, address, city, state, and zip code.

To begin creating the data table file, choose the **Tools**, **Merge**, **Define** option. The **Data Table Options** is selected and the Merge Codes (Table Data File) dialog box displays. Choose **Create a Table with Field Names.** The Field Names dialog box displays and each field name is entered separately in the File Name box. After selecting **OK**, a table displays with the field names in row 1 and empty cells in row 2. The data for each field of the first record is entered into the appropriate cells. When the **Tab** key is pressed after the last cell entry, a new row displays. When the data for all recipients are typed, the data table is saved and the file can be closed.

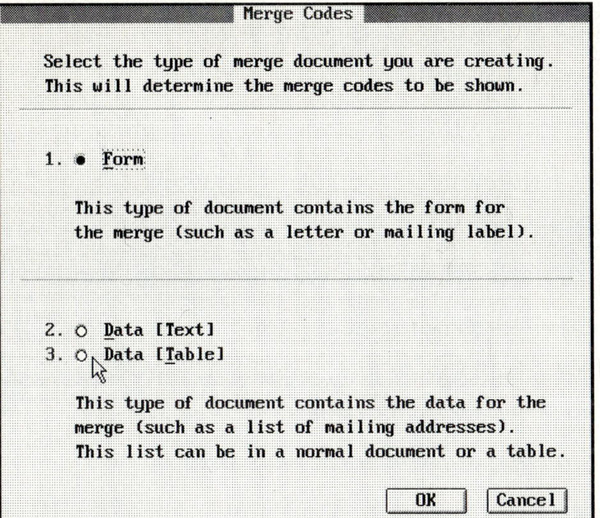

FIGURE 12.2

Merge Codes dialog box

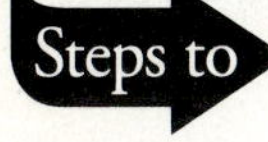

Steps to ▶ Create a Data Table File

1. Decide on a name for each field.

   For example, title, first, last, co, address, city, state, zip, and acct#.

2. Select **Tools, Merge, Define** {Shift and F9}.

   Note: The Merge Codes dialog box displays (see Figure 12.2).

3. Select **Data [Table]** {t}.

   Note: The Merge Codes (Table Data File) dialog box displays.

4. Select **Create a Table with Field Names** {n}.

   Note: The Field Names dialog box displays (see Figure 12.3).

5. Create each field as follows:

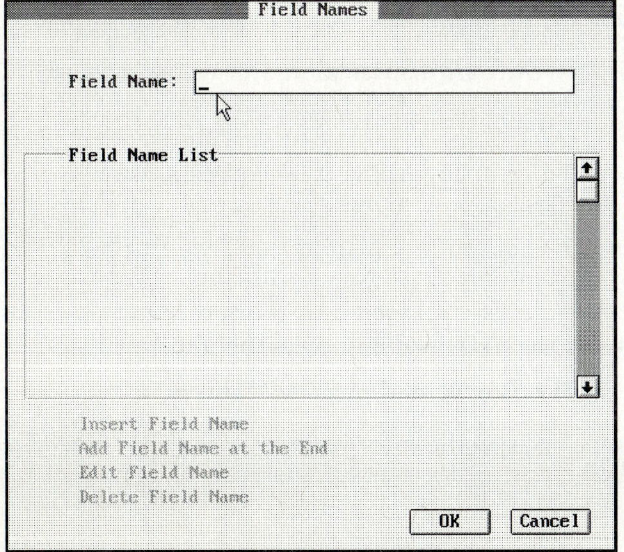

FIGURE 12.3

Field Names dialog box

a. Type the name of the first field in the Field Name box.

For example, type **title**.

b. Press **Enter** to display the field name in the Field Name List box.

c. Type the next field name in the Field Name box.

For example, type **first**.

d. Press **Enter** to display the field name in the Field Name List box.

6. Repeat Step 5a-d to add the remaining field names.

For example, add the field names **last, co, address, city, state, zip,** and **acct#**. (Do not type the final period.)

Note: If the field names are in a different order, that's OK.

7. Select **OK** {Enter twice}.

Note: The lowercase field names display in the first row of a two-row table. The cursor/insertion point is located in the first cell of row 2. The text may wrap around in the table cells.

8. Press **Home** and the up arrow key once and change the font to **Dutch 801 Roman (Speedo), 10-point**.

9. With the cursor/insertion point in the first cell of row 2, type the information for the first field.

For example, type the recipient's title: **Ms.**

10. Press the **Tab** key to move the cursor/insertion point to the next cell.

11. Type the information for the second field.

For example, type the recipient's first name and, if available, middle initial: **Roxanne E.**

12. Press the **Tab** key to move the cursor/insertion point to the next cell.

13. Type the information for the third field.

For example, type the recipient's last name: **Peterson.**

14. Press the **Tab** key to move the cursor/insertion point to the next cell.

15. Type the information for the next field.

For example, type the company name. If no company name is available, press the **Tab** key.

*Note: When information for a field is not available, press the **Tab** key to skip to the next cell.*

16. Type the information for the next field and press the **Tab** key.

For example, type **P.O. Box 96** and press the **Tab** key.

17. Repeat Step 16 and type the specific information for the city, state, zip, and acct# fields:

Cathlamet	Tab
WA	Tab
98612-0096	Tab
4182	Tab

*Note: When the **Tab** key is pressed after the last column entry, a new row displays.*

18. Repeat steps 9-17 and enter the field information for the following two records.

Mr.	Tab
Mark	Tab
Koch, Jr.	Tab
Abby, Inc.	Tab
25 Jones Lane	Tab
Mt. Juliet	Tab
TN	Tab
37122	Tab
3198	Tab

Ms.	Tab
Ester	Tab
Emerson	Tab
	Tab
40 E 56th St., #5	Tab
New York	Tab
NY	Tab
10022	Tab
2186	Tab

Finish-Up Instructions

❖ Use the filename **12drill1.dt** and save the file to your file disk.

❖ Close the document.

Create a Form File

A *form (primary) file* is a letter containing the information that remains the same in each letter (see Figure 12.4). The form file also includes the *field names* that correspond to the variable information that will print in each letter. Field names that exactly match the data file field names are placed in the form file to indicate the specific location for each field.

Since field information in a data file can vary, WordPerfect has provided special instructions that give the user more control over the varying information. Some fields in a data file can be empty; for example, a company field may not be needed in all

(insert dates code)

FIELD(FIRST) **FIELD**(LAST)
FIELD(CO)
FIELD(ADDRESS)
FIELD(CITY), **FIELD**(STATE) **FIELD**(ZIP)

Dear **FIELD**(NAME):

Thank you for your World Club card membership. Your account number is **FIELD**(ACCT#).

I want to take this opportunity to inform you of our new service, Account Registry. With this service, we will inform all of your card issuers in the event that your wallet is lost or stolen. You will only have to make one phone call.

A brochure describing the Account Registry program features and costs as well as an enrollment form are enclosed.

I urge you to take advantage of this convenient service and sign up today.

Sincerely,

Frazer M. Horwitz
Vice President

FMH/xx
12drill1.frm/diska

Enc.

form letters. Blank cells in the data table file indicate the fields that contain no data. When the data and form files are prepared for merging, **Data File Options** can be selected in the Run Merge dialog box (see Steps to Merge a Form File and Data Table File later in this chapter). When the **Remove Resulting Blank Line** option is chosen in the Blank Files box of the Run Merge dialog box, the hard returns that ordinarily result from a blank field will not be placed in the merged letter.

A form letter can be used over and over again with the date set up to change with each use. The date code is inserted in the form file at the location where the current date is to print. When the **Tools, Date, Code** is used in a document, the current date is automatically printed in the letter. The date code [Date…] can be viewed using Reveal Codes.

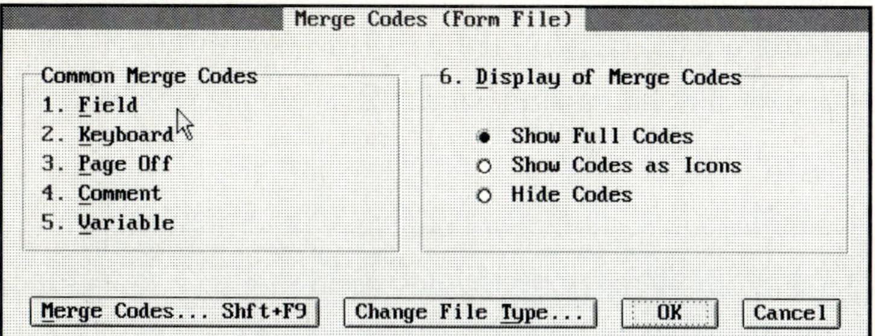

FIGURE 12.5

Merge Codes (Form File)
dialog box

Steps to ▶ Create a Form File

1. Select **Tools, Date, Code** to place the date code and the current date in the document {Shift and F5, c} and press **Enter** five times.

2. Select **Tools, Merge, Define** {Shift and F9}.

   Note: The Merge Codes dialog box displays.

3. Select **Form** {Enter}.

   Note: The Merge Codes (Form File) dialog box displays (see Figure 12.5).

4. Select **Field** {f}.

   Note: The Parameter Entry dialog box displays.

5. Select **List Field Names** {F5}.

   Note: The Select Data File for Field Names dialog box displays.

6. Press **F5** to select File List.

   Note: The Select List dialog box and the drive accessed displays in the Directory box. If necessary, type the disk drive letter followed by a colon.

7. Select **OK** {Enter}.

8. Double-click on the name of the desired data file {highlight the data filename, Enter}.

   For example, double-click on the data file named **12drill1.dt**.

   Note: A List Field Names dialog box displays with an alphabetized list of the field names created in the data file.

9. Double-click on the desired field name {highlight the field name, Enter}.

   For example, double-click on **TITLE** and press the **Spacebar** once.

   *Note: The **FIELD** code and field name TITLE display in the document window.*

10. Select **Tools, Merge, Define** {Shift and F9}.

11. Select **Field** {f}.

12. Select **List Field Names** {F5}.

13. Double-click on the desired field name {highlight the field name, Enter}.

   For example, double-click on **FIRST** and press the **Spacebar** once.

   Note: The FIELD code and field name first display in the document window.

14. Repeat Steps 10-13 and double-click on the next field name.

> For example, double-click on the field name **LAST** and press **Enter.**

15. Repeat Steps 10-13 and double-click on the next field name.

> For example, double-click on the field name **CO** and press **Enter.**

16. Repeat Steps 10-13 and double-click on the next field name.

> For example, double-click on the field name **ADDRESS** and press **Enter.**

17. Repeat Steps 10-13 and double-click on the next field name.

> For example, double-click on the field names **CITY**, **STATE**, and **ZIP**. Be sure to type a comma after the city field name and to press the **Spacebar** once between each field name. After the ZIP field has been selected, press **Enter** twice, type **Dear** and press the **Spacebar** once.

18. Repeat Steps 10-13 and double-click on the next field name.

> For example, double-click the field name **TITLE** and press the **Spacebar** once.

19. Repeat Steps 10-13 and double-click on the next field name.

> For example, double-click on the field name **LAST** and type a colon.

Finish-Up Instructions

❖ Continue to type the first paragraph of the letter body text shown in Figure 12.4. Repeat Steps 10-13 to create a field for **ACCT#**. Remember to place a space before the account field and to type a period after the account field. Press **Enter** twice before typing the second paragraph.

❖ Type the remaining letter body text.

❖ Place the cursor/insertion point at the top of the document (press the **Home** key three times and the up arrow key once) and change the top margin to **1.5"**; change the left and right margins to **1.25"**.

❖ Save the file as **12drill1.frm**.

❖ Close the document.

Merge a Form and Data Table File

Once the form and data files are created and saved, a new document window is obtained. Usually, the form and data files are closed, but can be open in other windows (see Chapter 17). To combine the form and data files, **Tools, Merge, Run** is selected and the name and location of the form and data files are placed in the Run Merge dialog box. If desired, **Data File Options** is selected in order to choose the option **Remove Resulting Blank Line**. When the form and data

   Chapter 12—Create a Form Letter and Mailing List

file are merged, if a blank field is encountered in the data file table and the **Remove Resulting Blank Line** option is selected, no blank line will display in the merged letter. The form and data files are merged by selecting **Merge**. All the merged letters display in the current window with each letter separated by a hard page break.

Each time WordPerfect is loaded and the Run Merge dialog box is accessed for the first time, a short version of the Run Merge dialog box displays. The disk drive letter where the form file is located and the form filename are typed in the Form File box, e.g., 12drill1.frm. After the **Enter** is pressed, the drive letter and filename of the data file automatically display. (If the filename displayed is not the desired name, delete the name in the Data File box and type the desired name.) The **Merge** option can be selected at this point; however, additional data file options are often desired. Once **Data File Options** is chosen, the expanded Run Merge dialog box displays (see Figure 12.6).

If **Merge**, **Run** is selected a second time, the expanded version of the Run Merge dialog box displays with the prior form and data filename and previously selected options automatically displayed. WordPerfect's ability to remember the previously requested merge information assists the user by saving time when the merge process is performed more than once.

If an addressed envelope is desired for each merged letter, **Generate an Envelope for Each Data Record** is selected in the Run Merge dialog box. See Chapter 13 for information on how to print mailing labels and envelope addresses.

Once the form and data files have been merged, check each of the merged letters for accuracy. If errors have occurred in any of the merged letters, close (but do not save) the merged file and access the form or data file to make corrections. Once the necessary corrections have been made, the form and/or data file is saved again; a new document window is obtained; and the form and data files are merged again. If desired, the merged letters can be saved; however, saving the merged letters is not recommended since the same information has previously been saved in the form and data files.

A copy of each letter is printed using the normal print feature. Since a hard page break is placed between each letter, each letter will print on a separate page. If only one or two of the merged letters are to be printed, see Steps to Mark and Merge Specific Data Records.

After the form file is merged with the data file, printed copies of the form and data files can be very useful for filing or reference purposes. If desired, the data file table text and structure can be changed to display the information in a more attractive and readable manner. For example, widening the columns, selecting a smaller font, and/or changing the table position to Full will assist in making the table easier to read.

Start-Up Instructions

❖   The form file **12drill1.frm** and the secondary file **12drill1.dt** must have been created and saved before beginning the Steps to Merge a Form File and Data Table File.

Steps to Merge a Form File and Data Table File

1. In an empty document window, select **Tools, Merge, Run** {Ctrl and F9, m}.

   Note: The short version of the Run Merge dialog box displays and the cursor is located in the Form File box. If **Merge, Run** *has previously been selected, skip to Step 7.*

2. Type the name of the form file (if necessary, include the disk drive letter followed by a colon).

   For example, type **a:12drill1.frm.**

3. Press the **Enter** key once.

   Note: After a moment, the name of the data file should display in the Data File box. If necessary, type the data filename.

4. Select **Data File Options** {press Tab, t}.

   Note: The expanded Run Merge dialog box displays (see Figure 12.6).

5. Select **Blank Fields in Data File** {b}.

6. Select **Remove Resulting Blank Line** {press the down arrow key once, Enter}.

7. Check that the **Page Break Between Merged Records** and **All Records** options are selected.

8. Select **Merge** {Enter}.

   Note: A message in the Status bar briefly displays, "Merging Record 1, 2," etc. After a few moments, all merged letters display on the screen. The cursor/insertion point is located after the last letter. A hard page break displays between each letter. Each letter will print on a separate page.

FIGURE 12.6

Run Merge dialog box (expanded)

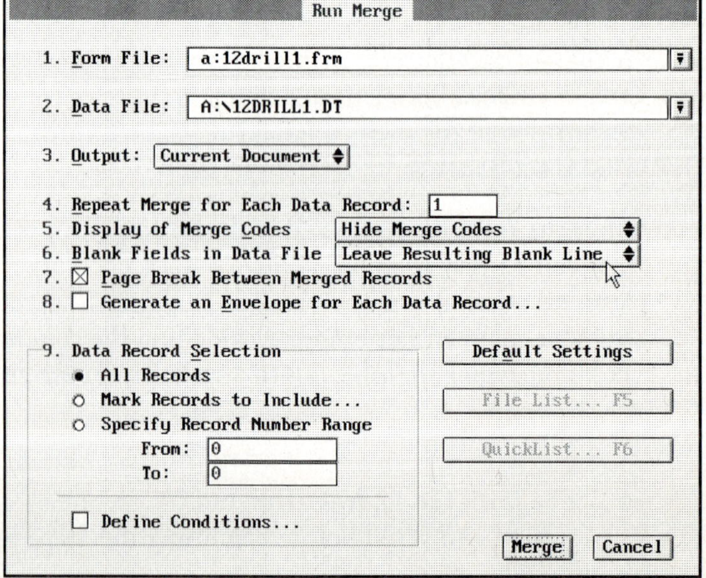

  Chapter 12—Create a Form Letter and Mailing List

- ❖ Press **Home** twice and the up arrow key once to locate the cursor/insertion point at the beginning of the first merged letter.

- ❖ Proofread the letters and check that the addresses, names, and variable information are placed correctly in the letter.

- ❖ Print the merged letters. A copy of each letter will be printed.

- ❖ Close the merged letter document.

Edit Data Table and Form Files

Often the information in a data table and/or form file must be altered. The data table file is changed by adding and/or deleting a record(s) or field(s). The data in any field can be updated or altered. A form file can also be changed by deleting or inserting fields and/or by changing the text of the document. The record information in the data table and the text of the form file can be altered using normal editing procedures. To add or delete a field(s) in a data table, select **Tools, Merge, Define** and make the necessary additions or deletions in the Table Edit dialog box. To add a field in a form file, select **Tools, Merge, Define** and follow Steps 10-13 of the Steps to Create a Form File to insert the new field name. An edited form or data file must be saved again before merging.

Once a form or data file is changed, all or specific data file records can be merged with the form file. The records can be viewed by a specific field name and the modified records marked and merged. If a specific range of records is to be merged, the **Specify Record Number Range** option is selected in the Run Merge dialog box, then the record (row) number of the first record to be merged is typed in the From box and the record (row) number of the last record to be merged is typed in the To box. For example, if records 2-4 are to be merged, 2 is typed in the From box and 4 is typed in the To box.

Start-Up Instructions

- ❖ The form file **12drill1.frm** and the secondary file **12drill1.dt** must have been created and saved before beginning the Steps to Edit a Data Table File.

Edit a Data Table File

1. The data table file to be edited should be displayed in the document window.

   For example, open the data table file named **12drill1.dt**.

2. Place the cursor/insertion point in the cell of the column or row to be edited.

   For example, place the cursor/insertion in any cell in the column with the field name **co**.

3. Select **Tools, Merge, Define** {Shift and F9}.

4. Select the desired option in the Table Edit box.

> For example, select **Delete a Column** {c}.

> *Note: The column is immediately deleted. If a mistake is made, select **Edit, Undo** before performing another action.*

5. Repeat Steps 2-4 as necessary to make other changes to the data table file.

> For example, place the cursor/insertion point in any cell in row 2.
> Select **Tools, Merge, Define**, and choose **Add a Row (above)**.
> Type the following record information into the new row cells:
> **Mr. A.D. Simmons, 2064 Maria Ave., Northbrook, IL 60062, 3956.**

6. When all the editing is complete, save the data table file again using the same filename.

> For example, save the file named **12drill1.dt**.

Edit a Form File

1. The form file to be edited should be displayed in the document window.

> For example, open the form file named **12drill1.frm**.

2. Delete or insert the desired text and/or fields.

> For example, block and delete **FIELD(co)** and the following hard
> return in the second line of the letter address fields.

3. When all the editing is complete, save the form file again using the same filename.

> For example, save the file named **12drill1.frm**.

Finish-Up Instructions

❖ Close all open documents.

Start-Up Instructions

❖ The form file **12drill1.frm** and the data file **12drill1.dt** must have been created and saved before beginning the Steps to Mark and Merge Specific Data Records.

Mark and Merge Specific Data Records

1. Select **Tools, Merge, Run** {Ctrl and F9, m}.

> *Note: If the files were previously merged, skip to Step 4.*

2. Type the name of the form file (if necessary, include the disk drive letter followed by a colon) and press **Enter**.

For example, type **a:12drill1.frm** and press **Enter**.

Note: The name of the data file should display in the Data File box. If necessary, type the data filename, 12drill1.df.

3. Select **Data File Options** {press Tab, t}.

    Note: The expanded Run Merge dialog box displays.

4. Select the desired option in the Data Record Selection box.

    For example, choose **Mark Records to Include** {s, m}.

    Note: If the files were marked previously, skip to Step 6.

5. Double-click on the field name to be used when viewing the records to be marked {press the down arrow key to highlight the desired field name, Enter}.

    For example, double-click on **LAST**.

6. Double-click on the record to be marked {highlight the record, press m}.

    For example, double-click on the **Simmons** record.

    Note: An asterisk displays to the left of the marked file(s).

7. When all desired records have been marked, select **OK** {press Tab, Enter}.

8. Select **Merge** {Enter}.

    *Note: After a moment, the marked/merged letter displays. If desired, press **Page Up** to display the top portion of the letter.*

Finish-Up Instructions

❖ Optional. Print the merged letter.

❖ Close the document (do not save the merged letter).

The Next Step

Chapter Review and Activities

FEATURES SUMMARY

FEATURES	ACTIONS	PAGE
Create a data table file	Decide on field names. Select **Tools**, **Merge**, **Define**, **Data Table**, **Create a Table with Field Names**. Type each field name followed by an **Enter**. Select **OK**. Type the field data into the appropriate cells (press the **Tab** key to move from cell to cell and row to row). Save the file.	321
Create a form file	If desired, select **Tools**, **Date**, **Code** to insert the current date into the form file and press Enter five times. Select **Tools**, **Merge**, **Define**, **Form**. Select **Field**, **List Field Names**. Press **F5** and select **OK**. Double-click on the desired data filename. Double-click on the desired field name. Continue selecting each field name desired, adding spacing, Enters, and text as needed. Save the file.	325
Merge a form and data table file	Select **Tools**, **Merge**, **Run**. Type the disk drive followed by a colon and the form filename. Press **Enter**. If necessary, select **Data File Options**, **Blank Fields in Data File**, **Remove Resulting Blank Lines**. Select **Merge**.	328
Edit a data table file	With the data table file on the screen, place the cursor/insertion point in the column or row to be edited and select **Tools**, **Merge**, **Define**. Select the desired action in the Table Edit box. Save the edited file.	329

Chapter 12—Create a Form Letter and Mailing List

FEATURES *(cont'd.)*	ACTIONS *(cont'.d)*	PAGE
Edit a form file	With the form file on the screen, insert or delete the text or fields to be changed. Save the edited file.	330
Mark and merge specific data records	Select **Tools, Merge, Run**, type the disk drive letter followed by a colon and the filename of the form file, press **Enter**. Select **Data File Options**, select **Mark Records to Include**. Double-click on the field name to use when viewing the record to be marked. Double-click on the record(s) to be marked. Select **OK**. Select **Merge**.	330

Self-Check Questions

True/False—Circle One

T F 1. A form letter is usually sent to more than one individual or company.

T F 2. A data file usually contains the field names and the records for each recipient.

T F 3. A field name is the filename given to the data table file.

T F 4. The form file contains the variable information for each record.

T F 5. To print the current date each time the form file is merged with the data table file, select **Tools, Merge, Code**.

Short Answer

1. State the difference between a record and a field.

2. List three examples of variable information.

3. The form file contains the letter text, ______________, spacing, and any other information that remains the same in each letter.

4. List the main advantages of using the date code in a letter.

5. Write down the name of the option in the Run Merge dialog box that omits a blank line that results from an empty data file field.

Enriching Language Arts Skills

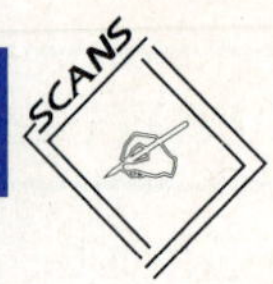

Spelling/Vocabulary Words

confirmation   the act of validating; establishing accuracy.

prime rate   the interest rate that banks use when loaning money to corporations.

virtually   just about; almost.

Nonrestrictive Clause

A nonrestrictive clause is a clause that is not essential to the meaning of the sentence and is, therefore, set off by a comma or commas.

Examples:

We will meet Tuesday at 1:30 for our monthly sales meeting, which was postponed last month.

Jim Clemens, who has good English and computer skills, can obtain well-paying jobs.

Activities

Activity 12.1—Create Data Table and Form Files and Merge

1. Use the following information and create a data table file.

    a. Select **Tools, Merge, Define, Data Table, Create a Table with Field Names.**

    b. Type each of the following field names and press **Enter** after each field name: **name, address, city, state, zip, salutation, child's name, and birthdate.**

    c. Select **OK.**

    d. Type the data for each table cell using the following information

        *Hint: Remember to press the **Tab** key after each entry including the last entry in each row. If desired, change the font to Dutch 801 Roman (Speedo), 11-point.*

Mr. and Mrs. Bob Otis	Ms. Carol A. Weber	Philip and Dawn Celaya
38 Nicholson Ave	280 Winton Ave #6	4806 Mission St
San Leandro	Hayward	Fremont
CA	CA	CA
94577	94545	94539
Mr. and Mrs. Otis	Ms. Weber	Philip and Dawn
Benjamin	Christine	Ernest
May 8	May 10	May 5

2. Save the data table file; use the filename **12act1.dt.**

3. Obtain a new document screen (select **File**, **New**).

4. Use the following information to create a form file.

    a. Change the top margin to 1.75"; change the left and right margins to 1.5".

    b. Insert the date using the date code.

    c. The form letter with place for field codes follows:

(Use date code)

FIELD(NAME)
FIELD(ADDRESS)
FIELD(CITY), **FIELD**(STATE) **FIELD**(ZIP)

Dear **FIELD**(SALUTATION):

I have read with interest the recent article in the newspaper about the birth of **FIELD**(CHILD'S NAME) on **FIELD**(BIRTHDATE) and extend to you my warmest best wishes and congratulations.

I would like to take this opportunity to join your family and friends in wishing you and **FIELD**(CHILD'S NAME) the best of health and much personal happiness in the years ahead.

If my office can be of service to you at any time, please contact me or my staff.

Sincerely,

Raymond T. Fletcher
Senator, 12th District

RTF/xx

---

5. Save the form file; use the filename **12act1.frm**.

6. Obtain a new document screen (select **File**, **New**).

7. Merge **12act1.frm** with **12act1.dt** (select **Tools**, **Merge**, **Run**; type **a:12act1.frm** in the Form File box; press **Enter**; if necessary, type **a:12act1.dt** in the Data File box; select **Merge**).

8. Print one copy of each merged letter.

9. Optional. Save the file of merged letters; use the filename **12act1.mr**.

10. Close all documents (select **File**, **Close** until a clear document window displays).

1. Use the following information and create a data table file.

   a. Select **Tools, Merge, Define, Data Table, Create a Table with Field Names**.

   b. Type each of the following field names and press **Enter** after each field name: **first/mid, last, address, city, state, zip, title, and amount**.

   c. Select **OK**.

   d. Type the data for each table cell using the following information.

      *Hint: Remember to press the **Tab** key after each entry including the last entry in each row. If desired, change the font to Dutch 801 Roman (Speedo), 11-point.*

Wanda B.	Lawrence	Ali R.
Chung	Aames	Ignacio
82 Main St., Apt. 16	6200 Baker Pl.	38 Sixth St.
Mesa	Seattle	Tenafly
AZ	WA	NJ
85201	98102	07670
Ms.	Mr.	Mr.
$5,000	$6,000	$6,000

2. Save the data table file; use the filename **12act2.dt**.

3. Obtain a new document screen (select **File, New**).

4. Use the following to create a form file.

   a. Change the left, right, and top margins to 1.5".

   b. Insert the date using the date code.

   c. The form letter with placement for field codes follows.

(Use date code)

FIELD(FIRST/MID) **FIELD**(LAST)
FIELD(ADDRESS)
FIELD(CITY), **FIELD**(STATE) **FIELD**(ZIP)

Dear **FIELD**(TITLE) **FIELD**(LAST):

Your UniCard credit line has been increased to **FIELD**(AMOUNT). You are a valued card member and because of your outstanding payment record, you have earned this additional purchasing power.

Your satisfaction with your UniCard is our highest priority. To help you get the most from your UniCard, our professional Customer Service representatives are available toll-free 24 hours a day to assist you and provide information about our exclusive card member services.

We appreciate the opportunity to serve you.

Sincerely,

Ginger T. Adams
President & CEO

GTA/xx

---

5. Save the form file; use the filename **12act2.frm**.

6. Obtain a new document screen (select **File, New**).

7. Merge **12act2.frm** with **12act2.dt** (select **Tools, Merge, Run**; type **a:12act2.frm** in the Form File box; press **Enter**; if necessary, type **a:12act2.dt** in the Data File box; select **Merge**).

8. Print one copy of each merged letter.

9. Optional. Save the file of merged letters; use the filename **12act2.mr**.

10. To edit the data table file, use the following information:

    a. If necessary, switch to the window that contains the data table file named **12act2.dt** (select **Window, Switch To**, select the filename desired).

    b. Change Wanda Chung's last name to Davis.

    c. Change the amount in Ali Ignacio's record to $7,000.

    d. Add a new record below the field name row (place the cursor/insertion point in any cell of row 2, select **Tools, Merge, Define**, select **Add a Row** (above). Type the new record information: **Keith J., Castro, 2390 New York Ave., Whiting, IN, 46394, Mr., $5,000.**

    e. Save the edited data table file using the same filename, **12act2.dt**.

11. Use the following information to view the records by field name and mark data records to be merged.

    a. Select **Tools, Merge, Run**.

    b. Type or check that the form filename **12act2.frm** and the data file filename **12act2.dt** display in the Form File and Data File boxes of the Run Merge dialog box.

    c. Select **Mark Records to Include**. (If necessary, select **Data File Options**).

    d. Select **LAST** in the List Field Name dialog box.

e. Double-click on the **Castro** and **Ignacio** records.

f. Select **OK**.

g. Select **Merge**.

   Note: Only the letters to Mr. Castro and Mr. Ignacio display.

h. Print one copy of the merged letters.

12. Close all documents (select **File, Close** until a clear document window displays).

    Note: It is not necessary to save the merged letters for Mr. Castro and Mr. Ignacio.

Activity 12.3—Create and Merge a Form and Data Table File with Blank Fields; Edit the Form and Data Files

1. Use the following information and create a data table file.

   a. Select **Tools, Merge, Define, Data Table, Create a Table with Field Names**.

   b. Type each of the following field names and press **Enter** after each field name: **first, last, company, address, city, state, zip, title, vendor, date, and amount**.

   c. Select **OK**.

   d. Type the data for each table cell using the following information.

      *Hint: Remember to press the **Tab** key after each entry including the last entry in each row. If desired, change the font to Dutch 801 Roman (Speedo), 11-point.*

Roy E.	Sharon	D. L.
Dunhill	Gaffney	Ibbaro
	McClure's Carpets	
6309 Clemens Ave.	7600 Third St.	2 S. Tenth Ave.
Ft. Lauderdale	Raleigh	Jacksonville
FL	NC	FL
36092	39016	33125
Mr.	Ms.	Mr.
Casual Foods	Timberline Associates	Abbey Shoes
October 25, 1993	December 31, 1993	November 20, 1993
15,000	8,000	12,000

2. Save the data table file; use the filename **12act3.dt**.

3. Obtain a new document screen (select **File, New**).

4. Use the following to create a form file.

   a. Change the left and right margins to **1.5"**; change the top margin to **2"**.

   b. Insert the date using the date code.

   c. The form letter with placement for field codes follows.

(Use date code)

FIELD(FIRST) **FIELD**(LAST)
FIELD(COMPANY)
FIELD(ADDRESS)
FIELD(CITY), **FIELD**(STATE) **FIELD**(ZIP)

Dear **FIELD**(TITLE) **FIELD**(LAST):

It is a pleasure to answer your recent letter requesting current information about **FIELD**(VENDOR). Credit was extended to **FIELD**(VENDOR) on **FIELD**(DATE), with a limit of $**FIELD**(AMOUNT).

Their invoices have always been paid promptly, many times taking advantage of the cash discount.

This information is to be held in strict confidence. We are glad to be of service to you. If you have any further questions, please do not hesitate to contact us.

Sincerely,

T. W. Loyden
Credit Division Manager

TWL/xx

---

5. Save the form file; use the filename **12act3.frm**.

6. Obtain a new document screen (select **File, New**).

7. Merge **12act3.frm** with **12act3.dt** (select **Tools, Merge, Run**; type **a:12act3.frm** in the Form File box; press **Enter**; if necessary, type **a:12act3.dt** in the Data File box, select **Blank Fields in Data File, Remove Resulting Blank Line**; select **Merge**).

8. Print one copy of each merged letter.

9. Optional. Save the file of merged letters; use the filename **12act3.mr**.

10. To edit the data table file, use the following information:

    a. If necessary, switch to the window that contains the data table file named **12act3.dt** (select **Window, Switch To**, select the filename desired).

    b. Change D. L. Ibbaro's name to **Daniel Louis Ibbaro**.

    c. Add the company name **Foodland, Inc.** to Roy E. Dunhill's record.

    d. Delete the column that contains dollar amounts (place the cursor/insertion point in the desired column, select **Tools**, **Merge**, **Define**, select **Delete a Column**).

    e. Save the data table file again using the same filename, **12act3.dt**.

11. To edit the form file, use the following information:

    a. If necessary, switch to the window that contains the form file named **12act3.frm** (select **Window**, **Switch To**, select the filename desired).

    b. Delete **FIELD(AMOUNT)** and replace with **14,000**.

    c. Save the file using the same filename, **12act3.frm**.

12. Obtain a new document screen (select **File**, **New**).

13. Merge **12act3.frm** with **12act3.dt** (if necessary, see Step 7 for specific instructions).

14. Print one copy of each merged letter.

15. Optional. Save the file of merged letters; use the filename **12act3.mr2**.

16. Close all documents.

Challenge Your Skills

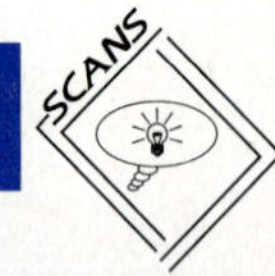

Skill 12.1—Create and Merge a Form and Data Table File; Edit Form and Data Files; Mark a Data Record

1. Use the following information and create a data table file.

    a. The field names for the data table file are:

       first, last, address, city, state, zip, title, date, and amounts

    b. The information for each record follows:

Lowell S.	Sharlene	Rudolph P.
Grizoffi	Kelterman	Lehman
72 Cobbs Creek Circle	572 Tiyunga Blvd	1370 North Avenue
New Gloucester	North Hollywood	Miami
ME	CA	FL
04260	91600	33139
Mr.	Ms.	Mr.
October 24, 199x	November 5, 199x	September 12, 199x
$15,000, $40,000, or	$25,000, $60,000, or	$10,000, $25,000, or
$65,000	$100,000	$50,000

2. Save the data table file; use the filename **12skill1.dt**.

3. Obtain a new document screen.

4. Create the following form file. Make decisions regarding:
>Margins
>Justification
>Fonts
>Tab settings for indention of enumerated items

(Insert date code)

FIELD(FIRST) **FIELD**(LAST)
FIELD(ADDRESS)
FIELD(CITY), **FIELD**(STATE) **FIELD**(ZIP)

Dear **FIELD**(TITLE) **FIELD**(LAST):

Thank you for your request for information on our special group term life plans. A brochure describing the special group life plans and an application for coverage are enclosed. In order for you to be eligible for the special group life rates, the enclosed applications must be received by **FIELD**(DATE). After that date, this special group plan will no longer be available.

Based on your age, there are three amounts of group term life insurance that you can apply for--**FIELD**(AMOUNTS). With the special group plan, you are guaranteed:

1. **No medical exam.** A medical exam is not automatically required--your insurability can usually be determined based on the information in your application.

2. **Personal rate protection.** Once your application has been accepted, the only time your rates will change is when you move into a different age group.

3. **Credit card convenience.** Your monthly premiums can be conveniently billed to your UniCard account. You will never have to worry about paying the premium on time.

Please fill out, sign, and return the enclosed application in the postage-paid envelope. Remember, the signed application must be received in our office by **FIELD**(DATE).

Sincerely,

Marshall K. Piazzola
Executive Vice President

MKP/xx

Enc.

---

5. Save the form file; use the filename **12skill1.frm**.

6. Obtain a new document screen.

7. Merge **12skill1.frm** with **12skill1.dt**.

8. Print one copy of each merged letter.

9. Optional. Save the file of merged letters; use the filename **12skill1.mr**.

10. Edit the data table file using the following information:

    a. Delete the AMOUNTS field column.

    b. Add two new rows above row 2. Type the additional record information shown below.

Peter N.	Art
Hurtado	Mansano
1469 Wilshire Blvd.	887 Hardow Drive
Los Angeles	Las Vegas
CA	NV
90023	89106
Mr.	Mr.
November 2, 199x	October 1, 199x

    c. Save the changed data file.

11. Edit the form file using the following information:

    a. Delete the entire second paragraph.

    b. Delete the last sentence in the last paragraph that begins "Remember..."

    c. Save the changed form file.

12. Mark and merge the two new records.

13. Print a copy of the two new merged letters and close all documents.

➥ Skill 12.2—Create and Merge a Form File and Data Table File with Blank Fields; Language Arts

1. Use the following information and create a data table file.

    a. The field names for the data table file are:

       title, first, lastname, address1, address2, city, state, zip, name, and amount

    b. The information for each record follows:

Mr.	Ms.	Mr.	Mrs.
Yohannes	Paige	Joseph R.	June A.
Wohlenberg	Ybarra	Nevitt	Penning
Gardenwood Terrace			Shore Apartments
36 Hill Rd., #16	2606 Auburn Way	313 36th St.	28 Addison Way, #6
York	Weatherford	Arlington	Springfield
PA	TX	VA	NJ
17403	76087	22203	07081
Yohannes	Paige	Joseph	June
5,000	7,000	6,000	5,000

2. Save the data table file; use the filename **12skill2.dt**.

3. Obtain a new document screen.

4. Create the following primary file. Make decisions regarding:

    Margins

    Justification

    Fonts

    Correct three spelling errors, two misused words, and two
       punctuation errors

    Reference initials, document identification, and enclosure notation

---

(Use date code)

FIELD(TITLE) **FIELD**(FIRST) **FIELD**(LASTNAME)
FIELD(ADDRESS1)
FIELD(ADDRESS2)
FIELD(CITY), **FIELD**(STATE) **FIELD**(ZIP)

Dear **FIELD**(TITLE) **FIELD**(LASTNAME):

First things first, **FIELD**(NAME). You can receive a credit card that is free forever.

You have been pre-approved to receive a Continental Omni card with a credit line of $**FIELD**(AMOUNT). All you need to do is use the card at least once a year and its yours free from annual fees for life. Simply apply by the expiration date on the enclosed confirmation card.

That's not the only savings you will receive. You can save on interest, to. Today 90 million people pay 16% or more in credit card interest. The Continental Omni card offers a variable Annual Percentage Rate that is only 15.4% (prime rate plus 9.4%). And if the prim rate drops, your interest rate drops, too.

Your Continental Omni card that includes your picture, is accepted worldwide. So you can shop, dine, travel and make calls--with one card. You will also have the only Omni card that comes with the TWT Customer Service network. You can reach us

anytime--24 hours a day, 365 days a year--from virtualy anywhere. And you will receive
the responsive, personal service you would expect from TWT.

The fastest way to receive your card is to call 1-800-555-8222 or complete and return
the enclosed confirnation card in the postage-paid envelope provided.

Sincerely,

Rachael G. Hunsberger
President

---

5. Save the primary file; use the filename **12skill2.frm**.

6. Obtain a new document screen.

7. Merge **12skill2.frm** with **12skill2.dt**.
    Hint: Remember to use the Remove Resulting Blank Fields option.

8. Print one copy of each merged letter.

9. Optional. Save the file of merged letters; use the filename **12skill2.mr**.

10. If you have completed your work, exit WordPerfect.

Create and Print Mailing Labels

Features Covered

- Create an envelope
- Create an envelope definition
- Create mailing labels
- Sort data table file records

Objectives

After successfully completing this chapter, you will be able to create an envelope using the **Envelope** button, create an envelope definition, and create mailing labels using pre-defined labels. In addition, you will be able to sort records in a data table file.

Chapter Introduction

Once a form file is merged with a data file, envelope addresses or mailing labels can be created for mailing each document. Using the existing data file addresses or the letter addresses to create envelope addresses or mailing labels can assist in expediting the process of setting up and printing addresses on envelopes or labels.

Create Envelope Addresses

Envelope addresses are easily created by selecting the **Envelope** button on the WPMAIN Button Bar or by using the **Layout**, **Envelope** command. However, the Envelope button can only be used if a mouse is available. When the **Enve-**

lope button or **Layout**, **Envelope** command is selected, WordPerfect determines if an envelope paper size has previously been defined. If no envelope paper size has been defined, a message displays prompting the user to create an envelope paper size (definition). If an envelope paper size has already been defined or after the user defines an envelope paper size, WordPerfect reviews the file in the current document screen and identifies the address information.

Once WordPerfect has identified the address information, the Envelope dialog box displays (see Figure 13.1). The address information displays in the Mailing Address area. If WordPerfect has incorrectly identified the address information, the correct address can be typed. If no address information is found in the current file, the Mailing Address area of the Envelope dialog box will be empty. Move the mouse pointer to the Mailing Address area, click once and type the desired address. Press **F7** to exit the Mailing Address box.

A previously typed return address may display in the Return Address box. A return address can be typed and saved as the default or can be omitted.

The U.S. Postal Service requests that mailing addresses be typed with vertical line spacing of one and no italic text or indented lines. For a large No. 10 envelope, the address is placed approximately 2 to $2\frac{1}{2}$ inches from the top edge and 4 to $4\frac{1}{2}$ inches from the left edge of the envelope. For many years, the Postal Service preferred addresses to be typed in all uppercase letters with no punctuation; however, the main concern of the Postal Service now is that the typed address be placed in an area easily read by OCR (optical character recognition) equipment. OCR equipment scans addresses electronically and sorts mail quickly, thus expediting the mail service. Word-Perfect automatically prints the envelope address in the appropriate location. Using uppercase letters and no punctuation or using lowercase letters with initial capitals and punctuation are now both considered acceptable forms for typing mailing addresses.

WordPerfect also has the capability of creating the PostNet bar code for any zip code. (The PostNet bar code is used by the U.S. Postal Service when routing mail.) The zip code is typed in the POSTNET Bar Code box. The bar code displays above the first address line when the envelope is inserted into the document or printed. If desired, **Setup** can be selected and the bar code can be automatically created, or manually entered, or the POSTNET Bar Code option can be removed from the Envelope dialog box.

Start-Up Instructions

❖   ■   Open the file named **13drill1.ltr**.

Steps to   Create an Envelope Address

Note: The WPMAIN Button Bar should be displayed. If necessary, select ***View***, ***Button Bar*** *Setup*, ***Select***, *and double-click on* ***WPMAIN***.

1. Select the **Envelope** button on the Button Bar {Alt and L, v or Alt and F12}. Wait momentarily.

        Chapter 13—Create and Print Mailing Labels

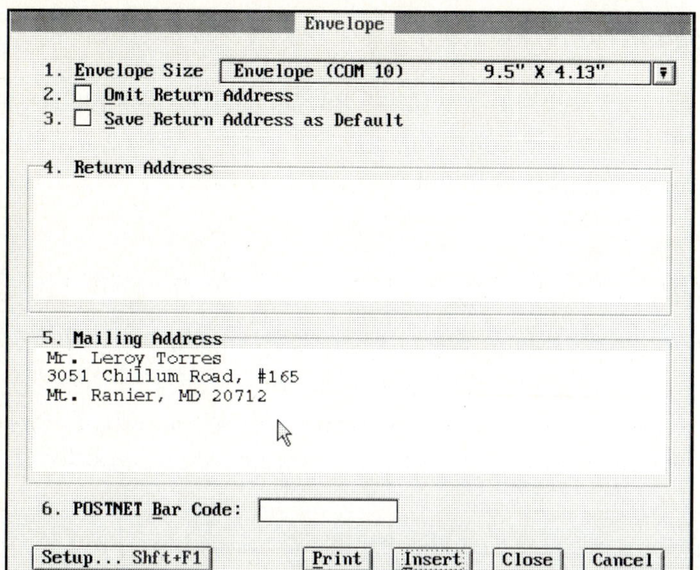

FIGURE 13.1

WordPerfect Envelope
dialog box

2. The Envelope dialog box displays (see Figure 13.1). Check that the address for the letter displays in the Mailing Address area. If a return address was typed at a prior time, the return address may also display in the Return Address area.

   Note: If a letter address is not displayed, click in the Mailing Address box and type the desired address. Press F7 to exit the Mailing Address box.

3. Click in the **Return Address** box {r}.

4. Type the desired return address.

   For example, type your name and return address information.

5. Press **F7**.

   Note: The Envelope Size box displays an available envelope and size. If the Envelope Size box is empty, see Steps to Create an Envelope Definition.

6. Check that an Envelope Size displays. If necessary, select **Envelope Size**, double-click on the down arrow at the right of the Envelope Size box, and select **Envelope 9.5" x 4.13"** {e, press the down arrow key to highlight Envelope 9.5" x 4.13", Enter}.

7. If desired, select the **POSTNET Bar Code** box and type the desired zip code {b, type zip code}.

   For example, select the **POSTNET Bar Code** box and type **20712**.

8. Select **Insert** {press Enter twice}.

   *Note: The envelope information will be placed at the end of the letter after a page break. If desired, select the **Preview** button to display the entire envelope on the screen; select **Close** to return to the document window.*

To Print an Envelope

9. The cursor/insertion point should be located on the page containing the envelope address and bar code.

10. Select the **Print** button {Shift and F7}.

11. Select **Page** {p}.

12. Select **Print** {Enter}.

    Note: A beep is heard and the printer pauses, allowing an envelope to be inserted in the printer or paper tray. Use of plain paper is OK for this practice activity.

13. *If using a dot matrix printer*, a message may display in the Status bar, "Press Shift and F7, 6." Press **Shift** and **F7**, select **Control Printer** {6}, press **g** (Go) to print the envelope.

    If using a laser printer, a message may display in the Status bar, "Press Shift and F7, 6." Press **Shift** and **F7**, select **Control Printer** {6}, press **g** (Go) to print the envelope. On the printer, press the *Resume* or *Continue* button. Some printers may require paper to be placed in a single sheet feeder slot before pressing the *Continue* button.

    Note: The address prints on the paper in the appropriate area.

14. Select **Close** {Enter}.

Finish-Up Instructions

❖ Use the new filename **13envel** and save the file. Close the document.

Create an Envelope Definition

Note: The following Steps to Create an Envelope Definition are for your information and your use if needed.

1. Select the **Envelope** button {Alt and L, v}.

2. Select **Setup** {Shift and F1}.

    Note: The Envelope Setup dialog box displays.

3. Select **Envelope Size** {e}.

4. Select **Create** {c}.

    Note: The Paper Size/Type dialog box displays.

5. Select **Create** again {c}.

    Note: The Create Paper Size/Type dialog box displays.

6. The Paper Name box is highlighted. Type a descriptive name for the paper.

    For example, type **small envelope** and press **Enter**.

7. Select **Paper Type** and double-click on **Envelope** {t, press the down arrow key to highlight Envelope, Enter}.

   Chapter 13—Create and Print Mailing Labels

8. Select **Paper Size** {s}.

9. Select **Other** {o}.

10. Type the desired size in the Define Paper Size box.

    For example, type **6.5**, press **Tab**, type **3.825**.

11. Select **OK** {Enter twice}.

12. Select **Paper Location** {L}.

13. Double-click on the desired paper location {use the up/down arrow keys to high-light the desired paper location, press s}.

    For example, double-click on **Continuous**.

14. If necessary, click on **Prompt to Load** to remove the X in the option box {p}.

15. Select **Orientation** {o}.

16. Double-click on the desired orientation {use the up/down arrow keys to high-light the desired orientation, Enter}.

    For example, double-click on **Landscape Font**.

    Note: The Orientation box displays the "A" in the landscape position.

17. Select **OK** {Enter}.

    Note: The message "Please wait" displays briefly and the small envelope option displays in the Paper Name box.

18. Select **Close** {F7}.

19. Double-click on the desired envelope size {use the up/down arrow keys to high-light the desired style}.

    For example, double-click on **small envelope**.

20. Select **OK** {Enter}.

21. Select **Print** {p}.

    Note: If necessary, see Step 13 in Steps to Create an Envelope Address

Mailing Labels

Mailing labels are short forms on which names and addresses are printed. Mailing labels come in various sizes. Two commonly used sizes are 4 by $1\frac{1}{3}$ inch and $2\frac{5}{8}$ by 1 inch. Generally, the labels are self-adhered to backing paper that is 11 inches in length. The self-adhesive mailing label is removed from the backing paper and placed on an envelope.

The mailing labels are usually designed with one, two, or three columns per page. Preferably the address is printed two to three spaces from the left edge of the form and starts on the second or third line.

Create Mailing Labels Using Predefined Labels

WordPerfect provides predefined label format for mailing labels, e.g., label size, number of labels per page, etc. The format for many common labels, such as Avery, 3M, etc. can be selected from the Labels dialog box (see Figure 13.2).

Once the mailing label format has been specified, the mailing labels can be created by typing the address information for each recipient followed by a hard page break. In the page mode view, the typed labels display in the document window in the same format as the labels will print. The **Preview** button can also be used to view the layout of the mailing labels on the page. If a laser printer is selected, the mailing labels will appear on a single page. With a dot matrix printer selected, each row of labels will appear as a separate page.

Mailing labels can also be created by using the Merge feature (see Chapter 12). The data file used to create form letters can be merged with a new form file that has been formatted using a predefined label format to create mailing labels.

Start-Up Instructions

❖　The page mode view should be active. If necessary, select **View**, **Page Mode**.

Create Mailing Labels Using a Predefined Label

1. Select **Layout, Page, Labels** {Shift and F8, p, L}.

   Note: The Labels dialog box displays (see Figure 13.2).

2. Scroll down the list of labels until the desired label name is highlighted {press the down arrow key repeatedly until the desired label name is highlighted}.

Labels dialog box

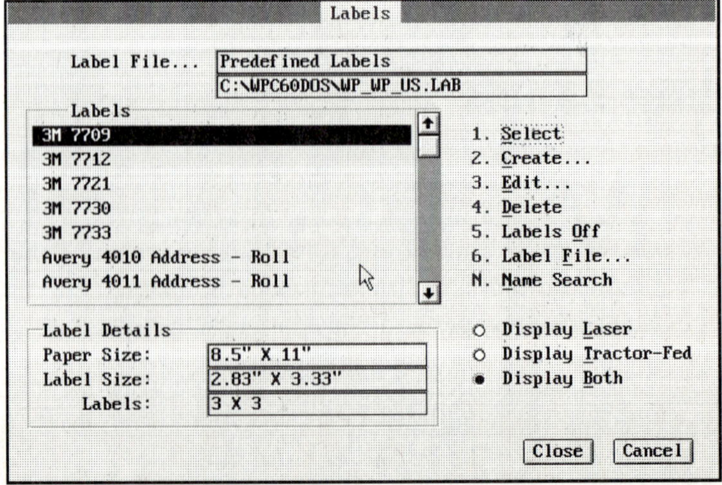

For example, *if using a dot matrix printer*, highlight **Avery 4144 Address**. *If using a laser printer*, highlight **Avery 5260 Address**.

3. Select **Edit** {e}.

   Note: The Edit Label dialog box displays.

4. Select **Printer Info** {i}.

   Note: The Labels Printer Info dialog box displays.

5. Select the desired location, i.e., Manual Feed or Continuous.

   For example, check that **Continuous** displays in the Location box. If necessary, select **Location**, and double-click on **Continuous** {L, highlight Continuous, Enter}.

   Note: Check that the Prompt to Load option is not selected (no X should appear in the box).

6. Select **OK** twice {Enter twice}.

   Note: The Labels dialog box displays.

7. Choose **Select** {s}.

   Note: The Page Format dialog box displays with the Paper Size/Type and Labels options both showing the label choosen.

8. Select **OK** {Enter}.

   Note: The document window displays with a gray area around the first place where a label can be typed.

9. Type the label information.

   For example, type the following label:
   NORA MARIE MURRAY
   220 N BOSWORTH APT 7
   CHICAGO IL 60613 {press **Ctrl** and **Enter**}

10. Repeat Step 9 to type the remaining labels.

    For example, type the following labels:
    STACEY L NAGATA
    P O BOX 543
    PLATTSBURG NY 12901 {press **Ctrl** and **Enter**}

    RICHARD MCDANIEL
    MCDANIEL'S GARAGE
    1050 BRANHAM LANE
    SAN JOSE CA 95123 {press **Ctrl** and **Enter**}

    LAUREL T KIRK
    NATIONAL TECHNOLOGY INC
    TWO INDUSTRIAL AVE
    LOWELL MA 01851

*Note: It is not necessary to press **Ctrl** and **Enter** after the last zip code.*

Finish-Up Instructions

- ❖ Use the filename **13drill2** and save the file.
- ❖ Select the **Preview** button to display the labels in three columns on the screen.

  *Note: If a laser printer is selected, the mailing labels will appear on a single page. With a dot matrix printer selected, each row of labels will appear as a separate page. If necessary, select the **PrevPage** or **NextPage** buttons to view additional labels.*

- ❖ Select **Close.**
- ❖ Print one copy.

  *Note: If the computer beeps, press **Shift** and **F7, 6, g** to resume printing.*

- ❖ Close the document.

Create Mailing Labels Using Form and Data Files

Mailing labels can be easily created using existing form and data files. The inside address field codes are copied to a new file from an existing form file (see Figure 13.3). A new document screen is obtained, the copied inside address field codes are inserted, and a label definition is installed. The new form label file is saved. A new document screen is obtained, and the new form label file is merged with an existing data file.

The Sort feature can be used to arrange the data file records in an assigned order. For example, the mailing label records can be presorted by zip codes in order to receive discounts on mail rates. To use the Sort feature, determine which field is to be used to sort the records. When sorting a data file, the number of the column is used to determine the number of the Sort field. After determining the column number of the Sort field, **Tools**, **Sort** is selected and the sort criteria are specified (see Figure 13.4). The Sort feature is discussed further in Chapter 16.

To obtain the sorted mailing labels a sorted data file is saved and merged with the desired form file. Labels can be viewed in the chosen label format by selecting the **Preview** button.

Start-Up Instructions

- ❖ The files named **12drill1.frm** and **12drill1.dt** created in Chapter 12 must be available.
- ❖ The default WPMAIN Button Bar should be displayed on the screen.

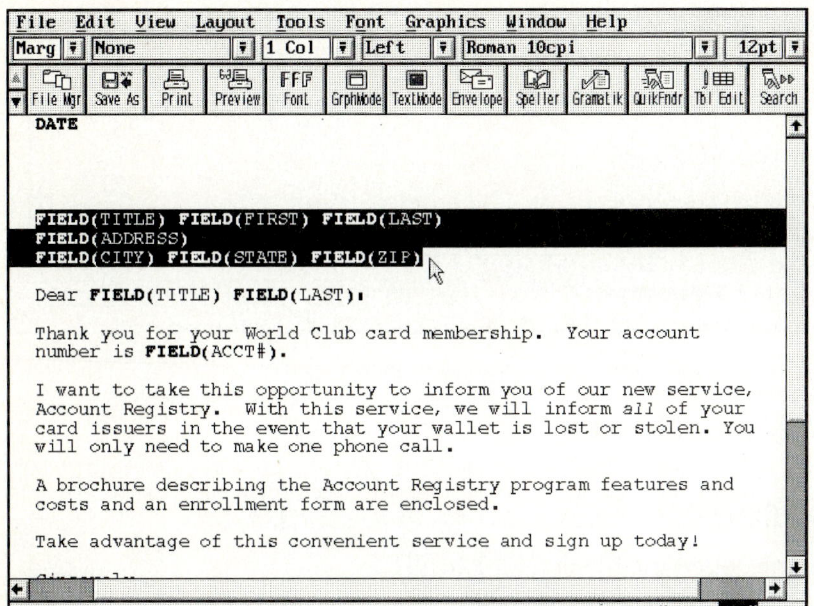

FIGURE 13.3

Field codes selected in a form file

Create Mailing Labels Using Existing Form and Data Files

1. Open the form file that contains the inside address field codes.

   For example, open **12drill1.frm**.

2. Block the inside address field codes (see Figure 13.3) and select **Edit, Copy** {Ctrl and c}.

3. Select **File, New** to obtain a new document screen {Alt and f, n}.

4. Select **Edit, Paste** to insert the copied inside address field codes {Ctrl and v}.

5. Move the cursor/insertion point to the top of the document.

6. Use the following information and repeat Steps 1-8 in the Steps to Create Mailing Labels Using Predefined Labels.

   a. If using a dot matrix printer, select **3M 7721** label.

   b. If using a laser printer, select **Avery 5161 Address** label.

   Note: The fields show in the label outline.

7. Save the new form label file.

   For example, use the filename **13drill3.frm** and save the form file.

Start-Up Instructions

❖ The form label file named **13drill3.frm** and **12drill1.dt** must be available.

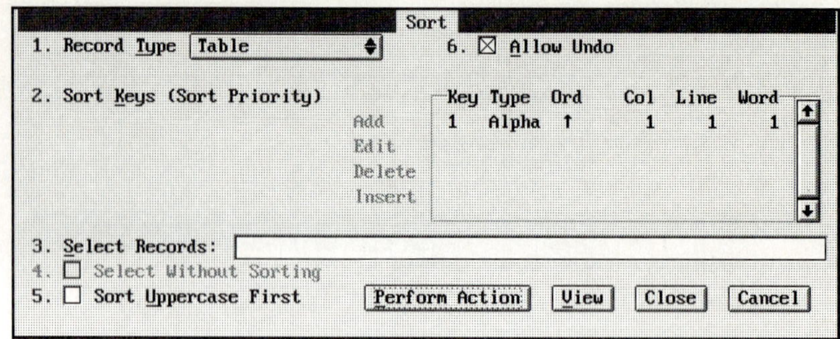

Sort the Records in a Data File

1. Open the data file that contains the records to be sorted.

   For example, open the file named **12drill1.dt**.

2. Determine the number of the column that will be used to sort records.

   For example, zip is column number 7.

   Note: The cursor/insertion point can be located in any table cell.

3. Select **Tools, Sort** {Alt and t, r}.

   Note: The Sort dialog box displays.

4. In the Record Type box, check that Table is displayed.

5. Select **Sort Keys (Sort Priority)** {k}.

6. Select **Edit** {e}.

7. Select the desired sort type, i.e., **Alpha** or **Numeric**.

   For example, select **Numeric** {t, n}.

8. Select **Column** and type the number of the column to be used for sorting records {c, type column number}.

   For example, select **Column** and type 7.

   Note: Your Sort dialog box should look similar to the one shown in Figure 13.4.

9. Select the desired sort order, i.e., **Ascending** or **Descending**.

   For example, check that **Ascending** is selected.

10. Select **OK** {Enter twice}.

11. Select **Perform Action** {press Tab twice, Enter}.

    Note: A message displays, "Sorting."

12. Save the sorted data table file.

    For example, use the filename **13drill3.dt** and save the file.

Merge a Label Form File and Sorted Data File

13. Select **File, New** to obtain a new document screen {Alt and f, n}.

14. Select **Tools, Merge, Run** {Ctrl and F9, m}.

    Note: The Run Merge dialog box displays.

15. Type the name of the form label file.

    For example, type **a:13drill3.frm**. (Do not type the final period.)

16. Press the **Tab** key.

17. If necessary, type the name of the existing data file.

    For example, if necessary, type **a:13drill3.dt**. (Do not type the final period.)

18. Select **Merge** {Enter}.

    Note: The labels display with the cursor/insertion point located after the last label, and the labels are arranged in ascending order by zip code.

Finish-Up Instructions

❖ Move the cursor/insertion point to the top of the document.

❖ Select the **Preview** button to view the labels on the screen.

   *Note: If a laser printer is selected, the two-column mailing labels appear on a single page. With a dot matrix printer selected, each row of labels appears as a separate page. If necessary, select the **NextPage** or **PrevPage** buttons to view additional labels.*

❖ Use the filename **13drill3.lab** and save the label file.

❖ Print one copy.

❖ Close all documents (select **File, Close** until a clear document window displays).

The Next Step

Chapter Review and Activities

FEATURES SUMMARY

FEATURES	ACTIONS	PAGE
Create an envelope address	Select the **Envelope** button; if necessary, click in the Mailing Address box and type the address, press **F7**. If desired, click in the **Return Address** box and type the address, press **F7**. Select the envelope size desired. Select **Insert** or **Print**.	346
Create a POSTNET bar code	Select the **POSTNET Bar Code** option in the Envelope dialog box. Type the address zip code, press **Enter**, select **Insert** or **Print**.	347
Create an envelope definition	Select the **Envelope** button, select **Setup**, **Envelope Size**. Select **Create** twice, type a name for the envelope. Select **Paper Type** and double-click on **Envelope**. Select **Paper Size**, **Other**, type desired size, select **OK**. Select **Paper Location**, double-click on the desired paper location. Select **Orientation**, double-click on the desired orientation. Select **OK**, **Close**. Double-click on the desired envelope style, select **OK**, **Print**.	348
Create mailing labels using predefined labels	Select **Layout**, **Page**, **Labels**, highlight the desired labels, choose **Select**, **OK**. Type the label mailing address, press **Ctrl** and **Enter** after typing each label (except the last label).	350

Sort records in a data table file	Open the data table file to be sorted and determine the number of the column to be used for sorting. With the cursor/insertion pointer in any cell in the data table, select **Tools**, **Sort**, select **Sort Keys**, **Edit**, **Column**, type the number of the column to be used for sorting, choose the desired sort type and sort order, select **OK**, **Perform Action**.	354

Self-Check Questions

True/False—Circle One

T F 1. Mailing labels are short forms that are self-adhered to backing paper.

T F 2. The inside address field codes from an existing form file can be copied and pasted in a new file to begin creating a form file for labels.

T F 3. When typing information in a mailing label using a predefined label, a hard page break (**Ctrl** and **Enter**) is inserted after each recipient's zip code.

T F 4. **File, Print Preview** is used to display the layout of mailing labels on a page.

T F 5. The records of a data file can only be sorted by the company name.

T F 6. U.S. Postal Service regulations require that mailing labels be printed with line spacing of two.

Short Answer

1. Name the key that is pressed to exit the Mailing Address box when the Envelope dialog box is displayed.

2. A large envelope is referred to as a No. _____ envelope.

3. A return address can be typed in the Envelope dialog box. List the other two options that can be selected for the return address.

4. List one advantage of using POSTNET bar codes.

Spelling/Vocabulary Words

warranty   a written agreement between a customer and manufacturer guaranteeing that the manufacturer will repair or replace a defective item or part.

components   individual parts of an item.

reliable   trustworthy; credible; dependable.

Subject-Verb Agreement

Verbs must agree in number with their subject. If a subject is singular (one), use a singular verb; if a subject is plural (more than one), use a plural verb.

Examples:

Bill and **Cindy** *are co-owners of the condominium.*

*Our **president**, as well as all staff members, **is** looking forward to developing a good relationship with all clients.*

To determine if a subject and verb are in agreement, omit the words between the subject and verb.

Examples:

*The **legs** of the chair **were** damaged.*
*(The **legs were** damaged.)*

***Anna**, together with her two daughters, **is** to arrive on an evening flight.*
*(**Anna is** to arrive on an evening flight.)*

Activities

Activity 13.1—Create Mailing Labels Using Predefined Labels

1. Choose **Layout, Page, Labels**.

2. Use the following information to select and use the desired label.

   a. *If using a dot-matrix printer*, highlight the **Avery 4144** label.

   b. *If using a laser printer*, highlight the **Avery 5260** label.

   c. Select **Edit, Printer Info**.

   d. Check the Location option. *If Continuous displays*, select **OK**. *If Manual Feed displays*, select **Location** and double-click on **Continuous**.

   e. Select **OK** twice.

   f. Choose **Select**.

g. Select **OK**.

3. Type the following names and addresses in uppercase letters with no punctuation. After each zip code, press **Ctrl** and **Enter** to obtain a hard page break.

MR NEIL LEONARD
4110 WEST 21ST PLACE
CHICAGO IL 60623

MS NICOLE OTTO
6500 E PRENTICE AVE
ENGLEWOOD CO 80171

MR GARTH KAHN
42 OLIVE STREET
ARLINGTON HEIGHTS IL 60005

MRS PAULA LANGENBERG
185 EAST ROCKS ROAD
NORWALK CT 06851

MR BERT ROTCHFORD
P O BOX 595
COLORADO SPRINGS, CO
80901-0595

4. Use the filename **13act1** and save the address labels.

5. Print the address labels.

6. Close the document.

■ Activity 13.2—Create Mailing Labels Using Existing Form and Data Files

*Note: The files named **12act1.frm** and **12act1.dt** must be completed from Chapter 12, Activity 12.1.*

1. Open the file named **12act1.frm**.

2. Block and copy the inside address field codes.

3. Open a new file and paste the inside address information into the new file.

4. Locate the cursor/insertion point at the top of the new file.

5. Select **Layout**, **Page**, **Label**, and use the following information to select and use the desired label.

   a. *If using a dot-matrix printer*, highlight the **3M 7721** label.

   b. *If using a laser printer*, highlight the **Avery 5161** label.

   c. Select **Edit**, **Printer Info**.

   d. Check the Location option. *If Continuous displays*, select **OK**. *If Manual Feed displays*, select **Location** and double-click on **Continuous**.

e. Select **OK** twice.

f. Choose **Select**.

g. Select **OK**.

6. Use the filename **13act2.frm** and save the new form label file.

7. Open a new file and merge **13act2.frm** with **12act1.dt** to create mailing labels.

8. Optional. Use the filename **13act2.lab** and save the mailing labels.

9. Print one copy and close the documents.

Activity 13.3—Create an Envelope Address

1. Type the following letter:

(Use current date)

Mr. Dennis Collins
200 Ramona St.
Yuma, AZ 85364

Dear Mr. Collins:

Recently you received a policy renewal notice. Now is a good time to review your insurance coverage limits and available optional coverages and deductibles.

Give me a call at 555-7007 or stop by the office. I look forward to seeing you.

Sincerely,

Alma Gossett

AG/xxx
collins.ltr/disk5

---

2. Use the filename **13act3** and save the file.

3. Select the **Envelope** button.

4. Check that the recipient's address is correct in the Mailing Address dialog box.

5. Click in the **Return Address** box; type your name and address in the return address box.

  Chapter 13—Create and Print Mailing Labels

6. Envelope 9.5" x 4.13" should be displayed in the Envelope Size box. If necessary, select the down arrow to locate the desired envelope size information.

7. Select **Insert** to place the envelope information at the end of the letter.

8. Optional. Print the envelope

9. Use the new filename **13act3e** and save the file. Close the document.

Challenge Your Skills

Skill 13.1—Create Mailing Labels Using Predefined Labels

1. Use the **Avery 5160** label (dot matrix) or **Avery 5260** label (laser) and create a label file using the information shown below.

   Note: When using 5160 labels on a dot matrix printer, change the font to Dutch or Roman 12 cpi or make a choice of your own. When using 5260 labels on a laser printer, change the font size to 11 points or make a choice of your own.

GEORGETTE HANSEN PERSONNEL MANAGER 1330 GREENWOOD PLACE LAKEWOOD CO 80226	LAURA RADDING INVERNESS INC 6534 75TH AVE FT COLLINS CO 80525	CHARLES CIMINO PERSONNEL DIRECTOR S & T SYSTEMS P O BOX 229 LAKE CITY FL 32056
DONG PHOUNG NGUYEN VICE PRESIDENT MICROCOMPUTER INC 460 UNIVERSITY AVE WESTERBURY NY 11590	MORT DEL SECCO P O BOX 7214 NASHVILLE TN 37221	DENNIS SUTTER 1023 POWERS TERRACE MARIETTA GA 30067
AMY R GONSALVES BUDGET DIRECTOR WESTERN SALES INC 445 S GRAND AVE LOS ANGELES CA 90071	RHONDA PLUMMER 160-20 91ST STREET HOWARD BEACH NY 11414	GARY ALMANZA 55 MARSHALL STREET ST PAUL MN 55102
DALE R ENGLEMAN P O BOX 502 HATTIESBURG MS 39401	SHANNON ANN TUNG 4030 PERSHALL DR #6B ST LOUIS MO 63131	DELOIS W TRUONG DWT INC P O BOX 60 LINCOLN NE 68588

2. Use the filename **13skill1.lab** and save the file.

3. Print the mailing labels.

4. Close the documents.

➥ Skill 13.2—Create Form and Data Table Files; Sort and Merge Mailing Labels; Language Arts

1. Read the following information including the form letter below and make decisions regarding the number of fields needed and the field names.

2. Create a data table file using the following information. Make a decision regarding a filename for the data file.

   a. Ms. Bonnie Avakian purchased a microwave range on the 15th of last month. The standard warranty will expire three years from the date of purchase. Ms. Avakian's mailing address is Box 168, Cobleskill, NY, 12043.

   b. Joseph L. Brownell, who resides at 310 Concord Street, Apt 8, Bloomfield, MI, 48304, purchased a refrigerator on the 20th of last month. The standard warranty will expire two years from the date of purchase.

   c. Russ Atkinson purchased a garbage compactor on the 24th of last month. The standard warranty will expire one year from the date of purchase. Mr. Atkinson resides at 2100 Indian Creek, Hood River, Oregon, 97031.

   d. Kip R. Carrillo, who resides at 68 Moorepark Ave., Tuscon, AZ, 85730, purchased a dishwasher on the 29th of last month. The standard warranty will expire three years from the date of purchase.

   e. Sort the data table file in ascending order by zip code.

   f. Save the data table file.

3. Use the traditional block letter style and create the following form file. Make decisions regarding:

   Margins
   Justification
   Fonts
   Correct three spelling errors, one misused word, and four punctuation/grammatical errors
   Reference initials
   Filename for form file

(Use date code)

{Inside
address
fields}

Dear {salutation field}:

Congratulations on the purchase of your new Vista {appliance field}. Thank you for placing your confidence in Vista products and service.

Years of Vista experience and quality workmanship has been built into your new {appliance field}, so you can expect many years of excellent performance.

Please take a few minutes to look for the "Use and Care" manual included with your purchase. It was written to address the questions most frequently asked by our customers about there new appliance. If you have additional service needs or questions we have also listed some phone numbers for your convenient reference.

Of course, the standard warrenty covering your appliance remains in force until {expiration field}. Should service be needed, repairs will cost you absolutely nothing while the warranty are in effect.

When your standard warranty runs out, you can continue protecting your {appliance field} with Vista's "Service Plan Plus". It covers all expenses for replacement parts and labor on repairs to operating componants that fail due to normal use. When you choose our extended service contract, you receive prompt, relieble service from our experienced personal as often as you need it.

We are proud that you are a Vista customer. Thank you again for giving us the opportunity to serve you!

Sincerely,

Trudy J. Carrigan
Director, Service Plan Plus

---

4. Merge the form letter file and data table file to create a personalized letter for each customer.

5. Optional. Print the merged letters.

6. Create a form file for labels (you determine an appropriate predefined label number to be used).

7. Merge the label form file and the data table file to create a mailing label for each customer.

8. Optional. Print the mailing labels.

9. If you have completed your work, exit WordPerfect.

Chapter 13—Create and Print Mailing Labels

Production Skill Builder Activities
Chapters 11-13

Production Activity 4.1—Create and Merge Form and Data Files; Create Mailing Labels

1. Create a data table file using the following information:

   a. The field names are: title, first, mid, last, jr/sr, address1, address2, city, state, zip, employee type, contact name, phone.

   b. The information for each recipient follows.

   Note: Remember, each record must contain the same number of fields. Be sure to create blank fields where no data is available.

Mr. Allen H. Nakakura Sr
Gardenwood Terrace
703 N Durant Apt. 105
Santa Ana, CA 92706
Mr. Nakakura is *an active* employee.
The contact name is *Carlos Lang*
who can be reached at *555-4004.*

Mr. Rick Mitchell
The Villages Community
20150 Burbank Blvd.
Woodland Hills, CA 91367
Mr. Mitchell is *a retired state*
employee. The contact name is *Beth
Adams* who can be reached at
555-6730.

Ms. Edith J. Montero
780 Debra Ave.
Sepulveda, CA 91343
Ms. Montero is *a public agency*
employee. The contact name is *John
Montalvo* who can be reached at
555-6800.

Mrs. Rose Marie Xavier
4500 Atlantic Blvd.
Long Beach, CA 90807
Mrs. Xavier is *a public agency*
employee. The contact name is *John
Montalvo* who can be reached at
555-6800.

2. Use the filename **4pact1.dt** and save the file.

3. Sort the data table file by zip codes.

4. Use the same filename and save the file again.

5. Create the following form letter file. Make decisions regarding:

> Margins
> Justification
> Fonts
> Bullet type and spacing for bulleted list
> Reference initials/document identification/enclosure notation

---

(Use date code)

FIELD(TITLE) **FIELD**(FIRST) **FIELD**(MID) **FIELD**(LAST) **FIELD**(JR/SR)
FIELD(ADDRESS1)
FIELD(ADDRESS2)
FIELD(CITY), **FIELD**(STATE) **FIELD**(ZIP)

Dear **FIELD**(TITLE) **FIELD**(LAST):

Last month the SERS (State Employees Retirement System) Board of Directors elected to freeze new enrollments in the Basic Diablo North/South Health Plans. This freeze applies to active as well as retired state and public Agency employees.

The SERS Board of Administration has negotiated a significant reduction in the rate of premium increases for most of our health plans with no reduction of benefits. The average premium increase for fifteen of our twenty Health Maintenance Organizations (HMOs) is 4.2 percent. The premium increases submitted by the Diablo Health Plans were over 9 percent.

In response to the excessive premium increase presented by Diablo, the SERS Board of Administration adopted the premium increases and imposed the enrollment freeze. This freeze does not affect employees and retirees who are currently enrolled in Diablo Health Plans.

The following types of transactions are **not** permitted:

- New enrollments in the basic Diablo Health Plans effective August 1, 199x, and later.

The following types of enrollment transactions **are** permitted:

- New enrollments in a Diablo basic plan effective July 1, 199x, or earlier.

- Enrollment changes in the Diablo Supplement to Medicare plans.

- Additions and deletions of eligible family members.

Refer to your "Health Plans" booklet for additional information about the state's Health Benefit Program.

As **FIELD**(EMPLOYEE TYPE) employee, please direct your inquiries to your health benefit officer, **FIELD**(CONTACT NAME), at **FIELD**(PHONE).

Sincerely,

Catherine L. Hawley
Assistant Executive Officer
Health Benefits Services

---

6. Use the filename **4pact1.frm** and save the file.

7. Merge the form letter file and the data table file to create personalized letters.

8. Print one copy of each letter.

9. Create a 2- or 3-column form label file. Select an appropriate label for your printer.

   Hint: Copy the inside address field codes from the form letter file.

10. Use the filename **4pact1.lab** and save the form label file.

11. Merge the form label file and the data table file to create a mailing label for each recipient. Print one copy of the mailing labels.

12. Close the documents.

Production Activity 4.2—Create a Résumé, Set Tabs, and Insert Special Characters

1. Use the following information to type the résumé shown.

   a. Change the top margin to .75" and the bottom margin to .5".

   b. Use the Tab Set dialog box and clear all tabs; set left tabs at .5 and .75 and set a right tab with dot leaders at 6.

   c. Make decisions on the use of bold, underline, and italic text attributes.

   d. Select a font of your own choice in a point size of 12.

   e. Use special characters to create the és in Résumé.

   f. Choose an appropriate bullet character to replace the asterisks shown.

Résumé
Robert N. Ortiz
341 Maple Ave.
Paterson, NJ 07509
(201) 555-4582

EMPLOYMENT EXPERIENCE

Crowe Communications, Inc., Wyckoff, New Jersey
- Technical Writer 10/91-Present
  Write and edit technical journals and procedure manuals for computer systems and applications on a contract basis.

Newpark Software, Boston, Massachusetts
- Copyeditor 5/87-10/91
  Copyedited documentation for software applications.

- Assistant Copyeditor 8/86-5/87
  Assisted with the copyediting of company newsletters, internal procedure manuals, and some advertising information. Was promoted to Copyeditor on May 1, 1987.

Law Offices of Adam T. Cusick, Takoma Park, Maryland
- Clerical Assistant (part-time) 1/85-5/86
  Duties included typing, photocopying, faxing, and mail distribution.

EDUCATIONAL BACKGROUND

Rutgers University, Newark, New Jersey (part-time) 2/91-Present
A.A. English, Montgomery Jr. College, Takoma Park, Maryland 9/84-5/86
High School Diploma, Denbigh High School, Denbigh, Virginia 6/84

REFERENCES

Jason Heller, Supervisor
Newpark Software
230 Franklin St., Suite 25
Boston, MA 02110
(617) 555-6721

Tom Yim, Paralegal
Law Offices of Adam T. Cusick
7629 Carroll Ave.
Takoma Park, MD 20912
(301) 555-3990

2. Use the filename **4pact2** and save the file.

3. Print one copy and close the document.

➤ Production Activity 4.3—Create a Letter and an Envelope; Language Arts

1. Use the traditional block letter style and create the following letter. Make decisions regarding:

> Margins
> Justification
> Fonts
> Date of letter
> Capitalization and punctuation for the letter address
> Salutation
> Text attributes
> Correct four spelling errors, 1 misused word, and two punctuation/
>   grammatical errors
> Reference initials/document identification/enclosure notation
> Capitalization and punctuation for the letter address

   a. Send the letter to Mr. Francisco T. Ayala, who resides at 210 Richneck Road, Williamsburg, VA 23185, should receive a 15% Savings Pass. Mr. Ayala's authorization must be received no later than 20 days after the date of the letter.

Dear (provide an appropriate salutation):

Once a year we choose a limited number of people to receive a pre-approved Armstrong Credit Card. You are one of those select people.

Armstrong Credit Card rates are among the lowest in the industry. Our rates are 3.5% above the prrime rate. Our company has instant and reliabel services that is provided through our toll-free number 24 hours a day, seven days a week.

To claim your card, simply sign and mail the enclosed Armstrong Certificate. Because this offer is a special pramotion, we need your authorization by (supply the date).

With your new card, you will receive excellent service, a low interest rate, and a (supply percent discount) One-Day Savings Pass. Also you will get a free Desk-Top Calculator when you make your first credit purchase.

If you send in your pre-approved certificate today, you no-annual-fee Armstrong Credit Card will be mailed to you within one week.

Sincerely,

Jamila R. Maldonado
Manager, Special Services

---

2. Print the letter.

3. Create and print an envelope for the letter (using a return address is optional).

4. Use a filename of your choice and save the file.

5. Close the document.

Part 5

A Step in the Right Direction

Advanced Documents and Features

Chapters 14-17

- Graphic lines
- Retrieve graphic images
- Position and size graphic images
- Page borders
- Rotate and enlarge graphic images
- Contour the flow of text around graphic images
- Word spacing and letterspacing
- Leading adjustment
- Initial font
- Append to file
- Superscripts and subscripts

- Equation Editor
- Styles
- Sorting
- Macros
- Title, cascade, maximize, minimize, move, and size document windows
- Document summary information
- Use File Manager
- QuickList
- Convert files
- Passwords
- Use DOS without exiting WordPerfect

Create a Letterhead, Flier, and Newsletter

- Create graphic lines
- Retrieve graphic images
- Position and size graphic boxes
- Create page borders
- Rotate and enlarge graphic images
- Flow text through a graphic box
- Copy graphic images
- Create Text boxes
- Adjust spacing around a graphic image
- Contour the flow of text around a graphic image

Objectives

After successfully completing this chapter, you will be able to use horizontal graphic lines and font changes to create a letterhead, to retrieve, position, and size graphic images and to place borders around an entire page in order to create a flier. You will also learn how to flow text through a graphic box in order to create a graphic with text overlay. In addition, you will rotate and enlarge a graphic image within a graphic box, adjust the spacing around a graphic box and contour the flow of text around a graphic image.

Note: The User Box does not have printed borders.

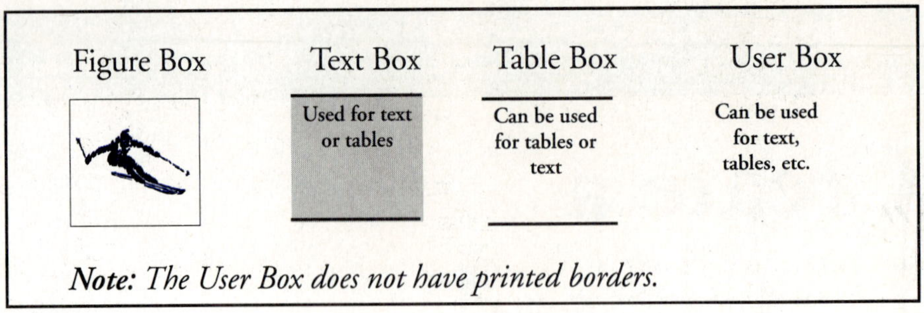

Chapter Introduction

WordPerfect's graphics features are used to illustrate an idea through a picture or to present text or data in an interesting and appealing manner. In addition, horizontal and vertical graphic lines can be used to separate text for a more pleasing appearance and to assist with easier reading.

Eight types of graphic boxes are available in WordPerfect, i.e., Figure, Text, Table, User, Button, Watermark, Equation, and Inline Equation. Each type of box is designed for a specific purpose and includes default settings for size, shading, and borders. Figure 14.1 shows samples of the border and shading settings for Figure, Text, Table, and User graphic boxes. Although the predesigned graphic boxes are designated for a specific item, most of the boxes can be used for other contents. For example, Table and User boxes can contain graphics, text, a table, or an equation.

WordPerfect provides 30 graphic images that can be retrieved into a document. When a graphic image is retrieved, WordPerfect automatically places the graphic image in a Figure box. If the graphics mode or page mode view is active, the graphic image displays on the screen. If the text mode view is active, an empty Figure box will display at the location of the graphic image on the screen. In addition to the graphic images provided by WordPerfect, graphic files created using many other graphic programs can also be retrieved into WordPerfect documents. Graphic images from other graphic programs must be saved in a format that can be interpreted by WordPerfect, such as PCX (PC Paintbrush) or PIC (Lotus 1-2-3).

Create a Letterhead

Aletterhead can be created by using different fonts, point sizes, and borders. Type the text for the letterhead unformatted. Once the letterhead text is typed, the fonts, point sizes, graphic lines, and alignment are selected.

To enhance the appearance of letterhead text, different fonts and point sizes as well as text attributes such as bold and italic can be used. The placement of letterhead text can be changed using the justification options. In addition, horizontal graphic lines can be placed above, below, or around the letterhead text.

❖ Type the letterhead information as follows:

    a. Type the business name in all uppercase letters, e.g., type **BASS IN-FORMATION SYSTEMS**. Press **Enter** once.

    b. Type the company address in uppercase and lowercase letters, e.g., **30 East Seventh Street**. Press **Enter** once.

    c. Type the city, state, and zip code in uppercase and lowercase letters, e.g., **St. Paul, Minnesota 55101**. Press **Enter** three times.

    d. Type the voice telephone number, e.g., **Voice:** (612) 555-1622.

    e. Press **Alt** and **F6** for Flush Right justification.

    f. Type the fax telephone number, e.g., **Fax:** (612) 555-3879. Press **Enter** once.

Steps to ▶ Create Graphic Lines

1. Place the cursor/insertion point at the location where the graphic line should be inserted.

   For example, move the cursor/insertion point to the blank line between the city, state, and zip and the phone numbers.

2. Select **Graphics, Graphics Lines, Create** {Alt and F9, L, c}.

   Note: The Create Graphics Line dialog box displays (see Figure 14.2). Notice that the default Line Orientation is Horizontal and the default Horizontal Position is Full.

3. To change the thickness of the graphic line, move the mouse pointer to the word **Thickness**, click once and select **Set** {t, s}.

4. Type the desired line thickness.

   For example, type **.020** in the Thickness box.

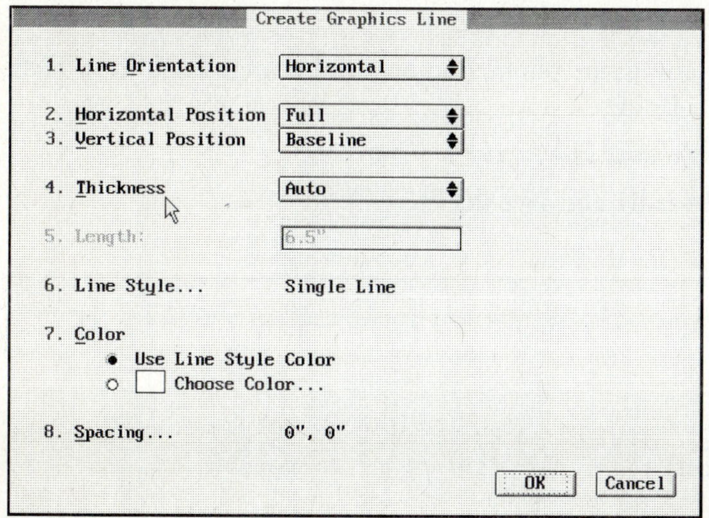

FIGURE 14.2

Create Graphics Line dialog box

Sample letterhead with graphic lines

BASS INFORMATION SYSTEMS
30 East Seventh Street
St. Paul, Minnesota 55101

Voice: (612) 555-1622   Fax: (612) 555-3879

5. Select **OK** {press Enter twice}.

6. Place the cursor/insertion point where the next graphic line should be located.

   For example, place the cursor/insertion point in the blank line below the phone numbers.

7. Select **Graphics, Graphics Line, Create** {Alt and F9, L, c}.

8. Move the mouse pointer to the words **Line Style** and click once {y}.

   Note: The Line Styles dialog box displays.

9. Move the mouse pointer to the desired line style and double-click {press the up or down arrow key to highlight the desired option, press Enter}.

   For example, double-click on **Thick Thin Line**.

10. Select **OK** {Enter}.

Finish-Up Instructions

❖ Block the company name, address, city, state, and zip information and choose **Center** justification.

❖ Block the company name and change the font to **Bodoni-WP Bold (Type 1), 14-point**.

❖ Block the address lines and change the font to **Helv-WP (Type 1), 12-point, Bold**.

❖ Block the line containing the phone numbers and change the font to **Helv-WP (Type 1), 10-point, Bold**.

   Note: Your letterhead should look similar to Figure 14.3.

❖ Use the filename **14drill1** and save the file.

❖ Print one copy.

❖ Close the document.

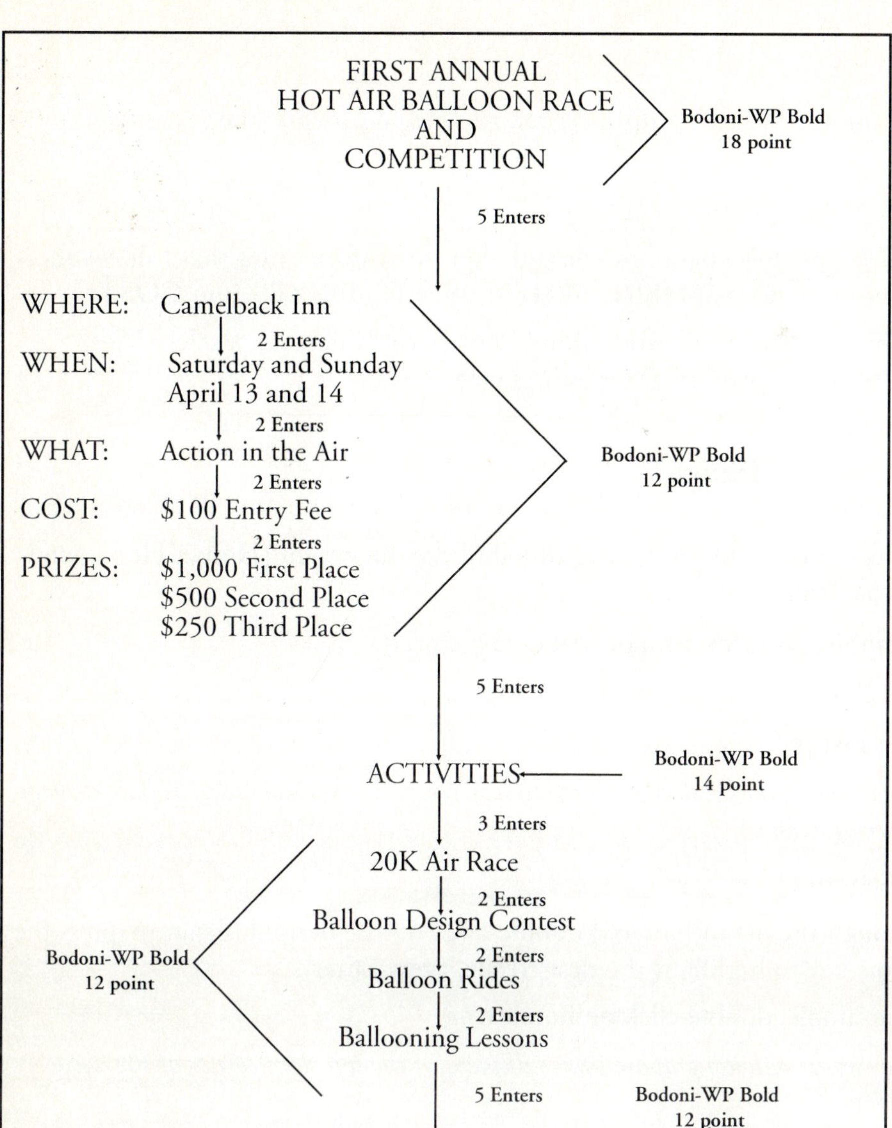

FIGURE 14.4

Flier text

Create a Flier with a Graphic Image

Creating a flier in WordPerfect is similar to creating a flier on a typewriter. However, the flier can include graphic lines, graphic images, and text printed in different font styles and point sizes (see Figure 14.6 on page 380).

Once the flier text is typed, the text is formatted with the desired fonts, point sizes, justification, and appearance. When a graphic image is retrieved, the image is placed in a graphic Figure box. If graphics or page view mode is active, the graphic image displays in the top right corner of the document screen. Graphics can be sized or re-positioned on the page, and the border lines around the graphic Figure box can be removed or changed. Also, a border can be placed around the entire page.

- ❖ Read and use the following information to type and format the text shown in Figure 14.4.

    a. Change the top margin to 1.25".

    b. Use the **Tab** key to indent and align the information that follows the heading lines **WHERE, WHEN, WHAT, PRIZES,** and **COST.**

- ❖ The graphics or page view mode should be active. If necessary, select **View, Graphics Mode** to turn on the graphics view.

Retrieve a Graphic Image

1. Place the insertion point at the beginning of the document (**Home, Home,** and the up arrow key).

2. Select **Graphics, Retrieve Image** {Alt and g, Enter}.

   Note: The Retrieve Image File dialog box displays.

3. Select **File List** {F5}.

   Note: The default WordPerfect graphics directory, e.g., C:\WP60\GRAPHICS, displays in the Directories box.

4. Select **OK** {Enter}.

5. Scroll through the list of files and double-click on the desired filename {press the down arrow key to highlight the desired file, press Enter}.

   For example, double-click on **hotair.wpg.**

   Note: The hot air balloon graphic image displays in the top right corner of the document window.

Finish-Up Instructions

- ❖ Use Reveal Codes to view the graphic code [Box (Para):1; Figure Box]. Wait momentarily until the graphic image is redrawn on the screen.

- ❖ Use the filename **14drill2** and save the file.

Start-Up Instructions

- ❖ The file named **14drill2** should be displayed on the screen.

Position a Graphic Box

1. Move the mouse pointer anywhere on the graphic image and double-click {Alt and F9, b; if necessary, type the graphic box number, e}.

   Note: The Edit Graphics Box dialog box displays (see Figure 14.5).

2. Select **Edit Position** {p}.

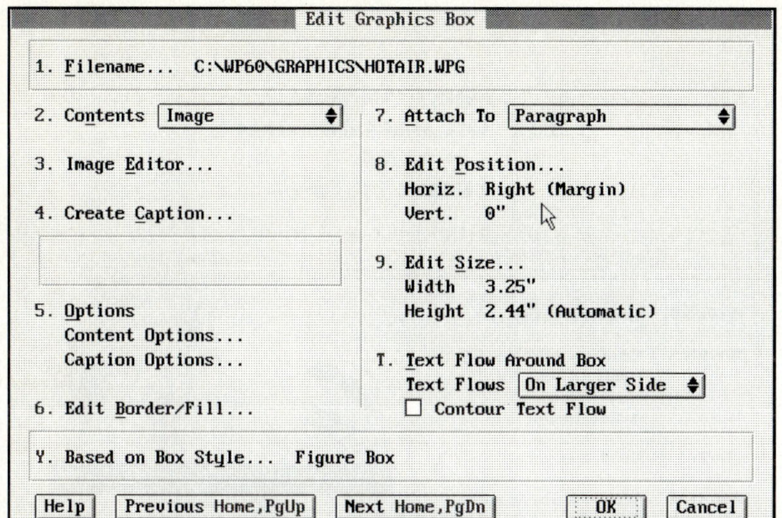

Edit Graphics Box dialog box

Note: The Paragraph Box Position dialog box displays.

3. Move the mouse pointer to the words **Horizontal Position** (located in the Horizontal Position of Box area) and click once {h}.

4. Select **Set** {s}.

5. Type the desired horizontal position for the graphic image.

   For example, type **4.25** to place the graphic image $4\frac{1}{4}$ inches from the left margin.

6. Click in the **Distance from Top of Paragraph** box {press Tab, d}.

7. Type the desired location for the graphic image.

   For example, type **1.25** to place the graphic image $1\frac{1}{4}$ inches below the first line of text.

8. Select **OK** {Enter twice}.

Remove the Border from a Graphic Box

9. Select **Edit Border/Fill** {b}.

10. Select **Based on Border Style** {y}.

11. Double-click on **None** to remove the graphic box border {press the up arrow key to highlight None, press Enter}.

12. Select **Close** {Enter}.

13. Select **OK** to return to the document screen {Enter}.

    Note: The graphics image displays at the new position, and the graphic box border has been removed. Your document should look similar to Figure 14.6.

Finish-Up Instructions

❖ Use the same filename, **14drill2**, and save the file.

Flier with a graphic image

FIRST ANNUAL
HOT AIR BALLOON RACE
AND
COMPETITION

WHERE: Camelback Inn

WHEN: Saturday and Sunday
April 13 and 14

WHAT: Action in the Air

COST: $100 Entry Fee

PRIZES: $1,000 First Place
$500 Second Place
$250 Third Place

Activities

20K Air Race

Balloon Design Contest

Balloon Rides

Ballooning Lessons

PROCEEDS WILL BENEFIT THE SCOTTSDALE YOUTH PROGRAM

Start-Up Instructions

❖ The file named **14drill2** should be displayed on the screen.

Steps to **Create a Page Border**

1. Select **Graphics, Borders, Page** {Alt and F9, o, a}.

2. Select **Border Style** {b}.

3. Move the mouse pointer to the desired border style and double-click {press the up or down arrow key to highlight the desired border, press Enter}.

    For example, double-click on **Thick Thin Border**.

4. Select **OK** {Enter}.

    *Note: To view the page border, select the **Preview** button or choose **View**, **Page Mode**. Your flier should look similar to Figure 14.6.*

     Chapter 14—Create a Letterhead, Flier, and Newsletter

- ❖ Use the new filename **14drill2.fin** and save the file.
- ❖ Print one copy.
- ❖ Close the document.

Graphic with Text Overlay

Text can easily be placed inside (overlaid) a graphic box by selecting the **Text Flow** option in the Edit Graphics Box dialog box and choosing **Through Box**. WordPerfect provides several graphic images that are suitable for creating documents with text overlays (see Figure 14.7).

After the Through Box option has been selected, text can be typed onto the page using the normal procedures for typing and editing text. However, it may be difficult to use the mouse to relocate the insertion point; instead use the up, down, left, and right arrow keys to move the insertion point to different locations in the document.

The actual content of a graphic image file cannot be changed in WordPerfect. However, the graphic image can be altered by rotating, sizing, and moving the image within the graphic Figure box.

Start-Up Instructions

- ❖ Change the top and bottom margins to .5".
- ❖ Press the **Enter** key five times. Type, center, and format the text as shown in Figure 14.7. Be sure and press the **Enter** key eight times after the last line of text.
- ❖ The graphics mode view should be active. If necessary, select **View**, **Graphics Mode**.
- ❖ Save the file; use the filename **14drill3**.

Steps to ▶ Create a Graphic with Text Overlay

1. Place the insertion point at the top of the document (press **Home** twice and the up arrow key).

2. Select **Graphics, Retrieve Image** {Alt and g, Enter}.

3. Select **File List** {F5}.

4. Select **OK** {Enter}.

5. Double-click on the desired graphic image filename {press the down arrow key repeatedly and highlight the desired filename, press Enter}.

   For example, double-click on **border7.wpg** .

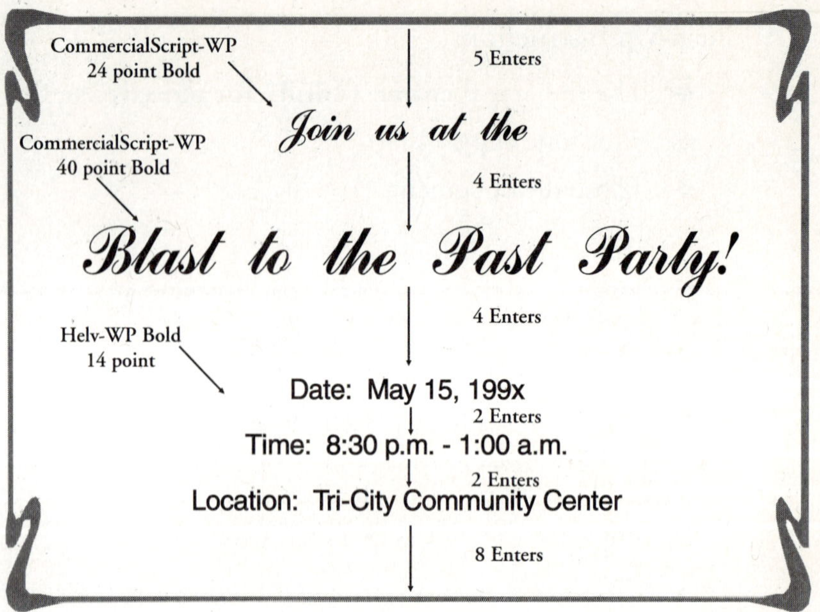

Note: The graphic image displays to the right of the text in the document window.

6. Double-click anywhere on the graphic image {Alt and g, b, e, Enter}.

   Note: The Edit Graphics Box dialog box displays.

7. Select **Edit Position** {p}.

8. Move the mouse pointer to the words **Horizontal Position** and click once {h}.

9. Select the desired horizontal position.

   For example, select **Full** {f}.

10. Select **OK** {Enter}.

Size a Graphic Box

11. Select **Edit Size** {s}.

12. Select the **Set Height** option and type the desired height for the graphic image {h, type size}.

    For example, type **4.5**. (Do not type the final period.)

13. Select **OK** {Enter twice}.

Remove Border Around Graphic Image

14. Select **Edit Border/Fill** {b}.

15. Select **Based on Border Style** {y}.

16. Double-click on **None** {press the up arrow key to highlight None, Enter}.

17. Select **Close** {Enter}.

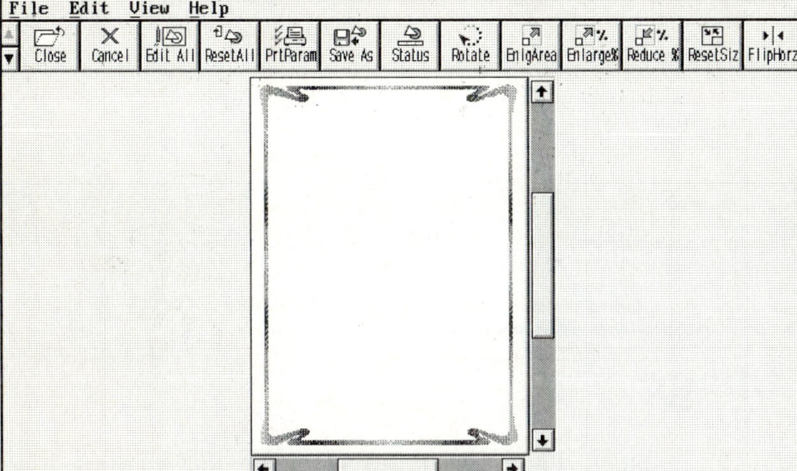

FIGURE 14.8

Image Editor window

Rotate Graphic Image Within a Graphic Box

18. Select **Image Editor** {e}.

    Note: The Image Editor window containing the graphic image displays (see Figure 14.8).

19. Click once in the **Rotation** option box located at the bottom of the window {o}.

20. Type the degree of rotation desired and press **Enter**

    For example, type **90** and press **Enter**.

    *Note: A graphic image can also be rotated by selecting the **Rotate** button and dragging the horizontal or vertical axis lines.*

Enlarge the Graphic Image Within the Graphic Box

21. Select the **Enlarge %** button to increase the size of the graphic image.

    For example, select the **Enlarge %** button 3-4 times.

    *Note: Each time the **Enlarge %** button is selected, the image becomes larger. If the Enlarge % button is selected too many times, select the **Reduce %** button to decrease the image size. If the **EnlgArea** button is selected in error, press the **Esc** key to deselect.*

22. Select the **Close** button to exit the Image Editor window {F7}.

Flow Text Through a Graphic Box

23. Move the mouse pointer to the option box beside the words **Text Flows**, press and hold down the mouse button to display a list of text flow options {t, f}.

24. Move the mouse pointer to the **Through Box** option and release the mouse button {t}.

25. Select **OK** to exit the Edit Graphics Box dialog box {Enter}.

Note: Wait a few moments until the border (border7.wpg) displays in the document window rotated and sized.

Finish-Up Instructions

❖ Save the file again using the same filename, **14drill3**.

❖ Print one copy.

Copy a Graphic Image

A graphic image can be blocked and copied into the same document or, if desired, into a different document. If all the text and graphic images in a document are to be copied, the **Edit, Select, Page** command can be used to ensure that everything in the document (e.g., text, margins codes, graphic box codes, etc.) is blocked. Once blocked, the text and graphic images can be copied by using any of the three methods of copying text discussed in Chapter 5, pages 117-119.

Start-Up Instructions

❖ The file named **14drill3** should be displayed on the screen.

Copy a Graphic Image and Text

1. Select **Edit, Select, Page** to block everything on the page {Alt and e, s, a}.

   Note: The entire text and graphic image are highlighted.

2. Select **Edit, Copy** {Ctrl and c}.

   Note: The highlighting has been removed from the text and the insertion point is located at the bottom of the document.

3. Select **Edit, Paste** {Ctrl and v}.

   Note: A copy of the graphic image and text is inserted into the document.

Finish-Up Instructions

❖ Select the **Preview** button to view the entire page. If necessary, select **Full Page**. Select **Close** to return to the document window.

❖ Press **Home**, **Home**, and the down arrow key once to move the insertion point to the bottom of the document. Delete the extra hard returns to remove the page break. (If necessary, turn on Reveal Codes to display and highlight the hard return [HRt] codes.)

❖ Use the new filename **14drill3.rev** and save the file.

❖ Print one copy and close the document.

Create a Newsletter

typical newsletter includes text columns, graphics, and borders. Different fonts and point sizes can be used for the newsletter text (see Figure 14.9). The heading portion (nameplate) of the newsletter is created by using the Text Box feature. The default settings for a Text box include a gray shading and horizontal graphic lines at the top and bottom of the box. If desired, the graphic lines or shading settings can be changed.

The newsletter body text is created using the **Column** button on the Ribbon to select the desired number of columns. (See Chapter 8, Steps to Create Newspaper Columns Using the Columns Button on the Ribbon on page 211.) Once the newsletter body text has been typed, graphic images can be placed in the document to add visual appeal.

Graphic boxes (e.g., Figure boxes, Text boxes, and User boxes) can be *attached* to a paragraph, a page, a fixed position on a page, or a character. A graphic box that is attached to a paragraph remains with the paragraph if the paragraph is relocated. A graphic box that is attached to a page remains at a fixed position on the page relative to the left and top margins/column. A graphic box that is attached to a fixed page position remains at a specific position on the page relative to the top and left edges of the paper. A graphic box attached to a character remains with the text on a line and is treated as a character. Usually, graphic boxes are attached to the page or a paragraph.

Text can be flowed around the edges of a graphic image by using the Contour Text Flow option. When **Contour Text Flow** is selected, the graphic box borders are automatically removed.

By default, a graphic box is surrounded by an area where text does not print (white space). The amount of space around the graphics box can be adjusted in order to create a visually appealing document.

A mouse can be used to change the position and/or size of a graphic box in the document window. In order to use the mouse to position or size a graphic box, the box must be selected. To select a graphic box, move the mouse pointer to the graphic image and click once. When selected, a dotted outline with black handles displays around the graphic box. A selected graphic box can be deleted by pressing the **Delete** key.

If desired, a vertical graphic line can be placed between columns in order to improve the readability of a multiple-column document. In order for the vertical graphic line to begin below the newsletter nameplate, the vertical graphic line code is placed in the document immediately after the column definition ([Col Def]) code (see Chapter 8, Steps to Place a Border Line Between Newspaper Columns on page 213).

Start-Up Instructions

❖ Change the top and bottom margins to .75".

❖   The newsletter nameplate information is shown in Figure 14.9.

Use a Text Box to Create a Newsletter Nameplate

1. Select **Graphics, Graphics Boxes, Create** {Alt and F9, b, c}.

   Note: The Create Graphics Box dialog box displays.

2. Select **Edit Position** {p}.

3. Move the mouse pointer to the words **Horizontal Position** (located in the Horizontal Position of Box area) and click once {h}.

4. Select **Full** {f}.

5. Select **OK** {Enter}.

6. Select **Create Text** {e}.

   Note: A clear document window displays on the screen. The words "Box: Press F7 when done. Press Alt+F9 to rotate" displays in the Status bar. Text can be typed and formatted in the document window.

7. Type the Text box information.

   For example, press the **Enter** key once and type the newsletter heading shown in Figure 14.9. The Text box information will be formatted in Step 8. After typing the date, press **Alt** and **F6** to use flush right alignment before typing the company name.

8. Format the Text box information.

   a. Block the first two lines and choose **Center** justification. Change the font to **Bodoni-WP Bold (Type 1), 14-point**.

   b. Block the last line and change the font to **Dutch 801 Roman, 10-point, Bold**.

9. Press **F7** to exit to the Create Graphics Box dialog box.

10. Select **Based on Box Style** {y}.

11. Double-click on the desired box style {press the up or down arrow key to highlight box style, press Enter}.

    For example double-click on **Text Box**.

12. Select **Edit Border/Fill** {b}.

    Note: The Edit Graphics Box Border/Fill dialog box displays. A sample of the default Text box borders and fill is shown.

13. To change the default lines, select **Lines** {L}.

14. Choose **Select All** {a}.

15. Move the mouse pointer to the desired type of border and double-click {press the up or down arrow key to highlight the desired border type, press Enter}.

                                        Chapter 14—Create a Letterhead, Flier, and Newsletter

Newsletter with Text box and contour text flow around a graphics image

For example, double-click on **Thick Thin Line**.

16. Select **Close** twice {press Enter twice}.

17. Select **OK** to return to the document window.

   Note: The Text box displays on the screen.

Finish-Up Instructions

❖ Press the **Enter** key once to move the insertion point two lines below the Text box.

❖ Save the file; use the filename **14drill4**.

 ❖ The file named **14drill4** should be displayed on the screen.

 ❖ The text for the newsletter is shown in Figure 14.9.

Create Newsletter Body Text

1. Select the **Columns** button on the Ribbon and double-click on the number of columns desired {Alt and F7, c, n, type the number of columns, Enter twice}.

    For example, double-click on **2 Cols.**

2. Set the font and point size for the body text of the newsletter.

    For example, select **Dutch 801 Roman, 12-point.**

3. Type the text for the newsletter columns (see Figure 14.9).

    Note: The graphic image will be placed in the document after all text, including the table, is typed.

Finish-Up Instructions

 ❖ Save the file again using the same filename, **14drill4.**

Start-Up Instructions

 ❖ Place the insertion point at the beginning of the first paragraph in the first column.

 ❖ Retrieve the graphics image named **Skier1.wpg** (see Steps to Retrieve a Graphic Image on page 378).

    Note: Since the last graphic box created was a Text box, the graphic image may display with the default Text box border and fill. The graphic box will be changed to a Figure box later.

 ❖ Move the mouse pointer to the graphic image and double-click to obtain the Edit Graphics Box dialog box (Alt and F9, b, e, 2, Enter}.

 ❖ Change the position and size of the graphic image and change box style. If necessary, see Position a Graphic on page 378 and Size a Graphic on page 382.

    a. Select **Edit Position** and change the horizontal position of the graphic image to **Left.** Click in the **Distance from Top of Paragraph** box and type **1.25.** Select **OK.**

    b. Select **Edit Size** and set the width of the graphic image to **2.25.** Select **OK.**

    c. Select **Based on Border Style** and change the box style to **Figure Box.**

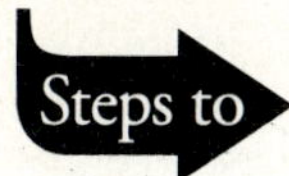 ## Contour the Flow of Text Around a Graphic Image

1. In the Edit Graphics Box dialog box, move the mouse pointer to the **Contour Text Flow** option and click {t, e}.

   Note: An X displays in the Contour Text Flow option box.

 ## Adjust Space Around a Graphic Box

1. In the Edit Graphics Box dialog box, select **Edit Border/Fill** {b}.

   Note: When the Contour Text Flow option was selected above, WordPerfect automatically removed the graphic box borders. The current setting for the Based on Border Style is Spacing Only (No Lines).

2. Select **Spacing** {s}.

   Note: An X appears in the Automatic Spacing box to indicate that this option is currently selected.

3. Select **Automatic Spacing** to turn off this option {a}.

4. Select **Outside, Set All** to change all the spacing around the graphic image {o}.

5. Type the desired amount of space to be placed between the graphics image and the text.

   For example, type .05.

6. Select **OK** twice {Enter three times}.

7. Select **OK** to exit the Edit Graphics Box dialog box and return to the document window {Enter twice}.

   Note: The graphic image displays in the first paragraph of text. The text flows around the shape of the graphic image with white space between the graphic image and the text.

Finish-Up Instructions

❖ If desired, place a vertical border line between the columns (select **Layout**, **Columns**, **Column Borders**, **OK** twice).

   Note: Your newsletter should look similar to Figure 14.9.

❖ Save the file again using the same filename, **14drill4**.

❖ If desired, select **File**, **Print Preview** to view the newsletter.

❖ Print one copy.

Start-Up Instructions

❖ The file named **14drill4** should be displayed on the screen.

 **Change the Size and Position of a Graphic Image Using the Mouse**

1. In the document window, move the mouse pointer to the graphic image and click once to select the graphic box.

   For example, move the mouse pointer to the skier graphic image and click once to select the graphic box.

   Note: A dotted rectangle with black handles along the edges and at the corners displays around the graphics image.

2. *To change the size of the graphic image,* move the mouse pointer to one of the black boxes on the dotted line until a two-headed arrow displays. Press and hold the mouse button and drag the dotted line to size the graphic box and image.

   For example, place the mouse pointer on the black handle at the bottom right corner of the skier graphic image, press and hold the mouse button and drag down and to the right approximately $\frac{1}{4}$". Release the mouse button.

3. *To change the position of the graphic image,* select the graphic box (see Step 1), move the mouse pointer within the graphic image. A four-headed arrow displays. Press and hold the mouse button and drag the graphic image to the new location.

   For example, drag the skier graphic image to the middle of the second paragraph in the first column and release the mouse button.

Finish-Up Instructions

- ❖ If desired, practice moving and sizing the graphic image using the mouse.
- ❖ Use the new filename **14drill4.rev** and save the file.
- ❖ Optional. Print one copy.
- ❖ Close the document.

The Next Step

Chapter Review and Activities

FEATURES SUMMARY

FEATURES	ACTIONS	PAGE
Create graphic lines	Select **Graphics, Graphics Lines, Create.** *To change the thickness of the graphics line*, move the mouse pointer to the word **Thickness** and click. Select **Set** and type the desired line thickness. *To change the line style*, move the mouse pointer to the words **Line Style** and click once, double-click on the desired style option. Select **OK.**	375
Retrieve a graphic image	Select **Graphics, Retrieve Image,** select **File List, OK,** double-click on the desired graphics filename.	378
Position a graphic box	Move the mouse pointer anywhere on the graphic image and double-click. Select **Edit Position.** Move the mouse pointer to the words **Horizontal Position** and click once. Select the desired position option. If desired, click in the **Distance from Top of Paragraph** box and type a desired location. Select **OK** twice to return to the document window.	378
Remove border from a graphic box	In the Edit Graphics Box dialog box, select **Edit Border/Fill,** select **Based on Border Style,** double-click on **None.** Select **Close, OK** to return to the document window.	379

| --- | --- | --- |
Create a page border	Select **Graphics, Borders, Page**, select **Borders Styles**, double-click on the desired border style. Select **OK**.	380
Size a graphic box	In the Edit Graphics Box dialog box, select **Edit Size**, select **Set Height** or **Set Width** and type the desired height or width. Select **OK** twice to return to the document window.	382
Rotate a graphic image	In the Edit Graphics Box dialog box, select **Image Editor**, click once in the **Rotation** option box, type the desired degree of rotation, and press **Enter**. To exit the Image Editor, select **Close**.	383
Enlarge a graphic image within a graphic box	In the Image Editor, select the **Enlarge %** button. To exit the Image Editor window, select **Close**.	383
Flow text through a graphic box	In the Edit Graphics Box dialog box, move the mouse pointer to the box beside the words **Text Flow**, press and hold down the mouse button, move the mouse pointer to the **Through Box** option and release the mouse pointer. Select **OK** to exit to the document window.	383
Copy a graphic image	Select **Edit, Select, Page, Edit, Copy, Edit, Paste**.	384
Create a Text box	Select **Graphics, Graphics Boxes, Create**. Select **Edit Position, Horizontal Position, Full, OK**. Select **Create Text**, type and format the text box information. Press **F7**. Select **Based on Box Style**, double-click on **Text Box**. If desired, change the border style by selecting **Edit Border/Fill, Lines, Select All**, double-clicking on desired line style. Select **Close** twice, select **OK** to return to the document window.	386
Contour the flow of text around a graphic box	In the Edit Graphics Box dialog box, move the mouse pointer to the **Contour Text Flow** option and click. Select **OK** to exit to the document window.	389
Adjust space around a graphic box	In the Edit Graphics Box dialog box, select **Edit Border/Fill**. Select **Spacing, Automatic Spacing, Outside, Set All**, type the desired amount of space, select **OK** three times to exit to the document window.	389
Position and size a graphic image using the mouse	Move the mouse pointer anywhere on the graphics image and click once. To move a graphic box, press and hold the mouse button and drag the graphic box to the desired location. To size a graphic box, place the mouse pointer on a black handle at the edge or corner of the graphic box, press and hold the mouse button, and drag to the desired size.	390

Chapter 14—Create a Letterhead, Flier, and Newsletter

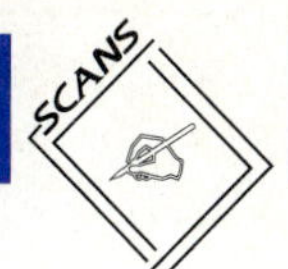

True/False—Circle One

T F 1. A horizontal graphics line can be created by selecting **Graphics**, **Graphics Line**, **Create**, choosing the desired line thickness and/or line style, and selecting **OK**.

T F 2. The border that appears around a graphic box cannot be removed or changed.

T F 3. In the Image Editor window, the **Enlarge %** button is selected to increase the size of the graphics image within the graphic box.

T F 4. In order for text to overlay a graphic, the Text Flows, Through Box option must be selected in the Edit Graphics Box dialog box.

T F 5. The vertical and horizontal position of a graphics box cannot be changed once a graphics image has been retrieved into a document.

T F 6. A horizontal graphics line can be placed below, above, or around a paragraph.

Short Answer

1. List the four steps to create a page border.

2. Write down the name of the directory where WordPerfect graphics files are stored on your system.

3. List the two main characteristics of the default setting for a graphic Text box. (**Hint:** See Figure 14.9.)

4. In the Edit Graphics Box dialog box, what option must be selected in order for text to flow through a graphics box?

Enriching Language Arts Skills

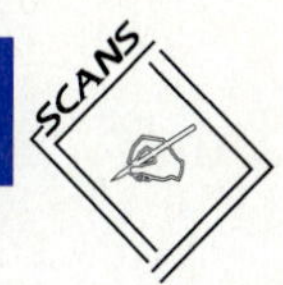

Spelling/Vocabulary Words

extensive   wide, broad; comprehensive.

HMO   Health Maintenance Organization. A term used by insurance companies that provide health care coverage; the client is seen by the HMO's selected doctor(s).

reputation   a measure of a person's or organization's character as viewed by others.

Initials Abbreviated

Periods or spaces are not placed after the letters of an acronym such as IRS (Internal Revenue Service), or TWA (Trans World Airlines).

Examples:

IRS (Internal Revenue Service)
TWA (Trans World Airline)

Activities

Activity 14.1—Create a Flier with Graphics

1. Type and center all text of the flier using the spacing shown in the flier on page 395.

2. Place the insertion point at the top of the document. Retrieve the graphics file named **hotrod.wpg** (select **Graphics, Retrieve Image, F5, OK**, double-click on **hotrod.wpg**).

3. Double-click on the graphic image and make the following changes:

   a. Select **Edit Position**, click in the **Distance from Top of Paragraph** and type **3.75**. Select **OK**.

   b. Select **Edit Size** and set the width of the graphics box to **3.75"**. Select **OK**.

   c. Remove the graphics box border (select **Edit Border/Fill, Based on Border Style**, double-click on **None**, select **Close** twice).

4. Select **OK**.

5. Place a Thick Thin border around the entire page (select **Graphics, Borders, Page, Border Style**, double-click on **Thick Thin Border, Close, OK**).

   Note: Your flier should look similar to the flier on page 395.

6. If desired, select the **Preview** button and view the flier on the screen.

7. Use the filename **14act1** and save the file.

8. Print one copy.

9. Close the document.

Chapter 14—Create a Letterhead, Flier, and Newsletter

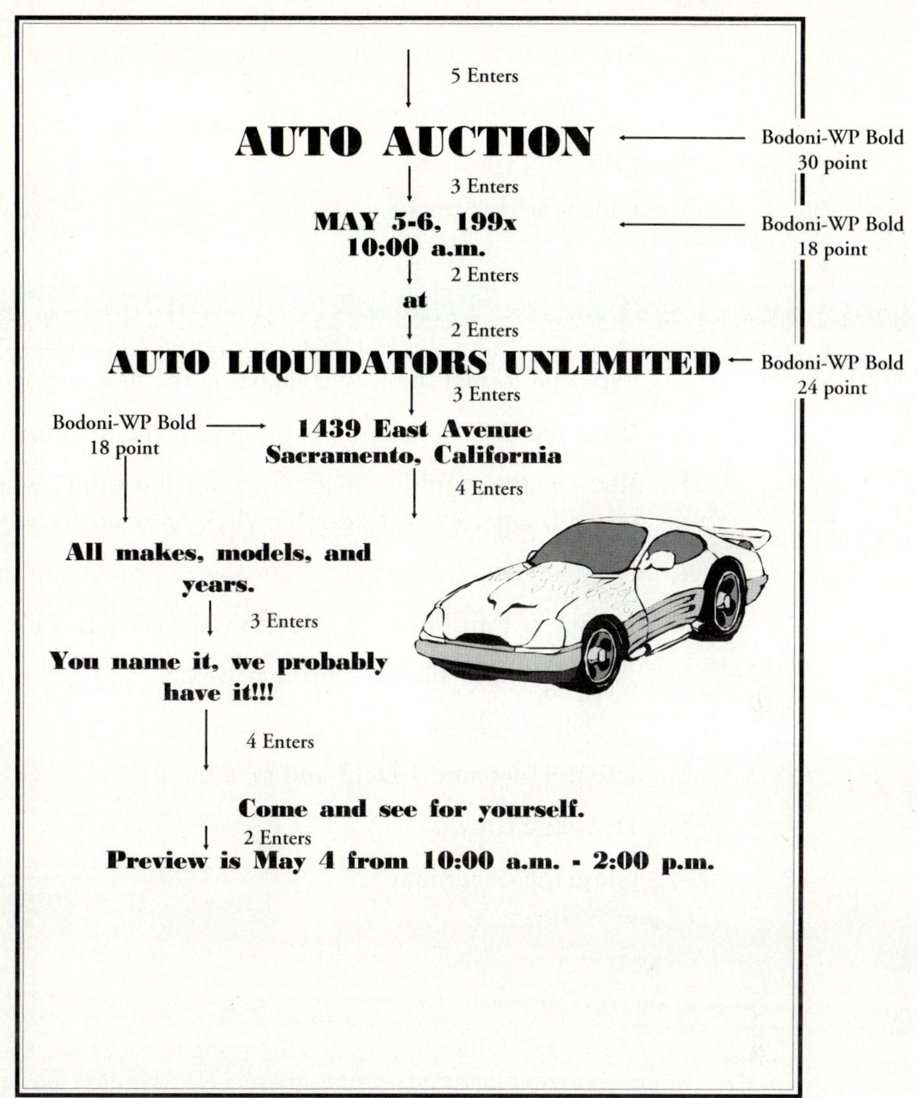

Activity 14.2—Create a Letterhead with Horizontal Graphics Lines

1. Create a letterhead using the following information. Use a style similar to
   the one shown in Figure 14.3.

Mountain Technology Services
P.O. Box 3002
Bellevue, WA 98009
Voice: (206) 555-4300
Fax: (206) 555-2364

2. If desired, select the **Preview** button to view the letterhead on the screen. Select **Cancel** to return to the document window.

3. Use the filename **14act2** and save the file.

4. Print one copy.

5. Close the document.

Activity 14.3—Create a Flier with a Graphic and Text Overlay

1. Type and format the text as shown in the flier on page 397.

2. Place the insertion point at the top of the document.

3. Retrieve the graphics image file named **overhd1.wpg** (select **Graphics, Retrieve Image, F5, OK**, double-click on **overhd1.wpg**).

4. Double-click on the graphic image and make the following changes:

   a. Select **Edit Position, Horizontal Position, Full, OK**.

   b. Select **Text Flows, Through Box**.

   c. Select **OK**.

5. Use the filename **14act3** and save the file.

6. Print one copy.

7. Close the document.

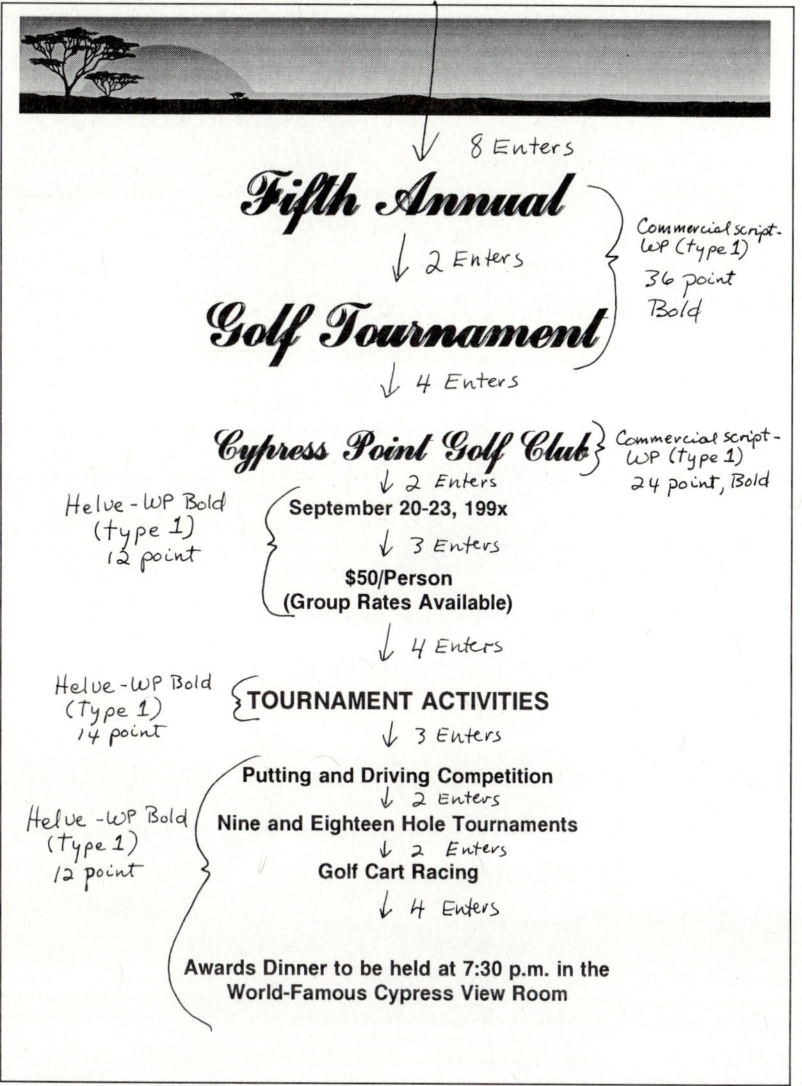

Activity 14.4—Create a Newsletter with a Graphic Image

1. Use the following information and the newsletter style shown in Figure 14.9 to create an employee newsletter for Campanella Systems.

   a. The text of the newsletter is shown on page 398.

   b. Create the nameplate using a Text box (if necessary, see page 386).

   c. Change the font for the table text to **Dutch 801 Roman (Speedo), 12-point**.

   d. Place the insertion point to the left of the first character in the first paragraph.

   e. Retrieve the graphics file named **skipper1.wpg**.

   f. Double-click on the graphic image and make the following changes:

CAMPANELLA'S

NEWS BULLETIN

February 199x   Campanella Systems, Inc.

EASTERN REGION

Our flagship account (MCI) has successfully upgraded to our new operating system and has also implemented the Flex program. We have had two teams assisting in these efforts: Monty Gillars and Belinda Fields (upgrade); Glenda King and Elvia Marshall (Flex). June Payton served as Account Manager with liaison responsibilities for both groups. Monty and Glenda are still involved there, integrating a new company into the system and assisting in year-end and flex tasks.

We have had two additions to our staff. Tom Burrnell joined us as the Eastern Region Sales Representative and Colleen Duke was hired as a Senior Consultant.

MIDWESTERN REGION

We have been fortunate to have several large projects in place. These have recently been supplemented by the University of Nebraska and Consumers Power of Michigan. Both of these accounts are using our mainframe operating system.

It was conference time again for several of our consultants. Amos Stenson attended the Canadian Human Resources conference in Toronto. Joanna Holt spent a day in Chicago at the Midwest Human Resources conference trying to discover the difference between the HR vendors and "GUIs." Ted Crutcher traveled to New Orleans to attend the Financial Users Conference. As a direct result of our conference efforts, we are in the process of closing sales with a couple of companies that we met in Toronto and Chicago.

WESTERN REGION

The Western region has added three new clients during the past month. With the addition of these new clients, the Western region is now serving 15 clients. We are well on our way to meeting our goal for serving 25 new western clients during this fiscal year.

---

g. Select **Edit Position** and set the Horizontal Position to **Left**. Click in the **Distance from Top of Paragraph** box and type **.75**. Select **OK**.

h. Select **Edit Size** and set the width to **1.75**. Select **OK**.

i. If necessary, select the **Based on Box Style** option and choose **Figure Box**.

j. Select the **Contour Text Flow** option.

k. Adjust the spacing around the graphic image (select **Edit Border/Fill**, **Spacing**, **Automatic Spacing**, **Outside**, **Set All**, type **.05**, **OK**, **Close**).

l. Select **OK**.

m. Place a column border between the two columns (select **Layout, Columns, Column Borders, OK**).

n. The newsletter should appear on one page. If necessary, adjust the size of the text fonts or change the top or bottom margins to fit the text on one page. Your newsletter should look similar to the newsletter on page 398.

2. If desired, select **File**, **Print Preview** to view the newsletter on the screen.

3. Use the filename **14act4** and save the file.

4. Print one copy and close the document.

Challenge Your Skills

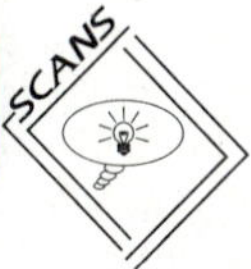

Skill 14.1—Create a Flier with Graphics

1. Use the following information and create a flier for the Pelican Beach Club vacation resort.

   a. The resort is located in the Grand Cayman Islands.

   b. A special vacation package including two nights' free lodging, a free glass-bottom boat ride, two days' car rental, and a visit to Grand Cayman Botanical Garden is available when a seven-day vacation is reserved.

   c. Eugenia McAllister of Global Travel Associates, (919) 555-6288, can assist with scheduling this special vacation package.

   d. Insert any *two* of the following graphics images:

   fishtrop.wpg   parrot.wpg
   humbird.wpg   summrcnr.wpg

2. Use the filename **14skill1** and save the file.

3. Print one copy.

4. Close the document.

Skill 14.2—Create a Newsletter with a Graphic Image and Table; Language Arts

1. Create a newsletter using the following information. Use a two-column style similar to the one shown in Figure 14.9.

   a. The text for the newsletter is on page 400.

   b. Insert the graphics image named **medical1.wpg** in the second paragraph. Adjust the size and position of the graphic box; contour the flow of text around the graphic image, and adjust the space around the graphic image as desired.

   c. Use a Text box to insert the NEWSFLASH information. Edit the border to specify a double-line border around all sides of the Text box.

d. Make decisions regarding:

> Fonts (a 10-12 point size is recommended for the newsletter
> body text)
> Justification
> Hyphenation
> Widow/Orphan protect
> Correct three spelling and three punctuation/grammatical errors

---

CLIENT RELATIONS NEWSLETTER

Vitacare Health Plan
158 Madison Avenue, Suite 240, New York, NY 10016

Winter 199x
(212)555-2666

ASU PURCHASES 20% SHARE OF VITACARE

The September 28, 199x, signing of ASU to purchase a 20-percent share of Vitacare represented a significant event in the history of Vitacare and an important step towards retaining large employer accounts.

G.A. Von Stetten, Senior Vice President of ASU's Eastern Region, stated that ASU's investment in Vitacare is based upon "confidence in its strong reputtation in the marketplace, its very solid and estensive provider network, and a firm commitment from its board and senior management". More than 95% of physicians and thirty-two hospitals have elected to participate.

ASU PRODUCTS

The ASU products to be offered are an EPO (Exclusive Provider Option) and a "point of service" product called CO (Controlled Options). The E P O is a plan that operates just like the Vitacare HMO. It is sold to employers as part of a package called IDO (Integrated Diverse Option) or a "tri-plan option." That means that the employer offers employees a choice of a guarantee pay plan, a physician choice plan, or an exclusive provider option.

The CO is sold to the employer as a "full replacement product." Under CO, an employee can make a choice at any time, i.e, at the "point of service," as to whether to seek care as directed by the primary care physician or to self-refer. All self-referrals result in the patient's paying a larger share of the service cost.

ASU sales representatives and Vitacare report a great deal of excitement in the marketplace about these products, which are aimed at large statewide or national employers. The products allow Vitacare to compete with other national and statewide insurers and will provide physicians with increased membership.

> ****NEWSFLASH****
>
> You may have heard about a recommendation that Vitacare along with other HOMs be dropped from the panel of HMOs that provide services to New York Employees Retirement System (NYERS). We are pleased to report that the recommendation has been rejected by the NYERS Board. In addition, the organization that prepared the report, H. Keith Wittenberger, an employee benefits consulting firm, acknowledged "a misunderstanding with Vitacare on certain key data included in the study."

---

2. Use the filename **14skill2** and save the file.

3. Print one copy.

4. If you have completed your work, exit WordPerfect.

Create Documents with Special Features

Features Covered

- Word spacing and letterspacing
- Leading adjustment
- Initial font
- Append to File
- Superscripts and subscripts
- Equation Editor

Objectives

After successfully completing this chapter, you will be able to change word spacing, letterspacing, and leading adjustment typesetting features to enhance the appearance of documents. You will also be able to use the Append to File feature in order to create new documents or to add text to existing files. In addition, you will learn how to create superscript and subscript text and how to create equations/formulas using the Equation Editor.

Chapter Introduction

After a document is typed, the document can be enhanced to present information that is more attractive and easier to read. For example, the space between letters, words, and paragraph lines can be precisely controlled. Also, documents can be developed by copying sections from existing documents. This eliminates the need to rekey information. Scientific/mathematical documents can be enhanced by the insertion of superscripts and subscripts, and the Equation Editor can be used to create complex formulas and equations.

Use Typesetting Features

WordPerfect provides advanced typesetting features to enhance the appearance of documents. These typesetting features include letterspacing (tracking), word spacing, and leading adjustment.

The letterspacing feature (also known as tracking) is used to increase or decrease the amount of space between *letters* in a selected block of text or an entire document. By tightening the letterspacing, more text can be condensed into the same amount of space. Word spacing is used to increase or decrease the amount of space between *words* in a selected block of text or in an entire document. By loosening the letterspacing and/or word spacing, words can be stretched out to create a special effect (see Figure 15.2).

WordPerfect automatically calculates the amount of space to be placed between lines of a paragraph (line height) based on the font and point size selected. For example, if Dutch 801 Roman (Speedo) 12-point is chosen, WordPerfect sets the line height to 0.194"—the size of the text (12 points = .167") plus 2 points (0.027) of vertical spacing (leading). If the point size is changed, WordPerfect adjusts the line height to accommodate the new point size.

At times, it is desirable to control the exact amount of spacing between lines of a paragraph. For example, if different font sizes are used in the same paragraph, WordPerfect adjusts the line height to accommodate the largest point size in each line. In order to make the line height uniform, the line height can be fixed at a specific amount. Once the line height between lines of a paragraph is uniform, a specific amount of additional space can be added between lines of a paragraph and between paragraphs by using the Leading Adjustment feature.

Start-Up Instructions

❖   🖫 Open the file named **15drill1**.

❖ The space between the lines of the indented paragraphs is not equal, because two different point sizes have been set. For example, you may notice that in the document on the screen, there is more spacing between the first and second lines than between the second and third lines in the paragraph that begins "Aim the extinguisher..." The *Steps to Set the Line Height* and the *Steps to Use Leading Adjustment* are used to correct this problem. Also, since additional changes will be made to the text, do not be concerned about the spacing and alignment at this time.

❖ The graphics mode view should be active.

Set the Line Height

1. Place the insertion point at the beginning of the text where the line height must be set.

<blockquote>For example, place the insertion point to the left of the first character in the first paragraph.</blockquote>

2. Select **Layout, Line** {Shift and F8, L}.

   Note: The Line Format dialog box displays.

3. In the Line Height box, select the **Fixed** option. If desired, change the amount of line height {h, f}.

   > For example, the default of 0.194 displays in the Fixed box. No change needs to be made.

4. Select **OK** {press Enter once or twice}.

   Note: The spacing between some of the lines of text on the screen is too small. This will be corrected using the following steps. If desired, use Reveal Codes and place the cursor on the [Ln Height] code to view the expanded line height code [Ln Height:0.194"].

➤ Use Leading Adjustment

1. Place the insertion point at the beginning of the text where the leading will be adjusted.

   > For example, place the insertion point to the left of the first character in the first paragraph.

2. Select **Layout, Other, Printer Functions** {Shift and F8, o, p}.

   Note: The Printer Functions dialog box displays.

3. Select **Leading Adjustment** {L}.

4. Type the desired adjustment.

   > For example, type **0.15**. (Do not type the final period.)

5. Select **OK** twice {press Enter as many times as needed to return the insertion point to the document window}.

   Note: Additional spacing has been placed between all lines of text. Notice that the spacing between lines of a paragraph are the same even if there are different font sizes within a paragraph. For example the space between the lines in the paragraph that begins "Aim the extinguisher..." is now the same.

Finish-Up Instructions

❖ Use the new filename **15drill1.fin** and save the file.

Start-Up Instructions

❖ The file named **15drill1.fin** should be displayed on the screen.

FIGURE 15.1

The Word Spacing and
Letterspacing dialog box

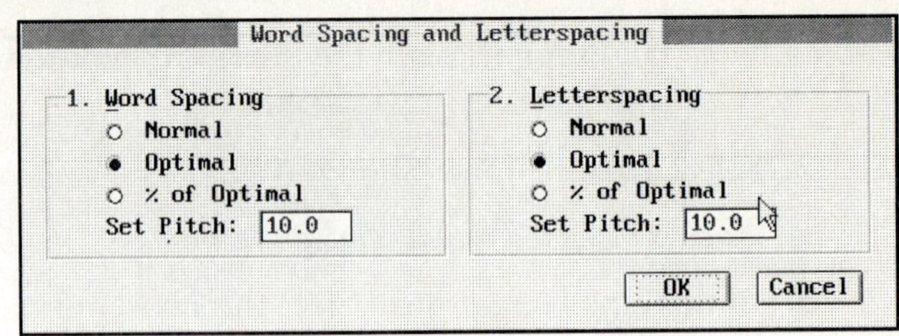

Steps to ▶ Change Letterspacing

1. Block the desired word(s) where letterspacing should be changed.

   For example, block the first lead word **Pull**.

2. Select **Layout, Other, Printer Functions** {Shift and F8, o, p}.

3. Select **Word Spacing and Letterspacing** {w}.

   Note: The Word Spacing and Letterspacing dialog box displays (see Figure 15.1).

4. Select the **Percent of Optimal** option in the Letterspacing box {L, p}.

5. Type the desired percentage of letterspacing.

   For example, to increase the amount of space between letters,
   type **150**. (Do not type the period.)

6. Select **OK** three times {press Enter four or five times}.

   Note: Additional space has been placed between each letter in the selected word. The paragraphs will align after completing the following instructions.

Finish-Up Instructions

❖ Repeat Steps 1–6 of the Steps to Change Letterspacing and change the optimal letterspacing for the words *Aim, Squeeze,* and *Sweep* to 150%.

❖ Check the alignment of the indented paragraphs. If necessary, add or delete indents in order to align all the paragraphs.

❖ Save the file again using the same filename, **15drill1.fin**.

Start-Up Instructions

❖ The file named **15drill1.fin** should be displayed on the screen.

Steps to ▶ Change Word Spacing

1. Block the desired words where word spacing should be changed

   For example, block the title *Emergency Procedures.*

2. Select **Layout, Other, Printer Functions** {Shift and F8, o, p}.

3. Select **Word Spacing and Letterspacing** {w}.

Chapter 15—Create Documents with Special Features

EMERGENCY PROCEDURES

Most fire extinguishers at Wabash Laboratories are type ABC all-purpose and can be operated using these instructions. However, it is important to read the label on the extinguisher used in your work area to be certain of its type and operation. Only fight fires if it is safe to do so and only after alerting the fire department to the situation. To operate a fire extinguisher, remember the following simple steps.

Pull — Pull the pin or plastic loop.

Aim — Aim the extinguisher so that it discharges at the base of the fire. Grip the handle and neck area for better control. Some units have a hose or horn.

Squeeze — Squeeze the handles together.

Sweep — Sweep the base of the fire using a side-to-side motion. The sweeping motion pushes the flames away from you.

Document created using leading adjustment, letterspacing, and word spacing

4. Select the **Percent of Optimal** option in the Word Spacing box {w, p}.

5. Type the desired percentage of word spacing.

   For example, to increase the amount of space between words, type **300**.

6. If desired, change the amount of letterspacing also by selecting the **Percent of Optimal** option in the Letterspacing box and typing the desired percentage of letterspacing {L, p, type percentage}.

   For example, change the letterspacing to **110%** of optimal.

7. Select **OK** three times {press Enter four or five times}.

   Note: Additional space has been placed beween the title words and between each letter in both title words. Your document should look similar to Figure 15.2.

Finish-Up Instructions

* Save the file again using the same filename, **15drill1.fin**.
* Print one copy.
* Close the document.

Change the Initial Font

When WordPerfect is installed, a printer is chosen and a printer initial font (default font) is automatically set. If desired, the initial (default) font for a document can be changed. The initial font can be changed for the current document or for all new documents. The advantage of changing the initial font is that the font change affects all document text including headers, footnotes, equations, page numbers, and text typed in graphics boxes. Changing the initial font can save time in formatting a document by reducing the number of times the font must be set.

Start-Up Instructions

-  Open the file named **15drill2**.

Steps to Change the Initial Font

1. Select **Layout, Document, Initial Font** {Shift and F8, d, f}.

   Note: The Initial Font dialog box displays.

2. Double-click on the desired font and size. Use the Font and Sizes boxes {f, highlight desired font, Enter; s, highlight desired size, Enter}.

   For example, double-click on **Dutch 801 Roman (Speedo)** and double-click on **11-point**.

3. In the "Change Initial Font for box," select **Current Document Only** or **All New Documents** {c or n}.

   For example, check that **Current Document Only** is selected.

4. Select **OK** twice {press Enter two or three times}.

   Note: The name of the initial font displays in the Status bar at the bottom left of the screen.

Finish-Up Instructions

- Create the following footer (if necessary, see Steps to Create a Footer in Chapter 10, page 272).

   DESIGN IDEAS   **Page #**

- Use the new filename **15drill2.if** and save the file. Print one copy and close the document.

Use Append to File

Text or graphics can be copied to a new file or added to the end of an existing file by using the Append to File feature. The Append to File feature is useful in creating new documents without having to rekey information. For example, to make overhead transparencies listing the major points in a report, the Append to File feature can be used to copy the main points from the report document to a new file. Once all main points have been appended to the new file, the new file is opened and formatted.

If WordPerfect is loaded through the WordPerfect Shell, text and graphics can also be appended to a clipboard (temporary memory). The contents of a clipboard can be retrieved into a new or existing document.

Start-Up Instructions

* 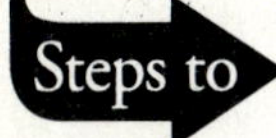 Open the file named **15drill3**.

Steps to ▶ Append Text to File

1. Block the first text to be appended to a new or existing file.

   For example, block **COMPUTER TERMINOLOGY** and the following two blank lines.

2. Select **Edit, Append, To File** {Alt and e, a, f}.

3. Type the drive letter and filename of the file to which the blocked text should be appended.

   For example, type **a:15append**. (Do not type the period.)

4. Select **OK** {Enter}.

5. Block the next text to be appended to the new or existing file.

   For example, block **Access** and the following blank line.

6. Select **Edit, Append, To File** {Alt and e, a, f}.

7. Type the drive letter and filename of the file to which the blocked text should be appended.

   For example, type **a:15append**. (Do not type the period.)

8. Repeat Steps 5-7 and append any other desired text to a new or existing file.

   For example, append the terms **Access Time, Back-up Drive, Back-up File, Buffer, Command, Execute, Kilobyte,** and **Mega-byte** to the existing file **15append**.

9. When all desired text has been blocked and appended to the new or exisiting file, close the document.

Finish-Up Instructions

* Open the file named **15append**.
* If necessary, center the title **COMPUTER TERMINOLOGY**.
* Change the font for all the text to **Helv-WP Bold (Type 1), 24-point**.
* Save the file using the same filename, **15append**.

❖   Print one copy of the file named **15append** and close the document.

Create Superscripts and Subscripts

Superscripts are characters that are printed a fraction above the line of type, and subscripts are characters that are printed a fraction below the line of type (see Figure 15.3). Superscripts and subscripts are used when printing chemical formulas, algebraic equations, degrees of temperature, etc.

When working with superscripts and subscripts, it is sometimes desirable to enlarge the display of text on the screen in order to better see the superscripted or subscripted text. With the Zoom feature, text and graphics can be displayed as large as 300% or as small as 50%. WordPerfect also provides Margin Width, Page Width, and Full Page zoom options. The Margin Width (Marg) option displays a complete line of text in the document window regardless of the font size selected. The Page Width (Wide) option displays the page including the margins within the document window. The Full Page (Full) option is similar to the Full Page view in Print Preview and displays the entire page. The Zoom feature can be accessed by selecting the **Zoom** button on the Ribbon (the first button on the left of the Ribbon) or by selecting **View, Zoom**.

Create a Superscript

1. Type the desired equation.

    For example, type **(x + 4)2**.

2. Block the character to be a superscript.

    For example, highlight the **2**.

3. Select **Font, Size and Position, Superscript** {Alt and o, z, p}.

    Note: The highlighted character displays as a superscript on the screen.

4. Before continuing to type, press the right arrow key once.

    For example, press the right arrow key once and then press the **Enter** key twice.

Create a Subscript

1. Type the desired formula.

    For example, type **NH4**.

2. Block the character to be a subscript.

    For example, highlight the **4**.

$(x + 4)^2$	NH_4
$(c - d)^2$	Na_2PO_4

3. Select **Font, Size and Position, Subscript** {Alt and o, z, b}.

   Note: The highlighted character displays as a subscript on the screen.

4. Before continuing to type, press the right arrow key once.

   For example, press the right arrow key once and then press the **Enter** key twice.

Use Zoom View

1. Select the **Zoom** button on the Ribbon (first button on the left of the ribbon) {Alt and v, z}.

2. Double-click on the desired view percentage or option {press the down arrow key repeatedly until the desired percentage is highlighted, press Enter}.

   For example, double-click on **200%**.

   Note: The Zoom button displays 200%, and the text in the document window is enlarged to 200%.

3. If desired, return to the normal Zoom view (Marg) by selecting the **Zoom** button and double-clicking on **Marg** {Alt and v, z, press the up arrow key repeatedly to highlight Marg, press Enter}.

Finish-Up Instructions

❖ Use the Steps to Create Superscripts and Steps to Create Subscripts and type the equation and formula in the second line of Figure 15.3. If desired, select **200% Zoom** view.

❖ Use the filename **15drill4** and save the file.

❖ Print one copy and close the document.

Use the Equation Editor

WordPerfect provides an Equation Editor window that can be used to type (but not solve) scientific and mathematical equations/formulas. When an equation/formula is created, the equation/formula is placed in either an Equation or Inline Equation graphic box. Both Equation and Inline Equation graphic boxes are defaulted to display and print without borders or shading. An equation box (like a Figure box or Text box) can be moved, sized, shaded, etc., and can be attached to a paragraph, page, or character. An Inline Equation box is inserted within a line of text and moves with that line of text when a document is edited.

When the Equation Editor is accessed, a separate window displays that is divided into three main sections: the *editing pane*, the *palette*, and the *display pane* (see Figure 15.4). The editing pane is the area in which an equation/formula is displayed as it is being created or edited. Text and/or numbers are typed in the editing pane and commands, functions, or symbols are either selected from the palette or are typed in order to build an equation/formula. The tilde (~) is used to insert space between characters instead of pressing the Spacebar.

The palette contains commands, functions, or symbols that are used to create a formula. For example, the SQRT command is selected to insert a square root ($\sqrt{}$) symbol. The left and right braces ({ }) are used to create a group that will act as a single unit. For example, to create $(\frac{2y}{4x})^2$, the following commands and text would be placed in the editing pane: { ({2y} OVER {4x}) } SUP 2. Also, commands, functions, and symbols can be typed directly into the editing pane. For example, to superscript text in the Equation Editor window, select the **SUP or ^** command or type **SUP** in the editing pane.

The display pane is the area in which WordPerfect shows the equation/formula as it will appear when printed. The **Redsplay** button is selected to view the formatted equation/formula. An error message (Syntax error) displays if an error is made when creating an equation/formula.

After the equation/formula is created, the **Close** button is selected in the Equation Editor window and **OK** is selected in the Create Graphics Box dialog box. WordPerfect places the equation/formula in an Equation box or Inline Equation box at the location of the insertion point in the regular document window. (*Note:* A graphics box is inserted even if the editing pane is empty when the **Close** button is selected.) To exit the Equation Editor window without inserting the equation and equation graphics box into the document screen, select **Close, Cancel.** The equation or formula can be edited by double-clicking on the equation/formula and by selecting **Edit Equation** to return to the Equation Editor window.

Create an Equation/Formula Using the Equation Editor

Note: The insertion point should be located in the document at the place where the equation/formula will be inserted. The graphics mode should be active.

1. Select **Graphics, Graphics Boxes, Create** {Alt and F9, b, c}.

2. Select **Based on Box Style** and double-click on **Equation Box** {y, press the down arrow key to highlight Equation Box, Enter}.

3. Select **Create Equation** {e}.

    Note: The Equation Editor window displays (see Figure 15.4).

4. Select or type the desired command {press the Tab key twice, press the down arrow key until the desired command is highlighted, press Enter}.

Chapter 15—Create Documents with Special Features

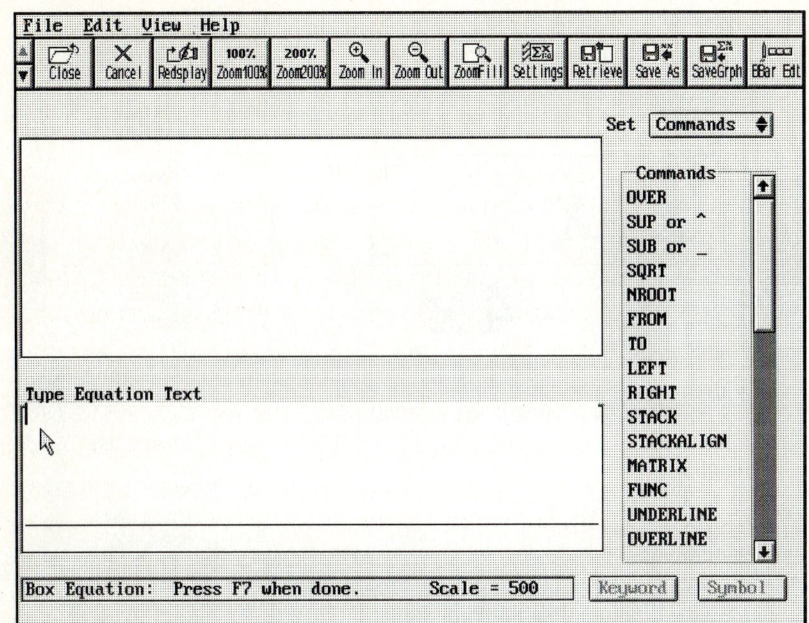

FIGURE 15.4

Equation Editor window

> For example, double-click on **SQRT** (square root) or type **SQRT**
> and press the **Spacebar** once.

5. Select or type the next command or text {press the Tab key twice, press the down
   arrow key until the left brace is highlighted, press Enter}.

   > For example, scroll down the list of commands and double-click
   > on the left brace ({) or type a left brace ({). Repeat to place a sec-
   > ond left brace in the editing pane.

6. Select or type the next command or text.

   > For example, type an **x**. Type a left parenthesis [(] followed by an-
   > other **x**.

7. Select or type the next command or text.

   > For example, double-click on the **SUP or ^** command or press
   > the **Spacebar**, type **SUP**, and press the **Spacebar** again.

8. Select or type the next command or text.

   > For example:
   >
   > a. Type a **2**. (Do not type the period.)
   > b. Type a tilde (~) to insert a space.
   > c. Type a hyphen (-) to represent a minus symbol.
   > d. Type a tilde (~) to insert a space.
   > e. Type a **y**.

9. Select or type the next command or text.

   > For example, double-click on the **SUP or ^** command or press
   > the **Spacebar** once, type **SUP**, and press the **Spacebar** again. Type
   > a **2** followed by a right parenthesis [)].

10. Select or type the next command or text.

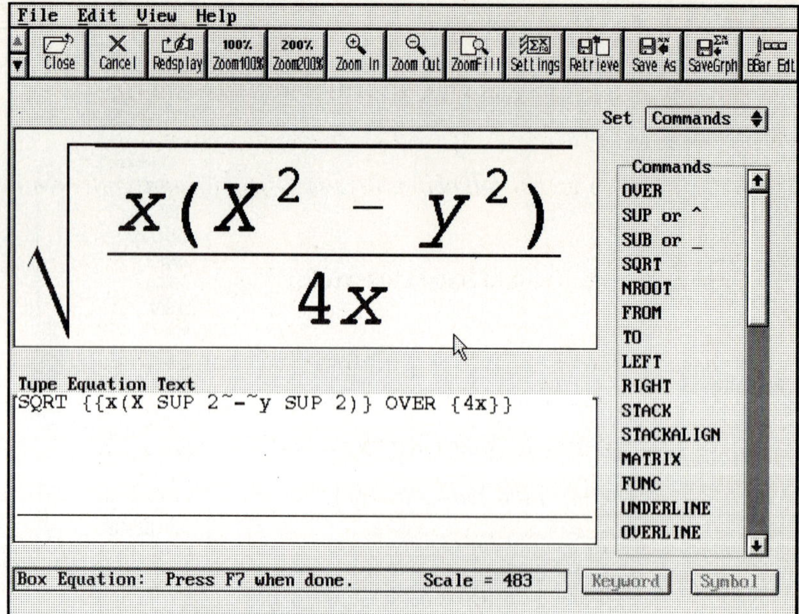

For example, scroll down the list of commands and double-click
on the right brace (}) or type a right brace (}).

11. Select or type the next command or text.

   For example, double-click on the **OVER** command or press the
   Spacebar once, type **OVER**, and press the **Spacebar** again.

12. Select or type the next command or text.

   For example, scroll down the list of commands and double-click
   on the left brace ({) or type a left brace ({). Type **4x**.

13. Select or type the next command or text.

   For example, scroll down the list of commands and double-click
   on the right brace (}) or type a right brace (}). Repeat to insert a
   second right brace.

   *Note: The equation displays on one line and should look similar to the equation shown
   in the editing pane in Figure 15.5.*

14. Select the **Redsplay** button {Ctrl and F3}.

   *Note: The formatted equation displays in the display pane. However, if the equation
   were entered incorrectly, an equation error message displays in the Status bar. If the commands were typed (and not selected from the palette), a blank space should both precede
   and follow the commands.*

15. Select the **Close** button to exit the Equation Editor window. Select **OK** to exit
   the Create Graphics Box dialog box and to place the equation in the regular
   document window {Enter}.

   *Note: The equation is located to the right of the insertion point and displays in the mid-
   dle of the document window.*

                                    Chapter 15—Create Documents with Special Features

❖ Use the filename **15drill5** and save the file.

❖ Print one copy and close the document.

Note: The following Steps to Edit an Equation/Formula are for your information.

 **Edit an Equation/Formula**

1. Move the mouse pointer to the equation in the document window and double-click {Alt and F9, b, e, press 1, type the desired box number, Enter twice}.

   Note: The Edit Graphics Box dialog box displays.

2. Select **Edit Equation** {e}.

   Note: The Equation Editor window and equation/formula display.

3. Make the desired changes.

4. Select the **Redsplay** button {Ctrl and F3}.

5. Select **Close** to exit the Equation Editor window {F7}. Select **OK** to exit the Edit Graphics Box dialog box {Enter}.

   Note: The corrected equation/formula displays in the document window.

Start-Up Instructions

❖ On a clear screen, type the following text that will precede the Inline Equation box:

   The formula for finding the area of a triangle when the lengths of the three sides are known is; press the **Spacebar** once after the last character.

Create an Inline Equation Graphic Box

1. Select **Graphics, Graphics Boxes, Create** {Alt and F9, b, c}.

2. Select **Based on Box Style** and double-click on **Inline Equation Box** {y, press the down arrow key to highlight Inline Equation Box, press Enter}.

3. Select **Create Equation** {e}.

4. Select or type the desired commands and text needed to create the desired equation.

   For example, create the equation $A=\sqrt{s(s-a)(s-b)(s-c)}$ by typing and selecting the following text and commands: **A= SQRT {s(s-a)(s-b)(s-c)}**. (A space should precede and follow the command(s).)

5. Select **Redsplay** {Ctrl and F3}.

6. Select **Close, OK** to return to the document window {F7, Enter}.

---

7. Continue typing any text that follows the Inline Equation box.

   For example, type a period (.) to complete the sentence.

Finish-Up Instructions

❖ Use the filename **15drill6** and save the file.

❖ Print one copy and close the document.

The Next Step

Chapter Review and Activities

FEATURES SUMMARY

FEATURES	ACTIONS	PAGE
Set line height	Select **Layout**, **Line**, **Fixed**. If desired, type a different amount of line height, select **OK**.	402
Use leading adjustment	Select **Layout**, **Other**, **Printer Functions**, **Leading Adjustment**, type the desired adjustment, select **OK** twice.	403
Change letterspacing or word spacing	Block the desired text, select **Layout**, **Other**, **Printer Functions**, **Word Spacing and Letterspacing**, select **Percent of Optimal** in the Letterspacing box and/or Word Spacing box, type the desired percentage of letterspacing/word spacing, select **OK** three times.	404
Change the initial font	Select **Layout**, **Document**, **Initial Font**, select the desired font and/or size, select **OK**.	406
Append to File	Block the desired text, select **Edit**, **Append**, **To File**, type the drive letter and filename of the file to which the blocked text should be appended, select **OK**.	407
Create a superscript	Block the character to be a superscript, select **Font**, **Size and Position**, **Superscript**.	408
Create a subscript	Block the text to be a subscript, select **Font**, **Size and Position**, **Subscript**.	408

Use zoom view	Select the **Zoom** button on the Ribbon, double-click on the desired view percentage or option.	409
Create an equation/formula	Select **Graphics**, **Graphics Boxes**, **Create**, choose **Based on Box Style** and double-click on **Equation Box** or **Inline Equation Box**. Select **Create Equation**. Type equation text and select or type the desired command, functions, and symbols. Select the **Redsplay** button to view the completed equation/formula. Select **Close**, **OK**.	410
Edit an equation/formula	Double-click on the equation/formula to be edited, select **Edit Equation**, make desired changes, select **Close**, **OK**.	413

Self-Check Questions

True/False—Circle One

T F 1. To set the line height, select **Layout**, **Line**, choose **Fixed** in the Line Height box and, if desired, change the amount of line height and select **OK**.

T F 2. Leading adjustment is also referred to as tracking.

T F 3. A superscript is a character that prints a fraction below the line of type.

T F 4. Once an equation has been created in the Equation Editor window, select **Close** and **OK** to place the formula/equation in the regular document window.

T F 5. Letterspacing is used to increase or decrease the amount of space between letters in a block of text.

T F 6. The **Zoom** button can be used to enlarge the display of text to 1000%.

Short Answer

1. List two advantages for changing the initial font of a document.

2. Expain the difference between word spacing and letterspacing.

3. Write an example in which you personally might use the Append to File feature.

4. List two advantages of using the Zoom feature.

Enriching Language Arts Skills

Spelling/Vocabulary Words

derogatory   tending to belittle, negative.

inclusion   the act of containing, encompassing, consisting of.

propaganda   information spread to help or harm a group, institution, or nation.

rendered   to have performed, to have done, supplied.

surreptitious   obtained or performed in a secretive or devious manner.

Independent Adjectives

Two adjectives that modify the same noun are separated by a comma.

> *Example:*
>
> *The small, blue chair will be used for guests when they visit the president.*

Activities

Activity 15.1—Set Initial Font and Use Leading Adjustment

1. Set the initial font for the current document to **Dutch 801 Roman (Speedo)**, **12-point**, or a font of your own choice (select **Layout**, **Document**, **Initial Font**, choose desired font, **OK**).

2. Use the following information and type the document shown.

    a. Press the **F4** key three times after typing the lead words **Medical Care**, **Rehabilitation**, and **Disability Income**.

    b. Bold the title and lead words.

    c. Press **Enter** only once after each paragraph.

NOTICE TO EMPLOYEES

If a work injury occurs, you are automatically entitled to workers' compensation. Texas law provides certain benefits to employees who are injured or become ill because of a job-related activity.

Medical Care   All medical treatment required to cure the injury or illness without cost to the employee. The employee chooses the physician and facility. The facility must be located within a reasonable geographical area. The employee should never see a bill since all costs are paid directly by the employer or its agents.

| **Rehabilitation** | If the injury or illness prevents return to the employee's usual job, the employee may receive vocational rehabilitation. All costs are paid by the employer. |
| **Disability Income** | Employees disabled by job injury or job illness receive disability income while unable to work. The payments are two-thirds of the employee's average weekly pay, up to a maximum set by state law. |

3. Use the filename **15act1** and save the file.

4. Change the font size to **24-point** for the title.

5. Change the word spacing for the title to 200% and letterspacing for the title to 150% of optimal (block the title, select **Layout, Other, Printer Functions, Word Spacing and Letterspacing,** choose **Percent of Optimal** in the Word Spacing box, type **200,** choose the **Percent of Optimal** in the Letterspacing box and type **150, OK** four times).

6. Select each lead word and change the font size to **18-point.**

7. Check the alignment of paragraphs and make adjustments as needed.

   Hint: Delete or insert indent code(s) between the lead words and indented paragraphs, as needed.

8. Locate the insertion point at the beginning of the first paragraph and set the line height to **Fixed** at **0.194** (select **Layout, Line, Fixed,** select **OK** three times).

9. Select **Layout, Other, Printer Functions, Leading Adjustment** and set the amount of adjustment to **.15.**

10. Use the filename **15act1.fin** and save the file.

11. Print one copy.

12. Close the document.

▣ Activity 15.2—Append to File

1. Open the file named **15act2.**

2. Block the title **PAID LEAVES** and the following two blank lines.

3. Select **Edit, Append, To File.** Type the filename **15act2.ovr.** Select **OK.**

4. Block the first heading **VACATION** and the following blank line.

5. Select **Edit, Append, To File.** Type the filename **15act2.ovr.** Select **OK.**

6. Block the next heading and the following blank line.

7. Select **Edit, Append, To File.** Type the filename **15act2.ovr.** Select **OK.**

8. Repeat Steps 6 and 7 to append the remaining headings to the filename **15act2.ovr.**

    Chapter 15—Create Documents with Special Features

9. When all of the remaining headings have been appended to the new file, close the document.

10. Open the filename **15act2.ovr**.

11. Format the text as an overhead transparency (use a large font size).

12. Save the file again using the same filename, **15act2.ovr**.

13. Print one copy.

14. Close the documents.

Activity 15.3—Use the Equation Editor

1. Use the Equation Editor (select **Graphics, Graphics Boxes, Create, Based on Box Style, Equation Box, Create Equation**) to type the following equations. Select **Close** and **OK** after completing each equation/formula to transfer the equation/formula to the document window. (The equations will each display on a separate line.)

$$\frac{3y}{5} \qquad\qquad \frac{3}{7}m = -21m \qquad\qquad \sqrt{25p^8} = 5p^4$$

Note: Below are the equations as displayed in the editing pane of the Equation Editor:

{3y} OVER 5   3 OVER 7 m~=~-21m   SQRT {25p SUP 8}~=~5p SUP 4

2. Use the filename **15act3** and save the file.

3. Print one copy.

4. Close the document.

Activity 15.4—Use Subscripts

1. Type and center the following text using subscripts as shown.

CHEMICAL FORMULAS--Aluminum

Aluminum Acetate: $Al(C_2H_3O_2)_3$
Aluminum Borohydride: $Al(BH_4)_3$
Aluminum Carbide: $Al_4(C_3)$

2. Use the filename **15act4** and save the file.

3. Print one copy.

4. Close the document.

Activity 15.5—Use Superscripts

1. Type and center the following text using superscripts as shown. A lower-case letter *o* is used to represent the degree symbol.

DEGREES OF TEMPERATURE

Celsius vs. Fahrenheit

$20^{o}C = 68^{o}F$
$30^{o}C = 86^{o}F$
$40^{o}C = 104^{o}F$

---

2. Use the filename **15act5** and save the file.

3. Print one copy.

4. Close the document.

Challenge Your Skills

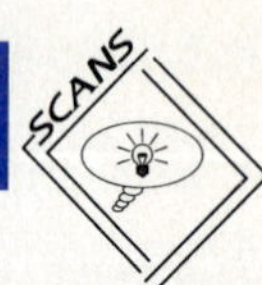

◘ Skill 15.1—Use Append to File

1. Open the file named **15skill1**.

2. Make decisions regarding:

    Margins
    Fonts
    Justification
    Footer text and placement

3. Save the file as **15skill1.fin** and print one copy.

4. Create an overhead transparency containing the title and headings by using the Append to File feature. Use the filename **15skill1.ovr**.

5. Open the file named **15skill1.ovr** and format the overhead transparencies. Make decisions regarding:

Fonts

Justification

Spacing between items

6. Save and print the overhead transparency file.

7. Close the document.

Skill 15.2—Superscripts and Subscripts

1. Create the following table. Make decisions regarding:

   Margins

   Fonts

   Table format (cell width, text justification, etc.)

OPERATING CONDITIONS			
Conditions	Soap Cleaner	Acid Etch	Nitric Acid Wash (HNO_3)
Concentration	6 oz./gal.	10% by volume	50% by volume
Temperature	$55°{-}60°C$	$60°{-}65°C$	Room temperature ($20°C$)
Time	5-7 minutes	2-4 minutes	45 seconds

2. Use the filename **15skill2** and save the file.

3. Print one copy.

4. Close the document.

Skill 15.3—Use the Equation Editor

1. Create the following equations.

(a) $\sqrt{x^4 y^{12}} = x^2 y^6$ (b) $\sqrt{\dfrac{25k^6}{36}} = \dfrac{5k^3}{6}$ (c) $\left(\dfrac{5x^3 y^5}{7mn}\right)^2$

Note: Below are the equations as displayed in the editing pane of the Equation Editor:

(a) SQRT {x SUP 4y SUP 12}~=~x SUP 2 y SUP 6
(b) SQRT {{25k SUP 6} over 36}~=~{5k SUP 3} over 6
(c) {(({5x SUP 3y SUP 5} over {7mn})} SUP 2

2. Use the filename **15skill3** and save the file.

3. Print one copy.

4. Close the document.

●ゃ ▣ Skill 15.4—Initial Font, Letterspacing, Word Spacing, and Leading Adjustment; Language Arts

1. Open the file named **15skill4**. Make decisions regarding:

   Margins (left and right margins of .75 or less are recommended)
   Fonts (set an initial document font)
   Justification
   Widow/Orphan protect
   Bold, underline, capitalization for the title and subheadings
   Word spacing and letterspacing for the title and headings
   Alignment of paragraphs
   Header or footer text and placement
   Correct five spelling and three punctuation errors

2. Use the filename **15skill4** and save the file.

3. Print one copy.

4. If you have completed your work, exit WordPerfect.

Create Documents Using Special Functions

Features Covered

- Edit, create, and apply styles
- Sort table rows, paragraphs, and lines
- Record and play macros

Objectives

After successfully completing this chapter, you will be able to edit, create, and apply styles in order to quickly format documents. You will also learn how to use the Sort feature in order to numerically and alphabetically sort table rows, paragraphs, and lines. In addition, you will learn to record and play macros in order to expedite your work.

Chapter Introduction

WordPerfect provides many special functions that can be used to expedite the production of documents and eliminate repetitious tasks. The Styles function can be used to quickly format documents. The Sort function makes alphabetical and numerical sorting easy and quick. Macros can be created to quickly and efficiently perform tasks that must be repeated on a regular basis.

Use Styles to Format Documents

A style is a set of formatting instructions that can be applied to related sections of text. For example, a style can be used to format the sideheadings of a report to print in 12-point Helve-WP Bold. The purpose of using styles is to save time and maintain a consistent format throughout a document. Time is saved by applying the same style repeatedly to the desired document text. Also, if the format of a style is changed, it automatically changes all text where the style has been previously applied.

There are three types of styles: Open, Paragraph, and Character. An Open style usually affects an entire document. For example, an Open style might change the margins and font type for the entire document. Paragraph and Character styles usually affect a portion of the document. For example, a Paragraph style could change the font and point size, set center justification, and bold the title of a report. A Character style might apply the bold and italic text attributes to text. To apply a Paragraph style, the cursor/insertion point can be located anywhere in the paragraph to be affected. To apply a Character style, however, block the text to be affected. When a Paragraph or Character style is applied to text, a code is placed at the beginning of the affected text to turn the style on and a second code is placed at the end of the affected text to turn the style off.

WordPerfect has several predefined styles that can be used to format outline levels, footnotes/endnotes, table of contents entries, etc. These predefined styles are referred to as WP System Styles. The [Open Style: InitialCodes] style that displays as the first item in the Reveal Codes screen of each WordPerfect 6.0 document is a WP System Style. WP System Styles can be edited but not deleted.

As needed, styles can be edited and new styles created. To edit or create styles, the Style List dialog box is accessed. The Style List dialog box shows a list of all styles available to format the document, including a minimal list of WP System Styles. WordPerfect System Styles are marked by a •. When editing or creating styles, all formatting codes for the style are placed in the Style Contents box of the Edit Style dialog box (see Figure 16.1). The formatting codes are inserted by selecting options in the Edit Styles dialog box. When a style is edited, any text in the current document that was previously formatted with the edited style is changed to reflect the new format specifications.

Once styles are created/edited, the styles are applied to the document text. To apply an Open or Character style, select **Layout**, **Styles**, and double-click on the desired style name, or highlight the style name and choose **Select**. To apply a Paragraph style, select the style name by using the **Style** button on the Ribbon.

In order to use the edited or new styles to format other documents, the styles must be saved in a style file. WordPerfect calls a style file a "style library." If the edited styles and new styles are not saved in a style library file, the styles can only be used to format the current document. If any of the WP System Styles, such as the Initial-Codes style, are modified, the user must tell WordPerfect to save both the User Created Styles and the WP System Styles.

Chapter 16—Create Documents Using Special Functions

In order to use the new or edited style library file to format another document, the style library file must be retrieved and the styles applied. If any WP System Styles were modified when the style library file was created, the user must tell WordPerfect to retrieve both the User Created Styles and the WP System Styles.

Start-Up Instructions

❖ ▪ Open the file named **16drill1**.

Steps to ▶ Edit a Style

1. Select **Layout, Styles** {Alt and F8}.

   Note: The Style List dialog box displays containing a list of existing styles. Styles that are marked by a • are WP System Styles.

2. Highlight the style to be edited {press the up or down arrow key to highlight desired style}.

   For example, highlight the style named **InitialCodes**.

3. Select **Edit** {e}.

   Note: The Edit Style dialog box displays.

4. Click in the **Style Contents** box {c}.

   Note: The options in the Edit Style dialog box change. The cursor is located in the Style Contents box and a list of options displays at the top of the dialog box (see Figure 16.1).

5. Use the options in the Edit Style dialog box to make the desired changes to the style.

   a. To change the font, press Ctrl and F8, select the desired font, choose OK.

      For example, select **Dutch 801 Roman (Speedo)**. Select **OK** {Enter twice} to exit to the Edit Style dialog box.

   b. To change the format for the style, press **Shift** and **F8** and choose the desired format option.

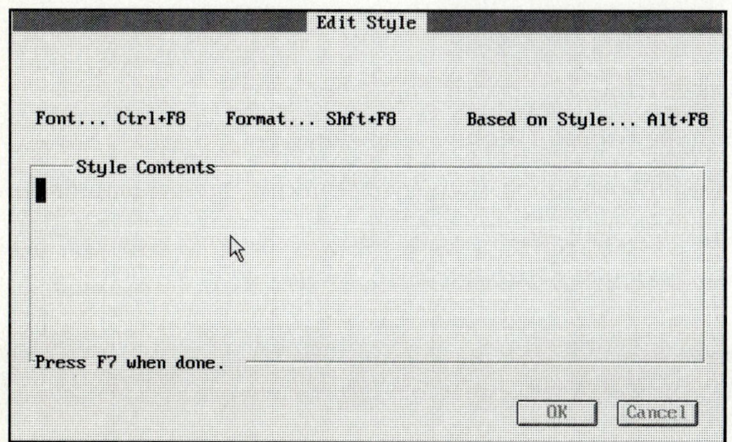

Style Edit dialog box after selecting Style Contents

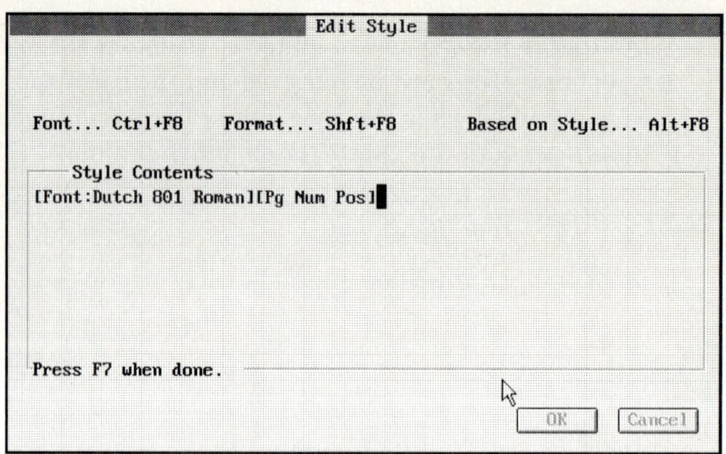

FIGURE 16.2

Edit Style dialog box with formatting codes

For example, to insert the page number at the bottom center of all pages, select **Page**, **Page Numbering**, **Page Number Position**, **Bottom Center**, and select **OK** three times, select **Close** {Shift and F8, p, n, p, c, press Enter four times}.

Note: As formatting options are selected, codes display in the Style Contents dialog box (see Figure 16.2).

   c. Press **F7** and select **OK** {Enter} to exit the Edit Style dialog box.

6. When all changes to the style have been made, select **Close** {Enter} to exit the Style List dialog box.

Note: The font for the document text will have been changed.

Start-Up Instructions

❖ The file named **16drill1** should be displayed on the screen.

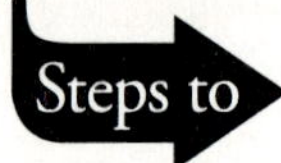

Create a New Paragraph Style

1. Select **Layout, Styles** {Alt and F8}.

2. Select **Create** in the Style List dialog box {c}.

   Note: The Create Style dialog box displays.

3. Type the desired style name in the Style Name box.

   For example, type **Report Title** and press **Enter**.

4. Select **Style Type** and choose the desired style option {t, press the up or down arrow key to highlight the desired type, press Enter}.

   For example, check that **Paragraph Style** is displayed in the Style Type box.

5. Select **OK** {Enter}.

   Note: The Edit Style dialog box displays.

6. Click in the **Description** box and type a description of purpose for the style {d}.

   For example, type **Style for report title.**

7. Click in the **Style Contents** box {press Tab, c}.

   Note: The cursor is located in the Style Contents box and a list of available options displays at the top of the dialog box (see Figure 16.1).

   a. To change the font, press **Ctrl** and **F8**, select the desired font style and size, and select **OK**.

      For example, change the font to **Helve-WP Bold (Type 1)** and the size to **14-point.**

   b. To change the justification for the style, press **Shift** and **F8**, select **Line**, and choose the desired justification, select **OK, Close** {Shift and F8, L, choose desired justification, Enter twice}.

      For example, choose **Center** justification.

   c. To change the amount of blank space below the paragraph, press **Shift** and **F8**, select **Margins, Paragraph Spacing**, type the desired number of blank lines to be inserted below the paragraph, and select **OK, Close** {Shift and F8, m, p, type number of blank lines, press Enter twice}.

      For example, type **3** in the Paragraph Spacing box to insert three blank lines below the title paragraph.

8. When all the formatting instructions have been selected, press **F7** and select **OK** to exit the Edit Style dialog box {F7, Enter}.

   Note: The Style List dialog box displays. The Report Title style name should be highlighted.

9. Use steps 2-8 to create any additional styles desired.

   For example, create the following styles:

   a. Style name: Sideheading
      Style type: Paragraph
      Description: Style for report sideheadings
      Font: Helve-WP Bold (Type 1), 12-point
      Paragraph Spacing: 2

   b. Style name: Company name
      Style type: Character
      Description: Changes font for company name
      Font: Dutch 801 Bold Italic (Speedo), 12-point

Save the Modified Styles and New Style

10. In the Style List dialog box, select **Save** to save the modified styles and the new style under a new style filename {v}.

11. Type the name of the new style file. If necessary, include the drive letter and directory where the style file should be saved.

> For example, type **a:16report.sty**. (Do not type the final period.)

12. Check that an X appears in the Save User Created Styles option box.

13. If changes have been made to WP System Styles, such as the InitialCodes style, select the **Save WP System Styles** option {s}.

> For example, since changes were made to the InitialCodes style, select the **Save WP System Styles** option.

14. Select **OK** {Enter}.

15. Select **Close** to exit the Style List dialog box {Enter}.

Steps to ▶ Apply the Styles

1. *To apply an Open style to the entire document*, place the cursor/insertion point at the top of the document (press **Home**, **Home**, and the up arrow key), select **Layout, Styles**, and double-click on the desired open style name {Alt and F8, press the up arrow key to highlight the open style name, press Enter}.

> For example, when the InitialCodes style was edited earlier in the chapter, the InitialCodes Open style went into effect immediately; therefore, skip to Step 2.

2. *To apply a Paragraph style*, place the cursor/insertion point between any two characters in the paragraph. Move the mouse pointer to the **Style** button in the Ribbon (second from the left) and click once. Double-click on the desired style name {Alt and F8, press the up or down arrow key to highlight the desired paragraph style, press Enter}.

> For example, place the cursor/insertion point between any two characters in the report title. Click on the **Style** button and double-click on the **Report Title** style name.

3. *To apply a Character style*, block the text to be affected, select **Layout, Styles**, and double-click on the desired character style name {Alt and F8, press the up or down arrow key to highlight the desired character style name, press Enter}.

> For example, block the company name, Hanford Consultants West, in the first paragraph of the report, select **Layout, Styles**, and double-click on the **Company name** style.

4. Use Steps 1, 2, or 3 and apply styles as needed to the document.

> For example, apply the Paragraph style named **Sideheading** to each of the sideheading paragraphs, i.e., *In-Situ Moisture Content and Dry Density, Percent Fines, Atterberg Limits, Shear Tests, Consolidation Tests,* and *R-Value.*

❖ Use the filename **16drill1.for** and save the document.

❖ Print one copy and close the document.

Start-Up Instructions

❖ 🖬 Open the file named **16rept2**.

Steps to ▶ Retrieve a Style File

1. Select **Layout, Styles** {Alt and F8}.

2. Select **Retrieve** {r}.

   Note: The Retrieve Styles dialog box displays.

3. In the filename box, type the name of the desired style file.

   For example type **a:16report.sty**. (Do not type the final period.)

4. Check that an X displays in the Retrieve User Created Styles box.

5. If the style file to be retrieved contains a changed WP System Style(s), select the **Retrieve WP System Styles** option.

   For example, since the InitialCodes style was modified, select the Retrieve WP System Styles option.

6. Select **OK** {Enter}.

   Note: A message displays "Style(s) already exist. Replace?"

7. Select **Yes** {Enter}.

8. Select **Close** {Enter}.

   Note: The styles created earlier—Report Title, Sideheading, and Company name—now display in the Style List dialog box and are available to format the document. The edited Initial Codes style is already in effect.

Finish-Up Instructions

❖ Place the cursor/insertion point in the report title and apply the Title *paragraph style* (if necessary, see Steps to Apply the Styles, Step 2).

❖ Block the company name in the first paragraph and apply the Company name *character style* (if necessary, see Steps to Apply the Styles, Step 3).

❖ Place the cursor/insertion point in the sideheading, Selection Committe Responsibilities, and apply the Sideheading *paragraph style* (if necessary, see Steps to Apply Styles, Step 2). Repeat for each sideheading, i.e., Screening Applicants, Interviews, Confidentiality.

❖ Use the new filename **16rept2.for** and save the file.

❖ Print one copy and close the document.

Create Alphabetically and
Numerically Sorted Text

The Sort function is used to arrange lines, paragraphs, and table rows in alphabetical or numerical order. A list of names can be sorted alphabetically, and a list of numbers can be sorted numerically.

Text can be selected to sort in *alpha* (alphabetical) or *numeric* (numerical) order. Text can also be listed either in descending or ascending order. Ascending order is listing A through Z, or the lowest number to the highest number. Descending order is listing Z through A, or the highest number to the lowest number.

If the first word in a line, paragraph, or table row begins with the same character, the character that follows is used to determine the correct order. For example, if there are two last names in a table that begin with the same letter, the next character is used to determine the alphabetical order.

Before sorting a document, all text to be sorted is selected. The Sort dialog box is used to choose the Record Type (Line, Paragraph, or Table) and Sort Key. The Sort Key box shows the sort criteria. If desired, the sort criteria can be changed by selecting **Sort Key**, **Edit** and choosing the desired sort options. Up to nine sort keys can be specified.

The sort can be undone by selecting **Edit**, **Undo**. The Undo command must be selected immediately after the sort before any other editing or formatting actions occur.

Start-Up Instructions

❖  Open the file named **16drill2**.

Steps to ▶ Sort Table Rows Numerically

1. Block the portion of the table to be sorted.

   For example, block all table cells except the table title or column heading cells.

2. Select **Tools, Sort** {Ctrl and F9}.

   Note: The Sort dialog box displays.

3. In the Record Type box, check that **Table** displays.

4. In the Sort Keys box, select the desired sort criteria.

   For example, edit the Sort Keys by selecting **Sort Keys, Edit** {k, e} and specify the following criteria:

Key:	1
Type:	Numeric
Order:	Descending

Chapter 16—Create Documents Using Special Functions

                Cell: 3 (to sort by the third column)
                Line: 1
                Word: 1

5. Select **OK** {Enter}.

    Note: The Sort Key criteria in the Sort dialog box show the new criteria.

6. Select **Perform Action** {Tab twice, Enter}.

    Note: After a few moments, the table (sorted by column 3) displays.

Finish-Up Instructions

❖ Use the new filename **16drill2.num** and save the file.

❖ Print one copy and close the document.

Start-Up Instructions

❖  Open the file named **16drill2**.

Steps to ▶ Sort Table Rows Alphabetically

1. Block the portion of the table to be sorted.

    For example, block all table cells except the table title or column heading cells.

2. Select **Tools, Sort** {Ctrl and F9}.

3. In the Record Type box, check that **Table** displays.

4. In the Sort Keys box, select the desired sort criteria.

    For example, if necessary, select **Sort Keys**, **Edit** and specify the following criteria:
                Key: 1
                Type: Alpha
                Order   ↑ (Ascending)
                Cell: 1
                Line: 1
                Word: 1

5. Select **OK** {Enter}.

6. Select **Perform Action** {Tab twice, Enter}.

Finish-Up Instructions

❖ Use the filename **16drill2.alp** and save the file.

❖ Print one copy and close the document.

❖   In a new document window, type the following information:

Tables:
Insert a row
Center text in a cell
Join cells
Move columns
Create a table
Shade a cell *(press Enter twice)*

Letters:
Form letters
Block style
AMS Simplified style *(press Enter twice)*

Merging:
Data file
Form file
Fields *(press Enter twice)*

Delete:
Delete a file
Block and delete text
Delete a table column or row
Delete a tab *(press Enter twice)*

❖   Use the filename **16drill3** and save the file.

❖   Print one copy.

Use Paragraph Sorting

1. Block all the paragraphs to be sorted

    For example, block all paragraphs in the document.

2. Select **Tools, Sort** {Ctrl and F9}.

3. Check that **Paragraph** displays in the Record Type box.

4. In the Sort Keys box, select the desired sort criteria.

    For example, check that the following are selected:
    Key: 1
    Type: Alpha
    Ord: ↑ (Ascending)
    Line: 1

Field:	1
Word:	1

5. Select **Perform Action** {Enter}.

Note: The text is sorted by the first line of each paragraph (section). For the purpose of sorting, a paragraph is defined as any text followed by two Enters (hard returns).

Finish-Up Instructions

❖ Use the new filename **16drill3.par** and save the file.

Start-Up Instructions

❖ The file named **16drill3.par** should be displayed on the screen.

Steps to ▶ **Use Line Sorting**

1. Block the lines of text to be sorted.

    For example, block the four lines under the heading "Delete."

2. Select **Tools, Sort** {Ctrl and F9}.

3. Check that **Line** displays in the Record Type box.

4. In the Sort Keys box, select the desired sort criteria.

    For example, check that the following are selected:

Key:	1
Type:	Alpha
Ord:	↑ (Ascending)
Field:	1
Word:	1

5. Select **Perform Action** {Enter}.

Finish-Up Instructions

❖ Repeat Steps 1–5 to sort the lines under each section in the document.

❖ Use the filename **16drill3.sor** and save the file.

❖ Print one copy and close the document.

Use Macros

Macros are shortcuts that eliminate repetitive action. Macros are especially useful when your actions involve selecting several menus, and submenus, as well as making changes in dialog boxes. For example, to create a horizontal graphic line with a thickness of .02 inches, the following must be selected: **Graphics, Graphics Lines, Create, Thickness, Set**, type **.02**, and choose **OK**. Using a macro, the instructions to create the horizontal graphics line could be reduced to only four steps.

WordPerfect supplies many macros, which are stored in the macros subdirectory and are identified by the filename extension *.wpm*. A supplied macro is played (activated) by selecting the desired macro and responding to prompts displayed on the screen. WordPerfect supplied macros can be used to create bulleted lists, memos, and letters; print a list of available fonts; convert footnotes to endnotes; and many other tasks.

In addition to the macros supplied by WordPerfect, new macros can be created. First, the macro is given a name, then every keystroke and mouse selection is recorded and, finally, the recording is stopped and automatically saved.

Since WordPerfect remembers each keystroke and mouse selection made while Record is turned on, plan the macro before selecting **Tools**, **Macro**, **Record**. Write down each step needed to create the macro. Once Record is turned on, Recording Macro displays in the Status bar. When all the desired keystrokes and mouse selections have been completed, the recording of the macro is stopped by selecting **Tools**, **Macro**, **Stop** and the macro is saved.

Once a macro is recorded, the macro can be played as often as needed by selecting **Macro**, **Play**, typing the desired macro filename, and selecting **OK**. The macro performs each recorded step. When all the recorded steps have been completed, you can edit, save, print, or close the file using normal procedures. Changes to a document created by a macro do not alter the macro. The macro can be used again and again.

Start-Up Instructions

- ❖   🖫 Open the file named **16drill4**.
- ❖   Block all document paragraphs except the title.

Use a Supplied Macro

1. Select **Tools, Macro, Play** {Alt and F10}.

   Note: The Play macro dialog box displays. The cursor is located in the Macro box.

2. Select **File List** {press **F5**}.

   Note: The Select List dialog box displays. The default directory for macros is shown in the Directory box, e.g., C:\WP60\MACROS.

3. Select **OK** {Enter}.

   Note: The File List dialog box containing the names of the WordPerfect macros (.wpm) files displays.

4. Double-click on the desired macro {press the down arrow key to highlight desired macro name, Enter}.

   For example, double-click on **BULLET.WPM**.

5. Wait a few moments, then respond to any prompts that display on the screen.

For example:

a. In the Bullet Inserter dialog box, select **Change Bullet** {c}.

b. In the Edit Bullet Character dialog box, select **User Defined** {u}.

c. Press **Ctrl** and **w** to access the WP Characters dialog box.

d. In the Set box, choose the **Iconic Symbols** character set {Tab, s, press the down arrow key to highlight Iconic Symbols, Enter}.

e. Click on either of the check mark characters {c, press the up, down, left, or right arrow keys to place the white outline around the desired character, Enter}.

f. Select **Insert**.

g. Select **OK** {press Enter twice}.
    Note: Wait a few moments.

h. Select **Insert Bullet** {i}.

Note: In a few moments, the macro inserts a bullet character (check mark) at the beginning of each selected paragraph. The macro is now finished.

Finish-Up Instructions

❖ Use the filename **16drill4.fin** and save the itinerary.

❖ Print one copy and close the document.

Steps to ▶ Record a Macro

1. In a clear document window, select **Tools, Macro, Record** {Ctrl and F10}.
    Note: The Record Macro dialog box displays.

2. In the Macro box, type the name of the macro (if necessary, include the drive letter and/or directory where the macro is located).

    For example, type **a:memohd.** (Do not type the period.)

3. Select **OK** {Enter}.

    *Note: The cursor/insertion point returns to the document window and the words **Recording Macro** display in the Status bar at the bottom of the screen.*

4. Perform the actions to be recorded.

    For example:

    a. Select **Layout, Margins** {Shift and F8, m}.

    b. Change the left, right, and top margins to **1.25"**.

    c. Select **Layout, Alignment, Center** {Shift and F6}.

    d. Change the font to **Dutch 801 Roman (Speedo), 12-point**.

    e. Type the word MEMORANDUM.

f. Block the text by pressing **Alt** and **F4** and **Home, Home,** left arrow key.

g. Select **Font, Bold** {Ctrl and b}.

h. Press **Home, Home, Home** and the right arrow key. Press the **Enter** key three times.

i. Type the word **DATE:;** press the **Tab** key once.

j. Select **Tools, Date, Code** to insert the date code in the document {Shift and F5, c}.

k. Press **Enter** twice.

l. Type the word **TO:.** Press the **Tab** key twice until the cursor/insertion point is aligned with the date. Press **Enter** twice.

m. Type the word **FROM:.** Press the **Tab** key once. Press **Enter** twice.

n. Type the word **SUBJECT:.** Press the **Tab** key once. Press **Enter** three times.

o. Select **Graphics, Graphics Lines, Create** {Ctrl and F9, L, c}.

p. In the Thickness box, choose **Set** and type **.02** {t, s, type desired line thickness}.

q. Select **OK** {Enter twice}.

r. Press **Enter** three times.

5. Select **Tools, Macro, Stop** {Ctrl and F10}.

   *Note: The macro was saved when **Tools, Macro, Stop** was selected.*

Finish-Up Instructions

❖ Close the document or select **File, New.**

Play the Recorded Macro

1. Select **Tools, Macro, Play** {Alt and F10}.

2. Type the desired macro name.

   For example, type **a:memohd.** (Do not type the period.)

3. Select **OK** {Enter twice}.

   Note: In a few moments, the top portion of the memorandum including the graphic line displays on the screen. The document can now be edited, saved, printed, etc. as any other document.

Finish-Up Instructions

❖ Type the text shown in Figure 16.3 to complete the memorandum.

❖ Use the filename **16drill4.mem** and save the file.

MEMORANDUM

DATE: (Current date)

TO: Will Cross

FROM: Rawley Ponce

SUBJECT: The Travel Program

Effective immediately, all travelers should call Harrison's Travel Service to make airline reservations. Our company representative at Harrison's Travel Service is Sid Khan. He can be reached at 1-800-555-6116.

If you have any questions, please contact me at extension 4434.

xx

Memorandum created using the memohd macro

❖   Print one copy and close the document.

The Next Step

Chapter Review and Activities

FEATURES SUMMARY

FEATURES	ACTIONS	PAGE
Edit a style	Select **Layout**, **Styles**, highlight the style to be edited, select **Edit**, **Style Contents**, make desired changes, press **F7**, select **Close**.	425
Create new styles	Select **Layout**, **Styles**, **Create**. Type the style name, select the **Style Type** (Open, Paragraph, or Character), and select **OK**. Type a description of the purpose of the style. Select **Style Contents**. Use options to specify the desired style format. When all formatting instructions have been selected, press **F7** and select **OK**. Select **Close**.	426
Save styles	In the Style List dialog box, select **Save**, type the name of the new style file. Check that an X appears in the **Save User Created Styles** option box. Select **Save WP System Styles**. Select **OK**, **Close**.	427
Apply styles	*To apply an Open style to the entire document,* place the cursor/insertion point at the top of the document. Select **Layout**, **Styles**, double-click on the desired style name. *To apply a Paragraph style,* place the cursor/insertion point anywhere in paragraph, move the mouse pointer to the **Style** button on the Ribbon, click once, double-click on the desired style name.	428

FEATURES *(cont'd.)*	ACTIONS *(cont'd.)*	PAGE
Apply styles *(cont'd.)*	*To apply a Character style*, block the text to be affected, select **Layout**, **Styles**, and double-click on the desired style name.	428
Retrieve a style file	Select **Layout**, **Styles**, **Retrieve**. Type the name of the desired style file. Check that an X displays in the **Retrieve User Created Styles** option box. If necessary, select **Retrieve WP System Styles**. Select **OK**, **Yes**, **Close**.	429
Sort table rows	Block the portion of the table to be sorted and select **Tools**, **Sort**. Check that Table displays in the Record Type box. Select the desired sort criteria. Choose **Perform Action**.	430, 431
Sort paragraphs	Block all paragraphs to be sorted and select **Tools**, **Sort**. Check that Paragraph displays in the Record Type box. Select desired sort criteria. Choose **Perform Action**.	432
Sort lines	Block the lines to be sorted and select **Tools**, **Sort**. Check that Line displays in the Record Type box. Select the desired sort criteria. Choose **Perform Action**.	433
Use a macro	Select **Tools**, **Macro**, **Play**, type the macro name or press **F5**, select **OK** and double-click on the desired macro name. If necessary, respond to prompts on the screen.	434
Record a macro	Select **Tools**, **Macro**, **Record**, type the name of the macro and select **OK**. Perform the desired actions to be recorded. Select **Tools**, **Macro**, **Stop**.	435

Self-Check Questions

True/False—Circle One

T F 1. Before a character style is applied, the desired text must be blocked.

T F 2. Text can be sorted in alphabetical or numerical order.

T F 3. Descending sort order is A through Z, or lowest to highest.

T F 4. The Record Macro dialog box is used to play a macro.

T F 5. To use a macro, select **Tools**, **Macro**, **Play**, type the desired macro name, and select **OK**.

T F 6. New and edited styles must be saved in a style library file before the styles can be used to format other documents.

1. List the three types of styles.

2. Describe a style and state two advantages of using styles.

3. State one reason for planning a macro before selecting **Tools, Macro, Record**.

4. Write one example of when you might create and use a macro.

Enriching Language Arts Skills

Spelling/Vocabulary Words

deferred   put off until another time.
integral   necessary for completeness.
acquisition   a purchase.

Apostrophe Used to Show Possession

If a noun is singular and used to show possession, add an apostrophe (') and an *s*. If the final letter in the noun is an s, the apostrophe is added after the *s*.

> *Examples:*
>
> *The secretary's table was misplaced.*
> *The brothers' house and the Lexis' garage are on the corner of Piedmont and High streets.*

Activities

▣ Activity 16.1—Retrieve, Apply, and Create Styles

*The file named **16report.sty** must have been created in order to accomplish this activity. If styles have not been created, use the steps shown on pages 425-428 to create the styles.*

1. Open the file named **16act1**.

2. Use the following information to format the report.

   a. Select **Layout, Styles, Retrieve**.

   b. Type the drive letter where the file disk is located followed by the style library name, **a:16report.sty**.

   c. Select **Retrieve WP System Styles.**

   d. Select **OK.** [If necessary, select **Yes** to Style(s) already exist. Replace?]

     *Note: The styles created in **16report.sty** will now be available for formatting.*

   e. Select **Close.**

     *Note: The **16report.sty** InitialCodes format is in effect. The font for the text has been changed to Dutch 801 Roman (Speedo).*

   f. Place the cursor/insertion point in the title of the report, **BANKING SERVICES.**

   g. Select the **Style** button on the Ribbon and double-click on **Report Title.**

   h. Block the company name in the first paragraph.

   i. Select **Layout, Styles,** and double-click on the **Company** name style.

   j. Place the cursor/insertion point in the the first sideheading, **CLIENT BANKING SERVICES.**

   k. Select the **Style** button on the Ribbon and double-click on **Sideheading.**

   l. Place the cursor/insertion point in the next sideheading, **SMALL BUSINESS ASSISTANCE.**

   m. Select the **Style** button on the Ribbon and double-click on **Sideheading.**

3. Place the cursor/insertion point in the first third-level heading, **Information about Banking Services.**

4. Create a new third level heading style.

   a. Select **Layout, Styles, Create.**

   b. In the Name box, type **3rd level.** Check that **Paragraph** style displays in the Style Type box. Select **OK.**

   c. In the Description box, type **Style for third-level headings.**

   d. Select **Style Contents.**

   e. Press **Ctrl** and **F8.** Set the font to **Dutch 801 Bold (Speedo).** Select **OK.**

   f. Press **Shift** and **F8,** select **Margins, Paragraph Spacing** and type 2. Select **OK, Close.**

   g. Press **F7.**

   h. Select **OK.** The style named 3rd level should be highlighted.

   i. Save the style file using the same style library filename, **16report.sty.** Be sure to select the **Save WP System Styles** option.

   j. Make sure that the new style, 3rd level, is highlighted. Choose **Select** to exit the Style List dialog box and apply the 3rd level style to the current paragraph.

k. Apply the 3rd level style to the remaining third-level paragraphs, i.e., *Client Data Reports, Electronic Banking, Small Business Ledger,* and *SBA-Guaranteed Loans.*

5. Save the formatted report as **16act1.for**.

6. Print one copy and close the document.

◘ Activity 16.2—Sort Table Columns

Part I

1. Open the file named **16act2**.

2. Block all table cells except the table title or column headings.

3. Select **Tools, Sort**.

4. Check that the following are selected.

Record Type:	Table
Key:	1
Type:	Alpha
Ord:	↑ (Ascending)
Cell:	1
Line:	1
Word:	1

5. Select **Perform Action**.

6. Use the filename **16act2.ven** and save the file.

7. Print one copy.

Part II

1. Block all table cells except the title and the column headings.

2. Select **Tools, Sort**.

3. Make the following selections in the Sort dialog box.

Record Type:	Table
Key:	1
Type:	Numeric
Ord:	↑ (Ascending)
Cell:	4
Line:	1
Word:	1

4. Select **Perform Action**.

5. Use the filename **16act2.amt** and save the file.

6. Print one copy and close the document.

1. Type the following information as shown.

MENUS FOR BANQUETS

Menu 1
CHICKEN FLORENTINE
$15.95 per person
Boneless Breast of Chicken
Artichoke Pasta Salad
Fresh Fruit

Menu 2
PRIME RIB DINNER
$19.95 per person
Prime Rib
Fresh Vegetable Sauté
Roasted New Potatoes

Menu 3
EGGPLANT PARMESAN
$12.95 per person
Thinly Sliced Eggplant
Layered with Marinara Sauce,
Ricotta, and Parmesan Cheese
Mixed Green Salad

---

2. Use the filename **16act3** and save the file.

3. Block all lines in the menus.

4. Select **Tools, Sort**.

5. To sort the menu selections by the cost per person, make the following selections in the Sort dialog box.

Record Type:	Paragraph
Type:	Numeric
Ord:	↑ (Ascending)
Line:	3
Field:	1
Word:	1

6. Select **Perform Action**.

7. After the menu selections have been sorted, renumber the selections.

8. Use the filename **16act3.sor** and save the file.

9. Print one copy and close the document.

■ Activity 16.4—Create a Macro to Change the Case and Use Bold and Italic Text Attributes

1. Open the file named **16act4**. (The WPMAIN Button Bar should be displayed and graphics mode should be selected.)

2. The insertion point should be placed to the left of the first character in the title of the report.

3. Select **Tools, Macro, Record**.

4. In the Macro box, type **a:casechg**. (Do not type the period.)

5. Select **OK**.

6. Press **Alt** and **F4**, and then press the **End** key to block the title of the report.

7. Select **Edit, Convert Case, Uppercase**.

8. Press **Alt** and **F4**, press the **Home** key and then press the left arrow key to block the title again.

9. Select the **Font** button.

10. Select the **Bold** and **Italic** appearance options. Select **OK**.

11. Select **Macro, Stop**.

12. Move the insertion point to the beginning of the desired text, e.g., move the insertion point to the first heading, *Research Grants....*

13. Select **Tools, Macro, Play**.

14. Type the macro name, **a:casechg**.

15. Select **OK**.

16. Repeat Steps 12–15 for each heading.

17. Use the filename **16act4.for** and save the file.

18. Print one copy and close the document.

Challenge Your Skills

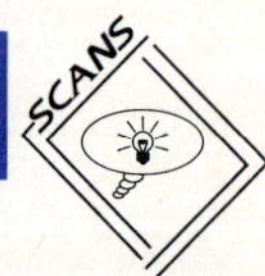

■ Skill 16.1—Paragraph Sorting

1. Open the file named **16skill1**.

2. Make decisions regarding margins, justification, and fonts.

3. Block all paragraphs except the report title.

4. Sort the paragraphs numerically in descending order by the first word (ballot number) of the first line of each paragraph.

5. Use the filename **16skill1.num** and save the sorted file.

6. Print one copy.

7. Block all paragraphs except the report title.

8. Sort the paragraphs alphabetically in ascending order by the second word of the first line of each paragraph.

9. Use the filename **16skill1.alp** and save the sorted file.

10. Print one copy and close the document.

Skill 16.2—Create and Apply Styles

1. Type the following unformatted presentation text.

WORDPERFECT 6.0
Features Presentation

1. BUTTON BAR
a. File Mgr
b. Save As
c. Print
d. Preview
e. Font
f. Grph Mode
g. Text Mode
h. Envelope
i. Speller
j. Gramatik
k. QuikFindr
l. Tbl Edit
m. Search
n. BBar Sel
o. BBar Opt

2. THE RIBBON
a. Zoom View
b. Style
c. Columns
d. Justification
e. Font Style
f. Size

3. MENU BAR
a. File
b. Edit
c. View
d. Layout
e. Tools
f. Font
g. Graphics
h. Window
i. Help

---

2. Use the filename **16skill2** and save the unformatted file.

3. Create the following styles.

Name:	P-Present
Type:	Open
Description:	Margins/font for presentations
Top margin:	1.25"
Left and right margins:	1.75"
Justification:	Left
Font:	Helve-WP Bold (Type 1), 14-point
Page Number:	Bottom Right

Name:	P-Title
Type	Paragraph
Description:	Title for presentations
Justification:	Center
Font:	Bodoni-WP Bold (Type 1), 18-point
Paragraph Spacing:	2

Name:	P-Subtitle
Type:	Paragraph
Description:	Subtitle for presentations
Justification:	Center
Font:	Bodoni-WP Bold (Type 1), 14-point
Paragraph Spacing:	3

Name:	P-Level 1
Type:	Paragraph
Description:	Topic level 1--presentations
Paragraph Spacing:	1.5

Name:	P-Level 2
Type:	Paragraph
Description:	Topic level 2--presentations
Special:	Press **F4** once to indent paragraphs

4. When all styles have been created, save the styles as **16skill2.sty**.

Chapter 16—Create Documents Using Special Functions

5. Apply the new styles to the document paragraphs. Remember to locate the cursor/insertion point at the top of the document when applying the P-Present style.

6. Use the filename **16skill2.for** and save the formatted presentation.

7. Print one copy and close the document.

Skill 16.3—Create a Macro with Font Changes, Date Code, and a Graphic Image

1. Create a macro that when played produces the fax cover sheet shown below.

    *Hints: Plan the macro by creating the document before selecting **Tools, Macro, Record**. Write down the steps needed to create the macro. When the graphic file (penpush.wpg) is retrieved, select Text Flows, Through Box so that the title will center correctly on the page. Use the Date Code so that the current date will be inserted each time the fax macro is played.*

2. When the macro is complete, close the document.

3. Play the macro and create a fax cover sheet using the following information:

TO:	Patti Zuecher
COMPANY:	Digital Microcomputer Products
PHONE:	512-555-6030
FAX:	512-555-2846

FROM:	A. R. Kieliszewski
COMPANY:	Verxion
PHONE:	612-555-1892
FAX:	612-555-7386
PAGES:	3
COMMENTS:	This report was also sent to your marketing group in Atlanta, attention Carmen Mistica.

4. Use the filename **16skill3.fax** and save the file.

5. Print one copy and close the document.

●◆ ▣ Skill 16.4—Sort Table Columns; Language Arts

1. Open the file named **16skill4**.

2. Make decisions regarding:

   Margins
   Justification
   Fonts (the final letter should fit on one page)
   Date of letter
   Table format (including cell widths, alignment of text, table borders)
   Correct four spelling and two punctuation errors
   Reference initials, document identification, and enclosure notation

3. Sort the table cells alphabetically by the item column.

4. Use the filename **16skill4.fin** and save the file.

5. Print one copy.

6. If you have completed your work, exit WordPerfect.

Chapter 16—Create Documents Using Special Functions

Document Window and File Maintenance

- Frame, cascade, tile, maximize, minimize, move, and resize document windows
- Create, revise, and print a document summary
- Use File Manager to copy, move, rename, locate, and delete files and create directories and subdirectories
- Use the QuickList
- Convert files to and from other word processing formats
- Assign passwords
- Use DOS without exiting WordPerfect

Objectives

After successfully completing this chapter, you will be able to cascade, tile, maximize, minimize, move, and resize document windows and create, revise, and print document summary information. You will also learn to use WordPerfect's File Manager to open, delete, rename, move, and locate files and to create and delete directories and subdirectories. In addition, you will learn to use WordPerfect's QuickList, file conversion, and Password features. Finally, you will learn to access DOS without exiting WordPerfect in order to perform tasks such as checking your hard disk or formatting a new disk.

Chapter Introduction

WordPerfect provides tools to manage, organize, access, and secure files. Files can be accessed or managed by using the Windows, Document Summary, File Manager, and QuickList features. Passwords can be created and used to secure files. Also, files from other word processing programs can be converted to or from the WordPerfect format.

If desired, WordPerfect can be temporarily exited in order for tasks to be accomplished at the DOS prompt.

The Windows in WordPerfect

The WordPerfect document window displays after the WordPerfect program is loaded. When a new file is created or an existing file is opened, a new window displays. Nine windows can be opened at one time. As each new file is opened, WordPerfect sequentially numbers the document windows, e.g., Doc1, Doc2, etc. The document number displays in the Status bar, and if the document window is framed it also displays in the Title bar. Any window can be framed, cascaded, tiled, maximized, minimized, moved, sized, or closed.

Start-Up Instructions

❖ Create five files as follows:

> a. In a new file, type **This is file 1.**; press **Enter** twice.
>
> b. Use the filename **file1** and save the file on your disk.
> *Note: Do not close the file(s).*
>
> c. Select **File, New**, type **This is file 2.**; press **Enter** twice.
>
> d. Use the filename **file2** and save the file on your disk.
>
> e. Select **File, New**, type **This is file 3.**; press **Enter** twice.
>
> f. Use the filename **file3** and save the file on your disk.
>
> g. Select **File, New**, type **This is file 4.**; press **Enter** twice.
>
> h. Use the filename **file4** and save the file on your disk.
>
> i. Select **File, New**, type **This is file 5.**; press **Enter** twice.
>
> j. Use the filename **file5** and save the file on your disk.

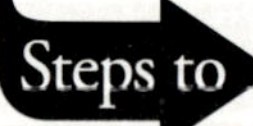

Frame a Document Window

1. Select **Window, Frame** {Alt and w, f}.

   Note: A Title bar (containing the window number, disk drive letter, and filename) displays below the Button Bar. The minimize and maximize buttons are located at the right of the Title bar, and the control box (which allows you to save and close a document) is located at the left of the Title bar (See Figure 17.1).

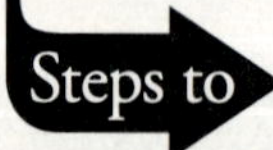

Cascade Document Windows

1. Select **Window, Cascade** {Alt and w, c}.

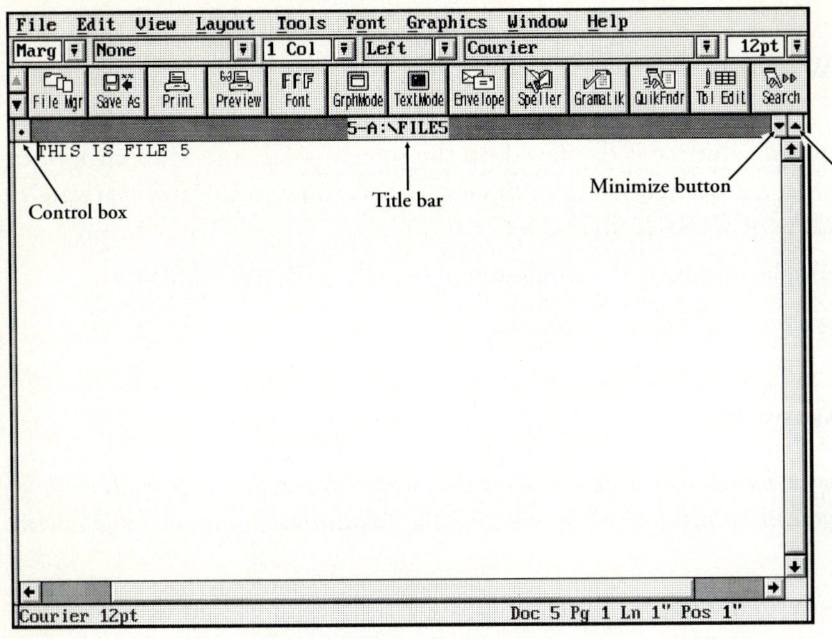

FIGURE 17.1

The framed document window with maximize and minimize buttons and control box

Note: When Cascade is selected, all open document windows overlap each other so that only the Title bar of each inactive window displays. The active window displays in front of the cascaded windows.

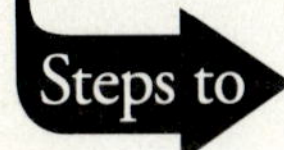 **Tile Document Windows**

1. Select **Window, Tile** {Alt and w, t}.

   Note: When Tile is selected, the open document windows are displayed so that all open windows are visible. The active window displays with a highlighted Title bar at the top or top left of the screen.

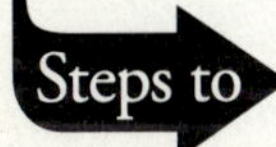 **Change the Active Window**

Note: The Title bar of an active window is highlighted.

1. Place the mouse pointer in the desired window and click once to activate the window {press the Home key, then press the desired window number, e.g., 1, 2, etc.}.

   For example, move the mouse pointer to the various open windows and click.

   *Note: If only one document window is displayed on the screen, select **Window, Switch To** and select the desired filename.*

The Windows in WordPerfect

Maximize a Window

1. If more than one window is displayed on the screen, select the **Maximize** button (up triangle) in the desired window to view the window in full size {activate the desired window; Alt and 2, m}.

   For example, maximize the window containing the file named **file4**.

   Note: The window will display in full size on the screen.

Minimize a Window

*Note: Minimizing a document window reduces the document window to a small rectangle. A document window can be minimized by selecting the **Minimize** button or by following the steps below.*

1. Activate the desired window, select **Window, Minimize** {Alt and w, i}.

   For example, minimize the window containing the file named **file4**.

   Note: The window returns to a small size.

Move a Window

Note: The window to be moved must be smaller than full size.

1. Locate the mouse pointer in the document window Title bar; press and hold the left mouse button {activate the desired window, Ctrl and F3, w, m}.

   For example, move the mouse pointer to the Title bar of the document window containing the file named **file2**, press and hold the mouse button.

   Note: A dashed outline appears around the document window, and the mouse pointer is a four-headed arrow.

2. Drag the dashed window outline to the desired position and release the mouse button {press the arrow keys to move the window to the desired location, press Enter}.

   For example, drag the dashed outline for the document window containing the file named **file2** to approximately the center of the screen and release the mouse button (see Figure 17.2).

Resize a Window

Note: The window must be smaller than full size.

1. Locate the mouse pointer on the document window left, right, or bottom edge until a double-headed arrow displays. Press and hold the left mouse button and drag

Chapter 17—Document Window and File Maintenance

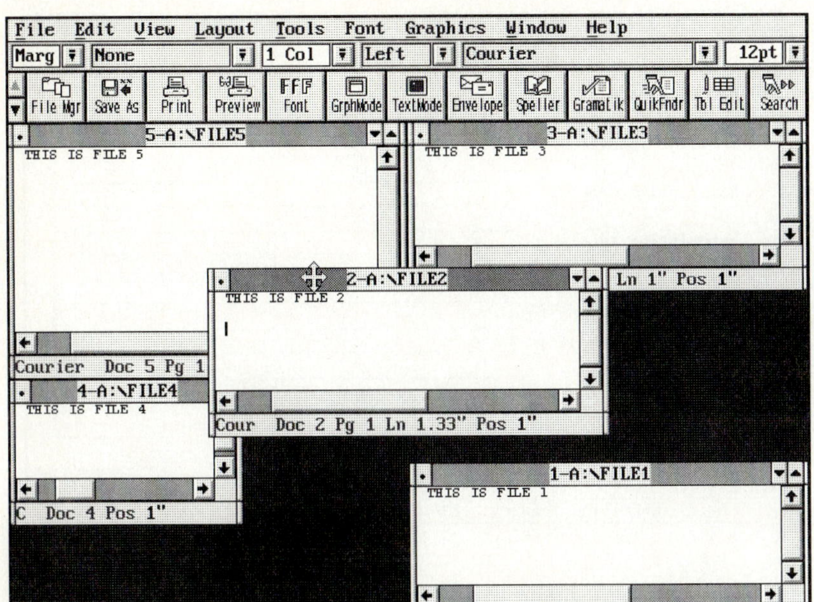

FIGURE 17.2

Moving a document window

the dashed outline to the desired size, release the mouse button {Ctrl and F3, w, s, press the up, down, left, or right arrow keys, press Enter}.

For example, move the mouse pointer to the bottom edge of the document window containing the file named **file2** and enlarge and reduce the window size.

Close All Windows

1. Select **File, Close** or select the **Control Box** (see Figure 17.1) at the left of the document Title bar {Alt and f, c}.

   For example, close the windows that contain file1, file2, file3, and file4.

   Note: When the document window is closed, the next opened window is displayed. However, if no other window has been opened, an empty screen with the words Doc 1 in the Status bar displays. Each open window must be closed separately one at a time.

Document Summary Information

A document summary can be created to provide specific information about a file, such as a descriptive name and document type and the name of the document author and typist (see Figure 17.3). The document summary is created by selecting **Layout, Document, Summary** and by typing the desired information into the option boxes in the Document Summary dialog box. If desired, Word-Perfect can be instructed to automatically display the Document Summary dialog box the first time a document is saved.

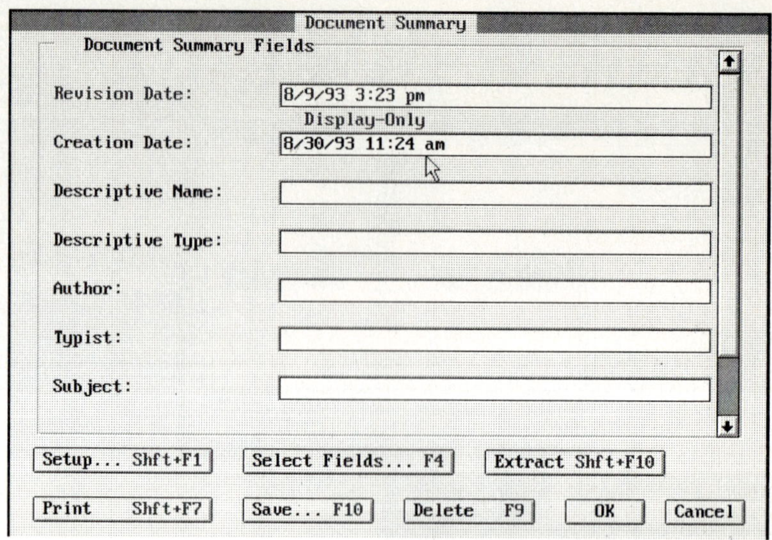

Once summary information is typed, the information can be changed and the up-dated information saved. If desired, the document summary can be printed. The document does not print when the document summary is printed.

Start-Up Instructions

❖ The file named **file5** should be displayed on the screen.

Create a Document Summary After a Document Is Saved

1. Select **Layout, Document, Summary** {Shift and F8, d, s}.

   Note: The Document Summary dialog box containing the revision and creation date displays. The current date displays in the Creation Date box to indicate the date the Document Summary was/is created. If desired, the Creation Date can be changed to an-other date. The Revision Date is the date the document was last revised. See Figure 17.3. This date is saved and updated automatically by WordPerfect and cannot be changed by the user.

2. Click in the Descriptive Name box and type words that identify the file {press Tab twice}.

   For example, type **This is a sample file**.

3. Click in the Descriptive Type box and type words that identify the document category {press Tab twice}.

   For example, type **Sample**.

4. Click in the Typist box and type the name of the typist.

   For example, type your name.

5. If desired, type any additional information into the desired option boxes.

6. Select **OK** twice {press Esc, Enter twice}.

Steps to ▶ Revise a Document Summary

1. Select **Layout, Document, Summary** {Shift and F8, d, s}.

2. Select the option(s) to be changed and type the updated information.

3. Select **OK** twice to save the updated document summary {press Esc, Enter twice}.

Steps to ▶ Print Document Summary Information

1. Select **Layout, Document, Summary** {Shift and F8, d, s}.

2. Select **Print** {Shift and F7}.

   Note: A message, "Print document summary?" displays.

3. Select **Yes** {press y}.

   Note: The document summary prints; the document does not print.

4. Select **OK** twice to return to the document window {press Esc, Enter twice}.

Steps to ▶ Make the Document Summary Dialog Box Display When Saving a Document

1. Select **Layout, Document, Summary** {Shift and F8, d, s}.

2. Select **Setup** {Shift and F1}.

3. Select the **Create Summary on Save/Exit** option {c}.

4. Select **OK** three times to return to the document window {Enter three or four times}.

   Note: If the Create Summary on Save/Exit option is selected, the Document Summary dialog box displays when a document is saved.

Finish-Up Instructions

❖ Close the document window.

Use the WordPerfect File Manager

The WordPerfect File Manager is used to open files, print multiple files, create directories and subdirectories, search for files by word(s) or name, and perform the usual disk maintenance tasks of copying, moving, renaming, and deleting files. The File Manager can also be used to look at the contents of a file without opening or retrieving the file to a document window.

The File Manager window is divided into two sections: the file list and a list of commands and options. The file list displays the names of the files and subdirectories in the current directory. When the File Manager window is accessed, the Current <Dir> name is highlighted. The current drive and directory are shown above the file list. The Parent <Dir> name can be selected to display a list of files or directories that are one level closer to the root directory.

The Find File and Find Word options allow you to quickly locate a file(s) by finding a file(s) by name or by finding a file(s) that contains certain words. Once the desired file(s) is found, the file(s) can be viewed, copied, opened, moved/renamed, deleted, or printed. (See Chapter 4 for information on printing from the File Manager window.)

Start-Up Instructions

❖   The files named **file1**, **file2**, **file3**, **file4**, and **file5** must be on your disk.

Access the File Manager Window

1. Select the **File Mgr** button on the Button Bar {F5}.

2. In the Specify File Manager List dialog box, type the desired drive letter and/or directory.

    For example, type the drive letter where your file disk is located (**a:** or **b:**).

3. Select **OK** {Enter}.

    Note: The File Manager window displays.

Look at the Contents of a File

1. In the File Manager window, highlight the desired filename.

    For example, highlight **File3**.

2. Select **Look** {L}.

    *Note: The Look window displays showing the filename (**a:\file3**), the name of the program used to create the file (WP 6.0), the date the file was revised, and the contents of the file. At the bottom of the Look window is a group of options that allows you to look at the next file or previous file, open the file to a document window, delete the file, mark the file, scroll through the document, and search for specific text within the document. See Figure 17.4.*

3. Select **Close** to return to the File Manager window {Enter}.

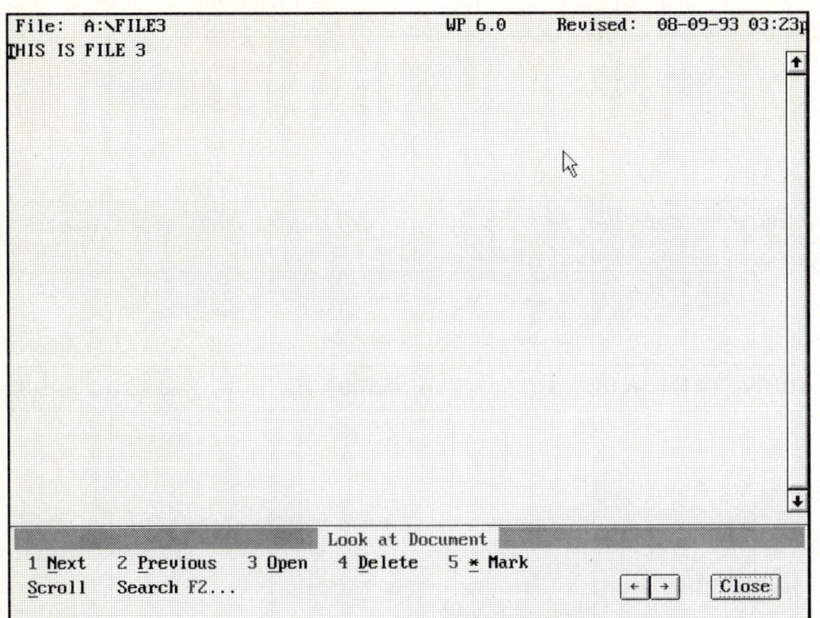

FIGURE 17.4

Document displayed in the
Look window

Print the List of Files

1. In the File Manager window, select **Print List** {t}.

   Note: Wait momentarily and a page listing the files in the current directory/drive will print.

Create a Directory

1. In the File Manager window, select **Change Default Dir** {h}.

   Note: The Change Default Directory dialog box displays with the New Directory indicating A:\ or B:\.

2. In the New Directory box, type the desired directory name.

   For example, type your last name (up to eight characters).

3. Select **OK** {Enter}.

   Note: A message "Create directory ...?" displays.

4. Select **Yes** {y}.

   Note: The new directory name displays in the File List followed by the word <DIR>.

Create a Subdirectory

5. In the File Manager window, select **Change Default Dir** {h}.

6. Click in the New Directory box and type the name of the directory followed by a backslash(\) and the desired subdirectory name, e.g., hart\andrew {press the right arrow key three times}.

Use the WordPerfect File Manager

> For example, type your last name, a backslash, and your first
> name (one to eight characters for each name).

7. Select **OK** {Enter}.

8. Select **Yes** {y}.

   Note: The subdirectory name does not display until you double-click on the directory name {highlight directory name and press Enter}.

Finish-Up Instructions

❖ Double-click on your last name directory to display the new first name subdirectory.

Start-Up Instructions

❖ Double-click on the Parent <Dir> to return the list of files in the root directory to the screen {highlight Parent <Dir> and press Enter}.

Mark and Copy Files

1. In the File Manager window, highlight the filename of the first file to be copied and press the **Spacebar** once to mark (*) the file.

   For example, highlight **file1** and press the **Spacebar** once.

   *Note: An asterisk displays beside the filename. If a file is marked by mistake, highlight the filename and press the **Spacebar** again to unmark the file.*

2. To mark additional files to be copied, highlight each filename and press the **Spacebar**.

   For example, mark the files named **file2**, **file3**, **file4**, and **file5**.

3. Select **Copy** {c}.

   Note: The message "Copy marked files?" displays.

4. Select **Yes** {y}.

   Note: The Copy dialog box displays.

5. Type the name of the directory (and, if necessary, the subdirectory) where the files are to be copied.

   For example, type your last name directory.

6. Select **OK** {Enter}.

   Note: Wait a few moments until the "Please Wait" message no longer displays.

Finish-Up Instructions

❖ When the copy process is completed, double-click on your last name directory to display a list of the copied files. If the message "Open marked files?" displays, select **No** {Enter}.

                                     Chapter 17—Document Window and File Maintenance

 Mark and Move Files

1. In the File Manager window, highlight the first file to be moved and press the **Spacebar** to mark (*) the file.

   For example, highlight the file named **file2** and press the **Spacebar**.

2. To mark additional files to be moved, highlight each filename and press the **Spacebar**.

   For example, mark the file named **file3**.

3. Select **Move/Rename** {m}.

   Note: A message "Move marked files?" displays.

4. Select **Yes** {y}.

5. Click after the last character displayed in the "Move Marked Files to" box {press the right arrow key repeatedly until the cursor is located after the last character}.

6. Type the name of the directory (and, if necessary the subdirectory) where the files are to be copied.

   For example, if necessary type your last name directory. Type a backslash (\) and your first name subdirectory.

7. Select **OK** {Enter}.

   Note: The filenames are removed from the list of files in your last name directory. Double-click on your first name subdirectory to display a list of the moved files.

 Delete Files

1. In the File Manager window, double-click on the directory (or subdirectory) that contains the files to be deleted.

   For example, if necessary, double-click on the first name subdirectory.

2. Mark the file(s) to be deleted by highlighting each filename and pressing the **Spacebar**.

   For example, mark the files named **file2** and **file3**.

3. Select **Delete** {d}.

   Note: The message "Delete marked files?" displays.

4. Select **Yes** {y}.

   Note: The messages "Marked files willl be deleted. Continue?" displays.

5. Select **Yes** {y}.

   Note: The selected filenames no longer display in the list of files for your first name subdirectory.

❖ Double-click on **Parent <Dir>** to return to your last name directory.

 ## Delete a Directory or Subdirectory

Note: A directory/subdirectory must be empty in order to be deleted.

1. In the File Manager window, highlight the name of the directory or subdirectory to be deleted.

   For example, highlight your first name subdirectory.

2. Select **Delete** {d}.

   Note: The message "Remove...?" displays.

3. Select **Yes** {y}.

   Note: The directory/subdirectory is removed from the file list. If the directory/subdirectory is not empty (files and/or subdirectories are listed under the directory/subdirectory name) when Delete is selected, a message, "Directory not empty. Cannot delete." displays. Delete any files or subdirectories and then delete the desired directory/subdirectory.

Rename a File

1. In the File Manager window, highlight the filename to be renamed.

   For example, highlight the file named **file5** in your last name directory.

2. Select **Move/Rename** {m}.

   Note: The Move/Rename File(s) dialog box displays showing the current drive, directory, and filename.

3. In the New Name box, type the new name for the file to replace the original filename.

   For example, type **2ndname**. (Do not type the period.)

4. Select **OK** {Enter}.

   *Note: The new name, **2ndname**, displays in your last name directory box and the filename **file5** no longer displays.*

❖ Double-click on **Parent <Dir>** to return to the list of files in the root directory of your file disk.

Find Files Containing Specific Word(s)

1. In the File Manager window, select **Find** {f}.

Note: The Find dialog box displays. The options in the Find dialog box are used to tell WordPerfect where to look for the text that will be specified in Step 3.

2. Select the desired option.

> For example, select **First Page** {p}.

Note: The Find Word in First Page dialog box displays.

3. In the Word pattern box, type the desired word(s)to be located.

> For example, type **This is file**. (Do not type the period.)

4. Select **OK** {Enter}.

Note: The Finding Files box displays indicating the number of files being searched. Then a list of the filenames containing the specified text displays. If no files are found that contain the specified text, a message "File not found" displays.

Finish-Up Instructions

> ❖ Double-click on **Parent <Dir>** to return to the list of files in the root directory of your file disk.

Find Files by Filename Using Search

1. In the File Manager window, select **Search** {F2 or e}.

   Note: The Search for Filename dialog box displays.

2. Type the name or partial name of the file(s) to be found.

   > For example, type **file*.*** to locate all filenames that begin with the word *file*.

   Note: The asterisks are DOS "wildcard" characters. The asterisk is a substitute for multiple characters. In this example, file.* instructs the search option to find all filenames that begin with the word "file" and end with any character(s).*

3. Select **Search** {F2}.

   Note: The first filename that contains the specified pattern is highlighted in the file list.

4. To continue the search, press **F2** twice.

5. Press **F2** repeatedly until the "Not Found" message box displays.

6. Select **OK** {Enter}.

Open Multiple Files Using the File Manager

1. In the File Manager window, mark the first file to be opened.

   > For example, mark the file named **file1** in the root directory of your file disk.

2. Repeat Step 1 to mark any additional files to be opened.

For example, mark the files named **file4** and **file5**.

Note: A maximum of nine files can be opened at one time.

3. Select **Open into New Document** {o}.

   Note: The message "Open marked files?" displays.

4. Select **Yes** {y}.

   Note: After a few moments, WordPerfect returns to the regular editing screen and opens each file into a separate document window.

Finish-Up Instructions

❖ Select **Window**, **Tile** to display all open document windows.

❖ Close all document windows.

The QuickList

The QuickList feature provides easy access to frequently used directories and subdirectories. Directories and subdirectories can be assigned descriptive names by using the QuickList feature. When opening or saving files, instead of typing the full path name for the desired directory/subdirectory, the descriptive name can be selected from the QuickList dialog box.

For example, letters authored by B. Smith of the Personnel Department might be saved in the subdirectory c:\persnl\letters\smith. A QuickList entry could be created that identified the subdirectory as B. Smith Letters. To open a file saved in the subdirectory c:\persnl\letters\smith, you would select QuickList in the Open Document dialog box, choose B. Smith Letters, and then the list of all the files in the subdirectory would display in the File Manager window.

The QuickList feature can be accessed from any dialog box where a filename can be typed, e.g., the Open Document, Save Document, Retrieve Document, and Specify File Manager List dialog boxes.

Create a QuickList Directory Entry

Note: The Steps to Create a QuickList Directory Entry can also be accomplished from the Save Document, Retrieve Document, and Specify File Manager List dialog boxes.

1. Select **File, Open** {Shift and F10}.

2. Select **QuickList** {F6}.

   Note: The QuickList dialog box displays.

3. Select **Create** {c}.

   Note: The Create QuickList Entry dialog box displays.

4. In the Description box, type a descriptive name of the directory (or subdirectory).

   For example, type **Sample Files**. (Do not type the period.)

5. Press the **Tab** key once.

6. Type the name of the directory to be added to the QuickList.

   For example, type **a:** or **b:** and your last name directory.

7. Select **OK** {Enter twice}.

   Note: The Sample Files entry has been added to the QuickList box.

8. Select **Close** {F7}.

9. Select **Cancel** {press Esc twice}.

Access a Directory Using the QuickList

1. Select **File, Open** {Shift and F10}.

2. Select **QuickList** {F6}.

   Note: The QuickList dialog box displays.

3. Double-click on the desired name in the QuickList box {use the up or down arrow key to highlight desired item, Enter}.

   For example, double-click on **Sample Files**.

   Note: The File Manager window displays showing the list of files in your last name directory. If desired, a file could be opened.

Finish-Up Instructions

❖ Select **Close, Cancel** {Esc three times} to exit the File Manager window and return to the document window.

Delete a QuickList Entry

Note: The Steps to Delete a QuickList Entry can also be accomplished from the Save Document, Retrieve Document, and Specify File Manager List dialog boxes.

1. Select **File, Open** {Shift and F10}.

2. Select **QuickList** {F6}.

3. In the QuickList box, highlight the name to be deleted {press the down arrow key to highlight the desired item name}.

   For example, highlight **Sample Files**.

4. Select **Delete** {d}.

   Note: The Delete QuickList Entry dialog box displays showing the description, filename/directory (path), and the message "Delete entry from QuickList?"

5. Select **Yes** {Enter}.

   Note: The Sample Files item no longer displays in the QuickList box.

6. Select **Close, Cancel** {Esc three times} to return to the document window.

Converting Files

WordPerfect for Windows provides a method to change the file format of a document. A document can be saved to another file format or can be converted from a different file format. For example, a document originally saved in the Word for Windows file format can be converted to a WordPerfect document. Also, a WordPerfect document can be saved in another format, such as WordStar.

Start-Up Instructions

❖   Open the file named **file1**.

Save a File in a Different File Format

1. Select the **Save As** button {F10}.

2. Type the desired filename in the Filename box.

   For example, **file1con.doc**. (Do not type the final period.)

3. Select the down arrow button in the Format box {press Tab, r}.

4. Scroll through the list of file formats and double-click on the desired file format {press the up or down arrow key until the desired file format is highlighted}.

   For example, scroll up the list of file formats and double-click on **MS Word for Windows 2.0b**.

5. Select **OK** {Enter twice}.

   *Note: The file named **file1con.doc** is now saved in the new MS Word for Windows format. The file named **file1** is still available on your file disk and is saved in the WordPerfect 6.0 file format.*

Finish-Up Instructions

❖   Close the document.

Open a File Created in a Different Program

1. Open the desired file.

   For example, open the file named **file1con.doc**.

2. Select **OK** {Enter}.

Note: The File Format dialog box displays. MS Word for Windows 2.0b is highlighted because WordPerfect attempts to determine the format of the file.

3. To select the file format, highlight the desired format and choose **Select** {Enter}.

    Note: A "Converting File" message displays. After a few moments the converted file displays. (The displayed file has been converted to the WordPerfect 6.0 format.)

File Security

Once a file is created, the file can be saved and given a password. Each time the saved file is opened, the password is requested. The password must be remembered by the user since there is no method available for finding a forgotten password. A password can be removed or changed at any time (but only if you remember the current password).

Start-Up Instructions

❖ Open a new file.

❖ Type the following sentence:

   This is a very secret file that no one but me should ever see.

Create or Change a Password

1. Select the **Save As** button {F10}.

2. Type the desired filename.

    For example, type **17secret.** (Do not type the final period.)

3. Select **Password** {F8}.

    Note: The Password dialog box displays.

4. Type the desired password.

    For example, type **007**. (Do not type the period.)

    Note: To ensure privacy, the typed characters are not displayed on the screen and the cursor does not move in the Password box. A password can be 1 to 23 characters and can contain spaces, uppercase and lowercase letters, and any characters found on the keyboard.

5. Select **OK** {Enter}.

    Note: A beep may be heard.

6. Retype the password to confirm.

7. Select **OK** {Enter}.

8. Select **OK** to save the file {Enter}.

❖ Close the document.

Open a File That Has Been Protected with a Password

1. Select **File, Open, File Manager**, if necessary, type the desired drive letter and select **OK** {Alt and f, o, F5, type drive letter, Enter}.

2. Select the desired filename.

   For example, double-click on **17secret**.

   Note: The Password dialog box displays.

3. Type the password exactly as typed when the password was created.

   For example, type **007**. (Do not type the period.)

   Note: As the password is typed, no characters display on the screen and the cursor does not move in the Password box.

4. Select **OK** {Enter}.

Remove a Password

1. Select the **Save As** button {F10}.

2. Select **Password** {F8}.

3. Select **Remove** {F6}.

4. Select **OK** {Enter}.

5. Save the file again using the same filename. Select **Yes** to replace the file.

   Note: If the file is not saved after the Password is removed, the password will still be needed to open the file.

Finish-Up Instructions

❖ Close the document window.

Using DOS Without Exiting WordPerfect

DOS commands such as format, chkdsk (check disk), dir (directory), date, erase, and diskcopy can be accessed without exiting the WordPerfect program by selecting **File, Go to Shell** and by choosing either the **Go to DOS** or **DOS Command** option. If the **Go to DOS** option is selected, the cursor will be taken back to the c:\ prompt. The desired DOS command(s) is typed and executed.

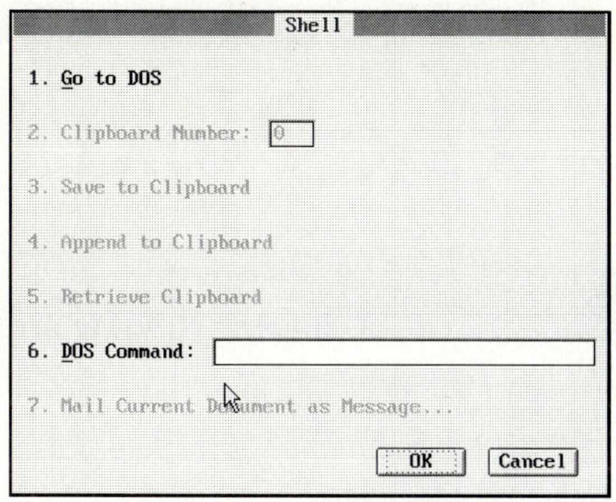

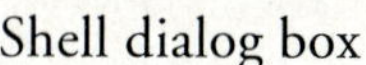

FIGURE 17.5

Shell dialog box

In order to return to the WordPerfect document window, the word **Exit** is typed and the **Enter** key is pressed. If the **DOS Command** option is chosen, the desired command is typed in the DOS Command Box and **Enter** is pressed to execute the command. The **Enter** key is pressed again to return to the WordPerfect document window.

Exit to DOS Using the Go to DOS Option

1. Select **File, Go to Shell** {Ctrl and F1}.

   Note: The Shell dialog box displays (see Figure 17.5).

2. Select **Go to DOS** {g}.

   Note: After a few moments, the DOS prompt displays.

3. Type and execute the desired DOS command.

   For example, type **ver** and press **Enter**.

   *Note: After typing **ver**, the number of the DOS version on the hard disk displays.*

4. If desired, type other DOS commands or type **exit** to return to the WordPerfect document window.

   For example, type **exit** and press **Enter**.

Access DOS Using the DOS Command Option

1. Select **File, Go to Shell** {Ctrl and F1}.

2. Select **DOS Command** {d}.

3. Type the desired DOS command.

   For example, type **ver**.

4. Press **Enter** to execute the command.

5. Press any key to return to the WordPerfect document window.

   For example, press **Enter**.

The Next Step

Chapter Review and Activities

FEATURES SUMMARY

FEATURES	ACTIONS	PAGE
Frame a document window	Select **Window**, **Frame**.	450
Cascade document windows	Select **Window**, **Cascade**.	450
Tile document windows	Select **Window**, **Tile**.	451
Change the active window	Place the mouse pointer in the desired window and press the left mouse button once.	451
Maximize a window	Select **Window**, **Maximize** or select the **Maximize** button in the desired window.	452
Minimize a window	Select **Window**, **Minimize** or select the **Minimize** button in the desired window.	452
Move a window	Locate the mouse pointer in the Title bar of the document window, press and hold the mouse button, drag the dashed outline for the document window to the desired location, release the mouse button.	452
Resize a window	Locate the mouse pointer on the left, right, or bottom edge of the document window, press and hold the mouse button, drag the dashed outline for the document window to the desired location, release the mouse button.	452

FEATURES *(cont'd.)*	ACTIONS *(cont'd.)*	PAGE
Close all windows	Select **File, Close** or select the **Control Box** for each open window.	453
Create a document summary	Select **Layout, Document, Summary**, type the desired document summary information, select **OK**.	454
Print a document summary	Select **Layout, Document, Summary, Print, Yes, OK** twice.	455
Display the Document Summary dialog box when saving a document	Select, **Layout, Document, Summary, Setup, Create Summary on Save/Exit, OK** twice.	455
Access the File Manager window	Select the **File Mgr** button, type the disk drive letter and/or directory, select **OK**.	456
Look at the contents of a file	In the File Manager window, highlight the desired filename and select **Look**. Select **Close** to return to the File Manager window.	456
Print the list of files	In the File Manager window, select **Print List**.	457
Create a directory/ subdirectory	In the File Manager window, select **Change Default Dir**; in the New Directory box, type the desired directory name (if a subdirectory, type the directory name followed by a \ and the subdirectory name); select **OK, Yes**.	457
Mark and copy files	In the File Manager window, mark each file to be copied by highlighting the filename and pressing the **Spacebar**, select **Copy, Yes**, type the name of the directory/ subdirectory where the files are to be copied, select **OK**.	458
Mark and move files	In the File Manager window, mark each file to be moved by highlighting the filename and pressing the **Spacebar**, select **Move/Rename, Yes**, type the name of the directory/ subdirectory where the files are to be moved, select **OK**.	459
Delete files	In the File Manager window, mark the files to be deleted, select **Delete, Yes, Yes**.	459
Delete a directory/ subdirectory	In the File Manager window, highlight the directory/ subdirectory to be deleted, select **Delete, Yes**.	460
Rename a file	In the File Manager window, highlight the file to be renamed, select **Move/Rename**, type the new filename, select **OK**.	460
Find files containing specific word(s)	In the File Manager window, select **Find**, select desired option, type the word(s) to be found, select **OK**.	460

| --- | --- | --- |
Find files by using Search	In the File Manager window, select **Search**, type the filename or partial filename, select **Search**. To continue the search, press **F2** twice.	461
Open multiple files	In the File Manager window, mark all files to be opened, select **Open into New Document, Yes.**	461
Create a QuickList directory entry	Select **File, Open, QuickList, Create**, type the descriptive name, type the name of the directory to be added to the QuickList, select **OK, Close, Cancel.**	462
Access a directory using the QuickList	Select **File, Open, QuickList**, double-click on the desired entry name.	463
Delete a QuickList	Select **File, Open, QuickList**, highlight the entry name to be deleted, select **Delete, Yes, Close, Cancel.**	463
Save a file in a different file format	Select the **Save As** button, type the desired filename, select the down arrow button in the Format box, double-click on the desired file format, select **OK.**	464
Open a file created in a different program	Select **File**, Open. If necessary, select **File Manager** to access a different directory, double-click on the desired filename. Check that the correct format is highlighted, choose **Select.**	464
Create or change a password	Select the **Save As** button, type the desired filename, select **Password**, type the desired password, retype the password, select OK twice to save the file.	465
Open a file protected by a password	Select **File, Open**, type desired filename, **OK**, type password, **Enter.**	466
Remove a password	Select the **Save As** button, select **Password, Remove, OK**, save the file again using the same filename.	466
Exit to DOS	Select **File, Go to Shell, Go to DOS**, type and execute the desired command, type exit to return to the document window. Select **File, Go to Shell**, DOS Command, type the desired command and press **Enter** to execute. Press **Enter** to return to the document window.	467

True/False—Circle One

T F 1. When multiple document windows are open, select **Window**, **Tile** to display all the documents on the screen.

T F 2. The **Maximize** button can be selected to reduce the size of a document window.

T F 3. A tiled document window can be moved but not resized.

T F 4. A document summary can be created or edited by selecting **Layout**, **Document**, **Summary**, typing/editing the desired information, and selecting **OK**.

T F 5. In the File Manager window, a file can be marked by highlighting the filename and pressing the **Spacebar** once.

Short Answer

1. List five tasks that can be accomplished by using the various options available in the File Manager window.

2. Write down the maximum number of document windows that can be open at one time.

3. List the seven steps to mark and move files.

4. Write down the maximum number of characters that can be used in a password.

5. List the four steps to access DOS using the DOS Command options.

Enriching Language Arts

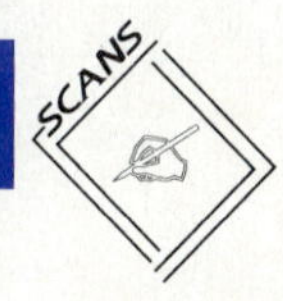

Proofreading Hints

When proofreading a document, read the document twice, once for content and meaning, and once to check grammar, spelling, and punctuation. When proofing your own work, place the original document/draft beside the screen and read across comparing line by line. Read aloud with a second person to compare the printed copy with the original document/draft.

Examples of types of errors to look for when proofreading:

Repeated words	The wedding reception will be held on Sunday *at the at the* Jamestown Country Club.
Misused or missing words	The transaction is *not* legal. The transaction is *now* legal.
Missing punctuation	The cost was *$2516.* (should be *$25.16*)
Misspelled names	Kathryn or Catherine
Transposed letters/ numbers	The *item* is 10:00 a.m. (*time*) The report is due October *21.* (should be October *12*)

Activities

Activity 17.1—Cascade, Tile, and Maximize Document Windows

1. Use the File Manager and open four of the files from your file disk.

2. Cascade the document windows.

3. Tile the document windows to observe all open windows.

4. Maximize one of the document windows.

5. Close all document windows.

Activity 17.2—Print a List of Files

1. In the File Manager window, print a list of all the files in the root directory of your file disk.

Activity 17.3—Create and Print a Document Summary

1. Open one of the files from your file disk and review the document to determine the document's subject.

2. Create a document summary for your chosen file. Fill in the Descriptive Name, Descriptive Type, and Typist boxes with the appropriate information.

3. Print the document summary.

4. Save and close the document.

 Chapter 17—Document Window and File Maintenance

Challenge Your Skills

Skill 17.1—Create and Delete Directories, Copy, Move, and Delete Files; Create a QuickList Entry

1. Create two directories on your file disk using the directory names **dir1** and **dir2**.

2. Mark and copy four **.wpg** files (WordPerfect graphics files) from the c:\wp60\graphics subdirectory to **dir1**. (If necessary, check with your instructor or instructional assistant for the drive and/or directory where the WordPerfect graphics files are located.)

3. Mark and move two of the graphics files from dir1 to dir2.

4. Optional. Print the list of files in the dir1 and dir2 directories.

5. Delete the files in the dir2 directory.

6. Delete the dir2 directory.

7. In the dir1 directory, rename one of the graphics files using the filename **graphics2.wpg**.

8. Optional. Print the list of files in the dir1 directory.

9. Create a QuickList entry for the dir1 directory.

10. If you have completed your work, exit WordPerfect

Production Skill Builder Activities
Chapters 14-17

Production Activity 5.1—Newsletter with Table and Graphics; Sorting

1. Use the following information to create the two-page newsletter shown on pages 476 and 477.

   a. Change the top and bottom margins to .75"; change the left and right margins to .5".

   b. Create a footer that includes the newsletter name, issue date, and page number.

   c. Use letterspacing and word spacing to adjust the spacing of the letters in the title.

   d. Use the bullet macro to insert the ☞ and ➡ characters that are located in the Iconic WordPerfect character set.

2. Optional. After completing the newsletter, sort the table of upcoming classes by class name or by date.

3. Optional. After completing the newsletter, use paragraph sorting to sort the locations of Bright Medical Center by name.

4. Use the filename **5pact1** and save the file.

5. Print one copy and close the document.

COMMUNITY HEALTH BULLETIN

Sunning Health Tips

Summer is almost here and it's time to start thinking about protecting your skin from burns and ultraviolet rays. Take a minute to review the following tips:

☞ Avoid being outside during midday hours (10 a.m. to 2 p.m.) on sunny days.

☞ Wear sunscreen for all outdoor activities year round. Apply sunscreen at least one hour before going out into the sun and again after swimming or perspiring heavily.

☞ If you are taking medication, check with your doctor before going out in the sun. Antihistamines, antibiotics, estrogen, tranquilizers, or birth control pills may cause a photosensitive skin reaction.

☞ Avoid using indoor sunlamps, tanning booths, sun reflectors, tan accelerators, or tanning pills.

Upcoming Health Education Classes

Bright Medical Center offers many health education classes. These classes are held at the Community Center. The fee to attend each class is $15. This fee covers handouts, a community health T-shirt, and refreshments. Your ideas for additional classes are welcome and can be sent to Dr. Deanna Berninger at Rose Valley Hospital. The following table shows a listing of upcoming classes.

CPR	4/14	7:30 p.m.
Food, Fitness & Fun	5/20	10:00 a.m. & 5:30 p.m.
Nutrition	6/11	6:00 p.m.
Senior Care Issues	4/20	3:00 p.m.
Anxiety & Phobias	5/15	7:00 p.m.
Cooking for a Healthy Heart	6/19	1:00 p.m.
Stop Smoking	6/10	6:30 p.m.
Sports Injuries	4/30	7:30 p.m.

Walking--The Right Exercise

Walking is becoming the exercise of choice by many people, mainly because it's so easy to do. Find a pair of comfortable shoes, a friend, and a park or walking trail and exercise your way to a healthier life.

What are the benefits of walking?

→ Improved cardiovascular fitness
→ Toned muscles
→ Reduced stress and tension
→ Reduced cholesterol
→ Increased metabolic rate, helping you to keep weight off

Carpal Tunnel Syndrome

Individuals who keyboard for long periods of time are at risk of developing the painful hand disorder known as "Carpal Tunnel Syndrome." Repetitive motions of the hand, such as excessive wrist movement or holding the wrists in a stationary position for long periods of time can irritate nerves, tendons and arteries in the narrow area of the wrist known as the "carpal tunnel." Carpal tunnel syndrome has been very prevalent in secretarial, word processing, data entry, and cashiering careers.

Although the actual injury occurs in the wrist area, the pain from the injury is usually felt in the hand. Carpal tunnel syndrome may also cause numbness in the fingers.

Below are a few suggestions for avoiding carpal tunnel syndrome:

☞ Maintain good posture--straight back, shoulders relaxed, elbows along side of the body, wrists straight, and arms parallel to the floor.

☞ Use a wrist rest to provide support for the wrists and to assist in maintaining the straight wrist position.

☞ Before beginning a job which requires repetitive wrist action, practice a few wrist stretching and strengthening exercises.

☞ Adjust the angle of the keyboard for comfort.

☞ Avoid over-reaching with fingers.

☞ Take frequent short breaks and perform other types of activities or practice wrist stretching exercises.

☞ Avoid pounding on the keys.

☞ Take advantage of computer program features that are designed to reduce repetitive keystrokes. Usually these features allow you to record a set of keystrokes, then play them back using only one or two keystrokes. Look for features with names such as "Recorder," "Macro," or "Playback."

Bright Medical Center Locations

For your convenience, Bright Medical Centers are located throughout the city. Please check for the location nearest you.

Clearlake Center   555-4200
1435 Clearlake Plaza, Suite 1000

Paradise Center   555-5800
4500 Paradise Road, Suite 255

Lakeport Center   555-4425
#525 Lakeport Mall

East Valley Center   555-7800
9900 Jefferson Avenue

1. Create the following document using superscripts, subscripts, and equations.

SUPERSCRIPTS, SUBSCRIPTS, AND EQUATIONS

COMPLEMENTARY ANGLES

40° 50°

35° 55°

27° 63°

10° 80°

CHEMICAL FORMULAS

Sodium Hydrosulfite = $Na_2S_2O_4$ Sodium Sulfite = Na_2SO_3

Sodium Phosphate = NaH_2PO_4 Sodium Ethylate = C_2H_5ONa

ALGEBRAIC EQUATIONS

$$\frac{1}{y}+\frac{1}{2}=\frac{1}{y-2} \qquad \frac{(2a^2c)^2}{5m} \qquad \sqrt{\frac{1}{20}} \qquad \sqrt{\frac{49a^2}{64b^2}}$$

---

2. Use the filename **5pact2** and save the file.

3. Print one copy and close the document.

1. Use the following information and create a flier similar to the one shown on page 479.

    a. The graphics file is named **pheasant.wpg** and is stored in the WP60\graphics directory.

    b. Use word spacing and letterspacing to adjust the spacing between the words and letters, if needed.

    c. Optional. Use Line Sort to sort the *General Information* items alphabetically.

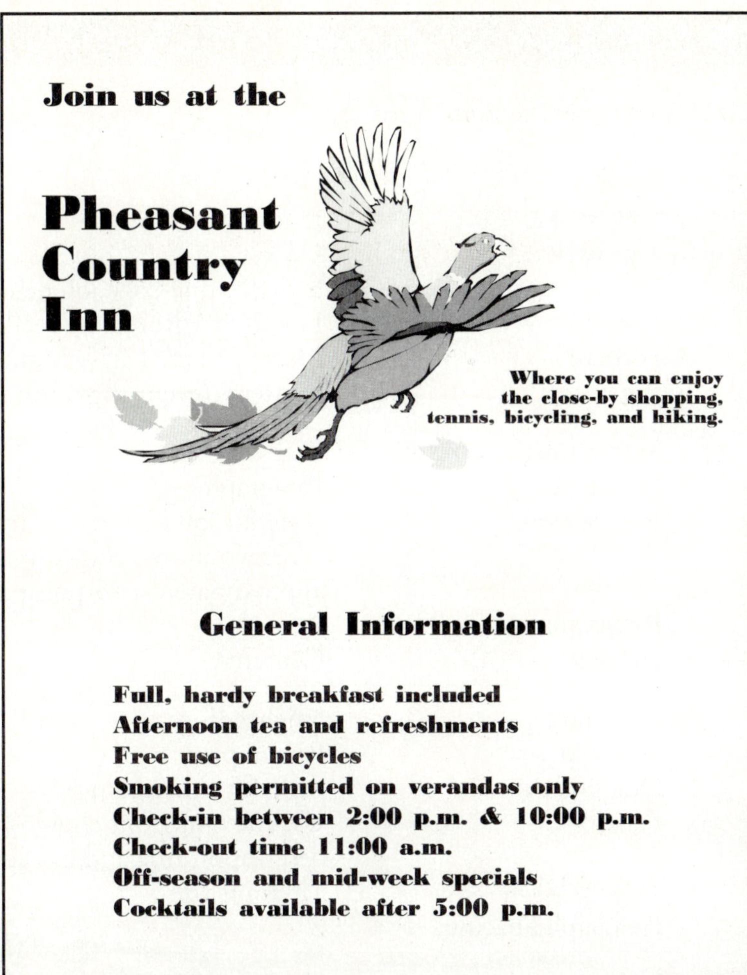

2. Use the filename **5pact3** and save the file.

3. Print one copy and close the document.

◧ Production Activity 5.4—Append to File

1. Open the file named **5pact4**.

2. Use the Append to File feature and create an overhead transparency containing the document title and sideheadings. Use the filename **5pact4.ovr.**

3. Open the file named **5pact4.ovr** and format the overhead transparency text, e.g., select a different font, use large size, and insert additional lines between the title and each sideheading.

4. Print one copy and close the documents.

1. Open the file named **5pact5**.

2. Create the following styles:

Style name:	Doc. style
Style type:	Open
Description:	Style for one-page job description
Font:	Dutch 801 Roman (Speedo), 12-point
Format:	Margins: Left 1.25"; Right 1.25"
Page:	Center Current Page (top to bottom)

Style name:	Doc. title
Style type:	Paragraph
Description:	Style for job description title
Font:	Make your own choice and use approximately a 14-point size
Paragraph Spacing:	2
Format:	Centered

Style name:	Sideheading
Style type:	Paragraph
Description:	Style for sideheadings
Font:	Use the same font chosen for the job description title and use approximately 12-point size
Paragraph Spacing:	2

Style name:	TV Prog Name
Style type:	Character
Description:	Changes TV program name font
Font:	Use Dutch 801 Bold, Italic (Speedo), 12-point

3. Save the new styles on your disk. Remember, an X should display in both the Save User Created Styles and Save WP System Styles option boxes. Use the filename **5pact4.sty**.

4. Apply the styles to the document, title, sideheadings, and TV program name.

5. Correct two spelling errors, two punctuation errors, and one repeated word error.

6. Use the new filename **5pact5.for** and save the formatted document.

7. If you have completed your work, exit WordPerfect.

Use Desktop Publishing

Chapters 18-20

- Landscape layout
- Shadow boxes
- Use the Advance feature
- Retrieve text into a graphic box
- Rotated text and reversed text
- Shadow text
- Unequal width columns
- Edit border line style settings
- Drop caps
- Automatically indent the first line of all paragraphs
- Graphic boxes that span multiple columns
- Convert typed characters to correct typography symbols
- Footers for odd and even pages
- Subdivide pages
- Watermarks
- Print a booklet

Use Special Desktop Publishing Features

Features Covered

- Landscape orientation
- Retrieve text into graphic boxes
- Shadow boxes
- Add captions to graphic boxes
- Rotated text
- Reversed text

Objectives

After successfully completing this chapter, you will be able to use landscape orientation, multiple columns, and graphic boxes to create a two-sided, tri-fold mailer brochure. You will also learn how to create special effects such as shadow boxes, rotated text, and reversed text.

Chapter Introduction

Brochures come in all shapes and sizes. One of the most common brochures is the tri-fold mailer. With a tri-fold mailer brochure, information is printed on both sides of the page. Generally, a three-column format is used, and the pages are printed in landscape orientation, i.e., 11 inches by 8.5 inches (see Figure 18.1). Often a tri-fold mailer will include graphic images, graphic lines and borders, and special effects such as shadow boxes, rotated text, and reversed text.

Mock-up of a tri-fold
mailer brochure

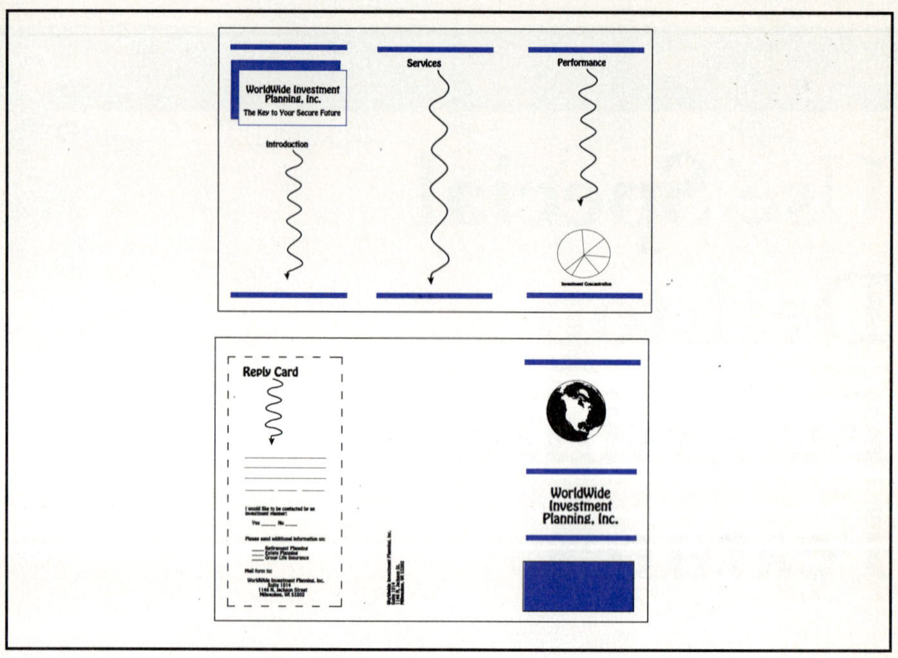

Format a Brochure

Before beginning to create a brochure in WordPerfect, it is a good idea to create a mock-up—a hand-drawn representation of how the final brochure will look. From the mock-up you can decide on the paper orientation (landscape or portrait), number of columns, margins, types of borders to be used, where graphic images will be placed, and what special effects will be used. The mock-up can also show where text will be placed in each column (see Figure 18.1).

One of the first decisions that must be made is what paper orientation will be used, i.e., portrait or landscape. Until now, all of the documents that have been created in this book have used portrait orientation, e.g., 8.5 inches by 11 inches. WordPerfect can also be used to create documents using landscape orientation, e.g., 11 inches by 8.5 inches (see Figure 18.2). When landscape orientation is selected, WordPerfect automatically rotates text when the document is printed so that text prints horizontally in relation to the long (11 inch) side of the page.

Once a decision has been made on the paper orientation, the number of columns is set. For example, if a tri-fold mailer is to be created, three columns are set. Margins can also be set. Small margins generally are used so that as much information as possible can be placed on the page. If a laser printer will be used to print the brochure, margins greater than .25 inch are used because the printer cannot place text closer than about $\frac{1}{4}$ of an inch from the edges of the page. (Note: The area that cannot be printed varies from printer to printer but generally a .25 inch margin can be used.)

Text can be typed directly into the brochure columns or, for design purposes, graphic boxes can be placed in each column to create column borders. Text can then be placed in graphic boxes to allow exact placement on the page. In this chapter, Table graphic boxes will be used to create borders at the tops and bottoms of columns. The

Chapter 18—Use Special Desktop Publishing Features

Portrait and landscape
orientation

brochure text will be retrieved into User boxes and placed in the desired column locations. When graphic boxes are used to create borders around or at the tops and/or bottoms of columns, the **Text Flows, Through Box** option is selected for the graphic boxes in columns 1 and 2. The **Text Flows, Neither Side** option is selected for the graphic box(es) in the third column. To create a second page, the **Ctrl** and **Enter** keys are pressed once or twice in order to insert a page break and to move the insertion point to the second page.

By default, the color of graphic lines/borders is black. However, the color of the graphic lines/borders can be changed if desired. The default color of borders/lines can be changed for all graphic boxes of a specific type, e.g., the top and bottom borders for all Table graphic boxes can be changed so that each time a Table graphic box is created in the document the new color is used. The color can also be changed for a single graphic box without affecting the default color.

When a graphic box is created, the **Attach To Page** option is selected, and the box is positioned relative to the desired column. The horizontal and vertical positions of the graphic box can also be specified.

Start-Up Instructions

- ❖ Select the **Columns** button on the Ribbon and double-click on **3 Cols**.
- ❖ Set the left, right, top, and bottom margins to .3".

Steps to ▶ Create Landscape Layout

1. Select **Layout, Page** {Alt and L, p}.

2. Select **Paper Size/Type** {s}.

3. Double-click on **Letter (Landscape)** {press the up arrow key to highlight Letter (Landscape) and press Enter}.

   Note: The Page Format dialog box redisplays and Letter (Landscape) is shown in the Paper Size/Type box.

4. Select **OK** {Enter}.

Define a Graphics Box for Each Column

1. Select **Graphics, Graphics Boxes, Create** {Alt and F9, b, c}.

2. Select **Based on Box Style** and double-click on the desired box type to be used {y, press the up or down arrow key to highlight box style, press Enter}.

   For example, to place a border line at the top and bottom of the column, double-click on **Table Box**.

Change the Default Color for Table Graphic Boxes

1. Select **Edit Border/Fill** {b}.

2. Select **Based on Border Style** {y}.

3. Select **Edit** {e}.

4. Select **Color** {o}.

5. Select **Choose One Color for All Lines** {c}.

6. Double-click on the desired color {press the up or down arrow key to highlight desired color, press Enter}.

   For example, double-click on **Blue**.

7. Select **OK** {press Enter}.

   Note: The new color for the border lines displays in a sample box.

8. To return to the Create Graphics Box dialog box, select **OK, Close, Close** {Enter three times}.

Set the Position of the Graphic Box

1. Select **Attach To** {a}.

2. Select **Page** {a}.

3. Select **Edit Position** {p}.

4. Select **Horizontal Position, Full** so that the graphic box will fill the entire width of the column {h, f}.

5. Select **Position Relative To** {r}.

6. Select *Column* and type the number of the column in which the graphic box will be placed {o, type number of column, Enter}.

For example, select *Column.* Notice that "1" (for column 1) displays in the box to the right of the word Column; no changes need to be made now.

7. Select **Vertical Position** {v}.

8. Select **Full** so that the graphic box will fill the entire length of the column {f}.

9. Select **OK** {Enter}.

10. Select **Text Flows, Through Box** {t, f, t}.

11. Select **OK** {Enter}.

*Note: A graphic box border line displays at the top of the first column. To view the entire column, select the **Zoom** button on the Ribbon and double-click on **50%** or select the **Preview** button to use Print Preview.*

Finish-Up Instructions

❖ Create a Table graphic box for column 2 using the following information:

    a. Attach the graphic box to the Page.

    b. Select **Edit Position** and set the **Horizontal Position** to **Full**.

    c. Set the **Position Relative To** to **Column** and type **2**.

    d. Select **Vertical Position** and choose **Full**. Select **OK**.

    e. Select **Text Flows, Through Box**. Select **OK**.

❖ Create a Table graphic box for column 3 using the following information:

    a. Attach the graphic box to the Page.

    b. Select **Edit Position** and set the **Horizontal Position** to **Full**.

    c. Set the **Position Relative To** to **Column** and type **3**.

    d. Select **Vertical Position** and choose **Full**. Select **OK**.

    e. Select **Text Flows, Neither Side**. Select **OK**.

❖ If desired, the three Table graphic boxes can be viewed by selecting the **Zoom** button and choosing **50%** or by selecting the **Preview** button.

❖ Save the file; use the filename **18drill1**.

Create a Shadow Box

The shadow box special effect is created by selecting the **Edit Border/Fill** option in the Create Graphics Box dialog box, choosing the desired border style, and selecting the **Shadow** option. The color and shading of the shadow can be changed if desired. Another special effect changes the corners of a graphic box from square to rounded. The corners of a graphic box are changed by selecting the **Edit Border/Fill** option in the Create Graphics Box dialog box, choosing the desired border style, selecting the **Corners** option, and choosing **Rounded**. When rounded corners are used, the radius of the curve can be set. The corners become more circular as the radius increases.

Start-Up Instructions

❖ The file named **18drill1** should be displayed on the screen. The insertion point can be located anywhere on page one.

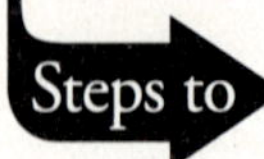

Create a Shadow Box

1. Select **Graphics, Graphics Boxes, Create** {Alt and F9, b, c}.

2. Select **Edit Border/Fill** {b}.

3. Select **Based on Border Style** {y}.

4. Double-click on the desired border style {press the up or down arrow key to highlight desired border style, press Enter}.

   For example, double-click on **Single Border**.

5. Select **Shadow** {h}.

6. Select the desired Shadow Type.

   For example, select **Upper Left** {t, u}.

7. To change the color of the shadow box, select **Shadow Color** {c}.

8. Highlight the desired color {press the up or down arrow key to highlight desired color}.

   For example, highlight **Blue**.

9. To change the shade of the shadow box color, select **Shade (% of Color)** and type the desired percentage {h, type percentage, Enter}.

   For example, select **Shade (% of Color)** and type **80**.

10. Choose **Select** {Enter}.

11. Select **OK** {Enter}.

Change Border Line Color of a Single Graphic Box

12. Select **Color** {o}.

13. Select **Choose One Color for All Lines** {c}.

14. Double-click on the desired color {press the up or down arrow key to highlight the desired color, Enter}.

   For example, double-click on **Blue**.

15. Select **OK** {Enter}.

16. Select **Close** {Enter}.

Place the Shadow Box

17. Select **Attach To** and choose **Page** {a, a}.

18. Select **Edit Position** {p}.

19. Select **Horizontal Position, Centered** {h, c}.

20. Select **Position Relative To,** *Column* and type the number of the column in which the shadow box will be placed {r, o, type the number of the column, Enter}.

     For example, select **Position Relative To,** *Column* and check that 1 (for column 1) displays.

21. Select **Vertical Position** {v}.

22. Choose the desired position or select Set and type a specific location on the page.

     For example, select **Set** and type .75 {s, .75, Enter}.

23. Select **OK** {Enter}.

24. Select **Text Flows, Through Box** {t, f, t}.

25. Select **Create Text** {e}.

26. Type and format the desired text.

     For example,

     a. Type and center the following:

        WorldWide Investment Planning, Inc. (Press **Enter** twice.)

        The Key to Your Secure Future

     b. Change the font to **Bodoni-WP**.

     c. Block **WorldWide Investment Planning, Inc.** and change the point size to **14 point**.

Finish-Up Instructions

❧ Continue to the Steps to Use Advance to Position Text.

Use Advance to Position Text

The Advance feature is used to position text at a specific location on the page or within a graphic box. The position of the text can be measured vertically and/or horizontally either from the location of the cursor or from the top/left edge of the page. The Advance feature is used instead of pressing the Enter, Spacebar, or Tab keys to change the location of the text.

❖ The file named **18drill1** should be displayed on the screen.

Use Advance to Position Text

1. Place the insertion point to the left of the first character in the text to be positioned.

   For example, place the insertion point to the left of the first W in WorldWide.

2. Select **Layout, Other** {Shift and F8, o}.

3. Select **Advance** {a}.

4. In the Vertical Position box, select the **Up from Cursor, Down from Cursor,** or **From Top of Page** option.

   For example, select **Down from Cursor** {d}.

5. Type the number of inches or fractions of inches that the text should be moved.

   For example, type **.20**. (Do not type the final period.)

6. Select **OK** twice {Enter three times}.

7. Press **F7** to return to the Create Graphics Box dialog box.

8. Select **OK** {Enter}.

❖ Use the same filename, **18drill1**, and save the file again.

Retrieve Text into a Graphic Box

When a graphic box is created, text can be typed into the graphic box or text can be retrieved from a previously saved file into the graphic box. When a previously saved file is retrieved into a graphic box, the original text file remains untouched and a copy of the text is placed into the graphic box. The text can be formatted and changed as desired in the graphic box.

In addition to text, graphic images created in many different graphic programs can be retrieved into graphic boxes. For example, a graph created in Lotus 1-2-3 (filename extension *.pic*) or a drawing created in PC Paintbrush (filename extension *.pcx*) can be retrieved into a graphic box and placed in a WordPerfect document.

When a graphic image saved in a format other than WordPerfect's graphic format (filename extension *.wpg*) is retrieved, WordPerfect converts the image to the .wpg format so that the graphic image can be placed in a WordPerfect document. Although WordPerfect can convert graphic images created in many different graphic programs, some of the original colors, shading, fonts, or other attributes may not be converted precisely as they appear in the original image.

Captions can be added to graphic boxes. The caption text is created by selecting the **Create Caption** option in the Create Graphics Box dialog box. WordPerfect automatically inserts a figure or box number in the Box Caption window. The figure or box number can be deleted, if desired, by pressing the **Backspace** key once. After the caption text is typed and formatted, press **F7** to return to the Create Graphics Box dialog box. The default position for the caption is below the graphic box. However, if desired, the position of the caption can be changed by selecting **Caption Options** in the Create Graphics Box dialog box.

Start-Up Instructions

❖   The file named **18drill1** should be displayed on the screen.

Place a Graphic Box Containing Text in a Column

1. Select **Graphics, Graphics Boxes, Create** {Alt and F9, b, c}.

2. Select **Based on Box Style** {y}.

3. Double-click on the desired box style {press the up or down arrow key to highlight box style, press Enter}.

    For example, double-click on **User Box**.

4. Select **Attach To, Page** {a, a}.

5. Select **Edit Position** {p}.

6. Select **Horizontal Position, Full** {h, f}.

7. Select **Position Relative To,** *Column,* and type the number of the column in which the graphic box will be located {r, o, type number of column, Enter}.

    For example, select **Position Relative To,** *Column,* and check that 1 displays.

8. Select **Vertical Position, Set**, and type the location in which the graphics box should be placed {v, s, type location, Enter}.

    For example, select **Vertical Position, Set** and type **2.5**.

9. Select **OK** {Enter}.

10. Select **Text Flows, Through Box** {t, f, t}.

Retrieve Previously Created Text into a Graphic Box

11. Select **Create Text** {e}.

12. Select **File, Retrieve** and type the location and name of the desired file {Alt and f, r, type the location and name of the file}.

    For example, retrieve the file named **18drill1.co1** from the data disk.

13. Select **OK** {Enter}.

   Note: Formatted text displays on the screen.

14. Press **F7** to return to the Create Graphics Box dialog box.

15. Select **OK** {Enter}.

Finish-Up Instructions

- ❖ Create a User graphic box for column 2 text using the following information:

   a. With the insertion point located anywhere on page one, repeat steps 1–6 of the Steps to Place a Graphic Box Containing Text in a Column.

   b. Select **Position Relative To, Column**, and type **2**. Select **Vertical Position, Set**, and type **.75**. Select **OK**.

   c. Select **Text Flows, Through Box**.

   d. Select **Create Text**.

   e. Select **File, Retrieve** and retrieve the file named **18drill1.co2** from the data disk.

   f. Select **Layout, Line, Tab Set, Clear All Tabs**. Set left tabs at .4 and .8.

   g. Press **F7** and select **OK**.

- ❖ Create a User graphic box for column 3 text using the following information:

   a. With the insertion point located anywhere on page one, repeat steps 1–6 of the Steps to Place Text in a Column.

   b. Select **Position Relative To, Column**, and type **3**. Select **Vertical Position, Set**, and type **.75**. Select **OK**.

   c. Select **Text Flows, Through Box**.

   d. Select **Create Text**.

   e. Select **File, Retrieve**, and retrieve the file named **18drill1.co3** from the data disk.

   f. Press **F7** and select **OK**.

- ❖ Use the new filename **18drill1.pg1** and save the file.

Start-Up Instructions

- ❖ The file named **18drill1.pg1** should be displayed on the screen. The insertion point can be located anywhere on page one.

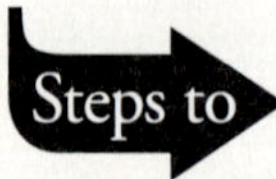

Insert a Graphic Box Containing a Lotus *Pic* File

1. Select **Graphics, Graphics Boxes, Create** {Alt and F9, b, c}.

2. If necessary, select **Based on Box Style** and double-click on **User Box** {y, highlight User Box, Enter}.

3. Select **Attach To, Page** {a, a}.

4. Select **Edit Position, Horizontal Position, Full** {p, h, f}.

5. Select **Position Relative To,** *Column*, and type the number of the column in which the graphic box is to be located {r, o, type column number, Enter}.

   For example, select **Position Relative To,** *Column*, and type **3**.

6. Select **Vertical Position** and choose the desired option {v}.

   For example, select **Set** and type **5.25**.

7. Select **OK** {Enter}.

8. Select **Filename**, type the location and name of the file to be retrieved, and select **OK** {f, type the name of the file, Enter}.

   For example, retrieve the file named **18pie.pic** from the data disk and select **OK**.

   Note: The File Format dialog box displays. The **Lotus .PIC Graphs** *format is highlighted.*

9. Choose **Select** {Enter}.

10. Select **Image Editor** {e}.

11. To enlarge the size of the graphic image within the graphics box, select the **Enlarge%** button.

    For example, select the **Enlarge%** button 2 or 3 times to increase the pie chart to fill the entire graphic box.

12. Select **Close** {F7}.

Create a Caption for a Graphic Box

13. Select **Create Caption** {c}.

    Note: A Box Caption window displays with a figure or box number showing in the upper left corner.

14. To delete the number, press the **Backspace** key.

15. Type and format the caption information.

    For example:

    a. Change the font to **Dutch 801 Bold, Italic, 10 point**.

    b. Type and center **Investment Concentration**.

16. Press **F7** to return to the Create Graphics Box dialog box.

    Note: The caption information displays below the Edit Caption option.

17. Select **OK** to return to the document window {Enter}.

Finish-Up Instructions

❖ Save the file again using the same filename, **18drill1.pg1**.

❖ If desired, print one copy.

❖ The file named **18drill1.pg1** should be displayed on the screen. The insertion point can be located anywhere on page one.

 **Create Page Two of the Brochure**

1. If necessary, select the **Zoom** button and choose **50%** so that the entire page can be viewed.

2. Press **Ctrl** and **Enter** repeatedly until a page break (a double horizontal line below the graphic box borders at the bottom of the page) displays and Pg 2 displays in the Status bar.

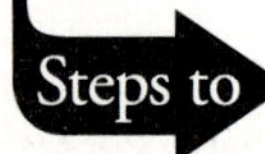 **Create a Dashed Box for a Tear Sheet**

1. Select **Graphics, Graphics Boxes, Create** {Alt and F9, b, c}.

2. Select **Edit Border/Fill** {b}.

3. Select **Based on Border Style** and double-click on **Dashed Border** {y, highlight Dashed Border, Enter}.

4. Select **Close** {Enter}.

5. Select **Attach To, Page** {a, a}.

6. Select **Edit Position, Horizontal Position, Full** {p, h, f}.

7. Select **Position Relative To,** *Column*, and type the desired column number {r, o, type column number, Enter}.

   For example, select **Position Relative To,** *Column* and check that 1 displays.

8. Select **Vertical Position, Full** {v, f}.

9. Select **OK** {Enter}.

10. Select **Create Text** {e}.

11. Select **File, Retrieve** and type the location and name of the file to be retrieved.

    For example, retrieve the file named **18drill1.co4** from the data disk.

12. Press **F7** to exit to the Create Graphics Box dialog box.

13. Select **OK** {Enter}.

❖ Use the new filename **18drill1.pg2** and save the file.

Rotated Text and Reversed Text

Two special effects that can be created using WordPerfect are rotated text and reversed text. WordPerfect can rotate text in 90° increments, e.g., 90°, 180°, 270°. In order to rotate text, the text must be placed in a graphic box.

Reversed text (white text on a dark background) is accomplished by choosing a black or dark solid fill for a graphic box, selecting Create Text, changing the color of the text to white, and typing the desired text. Many printers support reversed text; however, if you experience difficulty printing reversed text, choose **Print Job Graphically** in the Print dialog box. Reversed text is also referred to as "reversed type" or "reverses."

Start-Up Instructions

❖ The file named **18drill1.pg2** should be displayed on the screen. The insertion point can be located anywhere on page two.

Create Rotated Text

1. Select **Graphics, Graphics Boxes, Create** {Alt and F9, b, c}.

2. Select **Based on Box Style** and double-click on the desired box type.

    For example, double-click on **User Box** {y, highlight User Box, Enter}.

3. Select **Attach To, Page** {a, a}.

4. Select **Edit Position, Horizontal Position, Left** {p, h, l}.

5. Select **Position Relative To,** *Column*, and type the desired column number {r, o, type column number, Enter}.

    For example, select **Position Relative To,** *Column* and type **2**.

6. Select **Vertical Position, Bottom** {v, b}.

7. Select **OK** {Enter}.

8. Select **Create Text** {e}.

9. Type and format the desired text.

    For example:

    a. Change the font to **Bodoni-WP, 10 point**.

    b. Type and center the following:

    WorldWide Investment Planning, Inc.
    Suite 1014
    1146 N. Jackson St.
    Milwaukee, WI 53202

10. Press **Alt** and **F9**.

    Note: The Graphics dialog box displays.

11. Select **Rotate Box Contents** {c}.

12. Select the degree of rotation.

> For example, select **90° Rotation** {2}.

13. Select **OK** {Enter}.

> *Note: The text does not change rotation on the screen.*

14. Press **F7**.

15. Select **Edit Size** {s}.

16. Select **Set Width** and type the desired width of the graphic box {w, type desired width, Enter}.

> For example, type **1**.

17. Select **OK** twice {Enter twice}.

> *Note: To view the rotated text, select the **Zoom** button, choose **50%**, and use the scroll bars to display page two or select the **Preview** button.*

Finish-Up Instructions

❖ Save the file using the same filename, **18drill1.pg2**.

Start-Up Instructions

❖ The file named **18drill1.pg2** should be displayed on the screen. The insertion point can be located anywhere on page two.

▶ Steps to Create the Front Panel of the Brochure

1. Select **Graphics, Graphics Boxes, Create** {Alt and F9, b, c}.

2. Select **Based on Box Style** and double-click on the desired box style {y, highlight desired box style, Enter}.

> For example, double-click on **Table Box**.

3. Select **Attach To**, **Page** {a, a}.

4. Select **Edit Position, Horizontal Position, Full** {p, h, f}.

5. Select **Position Relative To**, *Column*, and type the number of the column in which the graphic box will be located.

> For example, select **Position Relative To**, *Column*, and type **3**.

6. Select **Vertical Position** and choose the desired option {v}.

> For example, choose **Full** {f}.

7. Select **OK** {Enter}.

8. Select **Text Flows, Through Box** {t, f, t}.

Import a Graphic Image

9. Select **Filename, F5, OK**.

10. Double-click on the desired graphic filename {highlight filename, Enter}.

   For example, double-click on **Globe.wpg**.

11. To position the graphic image within the graphic box, select **Image Editor** {e}.

12. *To move the graphic image vertically in the graphic box*, press the up or down arrow key.

   To move the graphic image horizontally in the graphic box, press the left or right arrow key.

   For example, press the up arrow key 5 or 6 times to move the graphic image up approximately 1" in the graphic box.

13. Select **Close** {F7}.

14. Select **OK** {Enter}.

Finish-Up Instruction

❖   Save the file again using the same filename **18drill1.pg2**.

Create Reversed Text

1. Select **Graphics, Graphics Boxes, Create** {Alt and F9, b, c}.

2. Select **Edit Border/Fill** {b}.

3. Select **Fill, Fill Style** {f, y}.

4. Scroll down the list and double-click on **100% Shaded Fill** {press the down arrow key repeatedly to highlight 100% Shaded Fill, press Enter}.

5. To change the color of the fill, select **Foreground Color** {c}.

6. Double-click on the desired color {press the up or down arrow key to highlight desired color, press Enter}.

   For example, double-click on **Blue**.

7. Select **OK** {Enter}.

8. Select **Close** {Enter}.

9. Select **Attach To, Page** {a, a}.

10. Select **Edit Position, Horizontal Position, Full** {p, h, f}.

11. Select **Position Relative To, *Column*,** and type the number of the column in which the graphic box will be located {r, o, type number of column, Enter}.

   For example, select **Position Relative To, *Column*** and type **3**.

12. Select **Vertical Position** and choose the desired option {v}.

For example, choose **Bottom** {b}.

13. Select **OK** {Enter}.

14. Select **Create Text** {e}.

15. Select the **Font** button {Ctrl and F8}.

16. Select **Color** and double-click on the desired color {c, press the up or down arrow key to highlight desired color, Enter}.

> For example, double-click on **White**. Also, change the font to **Bodoni-WP, 10 point**.

17. Select **OK** {Enter}.

18. Type and format the desired text.

> For example:

   a. Type and center the following:

   Suite 1014
   1146 N. Jackson St.
   Milwaukee, WI 53202
   414-555-8100

   b. Place the insertion point to the left of the S in Suite. Select **Layout, Other, Advance, Down from Cursor, .1, OK** twice {Alt and L, o, a, d, type .1, Enter three times}.

19. Press **F7**.

Finish-Up Instructions

❖ Create a graphic box using the following information:

   a. Use a Table box.

   b. Attach the Table box to the Page.

   c. Set the Horizontal Position to Full.

   d. Set the Position Relative To, Column, 3.

   e. Set the Vertical Position to 4.5.

   f. Create the following text: **WorldWide Investment Planning, Inc.** Change the font to Bodoni-WP, 24 point.

   g. If necessary, select **Center** alignment.

   h. Set an Advance Down from Cursor of .25 (**Layout, Other, Advance, Down from Cursor**, type **.25**, select **OK** twice, F7, OK).

❖ Use the new filename **18drill1.fin** and save the document.

❖ Print one copy of the tri-fold mailer brochure. Your final brochure should look similar to the tri-fold mailer shown on page 499.

Note: If you experience difficulties printing the reversed text, select **Print Job Graphically** *and reprint the brochure.*

WorldWide Investment Planning, Inc.

The Key to Your Secure Future

For over 25 years, WorldWide Investment Planning, Inc. has assisted individuals in developing a secure and prosperous financial future through sound investments.

WorldWide Investment Planning, Inc. strives to uphold a long tradition of superior quality investment opportunities for our clients. Our investments are high quality, widely diversified, and have good call protection--all key factors in sound risk management.

WorldWide Investment Planning, Inc. has over $3.5 billion in assets. The pre-tax return on assets for the last three years has averaged 8.95 percent.

Services

WorldWide Investment Planning, Inc. provides services to meet the needs of each individual.

- ✓ Retirement Planning
  - ✓ Tax-deferred annuities and pension plans
  - ✓ Pension administration for small businesses and individuals
- ✓ Estate Planning
  - ✓ Living trusts
  - ✓ Trust funds
  - ✓ Transfer of family business assets
  - ✓ Group Life Insurance

WorldWide Investment Planning, Inc. also provides a quarterly newsletter, *The Investment Report*, to keep our clients informed about investment opportunities and economic conditions that may affect their investments.

Performance

The management of WorldWide Investment Planning, Inc. constantly monitors the economic conditions around the world to ensure the best protection for our clients' investments. Currently, approximately 30 percent of our investments are in North America, 22 percent in Europe, 34 percent in the Pacific Rim, and 11 percent in Central and South America.

Our firm invests in a wide variety of products, industries, and services including banking, capital equipment, real estate, and investment-quality bonds.

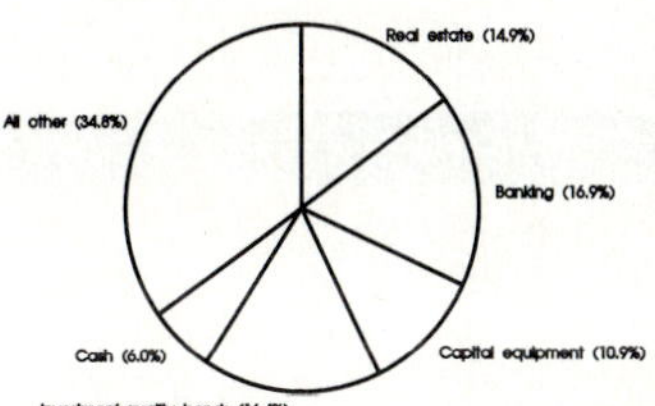

Investment Concentration

To receive additional information about WorldWide Investment Planning, Inc. or to be contacted by an investment planner, please complete and return this form.

Name _______________________

Address _______________________

City _________ State _____ Zip _____

Phone_______________________

I would like to be contacted by an investment planner:

     Yes ______ No ______

Please send additional information on:

    ______ Retirement Planning

    ______ Estate Planning

    ______ Group Life Insurance

Mail form to:

WorldWide Investment Planning, Inc.
Suite 1014
1146 N. Jackson Street
Milwaukee, WI 53202

WorldWide Investment Planning, Inc.
Suite 1014
1146 N. Jackson St.
Milwaukee, WI 53202

WorldWide Investment Planning, Inc.

Suite 1014
1146 N. Jackson Street
Milwaukee, WI 53202
414-555-8100

The Next Step

Chapter Review and Activities

FEATURES SUMMARY

FEATURES	ACTIONS	PAGE
Create landscape layout	Select **Layout**, **Page**, **Paper Size/Type**, double-click on **Letter (Landscape)**, **OK**.	485
Define a graphic box for a column	In the Create Graphics Box dialog box, select **Attach To**, **Page**. Select **Edit Position**, **Horizontal Position**, choose the desired position. Select **Position Relative To**, choose **Column**, type the number of the column in which the graphic box will be placed. Select **Vertical Position**, choose the desired position, select **OK**.	486
Change the default color for a graphic box	In the Create Graphics Box dialog box, select **Edit Border/Fill**, choose **Based on Border Style**, select **Edit**, **Color**, select **Choose One Color for All Lines**, double-click on desired color, select **OK** twice, select **Close** twice.	486
Create a shadow box	Select **Graphics**, **Graphics Boxes**, **Create**. Select **Edit Border/Fill**, **Based on Border Style**, double-click on the desired border. Select **Shadow**. Select the desired border shadow type. To change the shadow box color and shade of color, highlight the desired color, select **Shade (% of Color)** and type the desired percentage, choose **Select**, **OK**.	488

| --- | --- | --- |
Change border line color of a single graphic box	In the Create Graphic Box dialog box, select **Edit Border/Fill**, select **Color**, choose **One Color for All Lines**, double-click on the desired color. Select **OK**, **Close**.	488
Use Advance to position text	Locate the insertion point to the left of the first character in the text to be positioned. Select **Layout**, **Other**, **Advance**. In the Vertical Position box, select the desired cursor position, type the desired number of inches (or fractions) that the text should be moved, select **OK** twice.	490
Place a graphic box containing text in a column	Select **Graphics**, **Graphics Boxes**, **Create**, select **Based on Box Style**, and double-click on the desired box style. Select **Attach To**, **Page**. Select **Edit Position**, **Horizontal Position**, choose the desired position. Select **Position Relative To**, **Column**, type the number of the column in which the graphic box will be located. Select **Vertical Position**, choose the desired vertical position. Select **OK**. Select **Text Flows**, **Through Box**. To retrieve previously created text into a graphics box, select **Create Text** (in the Create Graphics Box dialog box). Select **File**, **Retrieve**, type the location and name of the desired file, **OK**.	491
Insert a graphic box containing a Lotus Pic file	Select **Graphics**, **Graphics Boxes**, **Create**. Select **Filename**, type the location and name of the file to be retrieved, select **OK**. Choose **Select**. Position, size, and edit the image as needed.	492
Create a caption for a graphic box	In the Create Graphics Box dialog box, select **Create Caption**. If desired, delete the existing number. Type the caption information, press F7, and select **OK**.	493
Create rotated text	In the Create Graphics Box dialog box, select **Create Text**, type the desired text, press **Alt** and **F9**, select **Rotate Box Contents**. Select desired rotation, select **OK**, and press F7. Edit the graphic box size and position the graphic box as desired.	495
Create reversed text	In the Create Graphics Box dialog box, select **Edit Border/Fill**, select **Fill**, **Fill Style**. Double-click on **100% Shaded Fill**. Select **Foreground Color**, double-click on the desired color. Select **OK**, **Close**. Select **Create Text**. Select the **Font** button, select **Color** and double-click on **White**, select **OK**. Type the desired text, **F7**, **OK**.	497

True/False—Circle One

T F 1. Information is printed on both sides of a tri-fold mailer brochure.

T F 2. When text is printed in landscape layout, the top of the page is the 11-inch side.

T F 3. Text can be typed directly into a brochure or text can be typed into a graphic box.

T F 4. The horizontal position of a graphic box can be specified; however, the vertical position cannot be changed.

T F 5. The corners of a graphic box can be changed from square to rounded.

T F 6. When a graphic box is created, text can be placed in the graphic box by typing the text or by retrieving text from a previously saved file.

Short Answer

1. Instead of pressing the Enter, Spacebar, or Tab key, the _______________ feature can be used to position text.

2. Create the shadow box effect by selecting **Edit Border/Fill** in the Create Graphics Box dialog box, choosing the border style, and selecting the ______ option.

3. List the steps to create a caption for a graphic box.

4. Before rotating text, the text must be placed in a _________ box.

Enriching Language Arts Skills

Spelling/Vocabulary Words

brochure   a small pamphlet, leaflet.

paramedic   person with medical training who responds to medical emergencies or assists physicians.

typography   a description of the features of a place or region; the art of graphically representing the physical features of a place or region.

Parentheses

Parentheses can be used to set off nonessential expressions that might otherwise confuse the reader. The information within the parentheses provides supplemental information that has no direct bearing on the main idea of the sentence or paragraph. Words, phrases, or clauses can be enclosed within parentheses. Unless a comma, colon, or semicolon is necessary to the text within a parentheses, place the punctuation outside the closing parenthesis. If the text within the parentheses is a complete sentence, the final period is placed within the parentheses.

Examples:

The actual gross sales for the quarter were $1,050,000 (compared with projected sales of $795,000).

If you are planning to attend the next sales conference (March 5), please contact the travel department immediately.

Several staff members will attend the sales conference next month. (The conference will be held in Hawaii.)

Activities

Activity 18.1—Create a Tri-Fold Mailer Brochure

1. Use skills learned in this chapter and the following information to create the tri-fold mailer brochure shown on page 504.

   a. Set all margins to .3". Set the number of columns to three.

   b. Change the paper orientation to Landscape (**Layout**, **Page**, **Paper Size/Type**, double-click on **Letter (Landscape)**, **OK**).

   c. Change the default color of Table boxes to blue. Create Table graphic boxes for each column on the first page of the brochure.

   d. The text for each column has been created and saved on the data disk. Retrieve the text files into User boxes.

Column 1	18act1.co1
Column 2	18act1.co2
Column 3	18act1.co3
Column 1, page 2	18act1.co4

   e. The graphic file in the third column of the second page is named **skipper.wpg** and is usually located in the WP60\GRAPHICS directory.

   f. Use the filename **18act1.fin** and save the final brochure.

   g. Print one copy.

Small Business Owners Forum

Fall Series

Nine years ago, the Small Business Owners Forum was developed to provide an information resource for local small businesses. The forum provides a setting in which valuable business relationships can be developed and information on common problems can be shared.

This fall's Forum series, entitled *Personal Development: Focus and Flexibility—Keys to Success*, will address many of the most challenging issues faced by small business owners including:

→   Defining and focusing on objectives
→   Meeting ever-changing economic and business challenges
→   Turning failures into successes
→   Finding the tools and resources needed to succeed

IF AT FIRST. . .

Learning to create new successes from past mistakes

October 8, 199x
Woodridge Clubhouse
3300 Woodridge Road
7:00 - 9:00 p.m.

Find reserves of energy, courage, and brilliance you never knew you possessed. Sharpen your focus and jump-start your motivation. Develop the skills to maintain your enthusiasm and motivation through the difficult times.

A panel of several local small business people will share their actual "near death" business experiences and recoveries. They will explain how it is that our attitude is often our biggest enemy or largest asset.

The panel moderator will be Deirdre Sacks, Vencon Technologies. Ms. Sacks will share management tips on how to turn around an ailing business and implement strategies for greater success.

AM I THERE YET?

Learn how to stay focused when all else is chaos

November 12, 199x
Woodridge Clubhouse
3300 Woodridge Road
7:00 - 9:00 p.m.

Phone calls, customer demands, production glitches, employee problems—how do you cope? How do you succeed? To find out, we have assembled a panel of local business people who know firsthand how to prioritize, organize, delegate, and SUCCEED.

Sheila Craighead, president of First Progressive Bank and chairperson of the Belle Mead Chamber of Commerce, will share with us how she keeps everything going.

Alfredo Belli, a customer relations consultant and owner of Belli Consultants, will share with us the common traits that lead to success.

Lucille Nugent, managing partner of Nugent, Dunkle, and Ponte, CPAs, works daily with owners of medium and small businesses. Nugent built her own successful business after having overcome several potentially lethal business circumstances. She will share with us what it takes for the entrepreneur to succeed.

Small Business Owners Forum

Registration

I plan to attend the following session(s):

____   October 8, 199x

____   November 12, 199x

Cost: $15.00 per session

Name: ______________________

Company: ____________________

Address: ____________________

City/State/Zip: ________________

Phone: ____________________

Make check payable to:

Belle Mead Chamber of Commerce

and mail to:

1428 Township Line Road
Belle Mead, NJ 08502

Belle Mead Chamber of Commerce
1428 Township Line Road
Belle Mead, NJ 08502

Small Business Owners Forum

Fall Series

1428 Township Line Road
Belle Mead, NJ 08502
201-555-3400

1. Use the following information to create the tri-fold mailer brochure shown on page 506.

   a. Make decisions regarding:

      Margins
      Number of columns
      Graphic boxes
      Color and shading for borders/lines and shadow
      Font sizes for text
      Correct three spelling and one parentheses error

   b. The text for columns 1, 2, 3, and 4 are saved on the data disk under the filenames **18skill1.co1**, **18skill1.co2**, **18skill1.co3**, and **18skill1.co4**.

   c. Rounded corners for the graphic boxes are created by selecting **Edit Border/Fill**, choosing the **Corner** option, selecting **Rounded**, and choosing **OK**.

   d. The graphics imaged is named **tree.wpg** and is usually located in the WP60\GRAPHICS directory.

2. Use the filename **18skill1.fin** and save the file.

3. Print one copy.

4. If you have completed your work in WordPerfect, exit the program.

Oak Hill--Douglas County Fire Protection District

Board of Directors
Robert Bradley, Chairperson
Vivian Baker
Terry Eliasen
Elena Morgan
Danny Griffin

Fire Chief
Arthur Bischoff

The District

The district serves all of Douglas County, an area of nearly 100 square miles. The population is approximately 20,000.

The district operates five fire stations, two of which are staffed by career personnel. Station 24 in Minden is staffed by a Captain and an Engineer assigned to Engine 24. Station 23 in Gardnerville is staffed by two Firefighters/Paramedics assigned to Medic 23. Stations 25, 26, and 27 in Genoa, Zephyr Cove, and Centerville, respectively, are staffed by volunteer personnel.

The district owns and operates five fire engines, one truck, one squad, one water tender, and one medic unit.

Insurance Service Office Rates the District

The district has received a new rating from the Insurance Service Office, which rates fire departments for insurance companies. We were previously rated as a 5 (on a scale of 1 to 10, 1 being the best for structures within 1,000 feet of a hydrant and 8 for structures farther than 1,000 feet from a hydrant. The new rating is 3 for structures within 1,000 feet of a hydrant and 5 for structures farther than 1,000 feet from a hydrant. This could mean a reduced insurance premium if your insurance company uses the ISO rating schedule.

Questions? Comments?

The Oak Hill Fire Protection District Board of Directors meet at 7:00 p.m. on the second Wednesday of each month at Station 24 in Minden. The public is encouraged to attend.

We welcome any comments/suggestions you may have. We can be contacted at the address and phone number listed on the front of this broshure.

New Engine in Service in Minden

Last year we purchased a new fire engine to be assigned at Minden Station 24.

The engine was placed in service at the end of the 1993 fire season. It was built by Hi Tech Fire Apparatus in Oakdale. The new machine features a 1,500 gallon per minute pump and all the tools necessary to combat structural and wildland fires. We feel it is an excellent addition to our organization.

The engine is different from what you might see on a city street. As you are well aware, the layout and topografy of the Oak Hill Fire Protection District offer many challenges to large trucks such as fire engines. The new engine is considerably shorter than most structural fire engines and features higher angles of approach and departure to accommodate our rough and narrow roads.

The new engine with its tools and equipment represent a $250,000 investment. We saved for a long time and paid for it in cash.

A Message from Medic 23

Two of the four firefighters on duty each day are Firefighters/Parimedics assigned to Medic 23 at Station 23.

Medic 23 is part of the Douglas County Emergency Medical System funded by County Service Area 16. Currently, there are six primary response medic units in service. All are operated by fire districts, and each district hires paramedics off a common hiring list.

Firefighters/Paramedics in the Service Area 16 system all have at least one year of paramedic experience prior to coming to Douglas County. Almost all come from areas that have very high call volumes.

Our system allows our medics to serve a dual role as firefighters. With the ability to use paramedics in any situation to which we respond, the public gets the most for its tax dollar.

Most of us came here to be part of the Douglas County community. We have chosen to live here for many of the same reasons that you have. We participate in community events, send our children to school here, and serve our communities as volunteer firefighters when not on duty.

We are proud to be part of your community and appreciate more than you know the support you give us.

Oak Hill--Douglas County
Fire Protection District
P.O. Box 684
Minden, NV 89423

OAK HILL--DOUGLAS COUNTY

Fire Protection District

Serving you 24 hours a day

P.O. Box 684
Minden, NV 89423
702-555-1000

Create a Magazine Article

Features Covered

- Use the shadow text attribute
- Create unequal column widths
- Edit border line style settings
- Create drop caps
- Indent the first line of all paragraphs automatically
- Create a graphic box that spans multiple columns
- Place (nest) a graphic box within a graphic box
- Use correct typography symbols for quotation marks and em dashes
- Create odd and even page footers

Objectives

After successfully completing this chapter, you will be able to use the shadow text attribute, create columns of unequal widths, edit border line styles, and create drop caps. In addition, you will learn to automatically indent each paragraph of a document, create a graphic box that spans multiple columns, "nest" a graphic box within a graphic box, and use typographical symbols for quotation marks and em dashes. Also, creating different footers for odd and even pages will be learned.

Chapter Introduction

WordPerfect 6.0 has continued to incorporate and enhance many of the functions that have traditionally been accomplished through the use of typesetting or desktop publishing programs. In this chapter, you will perform many desktop publishing functions that are used to enhance publications such as a magazine article.

Create a Magazine Article

Before beginning to create a magazine article, decisions need to be made regarding the graphic images to be included, the number of columns, and the widths of columns. Also, decisions will be made considering the use of special text attributes and other effects.

Many articles also include pull quotes and sidebars. A pull quote is a small portion of the article text that is excerpted from the article and placed in a separate box. The purpose of a pull quote is to attract attention to the article. Therefore, the font of the pull quote text is often changed and/or enlarged. Also, borders are usually placed above, below, or around the text to set the quote off from the article text.

A sidebar is a box or area that contains information that is related to the article text. The purpose of a sidebar is to further explain a subject covered in the article or to provide additional statistics or information that may interest the reader.

One of the main purposes of a magazine article's format is to entice people to read the article. Therefore, special text effects and attributes to add visual interest such as shadow text, rotated text, drop caps, and leading adjustments are used. Also, graphic images or pictures are often included in a magazine article to enhance page appearance or illustrate the article's key points.

Start-Up Instructions

- ❖   Open the file named **19drill1.txt** located on the data disk.
- ❖   Turn on widow/orphan protect (select **Layout, Other, Widow/Orphan Protect, OK**).
- ❖   Change the initial font to **Dutch 801 Roman** [select **Layout, Document, Initial Font, Font**, double-click on **Dutch 801 Roman (Speedo), OK** twice].

Use Shadow Text Attribute

1. Block the desired text.

   For example, block the words **Don't Knot Up**.

2. Select the **Font** menu on the Menu bar {Alt and o}.

3. Select **Shadow** {a}.

   Note: A gray shadow has been placed around the letters in the blocked text.

Increase Leading for Title and Subtitle Lines

4. Block the desired text.

   For example, block the title and subtitle lines.

5. Select **Layout, Other, Printer Functions** {Shift and F8, o, p}.

6. Select **Leading Adjustment** {L}.

7. Type the desired amount of additional space to be placed between the lines of the blocked text.

    For example, type **.15**. (Do not type the final period.)

8. Select **OK** twice {Enter four times}.

Finish-Up Instructions

❖ Insert a graphic image as follows:

   a. Select **Graphics, Graphics Boxes, Create.**

   b. Select **Filename, F5, OK.**

   c. Double-click on **humbird.wpg.**

   d. Select **Attach To, Page.**

   e. Select **Edit Position, Horizontal Position, Left.**

   f. Select **OK.**

   g. Select **Image Editor.**

   h. *To turn the graphic image around to face the opposite direction,* select the **FlipHorz** button located at the right of the Button Bar {h}.

   i. Select **Close** {F7}.

   j. Select **OK** {Enter}.

❖ Use the filename **19drill1.new** and save the file

Create Unequal Width Columns

Until now, only equal width newspaper columns have been created. However, it is also possible to create columns of different widths. When creating columns of different widths, it is important to remember that the total of the the widths of all columns and the space between columns should equal the width of the page minus the margins. For example, if default one-inch margins are used, the total of all columns and the space between columns should equal 6.5 inches.

Start-Up Instructions

❖ The file named **19drill1.new** should be displayed on the screen.

Create Unequal Width Columns

Note: If desired, select the text mode in order to avoid having the graphic image redraw to the screen.

1. Place the insertion point at the location where the columns are to begin.

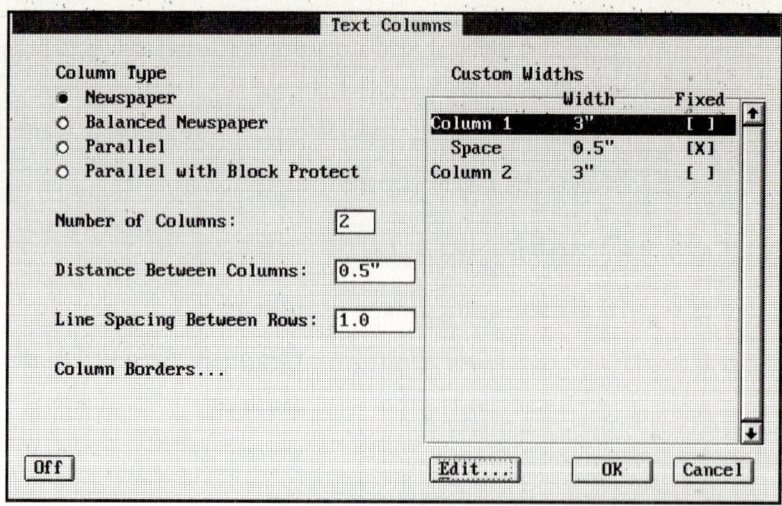

FIGURE 19.1

Text Columns dialog box with Custom Widths box displayed

For example, place the insertion point to the left of the C in Constant.

2. Select **Layout, Columns** {Alt and L, c}.

3. Select the **Custom Widths** option {w}.

   Note: The Text Columns dialog box is enlarged to include a Custom Widths box (see Figure 19.1). The current widths of each column and the space between each column display. Currently, column 1 and column 2 are each 3 inches wide with a space of .5 inches between columns.

4. Select **Edit** {e}.

   Note: The Column 1 dialog box displays (see Figure 19.2).

5. Select **Width** {w}.

6. Type the desired column width {type the desired width and press Enter once}.

   For example, type **2**. (Do not type the period.)

7. Select **Next** to display a dialog box for setting the width of the next column or the space between columns {n}.

   Note: A Space dialog box displays to set the space between columns 1 and 2.

8. Select **Width** {w}.

9. Type the desired space between columns {type the desired space and press Enter}.

   For example, type **.25**. (Do not type the final period.)

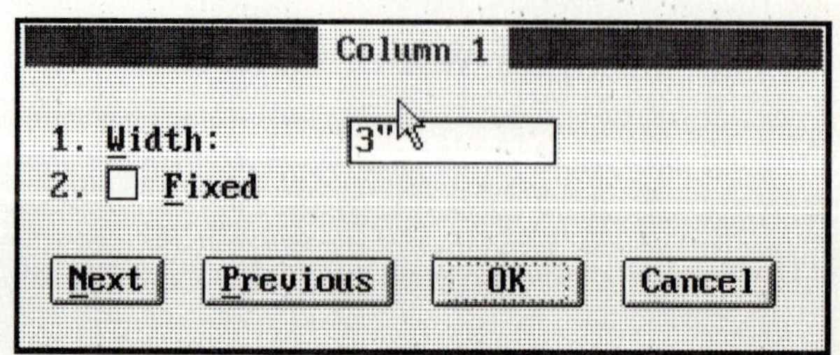

FIGURE 19.2

Column 1 dialog box

Chapter 19—Create a Magazine Article

10. Select **Next** to display a dialog box for setting the width of the next column or space between columns {n}.

    Note: The Column 2 dialog box displays.

11. Select **Width** {w}.

12. Type the desired column width {type the desired column width and press Enter}.

    For example, type **4.25**. (Do not type the final period.)

13. When all column widths have been set, select **OK** {Enter}.

    Note: The new column widths display in the Custom Widths area of the Text Columns dialog box.

14. Select **OK** to exit the Text Column dialog box {F7, Enter}.

    Note: The text displays in two columns on the screen.

Finish-Up Instructions

❖ Use the same filename, **19drill1.new**, and save the file again.

Edit Border Line Style Settings

Each graphic box type (Figure, Table, Text, etc.) contains settings for border lines (see Figure 14.1, page 374). For example, by default a Table box has a thick border line at the top and bottom of the box. If desired, the style of the border line(s) can be changed and/or the thickness of the border line(s) can be edited. For example, the top border line of a Table box can be changed to the thin-thick line style and the bottom border line can be changed to a thick-thin line style. Also, the thickness of each border line can be set and, if the border line style contains more than one line component, for example, a thin line and a thicker line, the space between the line components can be changed.

Start-Up Instructions

❖ The file named **19drill1.new** should be displayed on the screen.

Steps to ▶ Create a Graphic Box for Pull Quote Text

1. Select **Graphics, Graphics Boxes, Create** {Alt and F9, b, c}.

2. Select **Attach To, Page** {a, a}.

3. Select **Edit Position, Horizontal Position**, and choose the desired horizontal position {e, h, select desired position}.

    For example, select **Full** {f}.

4. Select **Position Relative To, Column**, and type the number of the column in which the pull quote will be located {r, c, type number of column, Enter}.

> For example, select **Position Relative To, Column**, and check that 1 displays.

5. Select **Vertical Position, Set**, and type the desired location for the pull quote {v, s, type desired location, Enter}.

> For example, type **4.25**. (Do not type the final period.)

6. Select **OK** {Enter}.

7. Select **Edit Size, Set Height**, and type the desired height {s, h, type height, Enter}.

> For example, type **5.3**. (Do not type the final period.)

8. Select **OK** {Enter twice}.

9. Select **Based on Box Style** and double-click on desired box style {y, highlight desired box style, Enter}.

> For example, double-click on **Table Box**.

10. Select **Create Text** {e}.

11. Type the desired pull quote text or select **File, Retrieve** and type the location and name of the file containing the pull quote text.

> For example, select **File, Retrieve** and retrieve the file named **19drill1.pul** from the data disk. Select **OK** {Alt and f, r, type filename, Enter}.

12. Press **F7**.

> *Note: The Create Graphic Box dialog box displays. Continue with the next steps to Change the Border Line Style Settings.*

Steps to ▶ Change Line Style Settings

1. Select **Edit Border/Fill** {b}.

2. Select **Lines** {L}.

3. Select **Top Line** {t}.

4. Highlight the desired line style.

> For example, highlight **Thin Thick Line**.

5. Select **Edit** {e}.

> *Note: The Edit Line Style dialog box displays (see Figure 19.3). On a color monitor, a red border displays around the line component that is currently selected. (On a monochrome monitor, a highlighted border displays around the currently selected line component).*

6. To change the thickness of the selected line component, select **Thickness**, type the desired line thickness, and press **Enter** once {t, type line thickness, Enter}.

> For example, select **Thickness**, type **.08**, and press **Enter**.

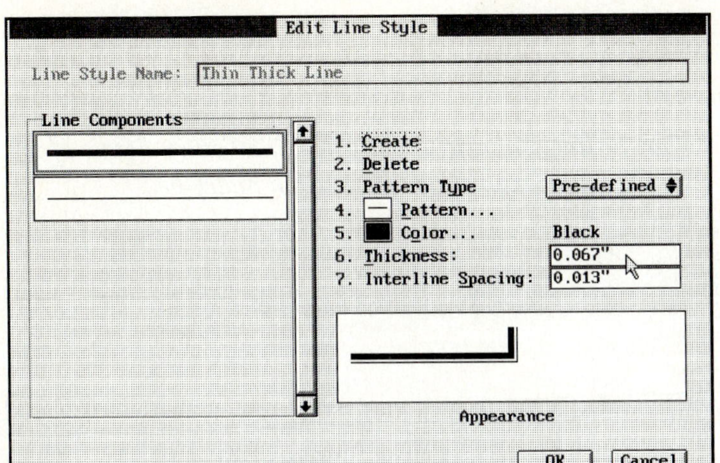

Edit Line Style dialog box

7. To change the amount of space between the two line components, select **Interline Spacing**, type the desired spacing, and press **Enter** {s, type desired spacing, Enter}.

   For example, select **Interline Spacing**, type **.04**, and press **Enter**.

8. To edit another line component, move the mouse pointer to the desired line component and click once {press the up or down arrow key to move the red border to the desired line component}.

   For example, move the mouse pointer to the second (thin) line component and click.

9. To change the thickness of the line component, select **Thickness**, type the desired line thickness, and press **Enter** {t, type desired line thickness, Enter}.

   For example, select **Thickness**, type **.04**, and press **Enter**.

10. Select **OK** {F7}.

11. Choose **Select** {Enter}.

12. To change the style of another line, select the desired line.

   For example, select **Bottom Line** {b}.

13. Highlight the desired line style.

   For example, highlight **Thick Thin Line**.

14. Select **Edit** {e} and repeat Step 9 to change the thickness of the selected line component.

   For example, change the thickness of the thin line to **.04**.

15. Repeat Step 7 to change the interline spacing.

   For example, select **Interline Spacing**, type **.04**, and press **Enter**.

16. Repeat Steps 8 and 9 to select the second line component and to change the line thickness.

   For example, change the line thickness of the thick line to **.08**.

17. Select **OK** {F7}.

18. Choose **Select** {Enter}.

19. Select **Close** {Enter}.

     Note: The new styles for the line components of the top and bottom border of the graphic box displays in the Edit Graphics Box Border/Fill dialog box.

20. Select **Close** {Enter}.

21. Select **OK** {Enter}.

Finish-Up Instructions

❖ Use the new filename **19drill1.lin** and save the file.

❖ If desired, select the **Zoom** button and choose **50%** view to displays the pull quote box. Select **Marg** view before continuing with the next section.

Create a Drop Cap

A drop cap is a special effect that is often used in the first paragraph of an article. The first character of the first word in the paragraph is enlarged. The A at the beginning of this paragraph is an example of a drop cap.

Start-Up Instructions

❖ The file named **19drill1.lin** should be displayed on the screen.

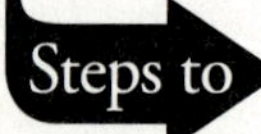

Create a Drop Cap

Note: If desired, select the text mode in order to avoid having the graphic image redraw to the screen.

1. Block and cut the letter that will become a drop cap.

     For example, block the letter **C** in Constant and select **Edit, Cut** {Ctrl and x}.

2. Select **Graphics, Graphics Boxes, Create** {Alt and F9, b, c}.

3. Select **Create Text** {e}.

4. Select **Edit, Paste** {Ctrl and v}.

5. Format the drop cap letter.

     For example, change the font to **Bodoni-WP Bold (Type 1), 48 point.**

6. Press **F7**.

7. Select **Edit Position, Horizontal Position, Left, OK** {p, h, L, Enter}.

8. Select **Edit Size** {s}.

9. Select the **Automatic Width Based on Box Contents Width** option {a}.

10. Select **Set Height** and type the desired height of the box to contain the drop cap {h, type desired height, and press Enter}.

   For example, type **.5.** (Do not type the final period.)

11. Select **OK** {Enter}.

12. Select **Based on Box Style** and double-click on **User Box** {y, press the up or down arrow key to highlight User Box and press Enter}.

Delete Space Around the Graphic Box

13. Select **Edit Border/Fill** {b}.

14. Select **Spacing** {s}.

15. Select **Automatic Spacing** to deselect the option. Select **Outside, Set All** {a, o, Enter}.

   Note: A zero displays in the Outside, Set All box.

16. Select **OK** {Enter}.

17. Select **Close** {Enter}.

18. Select **OK** {Enter}.

Finish-Up Instructions

❖ Use the same filename, **19drill1.lin**, and save the file again.

Automatically Indent the First Line of All Paragraphs

To save space, the first line of each paragraph is indented so that an extra blank line is not needed between paragraphs. The first line of each paragraph can be indented manually by moving the insertion point to the beginning of each paragraph and pressing the Tab key. However, WordPerfect can be instructed to automatically indent the first line of each paragraph. If the Tab key is pressed to indent the first line of a paragraph, the line is indented to the first tab stop. If the first line of a paragraph is automatically indented, the indention amount can be specified, e.g., .25 inches.

Start-Up Instructions

❖ The file named **19drill1.lin** should be displayed on the screen.

Indent the First Line of All Paragraphs Automatically

1. Place the insertion point to the left of the first character in the first paragraph to be indented.

   For example, place the insertion point to the left of the quotation mark (") that precedes the word **The** in the second paragraph of the document.

2. Select **Layout, Margins** {Shift and F8, m}.

3. Select **First Line Indent** {f}.

4. Type the desired indent amount.

   For example, type **.25**. (Do not type the final period.)

5. Select **OK** {Enter three times}.

   Note: Scroll through the document and notice that the first line of each paragraph is indented.

Finish-Up Instructions

- Press the **Page Down** key to move the insertion point to page 2 of the document.

- Create a graphic box for the first column of the second page using the following information:

  a. Select **Graphics, Graphics Boxes, Create**.

  b. Select **Attach To, Page**.

  c. Select **Edit Position, Horizontal Position, Full**.

  d. Select **Position Relative To, Column**, and check that 1 displays in the Column box.

  e. Select **Vertical Position, Full**. Select **OK**.

  f. Select **Based on Box Style** and double-click on **Text Box**.

  g. Select **Create Text**.

  h. Type and center the following:

     Millions overcome stress.
     You can too.

  i. Press **Alt** and **F9**, select **Rotate Box Contents**, and choose **90° Rotation**. Select **OK**.

  j. Place the insertion point at the beginning of the text and change the font to **Bodoni-WP Bold (Type 1), 30 point**.

  k. Press **F7**.

  l. Select **OK**.

- Use the same filename, **19drill1.lin**, and save the file.

Create a Graphic Box That Spans Multiple Columns

Until now, a graphic box in a multi-column document has been placed within a single column, e.g., position relative to column 1 or column 2. A graphic box can also be set to span (cover) more than one column. For example, if a two-column format is used, a graphic box can be set to span both columns.

Within a graphic box, multiple columns can be created. By creating a different number of columns in the graphic box than are on the page, a page can be created that contains a different number of columns.

A graphic box that spans more than one column in a magazine article can be used to hold a graphic image or sidebar information—or both. To place a graphic image in a graphic box that contains text, a second graphic box is created within the first graphic box. This is sometimes referred to as nesting a graphic box.

Start-Up Instructions

❖ The file named **19drill1.lin** should be displayed on the screen.

Steps to Create a Graphic Box That Spans Multiple Columns

1. Move the insertion point to the page on which the graphic box will be located.

   For example, press the **Page Down** key to move the insertion point to page 3 of the document.

2. Select **Graphics, Graphics Boxes, Create** {Alt and F9, b, c}.

3. Select **Attach To, Page** {a, a}.

4. Select **Edit Position, Horizontal Position, Full** {p, h, f}.

Place a Graphic Box Over Multiple Columns

5. Select **Position Relative To, Columns** {r, c}.

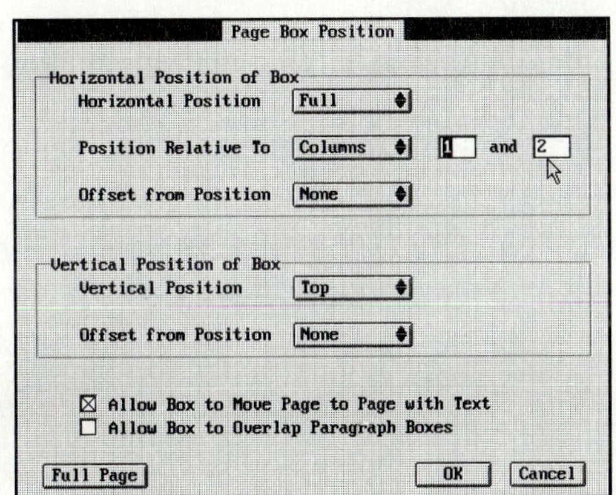

Note: When the Columns option is selected, two boxes display (see Figure 19.4) containing the number 1 (column 1) and the number 2 (column 2). These boxes are used to specify over which column(s) the graphic box will be located. Because this graphic box is to be placed over both columns, no change is necessary.

6. Select **OK** {Enter three times}.

7. Select **Edit Size, Set Height**, and type the desired height of the graphic box {s, h, type the desired height, Enter}.

   For example, type **5**. (Do not type the period.)

8. Select **OK** {Enter}.

9. Select **Based on Box Style** and double-click on the desired box style {y, highlight desired box style, Enter}.

   For example, double-click on **Table Box**.

10. Select **Create Text** {e}.

11. Type or retrieve the desired text.

    For example, select **File, Retrieve**, and retrieve the file named **19sbar.txt** from the data disk {Alt and f, r, type location and file-name, Enter}.

Create Multiple Columns Within a Graphic Box

12. Move the insertion point to the location where the multiple column layout should begin.

    For example, place the insertion point to the left of the T in the first word of the first paragraph.

13. Select **Layout, Columns** {Alt and L, c}.

14. Select the desired type of columns and type the number of columns in the Number of Columns box.

    For example, check that Newspaper columns is selected and type **3** in the Number of Columns box {n, 3}.

15. To change the amount of space between columns, select **Distance Between Columns** and type the desired amount of space between columns {d, type desired distance, Enter}.

    For example, select **Distance Between Columns** and type **.25**.

16. Select **OK** {Enter}.

Place (Nest) a Second Graphic Box Containing a Graphic Image Within a Graphic Box

1. Place the insertion point at the location where the graphic box will be inserted.

For example, press **Home, Home**, and the down arrow key to locate the insertion point on the blank line below the last paragraph.

2. Select **Graphics, Graphics Boxes, Create** {Alt and F9, b, c}.

3. Select **Filename** {f}.

4. To use a graphic image that has been placed into the document previously, select **Existing Images** {Shift and F5}.

5. Double-click on the desired filename {highlight the filename and press Enter}.

   For example, double-click on **c:\wp60\graphics\humbird.wpg**.

6. Select **Edit Position, Horizontal Position, Centered, OK** {p, h, c, Enter twice}.

7. If necessary, select **Based on Box Style** and double-click on the desired style.

   For example, select **Based on Box Style** and double-click on **User Box**.

8. Select **OK** to return to the Text box window {Enter}.

   Note: A second graphic box containing the humbird.wpg file has been placed within the graphic box containing the 19sbar.txt file.

9. Press **F7**.

10. Select **OK** {Enter}.

Finish-Up Instructions

❖ Use the same filename, **19drill1.lin**, and save the file again.

Correct Typography Symbols for Quote Marks and Em Dashes

In the past, when using a typewriter the quotation mark (") has been used in place of the correct opening (") and closing (") quotation marks. Also two hyphens (--) have been used to indicate a dash in place of the correct em dash (—). Because the ", ", and — characters are not available on keyboards, often " and -- are still used when creating text on the computer. However, the ", ", and — characters are available in the Typographic Symbols WP Characters set. WordPerfect can be instructed to search for the " or -- characters and replace the characters with the correct typography symbol.

Start-Up Instructions

❖ The file named **19drill1.lin** should be displayed on the screen.

 **Steps to** **Convert Typed Characters to Correct Typography Symbols**

1. Place the insertion point at the beginning of the text to be searched.

2. Select **Edit, Replace** {Alt and F2}.

3. Type the character(s) to be replaced.

   For example, type a quotation mark (") and press the **Spacebar** once so that WordPerfect will look for a " mark followed by a space.

4. Click in the **Replace With** box {Tab}.

5. To replace text with a character from a WordPerfect Character set, press **Ctrl** and **w** to display the WordPerfect Characters dialog box.

6. Move the mouse pointer to the down arrow located beside the Set box and press the mouse button. Point to the set that contains the desired character {press the Tab key, s, press the down arrow key to highlight the desired set, press Enter}.

   For example, choose **Typographic Symbols**.

7. Double-click on the desired character {3, press the arrow keys to move the rectangular outline to the desired character, press Enter}.

   For example, double-click on the " character (the last character in the second row). Press the **Spacebar** once.

8. If an X displays in the Find Whole Word Only box, select the **Find Whole Word Only** option to remove the X {press Tab, w}.

9. Select **Replace** {F2}.

10. Select **OK** {Enter}.

Finish-Up Instructions

❖ Place the insertion point at any location in the first paragraph of the document. Replace the remaining quotation marks (") with a " character by using the following information:

   a. Select **Edit, Replace**.

   b. In the Search For box, type a quotation mark (").

   c. In the Replace With box, press **Ctrl** and **W**; if necessary, select the **Typographic Symbols** set, and double-click on the " symbol (the first character in the third row).

   d. Select **Replace**. Select **OK**.

❖ Place the insertion point at any location in the first paragraph of the document. Replace the -- (hyphens) characters with an — (em dash) using the following information.

   a. Select **Edit, Replace**.

b. In the Search For box, type -- (two hyphens).

   Note: When the two hyphens are typed, the codes [-Hyphen][-Hyphen] display in the Search for box.

c. In the Replace With Box, press **Ctrl** and **w**; if necessary, select the **Typographic Symbols** set, and double click on the — (em dash) character (third character in the third row).

d. Select **Replace**. Select **OK**.

❖ Use the same filename, **19drill1.lin**, and save the file again.

Create Footers for Odd and Even Pages

Documents created in WordPerfect can contain one or two footers, i.e., Footer A and Footer B. If the same footer will appear on each page of a document, only one footer (Footer A) is created. If different footers are to appear on odd and even numbered pages, both Footer A and Footer B are created. For example, the Footer A option is used to create a footer that will appear on odd numbered pages (1, 3, 5, etc.), and the Footer B option is used to create a footer that will appear on even numbered pages (2, 4, 6, etc.). WordPerfect also has the capability to create different headers for odd and even pages (Header A, Header B).

Start-Up Instructions

❖ The file named **19drill1.lin** should be displayed on the screen.

Create Footers for Odd and Even Pages

Note: If desired, select the text mode in order to avoid having the graphic image redraw to the screen.

1. Move the insertion point to the page on which the footer is to begin.

   For example, move the insertion point to the top of the document.

2. Select **Layout, Header/Footer/Watermark** {Alt and L, h}.

3. Select **Footer A** {f, a}.

4. Select **Odd Pages** to create a footer for odd numbered pages (e.g., pages 1, 3, 5) {o}.

5. Select **Create** {c}.

6. Type and format the footer text.

   For example:

a. Change the font to **Bodoni-WP Bold (Type 1), 10 point**.

b. Type **Health Magazine Weekly**. (Do not type the period.)

c. Press **Alt** and **F6** to move the insertion point to the right margin.

d. Insert the page numbering code by selecting **Layout, Page, Page Numbering, Insert Formatted Page Number** {Alt and L, p, n, i, Enter twice}.

7. Press **F7** to exit the footer window.

8. Select **Layout, Header/Footer/Watermark** {Alt and L, h}.

9. Select **Footer B** {f, b}.

10. Select **Even Pages** to create a footer for even numbered pages {v}.

11. Select **Create** {c}.

12. Type and format the desired footer text.

For example:

a. Change the font to **Bodoni-WP Bold (Type 1), 10 point**.

b. Insert the page numbering code by selecting **Layout, Page, Page Numbering, Insert Formatted Page Number** {Alt and L, p, n, i, Enter twice}.

c. Press **Alt** and **F6** to move the insertion point to the right margin.

d. Type the article name, **Don't Knot Up**. (Do not type the period.)

13. Press **F7**.

Finish-Up Instructions

❖ Use the new filename **19drill1.fin** and save the file.

❖ Print one copy.

The Next Step

Chapter Review and Activities

FEATURES SUMMARY

FEATURES	ACTIONS	PAGE
Shadow text attribute	Block the desired text. Select the **Font** menu and choose **Shadow**.	508
Create unequal column widths	Place the insertion point at the desired location. Select **Layout, Columns, Custom Widths, Edit**. Select **Width** and type the desired column width. Select **Next, Width**, and type the desired space between columns. Select **Next, Width**, and type the desired column width. Select **OK** twice.	509
Change border line style settings	In the Create/Edit Graphics Box dialog box, select **Edit Border/Fill, Lines**. Select the desired line and highlight the desired line style. Select **Edit**. To change the thickness of the selected line component, select **Thickness** and type the desired line width. To change the spacing between two line components, select **Interline Spacing** and type the desired amount of space. Select **OK**. Choose **Select**. Select **Close** twice, **OK**.	512

| --- | --- | --- |
Create a drop cap	Block and cut the desired character. Select **Graphics, Graphics Box, Create, Create Text**. Paste the character. If desired change the font and size of the character. Press **F7**. Select **Edit, Position, Horizontal Position, Left, OK**. Select **Edit Size, Automatic Width Based on Box Contents Width**, select **Set Height**, type desired box height, **OK**. Select **Based on Box Style**, double-click on **User Box**. To delete space around the graphic box, select **Edit Border/Fill**, select **Spacing, Automatic Spacing, OK, Close, OK**.	514
Indent first line of paragraphs automatically	Place the insertion point at the beginning of the first paragraph to be indented. Select **Layout, Margins, First Line Indent**, type the desired indent amount, select **OK**.	516
Create a graphic box that spans multiple columns	Locate the insertion point on the page that will contain the graphic box. Select **Graphics, Graphics Boxes, Create, Attach To, Page**. Select **Edit Position, Horizontal Position, Full**. Select **Position Relative To, Columns, OK**. Select **Edit Size, Set Height**, type desired box height, **OK**. Select **Based on Box Style** and double-click on desired box style. Select **Create Text**. Type or retrieve desired text. Press **F7** and select **OK**.	517
Create multiple columns within a graphic box	In the Create/Edit Graphic Box dialog box, select **Create/Edit Text**. Type or retrieve desired text. Select **Layout, Columns**, select the desired columns type. Select **Number of Columns** and type the desired number of columns. Select **Distance Between Columns** and type the desired space between columns. Select **OK**.	518
Place (nest) a second graphic box containing a graphic image within a graphic box	In the Create/Edit Graphic Box dialog box, select **Create/Edit Text**. Type or retrieve the desired text. Place the insertion point at the location where the graphic box is to be inserted. Select **Graphics, Graphics Boxes, Create**. Select **Filename**. Retrieve the desired graphic image or select **Existing Images** and double-click on the desired filename to insert a graphic image that has previously been placed in the document. Position and size the graphic box as desired. Select **OK**.	518
Convert typed characters to correct typographical symbols	Place the insertion point at the beginning of the text to be searched. Select **Edit, Replace**, type the characters to be replaced. Click in the **Replace With** box. Press **Ctrl** and **w**. Select the desired WordPerfect Character Set (e.g., Typographic Symbols). Double-click on the desired symbol. Select **Replace, OK**.	520

| --- | --- | --- |
| Create footers for odd and Even Pages | Place the insertion point on the page where the footer is to begin. Select **Layout**, **Header/Footer/Watermark**. Select **Footer A**, **Odd Pages**, **Create**. Type and format the footer text. Press **F7**. Select **Layout**, **Header/Footer/Watermark**. Select **Footer B**, **Even Pages**, **Create**. Type and format the footer text. Press **F7**. | 521 |

Self-Check Questions

True/False—Circle One

T F 1. By default, a table box has a thick border line at the top and a thick thin border line at the bottom.

T F 2. The Interline Spacing option in the Edit Line Style dialog box is used to increase or decrease the space between two line components.

T F 3. The spacing around the graphic box that holds a drop cap character should be set to zero.

T F 4. Multiple columns cannot be created with a graphic box.

Short Answer

1. List the three steps to use the shadow text attribute.

2. The __________ option in the Text Columns dialog box is selected to create unequal column width.

3. List the five steps used to indent the first line of all paragraphs automatically.

4. A second graphic box created within another graphic box is often referred to as __________ a graphic box.

5. Choose the ______________ Symbols set to create typographically correct quotation marks.

6. Write a brief explanation of why two different footers would be used in a document.

Enriching Language Arts Skills

Spelling/Vocabulary Words

compatibility   able to exit together in harmony; consistent; suitable
promulgated   to have made known publicly; to have published; announced
standards   habits or customs established by an authority; example; paradigms

Em and En Dashes

The em dash (—), a typography symbol about the width of the character m, is often used in place of a comma. Press the hyphen key twice (--) to create a dash on a typewriter or computer keyboard. Many software programs provide a method to create correct typographic em dashes (see page 520). The en dash (–), a typography symbol about the width of the character n, is used as a hyphen or as a substitute for the word to, e.g., July–September. The correct typography symbols for em and en dashes have traditionally been used for books, newspapers, and advertisements and are recommended for use when creating a professional-looking document.

Example:

em dash   Our notebook sales have increased 20 percent since last year—from $10,000 to $12,000.

en dash   Joe's father–in–law was voted "Coach of the Year."

Activities

Activity 19.1—Create a Magazine Article

1. Open the file named **19act1.txt** from the data disk.

2. Select the title and choose the **Shadow** text attribute (select **Font**, **Shadow**).

3. Create a graphic box and retrieve the graphic image named **sound.eps**. The **sound.eps** file is located on the data disk (select **Graphics**, **Graphics Boxes**, **Create**, **Filename**, type the location and the filename **sound.eps**, and select **OK**).

4. Change the horizontal position of the graphic box to **Left** (select **Edit Position**, **Horizontal Position**, **Left**, **OK**).

5. Change the box style to a User box (select **Based on Box Style**, double-click on **User Box**).

6. Exit the Create Graphics Box dialog box (select **OK**).

7. Place the insertion point at the beginning of the first paragraph in the article and create two columns. Set the width of column 1 to **2.25"**. Set the space between columns to **.25"**. Set the width of column 2 to **4"**.

   Note: For assistance, see Steps to Create Unequal Width Columns on page 509.

8. Create a graphic box for the pull quote text using the following information.

   Note: For assistance, see Steps to Create a Graphic Box for Pull Quote Text on page 511.

   a. Select the Table box style.

   b. Attach the graphic box to the page and set the horizontal position to **Full**.

   c. Set the vertical position of the graphic box to **4"**.

   d. Set the height of the graphic box to **5.75"**.

   e. Change the line style for the top border line to **Thick Thin Line**. Change the thickness of the thin line to **.02"** and the Interline Spacing to **.03"**.

   f. Change the thickness of the thick line to **.04"**.

   g. Change the line style for the bottom border line to **Thick Thin Line**. Change the thickness of the thin line to **.02"** and the Interline Spacing to **.03"**.

   h. Change the thickness of the thick line to **.04"**.

9. Select the first character of the first paragraph in the article and create a drop cap.

   Note: For assistance, see Steps to Create a Drop Cap on page 514.

10. Automatically indent the first line of all the remaining paragraphs.

    Note: For assistance, see Steps to Automatically Indent the First Line of all Paragraphs on page 516.

11. Create a Text box in the first column of the second page using the following information.

    a. Place the insertion point on the second page and select **Graphics, Graphics Boxes, Create**.

    b. Select **Attach To, Page**.

    c. Select **Edit Position, Horizontal Position, Full**.

    d. Select **Position Relative to, Column**, and check that 1 displays.

    e. Select **Vertical Position, Full** and select **OK**.

    f. Select **Based on Box Style** and double-click on **Text Box**.

    g. Select **Create Text**.

    h. Type and center the following text:

Make music with your computer.
Or
Listen to a message from your boss.
It's all available with sound board technology.

    i. Press **Alt** and **F9**, **Rotate Box Contents**, **90° Rotation**, **OK**.

    j. Change the font to **Bodoni-WP Bold (Type 1), 24 point**.

12. Place the insertion point on the third page and create a graphic box that spans both columns. Retrieve the file named **19act1.bar** from the data disk.

    Note: For assistance, see Steps to Create a Graphic Box That Spans Multiple Columns on page 517.

13. Place the graphic image **sound.eps** in the sidebar graphic box.

    Note: For assistance, see Steps to Place a Second Graphic Box Containing a Graphic Image Within a Graphic box on page 518.

14. Create footers for the odd and even pages of the article using the following information:

    Note: For assistance, see Steps to Create Footers for Odd and Even Pages on page 521.

    a. Use Footer A to create the footer for odd pages. Change the font to **Bodoni-WP Bold (Type 1), 10 point**. The text for the footer follows:

    Today's PC Magazine   **Page (insert page number code)**

    b. Use Footer B to create the footer for even pages. Change the font to **Bodoni-WP Bold (Type 1), 10 point**. The text for the footer follows:

    Page (insert page number code)   **Sound Boards**

15. Convert the quotation marks (") contained in the document to typography quotation marks (" and ").

    Note: For assistance, see Steps to Convert Typed Characters to Correct Typography Symbols on page 520.

16. Use the filename **19act1.fin** and save the file.

17. Print one copy.

Challenge Your Skills

➥ ■ Skill 19.1—Create a Magazine Article

1. Open the file named **19skill1.txt** from the data disk. Review the text and determine appropriate pull quote text.

2. The graphic file named **fax.eps** is provided on the data disk for use in the article.

3. Make decisions regarding:

>   Initial font for the document
>   Font for article title, subtitle, and sideheadings
>   Leading adjustment for title
>   Number and widths of columns and space between columns
>   Placement and text for pull quotes
>   Use of drop cap
>   Indention for paragraphs
>   *Hint: If the first line of each paragraph will be automatically indented, remove the indention from sideheading paragraphs by blocking each paragraph and selecting **Layout, Margins, First Line Indent, 0 (zero), OK.***
>   Placement and format of sidebar information
>   Footers for odd and even pages of the article
>   Correct three spelling and four punctuation errors.

4. The sidebar text is contained in a file named **19skill1.bar**.

5. Use the filename **19skill1.fin** and save the file.

6. Print one copy.

7. If you have completed your work in WordPerfect, exit the program.

Create a Booklet

Features Summary

- Create subdivided pages
- Create a watermark
- Page numbering subdivided pages
- Print a booket

Objectives

After successfully completing this chapter, you will be able to subdivide a physical page into two or more logical pages, create a watermark that appears on all pages of a document, insert page numbers for subdivided pages, and print the subdivided pages in booklet form.

Chapter Introduction

WordPerfect's Subdivide Page feature is used to divide a physical page into two or more logical pages. Each logical page can contain text, graphics, a header and/or footer, a page number, etc. Subdividing pages is useful for creating booklets, tickets, or other documents that do not require a full page. WordPerfect also provides the capability to print subdivided pages in booklet form. WordPerfect's Watermark feature is used to print text or a graphic image in the background of pages in a document.

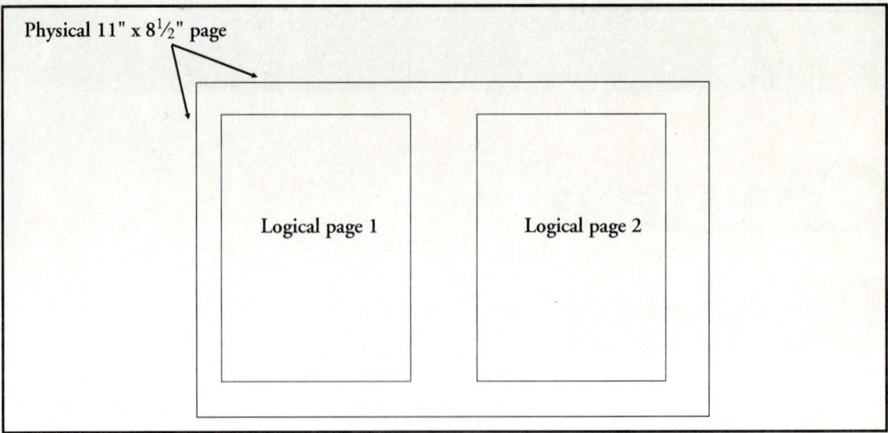

FIGURE 20.1

Physical page vs. logical pages

Subdivide Pages

WordPerfect Subdivide Page feature can be used to create documents such as booklets and programs. With the Subdivide Page feature, a single sheet of paper can be divided into multiple pages. The piece of paper is referred to as a *physical page*. The subdivided pages are referred to as *logical pages*. See Figure 20.1.

When subdivided pages are created, the physical page can be divided vertically (columns) and/or horizontally (rows). For example, when creating a booklet, the physical page is divided into two columns and one row. If tickets are being created, the physical page could be two columns and five rows to create ten tickets per physical page.

When pages are subdivided, each logical page is treated by WordPerfect as a separate page of the document and can contain headers and/or footers, page numbers, and other page items. Text can be centered vertically and horizontally relative to the margins of the logical page.

To view the logical pages on the screen side by side, the page mode is selected and a 50% or 75% zoom view is chosen. In graphics mode, the logical pages will display one at a time with a hard page break to show the division of the logical pages.

Start-Up Instructions

- ❖ 🖬 Open the file named **20drill1.txt** from the data disk.
- ❖ If necessary, switch to the page mode view.
- ❖ Change the initial font for the document to **Dutch 801 Roman (Speedo), 12 point** (select **Layout, Document, Initial Font, Font**, double-click on **Dutch 801 Roman**, select **OK** twice).

Create Subdivided Pages

1. Select **Layout, Page** {Alt and L, p}.

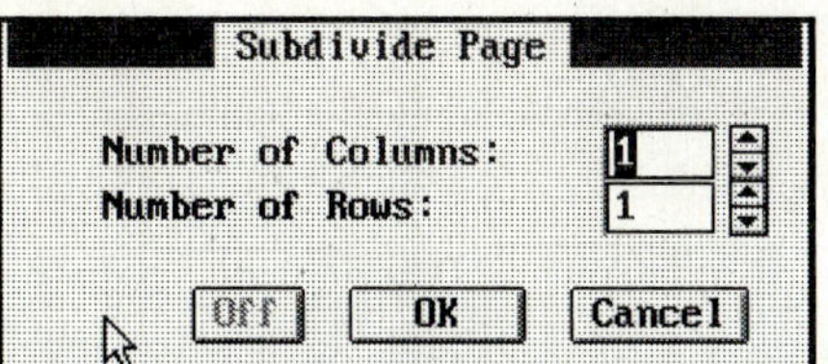

FIGURE 20.2

Subdivide Page dialog box

Note: The Page Format dialog box displays.

2. Select **Subdivide Page** {a}.

   Note: The Subdivide Page dialog box displays (see Figure 20.2).

3. Type the number of columns and/or rows that will be on one physical page of paper.

   For example, type **2** in the Number of Columns box.

4. Select **OK** {Enter twice} to return to the Page Format dialog box.

Change to Landscape Paper Type

5. In the Page Format dialog box, select **Paper Size/Type** {s}.

6. Double-click on the desired paper size/type.

   For example, double-click on **Letter (Landscape)**.

Center Text Vertically on All Pages

7. In the Page Format dialog box, select **Center Pages** {p}.

8. Select **OK** to exit the Page Format dialog box {Enter}.

Finish-Up Instructions

- ❖ Select the **Zoom** button and double-click on **50%** to view both logical pages.

- ❖ Use the following information and place the graphic image named **ecologo.wpg** on the first page of the document.

   a. Select **Graphics, Graphics Boxes, Create** {Alt and F9, g, b}.

   b. Select **Filename**, press **F5**, select **OK**, and double-click on **ecologo.wpg** {f, F5, Enter, highlight ecologo.wpg, Enter}.

   c. Select **Attach To, Page** {a, a}.

   d. Select **Edit Position, Horizontal Position, Centered** {p, h, c}.

   e. Select **OK** twice {Enter twice}.

- ❖ Use the new filename **20drill1.new** and save the file.

Create a Watermark

A watermark is a type of graphic box that is repeated on each page of a document. Text or a graphic image can be placed in a watermark box. The watermark text or graphic image is printed in a light gray on the page and other text and/or images can be placed on top of the watermark image. If a graphic image is used as a watermark, it may be necessary to lighten the image even more, so that overlying text can be easily read. The darkness of a graphic image can be changed by adjusting the contrast between the dark and light areas of the image. The contrast is changed by using the Image Editor, selecting the **Contrast** option, typing a number between -1 and 1, and pressing **Enter**.

Create a Watermark

Note: Select 75% zoom view.

1. Place the insertion point on the first page where the watermark is to be located.

   For example, place the insertion point to the left of the first character (F) in the first paragraph on logical page 2.

2. Select **Layout, Header/Footer/Watermark** {Alt and L, h}.

3. Select **Watermark A, Create** {w, a, c}.

   Note: An empty document window displays. The words "Watermark A: Press F7 when done" displays in the Status bar.

Place a graphic image in the watermark window

4. Select **Graphics, Graphics Boxes, Create** {Alt and F9, b, c}.

5. Select **Filename** {f}.

6. To select a graphic image that has previously been placed in the document, select **Existing Images** {Shift and F5}.

7. Double-click on the desired filename.

   For example, double-click on **ecologo.wpg**.

8. Select **Image Editor** to view the graphic image {e}.

   Note: Because the graphic image is in a Watermark graphic box, the image is a light gray.

Change the contrast between the light and dark areas of the graphic image

9. Select the **Contrast** option {c}.

10. Type the amount of contrast and press **Enter**.

    For example, type **.75** to lighten the image and press **Enter**.

Note: The graphic image is much lighter. In fact, it may be too light to read. However, the image will darken when printed.

11. To increase the width of the graphic image to fill the entire graphics box, select **Scale Width** {w}, type the desired amount of increase for the width, and press **Enter**.

    For example, type **1.06** and press **Enter**.

12. To increase the height of the graphic image the same amount as the width was increased, select **Scale Height** {g}, type the desired amount for the height, and press **Enter**.

    For example, type **1.06** and press **Enter**.

13. Select **Close** {F7}.

14. Select **OK** {F7}.

    Note: The graphic image displays in the watermark window.

15. Press **F7** to exit the watermark window.

    *Note: The watermark does not display in the document window. To view the watermark in logical page 2, select the **Preview** button; select **Close** to return to the document window.*

Finish-Up Instructions

❖ Use the same filename **20drill1.new** and save the file again.

Page Numbering Subdivided Pages

Page numbers can be added to subdivided pages using the normal procedure to insert page numbers. In the case of a booklet, the cover page generally is not included in the page numbering for the booklet. Therefore, the page numbering code is placed at the top of the second logical page and the page number can be reset to page 1. For page numbering purposes, page 2 is now page 1.

Start-Up Instructions

❖ The file named **20drill1.new** should be displayed on the screen.

Number Subdivided Pages

1. Place the insertion point on the page on which the first page number should be located.

    For example, place the insertion point to the left of the first character in the first paragraph on the second logical page.

2. Select **Layout, Page, Page Numbering** {Alt and L, p, n}.

3. To set a new starting page number, select **Page Number, New Number**, type the beginning page number, and select **OK** {n, n, type beginning page number, press Enter twice}.

   For example, type **1** and select **OK**.

4. Select **Page Number Position** and choose the desired position {p}.

   For example, select **Bottom Center** {c}.

5. Select **OK** three times.

Finish-Up Instructions

❖   If desired, scroll down to view the page numbers.

❖   Use the new filename **20drill1.fin** and save the file.

Print the Booklet

When a document has been created using the Subdivide Page feature, Word-Perfect can print the document in a booklet format. When the **Print as Booklet** option is selected, WordPerfect automatically arranges the pages in the correct order. For example, the first and last page of the booklet are printed on one piece of paper. If your printer supports duplex printing (both sides of the paper are printed at the same time), the **Double-sided Printing** option is chosen and the entire booklet is printed in one pass. Since most printers do not support duplex printing, only half of the logical pages will print. These pages are then reinserted into the printer and the other half of the pages are printed. When the second half of the pages have been printed, the pages can be folded in the middle to form a booklet.

Start-Up Instructions

❖   The file named **20drill1.fin** should be displayed on the screen.

Print the Booklet

1. Select the **Print** button {Shift and F7}.

2. Select **Multiple Pages** {m}.

3. Select **Print as Booklet** {b}.

4. Select **OK** {Enter}.

5. Select **Print** {Enter}.

   Note: As the first page prints, a beep may be heard from the printer and the message displays on the screen, "Press Shift+F7, 6 to resume printing."

6. When the first page(s) has been printed, place the printed page back into the paper tray.

   Note: Check with your instructor or aide for instructions on reloading the printed pages into your printer.

7. Press **Shift** and **F7**, **6**, and **g** to print the remainder of the booklet.

The Next Step

Chapter Review and Activities

FEATURES SUMMARY

FEATURES	ACTIONS	PAGE
Subdivide pages	Select **Layout, Page, Subdivide Pages**. Type the number of columns and/or rows that will be on one physical page. Select **OK**.	532
Create a watermark	Place the insertion point on the first page to contain the watermark. Select **Layout, Header/Footer/Watermark,** select **Watermark A, Create**. Place the desired text or graphic image in the watermark window. Press **F7** to exit the watermark window and return to the document.	534
Change the contrast between light and dark areas of a graphic image	In the Create/Edit Graphic Box dialog box, select **Edit Image**. Select **Contrast**, type the amount of contrast and press **Enter**. Select **Close, OK**.	535
Print booklet pages	Select the **Print** button. Choose **Multiple Pages, Print as Booklet, OK, Print**. When the first page(s) has been printed, place the printed page(s) back into the paper tray. Press **Shift** and **F7, 6, g** to print the remainder of the booklet.	536

True or False—Circle One

T F 1. A physical page can only be subdivided into two logical pages.

T F 2. Logical pages can be viewed side by side on the screen by selecting the page mode view and choosing **50%** zoom view.

T F 3. A watermark is a light gray when printed.

T F 4. Only a graphic image can be used as a watermark.

T F 5. In a document with subdivided pages, each logical page is treated as a separate page of the document.

T F 6. Page numbers cannot be printed on subdivided pages.

Short Answer

1. In two sentences, state the difference between the physical page and logical page(s).

2. In a document with subdivided pages, the piece of paper is referred to as the ____________ page.

3. List the seven steps to print a document with subdivided pages as a booklet.

4. Since a watermark graphic image or text prints in a light gray, why may it be necessary to lighten a watermark graphic image?

Enriching Language Arts Skills

Spelling/Voculary Words

coaching   providing instruction and direction.

evaluation   the appraisal of a person or thing; formal review of a person's job performance.

feedback   response to a question or request for information or input; e.g., information on the progress of meeting company goals.

Colons, Capitalization, and Punctuation for Bulleted and Enumerated Lists

Place a colon after an independent clause that introduces a bulleted or enumerated (numbered) list. An introductory clause frequently includes words such as "the following" and "as follows." When creating a bulleted or enumerated list, capitalize the first word and insert a final punctuation mark (period, question mark, or exclamation mark) after each item that is a complete sentence or phrase. Do not capitalize the first word or insert final punctuation when bulleted or enumerated items are not complete thoughts.

Example:

The following qualifications are suggested for an air conditioning mechanic applicant:

1. *high school or equivalent, plus three years' experience*

2. *hold a valid driver's license*

3. *successful compliance with job-related medical standards*

4. *proof of U.S. citizenship*

Activities

■ Activity 20.1—Create a Booklet

1. Open the file named **20act1.txt** from the data disk.

2. Subdivide the physical page into two logical pages using the following information:

   a. Select **Layout, Page.**

   b. Select **Subdivide Page**, type **2** in the Number of Columns box. Select **OK.**

   c. Select **Paper Size/Type** and double-click on **Letter (Landscape).**

   d. Select **Center Pages** to vertically center the text on all pages of the booklet.

   e. Select **OK.**

3. Use the following information to create a graphic box containing the graphic image named **ecologo.wpg.**

   a. Select **Graphics, Graphics Boxes, Create.**

   b. Select **Filename, F5, OK.**

   c. Double-click on **ecologo.wpg.**

   d. Select **Attach To, Page.**

   e. Select **Edit Position, Horizontal Position, Centered, OK.**

   f. Select **OK.**

4. Change the initial font to **Dutch 801 Roman** (select **Layout**, **Document**, **Initial Font**, **Font**, double-click on **Dutch 801 Roman**, select **OK** twice).

5. Create a watermark for the second and following pages using the **ecologo.wpg** graphic image.

   a. Move the insertion point to the left of the first character on the second page of the booklet.

   b. Select **Layout, Header/Footer/Watermark, Watermark A, Create**.

   c. Select **Graphics, Graphics Boxes, Create**.

   d. Select **Filename**.

   e. Select **Existing Images**.

   f. Double-click on **ecologo.wpg**.

   g. Select **Image Editor**.

   h. Select **Contrast** and type **.75**. Select **Close**.

   i. Select **OK** to return to the watermark window.

   j. Press **F7**.

6. Use the following information and place page numbers on the booklet pages.

   a. With the insertion point located on page 2 of the booklet, select **Layout, Page, Page Numbering, Page Number**.

   b. Select **New Number** and type **1**. Select **OK**.

   c. Select **Page Number Position** and choose **Bottom Center**.

   d. Select **OK** three times.

7. Print the document as a booklet (select the **Print** button, choose **Multiple Pages, Print as Booklet, OK, Print**).

   *Remember: After the first physical page of the booklet prints, reinsert the paper into the printer, press **Shift** and **F7**, **6**, and **g** to print the remaining booklet text.*

■ Activity 20.2—Create a Booklet

1. Open the file named **20act2.txt** from the data disk.

2. Subdivide the physical page into two logical pages using the following information:

   a. Select **Layout, Page**.

   b. Select **Subdivide Page** and type **2** in the Number of Columns box. Select **OK**.

   c. Select **Paper Size/Type** and double-click on **Letter (Landscape)**.

   d. Select **Center Pages** to vertically center the text on all pages of the booklet.

e. Select **OK**.

3. Use the following information to create a graphic box containing the graphic image named **hotrod.wpg**:

   a. Select **Graphics, Graphics Boxes, Create**.

   b. Select **Filename, F5, OK**.

   c. Double-click on **hotrod.wpg**.

   d. Select **Attach To, Page**.

   e. Select **Edit Position, Horizontal Position, Centered, OK**.

   f. Select **OK**.

4. Change the initial font to **Dutch 801 Roman** (select **Layout, Document, Initial Font, Font**, double-click on **Dutch 801 Roman**, select **OK** twice).

5. Create a watermark for the second and following pages using the **hotrod.wpg** graphic image.

   a. Move the insertion point to the left of the first character on the second page of the booklet.

   b. Select **Layout, Header/Footer/Watermark, Watermark A, Create**.

   c. Select **Graphics, Graphics Boxes, Create**.

   d. Select **Filename**.

   e. Select **Existing Images**.

   f. Double-click on **hotrod.wpg**.

   g. Select **Image Editor**.

   h. Select **Contrast** and type .75. Select **Close**.

   i. Select **OK** to return to the watermark window.

   j. Press **F7**.

6. Use the following information to place page numbers on the booklet pages:

   a. With the insertion point located on page 2 of the booklet, select **Layout, Page, Page Numbering, Page Number**.

   b. Select **New Number** and type 1. Select **OK**.

   c. Select **Page Number Position** and choose **Bottom Center**.

   d. Select **OK** three times.

7. Print the document as a booklet (select the **Print** button, choose **Multiple Pages, Print as Booklet, OK, Print**).

   *Remember: After the first physical page of the booklet prints, reinsert the paper into the printer, press **Shift** and F7, 6, and g to print the remaining booklet text.*

Challenge Your Skills

Skill 20.1—Create a Booklet

1. Create a booklet using the following information:

    a. The booklet text is contained in a file named **20skill1.txt** located on the data disk.

    b. Make decisions regarding:

    Initial font for the booklet
    Bold and alignment for the booklet title and headings
    Use and placement of appropriate graphic image(s)
    Use of watermark
    Page numbers for the booklet
    Conversion of dashes (--) to the correct typography em dash (—)
    Correct three spelling, errors, one misused word, and three
      punctuation errors

2. Save the file as **20skill1.fin**.

3. Print one copy of the document as a booklet.

Production Skill Builder Activities
Chapters 18-20

■ Production Activity 6.1—Create a Tri-Fold Brochure

1. Create a tri-fold brochure using the following information:

   a. The brochure describes the features of the Umpqua Lighthouse and Conference Center. A table graphic box should be placed in each column of page 1. Decide on a color for the border lines of the table boxes.

   b. The column text is contained in the following files that are located on the data disk:

Column 1	6pact1.co1
Column 2	6pact1.co2
Column 3	6pact1.co3
Column 1, page 2	6pact1.co4

   c. Make decisions regarding:

      Margins
      Font and point size for text
      Use of shadow boxes
      Use of rounded or square corners for shadow boxes
      Appropriate graphic image(s)
         (Suggested graphic images: lighths.wpg, humbird.wpg, or tree.wpg)
      Graphic boxes for first column on second page
      Rotated text for second column of page 2 (return address)
      Use of graphic image(s), reverse text, and borders for the third column of page 2 (the cover of the brochure)

2. Use the filename **6pact1.bro** and save the file.

3. Print one copy.

4. Close the document

Production Activity 6.2—Magazine Article (Group Project) 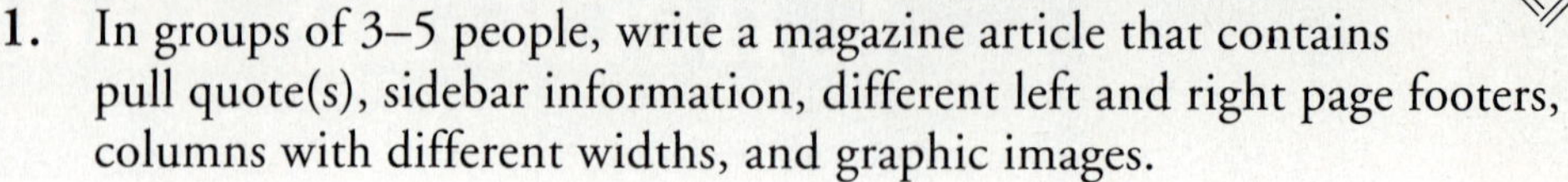

1. In groups of 3–5 people, write a magazine article that contains pull quote(s), sidebar information, different left and right page footers, columns with different widths, and graphic images.

2. Suggested article topics:

   Favorite features in WordPerfect 6.0 DOS
   WordPerfect 6.0 for Windows
   WordPerfect 6.0 vs. Word for Windows 6.0

3. Make decisions regarding:

   Margins
   Initial font for document
   Font and point size for article title
   Use of shadow text attribute
   Column widths
   Pull quote information, format, and placement
   Sidebar information, format, and placement
   Indention for first line of paragraphs
   Footer text

4. Save the final magazine article using the filename **6pact2.fin**.

5. Print one copy and close the document.

◆ ◼ Production Activity 6.3—Create a Booklet; Language Arts

1. Open the file named **6pact3.txt** from the data disk.

2. Make decisions regarding:

   Subdivided pages to create a booklet
   Paper size and type
   Page numbering
   Initial font for the document
   Font and point size for booklet title
   Graphic image for cover of booklet and watermark
   Use of correct typographical symbols for quotation marks and em dashes
   Text to appear on each page
   Correct four spelling errors, one misused word, three punctuation errors, and one missing parenthesis

3. Use the new file named **6pact3.fin** and save the file.

4. Print one copy as a booklet and close the document.

Part 7
A Final Step

Advanced Techniques

Chapters 21-26

- Split cells
- Formulas using spreadsheet-like functions
- Decimal alignment position
- Vertical alignment in a table cell
- Ignore cells when calculating
- Lock cells
- Header rows
- IFBLANK...ELSE...ENDIF merge command
- Select records when merging
- Form files that contain graphic images
- Import data into a text format data file
- Request user input in a merged letter
- Line numbering
- Strikeout, redline, and Compare Documents

- Comments and hidden text
- Bookmarks and hypertext
- Outlines
- Table of contents and index
- Create styles containing paragraph borders and graphic images
- Create styles based on existing styles
- Link styles
- Cross references
- Create, expand, condense, and save master documents
- Edit and correct (debug) macros
- Request user input in a macro
- Variables
- IF-ELSE statements in macros
- Glossary abbreviations

Advanced Tables

Features Covered

- Split cells
- Create a formula using a spreadsheet-like function
- Display negative numbers
- Set decimal alignment position
- Set vertical alignment in a table cell
- Ignore cells when calculating
- Lock cells
- Place a graphic image in a table
- Import a spreadsheet
- Create a header row
- Create a spreadsheet link

Objectives

After successfully completing this chapter, you will be able to create a form using the Tables feature. While creating the table form, you will learn to split cells, create a formula, display negative numbers between parentheses, and set the decimal alignment position from the right of the cell. In addition, you will learn to ignore cells when calculating, lock cells, and how to place a graphic image in a table using a Table box. You will also learn to import a spreadsheet and how to create a header row for a multiple-page table.

In addition to the basic table features that are discussed in Chapters 6 and 7, other functions are available to format and to display table numbers in cells. Also, a table can be enhanced by using any of the available WordPerfect graphics.

Create a Form Using the Tables Feature

Many business forms, such as expense reports and invoices, can be easily created using the Tables feature. Table cells can be split (horizontally and/or vertically), numbers in cells can be positioned and displayed in many different ways, and formulas can be used for calculating.

A single table cell can be split into columns or rows. Usually, a cell is split into two columns or rows but can be split in up to 60 columns/rows if space is available.

Formulas are created in a cell in which the result of a calculation is desired. The formulas created in WordPerfect include symbols that indicate various math functions. The math symbols used in formulas are as follows:

+ addition	- subtraction or negative number
* multiplication	/ division

When a column of numbers is added, a built-in, spreadsheet-like formula (called a function) is used as a shortcut to avoid typing each cell address of all cells to be added. For example, if cells B1 through B8 are to be added, the following built-in formula is typed: Sum(B1:B8). The cells shown in between the parentheses will be added and the result placed in the cell where the formula is located. The colon is used to indicate a block of cells, the word "Sum" is used to signify addition, and the parentheses are used to set apart the cell addresses from the word "Sum."

When a formula is used and the numbers in the cells are calculated, all cell numbers are included in the calculation. Sometimes numbers represent information that should not be included in a column/row calculation. For example, if the date 5/26/94 was placed in a cell in which the column is to be calculated, the date should not be included in the total amount. By using the **Ignore When Calculating** option in the Cell Format dialog box, cell information can be disregarded when calculated.

A minus sign (hyphen) is typed to indicate a negative number. The **Number Type** option in the Cell Format dialog box can be selected to obtain the Number Type Formats. Select the parentheses or the abbreviation CR/DR (credit or debit) option to indicate a negative number. If a number is aligned at the decimal point and the parentheses are used to display a negative number, the right parenthesis will wrap around to the next line. The **Decimal Align Position** option in the Column Format dialog box is used to set the amount of space (distance) between the decimal and the right side of the cell. The default is 0.1 inch and could be changed to 0.35 inch to allow ample space for two decimal places and the right parenthesis.

If the row height is increased, the cell text or numbers is defaulted to display at the top of the cell. Using the **Vertical Alignment** option in the Cell Format dialog box, the text numbers can be changed to display at the bottom or center of the cell.

Since a form will be used repeatedly, the information that remains constant in a table cell should be protected so that the cell contents will not accidentally be altered. Cells can be locked by selecting the **Lock** option in the Cell Format dialog box. The cursor/insertion point cannot be placed in a locked cell in the document window. Locked cells can be formatted, however, in the Table Edit window.

A table form can be enhanced by placing a graphic image in a table cell. A graphic can be inserted in any one of the graphic boxes. When placing a graphic image in a table, the User box style is often selected, because the User box style has no prede-fined borders.

Start-Up Instructions

- ❖   ■ Open the file named **21expens.uf1** from the data disk.
- ❖ Display the Tables Button Bar (select **View**, **Button Bar Setup**, **Select**, and double-click on **TABLES**).
- ❖ Select the **Tbl Edit** button to display the Table Edit window.

Split a Cell

1. Place the cursor in the cell to be split.

   For example, place the cursor in cell A9.

2. Select the **Split** option {s}.

   Note: The Split Cell dialog box displays.

3. Select the **Columns** or **Rows** option.

   For example, check that **Columns** is selected {c}.

4. In the "How many?" option box, type the number of times to split the cell.

   For example, check that **2** displays beside the "How many?" option.

5. Select **OK** {Enter}.

Finish-Up Instructions

- ❖ Repeat Steps 1–5 and split cell A9 into 2 rows.
- ❖ Select **Close** to exit the Table Edit window.
- ❖ Type **.29** (the payment rate for mileage) in cell B9.
- ❖ Use the same filename **21expens.uf1** and save the file.

- ❖ The file named **21expens.uf1** should be displayed on the screen.
- ❖ Select the **Tbl Edit** button to display the Table Edit window.

Create a Formula Using a Function

1. Locate the cursor in the cell in which the results of the formula are to be placed.

   For example, locate the cursor in cell C9.

2. Select **Formula** {f}.

   Note: The Table Formula dialog box displays.

3. Type the desired formula.

   For example, to multiply the number of miles by the mileage rate (.29), type **A10*B9**. (Do not type the period.)

4. Select **OK** {Enter twice}.

   *Note: The result of the multiplication formula zero (0) displays in cell C9 and the formula =A10*B9 displays in the Status bar.*

Finish-Up Instructions

- ❖ Repeat Steps 1–4 and type the formulas into the designated cells as follows:

Cell D11	sum(C5:C9)
Cell D16	sum(C12:C15)
Cell D17	sum(D3:D16)
Cell D19	D17+D18

  Note: The amount in cell C18 will be subtracted from the amount in cell C17 because the amount in C18 will be typed as a negative (minus) number.

- ❖ Continue with the Steps to Display Negative Number(s) Between Parentheses.

Start-Up Instructions

- ❖ The file named **21expens.uf1** should be displayed on the screen. The Table Edit window should also be displayed.

Display Negative Number(s) Between Parentheses

1. Place the cursor in the cell or block the cells in which a negative number(s) is to display between parentheses.

   For example, place the cursor in cell D18.

2. Select **Cell** {c}.

3. Select **Number Type** {t}.

4. Select **Parentheses** in the Negative Numbers box area {o, p}.

5. Select **OK** twice {press Enter twice}.

   Note: *No change displays on the screen at this time. The parentheses display only when a negative number is typed in the cell.*

Finish-Up Instructions

❖ Continue with the Steps to Set Decimal Alignment Position (From Right of Cell).

Start-Up Instructions

❖ The file named **21expens.uf1** should be displayed on the screen. The Table Edit window should also be displayed.

Set Decimal Alignment Position (From Right of Cell)

1. Place the cursor in any cell in the column in which the alignment position will be set.

   For example, place the cursor in any cell in column D.

2. Select **Column** {o}.

3. Select the **Distance** option in the Decimal Align Position (From Right of Cell) area and type the desired amount of space.

   For example, type **.35**. (Do not type the final period.)

4. Select **OK** {Enter}.

Finish-Up Instructions

❖ Continue with the Steps to Set the Vertical Alignment in a Table Cell.

Start-Up Instructions

❖ The file named **21expens.uf1** should be displayed on the screen. The Table Edit window should also be displayed.

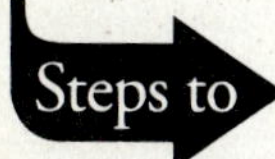

Set the Vertical Alignment in a Table Cell

1. Locate the cursor in the desired cell(s).

   For example, block all cells in row 2.

2. Select **Cell** {c}.

3. Select the desired Vertical Alignment option {v, b}.

   For example, select **Bottom** vertical alignment.

4. Select **OK** {Enter}.

Note: On some monitors, the cell contents will not display on the screen with the vertical alignment chosen. If desired, use Print Preview or print a copy of the table to see the vertical alignment selected.

Finish-Up Instructions

❖ Repeat Steps 1–4 in Steps to Set the Vertical Alignment in a Table Cell and set the vertical alignment to **Bottom** for cells B9 and C9.

❖ Continue with the Steps to Ignore Cells When Calculating.

Start-Up Instructions

❖ The file named **21expens.uf1** should be displayed on the screen. The Table Edit window should also be displayed.

 **Ignore Cells When Calculating**

1. Place the cursor in the cell or block the cells to be ignored when calculating.

   For example, place the cursor in cell D2.

2. Select **Cell** {c}.

3. Select the **Ignore When Calculating** option {i}.

4. Select **OK** {Enter}.

   Note: A quotation mark is placed in front of the cell address in the Status bar, e.g., "D2.

Finish-Up Instructions

❖ Continue with the Steps to Lock Cells.

Start-Up Instructions

❖ The file named **21expens.uf1** should be displayed on the screen. The Table Edit window should also be displayed.

 **Lock Cells**

1. Place the cursor in the cell or block the cells to be locked.

   For example, block the cells A2 through C2.

2. Select **Cell** {c}.

3. Select the **Lock** option {L}.

4. Select **OK** {Enter}.

   Note: Brackets are placed around the cell address in the Status bar, e.g., [A2].

❖ Repeat Steps 1–4 and lock the following cells:

    A3–A8   A9–B9   A11–A15

❖ Select **Close** to exit the Table Edit window.

❖ Use the new filename **21expens.uf2** and save the file.

Start-Up Instructions

❖ The file named **21expens.uf2** should be displayed on the screen.

Place a Graphic Image in a Table Using a User Box

1. In the document window, place the cursor/insertion point at the location where the graphic image is to be placed.

   For example, place the insertion point to the left of the "W" in the word Windmill in cell A1.

2. Select **Graphics, Graphics Boxes, Create** {Alt and F9, b, c}.

3. Select **Based on Box Style** {y}.

4. Double-click on the desired box style {highlight desired box style and press Enter}.

   For example, double-click on **User Box**.

5. Select **Filename** {f}.

6. Select **File List** {F5}.

7. Select **OK** {press Enter} to accept the directory C:\WP60\GRAPHICS*.*.

   Note: If your graphic images are located in a different directory, type the directory name.

8. Double-click on desired filename {highlight filename and press Enter}.

   For example, double-click on **WINDMILL.WPG**.

9. Select **Edit Size** {s}.

10. Select **Set Width** and type the desired amount {w, type desired amount, and press Enter}.

    For example, type **1.5**. (Do not type the final period.)

11. Select **Automatic Height, Based on Box Content Height** {u, Enter}.

12. Select **OK** {Enter}.

13. Select **Text Flows** option {t, f}.

14. Select **Through Box** {t}.

15. Select **OK** {Enter}.

Finish-Up Instructions

- ❖ If desired, change to the text mode so that the graphics image will not redraw to the screen after performing each of the following instructions:

- ❖ In the Table Edit window, block cells C3-D19 and set the cells for commas number type with 2 digits after the decimal; select **Decimal Align**.

- ❖ Place the cursor in cell A20 and change the row height to Fixed at **.6**.

- ❖ Join cells A11-C11.

- ❖ Join cells A16-C16.

- ❖ Join cells A17 and C17.

- ❖ Join cells A19-C19.

- ❖ Join the cells in row 21.

- ❖ Format cell D19 for currency number type.

- ❖ Block the cells in row 2 and change the fill to Button Fill Style and the bottom line style to Double (select **Lines/Fill**, **Fill**, **Fill Style**, scroll down the Fill Styles list, double-click on **Button Fill**, select **OK**, select **Bottom** and double-click on **Double Lines**, select **OK**, **Close**).

- ❖ Block cells D3–D19 and use 10% Shaded Fill (select **Lines/Fill**, **Fill**, **Fill Style**, scroll down the Fill Styles list, double-click on **10% Shaded Fill**, select **OK**, **Close**).

- ❖ Lock the following cells:

      A1   A16–A18   A19–A21

- ❖ Select **Close** to exit the Table Edit window.

- ❖ Use the new filename **21expens.for** and save the file.

- ❖ Type the following figures into the table cells:

      Cell D2 (Week Ending:)   9/24/9x
      Cell D3 (Lodging)   536.82
      Cell D4 (Meals)   138.93
      Cell C5 (Ground Transportation)   39
      Cell C6 (Car Rental)   157
      Cell C7 (Air Fare)   795.32
      Cell C8 (Parking)   39.87
      Cell A10 (Mileage)   565
      Cell C12 (Miscellaneous)   15.60
      Cell C13 (Shipping/Postage)   22
      Cell C14 (Telephone)   14.68
      Cell C15 (Copying/Faxing)   28.99
      Cell D19 (Advance Received)   -1800

- ❖ Select the **Tbl Calc** button on the Tables Button Bar.

- ❖ Use the new filename **21expens.924** and save the file.

- ❖ Print one copy.

❖   Close the document.

Import a Spreadsheet

spreadsheet file can be opened, retrieved, or imported easily into a WordPerfect document window. WordPerfect can open/import spreadsheet files from the following programs:

PlanPerfect (Versions 3.0 to 5.1)
Lotus 1-2-3 (versions 1A, 2.01, 2.3, 2.4, 3.0, and 3.1)
Excel (versions 2.1, 3.0, 4.0)
Quattro Pro (versions 3.0 and 4.0)
Quattro Pro for Windows (version 1)
Spreadsheet DIF

When a spreadsheet file is imported, *all* or *part* of the file information is copied into a WordPerfect document window. If a portion of a spreadsheet file is imported, a range (block of cells) can be typed to indicate the exact rows and columns to be copied. **Tools**, **Spreadsheet**, **Import** is used to import a spreadsheet file.

When a spreadsheet file is opened or retrieved *all* of the file information is copied into the document window. If the entire spreadsheet file is to be copied into an existing document, place the cursor/insertion point at the desired location and use either **File**, **Retrieve** or **Tools**, **Spreadsheet**, **Import**. If the entire spreadsheet file is to be copied into a new document window, use **File**, **Open**.

The spreadsheet can be imported as a table or as text. If the spreadsheet is imported as a table, WordPerfect copies the spreadsheet information (up to 64 columns) into a WordPerfect table. The formulas and spreadsheet format are converted to WordPerfect math functions and format; however, checking for accuracy is always recommended. If the spreadsheet is imported as text, WordPerfect copies the information into columns separated by tabs. No formulas are imported when the text option is selected.

When a spreadsheet file is opened or retrieved, the File Format dialog box displays. WordPerfect suggests the name of the spreadsheet file format being opened by highlighting the name. In the File Format dialog box, a message displays indicating that the file is not a WordPerfect 6.0 document and to select the correct file format. After the file format is confirmed or chosen, the entire file displays in a table format.

Once a file is imported, additional formatting may be desired. For example, the column widths may need to be increased or decreased and cells may need to be joined. Also, the number type can be changed to display a dollar sign, commas, etc., in column amounts.

❖ 💾 Open the file named **21ltr** from the data disk.

❖ Place the cursor/insertion point in the blank space between the two paragraphs.

❖ The Tables Button Bar should be displayed.

Steps to ▶ **Import a Spreadsheet**

1. Select **Tools, Spreadsheet** {Alt and F7, s}.

2. Select **Import** {i}.

3. Select **File List** {F5}.

4. Type the location where your spreadsheet file is located.

   For example, type the disk drive letter where the data disk is located (a: or b:).

5. Select **OK** {Enter}.

6. Double-click on the desired filename {highlight the filename and press Enter}.

   For example, double-click on the file named **21dril2f.xls**.

   Note: The Import Spreadsheet dialog box displays indicating the Range A1:E44. Check that the Import as Table option is selected under "Type."

7. Select **Import** {i}.

   Note: The "Please Wait" and "Importing Spreadsheet" messages display and in a few moments the imported spreadsheet displays in a WordPerfect Table format.

Finish-Up Instructions

❖ Locate the cursor/insertion point at the beginning of the document and change the left and right margins to .5 inch each.

❖ Place the cursor/insertion point in column 1 and select the **TColNarr** button approximately seven times. Scroll over to the last table column and check that the complete words and numbers display.

❖ Use the new filename **21drill2.ss** and save the file.

❖ Print one copy.

❖ Continue with the Steps to Create a Header Row(s).

Create a Header Row(s) for a Multiple-Page Spreadsheet

The second and following pages of a multiple-page spreadsheet should contain header information that identifies the spreadsheet and/or column titles. A row or consecutive rows from the first page of a multiple-page spreadsheet can be designated as a header row(s). A header row(s) prints as the top row(s) of the second and following pages of a multiple-page spreadsheet.

The **Header Row** option is selected from the Row option in the Table Edit window. An asterisk is placed to the right of the cell address in the Status bar to indicate that the cell is part of a row that will print as a header row.

Any row or consecutive rows can be selected as a header row(s). If more than one row is selected, however, the multiple rows must be consecutive.

Start-Up Instructions

❖   The file named **21drill2.ss** should be displayed on the screen.

Steps to Create a Header Row(s)

1. Select the **Tbl Edit** button {Alt and L, t, e}.
2. Block the row(s) to be used as a header row(s).

    For example, block rows 1–3.
3. Select **Row** {r}.
4. Select **Header Row** {h}.
5. Select **OK** {Enter}.

    Note: In the Status bar an asterisk displays to the right of the cell address.

Finish-Up Instructions

❖   Use the new filename **21ltr.ss** and save the file.

❖   Print one copy and close the document.

Create a Spreadsheet Link

A spreadsheet file can be imported and linked simultaneously. When a spreadsheet is linked, the copied spreadsheet information in the Wordperfect document is updated to reflect any changes that were made to the original spreadsheet file.

A link is created by selecting the **Spreadsheet** option from the **Tools** menu and choosing **Create a Link**. The filename of the spreadsheet to be imported and linked can be selected in the File List or typed in the Filename option box. When typing the filename, include the location of the file and the filename extension. For example, if the spreadsheet file is located on the disk in drive B, type b:\budget.xls. If only a portion of the spreadsheet is to be linked and imported, type the range of cells in the **Range** option box. The **Link & Import** option is selected to create a link and import the spreadsheet.

Comment codes display at the beginning and end of the imported/linked spreadsheet. The beginning comment code contains the location and name of the imported/linked spreadsheet, for example, [Link B:\budget.xls, A1:d40]. The ending comment code contains the message [End Code]. Comment codes do not print and can be hidden on the screen. To hide the comment codes, select **Spreadsheet** from the **Tools** menu, choose **Link Options**, and deselect **Show Link Codes**.

A linked spreadsheet can be updated automatically upon document retrieval or can be updated manually. To automatically update a linked spreadsheet, select **Tools, Spreadsheet, Link Options**. When the Spreadsheet Link Options dialog box displays, select **Update on Retrieve** and choose **OK**. To manually update a linked spreadsheet file, select the **Update All Links** option in the Spreadsheet Link Options dialog box.

The Next Step

Chapter Review and Activities

FEATURES SUMMARY

FEATURES	ACTIONS	PAGE
Split a cell	In the Table Edit window, locate the cursor in the desired cell, select **Split**, choose the **Columns** or **Rows** option, type the number of times to split the cell, and select **OK**.	551
Create a formula using a function	In the Table Edit window, place the cursor in the cell in which the results are to be located, type the desired formula, and select **OK**.	552
Display negative numbers between parentheses	In the Table Edit window, place the cursor in the cell (or block cells) in which a negative number is to display in parentheses. Select **Cell**, **Number Type**. Select **Parentheses**. Select **OK** twice.	552
Set decimal align position (from right of cell)	In the Table Edit window, place the cursor in any column cell, select **Column**, **Distance**, type the desired amount of space, and select **OK**.	553
Set the vertical alignment in a table cell	In the Table Edit window, place the cursor in the desired cell (or block cells), select **Cell**, select the desired Vertical Alignment option, and select **OK**.	553
Ignore cells when calculating	In the Table Edit window, place the cursor in the cell (or block cells), select **Cell**, **Ignore When Calculating**, and select **OK**.	554

FEATURES *(cont'd.)*	ACTIONS *(cont'd.)*	PAGE
Lock cells	In the Table Edit window, place the cursor in the cell (or block cells), select **Cell**, **Lock**, and choose **OK**.	554
Place a graphic image in a table	In the document window, place the cursor/insertion point at the location where the graphic image is to be placed, select **Graphics**, **Graphics Boxes**, **Create**. Select **Based on Box Style** and double-click on the desired box style. Select **Filename**, select **File List**, **OK**. Double-click on the desired filename. Select **Edit Size**, **Set Width**, and type the desired width for the graphic box. Select **Automatic Height, Based on Box Content Height**. Select **OK**. Select **Text Flows**, **Through Box**. Select **OK**.	555
Import a spreadsheet	Select **Tools**, **Spreadsheet**, **Import**. Select **File List**, type the location of the spreadsheet file and select **OK**. Double-click on the desired filename and select **Import**.	558
Create a header row(s)	Select the Table Edit button, block the row(s) to be used as a header row(s), select **Row**, **Header Row**, **OK**.	559

Self-Check Questions

True/False—Circle One

T F 1. If a cell is split into two columns, a formula cannot be used in either cell.

T F 2. The asterisk in the cell formula D8*E8 indicates multiplication.

T F 3. When typing a negative number into a table cell, first type a minus sign by pressing the hyphen key.

T F 4. When the row height is increased, text or numbers can be positioned at the top, center, or bottom of the cell.

T F 5. A locked cell can be formatted in either the document window or the Table Edit window.

Short Answer

1. List the three options available to display a negative number in a table cell.

2. List the four steps to set the decimal alignment position from the right of the cell.

3. Give two reasons for using the Ignore When Calculating option.

4. In three sentences or less, state the differences between importing a spreadsheet file and linking a spreadsheet file.

Enriching Language Arts

Spelling/Vocabulary Words

quarter   one of four parts into which something is divided; one-quarter of a year is three months, or $\frac{1}{4}$ of 12 months.

UPC   Universal Product Code; a series of black lines of different widths used on packages to mark prices for electronic checkout.

versus   as compared to; against. Common abbreviations are *v.* and *vs.*

Abbreviations in Table Column Headings

When creating tables and forms, abbreviations are often used in subtitles and/or column headings because of limited space. However, abbreviations should be used sparingly. If you are unsure of how to abbreviate a word, consult a dictionary.

Common abbreviations:

account	*acct.*	*department*	*dept.*
amount	*amt.*	*incorporated*	*inc.*
attention	*attn.*	*ounce*	*oz.*
dozen	*dz. or doz.*	*received*	*recd.*

Activities

Activity 21.1—Create and Format a Form Using the Tables Feature, Create Formulas

1. Using the Tables feature create a form similar to the form on page 564. Use your choice of fonts and font sizes.

2. Use the following information to format and place formulas in the form:

   a. Set the vertical alignment to bottom for the column heading rows.

   b. Right align cells in the columns below the Quantity and Stock No. column headings.

c. Set the number type to commas and two digits after decimal and use decimal alignment for the cells in the columns below the Unit Price and Total Price column headings.

d. In the bottom right cell, set the number type for currency and two digits after the decimal.

e. Create a formula in the first cell of the Total Price column to multiply the Quantity times the Unit Price (A6*D6). Copy the formula to the next two rows.

f. In the cell at the intersection of the Subtotal row and the Total Price column, create a formula to add the top three cells of the Total Price column, e.g., sum(E6:E8).

g. In the cell at the intersection of the Sales Tax row and the Total Price column, create a formula to multiply the subtotal times the sales tax. e.g., E10*.0825. (Do not type the final period.)

h. In the cell at the intersection of the Total row and the Total Price column, type a formula to add the subtotal and sales tax, e.g., E10+E11.

Purchase Order					P.O. No.:	Date:
ABC Discount Supply						
2018 Winter St.					Deliver To:	
Binghamton, NY 13909						
To:					Delivery Date:	
					Ship By:	
Quantity	**Stock No.**		**Description**		**Unit Price**	**Total Price**
						0.00
						0.00
						0.00
			Subtotal			0.00
			Sales Tax (8.25%)			0.00
			Total			$0.00

3. Use the filename **21act1.frm** and save the file.

4. Optional. Print one copy of the form.

1. Open the file named **21act1.frm** created in Activity 21.1.

2. Type the following information into the appropriate cells.

To:	Longman Construction Co.
	9822 Keystone Blvd.
	Pittsburgh, PA 15227
P.O. No.:	14022
Date:	Use current date (mm/dd/yy).
Deliver To:	Shane
Delivery Date:	Use a date one week from the current date.
Ship By:	UPS

Quantity	Stock No.	Description	Unit Price	Total Price
15	3455	Porcelain switches	1.50	
10	4822	Switch boxes	1.20	
50	4801	Switch plates	1.15	

3. Select the **Tbl Calc** button on the Button Bar to compute and display the results of the formulas in the form.

4. Use the new filename **21act2** and save the file.

5. Print one copy.

Challenge Your Skills

⊶ ▣ Skill 21.1—Import a Spreadsheet File and Edit the Spreadsheet; Language Arts

1. Open the file named **21skill1.mem** from the data disk.

2. Locate the cursor/insertion point on the second blank line below the first paragraph.

3. Import the Excel spreadsheet file named **21bando.xls**.

4. In the memo and spreadsheet, correct two spelling errors and one punctuation error.

5. Make the following changes to the table:

   a. Join all cells in rows 1 and 2; center the text in rows 1 and 2.

   b. In rows 1 and 5, use 10% shading.

   c. Set row 5 for a header row.

d. Use right alignment for the cells in columns A and E. Use decimal alignment for the cells containing amounts in columms D and H.

6. Insert page numbers at the bottom center.

7. Use the new filename **21skill1** and save the file.

8. Print one copy.

9. If you have completed your work in WordPerfect, exit the program.

Advanced Merging

Features Covered

- Use IFBLANK, ELSE, and ENDIF merge commands
- Merge a range of records
- Merge records based on conditions
- Form files with graphic images
- Output merged letters to a file or printer
- Import data
- User input in a merged letter

Objectives

After successfully completing this chapter, you will be able to use IFBLANK, ELSE, and ENDIF merge commands when merging a form and data file, and print selected records by using a range of records or by setting merge conditions. Also, you will learn to indicate the location of graphic images, to output merged letters to a file or printer, and to import data into a data text file. In addition, you will learn to place a KEYBOARD command in a form letter to allow user input as letters are merged.

Chapter Introduction

The basic structure of WordPerfect's merge program, which combines form files and data files to produce individualized letters and mailing labels, was introduced in Chapters 12 and 13. However, the merge program has options and commands that can make merged documents look more professional, make the merge operation more flexible and efficient, and allow WordPerfect to use data from mainframe or database programs.

FIELD(title) FIELD(firstname) FIELD(lastname)
FIELD(company)
FIELD(address)
FIELD(city), FIELD(state/province) FIELD(zipcode)
FIELD(country)

Dear FIELD(title) FIELD(lastname):

George Santana

2544 Morris Road
London,
England

Dear   Santana:

Improve the Appearance of Merged Documents

Many times data files will contain fields that are empty in some records. For example, Alan's Ads is a company that sends advertising for various clients to an international market. Their prospects' database contains the following fields: title, firstname, lastname, company, street address, city, state/province, country, zipcode, requestdate.

However, Alan soon finds out that some people omit checking the title box on their information form, some companies fill out the form without including a person's name, and some foreign countries do not use the state/province field. If the inside address in the form letter uses all fields, some letters will print with blank spaces as shown in Figure 22.1.

One way of eliminating a blank line was discussed in the example in Chapter 12, page 327. If the potentially blank field is by itself on a line, selecting the option **Remove Blank Lines** during the merge operation will eliminate the blank line when the field is empty. Similarly, a question mark after the field name, i.e., FIELD(company?) will eliminate a blank line. However, these techniques are not applicable to the title field, because the title field leaves blank horizontal spaces, not blank lines, if the title field is empty. Instead, WordPerfect uses merge commands, IFBLANK ...ELSE...ENDIF, to eliminate the blank space when a field is empty.

The IFBLANK command tells the Merge feature that: "If the field is empty (blank), print everything between here and the ELSE command that follows." An ELSE command is included to tell the Merge feature what to do if the field is not empty. The ENDIF command tells the Merge feature that this ends the IF statement. For an example of the IFBLANK, ELSE, and ENDIF merge commands, see Figure 22.3 on page 571. When an IFBLANK command is used, the ELSE and ENDIF commands must also be used to complete the command statement.

Another problem that occurs with large data files is that the computer may not have enough memory to store all the merged letters at one time. This can cause the merge process to stop before it has merged all the letters. Using the range of records method to limit the merge to specific records may be helpful, or it may be more efficient to use the **Output to File** or **Output to Printer** options to avoid an out-of-memory error.

Select a Range of Records

Specifying a range of records is useful in a situation where new records are added at the beginning or end of the data file. Also, selecting records that are grouped in a certain order can be useful, e.g., all records grouped by a specific zip code.

Start-Up Instructions

❖ Begin the merge operation by selecting **Tools**, **Merge**, **Run** {Ctrl and F9, m, r}.

❖ Type the location and name of the form file.

> For example, type **a:\22drill2.frm**.

❖ Click in the data file field, then type the location and name of the data file {Tab, then type the name of the data file}.

> For example, type **a:\22drill2.df**.

❖ If necessary, select **Data File Options** {t}.

 ## Select Range of Records When Merging

1. Check that the Blank Lines in Data File option is set to Remove Resulting Blank Lines.

2. In the Data Record Selection area, select **Specify Record Number Range** {s, r}.

3. In the From box, type the beginning number of the data record to be merged, then press **Enter**.

> For example, type 7 and press **Enter**.

4. In the To box, type the ending number of the data record to be merged, then press **Enter**.

> For example, type **9** and press **Enter**.

Note: Only records 7, 8, and 9 will merge with the form letter.

5. Select **Merge** {press Enter}.

Finish-Up Instructions

❖ Check that only records 7, 8, and 9 merged with the form file.

❖ Optional. Print one copy of the merged letters.

❖ Close all documents. (Do not save the merged letters.)

Select Records Based on Conditions

Another way to select records is to base the selection on a condition that occurs in the data file. For example, you might need to send a letter to everyone who lives in a certain geographical area, e.g., California. If the data file has been set up with the state as a separate field, it is easy to select only those records in which the state is CA.

Start-Up Instructions

❖ To begin the merge operation, select **Tools**, **Merge**, **Run** {Ctrl and F9, m, r}.

❖ Type the location and name of the form file.

> For example, type **a:\22drill3.frm**.

❖ Click in the data file field, then type the location and name of the data file {Tab, then type the name of the data file}.

> For example, type **a:\22drill3.df**.

❖ If necessary, select **Data File Options** {t}.

Select Records Based on Conditions When Merging

1. Check that the Blank Lines in Data File option is set to Remove Resulting Blank Lines.

2. Select **Define Conditions** in the Data Record Selection area {s, c}.

   Note: The Define Conditions for Record Selection dialog box displays.

3. Click on the "1" next to the first row {type 1}.

   Note: The List Field Names dialog box displays.

4. Double-click on the field name on which the condition will be based {press the up or down arrow key to highlight the field name, then press Enter}.

   > For example, double-click on **STATE/PROVINCE**.

   Note: The Define Conditions for Record Selection dialog box will reappear with state/province shown at the top of column 1 and the cursor in the first cell. (Some of the options for entering conditions are shown at the bottom of the dialog box.)

5. Type the conditions to be met.

   > For example, type **CA;NV** in the first box of the first row.

   Note: Any record with CA or NV in the state/province field will be merged.

Chapter 22—Advanced Merging

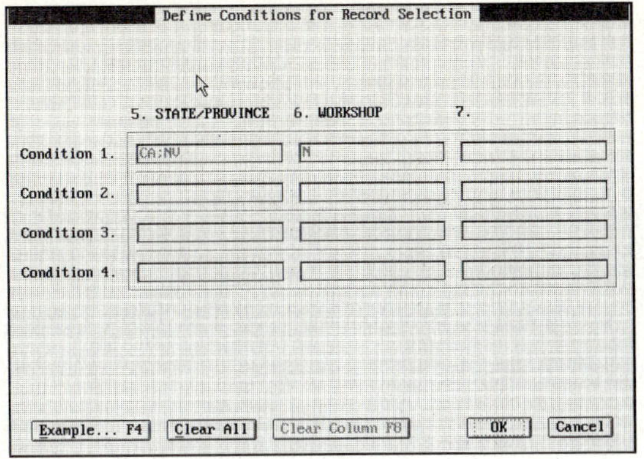

FIGURE 22.4

Define Conditions for
Record Selection dialog box

6. Press **Tab** once.

   Note: The List Field Names box displays.

7. Double-click on the field name on which the next condition will be based {press the up or down arrow key to highlight the field name, then press Enter}.

   For our example, double-click on **WORKSHOP**.

8. Type the conditions to be met before the record can be used in the merge.

   For example, type **N**.

   *Note: Your screen should look similar to Figure 22.4 . Conditions placed in the same row are AND conditions. That means the record must meet all of the conditions (the STATE/PROVINCE must be CA or NV **and** there must be an N in the WORKSHOP field). When conditions are placed in separate rows, an OR condition is created. For example, if the WORKSHOP field is shown in the second row, any record with CA or NV in the STATE/PROVINCE field **or** any record with the letter N in the WORK-SHOP field (regardless of the state) would be included in the merge.*

9. Select **OK** {Enter twice}.

10. Select **Merge** {Enter}.

Finish-Up Instructions

❖ Check that only records with CA and NV in the STATE/PROVINCE field **and** the letter N in the WORKSHOP field were merged with the form letters.

❖ Optional. Print one copy of the merged letters.

❖ Close all documents.

Form Files with Graphic Images

The merge operation will need less memory and less storage space if the option to use an Image on Disk has been selected in the Create/Edit Graphics Box dialog box. When this option is selected, each merged letter references the graphic file on the disk instead of saving a copy of the graphic within each letter.

❖  Open the form file **22drill3.frm** from the data disk.

Steps to ▶ Indicate the Location of a Graphic Image

1. Double-click on the desired graphic image {Alt and F9, b, e, Enter}.

   For example, double-click on the **globe** image.

   Note: The Edit Graphics Box dialog box displays.

2. In the Contents section, select the desired option {n, use up or down arrow key to highlight the desired option, Enter}.

   For example, check that Image on Disk is displayed.

3. Select **OK** to return to the document window.

Finish-Up Instructions

❖ Save the file using the same filename, **23drill3.frm**.

❖ Close the file.

Using Output Options

The output options can be used to reduce the memory needed during the merge operation. Normally, the output is set to "Unused Document," causing WordPerfect to open a new window and to place the merged letters in the new window.

Start-Up Instructions

❖ Select **Tools, Merge, Run.** Use the file on the data disk named **22drill3.frm** as the form file and the file named **22drill1.df** as the data file.

Steps to ▶ Output Merged Letters to a File

1. In the Run Merge dialog box, select **Output** {o}.

2. Select **File** {use the up or down arrow key to highlight File, Enter}.

   Note: The Merge Output File dialog box displays.

3. Type the location and filename for the merged letters, then select **OK** {press Enter}.

   For example, type **a:\22drill3.mr.** (Do not type the final period.)

4. Select **Merge** {press Enter}.

Note: The message, "Merging Record...," displays in the left corner of the Status bar. The merging message disappears when the merge is complete and nothing displays in the document window.

Finish-Up Instructions

❖ Open the file named **22drill3.mr** to display the merged letters.

❖ Optional. Print one copy.

❖ Close the document.

Start-Up Instructions

❖ Check that the printer is on and connected to the computer.

❖ Select **Tools, Merge, Run**. Use the file on the data disk named **22drill3.frm** as the form file and the file named **22drill1.df** as the data file.

Output Merged Letters to a Printer

1. In the Run Merge dialog box, select **Output** {o}.

2. Select **Printer** {p}.

3. Select **Merge** {press Enter}.

   Note: The message, "Merging Record...," displays in the left corner of the Status bar. The merging message disappears when the merge is complete and the letters are sent to the printer.

Finish-Up Instructions

❖ Check the letters as they print to make sure the letters are correct. Sending the merged letters directly to the printer can avoid some memory problems but should be used only with data files and form files that have been merged and checked previously. Otherwise, a lot of paper can be wasted!

Data Text Files

In addition to the data table file format, WordPerfect offers a data text file format for data files. One advantage of using the data text file format is to avoid difficulty reading table columns when each record has many fields or many characters in each field. Also, if the data file has numerous records and additional records are added periodically, the data text file format may be faster to work with than working with a large table. The data text file format was the only format available until WordPerfect 6.0 for DOS, so data files created using earlier versions of WordPerfect are in the data text file format. Also, WordPerfect automatically places data file information imported from other programs into the data text file format.

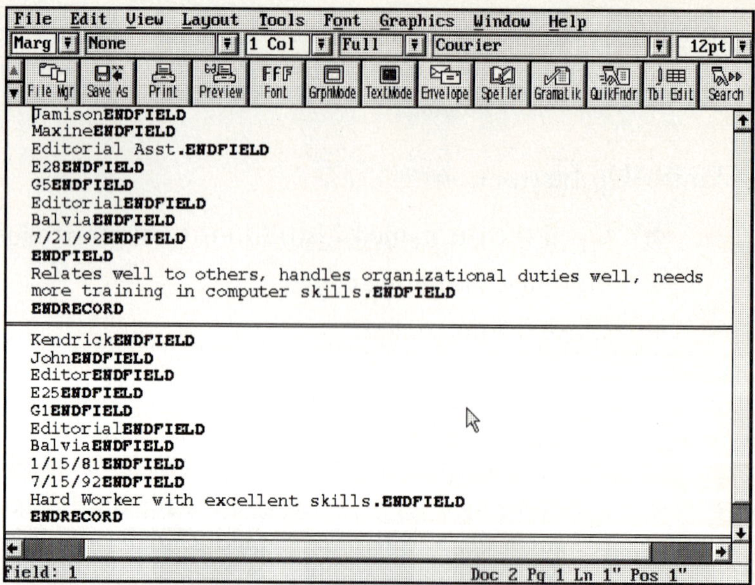

In a data text file, the field names are placed at the beginning of the document. The records are then typed with each field in the same order as they are shown at the beginning of the document. Each field in the record must end with an EndField code, and each record must end with an EndRecord code. If a field does not have any data—for instance, if there is no company name, the EndField code is placed on the line by itself (see Figure 22.5). As the cursor/insertion point scrolls through a data text file, the Status bar at the bottom of the screen will show the field name. Always check the Status bar frequently when typing data in a data text file to make sure that the correct field information is being entered.

Import Data

The data to be imported from the mainframe or database program must be in an ASCII (DOS) delimited file. Typically, each field in a delimited file is separated by a comma, each record ends with a CR/LF (carriage return/line feed), and character strings (text) are enclosed in quotation marks. Figure 22.6 shows a sample delimited file. When WordPerfect imports the delimited file, ENDFIELD and ENDRECORD codes will be inserted automatically. Before the data file can be merged with a form letter, however, field names must be added to the beginning of the file.


```
"Jamison","Maxine","Editorial Asst.","E28","G5","Editorial","Balvia",7/21/92,
"Kendrick","John","Editor","E25","G1","Editorial","Balvia",1/15/81,7/15/92,
"Leong","Wendell","Oper. Mgr.","E32","G1","Admin.","Peterson",3/25/77,9/15/91,
```

Import Data into a Data Text File

1. Select **File, Open** to open the file containing the data in ASCII delimited format {Shift and F10}.

2. Type the location and name of the desired file, then select **OK** {press Enter}.

   For example, type **a:\22drill4.txt**.

   Note: The File Format list displays.

3. Double-click on the appropriate File Format {press the up or down arrow key until the appropriate File Format is highlighted, then press Enter}.

   For example, double-click on **DOS Delimited Text**.

   Note: The Delimited Text Options dialog box displays.

4. In the Delimited Text Options dialog box, check that the appropriate characters are entered for the Field Delimiter, Record Delimiter, and Field Encapsulate Character options.

   For example, the WordPerfect defaults, shown in Figure 22.7, should be displayed.

5. Select **OK** to continue {press Enter once}.

   Note: Depending on the size of the data file, WordPerfect may take a few moments to format the imported data with ENDFIELD and ENDRECORD codes. The text will display on the screen in a form similar to that in Figure 22.5. However, no field names will display at the top of the document. Take a few moments to scroll through the document and check each record.

6. Select the **Save As** button.

7. Select the desired Format option and choose **OK**.

   For example, check that the WordPerfect 6.0 format option is selected and choose **OK**.

8. Type the location and new filename.

   For example, type **a:22drill4.df**.

FIGURE 22.7

Delimited Text Options
dialog box

---

9. Select **OK** {Enter}.

10. To add the field names to the data file, determine the field names and write down the exact order of the fields in a record.

    For example, the field names and order are: lastname, firstname, position, mailstop, grade, department, supervisor, startdate, last-promo, and evaluation.

11. Place the cursor/insertion point at the beginning of the document {Home, Home, up arrow}.

12. Select **Tools, Merge, Define** {Shift and F9}.

    Note: The Merge Codes (Text Data File) dialog box displays.

13. Select **Field Names** {n}.

    Note: The Field Names dialog box displays.

14. Type the field names in the order in which they appear in the data file, pressing **Enter** after each field name.

    For example, type the following:
    lastname
    firstname
    position
    mailstop
    grade
    department
    supervisor
    startdate
    lastpromo
    evaluation

    Note: If a mistake is made while typing the field names, click on the incorrect name in the Field Name List box and select Delete Field Name {press Tab to jump into the Field Name List box, then use the arrow keys to highlight the incorrect name, d}. To continue adding field names, click in the Field Name box {press Tab until the cursor appears in the Field Name box}.

15. When all the field names have been added and are in the correct order, select **OK** to display the field name in the document window {press Enter until the document window displays}.

Finish-Up Instructions

❖ Save the file again using the same filename, **22drill4.df**.

❖ Close the file.

    Note: The imported data can now be used with form files containing the same field names.

❖ Continue with the Steps to Request User Input in a Merged Letter.

Request User Input in a Merged Letter

Confidential data that may be used only one time in a document is often not saved in a data file. A special command, KEYBOARD, is inserted in the form file to instruct the program to pause and request the user to type the needed information. The KEYBOARD command is placed in the form file at the position in which the specific information will be located.

When the form file containing the KEYBOARD command is merged with a data file, the program will pause during the merging of each letter to allow the user to type the specific information. Once the information is typed, press **F9** to resume the merge operation.

Start-up Instructions

- ❖ Alan, of Alan's Ads, is giving a special bonus to various employees because of the work accomplished on the PCCA International campaign. Because the bonus is a one-time occurrence, it is not included in a data file.

- ❖ The data file created in the Steps to Import Data into a Data Text File on page 579 should be available (**22drill4.df**).

- ❖  Open the file named **22drill4.frm** from the data disk.

Steps to ▶ Request User Input in a Merged Letter

1. Place the cursor/insertion point at the location where the user will enter information.

   For example, place the cursor/insertion point in the first cell of the second row of the table.

2. Select **Tools, Merge, Define** {Shift and F9}.

3. Select **Keyboard** {k}.

   Note: The Parameter Entry dialog box displays. A KEYBOARD command is always followed by a prompt requesting information from the user.

4. Type the desired prompt message.

   For example, type **Enter vacation dates:**. (Do not type the final period.)

5. Select **OK** {Enter}.

Finish-Up Instructions

- ❖ Repeat Steps 1–5 to place a KEYBOARD code in the second cell of the second row. Type the prompt message, **Enter vacation resort:**. (Do not type the period.)

Maxine Jamison	August 1-7	Sunnyside Resort
John Kendrick	December 5-12	Lake Tahoe Bed & Breakfast
Wendell Leong	July 15-22	Cape Cod Anglers Inn

❖ Use the filename **22drill4.frm** and save the form letter on your disk.

Start-Up Instructions

❖ Merge the form file **22drill4.frm** with the data file **22drill4.df**. (If necessary, see the Steps to Merge a Form File and a Data Table File in Chapter 12 on page 328.)

Merge a Form File with User Input

Note: During the merging of the form file and the data file, the prompt will appear on the Status bar when a KEYBOARD command is reached.

1. When the prompt displays in the Status bar, type the requested information.

   For example, when "Enter vacation dates:" displays in the Status bar, type **August 1-7**.

2. Press **F9** to continue the Merge operation.

   Note: The next prompt displays in the Status bar.

Finish-Up Instructions

❖ Use the information in Figure 22.8 and continue to type the requested information at each prompt. To determine which letter is currently being merged, check the page number (1, 2, etc.) displayed in the Status bar.

❖ When all letters have been merged, the cursor/insertion point displays at the bottom of the final letter.

❖ Print one copy of each letter.

❖ Optional. Use the filename **22drill4.mr** and save the merged letter file.

❖ Close all documents.

The Next Step

Chapter Review and Activities

FEATURES SUMMARY

FEATURES	ACTIONS	PAGE
Insert the IFBLANK merge command	Select **Tools, Merge, Define, OK**. Select **Merge Codes**, double-click on the **IFBLANK** command, type the desired field name, select **OK**. Continue to insert desired fields and/or commands.	569
Insert the ELSE and ENDIF merge commands	Select **Tools, Merge, Define, OK**. Select **Merge Codes**, double-click on the desired command. Continue to insert desired fields and/or commands.	570
Select a range of records	Select **Tools, Merge, Run**, type the location and name for the form and data files. If necessary, select **Data File Options**. Select **Specify Record Number Range**, type the desired record numbers in the To and From boxes, and select **Merge**.	573
Select records based on conditions	Select **Tools, Merge, Run**, type the location and name for the form and data files. If necessary, select **Data File Options**. Select **Define Conditions**. Click on the number 1 in the first row, double-click on the desired field name, type the condition to be met, **Tab** once, if desired, create additional conditions to be met. Select **OK, Merge**.	574
Indicate the location of a graphic image	Double-click on the desired graphic image. In the Contents section, check that the Image on Disk option is displayed, select **OK**.	576

Self-Check Questions

True/False—Circle One

T F 1. The IFBLANK...ELSE...ENDIF commands are used in the form file to control extra spacing when fields are empty.

T F 2. When inserting commands in a form file, the commands can be *typed* or *selected* from the Merge Codes box.

T F 3. Data imported from a database or a mainframe program must be in an ASCII delimited file.

T F 4. Imported data can be placed in either a data table or data text file.

T F 5. A KEYBOARD command is used to request user input during the merge operation.

T F 6. A Parameter Entry dialog box appears whenever a Merge Code needs to be followed by a prompt or field name.

Short Answer

1. List the three options found in the Data Record Selection area for merging specific records.

2. Explain how to correct a mistake in the Field Name List box when entering field names for a data text file.

3. Give one example of using the KEYBOARD command in a form file.

4. List two options that could be used if the merge operation stopped because there was not enough memory to hold all the merged letters.

Enriching Language Arts Skills

Spelling/Vocabulary Words

bonus   money or other compensation given to an employee in addition to regular pay
suitable   acceptable, appropriate

Abbreviations for Time

Type a.m. and p.m. with lowercase letters and no spaces. Only one period is used if the abbreviation is the last element of a sentence.

Example: The planning meeting will begin at 9:00 a.m. and adjourn at 3:00 p.m.

Activity

Activity 22.1—Create a Form Letter with IFBLANK...ELSE...ENDIF Commands

1. Using the following guidelines, create the letter shown on page 586:

   a. The graphic image used for the PCCA International letterhead is **globe.wpg**.

b. Remember to select the **Image on Disk** option in the Contents section of the Edit Graphics Box dialog box.

c. Merge codes such as IFBLANK, ELSE, etc., cannot be typed into the document but must be placed in the form file using the Merge Codes list.

(Insert date code)

IFBLANK(TITLE)**FIELD**(FIRSTNAME) **FIELD**(LASTNAME)**ELSE FIELD**(TITLE)
FIELD(FIRSTNAME) **FIELD**(LASTNAME)**ENDIF**
FIELD(COMPANY?)
FIELD(ADDRESS)
FIELD(CITY)**IFBLANK**(STATE/PROVINCE), **FIELD**(COUNTRY)
FIELD(ZIPCODE)**ELSE** , **FIELD**(STATE/PROVINCE) **FIELD**(ZIPCODE) **ENDIF**

Dear **IFBLANK**(TITLE)Friend**ELSE FIELD**(TITLE) **FIELD**(LASTNAME)**ENDIF** :

The response to our workshops on SONIC Plumbing has been very exciting, and many of you have asked for additional opportunities to learn more about this new technology. You will be happy to know we have created a conference format with you in mind.

From July 22-25, 199x, we will be holding the first-ever SONIC Plumbing Professional Conference at the Sheraton Hotel in Washington, D.C. This conference is designed especially for those of you who have attended a SONIC Plumbing workshop and will include the following activities:

- Lectures and hands-on workshops by Nathan Hall and Peter Goodman, foremost developers of this technology.

- Peer panels and question/answer format lectures where you can talk with and ask questions of other technicians currently working with this technology.

- Exhibits by all major manufacturers of SONIC Plumbing equipment and fixtures.

Please return the enclosed registration card immediately so that your place will be reserved. Additional information on hotel rooms and transportation packages will be mailed to you as soon as we receive your registration.

Sincerely,

James McLaughlin
President
PCCA International

JM/xx
conf2.frm/diskA

Enc.

---

2. Save the form letter using the filename **22act1.frm**.

3. Merge the form letter **22act1.frm** with the data file **22drill3.df** using the following information:

    a. Use the **Define Conditions** option to select only those records with the letter **Y** in the WORKSHOP field.

    b. Check that the Blank Fields in Data File option is set to Remove Resulting Blank Lines.

    c. Set the Output option to merge the letters to a **File**. Use the filename **22act1.mr**. (Select **Output**, **File**, type location and name of file, select **OK**, **Merge**.)

4. Open the file named **22act1.mr** and check the merged letters. Make sure only those records with a Y in the WORKSHOP field were merged, and that all address and salutation information printed correctly. Print one copy of the merged letters

5. Close all documents.

Challenge Your Skills

◆ ▣ Skill 22.1—Create a Form File That Contains a KEYBOARD Command

1. Open the file **22drill4.frm**. Insert the following paragraph containing a KEYBOARD command after the table containing the vacation information. Correct two spelling and two punctuation errors.

    If you would rather have a cash bonus, your bonous would be **KEYBOARD(Enter cash bonus amount:)**. Please let me know by 5:00 PM on Friday whether you want the vacation or cash bonus and confirm that the vacation dates shown will be suitible.

2. Save the form file using the filename **22skill1.frm**.

3. Merge the form file **22skill1.frm** and the data file **22drill4.df** using the information below to respond to the prompts:

Maxine Jamison	August 1-7	Sunnyside Resort	$2,000
John Kendrick	December 5-12	Lake Tahoe Bed & Breakfast	$3,000
Wendell Leong	July 15-22	Cape Code Anglers Inn	$2,500

4. Print the merged documents.

5. Close all documents.

Advanced Editing Techniques and Hypertext

Features Covered

- Turn on line numbering
- Use strikeout and redline text attributes
- Compare Documents feature
- Insert a comment into a document
- Mark hidden text
- Create bookmarks
- Use hypertext
- Create a bookmark
- Create hypertext links

Objectives

After successfully completing this chapter, you will be able to turn on line numbering, use redline and strikeout text attributes to mark inserted/replaced and deleted text, and use the Compare Documents feature to mark the differences between two documents. You will also be able to use the Comments and Hidden Text features to insert notes into a document. Once you have learned to electronically mark a specific portion of text by using the Bookmark feature, you will then be able to link text by creating hypertext links.

Chapter Introduction

WordPerfect's line numbering feature can be turned on to print a line number beside each line of text in a document. This feature is often used when creating legal documents. The redline and strikeout text attributes can be used to mark inserted/replaced and deleted text as a document is edited. The Compare Documents feature is used to mark the differences between two documents. Redline, strikeout, and the Compare Documents feature are used to help track the changes made to a document. The Comments and Hidden Text features are used to insert notes into a document. These features are often used when a document is reviewed by more than one person. Each person that reviews the document inserts hidden text or comments that suggest changes, ask additional questions, or add remarks on the document's contents. The author of the document then reviews the comments or hidden text and determines the changes that need to be made to the document. Bookmarks are used to mark text, and hypertext links allow you to jump to and from the marked text.

Line Numbering

A number can be placed beside each line of text in a document. Line numbering is often used for legal documents and other documents in which text needs to be referenced by line numbers.

The Line Numbering Format dialog box is used to turn on line numbering and to control how line numbers are printed (see Figure 23.1). An illustration of the numbering format displays in the Sample Numbering box. If changes are made to the **Starting Line Number, First Line Number Printed, Numbering Interval**, or **Numbering Method** options, the illustration will reflect the changes.

The **Starting Line Number** option is used to change the number of the first line. For example, instead of beginning the line numbers at the number 1, line numbers can be set to begin at the number 100. Generally, WordPerfect begins printing line numbers at the line that contains the cursor/insertion point when line numbering is turned on. However, the **First Line Number Printed** option can be used to instruct WordPerfect to begin printing the line numbers on a line other than line 1. For example, if a document contains two blank lines at the top of the document, WordPerfect can be instructed to begin printing line numbers on line 3. A number can be placed beside each line of a document or at intervals. The **Numbering Interval** option is used to specify the interval at which numbers will be printed. For example, WordPerfect can be instructed to print line numbers at every fifth line. The default Numbering Method is Number (1, 2, 3). However, the **Numbering Method** can be changed to lowercase letters (a, b, c), uppercase letters (A, B, C), lowercase Roman numerals (i, ii, iii), or uppercase Roman numerals (I, II, III).

The position of the line numbers can also be changed. By default, line numbers are printed .6 inch from the left edge of the page. If margins are changed, it may be desirable to change the position of the line numbers. The position of the line numbers can be measured from the left edge of the page or from the left margin.

When the **Restart Numbering on Each Page** option is selected in the Line Numbering Format dialog box, the line numbers begin again on each page. If Restart Numbering on Each Page is not selected, the lines on all pages will be numbered continuously.

Blank lines can be counted or ignored when the lines in a document are numbered. If desired, the lines of each newspaper column can be counted. Finally, the font, color, or text attributes (bold, italic, etc.) for the line numbers can be changed.

When the line numbering has been turned on, the numbers can be viewed in either the graphics mode or page mode or by selecting the **Preview** button. In the graphics or page mode, it may be necessary to use the horizontal scroll bar to view the left margin of the page.

Start-Up Instructions

❖  Open the file named **23drill1.txt** from the data disk.

❖ The graphics view mode should be selected.

Steps to ▶ **Turn On Line Numbering**

1. Place the cursor/insertion point at the location at which the line numbering should begin.

    For example, place the cursor/insertion point at the top of the document.

2. Select **Layout, Line** {Shift and F8, L}

3. Select **Line Numbering** {n}.

    Note: The Line Numbering Format dialog box displays (see Figure 23.1).

4. Select **Line Numbering On** {L}.

5. Select any options desired.

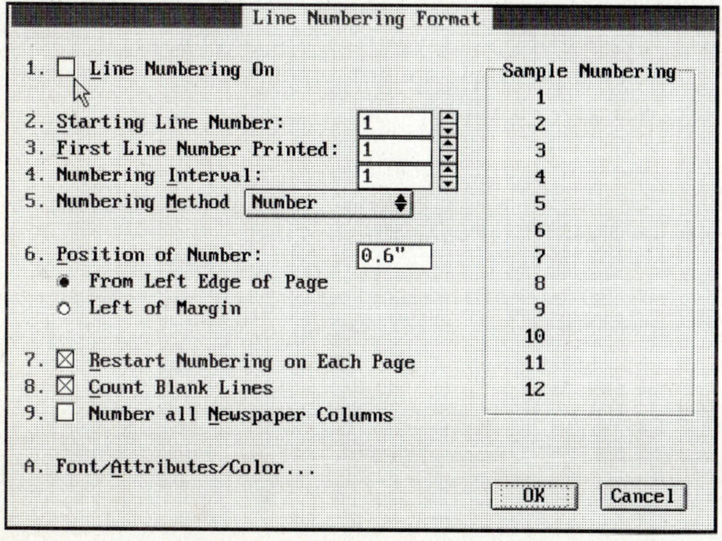

FIGURE 23.1

Line Numbering Format dialog box

6. Select **OK** twice {Enter three times}.

    *Note: To view the line numbers, use the horizontal scroll bar to scroll to the left. Line numbers can also be viewed by selecting the **Preview** button.*

Finish-Up Instructions

❖ Use the new filename **23drill1.num** and save the file.

❖ Print one copy.

❖ Close the document.

Redline and Strikeout

The redline and strikeout text attributes can be used to mark revision in a document. The redline text attribute is used to mark inserted or replaced text. The strikeout text attribute is used to mark text to be deleted. When text is formatted with the strikeout attribute, a line is placed through the text (i.e., ~~strikeout~~).

Depending on the monitor used, text marked with the redline attribute will display red or gray on the screen. Likewise, when redline text is printed, the text will print in gray with a shaded background and a dot beneath each character or the text will print in red.

The method of marking and printing redline text can be changed. For example, a vertical bar (|) placed in the left margin is often used to mark redline text. A redline character in the margin draws the reader's attention to the lines that contain inserted/replaced text.

After an edited document has been reviewed, the redline and/or strikeout marks can be removed. When redline marks are removed, the text changes to normal text (e.g., not red or gray). When strikeout marks are removed, the strikeout text is deleted from the document. At times, redline marks are not removed from a document so that inserted/replaced text is clearly identified.

Start-Up Instructions

❖ 📀 Open the file named **23drill1.txt** from the data disk.

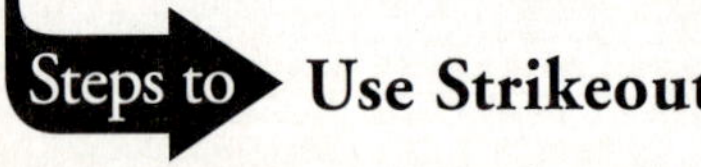

Use Strikeout

1. Block the desired text.

> For example, in the second sentence of the second paragraph,
> block the text from the first comma to the second comma (in-
> clude both commas in the block).

2. Select **Font, Strikeout** {Alt and o, s}.

   Note: A line is placed through the text.

Use Redline

1. Place the cursor/insertion point at the location at which text will be inserted.

   > For example, place the cursor/insertion point between the words
   > *state* and *may* in the first sentence of the third paragraph.

2. Select **Font, Redline** {Alt and o, r}.

3. Type the text to be inserted.

   > For example, type **composed of unrelated persons who live to-
   > gether for reasons of economy and safety.**

   *Note: The inserted text displays in red on color monitors and in gray on monochrome
   monitors.*

Finish-Up Instructions

❖ In the last paragraph, the text *one million* should be changed to *eight hundred
   thousand*.

   a. Block the text *one million* and select **Font, Strikeout**.

   b. Turn on Reveal Codes and press the right arrow key to move the high-
      light to the right of the [StkOut Off] code.

   c. Select **Font, Redline** and type **eight hundred thousand**.

❖ Use the new filename **23drill1.red** and save the file.

Start-Up Instructions

❖ The file named **23drill1.red** should be displayed on the screen.

Change the Method of Marking Redline Text

1. Select **Layout, Document** {Alt and L, d}.

2. Select **Redline Method** {r}.

3. Select the desired option.

   > For example, select **Left** to place a redline character in the left
   > margin beside each line that contains inserted/revised text {L}.

4. Select **OK** {Enter}.

Note: The redline character (vertical bar) has been placed in the left margin beside each line that contains revised/inserted text. Scroll to the left side of the document to view the redline character (|).

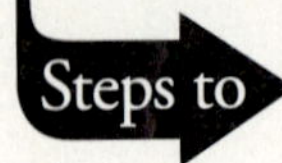 **Remove Strikeout Text**

1. Select **File, Compare Documents** {Alt and f, d}.

2. Select **Remove Markings** {r}.

3. Select **Remove Strikeout Text Only** {s}.

4. Select **OK** {Enter}.

   Note: The strikeout text has been deleted. However, redline characters still display to indicate where text has been inserted/replaced.

Finish-Up Instructions

❖ Use the new filename **23drill1.fin** and save the file.

❖ Print one copy.

❖ Select **Layout**, **Document**, **Redline Method**, **Printer Dependent**, and **OK** to return to the default redline setting {Shift and F8, d, r, p, Enter}.

❖ Close the document.

Compare Documents

The Compare Documents feature is used to mark the differences between the text in two files. When documents are compared, WordPerfect marks inserted/replaced text with the redline text attribute and marks deleted text with the strikeout text attribute. If text has been moved, a note "THE FOLLOWING TEXT WAS MOVED" displays before the moved text and a note "THE PRECEDING TEXT WAS MOVED" displays after the moved text. The notes are formatted as strikeout text.

WordPerfect can compare documents by **Word**, **Phrase**, **Sentence**, or **Paragraph**. Word, Phrase, Sentence, and Paragraph are defined as follows:

Word	Text that ends with a space, any punctuation mark, hard return, or hard page break.
Phrase	Text that ends with any punctuation mark, hard return, or hard page break.
Sentence	Text that ends with any final punctuation mark, a hard return, or a hard page break.
Paragraph	Text that ends with a hard return or hard page break.

SMALL CLAIM FILING INSTRUCTIONS

The small claim filing fee form is used to tell the Court how many filings you have had in the past 12 months. This information is used to determine your filing fee. If you have had less than 12 filings in the past 12 months, the charge is $6.00, if 12 or more the charge is $12.

This filing fee and a reasonable cost for serving the defendant are reimbursible to you if your case is rewarded with a judgment against the defendant. Reasonable cost of personal service is usually considered to be $14 per individual served. Amounts in excess of this amount may be denied at the discretion of the judge hearing the case.

FIGURE 23.2
Revised text

Using the Word option provides the most precise results because only the inserted, replaced, deleted, and moved text is marked. When the Phrase, Sentence, or Paragraph options are selected, whole segments of text may be marked making it unclear as to the specific word(s) that have been changed.

After the documents have been compared, the redline and/or strikeout text can be accepted by removing markings. When markings are removed, redline text is changed to normal text and strikeout text is deleted.

Start-Up Instructions

❖ 💾 Open the file named **23drill2.txt** from the data disk.

Steps to ➤ Use Compare Documents

1. Make desired revisions.

   For example, make the revisions shown in Figure 23.2.

2. Select **File, Compare Documents** {Alt and f, d}.

3. Select **Add Markings** {a}.

   Note: The Compare Documents dialog box displays.

4. Select the desired Compare by option.

   For example, select **Word** {c, w}.

5. Select **OK** {Enter}.

   Note: The Comparing Documents box displays showing the progress being made in checking the documents. In a moment, the document displays with redline and strikeout marks showing the inserted and deleted text.

- ❖ Use the new filename **23drill2.com** and save the file.
- ❖ Print one copy.

- ❖ The file named **23drill2.com** should be displayed on the screen.

Remove Strikeout Text and Redline Markings

1. Select **File, Compare Documents** {Alt and f, d}.

2. Select **Remove Markings** {r}.

3. Select **OK** to remove redline markings and strikeout text {Enter}.

   Note: The text that was marked with the strikeout attribute has been deleted and the text that was marked with the redline attribute has been changed to normal text.

Finish-Up Instructions

- ❖ Use the new filename **23drill2.fin** and save the document.
- ❖ Print one copy.
- ❖ Close the document.

Comments

Nonprinting notes (comments) can be placed within a document using the Comments feature. Comments can remind you of special formatting or printing requirements or other tasks that need to be accomplished when the document is created. For example, a comment might remind you to load letterhead paper into the printer before printing the document or to call to verify the title of the addressee before sending a letter. The Comments feature can also be used to collect the responses of people who review a document. For example, a proposal can be sent via e-mail (electronic mail) to several people asking for their input. The reviewers can insert their comments into the document and return the document to the originator (person who originally sent the document).

These comments can be edited and, if desired, converted to text and inserted into the document. To delete a comment, turn on Reveal Codes, highlight the [Comment] code and press the **Delete** key.

Start-Up Instructions

- ❖ 🔳 Open the file named **23drill3.txt** from the data disk.

  Note: A comment box displays in the document between the title and first paragraph.

 Insert a Comment

1. Place the cursor/insertion point at the location at which the comment should be inserted into the document.

   For example, place the cursor/insertion point after the final period in item number 1.

2. Select **Layout, Comment** {Alt and L, n}.

3. Select **Create** {c}.

4. Type the comment text.

   For example, type the following:

   I think this should be changed to three consecutive periods and 95% of sales objective.

   Also, should a copy of the meeting report be forwarded to the Personnel department to be placed in the sales representative's personnel record?

   (insert your name)

5. Press **F7** to exit to the document window.

   Note: The comment text is placed in a box below the number 1 paragraph.

Finish-Up Instructions

❖ Place the cursor/insertion point after the final period in item number 2.

❖ Repeat Steps 2–5 and create the following comment:

   Will a copy of the meeting report and written plan be forwarded to the Personnel department?
   (insert your name)

❖ Use the new filename **23drill3.cmt** and save the file.

❖ Close the document.

Hidden Text

The Hidden Text feature is useful for creating notes, questions, messages, or confidential information that can show (be visible on the screen and can be printed) or be hidden (not displayed on the screen and not printed). By using hidden text, a single document can be used for more than one purpose. For example, a list of employee names, departments, business phone numbers, home phone numbers, and home addresses can be created. The home phone numbers and home addresses can be marked as hidden text. The complete document, including the hidden text, can be printed for managers; a second document containing only the employee names, departments, and business phone numbers can be printed for everyone else.

❖ Open the file named **23drill4.txt** from the data disk.

 **Steps to** **Mark Hidden Text**

1. Block the text to be hidden.

   For example, block the column heading Minimum Price.

2. Select **Font, Hidden Text** {Alt and o, h}.

   Note: The Hidden Text dialog box displays. An X should display in the Show All Hidden Text box.

3. Select **Hidden Text** {h}.

4. Select **OK** {Enter}.

   Note: No change displays on the screen. Turn on Reveal Codes to view the [Hidden On] and [Hidden Off] codes around the words "Minimum Price."

Finish-Up Instructions

❖ Repeat Steps 1–4 and mark each price in the Minimum Price column as hidden text.

❖ Use the new filename **23drill4.hid** and save the file.

Start-Up Instructions

❖ The file named **23drill4.hid** should be displayed on the screen.

 **Steps to** **Hide Hidden Text**

1. Once text has been marked as hidden, select **Font, Hidden Text** {Alt and o, h}.

2. Select **Show All Hidden Text** to remove the X in the Show All Hidden Text box.

3. Select **OK** {Enter}.

   Note: The text marked as hidden is no longer displayed on the screen.

Finish-Up Instructions

❖ Print one copy.

1. Select **Font, Hidden Text** {Alt and o, h}.

2. Select **Show All Hidden Text** {s}.

3. Select **OK** {Enter}.

Finish-Up Instructions

❖ Print one copy.

❖ Close the document.

Bookmark Feature

The Bookmark feature enables you to electronically mark a specific portion of text in a document in a manner similar to placing a paper bookmark in a book to mark a reference or page. There is no limit to the number of bookmarks that can be placed in a document. Each bookmark is given a unique name. When a bookmark is created, WordPerfect automatically suggests the first 38 characters following the cursor/insertion point as the bookmark name. The suggested name can be changed by deleting the original characters and typing a new name. Once a bookmark is created, the cursor/insertion point can be moved (jumped) from any location in the document to the bookmark location.

Start-Up Instructions

❖  Open the file named **23drill5.txt** from the data disk.

Steps to **Create a Bookmark**

1. Place the cursor/insertion point at the location where the bookmark should be inserted.

   For example, place the cursor/insertion point at the beginning of the heading Apartment Complexes on page two of the document.

2. Select **Edit, Bookmark, Create** {Shift and F12, c}.

   Note: The text "Apartment Complexes" displays in the Bookmark Name box of the Create Bookmark dialog box. The bookmark name can be accepted or a different name can be typed.

3. Select **OK** to accept the bookmark name.

   Note: If desired, use Reveal Codes to display the [Bookmark] code.

* Place the cursor/insertion point at the beginning of the heading Shopping Malls on page three of the document.

* Repeat Steps 2 and 3 to create a bookmark named Shopping Malls.

* Place the cursor/insertion point at the beginning of the heading Light Industrial and Warehouse/Distribution Properties on page four.

* Repeat Step 2 and change the bookmark name to Light Industrial (in the Bookmark Name box, highlight the unneeded text and press the **Delete** key).

* Select **OK**.

* Use the new filename **23drill5.bkm** and save the file.

Start-Up Instructions

* The file named **23drill5.bkm** should be displayed on the screen.

Jump to a Bookmark

1. Select **Edit, Bookmark** {Shift and F12}.

2. Double-click on the desired bookmark name.

   For example, double-click on **Apartment Complexes**.

   Note: The cursor/insertion point moves to the heading Apartment Complexes on the second page of the document.

Finish-Up Instructions

* Repeat Steps 1 and 2 and jump to the Light Industrial bookmark.

Create Hypertext Links

The Hypertext feature is used to link a part of a document to another part of the same document (via a bookmark), to another document, or to a macro. In order to use hypertext to link sections of a document, bookmarks must be created. The Hypertext feature uses the bookmark names to establish a connection between sections in a document.

When creating a link, a portion of text is selected to function as *hypertext*. Text marked as hypertext displays bold and is underlined on the screen, or can be placed in a shaded box that resembles a button.

After all hypertext links have been established, the Hypertext feature must be activated in order to jump from the marked hypertext to the linked bookmark. After a hypertext jump has been made, the cursor/insertion point can be returned to the original position in the document by using the **Return from Jump** option. If the marked hypertext is to be edited, the Hypertext feature must be deactivated.

Start-Up Instructions

❖ The file named **23drill5.bkm** should be displayed on the screen.

Steps to ▶ Create Hypertext Links

1. Block the text to be used as a hypertext link.

   For example, in the first sentence of the document, block the words "**apartment complexes.**"

2. Select **Tools, Hypertext** {Alt and t, h}.

3. Select **Create Link** {c}.

4. Click in the box located beside the Go to Bookmark option.

5. Press **F5** to display a list of the bookmark names in the document.

6. Double-click on the desired bookmark name.

   For example, double-click on **Apartment Complexes**.

7. Select **OK** {Enter}.

   Note: The hypertext link text displays in bold and is underlined on the screen.

Finish-Up Instructions

❖ Block the text "shopping malls" in the first sentence of the document. Repeat Steps 2–7 and select the **Shopping Mall** bookmark.

❖ Block the text "light industrial and warehouse/distribution." Repeat Steps 2–7 and select the **Light Industrial** bookmark.

❖ Use the new filename **23drill5.hyp** and save the file.

Start-Up Instructions

❖ The file named **23drill5.hyp** should be displayed on the screen.

Steps to ▶ Use Hypertext

1. Select **Tools, Hypertext** {Alt and t, h}.

2. Select **Hypertext is Active** {a}.

3. Select **OK** {press Enter}.

4. Move the mouse pointer to the desired hypertext and click once {move the cursor/insertion point to the hypertext and press Enter}.

For example, move the mouse pointer to the hypertext "**apart-ment complexes**" and click.

Note: The cursor/insertion point moves to the location of the Apartment Complexes bookmark.

To Return the Cursor/Insertion Point to the Original Position in the Text

5. Select **Tools, Hypertext, Return from Jump** {Alt and t, h, r}.

Finish-Up Instructions

❖ Move the mouse pointer to the hypertext link "shopping malls" and click.

❖ Return the cursor/insertion point to the original position in the text.

❖ Move the mouse pointer to the hypertext link "light industrial and ware-house/distribution" and click.

❖ Return the cursor/insertion point to the original position in the text.

Turn Off Hypertext

1. Select **Tools, Hypertext** {Alt and t, h}.

2. Select the **Hypertext is Active** option {a}.

   Note: An X should not display beside the Hypertext is Active option.

3. Select **OK** {Enter}.

The Next Step

Chapter Review and Activities

FEATURES SUMMARY

FEATURES	ACTIONS	PAGE
Turn on line numbering	Place the cursor/insertion point at the location at which line numbering should begin. Select **Layout, Line, Line Numbering, Line Numbering On**. Select any desired options. Select **OK**.	591
Use strikeout	Block the desired text, select **Font, Strikeout**.	592
Use redline	Place the cursor/insertion point at the location where text will be inserted, select **Font, Redline**. Type desired text.	593
Change method of marking redline text	Select **Layout, Document, Redline Method**. Select desired option, **OK**.	593
Remove redline and/or strikeout marks	Select **File, Compare Documents, Remove Markings**. Select **Remove Strikeout Text Only** or **Remove Redline Markings and Strikeout Text**. Select **OK**.	594, 596
Use Compare Documents	Make revisions to a document. Select **File, Compare Documents, Add Markings**. Select the desired Compare by option, **OK**.	595
Insert a comment	Place the cursor/insertion point at the location at which the comments should be inserted. Select **Layout, Comment, Create**, type comment text, press **F7**.	597

FEATURES	ACTIONS	PAGE
Use hidden text:		
Mark hidden text	Block the text to be hidden, select **Font, Hidden Text.** Choose **Hidden Text** and select **OK.**	598
To hide hidden text	Select **Font, Hidden Text.** Choose **Show All Hidden Text** to deselect the option. Select **OK.**	598
To display hidden text	Select **Font, Hidden Text.** Choose **Show All Hidden Text.** Select **OK.**	599
Create a bookmark	Place the cursor/insertion point at the location at which the bookmark should be inserted, select **Edit, Bookmark, Create.** Type a bookmark name or select **OK** to accept the bookmark name.	599
Jump to a bookmark	Select **Edit, Bookmark,** double-click on desired bookmark name.	600
Create hypertext links	Block the text to be used as a hypertext link. Select **Tools, Hypertext, Create Link.** Click in the box located beside the **Go to Bookmark** option, press **F5,** double-click on the desired bookmark name. Select **OK.**	601
Use hypertext	Select **Tools, Hypertext, Hypertext is Active, OK.** Move the mouse pointer to the desired hypertext line and click once.	601
	To return the cursor/insertion point to the original position in the text, select **Tools, Hypertext, Return from Jump.**	602
	To turn off hypertext, select **Tools, Hypertext, Hypertext is Active, OK.**	602

Self-Check Questions

True/False—Circle One

T F 1. The position of line numbers cannot be changed.

T F 2. The redline text attribute can be used to mark inserted/replaced text.

T F 3. To remove strikeout text only, select **File, Compare Documents, Remove Markings, Remove Strikeout Text Only,** and **OK.**

T F 4. WordPerfect can compare documents by Word, Phrase, or Paragraph, but not
by Sentence.

T F 5. Comments created using WordPerfect's Comments feature can be printed.

Short Answer

1. List the five formats for line numbers.

2. List the four steps to change the method of marking redline text.

3. Write a brief description of how you might use the Hidden Text or Comments
feature.

4. Which Compare by option is used to obtain the most precise results when using the Compare Documents feature?

5. In order to use hypertext to link sections of a document, _____________ must be
created.

Enriching Language Arts Skills

Spelling/Vocabulary Words

mentor   a teacher or guide

demonstrate   to prove; to display or operate

realistic   practical, obtainable

Contractions

An apostrophe is used to indicate where a letter(s) has been omitted when two words
are combined to form a verb contraction. Generally, contractions are not used in formal business writing. Contractions can be used in personal letters or informal business documents.

Examples:

it's (it is)	*you're (you are)*
I've (I have)	*don't (do not)*
we'll (we will)	*they're (they are)*

Activities

Activity 23.1—Use Line Numbering

1. Open the file named **23act1.txt** from the data disk.

2. Turn on line numbering at the top of the document. Change the font for line numbers to **Helv-WP (Type 1), 10 point**.

3. Use the new filename **23act1.num** and save the file.

4. Print one copy.

5. Close the document.

Activity 23.2—Use Redline and Strikeout

1. Open the file named **23act2.txt** from the data disk.

2. Make the changes shown. Use the redline attribute to mark inserted/replaced text. Use the strikeout attribute to mark text to be deleted.

A current challenge in offices today is the need to provide individuals with a sense of accomplishment and a feeling of control over how their job is performed.

One solution is to ensure that the system increases the user's capability by delivering professional results and functions needed for the job. For example, voice has been overlooked in many systems; telephone integration and voice mail are being added to office systems.

A second solution is to give the user more control over the system resources by providing personal tools. Personal computers are turning out to be a ~~most~~ powerful motivator for office personnel. A laptop computer especially provides flexibility for travel and home use as well as connecting easily to the company's local area network.

Individual satisfaction and motivation are the critical components of working life quality and productivity improvement. Computers and software applications that are designed to provide ~~Design that addresses the user's personal concerns by providing~~ intuitive and efficient interfaces, needed functions, and resource control can improve job satisfaction and motivation.

3. Use the new filename **23act2.red** and save the file.

4. Print one copy.

Chapter 23—Advanced Editing Features

5. Remove the strikeout text (select **File, Compare Documents, Remove Markings, Remove Strikeout Text Only, OK**).

6. Change the redline method to Left (select **Layout, Document, Redline Method, Left, OK**).

7. Save the document again.

8. Print one copy.

9. Close the document.

■ Activity 23.3—Create Bookmarks and Hypertext Links

1. Open the file named **20act1.txt** from the data disk.

2. Create the following bookmarks:

    a. Place the cursor/insertion point at the beginning of the heading **Trips, Falls, and Slips** on page three of the document.

    b. Select **Edit, Bookmark, Create**. Select **OK** to accept the suggested bookmark name.

    c. Place the cursor/insertion point at the beginning of the heading **Back Injuries** on page four of the document.

    d. Select **Edit, Bookmark, Create**. Select **OK** to accept the suggested bookmark name.

3. Create the following hypertext links:

    a. Highlight the text "**trips, falls, and slips**" in the first paragraph under the heading Introduction.

    b. Select **Tools, Hypertext, Create Link**.

    c. Click in the box beside the Go to Bookmark option.

    d. Double-click on the **Trips, Falls, and Slips** bookmark name.

    e. Select **OK**.

    f. Highlight the text "**back injuries**" in the first paragraph under the heading Introduction.

    g. Select **Tools, Hypertext, Create Link**.

    h. Click in the box beside the Go to Bookmark option.

    i. Double-click on the the **Back Injuries** bookmark name.

4. Turn on Hypertext (select **Tools, Hypertext, Hypertext is Active, OK**).

5. Move the mouse pointer to the hypertext line "**back injuries**" and click to jump to the Back Injuries bookmark. Return from the jump (select **Tools, Hypertext, Return from Jump**).

6. Use the new filename **23act3.hyp** and save the file.

Challenge Your Skills

➥ Skill 23.1—Use Compare Document; Language Arts

1.   Type the following document.

2.   Make decisions regarding:

> Margins
> Fonts
> Indention for enumerated items
> Correct three spelling errors, two contractions, and two punctuation errors.

STEPS TO ATTRACT A MENTOR

Attracting the support and encouragement of older professionals in your career field is the basis of mentoring. A good menter offers excellent insights and introductions to people higher up. It's a great way to learn about a companys unspoken rules. You will need to develop several skills in order to attract a mentor.

1. Learn how to listen. Never interrupt others before they have completed their comments. Look for opportunities to deminstrate that you're listening carefully.

2. Develop a presentation that demonstrates your personal pride. Walk straight, keep your head up, shake hands firmly and establish eye contact whenever you are in a conversation.

3. Be persistent. People who persist develop excellence in their fields faster than those who settle for second best.

4. Be willing to accept failure as easily as you accept success. Learn from your mistakes.

5. Set realitic career goals. Without a career map, it is easy to drift aimlessly from one job to another.

---

3.   Use the filename **23skill1.txt**.

4.   Print one copy.

5.   Make the following changes. (Do not save the changes at this time.)

Attracting the support and encouragement of ~~older professionals~~ *a more experienced professional* in your career field is the basis of mentoring. A good menter offers excellent insights and introductions to ~~people higher up.~~ *individuals in leadership positions* It's a great way to learn about a companys unspoken rules. You will need to develop several skills in order to attract a mentor.

1. Learn how to listen. Never interrupt others before they have completed their comments. ~~Look for opportunities to deminstrate that you're listening carefully.~~ *Learn listening skills by observing other good listeners.*

2. Develop *body language that demonstrates self-confidence.* ~~a presentation that demonstrates your personal pride.~~ Walk straight, keep your head up, shake hands firmly and establish eye contact *when conversing with others.* ~~whenever you are in a conversation.~~

3. Be persistent. People who persist develop excellence in their fields faster than those who settle for second best.

4. Be willing to accept failure as easily as you accept success. Learn from your mistakes.

5. Set realitic career goals. *Setting specific career objectives will enable you to make decisions that lead to your desired goal.* ~~Without a career map, it is easy to drift aimlessly from one job to another.~~

6. Use Compare Documents to show inserted/replaced and deleted text.

7. Print one copy.

8. Remove all redline and strikeout markings to accept the changes to the document.

9. Use the new filename **23skill1.fin** and save the edited document.

10. Print one copy.

11. If you have completed your work, exit WordPerfect.

Create an Outline, Table of Contents, and Index

- Outline styles
- Outline body text
- Outline numbering
- Hide/show an outline family
- Hide/show body text
- Move, cut, and copy outline families
- Mark, define, and generate a table of contents and an index

Objectives

After successfully completing this chapter, you will be able to display the Outline Bars and create, number, and edit an outline. In addition, you will learn to mark, define, and generate both a table of contents and an index.

Chapter Introduction

Creating an outline is often very useful when writing reports, manuscripts, or other multiple-page documents. An outline assists a writer in organizing thoughts and grouping related information. Once a document is written, WordPerfect provides tools to assist the writer in creating a table of contents and/or an index.

Sample Outline

3 Enters

I.　Level one--first major idea
　A.　Level two
　B.　Second idea at level two
　　1.　Level three
　　　a.　Level four
This is an example of body text in an outline. The body text is not numbered.
　　　　(1)　Level five
　　　　　(a)　Level six
　　　　　(b)　Second idea at level six
　　　　　　i)　Level seven
　　　　　　　a)　Level eight
　　　　　　　b)　Second idea at level eight

2 Enters

II.　Level one--second major idea

Outline Styles

WordPerfect provides predefined outline styles for numbering outlines, paragraphs, legal documents, and documents with headings. The outline styles are predefined formats that are selected from the **Style** button on the Outline Bar. An outline description displays the type of numbering for the style chosen. The predefined outline style for an outline is illustrated in Figure 24.1.

Create an Outline

An outline is a list of ideas expressed in phrases or sentences. The outline can provide a brief summary for writing a document such as a report. The ideas in an outline are enumerated in levels. WordPerfect's outline numbering feature can automatically number eight outline levels. In addition, body text (text that is not numbered) can be included in an outline style. An example of a WordPerfect enumerated outline style with body text and eight levels is shown in Figure 24.1.

An Outline Bar and an Outline Button Bar can be displayed on the screen (see Figure 24.2). The Outline Bar and Outline Button Bar provide buttons that can be used to quickly access and use the many outline features such as formatting and editing the outline displayed. Many of the buttons on the Outline Bar and Outline Button Bar access the same functions. For example, the **Options** button on the Outline Bar and the **Out lnOpt** button on the Outline Button Bar both access the Outline Options dialog box.

Once an outline is created, a different outline style can be selected and immediately applied to the outline displayed on the screen. For example, a legal style outline can be converted to a bullets style outline.

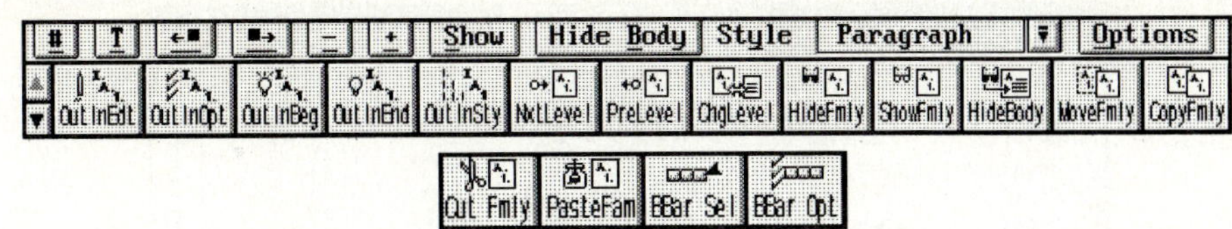

An idea and indented related ideas and body text below the idea are a *family*. A family can consist of one or more ideas (levels). An outline family can be hidden or shown on the screen, moved, copied, or cut (deleted). When an outline family is moved or cut, any outline ideas below the moved or cut family are automatically renumbered.

Outline families can be hidden so only the first item in a family is visible. Hiding the related ideas assists a writer in organizing main ideas. If a main idea is moved, cut, or copied, the hidden family(ies) is also moved, cut, or copied. Families can be hidden on an individual level or can be hidden by level for the entire outline. For example, to hide all families below level three, select the **Show** button on the *Outline Bar* and choose **3**. Families are hidden on an individual level by choosing the **HideFmly** button on the *Outline Button Bar*. The capability to hide and show outline families is often referred to as collapsible outlining.

Start-Up Instructions

❖ Use the graphics view mode.

❖ Change the font to **Dutch 801 Roman (Speedo)**.

❖ Type the outline title **Sample Outline Levels**. Press **Enter** three times. Center the title.

Display the Outline Bar and Outline Button Bar

1. Select **View, Outline Bar** {Alt and v, o}.

2. Choose **View, Button Bar Setup, Select** {Alt and v, s, s}.

3. Double-click on **Outline** {highlight Outline and press Enter}.

   Note: The Outline Bar and Outline Button Bar display on the screen. See Figure 24.2.

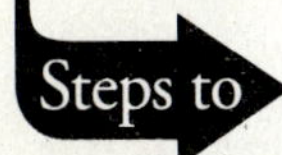

Create an Outline

1. Select the **Out lnBeg** button on the Outline Button Bar {Ctrl and F5, b}.

   Note: The Outline Style List dialog box displays (see Figure 24.3).

2. Double-click on the name **Outline** {highlight Outline and press s}.

   *Note: The Roman numeral I displays and the insertion point is located at the first default tab. Also, Level 1 displays in the **Style** button on the Ribbon. Turn on Reveal Codes (**Alt** and **F3**) to view the outline codes, [Outline][Para Style:Level1;].*

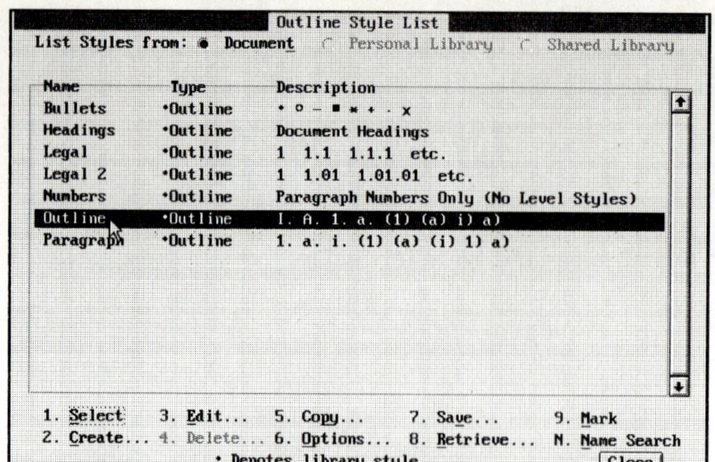

FIGURE 24.3

Outline Style List dialog box

3. Type the desired information.

> For example, type **Level one--first major idea**. (Do not type the period.) Press **Enter** twice.

Note: *The Roman numeral II displays.*

4. Press the **Tab** key once or select the **NxtLevel** button on the Outline Button Bar.

Note: *An A is displayed, replacing the Roman numeral II. Level 2 displays in the* **Style** *button on the Ribbon.*

5. Type the desired information.

> For example, type **Level two**. (Do not type the period.) Press **Enter** once.

Note: *The letter B displays.*

6. Type the desired information.

> For example, type **Second idea at level two**. Press **Enter** once.

Note: *The Letter C displays.*

7. Press the **Tab** key once or select the **NxtLevel** button on the Outline Button Bar.

Note: *The number 1 displays, replacing the letter C.*

8. Type the desired information.

> For example, type **Level three**. Press the **Enter** key once.

9. Press the **Tab** key once or select the **NxtLevel** button on the Outline Button Bar.

Note: *The lowercase "a" displays.*

10. Type the desired information.

> For example, type **Level four**. Press **Enter** once.

To Create Outline Body Text

11. Select the **T** (Text button) on the Outline Bar {Ctrl and t}.

 Chapter 24—Create an Outline, Table of Contents, & Index

12. Type the body text.

> For example, type **This is an example of body text in an outline. The body text is not numbered.** Press the **Enter** key once.

To Return to Outline Numbering

13. Select the **Options** button on the Outline Bar {Ctrl and F5}.

14. Select **Insert Outline Level (1-8)** {i}.

15. Type the desired level.

> For example, type **5.**

> *Note: A (1) displays.*

16. Type the desired information

For example, type **Level five.** Press the **Enter** key once.

17. Press the **Tab** key once or select the **NxtLevel** button on the Outline Button Bar.

Note: An (a) displays.

18. Type the desired information.

> For example, type **Level six.** Press the **Enter** key once.

Note: A (b) displays.

19. Type the desired information.

> For example, type **Second idea at level six** and press the **Enter** key once.

20. Press the **Tab** key once or select the **NxtLevel** button on the Outline Button Bar.

Note: An i) displays.

21. Type the desired information.

> For example, type **Level seven.** Press the **Enter** key once.

22. Press the **Tab** key once or select the **NxtLevel** button on the Outline Button Bar.

Note: An a) displays.

23. Type the desired information.

> For example, type **Level eight.** Press the **Enter** key once.

24. Type the desired information.

> For example, type **Second idea at level eight.** Press the **Enter** key twice.

25. To return the insertion point to the left margin, select the **Options** button in the Outline Bar, select **Insert Outline Level**, and type **1** {Ctrl and F5, i, 1}.

Note: The Roman numeral II displays.

26. Type the desired information.

> For example, type **Level one--second major idea.**

27. Select the **Out lnEnd** button on the Outline Button Bar {Ctrl and F5, e}.

*Note: Press the **Enter** key once and notice that no new Roman numeral displays.*

Finish-Up Instructions

❖ Optional. Place the insertion point in front of the first word "This" in the body text. Press **F4** twice to indent the body text under Level three.

❖ Use the filename **24drill1** and save the file.

❖ Optional. Print one copy.

❖ Close the document.

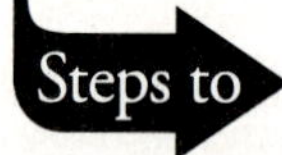

Change an Outline Style

1. Place the insertion point in any line below the first item of the outline.

2. Select the **Style** button on the Outline Bar; double-click on the desired style {Ctrl and o, y, press the up or down arrow key to highlight desired style, press Enter, F7}.

For example, double-click on **Legal**. Select the **Style** button again and double-click on **Bullets**.

Note: Your outline with Bullets style should look similar to Figure 24.4.

Insert a New Item(s) in an Outline

1. Place the insertion point to the right of the final character in the item that will precede the new item.

For example, place the insertion point to the right of the "r" in four.

2. Press **Enter** once to obtain the next outline number.

<table>
<tr><td>

FIGURE 24.4

Outline using Bullets style

</td><td>

```
                        Sample Outline


  •      Level one--first major idea

      o      Level two
      o      Second idea at level two
         -      Level three
            ■      Level four
      This is an example of body text in an outline.  The body text is not
      numbered.
               *      Level five
                  +      Level six
                  +      Second idea at level six
                     '      Level seven
                        x      Level eight
                        x      Second idea at level eight
  •      Level one--second major idea
```

</td></tr>
</table>

   Chapter 24—Create an Outline, Table of Contents, & Index

*Note: If necessary, select the **PreLevel** or **NxtLevel** button to obtain the desired outline level.*

3. Type the desired outline item.

   For example, type **Second idea at level four.** (Do not type the period.)

Steps to ▶ Hide or Show an Outline Family

1. Place the insertion point in the first item of the family to be hidden.

   For example, place the insertion point in Level five.

2. Select the **HideFmly** button on the Outline Button Bar {Ctrl and o, press the hyphen key, press F7}.

   Note: All indented items below Level five no longer display on the screen.

3. To show a hidden family, place the insertion point in the desired family item and select the **ShowFmly** button {Ctrl and o, press the + key, press F7}.

   For example, place the insertion point in Level five; select the **ShowFmly** button.

Steps to ▶ Hide or Show Outline Body Text

1. Place the insertion point in any line of the outline.

2. Select the **Hide (Show) Body** button in the Outline Bar or Outline Button Bar {Ctrl and F5, h, b}.

   *Note: The body text is hidden if the **Hide Body** button in the Outline Bar is selected. The body text is removed temporarily from the screen and the **Show Body** button displays. If the **Show Body** button is selected, the body text is displayed on the screen and the **Hide Body** button displays. The **Hide Body** Button in the Outline Button Bar functions the same way as the **Hide (Show) Body** button in the Outline Bar except the button name does not change. To show **all** hidden text, select the **Show** button in the Outline Bar and select **All**.*

Steps to ▶ Move an Outline Family

1. Place the insertion point in the first item of the family to be moved.

   For example, place the insertion point in Level seven.

2. Select the **MoveFmly** button on the Outline Button Bar {Ctrl and F5, m, m}.

   Note: Level seven and all indented items below Level seven are removed from the screen.

3. Locate the insertion point in the first item of the family where the moved item(s) is to be placed.

   For example, place the insertion point in Level 2.

4. Press **Enter** to complete the move.

   Note: The family of Level seven is moved to Level two.

Cut (Delete) an Outline Family

1. Place the insertion point in the first item of the family to be deleted.

   For example, place the insertion point in the "Level seven" family that is now located in Level two.

2. Select the down triangle on the left side of the Outline Button Bar to display the **Cut Fmly** button; select the **Cut Fmly** button {Ctrl and F5, m, t}.

   *Note: Select the up triangle on the left side of the Outline Button Bar to no longer display the **CutFmly** button.*

Copy an Outline Family

1. Place the insertion point in the first item of the family to be copied.

   For example, place the insertion point in Level two.

2. Select the **CopyFmly** button on the Outline Button Bar {Ctrl and F5, m, c}.

3. Locate the insertion point where the copied family is to be placed.

   For example, move the insertion point below Level one--second major idea. Turn on Reveal Codes and press the left arrow key to locate the cursor on the [Outline] code.

4. Select the down triangle on the left side of the Outline Button Bar to display the **PasteFam** button; select the **PasteFam** button {Ctrl and F5, m, p}.

   Note: Because there are no indented family items directly below the Level two item, only the Level two item displays.

Finish-Up Instructions

❖ Select the up triangle on the left side of the Outline Button Bar to no longer display the **PasteFam** button.

❖ Use the new filename **24drill1.rev** and save the file.

❖ Optional. Print one copy.

❖ Close the document.

Change an Outline Level

Note: The following steps are for your information only.

1. *To demote an item,* select the **NxtLevel** button on the Outline Button Bar or press the **Tab** key.

2. *To promote an item,* select the **PreLevel** button on the Outline Button Bar or press the **Shift** and **Tab** keys.

Create a Table of Contents

A table of contents lists the main topics that are written in a report, newspaper, book, etc. The topic is usually followed by *leader characters* (periods) and the page number where the topic is located (see Figure 24.5). Buttons on the Tools Button Bar provide easy access to many of the table of contents commands.

Creating a table of contents is a four-part process:

1. The document is typed.

2. The table of contents entries are marked.

3. The table of contents is defined.

4. The table of contents is generated.

The table of contents entries are identified (marked) in a document that has been previously typed. In the document, the main topics are usually typed centered or at the left margin and are referred to as major headings. Under each major heading, there can be one or more subheadings.

Table of contents entries are marked by selecting the **MarkText** button on the Tools Button Bar and by choosing the appropriate table of contents level. When all the table of contents entries have been marked, the table of contents is defined. Usually, a table of contents is placed on a separate page at the beginning of the document. The insertion point is moved to the top of the document and a new page is created by pressing **Ctrl** and **Enter**. After **Ctrl** and **Enter** are pressed, the page number must be reset to 1 so that the table of contents will show the correct page numbers. The insertion point is then moved to the new first page and the table of contents title is typed. In the Define Table of Contents dialog box, the table of contents is defined by typing the number of levels in the table of contents. If desired, the numbering mode (format) for each level of the table of contents can be selected. WordPerfect places a table of contents definition code ([Def Mark]) in the document at the location of the insertion point.

CONTENTS

PRESIDENT'S ANNOUNCEMENT 1
   Operation Changes 1

A JOINT VENTURE 1
   Market Conditions 2

RAW LAND 2
   Raw Land/Joint Ventures 2

FIGURE 24.5

Sample table of contents

When the table of contents is generated by selecting the **Generate** button on the Tools Button Bar, the table of contents text is placed at the location of the table of contents definition code. When the default table of contents numbering mode is used, the table of contents text displays with dot leader characters and the page number aligned at the right margin. Second-level entries are indented .5 inches from the left margin.

If a document is modified after the table of contents has been generated, the table of contents can be updated to show new page numbers. Also, new table of contents entries can be marked or existing entries can be deleted. When all changes to the document and entries have been completed, the document is saved and the **Generate** button is selected again. The original table of contents is replaced by the updated table of contents.

Display the Tools Button Bar

1. Select **View, Button Bar Setup, Select** {Alt and v, s, s}.
2. Double-click on **Tools** {highlight Tools and press s}.

   Note: The Tools Button Bar displays on the screen.

Start-Up Instructions

❖   Open the file named **24drill2.txt** from the data disk.

Mark Table of Contents Entries

1. Select a major heading.

   For example, block the heading **PRESIDENT'S ANNOUNCEMENT**.

2. Select the **MarkText** button on the Tools Button Bar {Alt and F5}.
3. Select **Table of Contents** {c}.

   Note: The Mark Text dialog box displays and the number 1 Level is highlighted (see Figure 24.6).

FIGURE 24.6

Mark Text dialog box

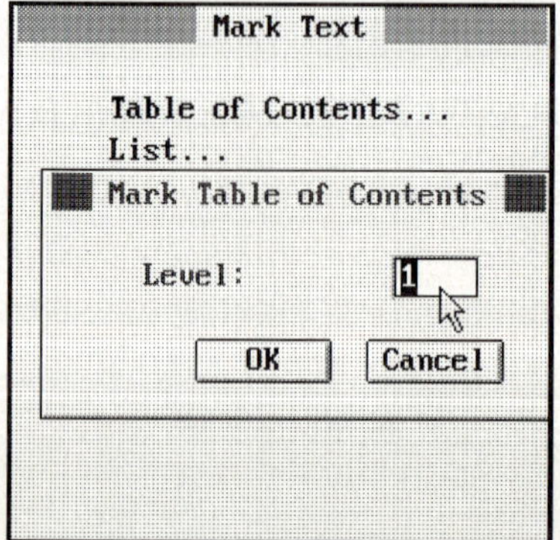

4. Type the desired table of contents level number.

   For example, check that the number 1 is displayed.

5. Select **OK** {Enter}.

   Note: The text is no longer highlighted. Use Reveal Codes to view the table of contents codes, [Mrk Txt ToC Begin] and [Mrk Txt ToC End]. Turn off Reveal Codes if desired.

6. Select a subheading.

   For example, select **Operation Changes**.

7. Select the **MarkText** button on the Tools Button Bar; select **Table of Contents** {Alt and F5, c}.

8. Type the desired table of contents level.

   For example, type **2**.

9. Select **OK** {Enter}.

Finish-Up Instructions

❖ Repeat Steps 1–5 to mark the remaining major headings, **A JOINT VENTURE** and **RAW LAND**, as table of contents Level 1 entries.

❖ Repeat Steps 6–9 to mark the remaining subheadings, **Market Conditions** and **Raw Land/Joint Ventures**, as table of contents Level 2 entries.

❖ Use the filename **24drill2.mk** and save the file.

Start-Up Instructions

❖ The file named **24drill2.mk** should be displayed on the screen.

❖ If a mouse is available, the Tools Button Bar should be displayed.

Steps to ▶ Define a Table of Contents

1. Move the insertion point to the top of the document.

2. Press **Ctrl** and **Enter** to insert a hard page break at the top of the document to create a new page for the table of contents.

   Note: Page 1 of the original document is now page 2 and must be renumbered to become page 1 again.

3. Select **Layout, Page, Page Numbering** {Alt and L, p, n}.

4. Select **Page Number**, choose **New Number**, and type **1** {n, n, 1}.

5. Select **OK** three times {Enter four times}.

   Note: Pg 1 displays in the Status bar.

6. Press the up arrow key to move the insertion point to the new page.

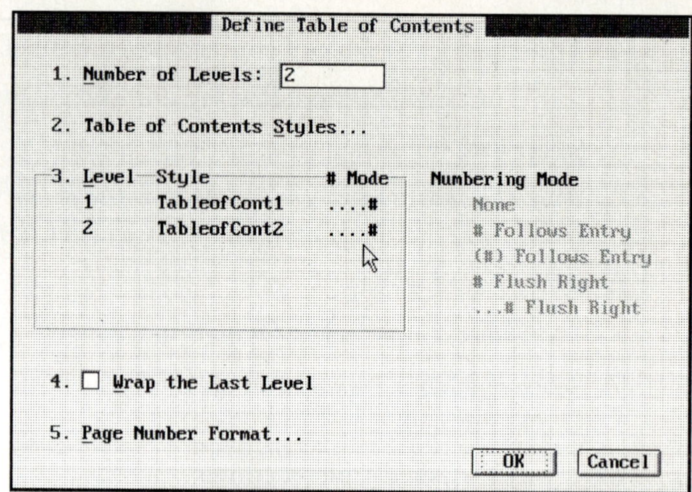

7. Type and center the table of contents page title, e.g., **CONTENTS**. Press **Enter** once. Select **Left** justification; press **Enter** twice.

   Note: The table of contents definition code must be located below the justification code.

8. Select **Tools, Table of Contents, Define** {Alt and F5, d, c}.

   Note: The Define Table of Contents dialog box displays.

9. Select **Number of Levels** {n}.

10. Type the number of table of contents levels used when marking the document.

    For example, type **2** and press **Enter** once.

    Note: Level 1 and Level 2 are now active and display in the Level, Style, and # Mode area. The # Mode displays the number style, i.e., . . .# (see Figure 24.7).

11. Select **OK** {Enter}.

    Note: The dialog box is removed from the screen. Use Reveal Codes to view the Table of Contents definition code, [Def Mark]. When the table of contents is generated, the table of contents will be placed after the definition code.

Finish-Up Instructions

❖ Save the file again using the same filename **24drill2.mk**.

Start-Up Instructions

❖ The file named **24drill2.mk** should be displayed on the screen.

❖ The table of contents entries must be marked and the table of contents format and location defined before the table of contents can be generated.

❖ If a mouse is available, the Tools Button Bar should be displayed.

 Generate a Table of Contents

1. Select the down triangle on the left side of the Tools Button Bar to display the **Generate** button. Select the Generate button {Alt and F5, g}.

   Note: The message, "Existing tables, lists, and indexes will be replaced if you continue." displays.

2. Select **OK** {Enter}.

   Note: Generate in Progress displays briefly. Then the table of contents displays at the location of the table of contents definition code.

Finish-Up Instructions

❖ Use the filename **24drill2.toc** and save the file.

❖ Print one copy.

❖ Close the document.

Create an Index

An index is an alphabetical listing of topics contained in a document. Entries in the index usually include a page number to indicate the location of the topic. Once a document is typed, main index heading and subheading entries can be marked, the index number mode defined, and the index generated. The Tools Button Bar can be used to access many of the index commands.

Once the main index heading and subheading entries have been marked, the index format is defined. Usually, an index is placed on a separate page at the end of the document. A hard page break is inserted at the end of the document and an index page title is typed. When the numbering format of the index is defined, an index definition code, [Def Mark], is inserted at the location of the insertion point in the document.

After the main index heading and subheading entries have been marked and the index numbering format defined, the index is generated. The generated index organizes all topics alphabetically and inserts the page number where the topic is located in the document. The generated index displays at the location of the index definition code.

If a document is modified after the index has been generated, the index can be updated to show new page numbers. Also, new main heading and subheading entries can be marked. When all changes to the document and entries have been completed, the document is saved and the **Generate** button is selected again. The original index is replaced by the updated index.

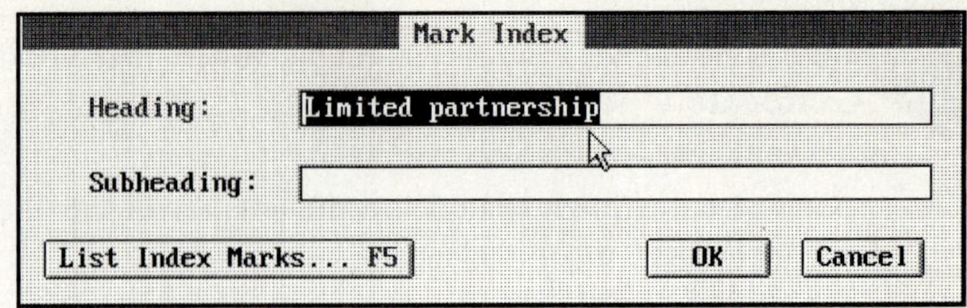

FIGURE 24.8

Mark Index dialog box

❖  Open the file named **24drill2.txt** from the data disk.

❖ If a mouse is available, the Tools Button Bar should be displayed.

Steps to ▶ Mark Index Entries

1. Select the text to be a main index heading entry.

   For example, select **limited partnership** in the first sentence of the first paragraph.

2. Select the **MarkText** button on the Tools Button Bar {Alt and F5}.

3. Select **Index** {i}.

   Note: The Mark Index dialog box displays and the selected text is shown in the Heading box (see Figure 24.8).

4. Select **OK** {press Enter three times}.

   Note: The text is no longer highlighted. Use Reveal Codes to view the Index code, [Index].

5. Select the text to be a main index heading entry.

   For example, select **joint venture** in the first sentence of the third paragraph.

6. Select the **MarkText** button on the Tools Button Bar; select **Index** {Alt and F5, i}.

7. Select **OK** {Enter three times}.

Mark an Index Subheading

8. Select the text to be an index subheading.

   For example, select the words **form of partnership** located in the first sentence of the third paragraph.

9. Select the **MarkText** button on the Generate Button Bar; select **Index** {Alt and F5, i}.

   Note: The selected text "Form of partnership" is highlighted in the Heading box. "Form of partnership" will be a subheading index entry under the main heading, Joint venture.

10. Type the main index heading entry.

    For example, type **Joint venture**.

    Note: When the main index heading entry is typed in the Heading box, WordPerfect places the selected text, "form of partnership," in temporary memory.

11. Press the **Tab** key to move the insertion point to the Subheading box.

   Note: WordPerfect automatically inserts the selected text in the Subheading box.

12. Select **OK** {Enter twice}.

Finish-Up Instructions

❖ Select the heading **Market Conditions**. Repeat Steps 2–4 to mark the selected text as a main index heading. The "C" in *Conditions* should be changed to lower case.

❖ Select the words **raw land** in the first sentence of the last paragraph. Repeat Steps 8–12 to mark the selected text as an index subheading under the main heading, *Joint venture.*

❖ Use the filename **24drill3.ind** and save the file.

Start-Up Instructions

❖ The filename **24drill3.ind** should be displayed on the screen.

❖ If a mouse is available, the Tools Button Bar should be displayed.

Steps to ▶ Define an Index

1. Move the insertion point to the bottom of the document.

2. Press **Ctrl** and **Enter** to insert a hard page break.

3. Type and center the index page title, e.g., **INDEX**.

4. Press **Enter** once and select **Left** justification. Press the **Enter** key twice.

5. Select **Tools, Index, Define** {Alt and F5, d, i}.

   Note: The Define Index dialog box displays (see Figure 24.9).

6. Select the desired Numbering Mode.

```
                        Define Index
 ┌Level──────────Current Style──┐  ┌Numbering Mode─────────┐
 │ Heading        Index1        │  │ 1. ○  None            │
 │ Subheading     Index2        │  │ 2. ○  # Follows Entry  │
 │                              │  │ 3. ○  (#) Follows Entry│
 │                              │  │ 4. ○  # Flush Right    │
 6. Index Level Styles...          │ 5. ●  ...# Flush Right │
                                   └───────────────────────┘

 7. ⊠ Combine Sequential Page Numbers (Example: 51-62)

 8. Page Number Format...

 9. Concordance Filename: [                              ]

 [ File List... F5 ]  [ QuickList... F6 ]       [  OK  ]  [ Cancel ]
```


Define Index dialog box

For example, select the **# Follows Entry** option {f}.

7. Select **OK** {press Enter}.

   Note: WordPerfect inserts an Index definition code into the document. Use Reveal Codes to view the index definition code, [Def Mark]. When the index is generated, the index text will be placed at the location of the index definition code.

Finish-Up Instructions

❖ Save the file again using the same filename.

Start-Up Instructions

❖ The file named **24drill3.ind** should be displayed on the screen.

❖ The index entries must be marked and the index format and location defined before the index can be generated.

❖ If a mouse is available, the Tools Button Bar should be displayed.

Generate an Index

1. Select the **Generate** button on the Tools Button Bar {Alt and F5, g}.

   Note: The message, "Existing tables, lists, and indexes will be replaced if you continue." displays.

2. Select **OK** {Enter}.

   *Note: The Generate in Progress box displays briefly. Then the index displays at the location of the index definition code. If necessary, press **Ctrl** and **End** to view the index at the bottom of the document.*

Finish-Up Instructions

❖ Place the insertion point at the top of the index page and change the line spacing to one.

❖ Use the filename **24index** and save the file.

❖ Print one copy of the index page only.

❖ Close the document.

The Next Step

Chapter Review and Activities

FEATURES SUMMARY

FEATURES	ACTIONS	PAGE
Display the Outline Bar and Outline Button Bar	Select **View**, **Outline Bar**; choose **View**, **Button Bar Setup**, **Select**, double-click on **OUTLINE**.	613
Create an outline	Select the **Out lnBeg** button, double-click on the name **OUTLINE**, type desired information, press **Tab** or select the **NxtLevel** button.	613
Create outline body text	Select the **T** button on the Outline Bar, type the desired text.	614
Return to outline numbering	Select the **Options** button, select **Insert Outline Level**, type desired level number.	615
Change an outline style	Select the **Style** button on the Outline Bar, double-click on the desired style.	616
Insert a new item(s) in an outline	Place the insertion point to the right of the final character in item that will precede the new item, press **Enter** once, select **NxtLevel** or **PreLevel** button for desired level number, type the new outline item.	616
Hide/show an outline family	Place the insertion point in the first item of the family to be hidden, select the **HideFmly** button. To show a hidden family, place the insertion point in the desired family item and select the **ShowFmly** button.	617

| --- | --- | --- |
Hide/show outline body text	Place the insertion point in any line of the outline, select the **Hide (Show) Body** button on the Outline Bar.	617
Move an outline family	Place the insertion point in the first item of the family to be moved, select the **MoveFmly** button; locate the insertion point in the first item of the family where the moved item(s) is to be placed, **Enter**.	617
Cut (delete) an outline family	Place the insertion point in the first item of the family to be deleted, select the down triangle on the left side of the Outline Button Bar, select the **CutFmly** button.	618
Copy an outline family	Place the insertion point in the first item of the family to be copied, select the **CopyFmly** button. Locate the insertion point where the copied family is to be placed, select the down triangle on the left side of the Outline Button Bar, and select the **PasteFam** button.	618
Demote an outline item	Select **NxtLevel** button.	618
Promote an outline item	Select **PreLevel** button.	618
Create a table of contents:		
Mark table of contents entries	Select a major heading, select the **MarkText** button, select **Table of Contents**, type the desired table of contents level number, **OK**.	620
Define a table of contents	Move the insertion point to the top of the document, press **Ctrl** and **Enter**, select **Layout**, **Page**, **Page Numbering**, select **Page Number**, **New Number**, type desired page number, select **OK** three times; press up arrow key once, type **CONTENTS**, press **Enter** once, select **Left** justification, **Enter** twice, select **Tools**, **Table of Contents**, **Define**, select **Number of Levels**, type the number of levels used when marking text, **OK**.	621
Generate a table of contents	Select the down triangle on the left side of the Tools Button Bar, select the **Generate** button, **OK**.	623
Create an index:		
Mark main index headings	Block the text to be a main index heading entry, select the **MarkText** button, select **Index**, **OK**.	624
Mark index subheadings	Block the desired text, select the **MarkText** button, type the main index heading entry, press **Tab**, **OK**.	624

Self-Check Questions

True/False—Circle One

T F 1. WordPerfect can number nine outline levels automatically.

T F 2. Legal is one of WordPerfect's predefined formats for numbering paragraphs.

T F 3. To obtain the next outline level, press the **Tab** key.

T F 4. If items are deleted or inserted in an outline, WordPerfect automatically renumbers the outline.

T F 5. After the text is marked and the table of contents is defined, the generated table of contents will be placed at the location of the table of contents definition code.

T F 6. All items in a numbered outline, including body text, are numbered.

Short Answer

1. List the four steps to move an outline family.

2. Creating a table of contents is a four-part process. List the four processes.

3. A generated index is usually placed on a separate page at the _________ of a document.

4. List the five steps to mark an index subheading.

Enriching Language Arts Skills

Spelling/Vocabulary Words

dissolution   the act of breaking apart or terminating.

irrevocable   not to be canceled or reversed.

valid   sound, authentic, just.

appreciation   the increase in the value of property or goods.

Percentage Amounts

Use figures for numbers that are followed by the word *percent*. Spell out the word *percent* unless the percentage amount is used in a table that contains statistical information or is used in a headline/title.

Examples:

Salaries are 30 percent of the total budget. (Percent spelled out)

Percentage of Males and Females		
Age Group	Male	Female
20-29	68.0%	65.0%
30-39	18.5%	19.5%
40-49	13.5%	15.5%

PRICES ARE SLASHED 40% STOREWIDE!!! (Headline information)

Activities

Activity 24.1—Create an Outline

1. Display the Outline Bar and the Outline Button Bar.

2. Type and center the following outline title:
   ESTATE AND FINANCIAL MANAGEMENT PLANNING

3. Press **Enter** three times and select **Left** justification.

4. Define and create the following outline. (If necessary, see the Steps to Create an Outline on pages 613-616).

I.   Tools of estate planning
      A.   Financial
      B.   Legal

II.   Estate planning is money
      A.   Creation/investment
      B.   Reinvestment
      C.   Distribution

III. Why financial planning?
      A.   Financial security
            1.   Obstacles
            2.   Concerns
      B.   Financial life improvement
            1.   Lower income taxes
            2.   Investments
            3.   Retirement income
                  a.   Early retirement
                  b.   Retirement at age 65

IV.   Financial security
      A.   Financial check-up
      B.   Professional consultation

5. Use the filename **24act1** and save the file.

6. Print one copy.

7. Close the document.

◼ Activity 24.2—Create a Table of Contents and Index

1. Display the Tools Button Bar.

2. Open the file named **24act2.txt** from the data disk.

3. Change the vertical line spacing to two.

4. Mark all sideheadings for the table of contents entries (select the sidehead-ing, choose the **MarkText** button, select **Table of Contents**, **OK**).

5. Mark the first occurrence of the following index entries. If necessary, see Steps to Mark Index Entries and Mark an Index Subheading on page 624.

      Member meetings
        annual meetings
        special meetings
      Executive Committee
      Proxies
      Quorum

6. Move the insertion point to the top of the document and create a new page for the table of contents (press **Home** three times, press the up arrow key once, **Ctrl** and **Enter**).

7. With the insertion point on page 2, reset the page number to 1 (select **Layout**, **Page**, **Page Numbering**, select **Page Number**, choose **New Number**, type 1, select **OK** three times).

8. Press the up arrow key to move the insertion point to the new page. Type and center the title **CONTENTS**. Press **Enter** once and select **Left** justification. Press **Enter** twice.

9. Define the table of contents (select **Tools**, **Table of Contents**, **Define**, select **Number of Levels**, type 1, **OK**).

10. Move the insertion point to the bottom of the document (press **Home** twice and the down arrow key once). Insert a hard page break to create a new page for the index (**Ctrl** and **Enter**).

11. Change the line spacing to one for the index page.

12. Type and center the title **Index**. Press **Enter** once and select **Left** justification. Press **Enter** twice.

13. Define the index (select **Tools**, **Index**, **Define**, choose **# Follows Entry**, **OK**).

14. Use the filename **24act2.fin** and save the file.

15. Generate the table of contents and index (select the down arrow on the left side of the Button Bar, select the **Generate** button, **OK**).

16. Save the file again using the same filename.

17. Print one copy.

18. Close the document.

Challenge Your Skills

Skill 24.1—Create and Edit an Outline

1. If necessary, display the Outline Bar and Outline Button Bar.

2. Use the Outline style and create the following outline. The paragraphs have been indented to show levels for outline numbering. Make decisions regarding:

   Margins
   Justification
   Fonts (**Hint:** *Use Dutch 801 Roman or similar font.*)
   Outline numbering and spacing

    Chapter 24—Create an Outline, Table of Contents, & Index

Bankcroft Owners' Conditions and Restrictions

Definitions
  Association
  Owner

Property rights
  Owner's easements of enjoyment
  Parking rights
  Easements
        For private sidewalk, yard, and patio use
        For encroachments of overhanging eaves and decks

Annual and special assessments
  Liens and personal obligations of assessments
  Maximum annual assessments
        No more than 15 percent increase without a vote
        Increased assessments with a written consent of 60 percent of members
  Due dates for assessments
        Approved operating budget 60 days before beginning of year
              Estimate revenue and expenses on accrual basis
              Identify total cash reserves
        Financial statements prepared with accepted accounting principles

Exterior maintenance
  Common area maintenance
  Exterior maintenance on lots

---

3. Use the filename **24skill1** and save the file.

4. Edit the outline as follows:

    a. Insert the following items:

       Under item I:

       C.   Properties
       D.   Common areas

    b. Insert the following first level and second level items above Roman numeral III (Annual and special assessments):

       Membership and voting rights

           Every lot owner is an Association member
           All owners are entitled to one vote

    c. Hide the outline family now numbered IV. B.

    d. Select the Bullets style outline.

5. Once changes are made, use the filename **24skill1.rev** and save the file again.

6. Print one copy.

7. Close the document.

➡ ▪ Skill 24.2—Create and Edit a Table of Contents and an Index; Language Arts

1. Display the Tools Button Bar.

2. Open the file named **24skill2.txt** from the data disk and make decisions regarding:

   Margins
   Justification
   Fonts
   Widow/Orphan control
   Footer text and placement
   Spacing before and after headings and subheadings
   Bold, underline, capitalization of title, headings, and subheadings
   Format of table of contents
   Format of index
   Correct two spelling errors, one misused word, one percent error, and
     two punctuation errors.

3. The title of the document is Pocatello College Agreement.

4. Mark the first- and second-level table of contents entries.

5. Mark all occurrences of the following main index heading and subheading entries.

   Hint: Use the Search command to locate index entry text. If the index entry text appears in a paragraph more than once, only mark the first occurrence of the text.

   Preamble
   Recognition
   Leaves
       Sick leave
       Industrial accident or illness leave
       Jury duty
   Transfers and Reassignments
   Professional Education Program
       Multicultural program
       Learning styles program
   Layoffs
   Performance Evaluation Procedures
       Contract employees
       Regular employees

6. Define the table of contents and index.

   Hint: Remember to reset the page number for the first page of the document (after the table of contents page) to page 1.

          Chapter 24—Create an Outline, Table of Contents, & Index

7. Use the filename **24skill2.fin** and save the file.

8. Generate the table of contents and index.

9. Print one copy.

10. Revise the document as follows:

   a. Insert the following paragraph after the first paragraph under the "LEAVES" heading:

      Immediate Family Illness Leave

      An employee may be granted three (3) days of paid leave per year in the event of the serious illness of a member of his or her immediate family.

   b. Insert the following paragraph after the first paragraph under the "RECOGNITION" heading.

      ORGANIZATIONAL RIGHTS

      The Union shall have the right to use institutional bulletin boards and mail services, subject to reasonable regulations, and the right to use institutional facilities for the purpose of conducting Union business.

   c. Determine the appropriate table of contents and index entries for the inserted text and mark those entries.

      Hint: To mark the new table of contents and index entries, use the index and table of contents entries structure described in Steps 4 and 5 on page 634.

11. Use the filename **24skill2.rev** and save the document.

12. Generate the table of contents and index.

13. Use page numbering to insert a Roman numeral for the table of contents page.

14. Save the file again and print one copy.

15. Close the document.

Advanced Features and Master Documents

Features Covered

- Create a paragraph style containing a paragraph border and graphic image
- Create a style based on an existing style
- Link styles
- Create cross references
- Create a master document
- Expand and condense a master document
- Use cross references in a master document
- Save a master document and subdocuments

Objectives

After completing this chapter, you will be able to create a paragraph style containing a paragraph border and a graphic image. You will also be able to create a style based on an existing style as well as be able to link styles. You will learn to create cross references and master documents. In addition, you will expand, condense, and use cross references in a master document as well as save the master document and subdocuments.

Chapter Introduction

In addition to formatting codes (see Chapter 16), text and graphic elements can be included in styles. Using styles can assist you in creating documents with a consistent and professional appearance. Also, WordPerfect's Cross Referencing and Master Document features promote easy use when creating multiple-page documents.

Advanced Styles

In Chapter 16, basic styles that contain formatting such as margins, font changes, and justification were created. In addition, many other formatting elements such as graphic lines, borders, and graphic images can also be incorporated into a style. Also, if desired, text that is used often can be inserted into a style. For example, a letterhead style can be created that contains text, font changes, graphic lines, and/or a graphic image. The letterhead style can be saved in a style library file and can be used each time a letter is being created.

Styles that contain graphic elements such as graphic lines, page/paragraph borders, and graphic boxes can be created. Graphic elements are inserted into a style similar to creating a graphic element in a regular document window. Within the Style Contents box of the Edit Style dialog box, **Alt** and **F9** are pressed to access the graphic commands. (The Graphics menu cannot be used when creating a style in the Edit Style dialog box.)

In addition to creating styles by placing codes in the Style Contents box of the Edit Style dialog box, styles can be created based on an existing style or based on formatting codes within the text. Creating styles based on an existing style or based on existing text formatting can greatly expedite the process of creating styles.

When creating a new style based on another style, the name of the existing style displays in the Style Contents box. Additional formatting options are selected to modify the new style. For example, the font or justification of the new style may be changed. To create a style based on existing formatting codes, place the cursor/insertion point at the location of the desired code(s), select **Layout**, **Styles**, **Create**, type a style name, and select **Paragraph** or **Character** style type. The **Create From Current Paragraph** or **Create From Current Character** option is then selected.

A style can be linked to another style. When styles are linked, the first style is in effect until the **Enter** key is pressed. When the **Enter** key is pressed, the first style is turned off and the next (linked) style is turned on.

Once styles have been created, save the styles in a style library file so that the created styles are available when formatting other documents (see Chapter 16). Styles can be saved in a personal or shared style library file. There is no difference between a personal or shared library file except when WordPerfect is being run on a local area network (LAN). When WordPerfect is being run on a LAN, shared style library files are used so that all users of the network can access the same styles.

Start-Up Instructions

❖ 💾 Open the file named **25drill1.txt** from the data disk.

 Create a Paragraph Style Containing a Paragraph Border

1. Place the cursor/insertion point in the paragraph where the new style will be applied.

    For example, place the cursor/insertion point in the first side heading, Always Ask Questions.

2. Select **Layout, Styles** {Alt and F8}.

3. Select **Create** {c}.

4. Type a name for the new style.

    For example, type **side heading**. (Do not type the period.)

5. Check that Paragraph Style displays at the Style Type option.

6. Select **OK** {Enter}.

7. Click in the Description box and type a description of the style {d}.

    For example, type **style for side headings**. (Do not type the period.)

8. Click in the Style Contents box {Tab, c}.

9. To change the font, appearance, or size, press **Ctrl** and **F8**, make the desired changes, and select **OK**.

    For example, change the appearance to **Bold** and select **OK**.

To Place a Paragraph Border Below the Paragraph

10. Press **Alt** and **F9** to access the Graphics dialog box.

11. Select **Paragraph** in the Borders area {o, p}.

    Note: The Create Paragraph Border dialog box displays. By default, a single line border is placed around all sides of a paragraph. This default can be accepted by choosing OK, or the paragraph border settings can be changed by choosing the Customize option.

12. Select **Customize** {c} and make desired changes.

    For example:

    a. Select **Lines** {L}.

    b. Select **None** for the Left Line, Right Line, and Top Line options.

    c. Select **Close** twice {Enter twice}.

13. Select **OK** {Enter}.

14. Press **F7**.

15. Select **OK** {Enter}.

    Note: The new style for side headings displays in the Style List dialog box.

16. Choose **Select** {s} to apply the new style to the paragraph containing the cursor/insertion point.

Finish-Up Instructions

❖ Place the cursor/insertion point in the side heading *Listen to Advice But Make Your Own Decision.*

❖ Move the mouse pointer to the **Style** button on the Ribbon and click once.

❖ Scroll down the list of styles and double-click on the **side heading** style name to apply the style to the side heading paragraph.

❖ Place the cursor/insertion point in the side heading *There are No Shortcuts to Success.*

❖ Move the mouse pointer to the **Style** button on the Ribbon and click once.

❖ Scroll down the list of styles and double-click on the **side heading** style name to apply the style to the side heading paragraph.

❖ Use the filename **25drill1.for** and save the file.

Start-Up Instructions

❖ The file named **25drill1.for** should be displayed on the screen.

Create a Paragraph Style Containing a Graphic Image

1. Place the cursor/insertion point in the paragraph to be formatted with the new style.

   For example, place the cursor/insertion point in the first paragraph that begins "To succeed as an entrepreneur. . ."

2. Select **Layout, Styles** {Alt and F8}.

3. Select **Create** {c}.

4. Type a name for the new style.

   For example, type **graphic par**.

5. Check that Paragraph Style displays at the Style Type option.

6. Select **OK** {Enter}.

7. Click in the Description box and type a description of the style {d}.

   For example, type **style that contains a graphic image**.

8. Click in the Style Contents box {Tab, c}.

9. Press **Alt** and **F9** to access the Graphics dialog box.

10. Select **Create** in the Graphics Boxes area {b, c}.

11. Select **Filename, File List, OK** {F, F5, Enter}.

12. Double-click on the desired filename {highlight filename, press Enter}.

    For example, double-click on **PENPUSH.WPG**.

13. Select **Edit Position** and choose the desired horizontal position {p, h, select desired alignment}.

    For example, in the Horizontal Position box, select **Left** {L}.

14. Select **OK** {Enter twice}.

15. Select **Edit Size** and type the desired width for the graphic box {s}.

    For example, type **.5** in the Set Width box.

16. Check that the Automatic Height, Based on Box Content Height option is selected.

17. Select **OK** {Enter twice}.

18. Select **Based on Box Style** and double-click on the desired box style {y, highlight desired style, Enter}.

    For example, double-click on **User Box**.

19. Select **OK** {Enter}.

20. Press **F7**.

21. Select **OK** {Enter}.

22. Choose **Select** {Enter} to apply the new style to the paragraph that contains the cursor/insertion point.

Finish-Up Instructions

- ❖ Move the cursor/insertion point to the paragraph that begins "The successful entrepreneur. . ."
- ❖ Move the mouse pointer to the **Style** button on the Ribbon and click.
- ❖ Double-click on the **graphic par** style name.
- ❖ Move the cursor/insertion point to the paragraph that begins "A successful entrepreneur. . ."
- ❖ Move the mouse pointer to the **Style** button on the Ribbon and click.
- ❖ Double-click on the **graphic par** style name.
- ❖ Use the same filename **25drill1.for** and save the file.

Start-Up Instructions

- ❖ The file named **25drill1.for** should be displayed.
- ❖ Create a title style using the following information.

    a. Move the cursor/insertion point to the top of the document.

    b. Select **Layout, Styles, Create** {Alt and F8, c}.

c. Type the style name **title** in the Style Name box and check that Paragraph Style displays in the Style Type box. Select **OK**.

d. In the Description box, type **style for title**.

e. Click in the Style Contents box.

f. Press **Ctrl** and **F8** and change the font to **Bodoni-WP Bold (Type 1), 14 point**. Select **OK**.

g. Press **Shift** and **F8** and select **Line**. Change the justification to **Center** and select **OK**.

h. Press **Enter** twice.

i. Press **F7** and choose **OK**.

❖ Continue with the Steps to Create a Style Based on an Existing Style.

Create a Style Based on an Existing Style

1. In the Style List dialog box, select **Create** and type the name for the new style {c}.

   For example, type **subtitle**.

2. Select **OK** {Enter}.

3. In the Description box, type a description of the style {d}.

   For example, type **style for subtitle paragraphs**.

4. Click in the Style Contents dialog box {Tab, c}.

5. To select the Based on Style option, press **Alt** and **F8**.

   Note: The Style List dialog box displays.

6. Double-click on the style to be used as the basis for the new style.

   For example, double-click on the style name **title**.

   Note: The code [Para Style:title;] displays in the Style Contents box.

7. Make additional selections in the Style Contents box to modify the new style.

   For example, press **Ctrl** and **F8** and change the size to **12 point**.
   Select **OK**.

8. When all modifications are complete, press **F7**.

9. Select **OK** {Enter}.

Finish-Up Instructions

❖ Continue with the following Steps to Link Styles.

 Link Styles

1. In the Style List dialog box, highlight the name of the style that will be linked to another style.

   For example, highlight the style named **title**.

2. Select **Edit** {e}.

3. Select the **Enter Key Action...Off/On** option {e}.

4. Select the **Turn Style Off and Link to** option {t}.

   Note: A list of style names displays.

5. Scroll through the list of style names and double-click on the style to be linked {highlight the desired style name and press Enter}.

   For example, double-click on **subtitle**.

6. Select **OK** twice {Enter twice}.

Finish-Up Instructions

❖ Save the new styles using the filename **25drill1.sty**.

   a. In the Style List dialog box, select **Save**.

   b. Type the name of the new style file including the drive letter and/or directory name. For example, type **a:25drill1.sty**.

   c. Check that an X appears in the Save User Created Styles option box.

   d. Select **OK**.

   e. Select **Close** to exit the Style List dialog box.

❖ At the top of the document, type the following text:

   Becoming a Successful Entrepreneur (do not press Enter).

❖ Move the mouse pointer to the **Style** button on the Ribbon and click once. Double-click on the **title** style name.

❖ Press **Enter**.

*Note: The style name subtitle displays in the **Style** button on the Ribbon.*

❖ Type the following text.

   Key Points to Remember

❖ Press **Enter** once.

❖ Use the new filename **25drill1.fin** and save the document.

❖ Print one copy.

Create Cross References

The Cross Reference feature is used to *direct* readers from one area of a document to another area of the document. For example, in this textbook, cross references are often used to direct readers from the text to a related figure. Cross references can be connected to pages, figures, notes, captions, etc.

Creating a cross reference requires two parts: a reference and a target. The *reference* is the location in the document where the cross reference information is inserted. The *target* is the location in the document where the reader is directed. For example, in the cross reference information "See Table 3 on page 596," the reference is the location where the page number is inserted and the target is the table that appears on page 596.

A target is identified by a target name. A single target name can be used for cross referencing multiple references. For example, a target name given to a figure can be used to reference the figure one or more times.

A reference can be linked to multiple targets, e.g., see pages 22, 30, and 46. When the cross reference is created for multiple tables, each target is marked separately using the same target name.

When a cross reference is created, the reference information is automatically placed at the location of the insertion point. If any target(s) is moved to a different page or deleted, the Generate feature must be used to update the cross reference(s).

Start-Up Instructions

❖   💾   Open the file named **25chap1.sub** from the data disk.

Create a Cross Reference

1. Place the cursor/insertion point where the reference is to be located in the document.

   For example, place the cursor/insertion point directly to the left of the period in the last sentence in the Chapter 1 subdocument.

2. Select **Tools, Cross-Reference, Both** {Alt and F5, m, b}.

   Note: The Mark Cross-Reference and Target dialog box displays.

3. Select the desired Tie Reference to option.

   For example, check that the Page option is selected.

4. Select **Target Name** {t}.

5. Type the desired target name.

   For example, type **first figure**.

6. Select **OK** {Enter twice}.

Note: A different Mark Cross-Reference and Target dialog box displays. The cursor/insertion point is positioned at the location where the reference will be placed. The cursor/insertion point is then moved to the target location.

7. Move the cursor/insertion point to the desired target location.

   For example, press the down arrow key approximately four times to locate the cursor/insertion point below the captioned box.

8. Press **Enter** to insert the target.

   Note: The cursor/insertion point returns to the document window. The page number where the target is located displays at the reference in the document.

Finish-Up Instructions

❖ Save the file using the same filename **25chap1.sub**.

❖ Open the file named **25chap2.sub** that is located on your data disk.

❖ Create a cross reference using the following information:

   a. Place the cursor/insertion point to the left of the period in the last sentence of the Chapter 2 subdocument.

   b. Repeat Steps 1–8. Use the target name **second figure**.

❖ Save the file using the same filename, **25chap2.sub**.

Generate the Cross Reference

Note: The following steps are for your information only.

1. With a document containing cross references on the screen, select **Tools, Generate** {Alt and t, g}.

   Note: The Generate dialog box displays.

2. Select **OK** {Enter}.

Create a Master Document

The Master Document feature in WordPerfect is useful for managing large documents such as a book with chapters. The master document is a file containing codes that connect other files (called subdocuments) to the master document file. The master document file also includes any formatting codes that will apply to the entire document. The subdocuments are the files that will be placed together with other files to become one (master) document. The subdocuments are saved as separate files and when desired are assembled together into one (master) file.

After the subdocument files are created and saved, the master document file is created. First, the formatting that applies to the entire document such as page numbering, margins, font type, and size are placed in the new document. If a title page is desired, the title information is typed. Usually a hard page break is placed after the title. Second, the subdocument links are inserted. A subdocument link displays in a comment box and contains the drive letter location and filename of the subdocument.

To display or print the subdocument text, the master document must be *expanded*. When the master document is expanded, the text of each subdocument displays between *Subdoc Begin:* and *Subdoc End:* codes.

After displaying or printing the expanded master document, the document can be *condensed* to remove the subdocument text and the begin and end codes. Also, after the expanded document is condensed, the original subdocument links are returned to the screen. The advantage of a condensed document is the saving of space on a disk, because the text of the subdocuments is not saved with the master document.

Formatting and editing changes can be made to a subdocument or master document. A format code remains in effect until WordPerfect encounters a new code. A subdocument must be expanded, however, for a format or editing change to take effect in a master document.

Changes made to the text in the master document and subdocuments can be saved. A master document, however, must be condensed before saving.

Start-Up Instructions

- ❖ Open a new document window.
- ❖ Type and center the title **WordPerfect 6.0 Made Easy.**
- ❖ Select the type and change the font to **Bodoni-WP Bold, 18 point.**
- ❖ Center the current page vertically (top to bottom). (Select **Layout, Page, Center Current Page, OK.**)
- ❖ Insert page numbers at the bottom center; suppress the page number on page one.
- ❖ Press **Ctrl** and **Enter** to create a hard page break.

Steps to ▶ **Create a Master Document**

1. Select **File, Master Document** {Alt and F5, a}.

2. Select **Subdocument** {s}.

3. Select **File List** {F5}.

4. Type the location where the subdocuments are located.

   For example, type the disk drive letter followed by a colon where the data disk is located (a: or b:).

5. Select **OK** {Enter}.

6. Double-click on the desired filename {highlight the filename and press s}.

   For example, select **25chap1.sub.**

Note: The code Subdoc:... displays in a comment-type box.

7. To place the next subdocument (chapter) of the master document on a separate page, press **Ctrl** and **Enter**.

   *Note: Since **Ctrl** and **Enter** will create a new page, a new sheet of paper will feed through the printer when printed. Do not press **Ctrl** and **Enter** after the last subdocument code.*

Finish-Up Instructions

❖ Repeat Steps 1–7 and select the following subdocuments:

> 25chap2.sub
> 25chap3.sub
> 25chap4.sub
> 25chap5.sub

❖ Use the filename **25master.doc** and save the file.

Start-Up Instructions

❖ The file named **25master.doc** should be displayed.

Expand a Master Document

1. With the master document in the document window, select **File, Master Document** {Alt and F5, a}.

2. Select **Expand** {e}.

   Note: The Expand Master Document dialog box displays with a list of the subdocuments marked, showing the file location of each subdocument.

3. Select **OK** {Enter}.

   Note: The message "Expand marked subdocs?" displays.

4. Select **Yes** {Enter}.

   *Note: The message "Expanding. . ." briefly displays. Each of the subdocuments displays in the document window; press **Home** twice and the up arrow key once to see Chapter 1. The Subdoc Begin: code box displays above each of the expanded chapters and the Subdoc End: code box displays below each of the expanded chapters.*

Finish-Up Instructions

❖ Use Print Preview to view each page of the document.

   Note: The cross references in Chapters 1 and 2 will display incorrect page references at this time. This problem will be corrected in a later step.

Start-Up Instructions

❖ The expanded master document named **25master.doc** should be displayed.

Steps to ▶ Condense a Master Document

1. With the expanded master document in the document window, select **File, Master Document, Condense** {Alt and F5, a, c}.

    Note: The Condense Master Document dialog box displays.

2. Select **OK** {Enter}.

    Note: A message "Condense marked subdocs?" displays.

3. Select **Yes** {Enter}.

    Note: In a moment only the document codes and the title page remain in the document window.

Cross Referencing in a Master Document

To use the Cross Reference feature to reference items in different documents, the files that will contain references and targets must be subdocuments in a master document. Also, when the documents that contain references are used as subdocuments of a master document, the Generate feature is used to update the cross references to reflect the correct page number in the master document.

Start-Up Instructions

❖ Expand the master document named **25master.doc** (select **File, Master Document, Expand**).

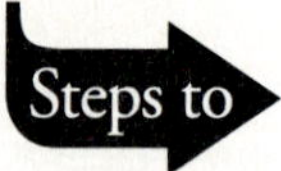

Steps to ▶ Create a Cross Reference in a Master Document

1. With the expanded master document on the screen, place the cursor/insertion point at the location at which the cross reference is to be inserted.

    For example, in the Chapter 3 subdocument, place the cursor/insertion point to the left of the period in the final paragraph.

2. Create a cross reference:

    a. Select **Tools, Cross-Reference, Both** {Alt and t, f, b}.

    b. Select the desired Tie Reference to option. For example, check that Page is selected.

    c. Place the cursor/insertion point in the target name box and type the desired target name. For example, type **business letters**.

    d. Select **OK** {Enter twice}.

Chapter 25—Advanced Features and Master Documents

e. Move the cursor/insertion point to the desired location. For example, move the cursor/insertion point to the left of the final period in the last paragraph in the Chapter 4 subdocument.

f. To insert the target, press **Enter**.

Finish-Up Instructions

❖ Use the Steps to Generate the Cross Reference on page 645 to update the cross reference page numbers.

Note: When the Generate dialog box displays, check that an X displays beside Save Modified Subdocuments.

❖ Optional. Print the master document.

Save an Edited Master Document and Subdocuments

1. Select **File, Save**.

   Note: The message "Document is expanded. Condense?" displays.

2. Select **Yes** {y}.

   Note: The Condense Master Document dialog box with the marked subdocuments displays.

Save Edited Subdocument

3. Highlight a subdocument name {press Tab twice}.

4. Select **Save All** {a}.

5. Select **OK** {Tab, Enter}.

   Note: The message "Condense marked subdocs?" displays.

6. Select **Yes** {Enter}.

   Note: The message "Condensing. . ." displays.

Save the Master Document

7. Type the location and name for the master document.

   For example, type the drive letter where your disk is located followed by a colon and the filename **25master2.doc**.

8. Select **OK** {Enter}.

The Next Step

Chapter Review and Activities

FEATURES SUMMARY

FEATURES	ACTIONS	PAGE
Create a paragraph style containing a paragraph border	Place the cursor/insertion point in the paragraph where the new style will be applied. Select **Layout**, **Styles**, **Create**, type desired name, **OK**; type a description in the Description box; click in the Style Contents box, make any desired format changes. Press **Alt** and **F9**, select **Paragraph** in the Borders area, select **Customize** and make the desired changes, select **OK**, press **F7**, **OK**; choose **Select** to apply the new style.	639
Create a paragraph style containing a graphic image	Place the cursor/insertion point in the paragraph to be formatted with the new style. Select **Layout**, **Style**, **Create**, type a name for the new style, select **OK**; type a description in the Description box; click in the Style Contents box, press **Alt** and **F9**, select **Create**, select **Filename**, **File List**, **OK**; double-click on the desired filename; make any desired changes to the size and position of the graphic, select **Based on Box Style**, double-click on **User Box**, **OK**, **F7**, **OK**; choose **Select** to apply the new style.	640
Create a style based on an existing style	In the Style List dialog box, select **Create** and type the new style name, select **OK**; type a description in the Description box, click in the Style Contents dialog box, press **Alt** and **F8**, double-click on the style to be used as the basis for the new style, make any desired changes to modify the style, press **F7**, **OK**.	642

| --- | --- | --- |
Link styles	Select **Layout, Styles, Create**, type a style name and a style description. In the Style List dialog box, highlight the name of the style that will be linked to another style, select **Edit**. Select the **Enter Key Action... Off/On** option, select **Turn Style Off and Link to** option, double-click on the desired style to be linked, **OK**.	643
Create a cross reference	Place the cursor/insertion point where the reference is to be located in the document, select **Tools, Cross-Reference, Both**, select the desired Tie Reference to option, select **Target Name**, type the desired name, select **OK**; move the cursor/insertion point to the desired target location, press **Enter** to insert the target.	644
Generate the cross reference	With a document containing cross references on the screen, select **Tools, Generate**, select **OK**.	645
Create a master document	Create the title page and any desired text, select **File, Master Document, Subdocument, File List**, type the drive letter followed by a colon where the subdocument files are located, select **OK**, double-click on the desired filename; if necessary, press **Ctrl** and **Enter** to begin a new page.	646
Expand a master document	With the master document in the document window, select **File, Master Document, Expand, OK, Yes**.	647
Condense a master document	With the expanded master document in the document window, select **File, Master Document, Condense, OK, Yes**.	648
Create a cross reference in a master document	With the expanded master document in the document window, place the cursor/insertion point at the location where the cross reference is to be inserted, select **Tools, Cross-Reference, Both**, select the desired Tie Reference to option, type the desired target name in the target name box, select **OK**; move the cursor/insertion point to the desired location, press **Enter** to insert the target.	648
Save an edited master document and subdocuments	Select **File, Save, Yes**; highlight a subdocument name, select **Save All, OK, Yes**; type the location and name for the master document, select **OK**.	649

True/False—Circle One

T F 1. Use **Alt** and **F9** to access the graphic commands when using the Style Contents box of the Edit Style dialog box.

T F 2. The target is the location in a document where the cross reference information displays.

T F 3. A reference cannot be linked to multiple targets.

T F 4. A master document must be expanded before the document is printed.

T F 5. A condensed master document contains the text and codes of the subdocuments.

Short Answer

1. When styles are linked, the first style is in effect until the _________ key is pressed.

2. List the six steps to link styles.

3. Creating a cross reference requires two parts: a _________ and a _________.

4. List the six steps to create a cross reference.

5. Define a subdocument.

Enriching Language Arts Skills

Spelling/Vocabulary Words

cuisine   a style of cooking or preparing food

duty-free   free from a government tax that is usually applied to imports

traditional   of or pertaining to the statements, beliefs, customs, etc., that are handed down through oral communication from one generation to another

Basic Rules for Numbers

Generally, numbers one through ten when used in writing are spelled out. Also, numbers used in approximation, at the beginning of a sentence, or numbers that are rounded are usually spelled out. Related numbers in the same document should be expressed in the same form, i.e., numbers one through ten are written as figures when used with related numbers above ten.

Examples:

We will pick up eight additional passengers at the next bus stop. (Numbers one through ten spelled out.)

Thirty-one people are enrolled in the television course for Real Estate Appraisals. (Spell out a number at the beginning of a sentence.)

Samuel reported that around sixty people attended the luncheon. (Spell out a number used in approximation.)

Out of the 23 questionnaires returned, 7 indicated that new stereo systems would be purchased this year. (Related number is written as a figure when used with a number above ten.)

Activities

■ Activity 25.1–Master Document and Cross Reference

1. Open a new document window.

2. Type and center the title **Tips for Saving the Environment**; use **Bodoni-WP Bold, 24 point**.

3. Center the current page vertically (select **Layout, Page, Center Page, OK**).

4. Insert page numbers at the bottom center; suppress the page number on page one.

5. Press **Ctrl** and **Enter** to create a hard page break.

6. Create a master document using the following subdocuments that are located on the data disk. Remember to place a hard page break between each subdocument. If necessary, see the Steps to Create a Master Document on page 646.

   25sub1.act
   25sub2.act
   25sub3.act
   25sub4.act

7. Use the filename **25act1.mtr** and save the master document.

8. With **25act1.mtr** in the document window, expand the master document. If necessary, see Steps to Expand a Master Document on page 647.

9. Create the following cross references:

    a. Place the cursor/insertion point to the left of the period in the last paragraph of Chapter 1.

    b. Select **Tools, Cross-Reference, Both**. Check that the Page option is selected.

    c. Select **Target Name** and type **energy**; select **OK**.

    d. Move the cursor/insertion point to Chapter 3 and place the cursor/insertion point after the period in the first sentence.

    e. Press **Enter** to insert the target.

    f. Press the **Spacebar** once, type the word **and**. Press the **Spacebar** again.

    g. Repeat Steps b–d and create the cross reference using the same target name, **energy**.

    h. Move the cursor/insertion point to Chapter 4 and place the cursor/insertion point after the second sentence in the first paragraph.

    i. Press **Enter** to insert the target.

10. Create the following cross reference:

    a. Place the cursor/insertion point to the left of the period in the last sentence of the first paragraph in Chapter 4.

    b. Select **Tools, Cross-Reference, Both**. Check that the Page option is selected.

    c. Select **Target Name** and type **table**; select **OK**.

    d. Move the cursor/insertion point below the table on the following page.

    e. Press **Enter** to insert the target.

11. Print one copy.

12. Select **File, Save** and select **Yes** (to condense the document).

13. Highlight the first subdocument name and select **Save All**, select **OK, Yes**.

14. Use the same filename **25act1.mtr** and save the file on your file disk; select **OK**.

Activity 25.2–Create Advanced Styles in a Master Document

1. Open the master document named **25act1.mtr** that was created in Activity 25.1.

2. Expand the master document. If necessary, see the Steps to Expand a Master Document on page 647.

3. Create a chapter heading style using the following:

    a. Place the cursor/insertion point at any position in the title, Chapter 1—Save Energy.

Chapter 25— Advanced Features and Master Documents

b. Select **Layout, Styles, Create.**

c. In the Style Name box, type **chapter head** and select **OK.**

d. In the Description box, type **style for chapter opening.**

e. Click in the Style Contents box and change the font to **Bodoni-WP Bold, 14 point.**

f. Press **Shift** and **F8,** select **Line,** choose **Center** justification, **OK, Close.**

g. Press **Alt** and **F9,** select **Paragraph** borders, **Customize, Lines,** and select **None** for Left and Right lines and choose **Thick** for Top and Bottom lines; select **Close.** Select **Spacing** and choose **Automatic Spacing** (to deselect). In the Top and Bottom Outside spacing boxes type .25 and in the Top and Bottom Inside spacing boxes type .2; select **OK, Close, OK.**

h. Press **F7,** select **OK,** and choose **Select.**

4. Create a style that contains a graphic image.

a. Place the cursor/insertion point at any location in the first paragraph.

b. Select **Layout, Styles, Create.**

c. In the Style Name box, type **graphic par** and select **OK.**

d. In the Description box, type **style for paragraph containing a graphic image.**

e. Click in the Style Contents box.

f. Press **Alt** and **F9.**

g. Select **Create** in the Graphics Boxes area.

h. Select **Filename, File List, OK** {F, F5, Enter}.

i. Double-click on the filename **tree.wpg.**

j. Select **Edit Position** and choose Left for the horizontal position.

k. Select **OK.**

l. Select **Edit Size** and type .5 in the Set Width box. Check that the Automatic Height, Based on Box Contents Height option is selected.

m. Select **OK.**

n. Select **Based on Box Style** and double-click on the User Box style.

o. Select **OK.**

p. Press **F7.**

q. Choose **Select** {Enter}.

5. Save the style library file; select **Save** in the Style List dialog box. Type the name of the new style file including the drive letter and/or directory name. Use the filename **25act2.sty.** Select **OK, Close.**

---

6. Apply the **graphic par** and **chapter head** styles to Chapters 2, 3, and 4.

7. Print one copy of the master document.

8. Use the Steps to Save an Edited Master Document and Subdocuments on page 649. Use the filename **25act2.mtr**.

9. Close the document.

Challenge Your Skills

➥ ▣ Skill 25.1—Create a Master Document, Cross References, and Advanced Styles; Language Arts

1. Open the file named **25skill1** from the data disk.

2. Insert page numbers at the bottom of each page; suppress the page number on page one.

3. With the cursor/insertion point on page two, create a master document using the following subdocuments:

    > 25sub1.skl
    > 25sub2.skl
    > 25sub3.skl
    > 25sub4.skl

4. Use the filename **25skill1.mtr** and save the file.

5. Expand the master document.

6. Correct two spelling, two punctuation, and two number rule errors.

7. Create cross references for the four sentences on the title page and for the cross reference in section 3.

8. Print one copy.

9. Create a section title style. Make decisions for the style name, font type, size, alignment, and paragraph borders. Apply the title style to each of the four section titles.

10. Create a style that contains a graphic image of your choice. Make decisions for the style name, graphic position and size, and the type of graphic box to use. Apply the graphic style to each of the four sections.

11. Print one copy.

12. Save and condense the master document. Use the same filename, **25skill1.mtr**.

Advanced Macros

26

- Edit macros
- Correct (debug) macros
- Macro commands, syntax, and parameters
- Record keystrokes while editing a macro
- User input in a macro
- Using variables in a macro
- Using a conditional statement in a macro
- Test a macro
- Use the glossary macro

Objectives

After successfully completing this chapter, you will be able to better understand macro terminology, edit a macro using the Edit Macro mode, and record keystrokes while editing a macro. You will also learn how to find the correct syntax and parameters for macro commands and how to use input, variables, and a conditional statement while editing a macro. In addition, you will learn to debug (correct) macro errors and learn to "test" a macro. Also, you will learn to set up and use the glossary macro.

Chapter Introduction

Macros can be a useful tool to avoid repetitious keystrokes, to ensure that work is accurate, and to set up tasks to be accomplished automatically. In addition to using the macros supplied by WordPerfect and recording simple keystroke macros, macros can be created from scratch or created using a combination of *direct* editing and recording.

Useful Terminology

WordPerfect uses a macro language that is based on commands. Other terminology is used to create and edit the macro. A brief explanation of key macro terms that will assist in a better understanding of macros is shown in Figure 26.1 and Figure 26.3.

Suggestions for Writing and Editing Macros

Use spaces, tabs, indents, and hard returns to make the macro easier to read. "White space" is ignored by the macro, which sees spacing commands only when they are in character strings, enclosed in quotation marks. DO NOT put spacing codes or characters in the middle of command names, parameter names, or parameter values. If you need to put a space in a long command so that WordPerfect can wrap the line, place it after a semicolon.

Many times macros printed in magazines or books will have numbered lines. These numbers are for reference only and are not typed in the macro.

Comments are explanations about the macro and should be used liberally when you are creating or editing a macro. Inserting comments will make it much easier to change or update the macro, and are very helpful if someone else must figure out how the macro works. To place a comment in the macro, start the line with two slashes (//). The comment will end at the next hard return.

Editing a Macro

Many times macros must be changed after they have been created. For instance, you might have a macro that prints your name and return address to create personal stationery. When you move or change your name, the macro must be changed. While you could re-record the macro (saving it under the same filename), editing the macro is often easier, particularly if the change is small and the macro is complex.

Start-Up Instructions

❖ The file named **namehead.wpm** should be available on the data disk. If necessary, see your instructor. (Do not open the file.)

MACRO TERMINOLOGY

COMMAND
A macro command tells the program to take a certain action. The command must be typed with the correct spelling, but it does not matter whether the command is in all uppercase letters or a combination of upper and lowercase letters. Many times commands will be placed in uppercase letters to make it easier to see them when the macro is edited.

PARAMETER
If there are two or more actions that can be directed by one command, the command must have a parameter to specify which action to take. The parameter will be in parentheses after the command.

ENUMERATED TYPE
A parameter that is a word followed by an exclamation point. For example, the command DisplayMode has three parameters: Text!, Graphics!, and FullPage! If any other word follows the DisplayMode command, an error message will be displayed when the file is saved.

NUMERIC EQUIVALENT
A number that can be used in place of an Enumerated Type or the ASCII value of a character. The Help screen for each command shows the parameters with both the Enumerated Type and the Numeric Equivalent listed. A chart of the ASCII value of characters and keystrokes is available in the Macro Help Appendices.

OPERATOR
A symbol or word that performs a function on one or more items in a command statement. For example, the equals sign (=) is used in many statements to compare two items and asks "Are they equal?".

VARIABLE
A variable represents a place in memory where information is stored. Variables are often used to keep track of words, numbers, and measurements that change while the macro plays.

CHARACTER STRING or CHARACTER EXPRESSION
Any text that is not a command or a parameter must be enclosed in quote marks so that the program will recognize it as text. This is commonly referred to as a character string or character expression.

COMPILE
Compiling is a process that changes the typed or recorded commands and keystrokes into the binary code that the computer uses. The compiler program also checks for various types of errors.

Steps to ▶ Edit a Macro Using the Edit Macro Mode

1. Select **Tools, Macro, Record** {Ctrl and F10}.

   Note: The Record Macro dialog box displays.

2. Select **Edit Macro** {press Tab, Enter}.

   Note: An X displays beside the Edit Macro option.

3. Type the location and macro name (the *.wpm* filename extension does not need to be typed).

> For example, type the drive letter where the data disk is located followed by a colon and the filename **namehead**.

Note: If a blank screen displays, close the document and repeat Steps 1 and 2.

4. Select **OK** {Enter}.

Note: The macro is now displayed in an Edit Macro window. The message "Edit Macro: Press Shift+F3 to Record" displays in the Status bar. Each keystroke previously recorded has been translated into a WordPerfect macro command or a character to be typed. The characters in the name and address are in quotes to tell WordPerfect not to interpret them as commands and they are enclosed in parentheses to indicate that they are a "parameter" for the command TYPE.

5. Make the desired changes to the macro.

> For example, replace the name and address shown in the macro with your name and address being careful not to delete the quotation marks or parentheses.

6. Select the **SaveAs** button and use a new filename to save the edited macro.

> For example, select the **Save As** button and type the location of your file disk followed by your initials and **.wpm** (a:kl.wpgm).

Note: The message "Compiling macro" will appear briefly and the usual "Saving filename" message will appear if the compilation is successful. If a mistake has been made, the macro can be corrected using the Steps to Correct (Debug) Macro Errors. (Do not stop the macro record at this time.)

Finish-Up Instructions

❖ Continue with the following Start-Up Instructions in the Correct (Debug) Macros section that follows.

Correcting (Debugging) Macros

Compiling is the process of converting the commands and text recorded or keyed into codes that the computer can understand. Some errors are identified by the compiler program. For example, if the command TYPE is keyed as TIPE or if the beginning parenthesis is missing after the command TYPE, the compiler will stop and ask if you want to Edit the macro or Save Anyway.

When an error is identified, the macro can be corrected. Correcting a macro is often referred to as "debugging". There are some types of errors the compiler cannot recognize, such as the following:

> a. Logic errors--for instance, forgetting to select a needed menu item.

b. Typographical or grammatical errors in text to be entered or displayed on the screen.

c. Errors that cause the program to do something unintended but perfectly valid from the program's viewpoint. For example, many options toggle on/off, so a macro that selects the option the first time it is played will deselect it on the second run.

Start-Up Instructions

❖ The macro file that is named with your initials should be open in the Edit Macro window.

❖ To make an error in the macro, delete the left parenthesis to the right of the word "DISPLAY" in the first line of the macro.

❖ Save the file using the same filename.

❖ The message "Compiling macro" will appear briefly. The Macro compiler error dialog box displays with the message "Syntax error." Continue with the Steps to Correct (Debug) Macro Errors.

Correct (Debug) Macro Errors

1. Select **Save Anyway** {s}.

   Note: Saving with an error is OK, because you will not lose the information that is correct and you will have the opportunity to correct any error(s).

2. The cursor/insertion point will be located where the compiler recognized an error. Make the necessary correction(s).

   Note: The cursor/insertion point is sometimes located several lines after the actual error. If necessary, move the cursor/insertion point to the position of the actual error.

   For example, if necessary, move the cursor/insertion point to the location where the parenthesis was deleted (after the word display in the first line) and type a left parenthesis.

3. Save the file using the same filename.

   Note: No error message should display.

Finish-Up Instructions

❖ Optional. Replace the "y" in the Type command in the second line with an "i," so the command is misspelled. Save the file and select **Save Anyway**.

   Note: The warning message displays, "LABEL name not found. . ." and then the cursor/insertion point displays at the location of the error.

❖ Correct the error by following the Steps to Correct (Debug) Macro Errors, then save the file again using the same filename.

❖ Close the document.

❖ Play the macro that was named with your initials (select **Tools**, **Macro**, **Play**, type the disk drive letter where your macro file is located followed by a colon and the name, e.g. a:nkl).

Note: Your name and address display centered at the top of the document window.

❖ Close and don't save the document.

Understanding Macro Commands

Each macro command tells the program to take some action. Some commands, such as HardReturn, have only one possible action. Other commands have several possible actions; therefore a parameter or several parameters must be included with the macro command to specify which of the possible actions is intended. For example, *AttributeAppearanceOn* has 10 possible actions (also called its Enumerated Types): Bold!, Underline!, SmallCaps!, Italics!, Shadow!, Redline!, Double Underline!, Strikeout!, Outline!, Every!. If the AttributeAppearanceOn command is placed in a macro without any of these parameters, the program has no way to know what it is supposed to do, and a compiler error will occur. The parameters are typed with an exclamation point at the end to distinguish them from variables and operators.

The macro command must be typed in an exact format so that the program recognizes it. This is called the *syntax* of the command. Capitalization is usually not important, but may be used to make it easier to spot commands when the macro is being created, edited, or corrected. However, spelling and the parentheses around the parameters are very important. The AttributeAppearanceOn(Bold!) command must be typed just as it is shown, without spaces separating the words, and in that exact order. The program will not recognize AppearanceAttributeOn(Bold!), Attribute Appearance On(Bold!), or AttributeAppearanceOnBold.

Start-Up Instructions

❖ A new document window should be displayed. If necessary, open a new document.

Find a Command's Syntax and Parameters

1. Select **Help, Macros** {Alt and h, m}.

2. Double-click on the desired topic {press down arrow to highlight the desired topic, press Enter}.

   For example, double-click on **Macro Commands Index M-Z**.

3. Select the **Name Search** button {n}, type the first few letters of the item to be located, and press Enter.

   For example, type **swi** and press **Enter**.

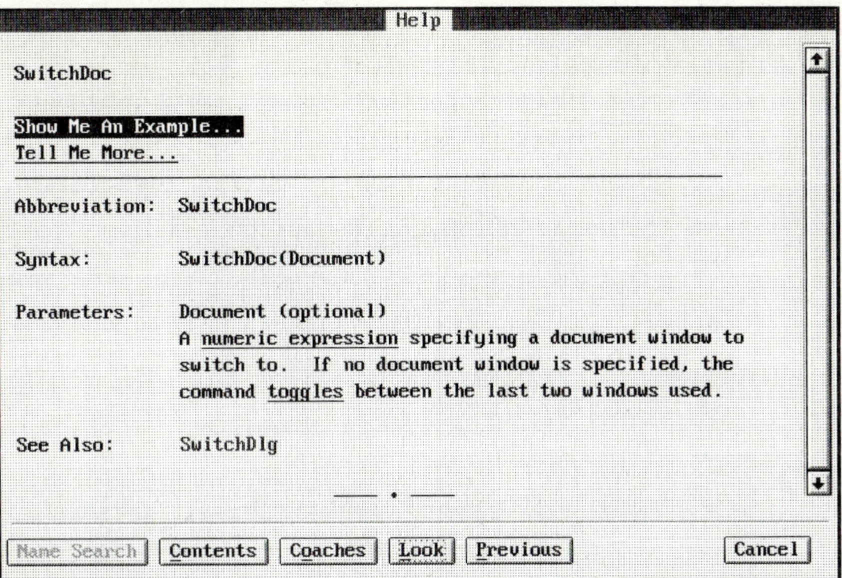

4. If necessary, press the up or down arrow key to highlight the desired item.

    For example, press the down arrow until **SwitchDoc** is high-lighted.

5. Double-click on the desired item {Enter}.

    For example, double-click on **SwitchDoc**.

Note: The Macro Help screen showing an explanation of the command, the correct syntax, and the possible parameters for the command displays (see Figure 26.2).

Finish-Up Instructions

❖ To return to the Macro Help Index, select **Previous** {p}. If desired, other topics can be selected to learn more about WordPerfect macros.

❖ To exit the Macro Help function, select **Cancel** or press **Esc**.

Additional Editing Techniques for Macros

In addition to changing characters in a macro, commands may be added, and you can switch to Record mode to record additional keystrokes. This is very helpful because recording commands, particularly infrequently used commands, is often faster and more accurate than typing the commands. However, there are some commands that must be typed, such as commands requesting the user to answer a prompt or to enter information.

- ❖ The macro being created will add a client's name to an existing data file and will provide the option of creating new client letters.
- ❖ Begin creating the macro by selecting **Tools, Macro, Record** {Ctrl and F10}.
- ❖ Select the **Edit Macro** option {Tab, Enter}.
- ❖ Type the location and name of the macro to be created.

  For example, type the drive letter where your file disk is located followed by a colon and **newclnt** (a:newclnt).

- ❖ Select **OK** {Enter}.
- ❖ Type the following commands:

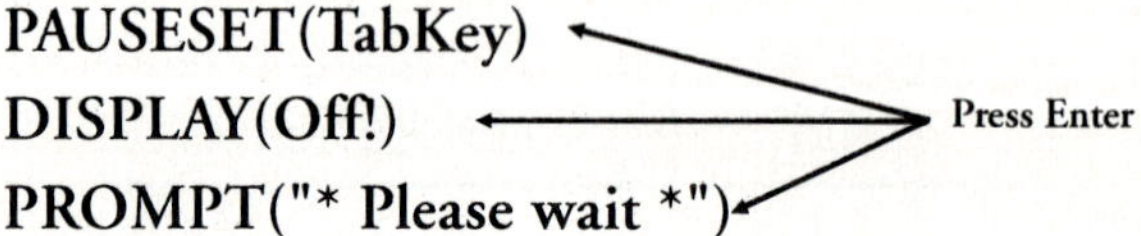

```
PAUSESET(TabKey)
DISPLAY(Off!)
PROMPT("* Please wait *")
```


Note: An explanation of the PAUSESET, DISPLAY, and PROMPT commands is shown in Figure 26.3.

Record Keystrokes While Editing a Macro

1. The Edit Macro window with the message "Edit Macro: Press Shift+F3 to Record" in the Status bar should be displayed.

2. Press **Shift** and **F3** to go into the Recording Macro window.

   Note: WordPerfect opens an empty "Recording Macro" window and places the cursor/insertion point at the top left of the window.

3. Each keystroke will now be recorded.

   For example, we will open an existing data file, move the cursor/insertion point to the second row of the table, and insert a new row as follows.

   a. Select **File, Open.**

   b. Type the drive letter where your file disk is located followed by a colon and the filename **clients.df.** Select **OK** {Enter twice}.

   c. Press the down arrow key until the cursor/insertion point is in the first cell of the second row of the table.

      Note: Remember, use the arrow keys only. Do not use the mouse to move the cursor/insertion point.

   d. Select **Layout, Tables, Insert, Row.**

4. Press **Shift** and **F3** to return to the Edit Macro window.

   Note: The steps just recorded will already be inserted at the end of the macro. If desired, the commands can be changed to uppercase.

PAUSESET	By default, after an INPUT or PAUSE command the macro waits to resume until the user presses Enter. In this macro, we will be working in a table, so we want the user to press the Tab key, just as they would if they were entering the data into the table manually. The PAUSESET command changes the "trigger" to the key used as the parameter. A list of the keys and their associated formats to be used in commands such as this is found in the Macro Help Appendices.
DISPLAY	The DISPLAY command controls whether or not WordPefect will update the screen display. As a general rule, the screen display should only be updated when it will be useful to the user to see the information, since updating the screen slows down the macro's operation.
PROMPT	PROMPT displays the text shown as a parameter on the Status bar. Showing the message "Please wait" lets the user know the macro is functioning even though nothing on the screen is being updated.
WAIT	The WAIT command halts the macro for the time specified in the parameter. The time is in tenths of a second. It is placed here to give the user time to read the instruction before beginning the data entry.
INPUT	This command displays the text string in the parameter on the Status bar, and places the keystrokes typed by the user in response into the document.
TabKey	The TabKey command is the same as pressing the Tab key. Although the user presses the TabKey when finished with the title or name, that keystroke only tells the macro to resume. (It is this TabKey command that actually moves the cursor/insertion point to the next column of the table.)
PAUSE	The PAUSE command stops the macro until the user presses the trigger key—in this case the Enter key (HardReturn) set by the PAUSESET command. This allows the user to review the entries and to make any corrections (as long as they do so without pressing Enter).
SAVE	Saves the current document. The document must already exist because this command does not have a parameter for the filename. If the document does not already exist, the FileSave(filename;type) command would be used.
CLOSE	Closes the current document.
CHAR	The command CHAR can be followed by a variable name (in this case "CreateVar" placed in parentheses) and optionally by a prompt (shown in quote marks after a semicolon) to give the user information on what key to press. Instead of storing the actual characters, the CHAR command converts them to their numerical equivalents. The list of characters and their numerical equivalents is available in the Macro Help section under Appendices.

Finish-Up Instructions

❖   Continue with the Steps to Request User Input in a Macro.

Requesting User Input in a Macro

In many macros, it is convenient to have the user input specific information. This can be the name of a file to open or retrieve, a Yes or No response to a question to determine what the user wants to do, or what action the macro is to take, or, in our example, the client's name, address, and other personal information. There are several macro commands that allow user input, and act on it in different ways. We will use two of the macro commands: INPUT and CHAR.

Start-Up Instructions

- ❖ The keystrokes recorded in the Steps to Record Keystrokes While Editing a Macro should be displayed on the screen in the Edit Macro window.
- ❖ The cursor/insertion point should be located at the end of the macro.
- ❖ To insert a blank line, press **Enter**.

Request User Input in a Macro

1. Type the following information, being sure to enter all parentheses and quotation marks exactly as shown.

   *Note: Press **Enter** only at the end of a command and its associated parameters. WordPerfect automatically wraps any command that extends over multiple lines.*

   ```
   PROMPT("Enter client information. Press Tab after each entry.")
   WAIT(75)
   INPUT("Enter title:")
   TabKey
   INPUT("Enter first name:")
   TabKey
   INPUT("Enter last name:")
   TabKey
   INPUT("Enter street address, including apartment #:")
   TabKey
   INPUT("Enter city:")
   TabKey
   INPUT("Enter state:")
   TabKey
   INPUT("Enter zip code:")
   TabKey
   INPUT("Enter phone number:")
   TabKey
   INPUT("Enter charges for today's work:")
   TabKey
   INPUT("Is this a new client? Y/N")
   PAUSESET(HardReturn)
   ```

PROMPT("Check your entry, make corrections, then press En-
ter to continue.")
PAUSE
SAVE
CLOSE

2. Press the **Enter** key once after the last line of the macro. Carefully proofread each line.

   Note: See Figure 26.3 for an explanation of the macro commands.

3. Save the macro file using the same filename, **newclnt.wpm**. The macro will be immediately compiled. If the compilation is completed, a message displays briefly that the file has been saved. If the compiler finds an error, use the Steps to Correct (Debug) Macro Errors and correct the error before continuing.

   Note: If the macro is played at this time, the macro will open the data file, ask for the user to input the client information, and find out whether the client is new. The next step is to determine whether the user wants to create and print the new client letters now, and will store the user's response.

Finish-Up Instructions

❖ Continue with the following Steps to Use a Variable.

Understanding and Using Variables

Storing small pieces of information to be used within the same macro is done through the use of variables. A variable is a small portion of memory that Word-Perfect sets aside to hold a piece of information. Once information has been stored in a variable, the variable and the information in it can be used elsewhere in the macro. Think of a variable as a scratch pad that the computer uses to hold information, just as you might jot down a name or phone number to use in a few minutes. A variable is given a name and then referred to by that name. The name should be something easy to remember and should relate to what is stored in the variable. When variable names are used in a parameter, they are not placed in quotes.

The command we will use is the CHAR command. CHAR automatically sends the next character pressed to be stored in a variable.

Start-Up Instructions

❖ The macro file named **newclnt.wpm** should be displayed in the Edit Macro window.

❖ If necessary, locate the cursor/insertion point below the last line of the macro.

1. Type the following command:

   For example, type **CHAR(CreateVar;"Do you want to create new client letters now? Y/N")** and then press the Enter key to move the cursor/insertion point to a new line.

   *Note: The **Enter** key should not be pressed **within** a character string (text within quotation marks). For an explanation of the CHAR command, see Figure 26.3.*

2. Save the macro file using the same filename, **newclnt.wpm**.

Finish-Up Instructions

❖ Continue with the Steps to Create an IF-ELSE Statement in a Macro.

Using a Conditional Statement in a Macro

Aconditional statement is one that allows the macro to take different actions based on some condition. There are several types of conditional statements, but the most common one is generally referred to as an IF statement, IF-THEN statement, or an IF-ELSE statement.

An IF statement in a WordPerfect macro will have three parts:

> IF
> ELSE
> ENDIF

The IF portion sets up some type of condition. In this case, we will compare the information stored in the variable named CreateVar with the numerical equivalents of the possible yes responses (Y = 121 and y = 90). The program will evaluate this IF statement, and if it finds the IF statement to be true, it will continue to read the command under the IF statement.

The ELSE portion of the macro tells the program what to do when it evaluates the IF statement and finds that it is false. If, for example, the user presses N or any other key except Y and y, the IF statement will be false because the number stored in the variable will not be 121 or 90. When the statement is false, the program skips to the ELSE statement and reads the commands under it.

The ENDIF command tells the macro that the IF statement is finished, and that it should resume reading each command and acting upon it.

❖   The macro named **newclnt.wpm** should be displayed in the Edit Macro window.

Steps to ▶ **Create an IF-ELSE Statement in a Macro**

1. Type the desired IF statement.

   For example, type the following IF statement as shown:
   IF(CreateVar = 90 OR CreateVar = 121). (Do not type the final period.)

2. Switch to Record mode by pressing **Shift** and **F3**.

3. Record the following steps to merge the form and the data file, and print letters ONLY for those clients who have a Y or y in the NEW? column.

   a. Select **Tools, Merge, Run** {Alt and t, e, r}.

   b. Type the drive letter where your file disk is located followed by a colon and the name of the form file (**a:\form1.pf**); press **Tab**.

   c. Type the drive letter where your file disk is located followed by a colon and the name of the data file (**a:\clients.df**); press **Tab**.

   d. Select **Data File Options** {t}.

   e. Select **Blank Fields in Data File, Remove Resulting Blank Lines** {b, r}.

   f. Select **Data Record Selection** {s}.

   g. Select **Define Conditions** {c}.

   h. Click once on the number **1** {press the number 1}.
   Note: A list of the fields in the data file displays.

   i. Select the field on which the condition is to be based {press down arrow until the field is highlighted}.

      For example, double-click on the **NEW?** field.

      Note: The NEW? field displays at the top of the first column, and the cursor/insertion point is located in the first cell of column 1.

   j. Type the condition to be met. If more than one true condition exists, type each with a semicolon between them.

      For example, type **Y;y**. (Do not type the period.)

   k. Select **OK** {press Enter twice}.

   l. Select **Merge** {press Enter}.

      Note: The merge operation will take place and create merged letters for the new clients. Wait until the merge operation is finished to continue with the next step. The insertion point is located at the end of the first letter.

   m. Use the filename **macro.if** and save the file of merged letters.

      Note: The saved file will be overwritten each time the macro is run.

4. Press **Shift** and **F3** to return to the Edit Macro window.

5. Complete the IF statement by typing the following:

> **PROMPT("New Client letters have been merged. Press Enter to clear screen.")**
> **PAUSE**
> **ELSE**
> **PROMPT("Client has been added to data file. Press Enter to clear screen.")**
> **PAUSE**
> **ENDIF**
> **CLOSE**

6. Save the macro file using the same filename. If the compiler finds any errors, use the Steps to Correct (Debug) Macro Errors to find and correct the error(s).

Finish-Up Instructions

- ❖ Close all open documents.

- ❖ Play the **newclnt.wpm** macro (select **Tools**, **Macro**, **Play**, type the drive letter where your disk is located followed by the macro name **newclnt**).

- ❖ As the macro plays, follow the prompts in the Status bar, press the **Tab** key to move from column to column and enter the following information:

    a. Mr. Rick Spences
    5903 Oak Creek Dr.
    Hayward, CA 94541
    555-4484
    $45
    Y (Press **Tab** and then press the **Enter** key to save the new client record.)

    b. The message displays "Do you want to create new client letters now? Y/N".

    c. Press **Y** to create new client letters now.

       Note: After the merging message no longer displays in the Status bar, a letter for each client that contained a Y in the "NEW" field displays.

- ❖ Optional. Print the merged letters.

- ❖ Press Enter to clear the screen.

Testing the Macro

Although the macro compiles without an error message, errors may still exist in the macro. Always test a macro by running it under all the conditions that you can imagine a user will select. For example, in the macro just created, you would want to test the following:

Scenario A: A client does not have a phone number. Pressing **Tab** without typing anything else should move the cursor/insertion point to the next column.

Scenario B: The user responds "Y" to merge and print the new letters.

Scenario C: The user responds "y" to merge and print the new letters.

Scenario D: The user responds "N" to leave the macro without merging the letters.

Scenario E: The user responds "n" to leave the macro without merging the letters.

Scenario F: The user accidentally presses any other key on the keyboard. The macro should respond as though the user pressed N.

As the macro becomes more complex, testing to make sure it will work under most normal conditions also becomes more complex. The amount of time spent developing and testing a complex macro must be weighed against the time saved or the increased accuracy or efficiency possible when the macro is available.

WordPerfect Supplied Macros

WordPerfect includes 13 macros with WordPerfect DOS 6.0 program. To find out all about these macros, select Help, Macros, List of Shipping Macros. In addition to using these macros, printing them and examining them will help you understand more about how WordPerfect macros work, and how to create your own.

Two of the shipping macros are particularly useful: GLOSSARY.WPM and ALLFONTS.WPM. The ALLFONTS macro prints a list of the fonts available for the currently selected printer with a sample of each font. This is a very useful reference list, and you will probably want to print it whenever you use a new printer.

GLOSSARY.WPM lets you set up a list of shortcut abbreviations to type in place of longer words or groups of words. For example, the company name Amalgamated Metals and Shipping might be set up in the glossary as *ams*. Whenever documents contain the company name, you could type *ams*, then select Tools, Macro, Play, and type glossary. WordPerfect's glossary macro would automatically expand the abbreviation into the full company name.

Set Up and Use a Glossary Abbreviation

1. Open a new document.

2. Select **Tools, Macro, Play** {Alt and F10}.

3. Type **glossary**.

4. Select **OK** {Enter}.

Note: In a few moments, the Glossary Definition dialog box displays.

5. Select **Create** {c}.

6. In the Abbreviation field, type the abbreviated form of the word or group of words.

   For example, type **ams**. (Do not type the final period.)

7. Place the insertion point in the Expanded Form field and type the word or group of words as they are to appear in the final document (up to 40 characters) {Tab, type the expanded text}.

   For example, type **Amalgamated Metals and Shipping**. (Do not type the final period.)

8. Select **OK** twice {press Enter three times}.

Use a Glossary Abbreviation

9. Type the abbreviated form of the word or group of words.

   For example, type **ams** (do not insert any punctuation and do not move the cursor/insertion point; the cursor/insertion point must be next to or in the abbreviation).

10. With the cursor/insertion point located directly after the abbreviation, select **Tools, Macro, Play** {Alt and F10}.

11. Type **glossary**.

12. Select **OK** {press Enter}.

    Note: The glossary program will automatically replace the characters "ams" with the expanded version of the glossary item.

Finish-Up Instructions

* The glossary items are saved on the hard disk in a file called WP{WP}GL.WPM in the WordPerfect directory. This file is created the first time a glossary item is created. This file should be deleted so that the next student performing the Steps to Set Up and Use a Glossary Abbreviation will be able to create the *ams* abbreviation. Ask your instructor or instructional assistant if you are to delete the file.

* Use the following information to delete the file containing the glossary items:

   a. Select **File, File Manager** {F5}.

   b. Select **Directory Tree** {F8}.

   c. Double-click on the directory containing the WordPerfect files (usually WP60) {press the up or down arrow until the directory containing the WordPerfect files is highlighted, press Enter}.

   d. Select the file **WP{WP}GL.WPM** {press the up or down arrow until the file WP{WP}GL.WPM is highlighted}.

   e. Select **Delete** {d}.

   f. Select **Yes** {y}.

The Next Step

Chapter Review and Activities

FEATURES SUMMARY

FEATURES	ACTIONS	PAGE
Edit a macro using the Edit Macro mode	Select **Tools, Macro, Record, Edit Macro.** Type the location and name of the macro. Select **OK.** Make the desired changes. Select **Save As** and type the desired filename. If desired, close the document or select **Tools, Macro, Stop.**	659
Correct (debug) macro errors	When saving a macro that contains an error(s), the Macro Compiler Error dialog box will display. Select **Save Anyway.** Locate the cursor/insertion point at the error and make necessary corrections. Save the macro again.	661
Find a command's syntax and parameters	Select **Help, Macros,** double-click on the desired topic, select the **Name Search** button, type the first few letters of the command to be located and press **Enter.** Press the up or down arrow key to highlight the desired topic. Double-click on the item to display the topic information.	662
Record keystrokes while editing a macro	To begin editing the macro, select **Tools, Macro, Record, Edit Macro,** type the location and name of the macro, and select **OK.** Type any desired macro commands. In the Edit Macro window, press **Shift** and **F3** (each keystroke will be recorded). Perform the actions to be recorded. Press **Shift** and **F3** to return to the Edit Macro window. If desired, save and/or close the macro file.	664

Self-Check Questions

True-False—Circle One

T F 1. The only way to create a macro is to record the keystrokes.

T F 2. When a macro is saved, it is automatically compiled.

T F 3. A macro command instructs the program to perform some type of action.

T F 4. An INPUT command can be used to ask the person running the macro for information.

T F 5. To switch from the Edit Macro window to the Record mode, press **F3**.

T F 6. The compiler converts the keystrokes and commands in a macro into codes that the computer can understand.

Short Answer

1. Describe the three parts of a macro IF statement.

2. List one reason why it is necessary to test a macro even though the compiler finds no errors.

3. Where would you begin looking for an error if the Macro Compiler Error dialog box appears while trying to save the macro?

4. Write a statement that describes the difference between the PROMPT command and the INPUT command.

Activities

Activity 26.1—Create a Macro with User Input and IF-ELSE Statement

1. Use the following information to create a macro that will ask a question and "type" a letter closing:

   a. Mr. John Wilson, Operations Manager, and Ms. Lucy Arpon, Systems Engineer, share an assistant, David Clark, who is responsible for both of their word processing needs. Create a macro for David to use that will ask him who will sign the letter, then place an appropriate complementary closing, signature line, and reference initials in the document.

   b. Make the user input as short as possible (Y/N or one initial of the person's name). Longer input is more likely to be mistyped.

   c. Use an IF statement.

   d. Record the keystrokes for the text and spacing between lines.

2. Print a copy of the macro.

Challenge Your Skills

1. Use the following information to create a macro that prints and formats the company named using the company format policy.

    a. Your supervisor gives you a document written by several different people. Each person has spelled the company name in a different way. In addition, the company policy is to bold and italicize the name. Moreover, this is going to be a monthly project. Create a macro that will put in the correct company name (Meunneres Villarosa) and format it according to company policy. The document is saved on the data disk with the filename **26skill1**.

    b. Open the file named **26skill1**.

    c. Start the macro after the text to be replaced is selected.

    d. Optional. Use the REPLACE and a WHILE/ENDWHILE statement to actually find each occurrence of the company name. Look up the commands, syntax, and parameters in the Macro section of Help.

2. Print a copy of the macro.

3. Run the macro and print one copy of the corrected document.

Checking Your Step
Part 7

Production Activity 7.1—Create a Macro with a Table and Formulas

1. Use the following information to create a macro that produces the product report shown on page 678 when played. Remember, before creating a macro, always write down each step by creating the document *before* selecting Macro, Record.

    a. Use the macro name **report**.

    b. Increase Column A so that the column displays approximately the same size as shown.

    c. Join the cells in Row 1. (When recording a macro, use **Alt** and **F4** to block and press the up, down, left, or right arrow key to highlight multiple cells.)

    d. Use decimal align and commas number type with two digits after the decimal for cells B2-B6.

    e. When creating the table, a formula should be placed in cell B4 that subtracts the actual sales from the projected sales (B3 - B2). Also, a formula should be placed in cell B5 that calculates the percentage increase or decrease of actual units sold over the projected unit sales (B4/B2*100).

    Note: In cell B4 a zero displays and in cell B5 two questions marks display because the required calculation cannot be performed until data is entered in the cells.

<table>
<tr><td colspan="2" align="center">PRODUCT REPORT
Product Line:</td></tr>
<tr><td>Total Projected Unit Sales</td><td></td></tr>
<tr><td>Total Actual Units Sold</td><td></td></tr>
<tr><td>Total Units Over/Under</td><td align="right">.00</td></tr>
<tr><td>% Increase/Decrease of Projected Sales</td><td align="right">??</td></tr>
<tr><td>Next Year's Projected Unit Sales</td><td></td></tr>
</table>

2. After the Record Macro is stopped, clear the screen. Do not save this document.

3. Open a new file and play the product report macro. Create a product report using the following information:

Product Line:	Cheese Crackers
Projected Sales:	234,680
Actual Sales:	238,200
Next Year's Projected Sales:	239,100

*Note: In order to obtain the Total Units Over/Under and the % Increase/Decrease of Projected Sales, select **Layout, Tables, Calculate** or use the **Tbl Calc** button.*

4. Press **Enter** three times and run the product report macro. Create a product report using the following information:

Product Line:	Yummy Bars
Projected Sales:	219,230
Actual Sales:	215,400
Next Year's Projected Sales:	220,900

*Note: Remember to select **Layout, Tables, Calculate** to obtain the Total Units Over/Under and the % Increase/Decrease of Projected Sales.*

5. Press **Enter** three times and run the product report macro. Create a product report using the following information:

Product Line:	Pecan Snacks
Projected Sales:	250,600
Actual Sales:	253,300
Next Year's Projected Sales:	255,500

6. Press **Enter** three times and run the product report macro. Create a product report using the following information:

Product Line:	Potato Skin Crunchies
Projected Sales:	226,660
Actual Sales:	224,540
Next Year's Projected Sales:	226,950

7. Use the filename **7pact1.rpt** and save the report.

8. Print one copy.

9. Close the document.

■ Production Activity 7.2—Master Document with a Cross Reference, Advanced Styles, Table of Contents, and Index

Note: If desired, this activity can be assigned as an individual project or as a group project with one group completing Part 1, the master document and cross reference, a second group completing Part 2, creating and applying styles to the master document, and a third group completing Part 3, creating a table of contents and index.

Part 1—Create a Master Document and a Cross Reference

1. Create a master document using the following information:

   a. Open a new document.

   b. Type and center the master document title: Today's Health. Make decisions regarding a font and point size, justification, and centering the title vertically on the page.

   c. Insert page numbers. Make decisions on suppressing the page number on page one and on the location of the page numbers.

   d. Place the following subdocuments into the master document. Each subdocument should be placed on a separate page. The following files are on the data disk.

      7psub1.txt
      7psub2.txt
      7psub3.txt
      7psub4.txt

   e. Use the filename **7pact2.mtr** and save the master document.

2. Expand the master document.

3. Create a cross reference for the table referenced on the first page of the Part 3 subdocument.

4. If desired, print one copy.

5. Save and condense the master document using the same filename, **7pact2.mtr**.

   Hint: Remember to also save the subdocuments.

Part 2—Create and Apply Styles to the Master Document

1. Expand the master document named **7pact2.mtr** and create appropriate styles for the part headings and text. Make decisions on the following:

Use and placement of a graphic image in a style
Use of graphic lines or paragraph borders in a style
Style names and descriptions
Fonts
Justification

2. Apply the styles to each of the four subdocuments in the master document.

3. If desired, print one copy.

4. Save and condense the master document using the same filename,
    7pact2.mtr.

    Hint: Remember to also save the subdocuments.

Part 3—Create a Table of Contents and Index for the Master Document

1. With the master document named **7pact2.mtr** displayed and expanded in
    the document window, mark appropriate table of contents entries and de-
    fine the table of contents location and levels. (If necessary, see Chapter 24
    for instructions on marking and defining a table of contents.)

2. Mark the following index entries. Also, define the location and format for
    the index.

    Health Insurance Plan of Missouri
    immunization
    osteoporosis
    calcium
    exercising

3. Generate the table of contents and index.

4. Print one copy.

5. Save and condense the master document using the same filename,
    7pact2.mtr.

    Hint: Remember to also save the subdocuments.

Appendices

WordPerfect Setup and Customizing the Button Bar

WordPerfect Setup

The WordPerfect setup option helps the user establish different settings for the computer hardware, e.g., the mouse, keyboard, disk drives, and monitor display. WordPerfect creates settings (defaults) that are suitable for most word processing users. However, by using the Setup feature, the settings are easily changed to accommodate the users' specific needs.

Setup is selected from the **File** menu (**Shift** and **F1**). The different hardware components settings that can be changed using Setup include the Mouse, Display, Environment, Keyboard Layout, Location of Files, and Color Palette options.

The mouse type, location, and functions of the mouse can be changed in the Mouse dialog box (select **File**, **Setup**, **Mouse**). The mouse type is the brand of mouse, e.g., Microsoft Mouse. When the brand name of the mouse is selected, WordPerfect accesses the mouse drive (file) that assists WordPerfect in communicating with your mouse.

The communication port where the mouse is plugged in can be selected by choosing *Port 1* or *2*. The mouse *Double-click Interval* option sets the time allowed between two clicks of the mouse. The *Acceleration Factor* is the time between the pointer movement on the screen and the movement of the mouse. When the *Left-handed Mouse* option is selected, a user can click with the right mouse button rather than the left mouse button.

The *Display* setup option is used to select the video driver (file). (The video driver is used to set up your screen for the graphics, page, or text modes.) The video driver can be either selected automatically or manually.

The *Environment* setup option is used to customize settings for many of the distinctive WordPerfect features. The *Backup* option allows the selection of a timed backup and the minutes that will elapse between backups. Also, when saving or exiting WordPerfect, the Backup file option can be selected to always save a copy of the original file and use the filename extension .BK! for the file. The *Beep* option can be turned on or off for a Beep on Error, Beep on Hyphenation, and/or Beep on Search Failure.

The *Cursor Speed* option is used to control the speed at which the cursor moves across the screen when the arrow keys are used.

The *Allow Undo* option allows the last formatting or editing change to be reversed. When Undo is turned off, some features, such as Sort, will perform more quickly.

The *Format Document for Default Printer on Open* option uses information about the currently selected printer to format a document when a file is opened. For example, if a document was saved with a different printer selected, the fonts available for the currently selected printer will be applied to text when the document is opened.

The *Prompt for Hyphenation* option can be set to Never, When Required, or Always (see Chapter 8).

The *Units of Measure* option is selected to change the system of measurement used by WordPerfect. WordPerfect supports many systems of measurement including inches (i or "), centimeters (c), and points (p).

The *Language* option is used to select a different installed language.

The *WordPerfect 5.1 Keyboard* option changes the function of keys to simulate the keystrokes used in the 5.1 version of WordPerfect.

The *Autocode Placement* option is used to automatically place certain formatting codes at the beginning of a page or paragraph. For example, when Autocode Placement is on, a page numbering or page size code is placed at the beginning of a page and a justification or tab set code is placed at the beginning of a paragraph.

The *WordPerfect 5.1 Cursor Movement* option, if selected, will provide the capability of simulating the cursor movements used in WordPerfect 5.1.

The *Delimited Text* options are used when retrieving spreadsheet or database information from other applications into a WordPerfect merge data file.

The *Keyboard Layout* option is used to change keystrokes in an existing keyboard, to create a new definition, or to select an alternative keyboard. For example, if the WordPerfect for Windows 5.2 keyboard keystrokes are desired, select the CUAWPW51 keyboard layout.

The *Location of Files* option is used to designate the drive and/or directory where files are located for backups, printers, styles, graphics, macros, etc. The location of files can be changed by selecting the file type and by typing a new drive/directory. For example, if documents are to be placed in a drive and/or directory other than the default directory, c:\wpdocs, select **Documents** and type the new drive letter followed by a colon, a backslash, and a directory name, e.g., n:\letters.

The *Color Palette* option provides the user with a color printing palette that has millions of colors that can be used to print text, graphic lines, borders, fills, etc.

Customizing the Button Bar

There are seven Button Bars provided by WordPerfect, namely FONT, LAYOUT, MACROS, OUTLINE, TABLES, TOOLS, and WPMAIN. A new Button Bar can be created and/or any of the buttons on any Button Bar can be changed. Also, a Button Bar can be rearranged, relocated, and/or displayed differently in the document window. A Button Bar name can be changed, or an entire Button Bar can be deleted.

To create a new Button Bar or to edit an existing Button Bar, use the **Add Feature** in the Edit Button Bar dialog box. In addition, use the **Delete Button** or **Move Button** option in the Edit Button Bar dialog box to change an existing Button Bar. Buttons on a Button Bar can be used to access menu commands, features, macros, and other Button Bars. *(**Note:** When a button that represents a Button Bar is selected, the displayed Button Bar is replaced with the selected Button Bar.)*

Add a Button

1. Select **View, Button Bar Setup, Edit** {Alt and v, s, e}.

   Note: The Edit Button Bar dialog box displays.

2. Select **Add Menu Item** {e}.

   Note: The File menu name is highlighted on the screen and a box with the message "Press F7 when finished adding buttons..." displays.

3. Use the arrow keys to locate and highlight the menu name and option desired, click once {Enter}.

4. When all desired options are selected, press **F7**.

5. Select **OK** {Tab, Enter}.

Delete a Button

1. Select **View, Button Bar Setup, Edit** {Alt and v, s, e}.

2. Select and highlight the Button Bar option to be deleted.

3. Select **Delete Button** {d}.

4. Select **Yes** {y} to delete the Button Bar option.

 **Move a Button**

Note: A button can be moved to a new location on the same Button Bar.

1. Select **View, Button Bar Setup, Edit** {Alt and v, s, e}.

2. Select and highlight the button to be relocated.

3. Select **Move Button** {m}.

4. Double-click on the button name that will be located to the right of the moved button {press the up or down arrow key to highlight the desired button name, Enter}.

5. Select **OK** {Tab, Enter}.

 **Relocate a Button Bar in the Document Window**

1. Select **View, Button Bar Setup, Options** {Alt and v, s, o}.

2. Select the desired position.

3. Select **OK** {Enter}.

 **Change the Picture/Text on the Buttons of a Button Bar**

1. Select **View, Button Bar Setup, Options** {Alt and v, s, o}.

2. Select the desired style.

3. Select **OK** {Enter}.

Create a Button Bar

1. Select **View, Button Bar Setup, Select** {Alt and v, s, s}.

2. Select **Create** {c}.

3. Type a name for the Button Bar.

4. Select **OK** {Enter}.

5. Select and use any of the following items:

> **Add Menu Item**
> **Add Feature**
> **Add Macro**
> **Add Button Bar**

6. When all the desired options have been chosen, select **OK** {Enter} to create the new Button Bar.

WordPerfect Customer Support

If you encounter difficulties installing, setting up, or using any WordPerfect feature, WordPerfect's Customer Support is available to assist you at the following numbers (these customer support numbers are for users within the United States, U.S. territories, or Canada).

Installation	800-228-9012 801-228-9954 (toll)
Equations, Graphics, Sound, Tables	800-228-9006 801-228-9952 (toll)
Macros, Merge	800-228-9013 801-228-9951 (toll)
All other features	800-228-9038 801-228-9950 (toll)
Laser or PostScript printers	800-228-9027 801-228-9955 (toll)
Dot matrix printers and other printers	800-228-9032 801-228-9956 (toll)
Networks	800-228-9019 801-228-9953 (toll)
Customer support fax number	801-222-4377 (toll)
After hours customer support number	801-222-9010 (toll)

QuickFinder

by Jeanette Hart

WordPerfect provides a special file indexing program called QuickFinder which is particularly useful if you create many documents and letters and need to find specific files quickly. QuickFinder has two advantages over the Find function in File Manager:

1. QuickFinder creates a special, compressed index of every word in the document, so the search for a specific word or group of words is many times faster than the File Manager's search. (The File Manager actually looks in each document and tries to match the search criteria.)

2. QuickFinder can index documents in multiple directories and drive paths, so only one search is needed to find the document.

One of the drawbacks of a true electronic filing system (a filing system that has no hard copies) is the difficulty of retrieving documents. QuickFinder gives an office a step towards a true electronic filing system by making document retrieval much simpler. For instance, an office could implement an archival system in which all files over six months old are transferred to an optical disk or other storage medium. QuickFinder could then be used to index the archival disk, and documents on the disk could be searched for by name, subject, or by any word in the document. The search would be very fast, and the files that matched the search criteria would then be displayed in the File Manager. The File Manager tools could then be used to view or open the documents.

Creating a QuickFinder Index

Before QuickFinder can be used to find documents, the indexes must be created. More than one index can be created using different criteria, such as the drives or directories to be indexed and the types of files to include in the index. The QuickFinder File Indexes Setup dialog box is used to define and create the indexes.

1. Select the **QuikFndr** button on the WPMAIN Button Bar.

   Note: The QuickFinder File Indexer dialog box displays. If indexes have been previously created, the last index used will display in the Index field.

2. Select **Setup**.

   Note: The QuickFinder File Indexes Setup dialog box displays.

3. Select **Location of Files**.

4. Click in the field next to the word "Personal Path," then type the path to the directory in which the QuickFinder Indexes are to be located.

   Note: Normally the WP60 directory is used, but the indexes can be placed in any directory.

5. Select **OK**.

6. Check that **Personal** is selected at the List Indexes from option.

   Note: Shared indexes are used if you are indexing a network or workgroup drive that is shared with other people.

7. Select **Create Index Definition**.

   Note: The Create Index Definition dialog box displays.

8. Type a descriptive name for the index, then press **Enter** or **Tab** to move to the next field.

9. In the Index Filename field, the first eight characters of the descriptive name will automatically appear. If this is an appropriate filename for the index, press **Enter** to continue.

   *Note: If the filename is not an appropriate filename or is a duplicate of a filename already in use, enter a new filename, including the path where the file is to be located. Press **Enter** to continue.*

10. Select **Add**.

    Note: The Add QuickFinder Index Directory Pattern dialog box displays.

11. In the Filename Pattern field, type the path to the directory that is to be indexed and the *.* if all files are to be indexed, e.g., **a:*.***.

    *Note: When *.* is used, WordPerfect will automatically exclude files with the filename extensions .exe and .com.*

12. Select **OK** to return to the Create Index Definition dialog box.

13. If there are filename extensions other than *.exe* and *.com* that you want to exclude from the index, select **Options**.

    Note: The QuickFinder Index Options dialog box displays.

14. Click in the Exclude Files field, press **End**, then type **; *.bat**.

Note: The semicolon separates the filename extensions. Files with the extension .bat are batch programs used to start programs or to set up paths and do not need to be included in the document index.

15. Select **OK** to return to the Create Index Definition dialog box.

16. Select **OK** to return to the QuickFinder File Indexes Setup dialog box.

17. If the newly created index is the only one listed, it will be highlighted and displayed with an asterisk, indicating that it must be generated. If an asterisk does not display, highlight the filename, then select **(Un)Mark to Regenerate**.

18. Select **Generate Marked Indexes**.

    Note: The screen will display blank for a moment, then WordPerfect will display a message showing the progress of the generation. Do not touch the keyboard while WordPerfect is generating the index.

19. When the index generation is completed, the message, "Generation Complete, Press Any Key" displays. Press any key to return to the QuickFinder File Indexes Setup dialog box.

    Note: The index is now ready to be used.

20. Select **Close**, then **OK** to return to the document screen.

Using a QuickFinder Index

Once a QuickFinder Index has been created, WordPerfect can use the index to locate documents by any word or group of words that are contained in the desired documents. There are many options to make searches more flexible and to customize QuickFinder indexes. For additional information, see QuickFinder in the WordPerfect Reference manual.

Use a QuickFinder Index

1. Select the **QuikFndr** button on the WPMAIN Button Bar.

2. Select the desired index.

   Note: The last index used (or the only existing index) displays in the Index field. To select another index, click on the arrow next to the Index field and double-click on the desired index.

3. The cursor/insertion point should automatically move to the Word Pattern field.

   Note: If the cursor/insertion point does not automatically move to the Word Pattern field, click in the Word Pattern field and type the search criteria.

4. Select **OK** to start the search.

   Note: A brief message will display showing the status of the search.

5. All files found that match the criteria will be displayed in a special File Manager window. This window has most of the options that are available in the regular File Manager window, and the File Manager tools can be used to view or retrieve a document. For example, highlight the first filename in the list and select **Look** to view the document.

6. Select **Close** twice to return to the document window.

Using Fax/Modems and E-Mail with WordPerfect

By Michele Woggon

WordPerfect 6.0 includes a fax capability called Fax Services as well as an electronic mail (E-Mail) feature called Message Board. These two communications tools, as well as basic information on fax technology and fax devices are presented in this appendix.

Fax Technology

Fax technology allows an exact copy of a document to be transmitted over the telephone system from one fax device to another. Fax, which was originally called facsimile, made its debut at the beginning of the 1930s.

The first fax devices were machines that sent copies of documents using analog signals. The analog method was very slow. In the 1980s digital signals replaced analog signals for the transmission of faxes. Digital fax transmission is much faster than analog transmission and is one of the fastest growing communications tools now available.

Fax Machines

A stand-alone fax machine is a device that transmits an exact copy of a document to a fax device in a distant location using the telephone system. A hard copy of the document is scanned by the fax machine, which digitizes the document so that it can be transmitted electronically.

Fax Modems

A fax modem is a computer hardware device that allows the computer user to send and receive computer data and documents using a computer and the telephone system. Fax modems, which are also called fax boards, function both as a regular data modem for communicating with other computers and for sending documents as faxes to distant fax machines and other fax modems.

Fax modems require software to control and facilitate their operation. Although fax modem software is usually included with the fax modem, WordPerfect 6.0 now provides software that permits faxing documents directly from the WordPerfect program.

WordPerfect Fax Services

The Fax Services feature allows the faxing of WordPerfect documents and other computer files directly from WordPerfect 6.0. To fax documents from WordPerfect, it is necessary to have a fax modem or a fax machine connected to the computer or network.

Fax Options

Fax Services offers numerous options for sending computer files as faxes. It is possible to send WordPerfect documents or other computer files as faxes without converting them to WordPerfect documents. All or part of a document can be faxed with or without a cover sheet. Faxes may be sent immediately or scheduled for sending at a later time and date. Options for selecting fax resolution, priority, routing, and billing are also available. These fax options are presented in the Send Fax dialog box.

Numerous options are available in Fax Services. To use the Fax Services options, select **File**, **Print/Fax**, and select **Fax Services**. If the Fax Services option is gray (not available), see Installing Fax Services on the next page.

Installing Fax Services

Fax Services must be installed from the WordPerfect 6.0 Install disks. If Word-Perfect 6.0 is already installed on the computer, select **File, Print/Fax**. If the Fax Services option is gray, Fax Services are not available. It is then necessary to install Fax Services by loading the WordPerfect 6.0 disk labeled Install 1, and by selecting **Miscellaneous Options 4 - Device Files (Sound, Graphics, Fax, Printer)**.

Note: To use the Fax Services feature in WordPerfect 6.0, a fax device and a fax software program must be installed on your computer or network.

Send a WordPerfect Document as a Fax

1. Select **File, Print/Fax** or press **Shift** and **F7**.

2. Select **Fax Services**.

3. Select **Manual Dial**.

4. Type the name of the recipient of the fax and press **Enter**.

5. Type the recipient's fax telephone number and press **Enter** twice.

6. To send the full document with a cover sheet press **Enter**.

7. To monitor the progress of the fax or to cancel the fax, select **Fax Activity**. If you want to cancel the sending of the fax, select **Cancel Current Fax** before the send process is complete.

   Note: If desired, press Esc repeatedly to exit Fax Services and to return to the WordPerfect document screen.

Send a Computer File as a Fax

1. Select **File, Print/Fax** or press **Shift** and **F7**.

2. Select **Fax Services**.

3. Select **Manual Dial**.

4. Type the name of the recipient of the fax and press **Enter**.

5. Type the recipient's fax telephone number and press **Enter** twice.

6. From the Send Fax screen select **Document on Disk**.

7. Type the path, filename, and file extension of the file to be faxed and press **Enter**.

   Note: The Print Multiple Pages screen displays.

8. Press **Enter** to send all pages.

9. Press **Enter** to send the fax.

10. To convert the file to a WordPerfect 6.0 document, press **Enter** to select ASCII Text (Standard).

*Note: To monitor the progress of the fax or to cancel the sending of the fax, select **Fax Activity**. To cancel the fax, select **Cancel Current Fax** before the send process is complete.*

Creating a Phonebook

The Phonebook feature is an electronic telephone directory of names and fax telephone numbers for individuals or groups to whom faxes are sent. Using Phonebook it is possible to create, edit, or delete individual or group entries.

Create a Phonebook Entry

1. Select **File, Print/Fax** or press **Shift** and **F7**.

2. Select **Fax Services**.

3. Select **Phonebook**.

4. Select **Create Entry**.

5. Type the name of the person to whom the fax will be sent and press **Tab**.

6. Type the fax telephone number of the person to whom the fax will be sent and press **Tab**.

7. Optional. Type the voice telephone number and press **Tab**. (Press **Tab** to skip this step.)

8. *To change the Destination Fax Machine settings,* press **Enter**. Press **Enter** to toggle the X to select the resolution desired and to determine whether the fax is a binary file.

9. *To make changes,* press **Tab** to highlight the item(s) to be changed and type the changes. When finished making changes, press **Tab** to move to OK.

10. Press **Enter** to save the Phonebook entry.

Canceling a Fax

Canceling a fax is possible so long as the send fax process has not been completed. To cancel a fax when using Fax Services, select **Fax Activity** and then choose **Cancel Current Fax**. How to cancel a fax is shown in Steps to Send a WordPerfect Document as a Fax and in Steps to Send a Computer File as a Fax on page C-3.

The WordPerfect Message Board

The Message Board feature in the WordPerfect 6.0 Shell permits the creating, sending, and storing of electronic mail messages. The messages can be notes to yourself, or, if your computer is part of a network, messages can be sent to other people's computers on the network. It is possible to create, send, read, reply to, and delete messages. It is also possible to attach computer files to send along with messages.

Using the Message Board

The Message Board is a part of the WordPerfect Shell. It is not available in the word processing part of WordPerfect. To use the Message Board, it is necessary to start the WordPerfect Shell. It is also necessary to know the location as well as the drive and the directory of the SHELL.EXE file.

If the drive and directory in which the SHELL.EXE is located is added to the path in your AUTOEXEC.BAT file, you can type **shell** at the DOS prompt to load the WordPerfect Shell.

If the Shell does not appear on your screen after completing the Steps to Start Word-Perfect Shell, see the *WordPerfect Shell Version 4.0 User's Guide* for directions on installing and starting the Shell.

*Note: Pressing the **Tab** key activates functions and is used to move between options in the Message Board.*

Start WordPerfect Shell

1. Change to the drive and directory that contains the SHELL.EXE file.

   Note: The SHELL.EXE may be in the directory WPC60DOS on the drive in which WordPerfect 6.0 resides, e.g., C:\WPC60DOS.

2. Type **shell** and press **Enter**. (It is also possible to type **mc shell** and press **Enter** to load the macro engine to start the Shell.)

   *Note: To exit the WordPerfect Shell, press **F7** and then press **Enter**.*

Setting Up the Message Board

It is necessary to make a directory for messages on the Message Board. Messages are saved as files in the directory created for the message board. The directories for message boards are like DOS directories but are created from within the WordPerfect Shell (see the following Steps to Set Up a Personal Message Board and the Steps to Set Up a Shared Message Board).

Creating a Sub-Message Board is similar to creating a subdirectory to a DOS directory, but it is created from within the WordPerfect Shell (see the Steps to Set Up a Sub-Message Board).

When assigning directory names, follow DOS filename conventions, i.e., only eight characters in a name, etc. If the DOS filename is not correct, no directory is created and there is no message explaining that the directory was not created.

There are two types of message boards, personal message boards and shared message boards. A personal message board is for writing messages to yourself. It is possible to have a personal message board using either a stand-alone computer or a computer on a network. A shared message board is for sending messages to people using other computers on the network.

Set Up a Personal Message Board

1. Select **File, Setup, Location of Files**.

2. In the Location of Files dialog box, select **Messages** if using a stand-alone computer or select **Messages** and then **Personal Directory** if using a networked computer.

3. Type the path for the directory to be used for messages.

4. Press **Enter**.

5. If creating a new directory, type **y** to respond "Yes" to Create Directory.

   *Note: If desired, press **Enter** to return to the Setup menu, press **Enter** to close and return to the WordPerfect Shell, or press **F7** and press **Enter** to exit the WordPerfect Shell.*

Set Up a Shared Message Board

1. Select **File, Setup, Location of Files**.

2. In the Location of Files dialog box, select **Messages, Shared Directory**.

3. Type the path for the directory to be used for the messages.

4. Press **Enter**.

5. Type **y** to answer "Yes" if creating a new directory.

Appendix C–Using Fax/Modems and E-Mail with WordPerfect

Set Up a Sub-Message Board

1. Select **File, Other Directory** and press **Enter**.

2. Type the path for the message board directory including the subdirectory and press **Enter**.

3. Select **Yes** to create the new subdirectory.

4. To display the new sub-message board name, select **Tools, Message Board**.

Naming Message Boards

The User Name function is used after setting up a message board to create a name that will identify the sender of messages. The User Name of your choice is inserted automatically after "From:" each time a message is created.

Set Up a Message Board User Name

1. Select **Tools, Message Board**, and press **Enter**.

2. Select **User Name**, type the name of your choice, and press **Enter**.

Creating a Message

There are two methods for creating messages to send to a personal or shared message board. The first method is available by selecting **Tools, New Message**, which takes you to the New Shell Message dialog box.

The second method is available by selecting **Tools, Message Board, Add**, which takes you to the Add Message screen.

Only the second method offers the option of including an attachment. An *attachment* is a computer file that can be sent with the message.

Press the **Tab** key to activate functions and to move around the New Shell Message screen and the Add Message screen.

Create a Message Using the New Message Option

1. Select **Tools, New Message**, and press **Enter**.

2. Type the subject of the message and press **Enter** to move to the Message area of the screen.

3. Type the message.

4. To make any changes after typing the message, press **Tab** to move to From, Subject, or Message and type changes.

5. When finished preparing the message, press **Tab** to move to OK, and press **Enter** to send the message and return to the WordPerfect Shell.

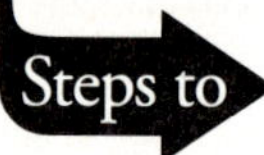
Create a Message with an Attachment Using the Add Message Option

1. Select **Tools, Message Board, Add**.

2. Type the subject of the message and press **Enter**.

3. Press **Tab** to move to the Message area of the screen.

4. Type the message.

5. To make any changes, press **Tab** to move to From, Subject, or Message and type changes.

6. To send a computer file with the message, select **Attachment**.

7. Type the path including the filename and file extension and press **Enter**.

8. Press **Enter** to send the message and return to the WordPerfect Shell.

Reading a Message

Whenever a message is sent, its name and subject is added to a list of all messages. From this message list it is possible to select messages to be read. To read a message, it is necessary to scroll through the message list and to highlight the name of the message to be read.

To locate a message, the Search function (F2) can be used when the message list is shown on the screen. The Search function makes it possible to locate messages by name or subject. After pressing **F2**, it is possible to type the name or subject to be searched. To search the entire list, it is necessary to highlight the first message in the list.

After a message has been read, a reply can be sent. Also, any files attached to the message can be viewed by pressing **Alt** and **F3**.

Read a Message

1. Select **Tools, Message Board**, and press **Enter**.

Note: If using a network, select the message board that has the message to be read.

2. Use the up or down arrow keys and highlight the name of the message to be read. ·

3. Press **1** to read the message.

   *Note: To view an attachment, press **Alt** and **F3**. Press **Enter** when finished viewing the attachment.*

Options for Saving a Message

The Message Board options allow messages to be saved as text, as a WordPerfect 6.0 document, or as a computer file with the drive, directory, and filename of your choice. It is also possible to save a message to the Clipboard and to paste it in other documents.

To use any of the Save options, select **Tools, Message Board**. Highlight the message to be saved and select **Save Msg**. The Save Message dialog box presents the various Save options. Use the **Tab** key to move around the screen to indicate the option to be selected, and press **Enter** to select.

Copying an Attachment

The Copy Attachment function can be used to find the location of and to copy a file attached to a message. The attachment can be given a new path and file-name or it may be saved to the Clipboard.

Copy an Attachment

1. Select **Tools, Message Board**.

   Note: If using a network, select the message board that has the attachment to be copied.

2. Use the up or down arrow keys to highlight the name of the message containing the attachment to be copied.

3. Press **5** to copy the attachment.

4. Type the path, including the filename and file extension where the attachment is to be copied, and press **Enter**.

Mark and Unmark Options

When the Shell Message Board screen is displayed, there are two options: * (Un)mark and Home,* (Un)mark All. The Mark option is used to select multiple files to be deleted, to be saved to another location, or to be copied as an attachment.

* (Un)mark means that an asterisk (*) displayed before a highlighted message name marks the file. Once a file is marked, typing an asterisk again unmarks the file.

Home,* (Un)mark All means that by pressing the Home key once and then typing an asterisk that all the files in the message list will be marked. If all the files are marked with an asterisk, pressing Home once and then typing the asterisk again will unmark all the files.

Sound Boards

by Darrel Dorsett

A sound board converts the computer's discrete digital signals to continuous analog signals. This process uses circuitry called a Digital Analog Converter (DAC). The quality of the sound depends on the digital input, the design of the board, and the audio amplifiers. Better sound usually means more bytes (megabytes) of digital data (larger files) and more expensive cards and amplifiers.

Sound is converted into digital signals from analog signals through software using circuity called an Analog Digital Converter (ADC). Not all sound boards can perform this function, but most boards today do so. The choice of which sound board to buy will depend on your current and future use of the board as well as how much money you want to invest.

Sound boards may interface with a Musical Instrument Digital Interface (MIDI). This is a standard interface initially created by Kawai, Korg, Roland, Sequential Circuits, and Yamaha. The MIDI interface allows the computer to generate music in a manner similar to earlier analog synthesizers, but much less expensively.

Sound boards usually have a joystick port because it was the support of sound in games that provided the market that brought about the proliferation of less expensive, more capable sound boards.

Many sound boards also provide support for CD-ROMs. This allows music and other sound sources to be integrated into programs and attached to data files in the computer. CDs with a library of sounds and sound effects are available.

Install and Configure the Sound Board

The first step in installing a sound board is to follow the instructions from the maker of the board. If two sets of connector fingers are on the bottom of the sound board, the board should be placed into a motherboard slot with two openings (a 16-bit slot). In general, the default values that the manufacturer has set up are used. The IRQ (interrupt request) value is often 5 or 7. The base I/O address is often 220H or 240H. The DMA (direct memory access) is usually 1. Generally, the sound board has accompanying diagnostic software to help set the correct values if conflicts are experienced. Try using several of the board capabilities with its own software before trying to access the board through WordPerfect. Always *write down* the settings you use for the sound board.

Once the sound board is installed, you must configure your software programs to work with the sound board. Software drivers (files) for various sound boards are provided with the WordPerfect 6.0 program.

After the sound board is working with its own software, WordPerfect must identify the board.

Identifying the Board for WordPerfect

1. Select Tools, Sound Clip, Sound Setup.

2. Choose Type, Select.

   Note: If your board is not on the list, choose one of the board types that your board emulates. If this does not work, try another board type. If other board types do not work, contact the board manufacturer and/or WordPerfect to find your board type. WordPerfect 6.0 must have the board properly identified before it will function.

3. In the Sound Setup dialog box, select Hardware Setup.

4. Select Hardware Interrupt Level and set the proper IRQ that was used during the board configuration.

5. To set the Base I/O, use the same base address that was used when the board was set up (configured).

6. Press Enter twice to return to the document window.

Test the Sound Board with WordPerfect 6.0

One of the simplest ways to test the sound board is to access and play a prerecorded sound file (sound clip) from a document in WordPerfect. WordPerfect includes a few MIDI sound files in the GRAPHICS directory. These files have a .MID filename extension. The file named FANFARE1.MID is a good file to use for testing your sound board.

Test the Sound Board with WordPerfect

1. Select **Tools, Sound Clip, Play**.

2. Select **Add Clip**.

3. Use the File List or QuickList options to locate the file named FANFARE1.MID. (It should be in the GRAPHICS directory.) If necessary, move the cursor to WPDOCS and change it to WP60\GRAPHICS. The directory should now show C:\WP60\GRAPHICS*.*.

4. Press **Enter**.

5. Use the down arrow and highlight **FANFARE1.MID**. Press **Enter**.

6. Check that FANFARE1.MID displays as the filename.

7. Select **Link to File on Disk**.

8. Press **Enter** or select **OK**.

9. Select **Play**.

   *Note: If no sound is heard, increase the volume. Use 100%. If necessary, select **Exit** and try the above steps again. If it still doesn't work, check all of your installation settings.*

   Note: If you run WordPerfect 6.0 as a DOS application from Windows in the enhanced mode, you will not be able to Play or Record; you will be able to add and delete clips only.

Use an Existing Sound File Linked to a WordPerfect 6.0 Document File

Using a separate sound file linked to the document is an efficient method because the size of the document file can be minimized. It also allows easy reuse of the sound file in other documents. A directory holding a library of sound clips is similar to the directory of graphics.

♪ **Sound (Ctrl+S):** Clip #1

Sound clip box

One disadvantage of an external sound clip file is the security of the sound file contents. Placing the sound clip file inside the document allows the clip to be saved and moved with the document. This also eliminates the necessity of moving external sound files with a document.

When you insert or link a sound file into the document, a sound clip box will appear in the document similar to Figure D.1.

 **Steps to** **Link the Sound to a Document on Disk**

1. Place the cursor at the location in the document where the sound clip is desired.

2. Select **Tools, Sound Clip, Add**.

3. Locate the desired sound file using the File List or QuickList options. Double-click on the desired filename.

4. Select **Link to File on Disk**.

5. Select **OK** or press **F7**.

Record Sounds or Voice in a WordPerfect 6.0 Document File

Plug the microphone into the phone input jack. Check that the on/off switch is in the On position. Beacuse a proper microphone is vital, many board manufacturers include a microphone with their sound board.

 **Steps to** **Record Sounds or Voice in a Document File**

Method 1

1. Select **Tools, Sound Clip, Record**.

2. Select **Rec** and speak into the microphone while holding the microphone 6 to 10 inches from your mouth.

3. Select **Stop** when finished.

   *Note: Use the Play, Pause, Rewind, and Fast Forward options to check your recording. If necessary, select **Edit Desc** to modify the text description for the clip.*

4. Select **Insert** to make the sound clip locator box in the document and to place the digital sound within the document; or select **Save** to write the digital sound as a separate file to be saved on the disk and link that file to the document.

5. Select **Exit** or press **F7**.

Method 2

1. Press **Ctrl** and **d** (for Dictation).

2. Select **Rec** and speak into the microphone while holding the microphone 6 to 10 inches from your mouth.

3. Select **Stop** when finished.

    *Note: Use the Play, Pause, Rewind and Fast Forward options to check your recording. If necessary, select **Edit Desc** to modify the text description for the clip.*

4. Select **Insert** to make the sound clip locator box in the document and to place the digital sound within the document.

    Note: There is no choice offered for saving a sound clip to a separate file if the Ctrl and d method is used.

Play the Sound Clip

1. Select **Tools, Sound Clip, Play**.

2. Move the cursor to highlight the desired clip to be played.

3. Select **Play/Pause**.

4. Select **Exit** or press **F7**.

Use Sound to Create a Text Description

1. Press **Ctrl** and **F7**, select **Sound Clip, Record**; or press **Ctrl** and **d** (for Dictation).

2. Select **Rec** and speak into the microphone while holding the microphone 6 to 10 inches from your mouth.

3. Select **Stop** when finished.

    Note: You should use the Play, Pause, Rewind, and Fast Forward options to check your recording.

4. Select **Edit Desc** to modify the text description for the clip.

5. Press **Enter** twice.

6. Select **OK** twice.

Sound File Storage Information

Sound files may use much of your storage resources, both memory and disk space. Digital audio files (sound converted to a digital format) are usually stored in the way that the board generated the bytes representing the sound. Two common voice file formats are .WAV and .VOC, which basically differ in their headers. The headers (initial sectors) indicate the characteristics of the recorded data, voice or wave, stereo or mono, for the particular file format, i.e., .WAV and .VOC.

Sampling sizes (8- or 16-bit) and *rates* help to determine the quality of the recorded sound as well as the size of the files. Eight-bit cards can produce one-byte (8-bit) samples. Sixteen bit cards store two-byte samples. An 8-bit card can generate 256 discrete steps. Four bits (a nibble) can represent 16 possibilities; 8-bits can represent two 16-possibility groups (16 x 16 is 256). A 16-bit card can represent 65,536 (256 x 256) possibilities or steps in the sound range. If the sampling rate is 6,000 hertz (Hz), 6,000 samples are taken per second. This restricts the recording upper frequency limits. Higher quality boards are now sampling at the rate of 44,100 in order to provide 22,050 sample rates for each of the two stereo channels. Six thousand hertz (the upper range of a typical male voice) for 60 seconds essentially uses an entire 360K floppy disk. A 20-MB hard disk is filled with 7.7 minutes of stereo at 22,050 Hz. The space used is the same for both disk and memory storage.

Sound files can be compressed to take less space on the disk. Generally, compressed files present degradation in the sound quality. Compressed files cannot be converted to other formats and are not easily edited. Compression techniques, somewhat similar to the methods of data compression used to store larger files or to increase effective disk space, are also used. Although LHARC, PKZIP, STACKER, DOUBLESPACE and other programs can make great reductions in data files, such large reductions in the voice files is not as easily done. The speed needed for sound files requires rapid file decompression. The complex algorithms of extreme data compression have not been able to provide this speed.

APPENDIX E

WordPerfect 6.0 Graphic Images

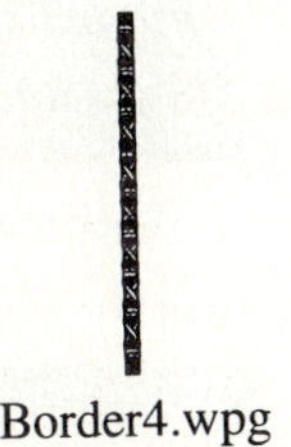

Border4.wpg

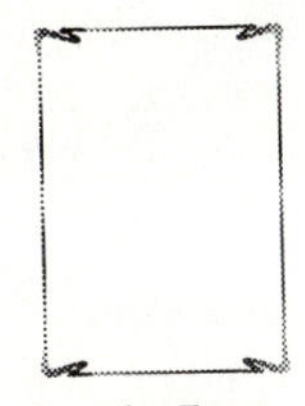

Border7.wpg

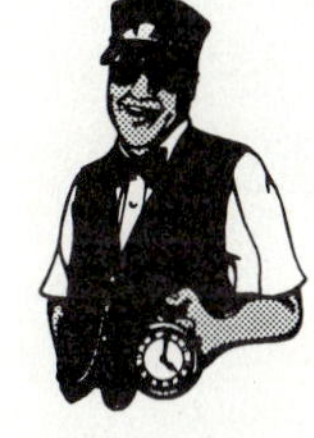

Conduct.wpg

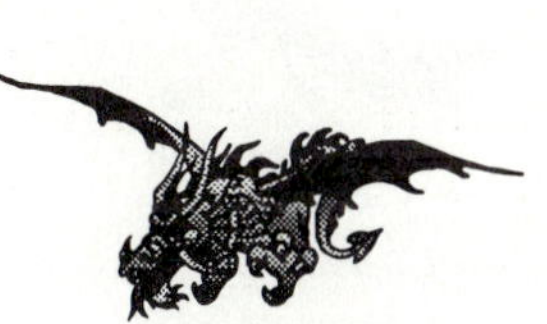

Dragon.wpg

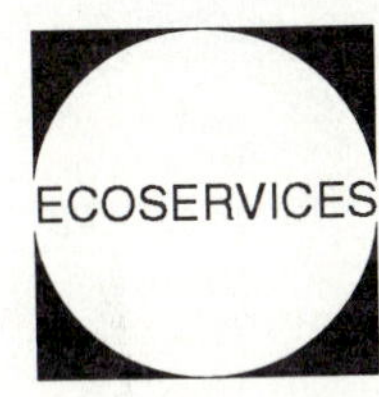

Ecologo.wpg

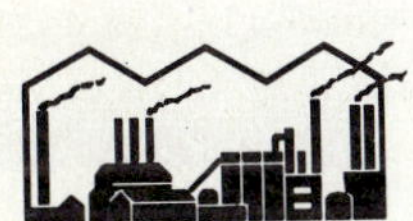

Factory.wpg

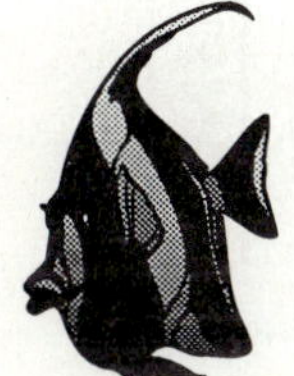

Fishtrop.wpg

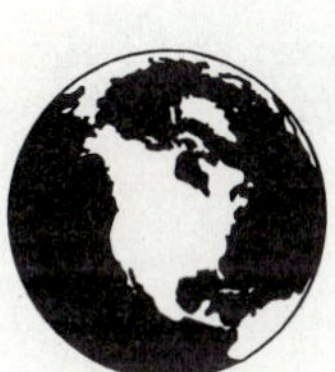

Globe.wpg

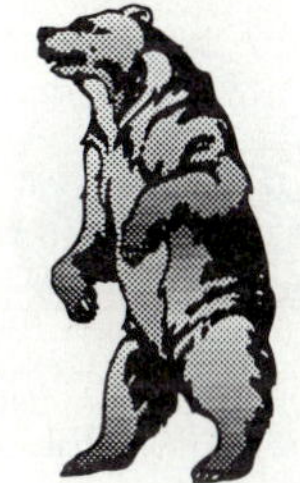

Grizzly.wpg

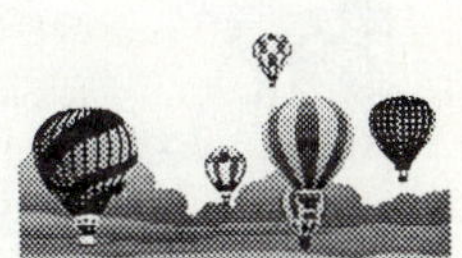

Hotair.wpg

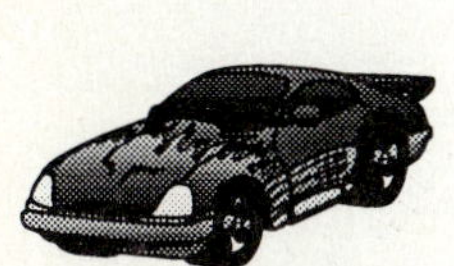

Hotrod.wpg

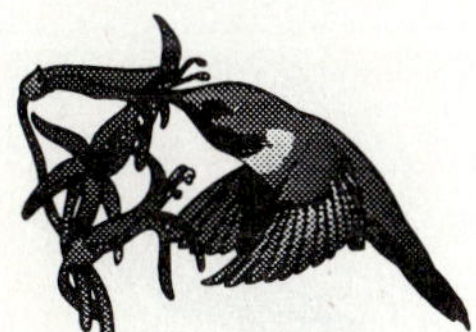

Humbird.wpg

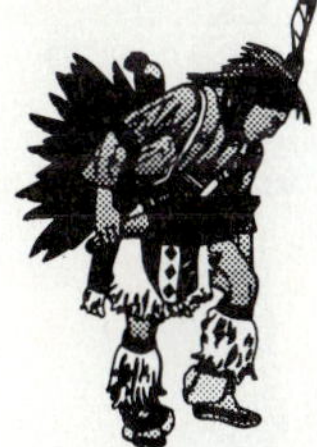

Indance.wpg

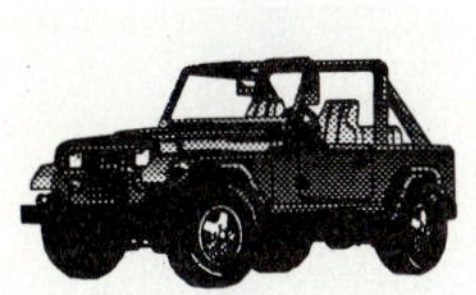

Jeep.wpg

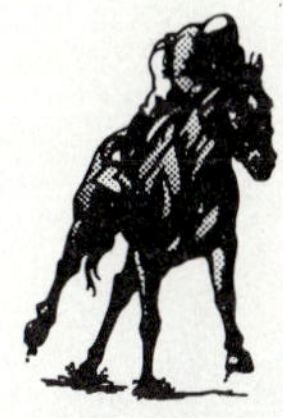

Jockey.wpg

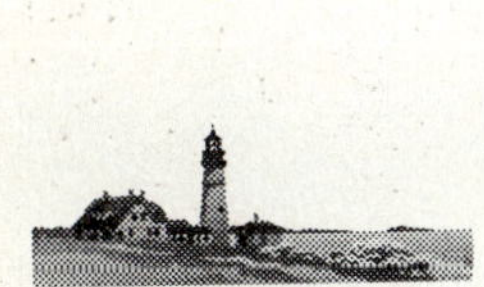

Lighths.wpg

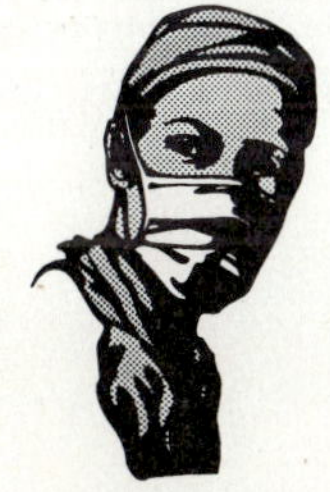

Medical1.wpg

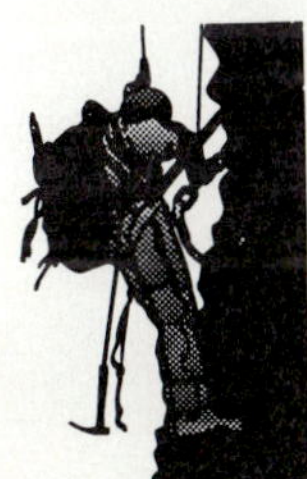

Mtnclimb.wpg

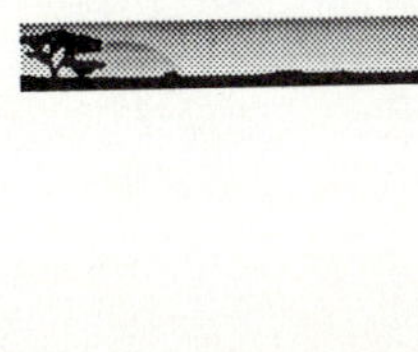

Overhd1.wpg

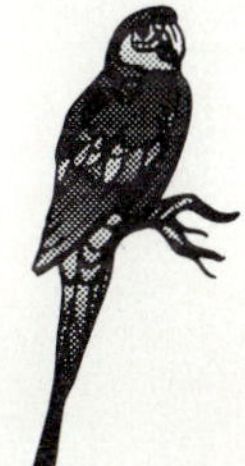

Parrot.wpg

Penpush.wpg   Pheasant.wpg   Plan2.wpg   Skier1.wpg   Skipper.wpg

Summrcnr.wpg   Tigerhd.wpg   Tree.wpg   Water4.wpg   Water7.wpg

Windmill.wpg   Winrace.wpg   Wizard.wpg   Wskier.wpg

Features Summary

FEATURES	ACTIONS	PAGE
Advance feature	Select **Layout, Other, Advance**.	490
Append to File	Select **Edit, Append, To File**.	407
Block text: Using the Edit, Select command	*To block a sentence,* choose **Edit, Select, Sentence**. *To block a paragraph,* choose **Edit, Select, Paragraph**. *To block a page,* choose **Edit, Select, Page**.	39
Using the keyboard:	Press **Alt** and **F4**. Use any of the following keystrokes: **Left** or **right arrow** key = one character left or right **Up** or **down arrow** key = one line up or down **End** = end of the current line **Home, Home, left arrow** key = beginning of line **Home, Home, down arrow** key = end of document **Ctrl** and **left** or **right arrow** key = one word left or right **Ctrl** and **up** or **down arrow** key = one paragraph up or down	40
Using the mouse: Drag method:	Move the mouse pointer to the beginning of the text to be blocked, press and hold the left mouse button while dragging the mouse to highlight the desired text, release the mouse button.	39
To block a word:	Move the mouse pointer to any character in the desired word and double-click.	39
To block a sentence:	Move the mouse pointer to any word in the desired sentence and triple-click.	39
To block a paragraph:	Move the mouse pointer to any location within the paragraph and click four times.	39

| --- | --- | --- |
Compare Documents	Select **File, Compare Documents, Add Markings.** Select the desired Compare by option, **OK.**	595
Convert case	Block text, select **Edit, Convert Case,** select **Uppercase, Lowercase,** or **Initial Caps.**	303
Copy text: Edit, Copy and Paste	Block the text to be copied, select **Edit, Copy and Paste,** move the insertion point to the desired location, press **Enter.**	117
Edit, Copy and Edit, Paste	Block the text to be copied, select **Edit, Copy,** move the insertion point to the desired location, select **Edit Paste.**	118
Drop and drag	Block the text to be copied, move the mouse pointer into the highlighted text, press and hold the mouse button and drag the mouse pointer to the desired location, press the **Ctrl** button as the mouse button is released.	119
Cross reference: Create	Select **Tools, Cross-Reference, Both,** select the desired Tie Reference to option, select **Target Name,** type the desired name, select **OK;** move the insertion point to the desired target location, press **Enter** to insert the target.	644
Generate the cross reference	Select **Tools, Generate,** select **OK.**	645
Date Code	Select **Tools, Date, Code.**	325
Date Text feature	Select **Tools, Date, Text.**	60
Delete text	Blocked desired text and press **Delete** (Del).	40
Disk drive (accessing)	Select the **File Mgr** button, press the = key, type the drive letter where the file disk is located, select **OK,** select **Cancel.**	19
Display modes	Select **View,** choose desired display mode.	13
Document Information	Select **Tools, Writing Tools,** select **Document Information.**	239
Document summary: Create	Select **Layout, Document, Summary,** type the desired document summary information, select **OK.**	454
Display the Document Summary dialog box when saving a document	Select, **Layout, Document, Summary, Setup, Create Summary on Save/Exit, OK** twice.	455
Print a document summary	Select **Layout, Document, Summary, Print, Yes, OK** twice.	455
DOS (exit to)	Select **File, Go to Shell, Go to DOS.**	467
	Select **File, Go to Shell, DOS Command.**	

FEATURES *(cont'd.)*	ACTIONS *(cont'd.)*	PAGE
Double indent	Select **Layout, Alignment, Indent** → ←.	125
Endnotes	Select **Layout, Endnote, Create**, press the **Tab** key, type the endnote information, press **F7**.	277
Envelopes:		
Create an envelope address	Select the **Envelope** button. Select the envelope size desired. Select **Insert** or **Print**.	346
Create an envelope definition	Select the **Envelope** button, select **Setup, Envelope Size**. Select **Create** twice, type a name for the envelope. Select **Paper Type** and double-click on **Envelope**. Select **Paper Size, Other**, type desired size, select **OK**. Select **Paper Location**, double-click on the desired paper location. Select **Orientation**, double-click on the desired orientation. Select **OK, Close**. Double-click on the desired envelope style, select **OK, Print**.	348
Create a POSTNET bar code	Select the **POSTNET Bar Code** option in the Envelope dialog box. Type the address zip code, press **Enter**, select **Insert** or **Print**.	347
Equation/formula:		
Create	Select **Graphics, Graphics Boxes, Create**, choose **Based on Box Style** and double-click on **Equation Box** or **Inline Equation Box**. Select **Create Equation**. Select the **Redsplay** button to view the completed equation/formula. Select **Close, OK**.	410
Edit an equation/formula	Double-click on the equation/formula to be edited, select **Edit Equation**.	413
Exit WordPerfect	Select File, **Exit WP**.	26
File Manager:		
Access File Manager and display a directory	Select the **File Mgr** button, type the disk drive letter and/or directory, select **OK**.	456
Create a directory/subdirectory	In the File Manager window, select **Change Default Dir**, in the New Directory box.	457
Delete a directory/subdirectory	Highlight the directory/ subdirectory to be deleted, select **Delete, Yes**.	460
Delete files	Mark the files to be deleted, select **Delete**, and select **Yes** twice.	459
Find files by using Search	Select **Search**, type the filename or partial filename, select **Search**. To continue the search, press **F2** twice.	461
Find files containing specific word(s)	Select **Find**, select desired option, type the word(s) to be found, select **OK**.	460
Look at the contents of a file	Highlight the desired filename and select **Look**.	456
Mark and copy files	Mark each file to be copied, select **Copy, Yes**, type the name of the directory/ subdirectory where the files are to be copied, select **OK**.	458

File Manager *(cont'd.)*		
Mark and move files	Mark each file to be moved, select **Move/Rename, Yes**, type the name of the directory/ subdirectory where the files are to be moved, select **OK**.	459
Open multiple files	Mark all files to be opened, select **Open into New Document, Yes**.	461
Print multiple files	Mark each file to be printed and select **Print, Yes, OK**.	93
Print the list of files	Select **Print List**.	457
Rename a file	Highlight filename, select **Move/Rename**, type new filename, **OK**.	460
Flush Right alignment	Select **Layout, Alignment, Flush Right** or press **Alt** and **F6**.	22
Font:		
Change font name and/or size	Select the **Font** button. Select desired font and/or size. Select **OK**.	88
Change the initial font	Select **Layout, Document, Initial Font**, select the desired font and/or size, select **OK**.	406
Create footnotes	Select **Layout, Footnote, Create**, type the footnote information, press **F7**.	275
Glossary abbreviation	Select **Tools, Macro, Play**, type **glossary** and select **OK**. Select **Create** and type an abbreviation for the desired words. Place the insertion point in the Expanded Form field and type out the word(s). Select **OK** twice.	671
	To use the glossary abbreviation, type the glossary abbreviation, select **Tools, Macro, Play**, type **glossary** and select **OK**.	672
Grammatik	Select the **Gramatik** button, select **Interactive Check**, select the desired option(s), select **Quit Grammatik**. Save the changed file.	245
Graphics:		
Adjust space around a graphic box	Select **Edit Border/Fill**. Select **Spacing, Automatic Spacing, Outside, Set All**, type the desired amount of space.	389
Change border line style settings	Select **Edit Border/Fill, Lines**. Select the desired line and highlight the desired line style. Select **Edit**.	512
	To change the thickness of the selected line component, select **Thickness** and type the desired line width.	
	To change the spacing between two line components, select **Interline Spacing** and type the desired amount of space.	
Change border line color of a single graphic box	Select **Edit Border/Fill**, select **Color**, choose **One Color for All Lines**, double-click on the desired color. Select **OK, Close**.	488

FEATURES	ACTIONS	PAGE
Graphics *(cont'd.):*		
Change the contrast between light and dark areas of a graphic image	Select **Edit Image**. Select **Contrast**, type the amount of contrast and press **Enter**. Select **Close**, **OK**.	535
Change the default color for a graphic box	Select **Edit Border/Fill**, choose **Based on Border Style**, select **Edit**, **Color**, select **Choose One Color for All Lines**, double-click on desired color.	486
Contour the flow of text around a graphic box	Select **Contour Text Flow**. Select **OK**.	389
Copy a graphic image	Select **Edit**, **Select**, **Page**, **Edit**, **Copy**, **Edit**, **Paste**.	384
Create a caption for a graphic box	Select **Create Caption**. Type the caption information, press **F7**, and select **OK**.	493
Create a drop cap	Block and cut the desired character. Select **Graphics**, **Graphics Box**, **Create**, **Create Text**. Paste the character. If desired change the font and size of the character. Press **F7**. Select **Edit**, **Position**, **Horizontal Position**, **Left**, **OK**. Select **Edit Size**, **Automatic Width Based on Box Contents Width**, select **Set Height**, type desired box height, **OK**. Select **Based on Box Style**, double-click on **User Box**. To delete space around the graphic box, select **Edit Border/Fill**, select **Spacing**, **Automatic Spacing**, **OK**, **Close**, **OK**.	514
Create a graphic box that spans multiple columns	Select **Graphics**, **Graphics Boxes**, **Create**, **Attach To**, **Page**. Select **Edit Position**, **Horizontal Position**, **Full**. Select **Position Relative To**, **Columns**, type the number of columns to span, **OK**.	517
Create a shadow box	Select **Graphics**, **Graphics Boxes**, **Create**. Select **Edit Border/Fill**, **Based on Border Style**, double-click on the desired border. Select **Shadow**. Select the desired border shadow type.	488
Create a Text box	Select **Graphics**, **Graphics Boxes**, **Create**. Select **Edit Position**, **Horizontal Position**, **Full**, **OK**. Select **Create Text**, type and format the text box information. Press **F7**. Select **Based on Box Style**, double-click on **Text Box**.	386
Create a page border	Select **Graphics**, **Borders**, **Page**, select **Borders Styles**, double-click on the desired border style. Select **OK**.	380
Create graphic lines	Select **Graphics**, **Graphics Lines**, **Create**. *To change the thickness of the graphics line*, select **Thickness**. Select **Set** and type the desired line thickness. *To change the line style*, select **Line Style** and double-click on the desired style option.	375
Create reversed text	In the Create Graphics Box dialog box, select **Edit Border/Fill**, select **Fill**, **Fill Style**. Double-click on **100% Shaded Fill**. Select **Foreground Color**, double-click on the desired color. Select **OK**, **Close**. Select **Create Text**. Select the **Font** button, select **Color** and double-click on **White**, select **OK**. Type the desired text, **F7**, **OK**.	497

FEATURES *(cont'd.)*	ACTIONS *(cont'd.)*	PAGE
Graphics *(cont'd.)*:		
Create rotated text	Select **Create Text**, type the desired text, press **Alt** and **F9**, select **Rotate Box Contents**. Select desired rotation, select **OK**, and press **F7**.	495
Define a graphic box for a column	Select **Attach To, Page**. Select **Edit Position, Horizontal Position,** choose the desired position. Select **Position Relative To,** choose **Column,** type the number of the column in which the graphic box will be placed. Select **Vertical Position,** choose the desired position, select **OK**.	486
Enlarge a graphic image within a graphic box	In the Image Editor, select the **Enlarge %** button.	383
Flow text through a graphic box	Select **Text Flow, Through Box.**	383
Place a graphic box containing text in a column	Select **Graphics, Graphics Boxes, Create,** select **Based on Box Style,** and double-click on the desired box style. Select **Attach To, Page.** Select **Edit Position, Horizontal Position,** choose the desired position. Select **Position Relative To, Column,** type the number of the column in which the graphic box will be located. To retrieve previously created text into a graphics box, select **Create Text** Select **File, Retrieve,** type the location and name of the desired file, **OK**.	491
Position a graphic box	Double-click on the graphic image. Select **Edit Position**. Select **Horizontal Position**. Select the desired position option.	378
Position and size a graphics box using the mouse	Click on the graphic image. To move a graphic box, press and hold the mouse button and drag the graphic box to the desired location. To size a graphic box, place the mouse pointer on a black handle at the edge or corner of the graphic box, press and hold the mouse button, and drag to the desired size.	390
Remove border from a graphic box	Select **Edit Border/Fill,** select **Based on Border Style,** double-click on **None**.	379
Retrieve a graphic image	Select **Graphics, Retrieve Image,** select **File List, OK,** double-click on the desired graphics filename.	378
Rotate a graphic image	Select **Image Editor,** click once in the **Rotation** option box, type the desired degree of rotation, and press **Enter**.	383
Size a graphic box	Select **Edit Size,** select **Set Height** or **Set Width** and type the desired height or width.	382
Hard space	Press **Home, Spacebar.**	304
Header/Footer:		
Create	**Layout, Header/Footer/Watermark.** Select desired header/footer, **Create.** Type the information and press **F7**.	270, 272

FEATURES *(cont'd.)*	ACTIONS *(cont'd.)*	PAGE
Header/Footer *(cont'd.):*		
Create footers for odd and Even Pages	Select **Layout, Header/Footer/Watermark**. Select **Footer A, Odd Pages, Create**. Type and format the footer text. Press **F7**. Select **Layout, Header/Footer/Watermark**. Select **Footer B, Even Pages, Create**. Type and format the footer text. Press **F7**.	521
Delete headers or footers	With Reveal Codes on, highlight the header or footer code, press **Delete**.	273
Edit headers or footers	Select **Layout, Header/Footer/Watermark**, select **Headers** or **Footers**, select **Edit**, make the desired changes, press **F7**.	271
Suppress header on page one	Select **Layout, Page, Suppress**, select **Header A**.	271
Help:		
Access from a menu command or dialog box	Highlight the desired menu command or display the desired dialog box, press **F1**.	68
Access using the Contents command	Select **Help, Contents**, choose the desired topic, select **Look**.	68
Access using the How Do I command	Select **Help, How Do I**, choose the desired topic, select **Look**.	67
Use Coach	Select **Help, Coaches**, choose the desired topic, press Enter, respond to prompts that display on the screen.	69
Hidden text:		
Mark hidden text	Block the text to be hidden, select **Font, Hidden Text**. Choose **Hidden Text** and select **OK**.	598
To hide hidden text	Select **Font, Hidden Text**. Choose **Show All Hidden Text** to deselect the option. Select **OK**.	598
To display hidden text	Select **Font, Hidden Text**. Choose **Show All Hidden Text**. Select **OK**.	599
Hypertext	Block the text to be used as a hypertext link. Select **Tools, Hypertext, Create Link**. Click in the box located beside the **Go to Bookmark** option, press **F5**, double-click on the desired bookmark name. Select **OK**.	601
	Select **Tools, Hypertext, Hypertext is Active, OK**. Move the mouse pointer to the desired hypertext line and click once.	602
	To return the insertion point to the original position in the text, select **Tools, Hypertext, Return from Jump**.	602
	To turn off hypertext, select **Tools, Hypertext, Hypertext is Active, OK**.	

FEATURES *(cont'd.)*	ACTIONS *(cont'd.)*	PAGE
Hyphenation: Change the Prompt for Hyphenation option	Select **File, Setup, Environment**, Select **Prompt for Hyphenation** option, select desired option, select **OK.**	219
Turn on hyphenation	Select **Layout, Line, Hyphenation, OK.**	219
Indent	Press **F4.**	124
Indent first line of paragraphs automatically	Select **Layout, Margins, First Line Indent**, type the desired indent amount, select **OK.**	516
Create an index: Mark main index headings	Block the text to be a main index heading entry, select the **MarkText** button, select **Index, OK.**	624
Mark index subheadings	Block the desired text, select the **MarkText** button, type the main index heading entry, press **Tab, OK.**	624
Define an index	Select **Tools, Index, Define**, select desired **Numbering Mode, OK.**	625
Generate an index	Select the **Generate** button on the Tools Button Bar. Select **OK.**	626
Italicize text	Block the text to be italicized, select **Font, Italic.**	63
Justification	Select the **Justification** button on the Ribbon and double-click on the desired justification type.	62
Landscape layout	Select **Layout, Page, Paper Size/Type**, double-click on **Letter (Landscape), OK.**	485
Leading adjustment	Select **Layout, Other, Printer Functions, Leading Adjustment**, type the desired adjustment, select **OK** twice.	403
Letterspacing or word spacing	Select **Layout, Other, Printer Functions, Word Spacing and Letterspacing**, select **Percent of Optimal**, type the desired percentage of letterspacing/word spacing.	404
Line height	Select **Layout, Line, Fixed.** Type desired line height, select **OK.**	402
Line numbering	Select **Layout, Line, Line Numbering, Line Numbering On.** Select any desired options. Select **OK.**	591
Load WordPerfect	Type **cd wp60**, press **Enter**, type **wp**, press **Enter** again.	12
Margins	Select **Layout, Margins**, click once in the box located beside the margin to be changed, type the desired margin in inches. When desired margins have been changed, select **OK.**	85
Master document: Create	Select **File, Master Document, Subdocument, File List**, type the location where the subdocument files are located, select **OK,** double-click on the desired filename.	646

Master document *(cont'd.)*:		
Expand a master document	Select **File, Master Document, Expand, OK, Yes.**	647
Condense a master document	Select **File, Master Document, Condense, OK, Yes.**	648
Save an edited master document and subdocuments	Select **File, Save, Yes;** highlight a subdocument name, select **Save All, OK, Yes;** type the location and name for the master document, select **OK.**	649

Macros:		
Edit a macro using the Edit Macro mode	Select **Tools, Macro, Record, Edit Macro.** Type the location and name of the macro. Select **OK.** Make the desired changes. Select **Save As** and type the desired filename. If desired, close the document or select **Tools, Macro, Stop.**	659
Record a macro	Select **Tools, Macro, Record,** type the name of the macro and select **OK.** Perform the desired actions to be recorded. Select **Tools, Macro, Stop.**	435
Play macro	Select **Tools, Macro, Play,** type the macro name or press **F5,** select **OK** and double-click on the desired macro name.	434
Request user input in a macro	In the Edit Macro window, type the desired macro command (e.g., INPUT or PROMPT), followed by the desired input or prompt message. Place the input/prompt message between quotation marks and enclose between parentheses.	666

Mailing labels using predefined labels	Select **Layout, Page, Labels,** highlight the desired labels, choose **Select, OK.** Type the label mailing address, press **Ctrl** and **Enter** after typing each label.	350

Merging:		
Create a data table file	Select **Tools, Merge, Define, Data Table, Create a Table with Field Names.** Type each field name followed by an **Enter.** Select **OK.** Type the field data into the appropriate cells.	321
Create a form file	Select **Tools, Merge, Define, Form.** Select **Field, List Field Names.** Press **F5** and select **OK.** Double-click on the desired data filename. Double-click on the desired field names.	325
Edit a data table file	With the data table file on the screen, place the insertion point in the column or row to be edited and select **Tools, Merge, Define.**	329
Import data into a data text file	Select **File, Open,** and type the location and filename of the desired file. Double-click on the appropriate file format and check the Field Delimiter, Record Delimiter, and Field Encapsulate Character options. Select **OK.** Select the **Save As** button, select the desired Format option, type the location and new filename, select **OK.** Determine and write down the needed field names and order. Locate the insertion point at the beginning of the document and select **Tools, Merge, Define, Field Names.** Type in each field name followed by an **Enter.** Select **OK.**	579

Merging *(cont'd.)*:

FEATURES	ACTIONS	PAGE
Insert the IFBLANK merge command	Select **Tools, Merge, Define, OK**. Select **Merge Codes**, double-click on the **IFBLANK** command, type the desired field name, select **OK**.	569
Insert the ELSE and ENDIF merge commands	Select **Tools, Merge, Define, OK**. Select **Merge Codes**, double-click on the desired command.	570
Mark and merge specific data records	Select **Tools, Merge, Run**, type the location and name of the form file, press **Enter**. Select **Data File Options**, select **Mark Records to Include**. Double-click on the field name to use when viewing the record to be marked. Double-click on the record(s) to be marked. Select **OK**. Select **Merge**.	330
Merge a form and data table file	Select **Tools, Merge, Run**. Type the location and form filename. Press **Enter**. If necessary, select **Data File Options, Blank Fields in Data File, Remove Resulting Blank Lines**. Select **Merge**.	328
Merge a form file with user input	When the form and data files are in the merge process, type the requested information. Press **F9** to continue.	582
Output merged letters to a file	Select **Tools, Merge, Run**, type the location and filename for the form and data files. Select **Output, File**, type the location and desired filename for the merged letters, select **OK, Merge**.	576
Output merged letters to a printer	Select **Tools, Merge, Run**, type the location and filename for the form and data files. Select **Output, Printer, Merge**.	577
Request user input in a merged letter	Select **Tools, Merge, Define, KEYBOARD**, type the desired prompt message. Select **OK**.	581
Select a range of records	Select **Tools, Merge, Run**, type the location and name for the form and data files. If necessary, select **Data File Options**. Select **Specify Record Number Range**, type the desired record numbers in the To and From boxes, and select **Merge**.	573
Select records based on conditions	Select **Tools, Merge, Run**, type the location and name for the form and data files. If necessary, select **Data File Options**. Select **Define Conditions**. Click on the number 1 in the first row, double-click on the desired field name, type the condition to be met, **Tab** once, if desired, create additional conditions to be met. Select **OK, Merge**.	574
Sort records in a data table file	Open the data table file to be sorted and determine the number of the column to be used for sorting. Select **Tools, Sort**, select **Sort Keys, Edit, Cell**, type the number of the column to be used for sorting, choose the desired sort type and sort order, select **OK, Perform Action**.	354

FEATURES	ACTIONS	PAGE
Move text:		114
Edit, Cut and Paste	Block the text to be moved, select **Edit, Cut and Paste**, move the insertion point to the new location, press **Enter**.	
Edit, Cut and Edit, Paste	Block the text to be moved, select **Edit, Cut**, move the insertion point to the new location, select **Edit, Paste**.	115

Move text *(cont'd.)*:		
Drop and drag	Block the text to be moved, move the insertion point into the highlighted text, press and hold the left mouse button and drag the mouse pointer to the desired location, release the mouse button.	116

Move the insertion point:		
With the mouse	Move the mouse pointer to the desired location and click once.	24
With the keyboard	**Home, left arrow** — Left side of line **Home, right arrow** — Right side of line **Home, Home, up arrow** — First character of document **Home, Home, down arrow** — Last character of document **Home, up arrow** — Top of document window **Home, down arrow** — Bottom of document window **Ctrl and left arrow** — Left one word **Ctrl and right arrow** — Right one word **Page Down** — Top of next page **Page Up** — Top of previous page **Ctrl and Home, page #, Enter** — Go to another page	25

Open a file	Select **File**, **Open**, select the **File Mgr** button, type the drive letter where the disk is located, select **OK**, double-click on the desired filename.	38

Open a file created in a different program	Select **File**, **Open**. If necessary, select **File Manager** to access a different directory, double-click on the desired filename. Check that the correct format is highlighted, choose **Select**.	464

Outlines:		
Begin an outline	Select the **Out lnBeg** button, double-click on the name **OUTLINE**.	613
Create outline body text	Select the **T** button on the Outline Bar, type the desired text.	614
Copy an outline family	Place the insertion point in the first item of the family to be copied, select the **CopyFmly** button. Locate the insertion point where the copied family is to be placed and select the **PasteFam** button.	618
Cut (delete) an outline family	Place the insertion point in the first item of the family to be deleted and select the **CutFmly** button.	618
Demote an outline item	Select **NxtLevel** button.	618
Display the Outline Bar and Outline Button Bar	Select **View**, **Outline Bar**; choose **View**, **Button Bar Setup**, **Select**, double-click on **OUTLINE**.	613
Hide/show an outline family	Place the insertion point in the first item of the family to be hidden, select the **HideFmly** button. To show a hidden family, place the insertion point in the desired family item and select the **ShowFmly** button.	617
Hide/show outline body text	Select the **Hide (Show) Body** button on the Outline Bar.	617

Outlines *(cont'd.)*:

FEATURES	ACTIONS	PAGE
Insert a new item(s) in an outline	Place the insertion point to the right of the final character in the item that will precede the new item, press **Enter** once, select **NxtLevel** or **PreLevel** button for desired level number, type the new outline item.	616
Move an outline family	Place the insertion point in the first item of the family to be moved, select the **MoveFmly** button; locate the insertion point in the first item of the family where the moved item(s) is to be placed, **Enter**.	617
Outline style	Select the **Style** button on the Outline Bar, double-click on the desired style.	616
Promote an outline item	Select **PreLevel** button.	618
Return to outline numbering	Select the **Options** button, select **Insert Outline Level**, type desired level number.	615

Page numbering

FEATURES	ACTIONS	PAGE
Page numbering	Select **Layout**, **Page**, choose **Page Numbering**, select **Page Number Position**, choose the desired position.	266
Change the page number method	Select **Layout**, **Page**, **Page Number**, select **Numbering Method**, select the desired method.	267
Delete page numbers	With Reveal Codes on, highlight the page numbering code, press **Delete**.	268

Password (create or change)

FEATURES	ACTIONS	PAGE
Password (create or change)	Select the Save As button, type the desired filename, select **Password**, type the desired password, retype the password, select OK twice to save the file.	465
Open a file protected by a password	Select **File**, **Open**, type desired filename, **OK**, type password, **Enter**.	466
Remove a password	Select the **Save As** button, select **Password**, **Remove**, **OK**, save the file again using the same filename.	466

Printing:

FEATURES	ACTIONS	PAGE
Print booklet pages	Select the **Print** button. Choose **Multiple Pages**, **Print as Booklet**, **OK**, **Print**. When the first page(s) has been printed, place the printed page(s) back into the paper tray. Press **Shift** and **F7**, **6**, **g** to print the remainder of the booklet.	536
Print a document	Select **File**, **Print**, **Print** or select the **Print** button and choose **Print** or press **Shift** and **F7**, **Enter**.	20
Control Printer	Select the **Print** button, choose **Control Printer**.	94
Print blocked text	Block the text to be printed, select the Print button, select **Print**.	126
Print Preview	Select the **Preview** button. Select desired view.	90
Print specific pages	Select the **Print** button, choose **Multiple Pages**, select **Page/Label Range**, type the desired page numbers, select **OK**, choose **Print**.	280

FEATURES *(cont'd.)*	ACTIONS *(cont'd.)*	PAGE
QuickList:		
Access a directory	Select **File, Open, QuickList**, double-click on the desired entry name.	463
Create a QuickList directory entry	Select **File, Open, QuickList, Create**, type the descriptive name, type the name of the directory to be added to the QuickList, select **OK, Close, Cancel**.	462
Delete a QuickList	Select **File, Open, QuickList**, highlight the entry name to be deleted, select **Delete, Yes, Close, Cancel**.	463
Redline	Select **Font, Redline**. Type desired text.	593
Change method of marking redline text	Select **Layout, Document, Redline Method**. Select desired option, **OK**.	593
Remove redline and/or strikeout marks	Select **File, Compare Documents, Remove Markings**. Select **Remove Strikeout Text Only** or **Remove Redline Markings and Strikeout Text**. Select **OK**.	594, 596
Remove all text attributes	Block the text for which all text attributes are to be removed, select **Font, Normal**.	64
Replace text	Press **Insert** (Ins) to turn on Typeover, type the replacement text, press **Insert** again to turn off Typeover.	42
Replace text automatically	Select **Edit, Replace**, type the word(s) to be replaced in the Search For box, click in the **Replace With** box, type the new text, select desired options, select **Replace**.	122
Reveal Codes	Select **View, Reveal Codes** or press **Alt** and **F3**.	18
Ribbon	Select **View, Ribbon**.	15
Save a file	Select **File, Save**, type the filename, select **OK**.	20
Save a file in a different file format	Select the **Save As** button, type the desired filename, double-click on the desired file format, select **OK**.	464
Save and rename a file	Select the **Save As** button, type the new filename, select **OK**.	43
Search for codes	Select the **Search** button, choose **Codes**, double-click on the code, select **Search**.	279
Search for text	Select the **Search** button, type the word(s) to be found in the Search For box, select desired options, select **Search**.	120
Shadow text attribute	Block the desired text. Select the **Font** menu and choose **Shadow**.	508
Sort lines/paragraphs	Block the lines to be sorted and select **Tools, Sort**. Select the desired option in the Record Type box. Select the desired sort criteria. Choose **Perform Action**.	432-433

ecial characters	Select **Font, WP Characters**, choose the desired character set in the Set box, select the desired special character or bullet, choose **Insert**.	301
eller	Select the **Speller** button, press **Enter**.	91
rikeout	Block the desired text, select **Font, Strikeout**.	592
yles: Apply	*To apply an Open style to the entire document,* place the insertion point at the top of the document. Select **Layout, Styles**, double-click on the desired style name. *To apply a Paragraph style,* click in the paragraph, click on the **Style** button on the Ribbon, and double-click on the desired style name. *To apply a Character style,* block the text to be affected, select **Layout, Styles**, and double-click on the desired style name.	428
Create a paragraph style containing a paragraph border	Select **Layout, Styles, Create**, type desired name, **OK**; type a description in the Description box; click in the Style Contents box. Press **Alt** and **F9**, select **Paragraph** in the Borders area, select **Customize** and make the desired changes, select **OK**, press **F7, OK**.	639
Create a paragraph style containing a graphic image	Select **Layout, Style, Create**, type a name for the new style, select **OK**; type a description in the Description box; click in the Style Contents box, press **Alt** and **F9**, select **Create**, select **Filename, File List, OK**; double-click on the desired filename, **OK, F7, OK**.	640
Create a style based on an existing style	In the Style List dialog box, select **Create** and type the new style name, select **OK**; type a description in the Description box, click in the Style Contents dialog box, press **Alt** and **F8**, double-click on the style to be used as the basis for the new style, make any desired changes to modify the style, press **F7, OK**.	642
Create new styles	Select **Layout, Styles, Create**. Type the style name, select the **Style Type**, and select **OK**. Type a description of the style. Select **Style Contents**. Use options to specify the desired style format. Press **F7** and select **OK**. Select **Close**.	426
Edit a style	Select **Layout, Styles**, highlight the style to be edited, select **Edit, Style Contents**, make desired changes, press **F7**, select **Close**.	425
Link styles	Select **Layout, Styles, Create**, type a style name and description. In the Style List dialog box, highlight the name of the style that will be linked to another style, select **Edit**. Select the **Enter Key Action... Off/On** option, select **Turn Style Off and Link to** option, double-click on the desired style to be linked, **OK**.	643
Retrieve a style file	Select **Layout, Styles, Retrieve**. Type the name of the desired style file. Check that an X displays in the **Retrieve User Created Styles** option box. If necessary, select **Retrieve WP System Styles**. Select **OK, Yes, Close**.	429

FEATURES *(cont'd.)*	ACTIONS *(cont'd.)*	PAG
Styles *(cont'd.)*: Save styles	In the Style List dialog box, select **Save**, type the name of the new style file. Check that an X appears in the **Save User Created Styles** option box. Select **Save WP System Styles**. Select **OK, Close.**	427
Subdivide pages	Select **Layout, Page, Subdivide Pages**. Type the number of columns and/or rows that will be on one physical page. Select **OK**.	532
Subscript/Superscript	Block the text to be a subscript, select **Font, Size and Position, Subscript** or **Superscript**.	408
Tabs (set)	Select **Layout, Tab Set**. Select **Clear All** to delete existing tabs. Click in the **Set Tab** box and type the desired tab location or click at the desired location on the tab set ruler. Select the tab alignment type. Select **OK** when all tabs have been set.	305
Set evenly spaced tabs	Select **Layout, Tab Set**. Select **Clear All**. Click in the **Repeat Every** box and type the desired spacing between tabs, select **OK**.	308
Table of contents: Mark entries	Select desired text, select the **Mark Text** button, select **Table of Contents**, type the desired table of contents level number, **OK**.	620
Define	Select **Tools, Table of Contents, Define**, select **Number of Levels**, type the number of levels used when marking text, **OK**.	621
Generate	Select the **Generate** button on the Tools Button Bar, **OK**.	623
Tables: Calculate a column total (using a formula)	In the Table Edit window, locate the cursor in the cell where the formula and calculated total will be placed, select **Formula**, type the desired formula, select **OK**.	181, 552
Center table horizontally	Select the **Tbl Fmt** button on the Tables Button Bar, select **Position, Center**, select **OK**.	150
Center table vertically	Select **Layout, Page, Center Current Page, OK**.	153
Center text in multiple cells	In the Table Edit window, block desired cells, select **Cell, Center, OK**.	147
Change row height	In the Table Edit window, block the row(s) desired, select **Row, Fixed**, type desired height in inches, select **OK**.	149
Change table border	In the Table Edit window, select **Lines/Fill**, select **Border/Fill, Border Style**, double-click on desired border style, **OK**.	154
Change table lines	In the Table Edit window, block the desired cell(s), select **Lines/Fill**, select desired option, double-click on the desired line style.	155
Change table row margins	In the Table Edit window block the row(s) where margins are to be changed, select **Row**, type the desired margins in the option boxes, select **OK**.	177

Feature	Action	Page
Tables *(cont'd.)*:		
Convert existing tabbed text to a table	Block desired text, select **Tbl Crt** button on the Tables Button Bar, select **Tabular Text, OK**.	151
Copy a formula	In the Table Edit window, locate the cursor in the cell that contains the formula, select **Move/Copy, Cell, Copy, Down** or **Right**, type the number of cells the formula should be copied to, select **OK**.	185
Create a table	Select the **Tbl Crt** button on the Tables Button Bar, type the desired number of columns and rows, select **OK**.	142
Decimal align figures in a table	In the Table Edit window, block the cell(s) desired, select **Cell, Decimal Align** justification.	143
Decrease column width	Select the **TColNarr** button on the Tables Button Bar or press the **Ctrl** and left arrow key in the Table Edit window.	144
Delete a table	Turn on Reveal Codes, place the insertion point on or before the table definition code, block the entire table (including the table definition code), press **Delete**.	179
Delete a table column	Select the **Tbl Edit** button, place the cursor in the column to be deleted, select **Del**, select **OK**.	175
Delete a table row	Place the insertion point in any cell of the row to be deleted, select the **Del Row** button on the Tables Button Bar.	175
Delete tab set code	Press **Alt** and **F3** to turn on Reveal Codes, highlight the tab set code to be deleted, press **Delete**.	309
Display negative numbers between parentheses	In the Table Edit window, place the cursor in the cell (or block cells) in which a negative number is to display in parentheses. Select **Cell, Number Type**. Select **Parentheses**. Select **OK** twice.	552
Display the Table Edit window	Select the **Tbl Edit** button on the Tables Button Bar.	142
Header row(s)	Select the Table Edit button, block the row(s) to be used as a header row(s), select **Row, Header Row, OK**.	559
Ignore cells when calculating	In the Table Edit window, place the cursor in the cell (or block cells), select **Cell, Ignore When Calculating**, and select **OK**.	554
Import a spreadsheet	Select **Tools, Spreadsheet, Import**. Select **File List**, type the location of the spreadsheet file and select **OK**. Double-click on the desired filename and select **Import**.	558
Increase column width	Select the **TColWide** button on the Tables Button Bar or press the **Ctrl** and right arrow key in the Table Edit window.	144
Insert a table row	Select the **Ins Row** button on the Tables Button Bar.	146

Tables *(cont'd.)*:

FEATURES	ACTIONS	PAGE
Insert table column(s)	In the Table Edit window, select **Ins**, select **Columns**, type desired number of columns to be inserted, select **Before** or **After Cursor Position**, select **OK**.	148
Join table cells	In the Table Edit window, block cells to be joined, select **Join, Yes**.	147
Lock cells	In the Table Edit window, place the cursor in the cell (or block cells), select **Cell, Lock**, and choose **OK**.	554
Move a table colum/row	Select the **Tbl Edit** button, place the cursor in any cell in the column to be moved, select **Move/Copy**, select **Column** or **Row, Move**. Move the cursor to the desired location and press **Enter**.	173-174
Move cursor/insertion point from cell to cell	Press the **Tab** key, the **Shift** and **Tab** keys, or arrow keys.	142
Omit table lines and table border	Select the **Tbl Edit** button, block the desired cell(s), select **Lines/Fill**, select **Default Line** option, select **Line Style**, double click on **None, Close**. Select **Border/Fill**, select **Border Style**, double-click on **None, Close**.	186
Recalculate	Select the **Tbl Calc** or **Calc All** button on the Tables Button Bar.	183
Set decimal align position (from right of cell)	In the Table Edit window, place the cursor in any column cell, select **Column, Distance**, type the desired amount of space, and select **OK**.	553
Set number type and digits after the decimal	Select the **Tbl Edit** button, block the cell(s), select **Cell, Number Type** (option #6), select the desired format, click in the **Digits After Decimal** option, type the desired number of digits, select **OK**.	181
Set vertical alignment in a table cell	In the Table Edit window, place the cursor in the desired cell (or block cells), select **Cell**, select the desired Vertical Alignment option, and select **OK**.	553
Shade table cells	In the Table Edit window, block cell(s) to be shaded, select **Lines/Fill, Fill, Fill Style**, double-click on desired shaded fill, select **OK, Close**.	156
Sort table rows	Block the portion of the table to be sorted and select **Tools, Sort**. Check that Table displays in the Record Type box. Select the desired sort criteria. Choose **Perform Action**.	430, 431
Split a cell	In the Table Edit window, locate the cursor in the desired cell, select **Split**, choose the **Columns** or **Rows** option, type the number of times to split the cell, and select **OK**.	551
Total a table row	In the Table Edit window locate the cursor in the cell where the formula and total amount will be placed, select **Formula**, type the desired formula (cell address + cell address, e.g., B3+C3), select **OK**.	184
Underline or Double underline	In the Table Edit window, block desired cell(s), select Cell, choose **Underline** or **Dbl Underline, OK**.	188

Thesaurus	Select **Tools, Writing Tools, Thesaurus**, select the desired replacement word, select **Replace**.	243
Undelete deleted text	After text has been blocked and deleted, move the insertion point to a new location select **Edit, Undelete, Restore**.	44
Underline text	Block the text to be underlined, select **Font, Underline** (F8).	63
Undo deleted text	After text has been blocked and deleted, select **Edit, Undo**.	44
Watermark	Select **Layout, Header/Footer/Watermark**, select **Watermark A, Create**. Place the desired text or graphic image in the watermark window. Press **F7** to exit the watermark window.	534
Widow/Orphan Protect	Select **Layout, Other, Widow/Orphan Protect, OK**.	274
Window: Change the active window	Place the mouse pointer in the desired window and click once.	451
Cascade document windows	Select **Window, Cascade**.	450
Close all windows	Select **File, Close** or select the **Control Box** for each open window.	453
Copy text between windows	Select **Window, Switch to**; select the desired document; block the desired text, select **Edit, Copy**; select **Window, Switch to**; select the desired document; place the insertion point at the chosen location in the document, select **Edit, Paste**.	250
Frame a document window	Select **Window, Frame**.	450
Maximize a window	Select **Window, Maximize** or select the **Maximize** button in the desired window.	452
Minimize a window	Select **Window, Minimize** or select the **Minimize** button in the desired window.	452
Move a window	Locate the mouse pointer in the Title bar of the document window, press and hold the mouse button, drag the dashed outline for the document window to the desired location, release the mouse button.	452
Resize a window	Locate the mouse pointer on the left, right, or bottom edge of the document window, press and hold the mouse button, drag the dashed outline for the document window to the desired location, release the mouse button.	452
Tile document windows	Select **Window, Tile**.	451
Vertical line spacing	Select **Layout, Line**, move the mouse pointer to the box beside the words **Line Spacing** and click once, type the desired line spacing, select **OK**.	65
Delete the vertical line spacing code	Turn on Reveal Codes, move the mouse pointer to the line spacing code and click to select the code, press **Delete**.	86

Zoom view	Select the **Zoom** button on the Ribbon, double-click on the desired view percentage or option.	409

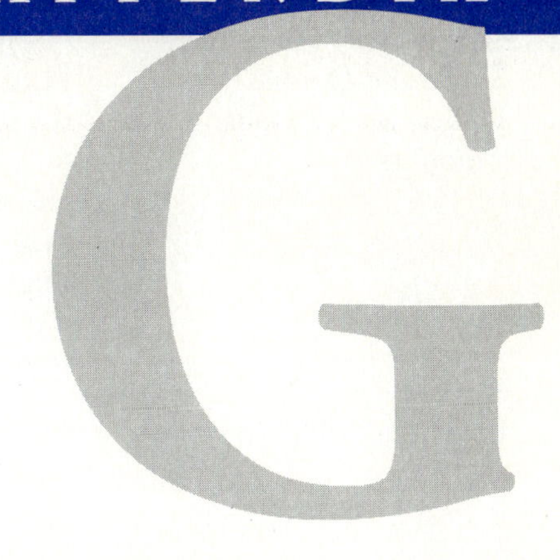

Summary of Enriching Language Arts Skills

PUNCTUATION/ GRAMMAR RULE	EXPLANATION	PAGE
Introductory Adverbs and Phrases	A comma often follows an introductory adverb or phrase because the word or phrase provides a transition from the previous sentence. Some common introductory words/phrases are: *however, for example, also, consequently, in other words.*	29
Introductory Clauses	A comma should follow a dependent clause. (A dependent clause has both a subject and verb but cannot stand alone as a sentence.) An introductory clause often begins with *if, in, when, since,* or *as.*	48
Appositives	Appositives are words that immediately follow a noun and further identify the noun but usually are not necessary to the meaning of the sentence. Appositives are set off by commas.	72
Coordinating Conjunctions	A comma is placed before a coordinating conjunction (*and, or, because*) that joins two independent clauses, i.e., clauses that are complete sentences. No comma is placed before a conjunction if one or both clauses are dependent.	97
Compound Adjectives	Hyphenate two words that precede and describe a noun and function as a single adjective.	130
Dollar Amounts Formats	Use a comma to separate the number digits into groups of thousands. No space is placed between a number and dollar sign unless the dollar signs are aligned in a column. If a column of numbers has even dollar amounts, the zeros are omitted. Even dollar amounts can either be right justified or decimal justified in a column in order to align the numbers on the right.	159

PUNCTUATION GRAMMAR RULE	EXPLANATION	PAGE
Single and Double Underlines for Dollar Amounts	Place a single underline below the last column amount and before the total amount. The single underline should extend the width of the amount that has the most characters, including the dollar sign. However, if any one of WordPerfect's number type options (other than General) is used, the spaces cannot be added to extend the single underline. In a table without lines or borders, a total amount is usually emphasized by placing double underlines beneath the total amount.	192
Using the Abbreviations *e.g.* and *i.e.*	The abbreviation *e.g.* is used in place of "for example" and is often used when one or more of many examples are listed. The abbreviation *i.e.* is used in place of "that is" and is used when all potential conditions are listed. A period follows each initial with no space between the period and the initials. The final period is followed by a comma.	228
Quotation Marks with Punctuation	Always place a comma or period inside a closing quotation mark. Place a question or exclamation mark inside a closing quotation mark if the question or exclamation pertains only to the quoted information. Place a question or exclamation mark outside the closing quotation mark if the question or exclamation pertains to the entire sentence. Semicolons and colons are placed outside the closing quotation mark.	284
Commas Used in a Series	Words and/or ideas listed in a series are separated by commas.	313
Nonrestrictive Clause	A nonrestrictive clause is a clause that is not essential to the meaning of the sentence and is, therefore, set off by a comma or commas.	334
Subject-Verb Agreement	Verbs must agree in number with their subject. If a subject is singular (one), use a singular verb; if a subject is plural (more than one), use a plural verb. To determine if a subject and verb are in agreement, omit the words between the subject and verb.	358
Initials Abbreviated	Periods or spaces are not placed after the letters of an acronym such as IRS (Internal Revenue Service), or TWA (Trans World Airlines).	394
Independent Adjectives	Two adjectives that modify the same noun are separated by a comma.	417
Apostrophe Used to Show Possession	If a noun is singular and used to show possession, add an apostrophe (') and an *s*. If the final letter in the noun is an s, the apostrophe is added after the *s*.	440
Parentheses	Parentheses can be used to set off nonessential expressions that might otherwise confuse the reader. The information within the parentheses provides supplemental information that has no direct bearing on the main idea of the sentence or paragraph. Words, phrases, or clauses can be enclosed within parentheses. Unless a comma, colon, or semicolon is necessary to the text within parentheses, place the punctuation outside the closing parenthesis. If the text within the parentheses is a complete sentence, the final period is placed within the parentheses.	503

Em and En Dashes	The em dash (—), a typography symbol about the width of the character m, is often used in place of a comma. Press the hyphen key twice (--) to create a dash on a typewriter or computer keyboard. Many software programs provide a method to create correct typographic em dashes (see page 520). The en dash (–), a typography symbol about the width of the character n, is used as a hyphen or as a substitute for the word to, e.g., July–September. The correct typography symbols for em and en dashes have traditionally been used for books, newspapers, and advertisements and are recommended for use when creating a professional-looking document.	526
Colons, Capitalization, and Punctuation for Bulleted and Enumerated Lists	Place a colon after an independent clause that introduces a bulleted or enumerated (numbered) list. An introductory clause frequently includes words such as "the following" and "as follows." When creating a bulleted or enumerated list, capitalize the first word and insert a final punctuation mark (period, question mark, or exclamation mark) after each item that is a complete sentence or phrase. Do not capitalize the first word or insert final punctuation when bulleted or enumerated items are not complete thoughts.	540
Abbreviations in Table Column Headings	When creating tables and forms, abbreviations are often used in subtitles and/or column headings because of limited space. However, abbreviations should be used sparingly. If you are unsure of how to abbreviate a word, consult a dictionary.	563
Abbreviations for Time	Type a.m. and p.m. with lowercase letters and no spaces. Only one period is used if the abbreviation is the last element of a sentence.	585
Contractions	An apostrophe is used to indicate where a letter(s) has been omitted when two words are combined to form a verb contraction. Generally, contractions are not used in formal business writing. Contractions can be used in personal letters or informal business documents.	605
Percentage Amounts	Use figures for numbers that are followed by the word *percent*. Spell out the word *percent* unless the percentage amount is used in a table that contains statistical information or is used in a headline/title.	630
Basic Rules for Numbers	Generally, numbers one through ten when used in writing are spelled out. Also, numbers used in approximation, at the beginning of a sentence, or numbers that are rounded are usually spelled out. Related numbers in the same document should be expressed in the same form, i.e., numbers one through ten are written as figures when used with related numbers above ten.	653

Spelling/Vocabulary Words
Chapters 1-26

accrual method	duty-free	profound
acquisition	enormous	promotional
adversely	euphoria	prompt
affiliation	evaluation	promulgated
alliances	existence	propaganda
amortized	extensive	quarter
analysis	feedback	realistic
antagonistic	HMO	regulation
appreciation	implement	reimbursement
attitude	incentive	reliable
biosphere	inclusion	rendered
bonus	initiative	reputation
brochure	integral	spiraling
coaching	irrevocable	standards
commendable	liability	strategic
compatibility	liquidation	suitable
compliance	mandatory	surreptitious
components	maturity	tailored
confirmation	mentor	telecommunications
cuisine	negotiations	traditional
deferred	nominated	typography
demonstrate	offensive	unkempt
depreciation	outweigh	UPC
derogatory	paramedic	valid
description	partnership	versus
dissolution	per diem	virtually
distinguished	phenomenon	warranty
dues	prime rate	wholesalers

Answers to Self-Check Questions

Chapter 1	Chapter 2	Chapter 3	Chapter 4	Chapter 5	Chapter 6	Chapter 7
1. F	1. F	1. T	1. T	1. T	1. F	1. F
2. T	2. T	2. T	2. T	2. F	2. T	2. T
3. F	3. T	3. F	3. T	3. T	3. F	3. T
4. T	4. T	4. F	4. T	4. T	4. F	4. F
5. F	5. T	5. T	5. T	5. F	5. T	5. T
					6. T	

Chapter 8	Chapter 9	Chapter 10	Chapter 11	Chapter 12	Chapter 13	Chapter 14
1. T	1. F	1. T	1. F	1. T	1. T	1. T
2. F	2. F	2. T	2. T	2. T	2. T	2. F
3. T	3. T	3. F	3. T	3. F	3. T	3. T
4. F	4. F	4. T	4. F	4. F	4. T	4. T
5. T	5. T	5. T	5. T	5. F	5. F	5. F
	6. F				6. T	6. T

Chapter 15	Chapter 16	Chapter 17	Chapter 18	Chapter 19	Chapter 20	Chapter 21
1. T	1. T	1. T	1. T	1. F	1. F	1. F
2. F	2. T	2. F	2. T	2. T	2. T	2. T
3. F	3. F	3. F	3. T	3. T	3. T	3. T
4. T	4. F	4. T	4. F	4. F	4. T	4. T
5. T	5. T	5. T	5. T		5. T	5. F
6. F	6. T		6. T		6. F	

Chapter 22	Chapter 23	Chapter 24	Chapter 25	Chapter 26
1. T	1. F	1. F	1. T	1. F
2. F	2. T	2. T	2. T	2. T
3. T	3. T	3. T	3. F	3. T
4. F	4. F	4. T	4. T	4. T
5. T	5. F	5. T	5. F	5. F
		6. F		6. T

Vertical line, *see* newspaper columns, border between columns
Vertical line spacing, 64
    Return vertical line spacing to default, 86
Vertical scrolling, *see* scrolling
View, *see* zoom view

Watermark, 534
Widow/Orphan lines, 273, 274
Windows in WordPerfect, *see* document windows
Word count, *see* document information
Word division guidelines, 220
Word spacing, 402, 404
WordPerfect 6.0, 6
WordPerfect customer service, A-5
WordPerfect graphic images, E1-E2
WordPerfect message board, C5-C10
WordPerfect setup, A1-A3
Wordwrap, 16
WP Characters, 301
WYSIWYG, 13

Zoom view, 409

WORDPERFECT 6.0 DOS BUTTON BARS

WPMAIN Button Bar

File Mgr | Save As | Print | Preview | Font | GrphMode | TextMode | Envelope | Speller | Gramatik | QuikFndr | Tbl Edit | Search | BBar Sel | BBar Opt

FONT Button Bar

Font | Normal | Bold | Underln | DblUndln | Italics | Fine | Small | Large | VryLarge | X Large | NormSize | Suprscpt | Subscrpt | Norm Pos | Outline | Shadow | SmallCap | Redline | Strkeout | PrtColor | WP Chars | BBar Sel | BBar Opt

LAYOUT Button Bar

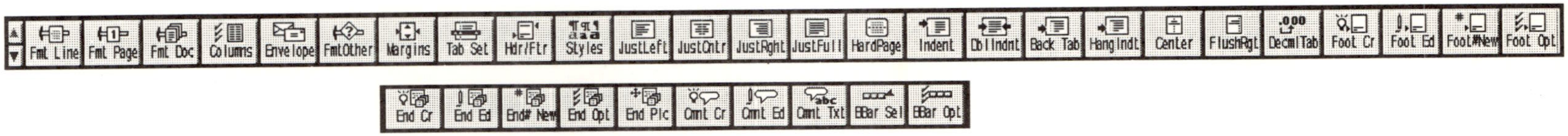

Fmt Line | Fmt Page | Fmt Doc | Columns | Envelope | FmtOther | Margins | Tab Set | Hdr/Ftr | Styles | JustLeft | JustCntr | JustRght | JustFull | HardPage | Indent | DblIndnt | Back Tab | HangIndt | Center | FlushRgt | DecmlTab | Foot Cr | Foot Ed | Foot#New | Foot Opt

End Cr | End Ed | End# New | End Opt | End Plc | Cmnt Cr | Cmnt Ed | Cmnt Txt | BBar Sel | BBar Opt

MACRO Button Bar

Mod_atrb | Initcaps | Pleading | Spacetab | Calc | Bullet | Memo | Editcode | Glossary | Notecvt | Allfonts | BBar Sel | BBar Opt

OUTLINE Button Bar

OutlnEdt | OutlnOpt | OutlnBeg | OutlnEnd | OutlnSty | NxtLevel | PreLevel | ChgLevel | HideFmly | ShowFmly | HideBody | MoveFmly | CopyFmly | Cut Fmly | PasteFam | BBar Sel | BBar Opt

TABLES Button Bar

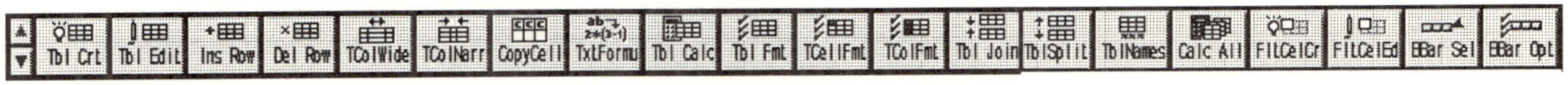

Tbl Crt | Tbl Edit | Ins Row | Del Row | TColWide | TColNarr | CopyCell | TxtFormu | Tbl Calc | Tbl Fmt | TCellFmt | TColFmt | Tbl Join | TblSplit | TblNames | Calc All | FltCelCr | FltCelEd | BBar Sel | BBar Opt

TOOLS Button Bar

Speller | Gramatik | Thesarus | Mac Play | Mac Rec | Mac Ctrl | MergeDef | MergeRun | Sort | DateText | DateCode | Date Fmt | MarkText | JustFull | HardPage | Indent | DblIndnt | Back Tab | HangIndt | Center | FlushRgt | DecmlTab | Foot Cr | Foot Ed | Foot#New | Foot Opt

SoundSet | BBar Sel | BBar Opt